PARAGON
ISSUES IN
PHILOSOPHY

PARAGON ISSUES IN PHILOSOPHY

FORTHCOMING TITLES

THE PARAGON ISSUES
IN PHILOSOPHY SERIES

At colleges and universities, interest in the traditional areas of philosophy remains strong. Many new currents flow within them, too, but some of these—the rise of cognitive science, for example, or feminist philosophy—went largely unnoticed in undergraduate philosophy courses until the end of the 1980s. The Paragon Issues in Philosophy Series responds to both perennial and newly influential concerns by bringing together a team of able philosophers to address the fundamental issues in philosophy today and to outline the state of contemporary discussion about them.

More than twenty volumes are scheduled; they are organized into three major categories. The first covers the standard topics—metaphysics, theory of knowledge, ethics, and political philosophy—stressing innovative developments in those disciplines. The second focuses on more specialized but still vital concerns in the philosophies of science, religion, history, sport, and other areas. The third category explores new work that relates philosophy and fields such as feminist criticism, medicine, economics, technology, and literature.

The level of writing is aimed at undergraduate students who have little previous experience studying philosophy. The books provide brief but accurate introductions that appraise the state of the art in their fields and show how the history of thought about their topics developed. Each volume is complete in itself but also complements others in the series.

Traumatic change characterizes these last years of the twentieth century; all of it involves philosophical issues. The editorial staff at Paragon House has worked with us to develop this series. We hope it will encourage the understanding needed in our times, which are as complicated and problematic as they are promising.

John K. Roth   Frederick Sontag
Claremont McKenna College   Pomona College

FOUNDATIONS OF COGNITIVE SCIENCE: THE ESSENTIAL READINGS

JAY L. GARFIELD

HAMPSHIRE COLLEGE
AMHERST, MASSACHUSETTS

FOUNDATIONS OF COGNITIVE SCIENCE:
THE
ESSENTIAL READINGS

PARAGON
ISSUES IN
PHILOSOPHY

PARAGON HOUSE • NEW YORK

FIRST EDITION, 1990

PUBLISHED IN THE UNITED STATES BY
PARAGON HOUSE
90 FIFTH AVENUE
NEW YORK, NY 10011

SERIES DESIGN BY KATHY KIKKERT

LIBRARY OF CONGRESS CATALOGING-IN-PUBLICATION DATA
FOUNDATIONS OF COGNITIVE SCIENCE : THE ESSENTIAL READINGS / JAY L.
    GARFIELD, EDITOR.—1ST ED.
        P.   CM.
    INCLUDES BIBLIOGRAPHICAL REFERENCES.
    ISBN 1-55778-257-1 : $17.95
    1. COGNITIVE SCIENCE.   I. GARFIELD, JAY L., 1955–
BF311.F.665   1990
153—DC20   89-78178
                                                          CIP

THE PAPER USED IN THIS PUBLICATION MEETS THE MINIMUM
REQUIREMENTS OF AMERICAN NATIONAL STANDARD FOR INFORMATION
SCIENCES—PERMANENCE OF PAPER FOR PRINTED LIBRARY MATERIALS,
ANSI Z39.48-1984.

MANUFACTURED IN THE UNITED STATES OF AMERICA
10 9 8 7 6 5 4 3 2 1

FOR RUTH AND LENI:
THE FOUNDATIONS OF COGNITIVE SCIENCE

CONTENTS

PART III. ARTIFICIAL INTELLIGENCE

PART IV. HUMAN INTELLIGENCE

ACKNOWLEDGMENTS

"Computation and Cognition: Issues in the Foundations of Cognitive Science" by Zenon Pylyshyn originally appeared in *Behavioral and Brain Sciences 3:1* (1980) pp. 154–169. It is reprinted by permission of Cambridge University Press.

"Epistemics: The Regulative Theory of Cognition" by Alvin Goldman originally appeared in *The Journal of Philosophy LXXV* (1978) pp. 509–523. It is reprinted by permission of *The Journal of Philosophy* and Alvin Goldman.

"Three Kinds of Intentional Psychology" by Daniel Dennett originally appeared in Healy, ed., *Reduction, Time and Reality*, New York: Cambridge University Press (1981) pp. 37–61. It is reprinted by permission of Cambridge University Press and Daniel Dennett.

"Computer Science as Empirical Enquiry: Symbol and Search" by Alan Newell and Herbert A. Simon was the tenth Turing Award Lecture, delivered to the annual conference of the Association for Computing Machinery in 1975 and published in *Communications of the Association for Computing Machinery 19* (1976) pp. 113–126. It is reprinted by permission of the Association for Computing Machinery.

"The Philosophical Significance of the Four Color Problem" by Thomas Tymoczko originally appeared in *The Journal of Philosophy LXXVI* (1979) pp. 57–84. It is reprinted by permission of *The Journal of Philosophy*.

"Lucas' Number Is Finally Up" by G. Lee Bowie originally appeared in *The Journal of Philosophical Logic 11* (1982) pp. 279–285. It is reprinted by permission of D. Reidel Publishing Co. I gratefully acknowledge Professor Bowie's preparation of a slightly revised and simplified version for publication in this anthology.

"Minds, Brains, and Programs" by John Searle originally appeared in *The Behavioral and Brain Sciences 3* (1980) pp. 417–424. It is reprinted by permission of Cambridge University Press and John Searle.

"Brains + Programs = Minds" by Bruce Bridgeman originally appeared in *The Behavioral and Brain Sciences 3* (1980) pp. 427–428. It is reprinted by permission of Cambridge University Press and Bruce Bridgeman.

"The Milk of Human Intentionality" by Daniel Dennett originally appeared in *The Behavioral and Brain Sciences 3* (1980) pp. 428–430. It is reprinted by permission of Cambridge University Press and Daniel Dennett.

"Searle on What Only Brains Can Do" by Jerry Fodor originally appeared in *The Behavioral and Brain Sciences 3* (1980) pp. 431–432. It is reprinted by permission of Cambridge University Press and Jerry Fodor.

"Programs, Causal Powers, and Intentionality" by John Haugeland originally appeared in *The Behavioral and Brain Sciences 3* (1980) pp. 432–433. It is reprinted by permission of Cambridge University Press and John Haugeland.

"Reductionism and Religion" by Douglas Hofstadter originally appeared in *The Behavioral and Brain Sciences 3* (1980) pp. 433–434. It is reprinted by permission of Cambridge University Press and Douglas Hofstadter.

"The Functionalist Reply" by William Lycan originally appeared in *The Behavioral and Brain Sciences 3* (1980) pp. 434–435. It is reprinted by permission of Cambridge University Press and William Lycan.

"The Causal Powers of Machines" by Zenon Pylyshyn originally appeared in *The Behavioral and Brain Sciences 3* (1980) pp. 442–444. It is reprinted by permission of Cambridge University Press and Zenon Pylyshyn.

"Modules, Frames, Fridgeons, Sleeping Dogs, and the Music of the Spheres" originally appeared in Pylyshyn, ed., *The Robot's Dilemma: The Frame Problem in Artificial Intelligence*. Norwood, N.J.: Ablex Publishers (1988). It is reprinted by permission of Ablex Publishers and Zenon Pylyshyn.

"Artificial Intelligence as Philosophy and as Psychology" originally appeared in Dennett, *Brainstorms*, Cambridge, MA: MIT Press/Bradford Books, pp. 109–128. It is reprinted by permission of MIT Press and Daniel Dennett.

"Ecological Optics" by J. Gibson originally appeared in *Vision Research 1* (1961) pp. 253–262. It is reprinted by permission of Permagon Press and Eleanor Gibson.

"How Direct Is Visual Perception: Some Reflections on Gibson's Ecological Approach" by Jerry Fodor and Zenon Pylyshyn originally appeared in *Cognition 9* (1981) pp. 139–196. It is reprinted (abridged) by permission of *Cognition*, Jerry Fodor, and Zenon Pylyshyn.

"Grammars, Psychology, and Indeterminacy" by Stephen Stich originally appeared in *The Journal of Philosophy VXXIX* (1972) pp. 799–818. It is reprinted by permission of *The Journal of Philosophy* and Stephen Stich.

"What the Linguist Is Talking About" by Noam Chomsky and Jerrold J. Katz originally appeared in *The Journal of Philosophy* LXXI (1974), pp.

347–367. It is reprinted by permission of *The Journal of Philosophy* and Noam Chomsky.

"The Role of TAU's in Narratives" by Michael Dyer originally appeared in the Proceedings of the Third Annual Conference of the Cognitive Science Society in Berkeley, California (August 1981) pp. 243–246. It is reprinted by permission of Michael Dyer.

"$RESTAURANT Revisited or Lunch with BORIS" by Michael Dyer originally appeared in the Proceedings of the Seventh International Joint Conference on Artificial Intelligence held in Vancouver, British Columbia (1981) pp. 234–236. It is reprinted by permission of Michael Dyer.

"An Introduction to Connectionism" by John Tienson originally appeared in *The Southern Journal of Philosophy XXVI* (1979) pp. 57–84. It is reprinted by permission of *The Southern Journal of Philosophy* and John Tienson.

"Moving the Semantic Fulcrum" by Terry Winograd originally appeared in *Linguistics and Philosophy 8* (1985) pp. 231–364. It is reprinted by permission of D. Reidel Publishing Co. and Terry Winograd.

"Understanding Natural Language" by John Haugeland originally appeared in *The Journal of Philosophy VXXVI* (1979) pp. 619–632. It is reprinted by permission of *The Journal of Philosophy* and John Haugeland.

PREFACE

This volume is intended as a companion to James Fetzer's book *Philosophy and Cognitive Science*, also in the *Paragon Issues in Philosophy* series of texts. The essays collected herein present alternative and sometimes conflicting positions on issues raised in that text. It is hoped that when these texts are used in tandem students will receive both a general introduction to a set of questions and problems and a taste of the primary literature and recent debate they occasion. While many of these essays are somewhat challenging, all are accessible to intermediate or advanced undergraduate students of philosophy or cognitive science. It would be folly to pretend either that every major topic in the foundations of cognitive science is represented, or that every significant position taken on the topics addressed is presented. The selection of essays was determined in part by the content of this anthology's companion text, in part by the availability of primary material accessible to students using that text, and, unfortunately, in part by the reasonableness of publishers in setting fees for permission to reprint scholarly articles. This last problem deserves some comment: In producing an anthology for textbook use, it is obviously essential to keep costs down, so that the resulting volume will be affordable to students. While many publishers recognize this, and charge modest fees, or no fees at all for permission, and while some others willingly modify their price structure in recognition of this problem, others ask such exorbitant fees that it is for all practical purposes impossible to reprint material originally published by them, even despite the requests of authors for abatement of fees. This, in my view, is a serious impediment to the dissemination of scholarly work, and to its use in the classroom. I urge all scholars before publishing articles, chapters, or books to pay close attention to the policies regarding the reprinting of their work, and to take steps to ensure its broad availability to scholars and students.

I thank the authors and publishers who granted permission to reprint the work contained herein, Don Fehr of Paragon House for editorial support and encouragement, and Ruth Hammen and Leni Bowen for administrative and secretarial support. Special thanks go to Kirsten Hekler, whose tireless, intelligent, and precise research, correspondence, filing, and editorial work made this project possible. I cannot imagine having completed the project without her. Thanks also to my family, Blaine Garson, Jonas Garson, Joshua Garfield, and Abraham Garfield, for putting up with my frequent physical and psychological absence while this volume was in preparation.

JAY L. GARFIELD

INTRODUCTION

Cognitive science is among the most exciting interdisciplinary fields to emerge in recent years. Though its intellectual territory is reasonably well demarcated, characterizing the field is not straightforward, for almost every plausible description involves some philosophical or methodological bone of contention within the field. One might, for instance, say with some justice that cognitive science is the study of the mind. But some cognitive scientists argue (with straight faces) that there are no minds; and while artificial intelligence is at the center of the domain of cognitive science, whether computers can have minds is hotly disputed even by those who are comfortable with the notion that humans, at least, have them. Or one might describe cognitive science as the study of information processing systems. But there are at least two problems with this characterization: First, many urge that it is inappropriate to characterize humans as information processing systems in the technical sense at stake. Second, the connectionist systems that have recently burst on the cognitive science scene are not, despite their computer implementations, information processing systems in that strict sense either. But cognitive psychology, linguistics, artificial intelligence, and the philosophy of mind—however their convergence is *described*—*have* clearly converged in a recognizable alliance. But that alliance is not reflected in theoretical unanimity. There is the ferocious theoretical disputation in cognitive science characteristic of a young field. Not only are specific models of cognitive processes or accounts of the nature of fundamental theoretical entities in dispute. Fundamental methodological questions concerning the structure of psychological theory, the nature of language, and the very existence of representations are still very much open. Despite this "wide open" character of the theoretical landscape in cognitive science, there is a recognizable methodological unity to the field.

Cognitive scientists are committed to the fruitfulness of a certain approach to understanding intelligent behaviors and capacities. That approach involves at least taking seriously (if only as a plausible target for subsequent refutation) the notion that intelligent behavior is, or at least is made possible by, the manipulation of symbolic representations. It involves taking seriously the notion that the operations on those representations can be described, at least at some theoretically useful level of analysis, as computations (perhaps serial—perhaps distributed). It involves trying to understand how these psychological or linguistic processes are realized in the biological or electronic substrata of brains or machines. It also involves characterizing the processes themselves in abstraction from their physical implementation. Finally, cognitive science involves taking seriously the possibility that such apparently diverse fields as linguistics, artificial intelligence, psychology, and the philosophy of mind and language each have important insights to contribute to each other. The essays in this volume and the exposition presented in the accompanying textbook are meant to explain and to demonstrate the nature and fruits of this collaborative exploration of the domain and questions characterized by this set of methodological assumptions.

Much (though by no means all) of what philosophers contribute to cognitive science concerns what has come to be known as "the foundations of cognitive science." While the contributions of philosophers certainly extend beyond such foundational concerns (and include important work in semantics, knowledge representation, the theory of perception, and logical theory), this volume and the text it accompanies focus on the foundations of cognitive science (which, as is amply demonstrated by the range of contributors to the present volume, is not the exclusive domain of philosophers). This subdomain is concerned primarily with methodological and ontological questions regarding the structure of cognitive theories and the nature of the entities they posit.

Among the debates that currently dominate the foundational scene are these: Are there actually mental representations? Eliminativists say, "No, there are only brain states (or some such thing)." Realists say, "Sure. There is a level of description of any cognitive system at which it manipulates representations, and that level has as much claim to reality as does the physical." Could computers think? AI proponents say, "Sure. Thinking is the manipulation of symbols. Computers manipulate symbols. So, of course, if we can get them to manipulate those symbols in the right way, they would be thinking." Opponents say, "No. Even were the behavior of a computer indistinguishable from that of a human, and even were the formal character of its processes isomorphic to that employed by humans, thinking is an essentially biological phenomenon, and so computers can at best simulate it." Still others would express doubts about the empirical possibility of computer thought, but would not argue for its conceptual impossibility. The explanation of human linguistic capacities also excites vigorous foundational debate: Orthodox

Chomskyans assert that our linguistic capacities reflect our innate knowledge of a "universal grammar" that characterizes all possible human languages. Opponents either doubt the explanatory necessity of such a set of rules, or doubt that the appropriate way to describe their role makes use of the concept of knowledge. This is but a sampler of the many fascinating problems addressed by cognitive scientists under the "foundations" rubric. I hope that it gives a feel for the vitality of this enterprise and for its centrality in the prosecution of empirical research in the field. I now turn to a brief introduction of the foundational issues with which the papers collected in this volume are concerned.

The concept of representation and its allied concepts—belief, perception, etc.—lie at the heart of cognitive science. For common to all noneliminativist accounts of psychology, of the nature of mind, and of linguistic behavior is the thesis that humans and other cognitively characterizable organisms manipulate representations (and what gets eliminativist accounts going in the first place is the commitment to attacking the reality of representations). Most of the interesting substantive debates get going when we ask just what those representations are, and how one could build them out of blind matter. Among those debates is that between naturalists and individualists regarding the ontology of representation. Individualists (Pylyshyn in this volume) argue that representations are to be identified with particular, determinate physical states or processes in the hardware or wetware out of which a cognitive system is built. While attention to the context in which the organism or machine functions may be necessary in order to *know* the representational content of a particular episode, the representation itself is in the end a particular state of the representer. Naturalists, on the other hand (Garfield in this volume) argue that representation is an essentially relational phenomenon, and that a representation is not an internal state of an organism or a machine, but rather a relation in which an organism or a machine stands to its environment. In much the same way, being a parent is not an internal state of a human being, but is rather a relation one bears to one's offspring. If one is interested in a theory of how humans, for example, manipulate representations, it matters very much whether one is interested in finding internal representational episodes or whether one wants to understand nonrepresentational capacities for entering into representations. In the first case, one would be interested in locating specific internal states of an organism—perhaps physical states of its brain—and determining their representational character and role. This might require a general theory of the psychosemantics of biological states. Or one might take classical artificial intelligence models wherein information is stored in discrete locations very seriously as cognitive models. On the other hand, naturalism might lead one to look for very general capacities of organisms—perhaps biological or computational—which, while themselves not representational, account in some way for the organism's ability to enter into particular kinds of relations to its environment—an approach akin, for instance, to that taken by Gibson and his followers in the theory of perception. This debate is hence of great importance to much of cognitive science.

Cognitive science finds itself in a methodological position unique among the empirical sciences. While cognitive science aims at the description, prediction, and explanation of natural phenomena whose status is in principle no different from those in the domains of such sciences as biology, chemistry, and physics, it finds itself using language that is shot through with *normative* content. The focus of this normative infection is the concept of **knowledge**. For knowledge, as ordinarily conceived, is not mere belief, or even mere true belief. For it is possible to adopt true beliefs for the wrong reasons—based upon incorrect information or faulty reasoning. Knowledge, we want to say, is *justified* true belief. And there's the rub: Justification is a normative notion. We are justified in believing some proposition when we *ought* to believe it (given whatever else we know, and what inferences we are in a position to draw). So, to the extent that cognitive science is concerned with *knowledge representation* or *linguistic knowledge*, it seems to face a dilemma: either produce a non-normative account of knowledge, or an account of the foundation of a science whose basic vocabulary is normative in this way. These and related issues are explored by Goldman in his contribution to this volume.

The problem goes still deeper though, and involves the very possibility of attributing representations to systems or organisms in a principled way. After all, attributing contents to the states, events, and processes in an organism's or machine's life is a form of interpretation. Those who do it are, in effect, providing a translation manual to guide them in translating physical states of the organism or machine into representations, statements, rules, or other such quasi-linguistic entities. And interpretation requires assumptions regarding the coherence, rationality, and prudence of the system being interpreted, and assumptions about what it *ought* to believe, given whatever else one has interpreted it as believing. A proposed interpretation according to which a person or an animal believed mostly false things, drew crazy inferences, and acted in a way that bore no discernible relation to the beliefs and desires the interpretation assigned it would obviously be a very bad interpretation. That is not, of course, to say that all representers are perfectly rational or omniscient. It is just to point out that the only evidence that could ever vindicate an interpretation would be the fact that under the interpretation most of the beliefs, desires, and behavior of the system turn out to "make sense." (This point has been made with exceptional clarity by Haugeland in [1978].) Interpretation is hence shot through with normative assumptions—assumptions about what an individual *ought* to believe, what inferences it *ought* to draw, etc The character of such intentional interpretation and the problems it poses are explored in Dennett's essay.

One respect in which the domain of cognitive science is unique is that it comprises computing machines as well as organisms. For cognitive science takes as its *prima facie* object of study systems that process and represent information. But just what role to assign the computer and computational models in the study of mind and mental processes is a vexing matter. The first two essays in the section on computation theory in the foundations of cognitive science come at this problem from two different perspectives. Newell and Simon urge that the proper domain of cognitive science is that of physical symbol systems, and that there is in principle no difference between machines and humans in their status as cognitive systems. They sketch a powerful and coherent vision of the structure of a science of just such objects. Tymoczko, on the other hand, explores one of the more interesting consequences of treating computing machines on the same footing as humans—that their intellectual achievements must then be understood as of a piece with human intellectual achievements. He explores the problems this raises in the context of mathematical discovery and proof.

Even more fundamentally, it is not clear whether it even makes sense to treat humans and machines as of a kind. Among the most salient fronts along which this battle has been fought has been that defined by the consequences of Gödel's incompleteness theorem for computing machines and for minds. In two diametrically opposed essays Tymoczko argues that Gödel's theorem demonstrates conclusively that human capabilities transcend those of machines, and Bowie argues that the theorem demonstrates no such thing. The outcome of this and related debates is crucial for the definition of the domain and structure of cognitive science. For if it turns out that humans and machines differ fundamentally in their computational and representational powers, regarding them as two instances of a single general type would become problematic. Moreover, the use of computational models as models of human cognitive processes would in each case require the assurance that the process at issue was indeed limited in the ways that Gödel's theorems show that machines are limited.

A very different question regarding the possibility and nature of artificial intelligence, and regarding the role of artificial intelligence models in cognitive science, is at stake between Searle and his critics. For Searle grants the possibility that the behavioral repertoire and computational capacities of humans and suitably programmed machines might be the same. But he denies that machines would on that account actually think, represent, or have a genuine mental life. Accordingly, he argues, while artificial intelligence may yield useful *models* of psychological processes, to treat the processes of artificially intelligent systems *as psychological* is to commit a serious error. Searle's argument has been both enormously influential and quite controversial in the foundations of cognitive science. It challenges the widespread assumption in the field that cognitive processes can be considered in abstraction from their physical implementation, and hence the assumption that humans and computing machines are, in a theoretically useful sense, of a kind. A range of replies to his position is reflected in the selection of responses to the essay reprinted in this volume.

If we grant—as even as ardent a critic of artificial intelligence as Searle does—that artificial intelligence has a genuine role in cognitive science, we must confront hard epistemological problems raised by the construal of computers as epistemic agents. The most massive problem is that known as the "frame problem." The frame problem is a vast and somewhat amorphous problem, and seems to many to lie in wait for any large-scale knowledge-based or general-purpose artificial intelligence system, and to force artificial intelligence systems, in order to be successful, to be narrow, tightly constrained, and distinctly nonhuman in character and in capacity. Put in too small a nutshell, the frame problem is this: How does one decide what concepts, what knowledge, and what capacities to mobilize in order to understand a situation or to solve a problem? How do we know what information about a situation is relevant to action? Given the vastness of information available about situations, texts, and problems, and the even greater vastness of potentially relevant information one could mobilize in comprehending or acting in any situation, the frame problem is mammoth. It is addressed by Garfield and Haugeland, and by Dennett and Fodor quite directly from interestingly different vantage points. The centrality and the daunting character of this problem make it one of the most important problems in the foundations of cognitive science. Its manifold connections to other philosophical problems (as all of these authors emphasize) issues in its fertility as a topic of foundational research for philosophers and in the prospect for artificial intelligence to contribute both to the empirical and to the conceptual sides of cognitive science.

Historically and conceptually, cognitive psychology lies at the center of cognitive science. And it is fair to say that it has more to say about more problems and projects in the field than do any of the other disciplines comprised by the alliance. Psychological research in cognitive science is responsible for the investigation of the nature of the embodiment of cognitive processes in human (or other animal) minds. In this volume two significant debates in the foundations of cognitive psychology are represented: that regarding the nature of the theory of perception and that regarding the nature of linguistic theory. Each, as are all of the debates addressed in this volume, and as is virtually every significant problem in the foundations of cognitive science, is intimately bound up with the nature and role of representation in cognition. The first debate is that between Gibsonian, or "Direct Perception" theorists and "orthodox" computationalist theorists. Direct Perception theorists urge that perception is to be understood as an immediate relation between an organism and its environment, where "immediate" means *unmediated by representations*. In particular, Direct Perception theorists argue that the mechanisms by means of which organisms interact perceptually with their environments do not involve computations defined over representations of distal objects, or of features of distal objects. Rather, they argue, information pertinent to action and cognition is "picked up" directly. The task of perceptual psychology, they urge, is to uncover those properties of an organism's environment and of the organism's perceptual/cognitive/motor apparatus in virtue of which these direct relations are made possible. In its thoroughgoing naturalism, this position has much in common with that adopted by other naturalists concerning representation (e.g., Garfield in this volume), though it is by no means the case either that all Direct Perception theorists are naturalists in that more general sense or that all naturalists subscribe to a Gibsonian theory of perception.

Against this view, many in cognitive science (including Fodor and Pylyshyn) argue that the very concept of direct perception is incoherent—that any account of the process by which information is acquired from the environment must make essential reference to representations. For, such opponents of direct perception argue, perception essentially involves a move by the organism from the detection of sensible properties of its environment to the knowledge that there are objects in the environment with particular properties. And such a move can only be understood as *inferential*. And inference only operates on propositional objects—that is on representations. So all perception must, these opponents argue, be representational, and in fact inferential—computational—in form.

While this debate over the status and role of representations in perception is different in many particular respects from the current debate over the status and role in linguistic performance of grammatical knowledge, these debates are recognizable cousins in outline. For Chomskyans (Chomsky and Katz in this volume) argue that grammatical rules are represented in the mind and are mobilized in the acquisition, understanding and production of language, and so that what a linguist studies—the *grammar* of languages—is in fact the structure and content of *knowledge*. Hence according to this view representations of rules are themselves necessary ingredients in the processing of language. Critics of this position (Stich in this volume) argue (on a variety of grounds) that this position gratuitously inserts a representation of rules into the explanation of linguistic performance. Such critics grant that grammars of the kind Chomskyans posit might accurately *describe* the output of linguistic processing. But, they argue, in virtue of the indefinitely many representationally distinct grammars that would do so, and in virtue of the fact that processes *described* by rules (*e.g*, the motion of the planets) are not necessarily *mediated by representations* of those rules, there is no warrant in the inference from the characterization of the grammar for a language (or even from the characterization of the grammatical form common to all languages) to the conclusion that such rules are represented in or mobilized by the mind in processing language. Debates such as that concerning the place of representations in human cognitive psychology, and of the role of the concept of representations or of computational models of processing in cognitive theory are among the most central in the foundations of cognitive science.

The entire constellation of foundational problems and debates we have surveyed revolves around the understanding of the role of representations in cognition. The most general of these problems, we noted, was the frame problem. As one surveys the most exciting recent developments in cognitive science—those that promise real theoretical revolution as opposed to advances within already well-understood paradigms—and as one considers the problems and prospects facing these new approaches, the significance of the frame problem as an impetus and as a possible obstacle emerges in stark relief. In the closing section of this collection, we encounter three such *prima facie* promising theoretical developments, and a general characterization of the difficulties they face. All are cast in terms of artificial intelligence models, but as artificial intelligence models of human cognitive performance that are inspired by epistemological models. They hence represent not only the theoretical frontiers of the science, but also the truly interdisciplinary character of research at the frontier.

The most direct assault on the frame problem (exemplified by Dyer's **BORIS**) involves the construction of a classical knowledge representation system that represents large bodies of real-world knowledge in a form sufficient to enable its retrieval and use at just the right time in on-line processing. The most ambitious and plausible attempts to date make use of the kinds of high-level meta-knowledge structures employed by **BORIS** to guide the system's use, revision, and representation of its base-level knowledge. Whether this form of direct assault will ultimately be successful it is too early to say, though Haugeland, in his essay, raises some significant *prima facie* problems for such approaches.

Since it is plausible that artificial intelligence systems with classical architectures are particularly subject to outbreaks of the frame problem in virtue of their commitment to the explicit representation of so much of the system's knowledge, and in virtue of the virtually unlimited scope of that knowledge, it is also plausible that a solution to the frame problem will require—instead of the enrichment of classical systems in **BORIS** fashion—that complete replacement of those architectures. That is the strategy proposed by Connectionism—a movement in cognitive science that has rapidly become one of the most active and controversial areas of current research. In connectionist systems, knowledge is not explicitly represented by particular data structures in memory, or by particular components of a stored program. Rather, all of the system's knowledge, and its capacities are "represented" holistically, in the dynamically varying activation levels and connection weights of the nodes and links of the connectionist network. In such systems, it is typically difficult—or perhaps impossible—to localize representation, to specify *exactly* the content of representations or to distinguish what is known from the program making use of knowledge. Much processing occurs in parallel. Connectionist systems are, of course, inspired by brain science, and connectionist architecture is in many ways strikingly similar to brain architecture (though there are many notable and perhaps crucial differences.)

One reason that some hope that connectionism will sidestep or solve the frame problem is just that: Brains don't suffer from the problem, and perhaps that is simply a consequence of their highly connected, continuous and dynamic architecture. A second reason for optimism derives from the "automatic" character of the spread of activation in connectionist networks, coupled with their capacity to "learn" and the simultaneity and diffuse character of connectivity in connectionist networks. The frame problem, one might say, arises just because a system must "know" what knowledge to activate next or which features of a situation to update, and which to leave alone; because it must have much of this knowledge "built-in"; and because of the fact that knowledge is typically organized in such a way that activation paths are serial and hierarchical in character. Connectionist systems suffer from none of these problems. Activation spreads in parallel, throughout much of the net in parallel, automatically, and has constant dynamic effects on the structure of the network, and consequently on the future patterns of activation diffusion. It is, of course, very much an open question whether such systems will in fact overcome the frame problem. But the evidence and the general theoretical considerations are suggestive.

A final approach to the frame problem—perhaps at the same time the most daunting and the most plausible—is to take seriously the line of argument proposed by Garfield and Haugeland and to adopt a thoroughly naturalistic approach to understanding representation and to modeling cognition. This approach in the domain of language processing is sketched by Winograd. All of these approaches are actively being pursued in cognitive science both by theorists of the foundations of cognitive science and by empirical and computational researchers. The frontiers are constantly moving, and the future shape of the field is hard to predict. But there are fruitful insights emerging from all quarters.

This volume provides only a glimpse of the questions being addressed and the debates being prosecuted in the foundations of cognitive science. And each question and debate represented is of necessity only partially represented. But I hope that this glimpse gives something of the character and shape of the field, exhibits the central role that the theory of representation has in cognitive science and in the foundations of cognitive science in particular, and encourages further reading and research.

PART ONE

CRITICAL
DISTINCTIONS

JAY L. GARFIELD

CONVENTION, CONTEXT, AND MEANING: CONDITIONS ON NATURAL LANGUAGE UNDERSTANDING

I

Convention—social agreement—determines linguistic meaning and practice at countless levels, including the fixation of lexical meaning; the adoption of particular syntactic options from among those permitted by universal grammar; the determination of politeness and felicity conditions; and most broadly, the determination of the character of the background of human activities and purposes against which most discourse takes place, and in the context of which it is intended to be interpreted. In assigning meaning to, or understanding, a particular utterance or inscription, it is frequently, if not always, the case that convention insinuates itself into the process at each of these levels, or so many philosophers of language and linguists have imagined. This view has, however, been recently challenged by theoreticians in the Artificial Intelligence (**AI**) community, who, under the banner of "Procedural Semantics" have argued, sometimes explicitly (Moore and Hendrix 1982, Miller and Johnson-Laird 1976), and sometimes merely implicitly (Winograd 1973) that the meanings of natural language expressions are to be identified with the computational procedures to which they give rise in successful artificial or biological interpreters, and that understanding an expression just constitutes executing the appropriate procedure in its presence. On this view, a language understander could be ignorant of and isolated from any social conventions ostensibly relevant to the semantics of the expressions upon which it operates.

The semantic ideology embodied by procedural semantics and the success of artificial intelligence research in understanding natural language have often been taken to be mutually supporting (see e.g., Winograd, op. cit., Fodor 1978). After all, if the meanings of words just are the programs they call, and if the compositional rules for computing the meanings of larger expressions just are rules for composing programs into larger programs, then, since computers are program runners and composers *par excellence*, there would be good reason to hope that computers could compute the meanings of any natural language expression. Conversely, if **AI** natural language understanding were successful, since that presumably requires the machines to represent the meanings of the expressions they understand, and since whatever machines represent is represented in *programs*, the meanings of words must be programs, and the compositional rules which operate on them must be rules for combining programs.

This semantic ideology receives further support, and perhaps in turn itself provides a buttress for the psychophysical ideology that currently dominates the cognitive science scene, from computational functionalism. According to this view, human psychological events, states, and processes are to be understood as (at least tokenly) identical to neurological events, states, and processes, related to them as the computational events, states, and processes of computing machines are related to their silicon substrata—roughly—as their functional characterizations. (The literature here is vast, and I don't propose to take a detour through discussions of the types, virtues, and vices of functionalist or computational models of mind. See Garfield 1983, 1985a, 1988, Burge 1979, 1982, 1987, Fodor 1981, Haugeland 1985, Lycan 1981, 1985, Searle 1980 for more discussion.) The link is provided by the intuition that if human psychological processes are at bottom computational, and if natural language understanding is a psychological process, it, too, must be computational. And, if to understand natural language is, *inter alia*, to represent meanings, then the representation of meaning must be simply a computational affair.

Now, despite these suggestive arguments, and despite the flourishing both of **AI** and of computational functionalism, few ideas have performed as much like lead balloons in the philosophical community as that of procedural semantics. Fodor (op cit.) sums up much of the (I think justified) criticism as follows:

. . . **PS** suffers from verificationism, operationalism, empiricism, reductionism, recidivism, atomism, compound fractures of the use/mention distinction, *hybris*, and a serious misunderstanding of how computers work. What, then, is *wrong* with **PS**? Basically that it confuses semantic theories with theories of sentence comprehension. (in 1981, p. 220)

(Much of what I have to say about **PS**, *per se*, follows Fodor's account. Much of what I have to say about major impediments to **AI** natural language understanding follows Haugeland's (1978, 1985) views. Any view for which *these* two can both be counted on for support *has* to be either right or incoherent, but at least unique.) Despite this criticism, however (or maybe because of it), **PS** (as well as other approaches that share with it the view that meanings are inner computational states or processes, and that understanding can hence be characterized without reference to human convention, and which for present purposes I lump together with it) is still alive and well in the **AI** community. So, I propose to take one more stab at it (and to draw some blood from functionalism on the backswing). But my sword will be double-edged. For while I will end up arguing both that **PS** and its cousins are misguided as semantic theories (though, following Fodor, not *necessarily* as psychological theory), and that there are principled problems posed for artificial natural language understanding systems by the role of convention in natural language semantics, I will also argue that though these problems may be *principled*, they are not insurmountable *in principle*. Moreover, I will argue, they do not issue in particular from the role of convention in *lexical* semantics, as has often been supposed (e.g., Tymoczko 1985) but rather from the complexity of the web of social conventions that forms the background for language understanding.

I will begin by discussing both the inadequacies of **PS** and its computational cousins as semantic theory, and its possible utility and even truth as psychological theory. In this context, I will argue that no merely computational facts about a system can constitute its understanding language, and that no computational procedures can constitute word meanings. But, I will argue that though what is required of such a system in order to enter such semantic epistemic states and to represent word meanings is its situation in a linguistic community, these facts constitute by themselves no grounds for believing that artificially intelligent computational systems are incapable of understanding natural language. For, I will argue, it may well be that the cognitive structures characterized by computational theories of language processing might themselves be what explains our capacity for citizenship in such a community.

However, I will argue, the prospects for artificial language understanders this argument suggests may not be as rosy as these considerations might lead one to believe. For, as philosophers from Heidegger to Haugeland have argued, and as recent developments in semantics—particularly, though not exclusively, in situation semantics (Barwise & Perry 1984)—have indicated, successful natural language understanding, and successful semantic algorithms, would require a solution to the infamous frame problem. And that, I will suggest, when properly generalized, just is the problem of constructing a machine fit not merely for language understanding, or for membership in a linguistic community, but one fit for human understanding, and for membership in the human community generally. The achievement of Artificial Intelligence in the full sense hence may require the achievement of artificial humanity, or artificial citizenship in the community of persons.

Finally, I will suggest that the difficulties that attend such a Herculean task can be understood as issuing in part from the essentially relational, contextual, and in part socially constituted nature of human psychological process generally. Seen in this light, I will claim, the open-ended nature of the enterprise of artifical natural language understanding is merely a special case of the open-ended nature of the enterprise of artificial intelligence generally, and this open-endedness is a consequence of the seamlessness of the web of natural and social, conventional and immutable, perceptual and meaning-inducing, relations into which intelligent organisms and systems must be located in order to manifest intelligence and understanding.

II

There is no great trick to demonstrating that the meaning of an expression cannot be identified with the internal procedures (whether computational, neurochemical, or magical) that it triggers, or that are, in some psychological sense, responsible for its comprehension. For we can certainly construct pairs of expressions which are interpreted in a computing system by means of procedures identical at a machine language level, but whose meanings, as determined by the larger contexts in which they occur, are quite different. Fodor and Rey (Fodor, op. cit.) have put this point nicely by pointing out that portions of a computer chess playing program and of a computer simulation of the Six Day War might receive identical machine language interpretations, which in the one case would interpret an expression whose meaning is that white's knight is under attack by black's pawn, and in the other that an Egyptian tank division is surrounded by Israeli infantry. Arguing in the opposite direction, we do not hold an expression to be indefinitely many ways ambiguous on the grounds that there are indefinitely many (perhaps isomorphic, in some sense) procedures that might successfully interpret it, or because there are a number of different psychological mechanisms that might account for our understanding it.

This is, of course, the by now shopworn point of Putnam (1975), *viz.*, that "meanings ain't in the head" (and, of course, made in different ways and in different contexts by Burge, op. cit., Wittgenstein 1958, Sellars 1956, and Kripke 1982 among others). Meanings are public entities, fixed by the conventions of the communities in which the expressions whose meanings they are not used. Some (e.g., Searle 1981, Tymoczko 1985) have inferred from the conventionality and communitistic character of meaning in this sense that artificial intelligence is not possible, since whatever representations are processed, constructed, or stored in a computing machine are, *ipso facto*, internal to that machine, and hence, presumably, hermetically sealed from the communities that alone could give them meaning. I will, in a moment, argue that this inference, an apparent cousin to the Private Language Argument, is fallacious.

But first, we need to ask what the considerable grain of truth in procedural theories of meaning is. When a meaning is grasped, when an expression is understood, *something* is going on in the head, and what is more, something connected in some way with that expression's meaning. And, if anything like contemporary cognitive theories of language comprehension are correct, that something is a complex computation. If that is so, then regardless of *what else* is going on, in or out of our heads, we might expect a successful language *processing theory*, e.g., like those envisioned by procedural semantics, to specify the appropriate interpretive algorithms designated (in the technical sense), or called by, particular expressions, or perhaps expression types, of natural language. And indeed, this is the goal of much important and productive research in computational psycholinguistics (see, e.g., Johnson-Laird 1983, Garfield 1987).

But it is important to see that even if we had such a language processing theory (and that is a very big "if," since there is not, nor has there ever been claimed to be, any sense in which the possibility of **PS** is *a priori* true, and since the best worked out theories along these lines are as yet both embryonic and difficulty-plagued), it would in no sense be a *semantic* theory. For while such a theory might tell us a good deal about how an organism (or a machine implementing the same set of algorithms) performs the processing tasks that are necessary for connecting linguistic tokens to their meanings, those processes themselves cannot, for the reasons discussed above, *themselves be* those meanings. At least some of us, even philosophers, talk about more than our own cognitive processes. The task of semantic theory, however the details are conceptualized, is to identify and characterize the objects associated as semantic values with linguistic items, and not merely, or even necessarily, to characterize the cognitive processes responsible for our grasping those semantic objects in the course of language processing.

Now, this impossibility of any theory that mentions only processes internal to a computational system to encompass a theory of meaning, and hence to provide a *complete* account of language understanding, has been taken by some to imply, together with the observation that the reason for this impossibilty has to do with the public, conventional, external nature of meanings, that no machine will ever understand language in the sense that we do (and that is the sense that is interesting, at least to a metaphysician, ethicist, or epistemologist). There is, of course, a further premise needed to raise this argument to the level of plausibility: All that there is to a complete theory of a machine—all that is of interest to it, *qua* computing device—is a specification of its internal workings, whether these be computationally or physically characterized. For if this premise is granted, and if no theory that adverts only to such internal processes could encompass a semantic theory, and if understanding language requires representing, or at least being connected in *some* epistemically interesting way to the meanings of the linguistic expressions understood, then there can be no theory of machine understanding. Hence any language understanding machine must be either magical or nonexistent.

But this argument is too powerful for comfort. For the same considerations would seem to apply, *mutatis mutandis*, to humans. For, assuming that there is some correct story of the internal processes that make our language comprehension possible, then insofar as this psychological story cannot encompass a semantic theory, and insofar as only our internal workings are of interest to it, such a theory would leave our language understanding unexplained, mysterious, magical. But that, to quote R. M. Nixon, would be wrong.

The difficulty is easy to pinpoint: There is far more of interest to any story about our language understanding than the specifications of the internal processing that *underlies the possibility of our entering into* the collectively constituted activity of speaking and understanding a natural language. For such processing is only of interest at all insofar as it underlies and makes possible our situation in this complex, conventionally instituted web of relations to our environment; our fellows; and the linguistic conventions themselves that govern our native tongue. Understanding our understanding hence requires not only an account of the nature of the sophisticated processing that makes this situation possible, but of the situation itself as well.

But when the difficulty is put in this way, it is clear that it exonerates machines, as well, of this particular charge of principled aphasia. For, supposing that they can be imbued with the same psycholinguistic procedures as yet to be discovered in us, then if the essential *privacy* (in the Wittgensteinian sense) of those processes in *us* does not issue in the impossibility of *our* participating in *our* linguistic community in large part in virtue of those processes, then there would seem to be no reason why it should issue in such impossibility in the case of the machines.

This conclusion is important for our present enterprise, for it means that the argument from the conventional nature of linguistic meaning and the nonconventional nature of machine language *processing* does not entail that machines cannot understand language, precisely because a theory of processing is only one component of a theory of understanding, one which stands in need of a semantically informed theory of the connection of that processing to public linguistic behavior and meaning in order to be complete. (This is the *real* point of the Private Language Argument.) And this is an augmentation no more problematic *in principle* for machines than for humans.

III

So far, I have defended the artificial intelligentsia against an attack on their enterprise grounded in the ineliminable conventionality of language. I now wish to raise what I see as the real threat from this quarter to the enterprise of artificial natural-language understanding.

To understand a language is to be, at least in a minimal sense, a member of a community of users of that language. One way of putting the problem that confronts us now, as we consider just what it would take for a machine to gain entrance into this community, is this: Can one join in a merely minimal sense? Could a machine, for instance, be a "language processing specialist," where by "language processing" we mean something like genuine understanding? I will argue that this question must be answered in the negative, for two reasons, one suggested by Haugeland (op. cit.), and one which has more directly to do with the nature of the conventions which determine the interpretations of linguistic expressions themselves.

Understanding language requires us to make use of a tremendous amount of general knowledge, or commonsense, in order to provide the interpretations for expressions we hear or read. So, for instance, examples like Haugeland's

(1) She put the raincoat in the bathtub because **it** was wet.

or Minsky's

(2) "He already has a kite. He will make you take **it** back."

(said to a child contemplating giving a kite as a birthday present) show that almost *any* item of general knowledge can become relevant at almost any point in a discourse to fixing the correct interpretation of such lexical items as pronouns, whose interpretation *must* be fixed if we are to understand. This, of course, is just the frame problem—the problem of how to organize knowledge about the world in such a way that the right bits are available when they are needed without an exhaustive or horrendously inefficient search of the listener's knowledge base. The frame problem is hard. It is the major stumbling block to progress in artificial intelligence of the philosophically interesting kind. It is, perhaps, the central problem of contemporary epistemology in the context of cognitive science. So far, we haven't a clue concerning what a solution to it would look like, or even whether there is a solution. (except that we know that *people* either don't suffer from it to anywhere near the degree that machines do, or, in other words, that, for most practical purposes, *we* have solved it.)

But there is another problem, perhaps best conceived of as a generalization of the frame problem, which derives directly from the nature of social convention, and the situation of linguistic conventions in their more general social context. Consideration of this larger problem may well shed light on the puzzling fact that whereas the frame problem is staggeringly difficult for current artificially intelligent machines, it isn't even noticed by naturally intelligent persons. The kernel of the generalized problem I have in mind is just this: Linguistic conventions do not comprise a set of neatly encapsulated practices. They cannot be carved off at any natural joint from the vast body of other social conventions. Just as at least extragrammatical linguistic knowledge—a major part of the knowledge required in order to *understand* language—cannot be segregated from all of the rest of our knowledge, issuing in the frame problem, linguistic convention—the set of conventions that determine the interpretation and use of linguistic expressions in communication—cannot be segregated from other human conventions. If this is so, then we might expect that just as a solution to the frame problem would involve the development of a knowledge representation system capable of representing all of the knowledge of a typical person, a solution to the generalized frame problem would involve the development of a machine capable of participating in an equally wide range of human conventions.

I said a moment ago that consideration of the generalized frame problem might shed some light on the ease with which persons surmount the frame problem as it arises in knowledge representation. What I had in mind was this: If our model of knowledge representation is constrained by the image of the computing machine, we think of knowledge as the kind of thing either explicitly represented in a data base, or derivable by an "inference engine" from what is already explicitly represented. When knowledge is conceived in this fashion, the frame problem forces us to ask how we could either construct and organize a data base vast and efficient enough to facilitate language understanding, or how we could build an inference engine clever and fast enough to operate on a more limited data base.

But if we cast our gaze not at machines, but instead at persons, we cannot help but be confronted by the possibility that much of what counts as our knowledge is not in any sense explicitly represented belief, let alone justified true belief. It rather appears to emerge from a network of adaptive habits, tendencies, and skills, which, together with what *is* explicitly represented, and together with our inferential mechanisms, enable us to function in our social and physical environments. Though this point is by no means entirely clear or anywhere near settled empirically, it is at least highly plausible that we "know" that a raincoat's being wet is a good reason to put it into a bathtub, but that a bathtub's being wet is a lousy reason to put a raincoat in it, *ceteris paribus*, probably without explicitly representing these facts, or any others from which we could derive them using an inference engine in real time. (I have no idea what the correct account might be of the behavioral, social, and biological underpinnings of our commonsense knowledge, but it is important to note that there is no evidence—either *a priori* or empirical—that should convince one that explicit declarative representation and logical inference are the only available options. There are, of course, affinities here to points made by Dreyfuss [1980] and, of course, Heidegger.)

But this has been somewhat of a digression. I now wish to sketch what I have called the generalized frame problem—the problem posed for those who would construct an artificial language understander by the inextricability of linguistic convention from other social conventions. In the discussion above of the place of procedural models of language understanding in the general enterprise of the explanation of linguistic activity, I was at pains to make two points: (1) what goes on *inside* a language understander may explain its *capacity to enter into and to conform to public conventions,* but, (2) any explanation of its linguistic activity *as meaningful* must advert to its participating in those conventions, regardless of *how it does this.* Now whereas the frame problem is a problem about what additional *knowledge* must be represented in order to mobilize successfully any specifically *linguistic* knowledge, the generalized frame problem is a problem about what additional *conventions* must be entered into in order to enter into any specifically *linguistic* conventions. Just as the answer to the central question posed by the frame problem seems to be "a vast and indefinitely large and complex body of knowledge," the answer to the central question posed by the generalized frame problem, I now want to suggest is "a vast and indefinitely complex web of social conventions."

Consider, for instance, what is surely among the most mundane uses of language, and attend not to the knowledge one would have to represent in order to produce "mental models" of the assertions made in such a context, but rather the conventions into which one would have to enter in order to participate in it, *viz.,* small talk at a Five College bus stop. The participants are a certain Professor Smith and a student, Mary.

SMITH: Lovely fall day, isn't it?

MARY: Yes, it is, Professor Smith.

SMITH: How are your classes going this year? Besides my **AI** course, I don't know what you're taking.

MARY: Well, of course I just love **AI**, especially writing that wonderful program for translating **BASIC** into **FORTRAN**. I think I see what you mean when you say we can just change a few parameters, add a dictionary, and turn it into an automatic Russian-English translator. Too bad we won't get to that part of the course.

SMITH: Yeah. But you know, except for you and maybe a few others, the students in the course just couldn't handle it. Well, here's my bus.

There are certainly some at least *prima facie* specifically linguistic conventions that Smith and Mary must enter in order to make this conversation, considered as a conversation, possible: They must adhere to the lexical semantic rules governing the words they use; they must use English syntax, and so forth. But these conventions alone will not suffice to explain the significance of their linguistic behavior. For the topic of the conversation is not, and arguably doesn't even include, in any interesting sense, meteorology. Smith's opening line, and Mary's reply, while sensitive in some respects to the weather (they would have been different in a downpour) are properly understood as "openers," and in order to "Get them right," the rules of American college small talk, and facts about relative status are relevant, though these are not explicitly mentioned (Smith doesn't use Mary's name, and if s/he did, it would be her first name; Mary uses "Professor Smith.") Or consider Smith's polite question about Mary's academic schedule, which Mary answers, quite satisfactorily, by praising Smith's course. One has a strong intuition that participating in this conversation does not require one to constantly change from topic to topic—from the weather to Mary's schedule, to Smith's course, to the oncoming bus. Rather the entire conversation is governed by a more or less unitary, seamless set of conventions regarding academic status, bus stops, small talk, and so forth. Participating in such conversations, which in this respect are typical of human communicative interactions—in the sense of understanding one's interlocutors' comments in any more than a trivial sense—and contributing to one appropriately—not merely, or even necessarily, truthfully—requires participation in this broader range of conventions as well as in the *simply* linguistic conventions governing the use of the expressions comprised by conversations.

There are two senses of "understanding" at work here. I am arguing that even if the difficulties posed by the frame problem as it arises in the context of knowledge representation were surmounted, and hence understanding of discourses in the more limited sense were achieved, the generalized frame problem would stand as a barrier to understanding in the second sense, which is what gives human communication its point. To understand a discourse in the first, more limited sense, is, roughly, to create a model of the assertions made in the discourse, as well as perhaps to construct the analogous model-theoretic entities corresponding to commands, questions, and so forth. So, for instance, a system that understood Mary's and Smith's conversation would represent the facts that the weather is lovely, that Smith is a professor and Mary a student, that Smith doesn't know what courses Mary is taking, that Mary loves **AI**, etc. To be sure, to achieve artificial discourse understanding in this sense would be no mean feat, and would require the construction of a remarkable knowledge representation system. (This is the kind of understanding that is the partially achieved goal of the programs of Schank

[1977] and Lehnert [1983], among others, and it is important to note the amount of knowledge required in order to drive this kind of system.) But even if it were achieved, understanding in the full sense would not thereby be achieved.

To understand in the second sense, and that more relevant to the purposes of human language, is to respond not only to the information contained directly by (suitably disambiguated) utterances comprised by the discourse, but also to that which is not asserted, but which is implied by the social context and relevant conventions that define the framework within which the discourse occurs, and which contribute to the information conveyed and received by its participants, information that is often even at odds with what is explicitly asserted or literally implied by even central utterances. It involves attention to implicature, presumed motives, stereotyped interactions, etiquette, and an unending web of similar nonlinguistic facts that nonetheless determine the significance of the linguistic events to be understood. It is this kind of understanding (hinted at by Haugeland [op. cit.] in his discussion of "existential holism" that humans achieve, and which arises from their participation in this web of meaning-inducing conventions, of which linguistic conventions are but a small, albeit crucial, and inextricable part.

To make this point in a somewhat different way, consider what it would be for a (possibly human) language processing system to carry on such a conversation guided only by a suitably powerful knowledge representation system and a grammar for the language in which the conversation is taking place, but not participating in any extralinguistic social conventions. It would have to *make small talk*—for this is a description satisfied by this and similar conversations, and one under which they arguably fall (or similar in the relevant respects to descriptions under which they fall) for social-scientific explanatory purposes—without conforming to the conventions governing that practice. It would have to be *polite*, without observing the conventions of etiquette, and on and on. These strike one immediately as conceptual impossibilities, and it is important to note that *these* conventions govern far more than specifically linguistic behavior. Conforming to them involves conforming a broad range of one's behavior to the norms they embody. And finally, such a language understanding system would have to understand its interlocutor's contributions, guided as they are by these conventions, without itself participating in them.

This point may be obvious (though it is easily obscured by too much attention to discourses comprising a single declarative sentence uttered by no one in particular to no one in particular, and whose sole point is to illustrate a semantic, computational, or psychological theory.) But its implications for natural language understanding are significant. The point is not that it is impossible in principle for a machine to participate in the full range of human social conventions, and therefore impossible for one to achieve genuine natural language understanding. (As Searle [1981] in an otherwise highly problematic article has pointed out, *we* are such machines, and *we* understand natural language.) Surely, systems capable of whatever internal processes make possible our entrance into this rich web of convention are at least in principle capable of manufacture. (They are not, however, for this reason, *a priori* possible to realize in digital silicon-based computers, though they might turn out to be in fact realizable in such devices. Of course, we are already acquainted with one way to manufacture such machines: human reproduction and child rearing. But it is an expensive, unreliable, and time-consuming approach.)

Instead, the point is that the creation of a machine capable of entering this entire web of convention is a necessary condition of creating one capable of entering into specifically linguistic convention. This is just so because of the seamless nature of human social convention, and the interpenetration of *prima facie* nonlinguistic conventions into the realm of natural language understanding in the full sense—*viz.*, representing not simply the truth-conditions of the declarative sentences occurring in the utterance, but the full range of information conveyed by declaration, by implication, and by implicature, where the unspoken premises that mediate these implications and quasi-implications derive from the larger human situations, goals, purposes, and propensities, in the contexts of which discourse occurs. Again, I am not arguing that it is impossible to achieve a knowledge representation and utilization system capable of this full range of language understanding. Rather, I am arguing that simply achieving the incredibly difficult task of representing the necessary commonsense knowledge about the world in a way which would surmount the frame problem would be insufficient. In addition, sufficient information to guide the participation in a full range of human intellectual and cultural conventions would be necessary. For it is only in this context that much language is meaningful at all.

IV

Up to now, I have been grounding an argument for the extreme difficulty of achieving artificial natural language understanding on observations about the nature of the information and background of practices that render language intelligible. I now want to get at the same conclusion from a slightly different perspective, in the hope that this binocular vision will grant a better view of the nature of the intelligence we are trying to achieve. An important fact about understanding language, though one easy to overlook when the questions in the foreground are primarily semantic, is that language processing is realized through a number of psychological events, states, and processes, including such things as belief, knowledge, inference, and the like, and that inasmuch as a language understander will be, *ipso facto* a subject of such phenomena, the necessary conditions of such subjectivity will also be necessary conditions on language understanding, at least of the philosophically interesting kind.

I now want to argue that these psychological properties, essential to natural language understanding, like such apparently nonlinguistic properties as moral properties, are acquired in virtue of the relations an organism or machine bears to a community of which is a member, and hence that any account of the psychology, including the psycholinguistics, of an organism which fails to take note of this social context, will be inadequate. That is, I want to suggest, that we can argue for the necessity of the general participation of a language understander in a social-linguistic community not only on semantic grounds, but on metapsychological grounds as well.

Corporations are persons for some purposes—they can make contracts, be sued, prosecuted, hold property, etc.—and nonpersons for others—they can't be the objects of homicide, they can be bought and sold, they can't leave wills, they can't vote; since *Roe v. Wade*, fetuses are not recognized to be persons in American law; but postviable fetuses may, in some jurisdictions, receive many of the same protections accorded to persons; in some cultures slaves have duties but no rights; in ours, infants and the deranged have numerous rights but no duties. Dead people can't vote, but they certainly have rights over the dispositions of their property.

The dead are particularly interesting. They have moral and legal rights, such as testamentary rights. But they are neither intelligent nor conscious. And it would be folly to assert that anything psychologically or behaviorally equivalent to a dead person, despite vast chemical differences (say a rock or a junked computer) was entitled to the same moral protection.

Why are the dead accorded such significant moral standing? Surely it has nothing to do with their computational capacities. To make what is a very long story very brief, it has to do with the complex and rather important ways in which the dead are connected to our social community, and to the interests the dead have in virtue of the interests they had when they were alive, and that we all have in matters after our deaths. Similarly, other borderline cases, such as very young children, corporations, and so forth, get their moral standing in virtue of their interests, capacities for benefit and suffering, and for action, and—in short—in virtue of their role in the community in which moral and personal predicates figure.

Just as we all, fully fledged persons, machines with genuine personality, and the Martians, acquire what social, moral, and epistemic standing we have in virtue of (1) our interests and (2) community relationships, which in our cases, of course, are quite substantial, we acquire, as I shall argue in a moment, our *psychological*, or *intentional* standing in virtue of such relationships, interests, and connections to our environment. This claim about what is relevant to personhood or psychological standing is noncommittal about the relevance of physical composition or computational complexity to the achievement of such interests and connections. As cognitive scientists have correctly emphasized, in typical cases a fair amount of complexity is required and is sufficient in order to have the right sorts of interests and community relationships. But relevant exceptional cases include wildly complex and successful, but hopelessly narrow in- and non-human, "expert systems"; severely intellectually handicapped humans; and, of course, the dead.

It is now time to note the most important consequence of the conventional nature of language and other social behavior, and the seamlessness of the conventional, *viz.*, that psychological states cannot be understood, or ascribed in isolation from the social, ecological, and linguistic contexts of their realizing tokens. Tokens that are internally identical, but relationally distinct, can differ significantly with respect to their psychological and semantic character. Every belief is a belief **that p,** for some **p.** Hence any belief, *qua* belief, is a *meaningful* state of its subject. In ascribing a belief that **p** to a candidate believer (including myself) I am *interpreting* its physical state, much as in ascribing significance to ancient marks on a stone, I am interpreting the physical state of the stone. But for a state, or an object, to have a meaning, as opposed to a characteristic cause or effect, is for it to play a particular role in a system of other such meaningful states and objects, manipulated according to rules that determine its meaning (as much as meaning can be determined). Compare for instance the meaningfulness of an inscription of "Harriet Loves Harry" written on a blackboard with the meaninglessness of an arbitrarily selected group of hydrogen atoms scattered across interstellar space, which happen to form the same shape, 45 light-years across, or compare the difference between the significance of the move of a knight on a chessboard when performed by a human chess player in a game, with the lack of significance of that same physical alteration when produced by a crow in the park (See De Vries and Garfield, Op. cit.) This is a point that has been made forcefully by such philosophers as Wittgenstein and Sellars, among others.

Hence having a belief in the sense in which *genuinely* intelligent creatures possess their beliefs requires one's situation in a community of language users. For to have a belief is to be in a state that plays a particular semantic role in that community and its linguistic practices. A belief is an element in a rule-governed symbolic system, and hence neither merely a state that, *were* it to be embedded in such a system in an appropriate way, *would* be a belief of a particular sort, as in the movement of a chess piece across a board, nor a state with characteristic causes and effects, which can hence serve to indicate them, regardless of the obtaining of any social conventions, like lightning, which "means" thunder.

To understand our psychological states hence essentially involves understanding the epistemological and linguistic communities to which we belong, their conventions, and the relations we bear to them. To attribute intelligence or psychological states to an organism or to a machine is to situate it appropriately relative to an epistemic and linguistic community. Just as in the case of moral standing, there may be gradations of intellectual standing. But just as in the case of moral standing, whatever intellectual standing we attribute to an organism must be a function not of its computational capacity or complexity *per se*, but of the relations in which it stands to the appropriate semantic environment. Of course, certain computational capacities are generally required, and are often sufficient, in order to be so situated in moral and epistemic communities. It is not, however, in virtue of these capacities that we have the psychological and moral properties we do, but rather in virtue of our situation in the communities into which these capacities allow us entrance.

This is not to say that only *Homo sapiens* is eligible for membership in epistemic and moral communities—that only we can think and have rights— that computing machines will never be eligible. That would indeed be human chauvinism. It is to say, however, that what matters most directly for moral standing and psychological capacity is not any feature of any organism or machine *per se*. No account that pays attention *only* to the computational complexity and capacity of the individual organism or machine to the neglect of its natural, cultural, conventional, and epistemic environment can possibly capture what is important about intelligence, thought, or moral personhood.

The frame problem is this: In understanding natural language, any old piece of commonsense knowledge, contained in any old "knowledge representation frame" might become relevant at any moment, and so there is no obvious way to implement or to activate selectively some limited portion of knowledge about the world without simultaneously dragging in everything else, and choking the system on its own data. The generalized frame problem, then, is this: In participating in the conventions requisite for understanding and producing language, any old social convention might come to govern our behavior or inform our understanding at any moment, and so there is no obvious way to construct a language user that implements or activates selectively some subset of human conventions. But if this is so, then to construct a language user, to achieve artificial intelligence, is to construct a person, an artificial citizen. While this is not in principle impossible, recognizing this strong necessary condition for true artificial intelligence may cause optimists in the **AI** community to revise upward their estimation of the difficulty of the task.

ZENON W. PYLYSHYN

COMPUTATION AND COGNITION: ISSUES IN THE FOUNDATIONS OF COGNITIVE SCIENCE

1. INTRODUCTION AND SUMMARY

The view that cognition can be understood as computation is ubiquitous in modern cognitive theorizing, even among those who do not use computer programs to express models of cognitive processes. One of the basic assumptions behind this approach, sometimes referred to as "information processing psychology," is that cognitive processes can be understood in terms of formal operations carried out on symbol structures. It thus represents a formalist approach to theoretical explanation. In practice, tokens of symbol structures may be depicted as expressions written in some lexicographic notation (as is usual in linguistics or mathematics), or they may be physically instantiated in a computer as a data structure or an executable program.

The "information processing" idiom has been with us for about two decades and represents a substantial intellectual commitment among students of cognition. The fields that share this view (notably, segments of linguistics, philosophy of mind, psychology, artificial intelligence, cultural anthropology, and others) have been increasingly looking toward some convergence as the "cognitive sciences." Several journals devoted to that topic now exist (including, to some extent, BBS), and a Cognitive Science Society has just been formed. There remains, however, considerable uncertainty regarding precisely what constitutes the core of the approach and what constraints it imposes on theory construction.

In this essay I shall present what I consider some of the crucial characteristics of the computational view of mind and defend them as appropriate for the task of explaining cognition. As in the early stages of many scientific endeavors, the core of the approach is implicit in scientists' intuitions about what are to count as relevant phenomena and as legitimate explanations of the underlying processes. Yet as we tease out the central assumptions, we will find room for refinement: not everything that is intuitively cognitive will remain so as the theory develops, nor will all processes turn out to be appropriate for explaining cognitive phenomena.

We begin with an informal discussion of the position that certain types of human behavior are determined by *representations* (beliefs, tacit knowledge, goals, and so on). This, we suggest, is precisely what recommends the view that mental activity is computational. Then we present one of the main empirical claims of the approach—namely, that there is a natural domain of inquiry that can be addressed at a privileged *algorithmic* level of analysis, or with a proprietary vocabulary.

The remainder of the paper elaborates various requirements for constructing adequate explanatory theories on this basis. First, however, we need to analyse the notions of "cognitive phenomenon" and "cognitive process" in the light of the evolving understanding of cognition as computation. Hence we take a detour in our discussion (sections 5 and 6) to examine the fundamental distinction between 1) behavior governed by rules and representations, and 2) behavior that is merely the result of the causal structure of the underlying biological system. A primary goal of the paper is to defend this as a principled distinction, and to propose a necessary (though not sufficient) empirical criterion for it. This methodological criterion (called the *cognitive impenetrability condition*) supports the maxim that to be explanatory, a theoretical account should make a *principled* appeal to a computational model. Exhibiting an algorithm and a representative sample of its behavior is not enough. One must, in addition, separate and independently justify two sources of its performance: its fixed (cognitively impenetrable) functional capacities (or its "functional architecture"), and the "effectiveness principles" underlying its capacity to perform as claimed.

2. THE COGNITIVE VOCABULARY AND FOLK PSYCHOLOGY

Most people implicitly hold a sophisticated and highly successful cognitive theory; that is, they can systematize, make sense of, and correctly predict an enormous range of human behavior. Although textbook authors are fond of pointing out the errors in folk psychology, it nonetheless far surpasses any current scientific psychology in scope and general accuracy. What is significant about this is the mentalistic vocabulary, or level of description, of folk psychology, and its corresponding taxonomy of things, behaviors, events, and so on.

Whatever the shortcomings of folk psychology (and there are plenty, to be sure), the level of abstractness of its concepts (relative to those of physics), and particularly its appeal to the way situations are *represented in the mind* (i.e., its appeal to what human agents think, believe, infer, want, and so on, as opposed to the way they actually are), seems precisely suited to capturing just the kinds of generalizations that concern cognitive psychology—e.g., the nature of our intellectual abilities, the mechanisms underlying intellectual performances, and the causal and rational antecedents of our actions.

It seems overwhelmingly likely that explanations of cognitive phenomena will have to appeal to beliefs, intentions, and the like, because it appears that certain regularities in human behavior can only be captured in such terms and at that level of abstraction. For example, when a person perceives danger, he will generally set about to remove himself from the source of that danger. Now, this generalization has an unlimited variety of instances. Thus, generally, if a person *knows* how to get out of a building, and *believes* the building to be on fire, then generally he will set himself the *goal* of being out of the building, and use his knowledge to determine a series of actions to satisfy this goal. The point is that even so simple a regularity could not be captured without descriptions that use the italicized mentalistic terms (or very similar ones), because there is an infinite variety of specific ways of "knowing how to get out of the building," of coming to "believe that the building is on fire," and of satisfying the goal of being out of the building. For each combination of these, *an entirely different causal chain* would result if the situation were described in physical or strictly behavioral terms. Consequently the psychologically relevant generalization would be lost in the diversity of possible causal connections. This generalization can only be stated in terms of the agent's *internal representation* of the situation (i.e., in mentalistic terms). For a different example, the laws of color mixture are properly stated over *perceived color*, or what are called "metameric" equivalence classes of colors, rather than over physically specifiable properties of light, since they hold regardless of how the particular color is produced by the environment—e.g., whether, say, the perceived yellow is produced by radiation of (roughly) 580 nm, a mixture of approximately equal energy of radiations of 530 nm and 650 nm, by a mixture of any complex radiations that metamerically match the latter two wavelengths, or even by direct electrical or chemical stimulation of the visual system. We might never be able to specify all the possible physical stimuli that produce a particular perceived color, and yet the laws of color mixture shall hold if stated over perceived color. Hochberg (1968) presents a variety of such examples, showing that the regularities of perception must be stated over *perceived* properties—i.e., over internal representations.

Similarly, when a particular event can be given more than one interpretation, then what determines behavioral regularities is not its physical properties, or even some abstract function thereof, but rather each agent's particular *interpretation*. The classical illustrations are ambiguous stimuli, such as the Necker cube, the duck-rabbit or the profiles-vase illusions, or ambiguous sentences. Clearly, what people do (e.g., when asked what they see or hear) depends upon which reading of the ambiguity they take. But all physical events are intrinsically ambiguous, in the sense that they are subject to various interpretations; so psychological regularities will always have to be stated relative to particular readings of stimuli (i.e., how they are internally represented).

Finally, if we include *goals* as well as beliefs among the types of representations, it becomes possible to give an account of a wide range of additional regularities. Behavior that is goal-directed is characterized by such properties as equifinality (i.e., its termination can only be characterized in terms of the terminating state, rather than in terms of the path by which the system arrived at that state—see the discussion in Newell and Simon 1972).

It is no accident that the systematicity of human behavior is captured in a vocabulary that refers to internal representations, for these are the terms in which we conceptualize and plan our actions in the first place. For example, as I write this paper, I produce certain movements of my fingers and hand. But I do that under control of certain higher level goals, or, as some people prefer to put it, I execute the behaviors under a certain "intended interpretation." I *intend* to make certain *statements* by my behavior. I do not intend to make marks on paper, although clearly I am doing that too. Although this hierarchical aspect of the behavioral description is part of my conceptualization of it, rather than an intrinsic part of the behavior itself, yet it is critical to how the behavior must be treated theoretically if the theory is to capture the systematicity of my actions. A theory that took my behavior to be an instance of finger movement could not account for why, when my typewriter broke, I proceeded to make quite different movements using pencil and paper. This is an instance of the "equifinality" property associated with goal-directed behavior.

Of course, to say that folk psychology has nonfortuitously settled on some of the appropriate terms for describing our cognitive activity is not to say that it is good scientific theory. It may be that this set of terms needs to be augmented or pruned, that many of the beliefs expressed in folk psychology are either false or empirically empty, and that many of its explanations are either incomplete or circular. But its most serious shortcoming, from the point of view of the scientific enterprise, is that the collection of loose generalizations that makes up this informal body of knowledge is not tied together into an explicit system. The way in which sets of generalizations are tied together in developed sciences is through a theory that shows how the generalizations are derivable in some appropriate idealization from a smaller set of deeper universal principles (or axioms). The categories of the deeper principles are typically quite different from those found in the broader generalization (e.g., pressure and temperature are reduced to aspects of kinetic energy in molecular theory.)

3. REPRESENTATION AND COMPUTATION

There are many characteristics that recommend computation as the appropriate form in which to cast models of cognitive processes. I have discussed some of them in Pylyshyn (1978a). For example, the hierarchical character of programs and the abstraction represented by the "information processing" level of analysis make it the ideal vehicle for expressing *functional* models of all kinds. These were the aspects of computation that led Miller, Galanter, and Pribram (1960) to propose the basic iterative loop (TOTE, or Test-Operative-Test-Exit) as the fundamental building block for psychological theory—to replace the reflex arc and even the cybernetic energy feedback loop.

What I wish to focus on here is what I take to be the most fundamental reason why cognition ought to be viewed as computation. That reason rests on the fact that computation is the only worked-out view of *process* that is both compatible with a materialist view of how a process is realized and that attributes the behavior of the process to the operation of rules upon representations. In other words, what makes it possible to view computation and cognition as processes of fundamentally the same type is the fact that both are physically realized and both are governed by rules and representations. Furthermore, they both exhibit the same sort of dual character with respect to providing explanations of how they work—and for the same reason.

As a physical device, the operation of a computer can be described in terms of the causal structure of its physical properties. The states of a computer, viewed as a physical device, are individuated in terms of the identity of physical descriptions, and its state transitions are therefore connected by physical laws. By abstracting over these physical properties, it is possible to give a *functional* description of the device. This is a description of the systematic relations that hold over certain (typically very complex) classes of physical properties—such as the ones that correspond to computationally relevant states of the device. While the transitions over states defined in this way are no longer instances of physical laws (i.e., there is no *law* relating state n and state m of an IBM machine, even though it is wired up so that state m always follows state n), they are nonetheless reducible to some complex function of various physical laws and of the physical properties of states n and m. Such a functional description of the device might, for example, be summarized as a finite state transition diagram of the sort familiar in automata theory. We shall see below, however, that this is not an adequate functional description from the point of view of understanding the device as a computer.

On the other hand, if we wish to explain the computation that the device is carrying out, or the regularities exhibited by some particular *programmed* computer, we must refer to objects in a domain that is the *intended interpre-*

tation or the subject matter of the computations, such as, for example, the abstract domain of numbers. Thus, in order to explain why the machine prints out the symbol "5" when it is provided with the expression "(PLUS 2 3)," we must refer to the meaning of the symbols in the expression and in the printout. These meanings are the referents of the symbols in the domain of numbers. The explanation of why the particular symbol "5" is printed out then follows from these semantic definitions (i.e., it prints out "5" because that symbol represents the number five, "PLUS" represents the addition operator applied to the referents of the other two symbols, etc. and five is indeed the sum of two and three). In other words, from the definition of the symbols (numerals) as representations of numbers, and from the definition of the "PLUS" as representing a certain abstract mathematical operation, it follows that some state of the machine after reading the expression will correspond to a state that represents the value of the function and (because of a further definition of the implicit printout function) causes the printout of the appropriate answer.

This is true of computation generally. We explain why the machine does something by referring to certain interpretations of its symbols in some intended domain. This is, of course, precisely what we do in describing how (and why) people do what they do. In explaining why a chess player moves some piece onto a certain square, we refer to the type of piece it is in terms of its role in chess, to the player's immediate goal, and to the rules of chess. As I suggested earlier, this way of describing the situation is not merely a way of speaking or an informal shorthand reference to a more precise functional description. Furthermore, it is not, like the functional description referred to earlier, an abstraction over a set of physical properties. There is a fundamental difference between a description of a computer's operation cast in terms of its states (i.e., equivalence classes of physical descriptions) and one cast in terms of what it is *about*, such as in the illustrative example above. The fundamental difference is that the former refers to intrinsic properties of the *device*, while the latter refers to aspects of some entirely different domain, such as chess. The former can be viewed as a syntactic description, while the latter is semantic, since it refers to the represented domain.

This dual nature of mental functioning (referred to traditionally as the functional or causal, and the intentional) has been a source of profound philosophical puzzlement for a long time (e.g., Putnam 1978). The puzzle arises because, while we believe that people do things because of their goals and beliefs, we nonetheless also assume, for the sake of unity of science and to avoid the extravagance of dualism, that this process is actually carried out by causal sequences of events that can respond only to the intrinsic physical properties of the brain. But how can the process depend both on properties of brain tissue and on some other quite different domain, such as chess or mathematics? The parallel question can of course equally be asked of computers: How can the state transitions in our example depend both on physical laws and on the abstract properties of numbers? The simple answer is that this happens because both numbers and rules relating numbers are *represented* in the machine as symbolic expressions and programs, and that it is the physical realization of these representations that determine the machine's behavior. More precisely, the abstract numbers and rules (e.g., Peano's axioms) are first expressed in terms of syntactic operations over symbolic expressions or some notation for the number system, and then these expressions are "interpreted" by the built-in functional properties of the physical device. Of course, the machine does not interpret the symbols as numbers, but only as formal patterns that cause the machine to function in some particular way.

Because a computational process has no access to the actual represented domain itself (e.g., a computer has no way of distinguishing whether a symbol represents a number or letter or someone's name), it is mandatory, if the rules are to continue to be semantically interpretable (say as rules of arithmetic), that all relevant semantic distinctions be mirrored by syntactic distinctions—i.e., by features intrinsic to the representation itself. Such features must in turn be reflected in functional differences in the operation of the device. That is what we mean when we say that a device *represents* something. Simply put, all and only syntactically encoded aspects of the represented domain can affect the way a process behaves. This rather obvious assertion is the cornerstone of the formalist approach to understanding the notion of *process*. Haugeland (1978) has made the same point, though in a slightly different way. It is also implicit in Newell's (1979) "physical symbol system" hypothesis. Many of the consequences of this characteristic of computation and of this way of looking at cognition are far-reaching, however, and not widely acknowledged [for a discussion, see Fodor, 1980].

By separating the semantic and syntactic aspects of cognition, we reduce the problem of accounting for meaningful action to the problem of specifying a mechanism that operates upon meaningless symbol tokens and in doing so carries out the meaningful process being modelled (e.g., arithmetic). This, in turn, represents an important breakthrough because, while one can see how the formal process can be realized by causally connected sequences of events (as in a computer), no one has the slightest notion of how carrying out semantically interpreted rules could even be viewed as compatible with natural law [cf. Fodor, 1980]. That is, as far as we can see there could be no natural law that says, for example, that when (and only when) a device is in a state that represents the number *five*, and applies the operation that represents the successor function, it will go into the state that represents the number *six*. Whatever the functional states that are being invoked, there is nothing to prevent anyone from consistently and correctly interpreting the same states and the same function as representing something quite different—say, producing the name of the next person on a list, or the location of an adjacent cell in a matrix, or any other consistent interpretation. Indeed, the very same physical state recurs in computers under circumstances in which very different processes, operating in quite different domains of interpretation, are being exectued. In other words, the machine's functioning is completely independent of how its states are interpreted (though it is far from clear whether this would still remain so if it were wired up through transducers to a natural environment). For that reason we can never specify the behavior of a computer uniquivocally in terms of a semantically interpreted rule such as the one cited above (which referred to the domain of numbers). This is what people like Fodor (1978), Searle (1979), or Dreyfus (1979) mean when they say that a computer does not know what it is doing.

The formalist view requires that we take the syntactic properties of representations quite literally. It is literally true of a computer that it contains, in some functionally discernable form (which could even conceivably be a typewritten form, if someone wanted to go through the trouble of arranging the hardware that way), what could be referred to as a code or an inscription of a symbolic expression, whose formal features mirror (in the sense of bearing a one-to-one correspondence with) semantic characteristics of some represented domain, and which causes the machine to behave in a certain way. Because of the requirement that the syntactic structure of representations reflect all relevant semantic distinctions, the state transition diagram description of an automaton is an inadequate means of expressing the functional properties of a computational system. Individual states must be shown as factored into component parts rather than as being distinct atomic or holistic entities. Some functionally distinguishable aspects of the states much correspond to individual terms of the representing symbol structure, while other aspects must correspond to such additional properties as the control state of the device (which determines which operation will be carried out next) and the system's relation to the representation (e.g., whether the representation corresponds to a belief or a goal). Components of the syntactic expressions must be functionally factorable, otherwise we could not account for such regularities as that several distinct representational states may be followed by the same subsequent state, or that rules tend to be invoked in certain systematic ways in relation to one another. Indeed, one could not represent individual *rules* in the state transition notation since individual rules affect a large (and in principle unbounded) set of different states. For example, the rule that specifies that one remove oneself from danger must be potentially evokable by every belief state a part of whose representational content corresponds to danger. By representing this regularity once for each such state, one misses the generalization corresponding to that one rule. In addition, of course, the fact that there are an unbounded number of possible thoughts and representational states makes it mandatory that the symbolic encoding of these thoughts or states be combinatoric—i.e., that they have a recursive syntactic structure. I mention all this only because there have been some who have proposed that we not view the content of states in terms of some articulation of what they represent (e.g., Davidson 1970)—i.e., that we avoid postulating an internal syntax for representations, or a "mentalese."

The syntactic, representation-governed nature of computation thus lends itself to describing cognitive processes in such a way that their relation to causal laws is bridgeable, at least in principle. But beyond that, the exact nature of the device that instantiates the process is no more a direct concern to the task of discovering and explaining cognitive regularities than it is in computation—though in both cases specifying the fixed functional architecture of the underlying system is an essential component of understanding the process itself. Given that computation and cognition can be viewed in these common abstract terms, there is no reason why computation ought to be treated as merely a metaphor for cognition, as opposed to a hypothesis about the literal nature of cognition. In spite of the widespread use of computational terminology (e.g., terms like "storage," "process," "operation"), much of this usage has had at least some metaphorical content. There has been a reluctance to take computation as a *literal* description of mental activity, as opposed to being a mere heuristic metaphor. In my view this failure to take computation literally has licensed a wide range of activity under the rubric of "information processing theory," some of it representing a significant departure from what I see as the core ideas of a computational theory of mind.

Taking a certain characterization literally carries with it far-reaching consequences. The history of science contains numerous examples of the qualitative changes that can come about when a community accepts a certain characterization as applying literally to phenomena. The outstanding example of this is the case of geometry. Our current scientific conception of physical space is a projection of Euclidean geometry onto the observations of mechanics. But plane geometry was well known and widely used by the Egyptians in surveying. Later it was developed into an exquisitely elegant system by the Greeks. Yet for the Egyptians it was a way of calculating—like an abacus— while for the Greeks it was a demonstration of the perfect Platonic order. It was not until two millennia later that Galileo began the conceptual transformation that eventually resulted in the view, that is so commonplace today that virtually no vestige remains of the Aristotelian ideas of natural motions and natural places. Everyone imagines space to be that empty, infinitely extended, isotropic, three-dimensional receptacle, whose existence and properties are quite independent of the earth or any other objects. Such a strange idea was literally unthinkable before the seventeenth century. In fact, not even Galileo completely accepted it. For him a straight line was still bound to the earth's surface. It was not until Newton that the task of "geometrization of the world" was completed (to borrow a phrase from Butterfield 1957).

The transformation that led to the reification of geometry—to accepting the formal axioms of Euclid as a literal description of physical space—profoundly affected the course of science. Accepting a system as a literal account of reality enables scientists to see that certain further observations are possible and others are not. It goes beyond merely asserting that certain things happen "as if" some unseen events were taking place. In addition, however, it imposes severe restrictions on a theory-builder, because he is no longer free to appeal to the existence of unspecified similarities between his theoretical account and the phenomena he is addressing—as he is when speaking metaphorically. It is this latter degree of freedom that weakens the explanatory power of computation when it is used metaphorically to describe certain mental functions. If we view computation more abstractly as a symbolic process that transforms formal expressions that are in turn interpreted in terms of some domain of representation (such as the numbers), we see that the view that mental processes are computational can be just as literal as the view that what IBM computers do is properly viewed as computation.

Below I shall consider what is entailed by the view that mental activity can be viewed literally as the execution of algorithms. In particular I shall suggest that this imposes certain constraints upon the theory construction enterprise. If we are to view cognition as literally computation, it then becomes relevant to inquire how one can go about developing explanatory theories of such cognitive processes in selected domains and also to consider the scope and limit of such a view. In other words, if computation is to be taken seriously as a literal account of mental activity, it becomes both relevant and important to inquire into the sense in which computational systems can be used to provide *explanations* of mental processes. Before turning to the general issue of what is entailed by a literal view of cognition as computation, I shall conclude this discussion of the formalist nature of this approach with one or two examples, suggesting that even proponents of this view sometimes fail to respect some of its fundamental constraints. One still sees the occasional lapse when the psychological significance or the psychological principles implicated in some particular computer model are being described. Thus, semantic properties are occasionally attributed to representations (for an animated discussion, see Fodor 1978), and even more commonly, principles of processing are stated in terms of the semantics of the representations.

For example, in arguing for the indeterminacy of forms of representation, Anderson (1978) proposed a construction by means of which a system could be made to mimic the behavior of another system while using a form of representation different from that used by the mimicked system. While I have already argued (Pylyshyn 1979b) that much is wrong with Anderson's case, one flaw that I did not discuss is that the mimicking model is required (in order to be constructable as in Anderson's "existence proof") to have access to the semantics of the original representations (i.e., to the actual objects being referred to) in the system it is mimicking—which, as we have seen, is not possible according to the computational view. This occurs in Anderson's construction, because in order to decide what representation to generate next, the mimicking model must first determine what the mimicked model would have done. It does this by first determining what representation the original system would have had at that point and what new representation it would have transformed it into. Then it is in a position to infer what representation it should generate in its mimicking process. But the only way the mimicking system could be assured of finding out what representation the target model would have had (and the way actually invoked in the proposed construction) is to allow it to find out which stimuli correspond to its current representation, and then to compute what the target model would have encoded them as in its own encoding scheme. This step is, furthermore, one that must be carried out "on line" each time an operation is to be mimicked in the mimicking model—it cannot be done once and for all in advance by the constructor itself, except in the uninteresting case where there are only a finite number of stimuli to be discriminated (not merely a finite number of codes). But finding out which real stimuli generate a certain code in a model is precisely to determine the semantic extension of a representation—something that a formal system clearly cannot do.

Similarly, in describing the principles of operation of a model, it is common to characterize them in terms of the represented domain. For example, when it is claimed that "mental rotation" of images proceeds by small angular steps (e.g., Kosslyn and Schwartz 1977; Anderson 1978), or that "mental scanning" of images proceeds by passing through adjacent places, one is appealing to properties of the represented domain. Phrases like "small angular steps" and "adjacent places" can only refer to properties of the stimulus or scene being represented. They are semantically interpreted notions. The representation itself does not literally *have* small angles or adjacent places (unless one wishes to claim that it is laid out spatially in the brain—a logical possibility that most people shun); it only *represents* such properties. Of course, it is possible to arrange for a process to transform a representation of a stimulus into a representation of the same stimulus in a slightly different orientation, or to focus on a part of the representation that corresponds to a place in the stimulus that is adjacent to another specified place, but in neither case is this choice of transformation principled [see Kosslyn et al.: "On the demystification of mental imagery," *BBS* 2(4) 1979]. In other words, there is nothing about the representation itself (e.g., its syntax or format) that requires one class of transformation rather than another—as is true in the situation being represented, where to physically go from one point to another, one *must* pass through intermediate adjacent points or else violate universal laws of (classical) physics. Thus the existence of such a constraint on permissible transformations in the imaginal case is merely stipulated. The choice of the transformation in that case is like the choice of a value for a free empirical parameter—i.e., it is completely *ad hoc*—in spite of the appeal to what sounds like a general principle. However, because the principle as stated applies only to the semantic domain, one is still owed a corresponding principle that applies to the representational or syntactic domain—i.e., which applies in virtue of some intrinsic property of the representation itself. This issue is discussed in greater detail in Pylyshyn (1979c).

4. ALGORITHMIC MODELS AND THE PROPRIETARY VOCABULARY HYPOTHESIS

We begin our discussion of how a literal computational view can provide an explanatory account of cognition by examining what sorts of questions a computational model might be expected to address. One of the discoveries that led to the development of computer science as a discipline is that it is possible to study formal algorithmic processes without regard to how such processes are *physically* instantiated in an actual device. What this means is that there is an interesting and reasonably well-defined set of questions concerning computational processes (e.g., what is the fastest or the least memory-consuming way of realizing a certain class of functions?), the answers to which can be given without regard to the material or hardware properties of the device on which these processes are to be executed. This is not to suggest, of course, that issues of material realization are uninteresting, or even that they are irrelevant to certain other questions about computation. It simply imples that in studying computation it is possible, and in certain respects essential, to factor apart the nature of the symbolic process from properties of the physical device in which it is realized. It should be noted that the finding that there is a natural domain of questions concerning the behavior of a system, which is independent of the details of the physical structure of the device—providing only that the device is known to have a certain general functional character—is a substantive one. Prior to this century there was no reason to believe that there was even a coherent notion of *process* (or of mechanism) apart from that of physical process. The new notion initially grew out of certain developments in the study of the foundations of mathematics, especially with the work of Alan Turing (1936).

Because of the parallels between computation and cognition noted earlier, the corresponding view has also been applied to the case of mental processes. In fact, such a view has a tradition in philosophy that, in various forms, predates computation—though it has received a much more precise formulation in recent years in the form known as the representational theory of mind, one of the most developed versions of which can be found in Fodor (1975). One way of stating this view is to put it in terms of the existence of a privileged or a proprietary vocabulary in which the structure of mental processes can be couched—*viz.* the vocabulary needed to exhibit algorithms.

More precisely, the privileged vocabulary claim asserts that there is a natural and reasonably well-defined domain of questions that can be answered solely by examining 1) a *canonical description* of an algorithm (or a program in some suitable language—where the latter remains to be specified), and 2) a system of formal symbols (data structures, expressions), together with what Haugeland (1978) calls a "regular scheme of interpretation" for interpreting these symbols as expressing the representational content of mental states (i.e., as expressing what the beliefs, goals, thoughts, and the like are about, or what they represent). Notice that a number of issues have been left unresolved in the above formulation. For example, the notion of a canonical description of an algorithm is left open. We shall return to this question in section 8. Also, we have not said anything about the scheme for interpreting the symbols—for example, whether there is any indeterminacy in the choice of such a scheme or whether it can be uniquely constrained by empirical considerations (such as those arising from the necessity of causally relating representations to the environment through transducers). This question will not be raised here, although it is a widely debated issue on which a considerable literature exists (e.g., Putnam 1978).

A crucial aspect of the assumption that there exists a fixed formal vocabulary for addressing a significant set of psychological questions is the view that such questions can be answered without appealing to the material embodiment of the algorithm, and without positing additional special analytical functions or relations which themselves are not to be explained in terms of algorithms. In fact, as I shall argue presently, one can take the position that this proprietary vocabulary or level of description *defines* the notion of cognitive phenomenon in the appropriate technical sense required for explanatory theories. It should, however, be emphasized that such a definition is presented in the spirit of a broad empirical hypothesis. This hypothesis would be falsified if it turned out that this way of decomposing the domain of cognitive psychology did not lead to any progress or any significant insights into human thought and human rationality. Thus when I spoke of this level as specifying a domain of questions, it was assumed that such a domain is a natural one that (at least to a first approximation) can be identified independently of particular algorithms—though, like the notion of a well-formed sentence, it will itself evolve as the larger theoretical system develops. The tacit assumption, of course, has been that this domain coincides with what we pretheoretically think of as the domain of cognition—i.e. with the phenomena associated with language, thought perception, problem-solving, planning, commonsense reasoning, memory, and so on. However, there may also turn out to be significant departures from the pretheoretical boundaries. After all, we cannot be sure in advance that our commonsense taxonomy will be coextensive with the scope of a particular class of theory—or that we have pretheoretically carved Nature exactly at her joints.

One of the main points of this article will be that the proprietary level hypothesis, together with certain intrinsic requirements on the use of algorithmic models to provide theoretical explanations, leads to certain far-reaching consequences. For the next two sections, however, I shall make a somewhat extensive digression to establish a number of background points. Discussions of cognition and computation frequently founder on certain preconceived views regarding what a cognitive phenomenon is and what a cognitive process is. Thus, for example, cognitive science is sometimes criticized for allegedly not being able to account for certain types of phenomena (e.g., emotions, consciousness); at other times, attempts are made to provide explanations of certain observations associated with thinking (e.g., reaction time, effect of practice) in terms of *ad hoc* mixtures of biological and computational mechanisms. In many of these cases what is happening is that inappropriate or unclear ideas concerning the notion of cognitive phenomenon or cognitive process are being invoked, to the detriment of theoretical clarity. Consequently it is important to our story that we first try to clarify these notions in the following digression.

5. WHAT IS A COGNITIVE PHENOMENON?

Many things happen when people are engaged in thinking or problem solving. For example, they may ask questions or report being puzzled, frustrated, or following false leads, they may get up and walk around or jot down notes or doodles, their attentiveness to environmental events may deteriorate, various physiological indicators such as skin resistance, peripheral blood flow, or skin temperature (as measured by GSR, plethysmograph, or thermometer) may change systematically, and finally, they may report what they believe is a solution. In addition, these various events may occur over time in certain systematic ways. Now, one might ask which, if any, of these observations could be explained by examining a canonical description of an algorithm, or, taking the position that algorithmic accountability defines the now technical notion "cognitive phenomenon," one might ask which of the above reports represents an observation of a cognitive phenomenon?

It seems clear that this question cannot be answered without bringing in other considerations. In particular, we must know how the observations are being interpreted in relation to the algorithm. For example, a cognitive model (of the kind I have been speaking about) would not account for people's ability to move their limbs in certain ways (e.g., in certain directions and at certain speeds) or for the spectral properties of the sounds they make, although it ought to be able to account in some general way for what people do (i.e., what intended actions they carry out) in moving their limbs or for what they *say* in making those sounds. Thus, even when a phenomenon is clearly implicated in the cognitive activity, its relevance is restricted to the case in which it is appropriately described or interpreted (and, as we noted earlier, the appropriate interpretation will generally correspond to what the people themselves intended when they performed the action).

But what of the other observations associated with the problem-solving episode, especially the physiological indicators, task-independent performance measures (such as measures of distractability), and the temporal pattern associated with these observations? Here the case has typically not been as clear, and people's intuitions have differed. Thus the manner in which we interpret measures such as the galvanic skin response (GSR) and time-of-occurence in relation to the algorithm depends on various methodological assumptions, and these are just beginning to be articulated as the methodological foundations of cognitive science evolve.

For example, it is clear that a cognitive model will not have values for blood flow, skin resistance, or temperature among its symbolic terms, because the symbols in this kind of model must designate mental representations (i.e., they must designate mental structures that have representational content— such as thoughts, goals, and beliefs). The calculation of temperature and resistance in this case does not itself represent a cognitive process, and the values of these parameters are simply intrinsic physical magnitudes—they themselves do not represent anything (see the further discussion of this in section 6, below). However, such measures can be (and often are) taken as indices of certain aggregate properties of the process. For example, they might be taken as indices of what could be thought of as "processing load," where the latter is theoretically identified with, say, the size and complexity of the data structures on which the model is operating. Whether such an interpretation of these observations is warranted depends on the success of the ancilliary hypotheses in accounting for the relation among observations in the past. In other words, the justification of subsidiary methodological assumptions is itself an empirical question. There is no room here for *a priori* claims that a cognitive theory *must* account for these (or any other observations, and hence that certain phenomena are necessarily (or analytically) "cognitive."

Consider the following example, in which the developing methodology of cognitive science has led to a gradual shift in the way an important aspect of observed behavior is interpreted. The example concerns what is probably the most widely used dependent measure in cognitive psychology, namely, reaction time. This measure has sometimes been interpreted as just another response, to be accounted for by a cognitive model in the same way that the model accounts for such response properties as which button was pressed. Since Donders's (1969) pioneering work (carried out in the 1860s), it has also been widely interpreted as a more-or-less direct measure of the duration of mental processes [see Wasserman and Kong, "The Absolute Timing of Mental Activities," *BBS* 2(2) 1979]. I have argued (e.g., in commenting on the Wasserman and Kong paper) that neither of these interpretations is correct in general—that, in general, reaction time can neither be viewed as the computed output of a cognitive process itself, nor as a measure of mental duration.

If reaction time were thought of as simply another response, then it would be sufficient if our computational model simply calculated a predicted value for this reaction time, given the appropriate input. But clearly that would not suffice if the computation is to be viewed as modelling the *cognitive process*. Contemporary cognitive theorists would not view a system that generated pairs of outputs, interpreted as the response and the time taken, as being an adequate model of the underlying process, no matter how well these outputs fit the observed data.

The reason for this intuition is significant. It is related to what people understand by the concept of a cognitive process, and to the evolving concept of strong equivalence of processes, to which we will return in section 6.1. As the construction and validation of computational models has developed, there has evolved a general (though usually tacit) agreement that the kind of input-output equivalence that Turing proposed as a criterion for intelligence is insufficient as a condition on the validity of such models. It was obvious that two quite different algorithms could compute the same input-output function. It gradually became clear, however, that there were ways to distinguish empirically among processes that exhibited the same input-output function, providing certain additional methodological assumptions were made. In particular, these additional assumptions required that one view certain aspects of the organism's behavior not as a response *computed* by the cognitive process, but rather as an independent indicator of some property of the algorithm by which the response was computed. There are, in fact, independent reasons for wanting to distinguish between the kind of behavior that is directly attributable to the symbolic process, and other kinds of behavior that are not viewed as "outputs" of the cognitive process. We shall return to these below when we examine the complementary notion of a cognitive process—a notion that is as much in a state of evolution as that of a cognitive phenomenon.

It has become customary in cognitive science to view reaction time in the same way that we view measures such as the GSR or plethysmograph records, or measures of distractability—namely as an index, or an observable *correlate*, of some aggregate property of the process. In particular, reaction time is frequently viewed as an index of what might be called "computational complexity," which is usually taken to correspond to such properties of the model as the number of operations carried out. A process that merely computed time as a parameter value would not account for reaction time viewed in this particular way, since the parameter would not express the computational complexity of the process.

Measures such as reaction time, when interpreted in this way, are extremely important to cognitive science, because they provide one possible criterion for assessing *strong equivalence* of processes. Thus, all processes that, for each input, produce 1) the same output, and 2) the same measure of computational complexity, as assessed by some independent means, are referred to as complexity-equivalent. The complexity-equivalence relation is a refinement of the input-output or the *weak equivalence* relation. However, it need not be identical to what we would call the relation of strong equivalence, since we must allow for the possibility that future methodologies or other theoretical considerations may refine the relation even further.

Nonetheless the complexity-equivalence relation remains a central one in cognitive science, and reaction time measures remain one of the primary methods of assessing complexity. Since complexity is a relative quality (e.g., it makes no sense to speak of the absolute complexity of a computation, only of its complexity in relation to other computations that utilize the same hypothetical operations), we are only concerned with measures of complexity up to a linear transform. Thus we would distinguish between two lookup processes if the complexity of one increased linearly with the number of items stored while the complexity of the other was independent of, or increased as the logarithm of, the number of items. However, we would not necessarily discriminate between two hypothetical processes if their complexity varied in the same way with the input, but one process took a constant number of steps more than the other or required a fixed amount of storage capacity more than the other, unless we had some independent calibration that enabled us to translate this difference into, say, absolute reaction-time predictions.

This idea of appealing to plausible methodological assumptions (which must in the long run themselves be justified by the success of the models to which they lead) in order to make finer discriminations among theoretical systems is exactly parallel to the situation that has developed in linguistics over the last two decades. Linguistic judgments made by competent speakers are not simply taken as part of the linguistic corpus. The methodological assumption is that these judgments provide an independent source of constraint on linguistic structures, defining the analogous relation of strong equivalence of grammars (cf. Chomsky 1975).

This view of the role of reaction-time measures takes it for granted that such measures cannot be interpreted as a direct observation of the duration of a mental process. A mental process does not possess the intrinsic property of duration, any more than it possesses the property of location, size, mass, electrical resistance, or concentration of sodium ions. Of course, the underlying brain events do have these properties, and we can, at least in principle, measure them. But one must be careful in drawing conclusions about properties of the cognitive process on the basis of such measurements.

Recall that we are examining the claim that there is a domain, roughly coextensive with the range of phenomena covered by our intuitive notion of cognition, that can be accounted for solely in terms of a canonical description of the symbol manipulation algorithm. Suppose we have some observations (duration being a case in point) of properties of the physical instantiation of the algorithm. The question is, can such evidence be treated as the measurement of a cognitive property? We have already seen how, with the aid of ancillary methodological hypotheses, it can be used as evidence in favor of one or another putative cognitive process or algorithm. We are now asking whether such measurements can be viewed as anything more than fallible correlates, whose validity in each case depends upon whether or not the ancillary hypothesis holds.

I have argued (e.g., in my commentary on the Wasserman and Kong paper, BBS 2(3) 1979, and in Pylyshyn 1979b) that the answer to this question must in general be *no*. There are many situations in which measurements of properties of the underlying physical events may tell us little about the algorithm. It may, instead, tell us either about the way in which the process is physically (i.e., neurophysiologically) instantiated, or it may tell us about the nature of the task itself. We will briefly consider these two cases since they reveal an important general point concerning the relations among cognitive phenomena, the task being carried out, the method the person is using, the fixed functional properties (or functional architecture) of the cognitive system, and the biological or physical properties of some particular (token) instantiation of that solution process.

Measurement such as reaction time are particularly unlikely to tell us much about the nature of the underlying biological mechanism in the case of what is often called a "higher-level cognitive function," in which the processing is not as closely tied to anatomical structures as it is, say, in certain parts of perception or motor coordination. While in many cases there would, no doubt, be a correspondence between the duration of some correlated physical measurements and such purely algorithmic properties as the number of steps carried out, which particular steps were carried out, whether parts of the algorithm were carried out serially or in parallel, and so on, this is not always the case. The explanation of some of the time differences (and every explanation of the absolute time taken) must appeal to some properties of the physical realization that are unique to that particular instantiation and therefore irrelevant to the algorithmic or process explanation in general. Such duration data may not make a valid discrimination among putative algorithms.

Using a computer as an example, we can readily see that some of the time differences might arise from the fact that a signal had farther to travel in some particular (token) occasion because of the way the machine was wired up and the way the algorithm was implemented in it: some might arise from variable delay physical effects, such as the distance that a moveable arm had to travel in making a disk access in that implementation; and some could even depend on physical properties of the noncomputational environment, as would be the case if real-time interrupts could occur. None of these properties bears on the nature of the algorithm, since they could be quite different for a different realization of the identical algorithm. Consequently, in this case, measuring such times would not help to distinguish different candidate algorithms. That is why time measurements alone cannot be taken as measurements of a property of the algorithmic process in the computer case. And for precisely the same reasons they cannot be taken literally as measurements of mental durations—only as indirect (as possibly false) indicators of such things as processing complexity, to be used judiciously along with other indirect sources of evidence in inferring underlying mental processes.

The other case in which the observations may tell us little about the cognitive process itself arises when the preliminary determinant of the behavior in question is what Newell and Simon (1972) call the "task demands" (which, incidentally, are not to be confused with such "experimental demand" factors as Kosslyn, Pinker, Smith, and Schwartz 1979 have tried to rule out in their defense of their interpretation of the "mental scanning" results). Consider, for example, the various observations associated with certain operations on mental images. A large number of these investigations (e.g., Shepard 1978; Kosslyn, 1980) have proceeded by measuring the time it takes to imagine a certain mental action, such as rotating an image or scanning with one's attention between two points on a mental image. But what the analysis of these results has consistently failed to do is to distinguish two different tasks that could be subsumed under the same general instructions to the subject. The first is the task of simply using a certain form of representation to solve the problem. The second is to imagine actually seeing certain of the problem-solving events taking place. In the latter case one would expect various incidental properties of the real events to be duplicated in the imagining. For example, suppose you are asked to imagine two different events: call them E_1 and E_2. If you know that, in reality, E_1 takes, say, twice as long as E_2, and if you interpret the task as requiring you to imagine yourself *seeing* the events happening (as seems reasonable, given the ambiguity of the instructions in this respect), then surely the task requires, by its very definition, that you spend more time in the act of imagining E_1 than in the act of imagining E_2 (in fact, twice as long—if you are capable of the psychophysical task of generating a time interval corresponding to a particular known magnitude). The crucial difference between these two tasks is that quite different success criteria apply in the two cases; although "using an image" does not require, as a condition for having carried out the task, that one reproduce incidental characteristics of some imagined event such as its relative duration, the task of "imagining seeing it happen" does demand that this be done.

This is, in fact, part of a very general difficulty that permeates the whole range of interpretations of imagery research findings that appeal to such things as "analogue media." I discuss this issue in detail elsewhere (Pylyshyn 1979c). For the present purposes we might simply note that a variety of determinants of observed phenomena, other than the structure of the cognitive process or the functional architecture of the underlying system, are possible. In order for observations such as, say, that reaction time varies linearly with the imagined distance, to have a bearing upon the cognitive theory itself (i.e., upon the structure of the algorithm or the functional architecture of the model), it would be necessary to further show that under certain prescribed conditions (such as when subjects report that their answers come from examining their image) the relation between distance and time is a *necessary* one (i.e., it is not determined by beliefs, tacit knowledge, or certain specific goals—such as to reproduce aspects of the event as it would have been perceived). To my knowledge this has not been demonstrated—and furthermore, some preliminary evidence from our own laboratory suggests that it is false in the case of mental scanning (see Pylyshyn 1979c). Clearly, in the case of a situation such as imagining a heavy stone being rolled as opposed to a light object being flipped over, any differences in the time taken would be atributed to the subject's knowledge of the referent situation —i.e., to the task demand. It is not clear how many of the reported time functions for mental operations fall into this category. I suspect that not only mental scanning, but also such findings as the relation between "size" of mental images and time to report details is explainable in this way, although perhaps some of the mental rotation results are not—but then it appears that the latter are not explainable as holistic analogue processes either (cf. Pylyshyn 1979a).

Whatever the ultimate verdict on the correct explanation of the observed reaction time functions, considerations such as these do illustrate that certain distinctions need to be made before we are free to interpret the observations.

For example, if we distinguish, as I suggested, between the case of applying operations to visual images of objects and the case of *imagining yourself seeing* operations physically applied to real objects, then it would follow that in at least the second of these cases the reaction time functions should to some degree (depending on subjects' capacity to carry out the required psychophysical task of generating appropriate outputs) mirror the real time functions of the corresponding events. Furthermore, on this view it is also not at all surprising that we cannot imagine (in the sense of imagining ourselves seeing) such things as four-dimensional space. Certainly this fact tells us nothing about the nature of the representation: It is a matter of definition that we cannot *imagine ourselves seeing* what is in principle not seeable! The important point is that, to the extent that task-demand factors can be viewed as the primary determinants of observations, such observations cannot be taken as having a bearing on the structure of our cognitive model.

We thus have another instance of the principle that whether or not some measurement turns out to be an observation of a "cognitive phenomenon" by our definition depends on how we interpret it. I have no doubt that we will refine our notion of "cognitive phenomenon," just as we refined our notion of "physical phenomenon" in the course of the development of our theories. It should not come as a shock to us, therefore, if certain ways of viewing phenomena ultimately end up as irrelevant to cognitive theory, even though they might have been part of our pretheoretic notion of cognition. As Chomsky (1964) has reminded us, it is not less true of cognitive science than of other fields that we start off with the clear cases and work out, modifying our view of the domain of the theory as we find where the theory works.

For example, Haugeland (1978) considers it a serious shortcoming of the computational view that it appears unable to explain such things as skills and moods. There are two assumptions here, for which little evidence exists at present, one way or the other. The first is that no aspect of skills or moods can be accounted for computationally. The second is that, under the appropriate interpretation, these are phenomena that we know *a priori* to be cognitive. Consider the case of skills. The popular view is that, at least in the case of motor skills, competence is built up by repeated practice (given the inherent talent) without any intellectual intervention. In fact, it is often believed that thinking about such skills impedes their fluency (recall the story about the centipede that was asked which foot it moved first). But there is now reason to believe that the acquisition and exercise of such skills can be enhanced by purely cognitive means. For example, imagined or "mental" practice is known to improve certain motor skills. Furthermore, a careful functional analysis of a skill such as juggling, in terms of its intrinsic hierarchical structure, can lead to methods for verbally instructing novices, which cuts the learning time to a fraction of what it would otherwise take (Austin 1974). Clearly, cognitive processes are relevant to motor skills. Equally clearly, however, certain aspects of their execution are purely biological and physical. How this problem will naturally factor will depend on what the facts are: it is not a question of which we can issue a verdict in advance.

The same goes for moods, emotions, and the like. It is very likely that there will be certain aspects of these phenomena that will resist functional analysis, and therefore computational explanation (as there have been aspects that have historically resisted every kind of analysis). For instance, the conscious feeling accompanying moods may not be susceptible to such analysis, except insofar as it has a cognitive component (e.g., insofar as it leads to people noticing that they are experiencing a certain mood). It would not even be surprising if the pervasive effects that moods have on cognitive activity (which Haugeland mentions) turn out to be outside the scope of computational explanation. We know that there are global changes in various aspects of cognitive activity that accompany biological development and endocrine changes. Such changes seem more akin to variations in the underlying functional architecture (a concept to which we shall return shortly) than to changes in the algorithm. Variations in such inner environments do not connect with mental representations the way variations in the perceived environment do: We do not perceive our hormonal levels and thus come to have new beliefs. The relation in that case does not appear to be of the appropriate type: It is biological and causal, rather than rational or cognitive. On the other hand, we cannot rule out the possibility that a broader view of computation might make it possible to subsume even these facts into a computational theory. The real mystery of conscious experience is that the fact that it appears to elude both functionalist (i.e., computational) and naturalist (i.e., identity theory) accounts. A possible approach to this dilemma (and one on which I have speculated in Pylyshyn 1979d) might be to allow cognitive states to have access (via internal transduction) to biological states (e.g., imagine a computer with a register whose contents correspond to its internal temperature or line voltage). Neither providing for a computational system to appeal directly to arbitrary causal properties of its physical instantiation, nor allowing it to alter its own functional architecture presents any difficulties in principle. In fact, we routinely do change the functional architecture of computers by means of programs—for example, by a process called *compiling*. Whether such methods will allow us to capture aspects of such global effects as those mentioned above is a question for future theories to answer.

6. WHAT IS A COGNITIVE PROCESS?

6.1 Cognitive simulation and strong equivalence. There is a systematic ambiguity in the use of the term "computer simulation" that occasionally causes confusion. Computers are said to simulate economic cycles, traffic flow, chemical reactions, and the motion of celestial bodies. They are also said to simulate aspects of human behavior as well as cognition. It is important, however, to understand the essential difference between the latter sense of simulation (as a psychological model) and the former. When we simulate, say, the motion of planets, the only empirical claim we make is that the coordinate values listed on the printout correspond to the ones that will actually be observed under the specified conditions. Which algorithm is used to compute these values is irrelevant to the veridicality of the simulation. In other words, for this purpose we do not distinguish among algorithms that compute the same input-output function. We have referred to such algorithms as being *weakly equivalent*.

The case of cognitive simulation, however, is quite different. As we have already noted, weak equivalence is not a sufficient condition for validity of a model. Intuitively, we require that the algorithm correspond in much greater detail to the one the person actually uses. The difficulty is, of course, that we cannot directly observe this algorithm, so we must discriminate among weakly equivalent processes on the basis of other considerations. We have already suggested how observations such as reaction time can be used as evidence for deciding among weakly equivalent algorithms. Such criteria help us to select a set of what I have referred to as complexity-equivalent processes. Other criteria, such as those that provide evidence for intermediate states and for factorable subcomponents of the process (cf. Pylyshyn 1978a), as well as endogenous criteria, such as minimizing redundancy through appropriate subroutinizing, and further methodological criteria yet to be developed, define a sense of equivalence I have referred to earlier as *strong equivalence*.

There is an important reason why strong equivalence is relevant to cognitive models, though not to other uses of computer simulation, such as those mentioned earlier. The reason was hinted at when we spoke of modelling the algorithm that the person "actually uses." The idea is that the appropriate way to functionally characterize the mental activities that determine a person's behavior is to provide an initial representational state—interpreted as representing beliefs, tacit knowledge, goals and desires, and so on—and a sequence of operations that transform this initial state, through a series of intermediate states, into the commands that are finally sent to the output transducers. All the intermediate states, on this view, are also representations which, in the model, take the form of expressions or data structures. Each of these has psychological significance: it must be interpretable as a mental representation. Thus all intermediate states of the model constitute claims about the cognitive process.

Contrast this with the case of simulating planetary motion. Clearly in this case no empirical claims whatsoever are being made about the intermediate states of the computation itself: only the outputs are interpreted as referring to the modelling domain. The ambiguity we spoke of earlier arises because of the use of the phrase "computer simulation" to refer to two quite different activities. In the case of planetary motion, chemical processes, traffic flow, and so on, what we call simulation is only a way of computing a series of values of a function, while in the psychological case, simulation refers to the execution of a hypothesized algorithm in a simulated (in the first sense) mechanism. In the computer industry the technical term for this kind of mimicry is *emulation:* one computer is sometimes made to emulate the functional capacities or functional architecture of another, so that programs originally written for the first can be run directly on the second. Thus, modelling cognitive processes must proceed in two phases. The first is to emulate the functional architecture of the mind, and the second is to *execute* the hypothetical cognitive algorithm on it (not to *simulate* the behavior of the cognitive process, for the algorithm represents a literal proposal for the structure of this process).

Notice that this discussion is relevant to the distinction made earlier, between observations directly attributable to the cognitive algorithm and ones that must be attributed to physical properties of the device, where we included GSR, plethysmograph, thermometer, and timing records in the latter category. Although, clearly, we could in principle compute values of these paramenters, and this computation itself would be some sort of process, yet it would not be a *cognitive* process. In computing these values we would, at best, be simulating the function of the biological mechanism not literally executing *its* algorithm on an emulated architecture. The intermediate states of this process would not be viewed as having empirical cognitive referents. To the extent that the body could be said to "compute" GSR, it clearly does not do it symbolically. If it could be said to compute at all, it would be by analogue means (we shall have more to say below about the important question of when an organism or device symbolically computes a function, as opposed to merely instantiating or exhibiting that function).

Another closely related reason why strong equivalence is demanded of cognitive models, but not of models of physical processes, is that the former are assumed to be governed by rules acting upon symbolic representations. While we do not assume that planets have a symbolic representation of their orbits (or of the laws governing their trajectory), we *do* claim that the appropriate explanation of cognitive processes must appeal to the organism's use of rules and explicit symbolic representations. The distinction between behavior being governed by symbolic representations and behavior being merely exhibited by a device in virtue of the causal structure of that device is one of the most fundamental distinctions in cognitive science. We shall therefore devote the next section to examining that distinction.

6.2 Representation-governed behavior. The question of whether we should explain the behavior of a certain organism or device by ascribing to it certain explicit symbolic *rules and representations*, or whether we should simply describe its *dispositions to respond* (i.e., its intrinsic input-output function) in any way we find convenient (including appealing to exactly the same rules, but without the assumption that they are represented anywhere other than in the theorist's notebook, and consequently without any concern for strong equivalence), is a central philosophical issue in the foundations of cognitive science. To some extent the issue is a conceptual one and relates to the question of whether psychology has a special (and less than objective status among the sciences (for example, Putnam 1978 has argued that cognitive theories are necessarily "interest relative" rather than being empirically determinate—see, however, Chomsky, 1980). In addition to this more general question, however, there is also a straightforward empirical side to this issue, to which I now turn.

Elsewhere (Pylyshyn 1978b) I have sketched some general conditions under which it would be reasonable to speak of behavior as being governed by rules and representations. The general position is that whenever behavior is sufficiently plastic and stimulus-independent, we can at least assume that it is somehow mediated by internal functional states. Such states may be further viewed as representational, or epistemic, if certain other empirical conditions hold. For example, we would describe the behavior as being governed by representations and rules if the relation between environmental events and subsequent behavior, or the relations among functional states themselves, could be shown to be, among other things, a) arbitrary with respect to natural laws, b) informationally plastic, or c) functionally transparent. We elaborate briefly on these conditions below.

The relation between an event and the ensuing behavior would be said to be arbitrary if there were no *necessary* intrinsic connection between them. More precisely, a relation between an environmental event, viewed in a certain way and a behavioral act, is said to be arbitrary if, *under that particular description of the event and the behavior*, the relation does not instantiate a natural law. For example, there can be no nomological law relating what someone says to you and what you will do, since the latter depends on such things as what you believe, what inferences you draw, what your goals are (which might include obeying totally arbitrary conventions), and, perhaps even more important, how you perceive the event (what you take it to be an instance of). Since all physical events are intrinsically ambiguous, in the sense that they can be seen in very many different ways, each of which could lead to very different behavior, the nonlawfulness of the link between these events and subsequent behavior seems clear. Systematic but nonlawlike relations among functional states are generally attributed to the operation of *rules* rather than natural laws.

The condition that I referred to as informational plasticity will play an important role in later discussion. For the present I introduce it to suggest that epistemic mediation is implicated whenever the relation between environmental events and behavior can be radically, yet systematically, varied by a wide range of conditions that need have no more in common than that they provide certain information, or that they allow the organism to infer that a certain state of affairs holds—perhaps one which, if it were actually perceived, would also produce the same behavior. For example, seeing that the building you are in is on fire, smelling smoke coming in through the ventilation duct, or being told by telephone that the building is on fire, can all lead to similar behavior, and this behavior might be radically different if you believed yourself to be performing in a play at the time.

The third condition, that of transparency of relations among representations, is, in a sense, the converse of the second condition. Whereas informational plasticity reflects the susceptibility of the process between stimulus and response to cognitive influences, the transparency condition reflects the multiple availability of rules governing relations among representational states. Wherever quite different processes appear to use the same set of rules, we have a *prima facie* reason for believing that there is a single explicit representation of the rules, or at least a common shared subprocess, rather than independent identical multiple processes. The case can be made even stronger, however, if it is found that whenever the rules appear to change in the context of one process, the other processes also appear to change in a predictable way. In that case we would say (borrowing a term from computer science) that the rules were being used in an "interpretive" or transparent, rather than a "compiled" or opaque mode.

Such seems to be the case with grammatical rules, since we appear to have multiple access to these rules. We appeal to them to account for production, for comprehension, and for linguistic judgments. Since these three functions must be rather thoroughly coordinated (e.g., a rule first available only in comprehension soon becomes effective in the other two functions), it seems a reasonable view that they are explicitly represented and available as a symbolic code (as I have argued elsewhere; Pylyshyn 1976). In other words, there are cases, such as grammar, in which rules can be used not only within some specific function, but in some circumstances they can even be referred to or *mentioned* by other parts of the system. These cases argue even more strongly that the system could not simply be behaving *as if* it used rules, but must in fact have access to a symbolic encoding of the rules. [Other arguments for the representational theory of mind are offered by Fodor (1975 and 1980) and Chomsky (1980).]

To summarize, then, a *cognitive process* is distinguished from a process in general inasmuch as it models mental events, rather than merely simulating some behavior. This means that the states of the process are representational, and that this representational content is hypothesized to be the same as the content of the mental states (i.e., tacit knowledge, goals, beliefs) being modelled. Thus the computational states do not *represent* biological states, unless by this we mean to suggest that the person being modelled is thinking about biology. The process is, however, realized or carried out by the fixed functional capacities provided by the biological substrate. These functional capacities are called the functional architecture. The decision as to whether or not a particular function should be explained by positing a cognitive process—i.e., by appeal to rules and representations—rests on certain empirical considerations. One sufficient (though not necessary) condition for a function being determined by representations is that it be influenceable by beliefs and goals—i.e., that it be cognitively penetrable. Hence only cognitively impenetrable functions constitute the fixed functional capacities, or the functional architecture, out of which cognitive processes are composed. We shall elaborate upon these conditions further in sections 8, 9, and 10.

7. COMPUTATIONAL MODELS AND EXPLANATIONS

We return to the theme raised in section 4, namely the question of how a computational model, in the form of a symbol-processing algorithm, can be used to provide an explanation of cognitive phenomena. In general, what is commonly referred to as a model can be used in various ways in explanation. These range from using it merely as an illustration or metaphorical object, to using it as a constitutive part of the theory. Computational models have been particularly free in the way the explanatory burden has been shared between the model and the theorist. There has, in other words, been very little constraint on what a theorist is warranted to say about an algorithm. But if the algorithm is to be taken as a literal description of a mental process, then much stronger constraints must be imposed on how it is used in the explanatory account. In particular, the appeal to the algorithm must be *principled*.

Notice that the parallel problem is not as serious in the case of mathematical models in psychology, or models in physics. Here a clear separation is made among the fixed universal constants, empirical parameters estimated from the data, variables, and functional forms. Although in formulating the model the theorist is relatively free to choose a function (subject to available mathematical notation and technique, as well as to certain other intrinsic constraints, such as the general prevalence of linear and inverse-square law effects), thereafter the theorist is, to a considerable extent, accountable for the way estimates of parameter values are revised in response to observations. This is done by monitoring the degrees of freedom in the model. To prevent a theorist from arbitrarily revising the cognitive model, a notion similar to this accountability is needed. While I don't see an exact analogue to the degrees-of-freedom ledger emerging in cognitive science, I think there is an analogue to the technique of factoring the sources of variability in the system. Part of the requirement that the appeal to the computational model be principled, then, is the demand that various sources of the model's behavior be factored apart and independently justified. This is, in fact, an instance of an extremely general scientific maxim, namely, that a central goal of explanatory theories is to factor a set of phenomena, a problem, or a system into the most general and perspicuous components, principles, or subsystems.

Apart from the general application of this principle in, say, factoring apart knowledge of a domain, various problem-specific heuristics, and resource-limited performance mechanisms, there are two major classes of factors that a computational theory must explicitly recognize when appealing to an algorithmic model. I refer to these as a) the *functional architecture*, or the fixed capacities of the system, and b) the *functional requisites*, or the effectiveness principles relating the system to the task. Partitioning the explanatory appeal to the computational model in this way places two special burdens on the theory-building enterprise. The first is that the basic functional mechanisms or computational building blocks out of which the model is constructed must be independently justified. The second is that one must be able to specify the characteristics of the model and the task in virtue of which the system is capable of carrying out that task or producing the behavior we are explaining. In other words, both the underlying architecture of the computational model, and the properties of the algorithm or task that enables the system to successfully carry it out, must be explicitly addressed in the explanatory story, and both must be independently justified.

The first factor, regarding assumptions about the underlying functional architecture, is the primary concern of most of the remainder of this paper, and hence a detailed discussion will be postponed until the next section. What is at issue is that the success of an algorithm in accounting for a certain domain of behavior must not be due merely to some quite fortuitous property of a particular computational architecture, which itself cannot be independently justified. For example (Winston 1975), some interest was once aroused by the fact that a certain artificial intelligence "blocks world" vision system [based on Guzman's (1968) program SEE] seemed to exhibit an effect very similar to the Muller-Lyer illusion (i.e., it took a line with arrows on its ends like ↔ to be shorter than a line with forks on its ends like ><), and thus to provide a possible account of this illusion. This particular effect was due to the fact that the system's line-recognizing procedure used a diameter-limited scanner, which scanned the line looking for evidence of certain types of terminating vertices. Evidence for an "arrow" vertex accumulates sooner in the scan than does evidence for a "fork" vertex, because the secondary arrow lines enter the scan region even before the actual point of intersection does. Thus the system recognizes the end of the line segment earlier in scanning toward it when the segment terminates with an arrow than when it terminates with a fork, hence yielding a lower estimate of its length in the former case. By adjusting the diameter of the scan region, this method can account for some quantitative properties of the illusion reasonably well. Now in this example it is very clear that the phenomenon is associated with the assumption of a diameter-limited line scan. Thus, whether this particular account of the illusion is classed as a valid serendipitous finding or merely a fortuitous coincidence depends very much on whether the assumption concerning the mechanism, or the architectural property of the detector, can survive empirical scrutiny.

Although this example may seem fanciful, it is nonetheless the case that *every* computational model, if it is taken literally, must take assumptions about the mechanism. These are frequently not taken to be empirical hypotheses, since it can easily escape our notice that some of the system's performance is attributable to certain assumed architectural features. Our experience with a rather narrow range of possible computational architectures can blind us to the fact that our algorithms are relative to such architectures (as we shall see in section 8). Furthermore, when the assumptions are exposed and analysed, they do not always seem so plausible. A particular case worth mentioning concerns the architectural assumptions underlying the successful use of lists and two-dimensional matrices to model aspects of reasoning and the spatial character of images. We shall examine these briefly later.

The second class of factors—those relevant to answering the question of why the algorithm exhibits the ability it does (or the ability claimed)—represents a further application of the injunction that explanatory appeals to a computational model must be principled. It is also an attempt to deal with the (often justified) criticism that a hypothesized algorithm is *ad hoc* in the sense that there is no independent reason for it to be the way it is, as opposed to some other way, other than because it was designed to duplicate a certain set of observations. Earlier I characterized design decisions, motivated solely by the need to account for certain observations, as being equivalent to fixing the value of a free empirical parameter. Such decisions are unmotivated by general principles or constraints on processes, except perhaps ones that are stated in terms of properties of the represented domain, which, we have argued, makes them descriptive but not explanatory. Explanatory principles must characterize the operation of a system in terms of endogenous structural or functional properties of that system.

The nature of the requirement, that we be able to state the principles in virtue of which the algorithm is capable of achieving the claimed skill, is best illustrated by the following example, based on the work of Shimon Ullman (1979). It is known that the shape of a moving object can be perceived even in highly impoverished circumstances—such as when the presentation consists of a silhouette projection of a rotating unfamiliar wire shape, or even random unconnected elements on the transparent surface of the rotating forms. This perceptual ability was first studied by Wallach and O'Connell (1953) under the title "kinetic depth effect." Now, suppose someone designed an algorithm (perhaps one using statistical methods) that recognized shape successfully in over ninety percent of the cases presented to it. Could we consider this algorithm to be a model of the underlying process? If we answer this question in the affirmative, we must then ask the further question: In virtue of what principle does it have the claimed competence to perceive form from motion? In fact, it turns out that the appropriate order to ask these two questions is the opposite to the one given above. For it is only by trying to discern the principle governing the alleged ability that we can be sure that the system does indeed have that ability—that it does more than to "account for variance" or to mimic some segment of the behavior without embodying the competence in question.

The problem of inferring shape from motion is not solvable in general without bringing in additional constraints, because three-dimensional shape is underdetermined by its two-dimensional orthographic projection. But the imposition of extrinsic constraints on this inference should be, as we have emphasized, principled. In particular, it should be such as to guarantee a unique solution in all cases where a unique interpretation occurs perceptually. Ullman (1979) proposed that the constraint be viewed as a warranted assumption made by the interpretation scheme. He calls it the rigidity assumption, because it enjoins the system to interpret the moving elements in the two-dimensional projection as originating from a rigid body in motion, and to fail if such an interpretation is not possible (i.e., as a first approximation, not to produce an interpretation of the elements as belonging to an elastic or fluid medium). This is analogous to an assumption of grammaticality made in interpreting natural language. In that case the system would be asked to interpret a string as an instance of a structure generated by the grammar, and to fail if such an interpretation is not possible. Of course, in both cases a more elaborate model might produce analyses of the deviant cases as well (i.e., nonrigid and nongrammatical interpretations). However, this would not be done by abandoning the assumption completely, but rather by considering systematic departures from the strict form of the assumption (even ungrammatical sentences must be analysed in terms of grammatical rules, rather than simply in terms of such considerations as what is usually true of the referents of the terms, otherwise we could not understand a sentence about anything unexpected).

The rigidity assumption is warranted by two further findings. The first is the mathematical result (called the *structure from motion theorem*), showing that a set of four noncoplanar points in a rigid configuration is uniquely determined by three distinct orthographic views. The second finding is that the interpretation is in fact computable by a reasonable locally parallel procedure, given the sorts of data available to the human visual system, and under approximately those conditions in which people do perceive three-dimensional shape.

The lesson of this example is that by first understanding what the demands of the task are, it is possible to specify constraints that must be met by any algorithm capable of successfully carrying out that task. This, in turn, makes it possible to answer the question *why* a certain algorithm has the claimed ability. Without this extra stage of theoretical analysis we would be unable to say *why* some *particular* algorithm appeared to work on the set of problems on which we tried it. What is even more serious, however, is that we could not even say, with any degree of precision or confidence, what the class of tasks was that the algorithm *could* handle. While this might not be considered a shortcoming if we were merely concerned to account for experimental variance (i.e., for observational adequacy), it would be a serious defect if our goal was to provide a theoretical *explanation* of some domain of competence (i.e., if we were concerned with explanatory adequacy). If we know neither what the scope of a model's abilities is, nor what the principles are in virtue of which it behaves as it does, we do not have the basis for explanation.

To develop the analogous point with respect to the other class of requirements on the explanatory use of computational models (viz., that the functional architecture be separately constrained), we shall first examine the notion of functional architecture itself.

8. THE INFLUENCE OF ARCHITECTURE AND NOTATION ON PROCESSES

Computation is generally understood to be completely independent of the particular way it is physically realized. After all, a program can be executed by an unlimited variety of quite different physical devices, operating on quite different physical principles and in radically different physical media, such as mechanical, optical, acoustical, fluid, or any other conceivable substance (even including a group of trained pigeons!). On the other hand, the way in which the device functions is critical in determining whether it is capable of executing an algorithm. The design of a physical system that can function as a computer is no simple matter. But in view of the unboundedness of the variety of physical forms it can take, one might well ask what it is about the structure of the device, or class of devices, that makes it a computer? To answer this question we must recognize a level of description of the device intermediate between its description as a physical system (governed by the appropriate physical laws that determine its physical state transitions) and its description as a representational system (in which its behavior is governed by the rules and representations it embodies). This is the level we have been calling the functional architecture.

This level of description lies somewhere between the physical and the representational, in the sense that, unlike the physical description, it is independent of the particular physical laws that characterize any one physical realization of the system, and, unlike the usual algorithmic or rules-plus-representations description, it is an uninterpreted rule schema that can be exploited, by an appropriate choice of initial expression and interpretation scheme, to actually carry out some intended algorithm. It thus serves as the interface between the two. The physics of the device, together with a specified mapping from classes of physical states onto expressions, defines the functional architecture. In the computer case we can then view the role of such utility software as assemblers, loaders, compilers, interpreters, and operating systems as providing various realizations of this mapping, and hence as defining (or emulating) different functional architectures.

The notion of functional architecture has a special role to play in computer science, where it is sometimes referred to as "the architecture of the underlying virtual machine." When writing programs for some particular computer, programmers only have the resources provided by some particular programming language available to them. They are (to a first approximation—neglecting such practical factors as cost and resource limits) unconcerned about how the real physical device operates at the hardware level, since what they can do with the system is fixed by the functional specification of the language. This specification consists of the sorts of things that are contained in the language user's manual—e.g., a list of the available operations and what they do, restrictions on how the operations can be put together, how the contents of memory can be accessed, how arguments are to be passed to functions, how control is transferred, and so on. This functional specification defines the programmer's *virtual machine*, which a programmer cannot distinguish from a real machine without approaching the device in a quite different mode (e.g., looking in the systems manual or examining the switches and lights on the console). As far as the programmer is concerned, the device may well be wired to function exactly as the language manual specifies (indeed, contemporary computers are frequently designed to execute programs in LISP or PASCAL or some other high-level programming language at very nearly the level of real hardware). Thus, even though there may in fact be several layers of program interpretation between the programmer and the actual hardware, only the properties of the virtual machine architecture are relevant to the user, because that is the only level to which the user has uniform access (i.e., any changes to the machine's functioning can be made only by utilizing the facilities defined by this virtual machine).

For the cognitive scientist a similar distinction between the functional architecture of the "cognitive virtual machine" and the mental algorithm is important, though the principle for distinguishing the two must be stated in a slightly different form, since it will ultimately depend on empirical criteria. The functional architecture is, by assumption, that part of the system that is fixed in a certain respect (which we shall specify in the next section when we examine the notion of cognitive architecture more closely), and that is also, hopefully, universal to the species. Mental algorithms are viewed as being executed by this functional architecture. In view of the fact that a valid cognitive model must execute the *same* algorithms as those carried out by subjects, and in view of the fact that (as we shall see below) *which* algorithms can be carried out (keeping in mind that algorithms are individuated according to the criterion of strong equivalence) depends on the functional architecture of the device, and furthermore, in view of the fact that electronic computers clearly have a very different functional architecture from that of minds, we would expect that in constructing a computer model the mental architecture will first have to be *emulated* (i.e., itself modelled) before the mental algorithm can be implemented.

Consider, for example, how we would go about using a computational system as a cognitive model. First of all, in order to describe an algorithm so it can be viewed as a literal model of a cognitive process, we must present it in some standard or canonical form or notation. Typically this means formulating it as a program in some programming language, but it might also include graphical presentation (as a flowchart) or even a discursive natural language description. Now, what is typically overlooked when we do this is the extent to which the class of algorithms that can even be considered is conditioned by the assumptions we make regarding what basic operations are possible, how these may interact, how operations are sequenced, what data structures are possible, and so on. Such assumptions are an intrinsic part of our choice of descriptive formalism, since the latter defines what we are calling the functional architecture of the system.

What is remarkable is that the range of computer architectures available for our consideration is extremely narrow, compared with what could in principle be considered. Virtually all the widely available architectures are basically of the Von Neumann type, or closely related to it. This goes for both hardware (which uses serially organized, stored-list programs and location-addressable memory) and software (see a discussion of the latter in Backus 1978). Because our experience has been with such a rather narrow range of architectures, we tend to associate the notion of computation, and hence of algorithm, with the class of algorithms that can be realized by architectures in this limited class. For example, we tend to think of flow diagrams as a neutral way of exhibiting algorithms. This is the idea behind the TOTE unit of Miller, Galanter, and Pribram (1960). But flow diagrams (and TOTE units) are totally inappropriate as a way of characterizing algorithms implemented on unconventional (non–Von Neumann) architectures—such as, for example, the less familiar architecture of production systems, Planner-like languages, or predicate calculus-based programming systems like PROLOG (see Bobrow and Raphael 1974 for a discussion of some of these languages). If we use the criterion of strong equivalence relation, which I referred to as complexity-equivalence) to individuate algorithms, we will find that different architectures are in general not capable of executing strongly equivalent algorithms.

This point is best illustrated by considering examples of several simple architectures. The most primitive machine architecture is no doubt the original binary-coded Turing machine introduced by Turing (1936). Although this machine is universal, in the sense that it can be programmed to compute any computable function, anyone who has tried to write procedures for it will attest to the fact that most computations are extremely complex. More importantly, however, the complexity varies with such things as the task and the nature of the input in ways that are quite different from the case of machines with a more conventional architecture. For example, the number of basic steps required to look up a string of symbols in such a Turing machine increases as the square of the number of strings stored. On the other hand, in what is called a register architecture (in which retrieving a symbol by name or by "reference" is a primitive operation) the time complexity can, under certain conditions, be made independent of the number of strings stored. A register architecture can execute certain algorithms (e.g., the hash-coding lookup algorithm) that are impossible in the Turing machine—in spite of the fact that the Turing machine can be made to be weakly equivalent to this algorithm. In other words, it can compute the same lookup *function*, but not with the same complexity profile, and hence not by using an algorithm that is complexity-equivalent to the hash-coding algorithm. Of course, it could be made to compute the function by stimulating the individual steps of the register machine's algorithm, but in that case the Turing machine would be *emulating* the architecture of the register machine and executing the algorithm in the emulated architecture, a very different matter from computing it directly by the Turing machine. The distinction between executing an algorithm and emulating a functional architecture is crucial to cognitive science, as we have already remarked, because it relates directly to the question of which aspects of the computation can be taken literally as part of the model, and which aspects are mere technical implementation details necessitated by the fact that at the level of actual hardware production-model electronic computers have a functional architecture different from that of brains.

Examples of the architecture-specificity of algorithms could be easily multiplied. For example, a register machine that has arithmetic operations and predicates among its primitive operations (and hence can use numerals as names—or, as they are more frequently called, "addresses") makes a variety of additional algorithms possible, including binary search (in which the set of remaining options is reduced by a fraction with each comparison, as in the game "twenty questions"). The existence of arithmetic primitives as part of the architecture also means that it is possible to specify a total ordering on names, and hence to primitively partition certain search spaces (as in an *n*-dimensional matrix data structure), so that search can be confined within a region while other regions are literally not considered—items in those regions are not even checked and discarded, as they would have to be if they were merely part of an unordered set of items. Such algorithms could not be implemented on a Turing machine architecture.

As we go to more unusual architectures, other algorithms—with quite different complexity profiles—become possible. For example, Scott Fahlman (1979) has proposed a design for an architecture (realizable only with unconventional hardware) that computes set intersection as a primitive operation (in time independent of set size). He argues that many otherwise complex combinatorial algorithms required for symbolic pattern recognition (i.e., for access to stored data through multiple descriptions) become simple in such an architecture. In other words, because this architecture allows interesting new classes of algorithms to be implemented, the locus of the difficulty of giving a computational account of a certain task domain is dramatically shifted. Fahlman also argues that the resulting complexity profiles of certain memory-retrieval processes in this architecture are more like those of "natural intelligence." Although he does not use the methodology of the psychological laboratory (viz. reaction times), the goal is similar. Along the same lines, Mitch Marcus (1977) has also proposed certain general architectural features of the processor associated with grammatical analysis, which have the interesting consequence that they provide a principled account of certain linguistic universals in terms of general architectural constraints.

As we have already remarked, even when information-processing theorists make no claims about the form of the functional architecture, and attempt merely to develop models of certain cognitive processes, they cannot in fact avoid making certain tacit assumptions about the underlying architecture. Furthermore, the implicit adoption of some particular architecture carries with it certain further assumptions about the nature of mental functions. To see exactly what is being further assumed tacitly when a certain architecture is adopted, it is useful to look at properties of the architecture in a more abstracted way, and to ask what it is about it that makes it possible to carry out certain functions in certain ways. A fruitful way to view this question is in terms of the formal or mathematical *type* of the primitive operations built into the virtual machine. For example, the primitive relation that we call *reference* (or the operation of retrieving a symbol given another symbol that serves as its name) is of the formal type *asymmetric*. It can be used to define operations for computing other relations such as, for example, the operation we might call AFTER, which computes a relation that is irreflexive, antisymmetric, transitive, and connected over some specified set of names. Such a syntactic operation in the functional architecture can be freely interpreted, at the level of interpreted rules, as any relation of the same formal type, for example the relation of being of higher rank, or older, or being a superset of (a relation frequently used in semantic hierarchies known as ISA trees). In making such an interpretation we automatically inherit the formal properties of these built-in primitive relations. Thus we do not need to *explicitly represent* properties such as the reflexivity, symmetry, transitivity, noncyclicality, and so on, of the relation in the interpreted domain—i.e., we do not need to represent symbolically a rule such as "If X is older than Y, and Y is older than Z, then X is older than Z," if we have chosen to represent "older" by a primitive relation of the architecture that is of the appropriate formal type.

In an architecture that has what we call an "arithmetic unit" (really only a set of functional properties that are useful for, among other things, representing the syntactic rules relating numerals under certain mathematically interpretable operations), as well as an ordering relation over symbols, there is an even richer set of formal types to exploit in constructing an interpreted system of rules. For example, certain formal properties of the Peano axioms for arithmetic, as well as the metric axioms, can be modelled in terms of these primitive "arithmetic" relations. This means that, in a sense, certain aspects of metric scales are available in such an architecture. In fact, since the axioms of Euclidean geometry have a model in the real numbers, such an architecture allows us to choose an interpretation scheme that makes geometric properties available without the need to represent geometric axioms symbolically (e.g., if we interpret pairs of numerals as locations of points in space and use the "arithmetic" operations to define distances and movements through this space). If we interpret primitive relations in this way, a variety of spatial and metric properties can be represented, changed, and their consequences inferred *without the need for symbolic computation.*

This sort of exploitation of the functional architecture of computational systems is central to computer science, as we have already noted. From the point of view of cognitive science, however, it is not only important to choose functional properties of the computational architecture in such a way as to accomplish certain tasks efficiently, but is is equally important to be explicit about *why* it works, and to justify these crucial properties independently. That is, it is important for the use of computational models in an explanatory mode, rather than simply a performance mode, that we not take certain architectural features for granted simply because they happen to be available in our computer language. We must first explicitly acknowledge that certain noncomputational properties originate with certain assumed properties of the functional architecture, and then we must attempt to empirically motivate and justify such assumptions. Otherwise important features of our model may be left resting on adventitious and unmotivated assumptions.

For example, people have occasionally suggested that objects do not need to have knowledge of concepts such as, by transitivity, in making certain inferences, as in the base-term series problems ("John is taller than Mary and John is shorter than Fred. Who is tallest?"), because all they have to do is arrange the three items in order (either in a list or in an image) and read the answer off. But, of course, the fact that one can solve the problem this way does not entail that tacit knowledge of formal properties (e.g., transitivity) of the relation "taller than" is not needed, since the decision to represent "taller" by something like "further on the list" must have been based on the implicit recognition that the two relations were of the same formal type (a list would not, for example, have been suitable to represent the relation "is married to"). Furthermore, while ordering three names in a list and then examining the list for the position of a particular name may seem straightforward and free from logical deduction, a little thought will show that the ability to carry out this operation mentally, as distinct from physically, presupposes a great deal about the available primitive mental operations. For example, in the mental case, if we have the items A, B, and C, and we place A and B in a certain order and then add C next in the sequence, we must assume (in this example) that: a) placing C next to B leaves the relation between A and B unchanged, and b) the relation of A to C (with B between them) is the same with respect to the relevant represented aspect (e.g., tallness) as that between A and B. But such assumptions are justifiable only if the agent in question implicitly understands the logical properties of *succession.* Consequently, even if list operations are part of the functional architecture (which, as we saw earlier, assumes that the architecture incorporates primitive operations of the appropriate formal type), one is still not entitled to assume that the use of this capacity requires no further appeal to tacit knowledge of logical constructs. Furthermore, as Piaget has suggested, it may well be that either the availability of the relevant primitive operation *or* the tacit knowledge relevant to its appropriate use may develop with the maturation of the organism. If this were so, we might then wish to represent a logical property like transitivity as an explicit logical rule, rather than building it into the architecture [see Brainerd: "The Stage Question in Cognitive-Developmental Theory" *BBS* 1(2) 1978].

To take another timely example, matrix data structures have frequently been used to represent the spatial properties of images (e.g. Kosslyn and Schwartz 1977; Funt 1977). This is a convenient way to represent spatial layout, partly because we tend to think of matrices in spatial terms anyway. In addition, however, this structure seems to make certain consequences available without any apparent need for certain deductive steps involving reference to knowledge of geometry. For example, when we represent the locations of imagined places in our model by filling in cells of a matrix, we can "read off" facts such as which places are adjacent, which places are "left of" or "right of" or "above" or "below" a given place, and which places are "in between" a given pair of places. Furthermore, when a particular object is moved to a new place, its spatial relations to other places need not be recomputed. In an important sense this is implicit in the data structure. Such properties make the matrix a much more natural representation than, say, a list of assertions specifying the shape of objects and their locations relative to other objects.

But, as in the case of the apparently noninferential consequences of using lists, such properties of matrices arise from the existence of certain formal properties of particular functional architectures. These properties would not, for instance, be available in a Turing machine architecture. In order for a matrix data structure with the desired properties to be realizable, the architecture must provide at least the primitive capacity to address the content of a representation by *place*—i.e., it must be. possible to *name* a location and to ask for the content of a named location. This itself may require, for instance, what is known as a register architecture (or some other kind of location-addressable store). Furthermore, it must be possible in this architecture to primitively generate the names of places adjacent to a given place (i.e., it must be possible to do this without appealing to other representations or to tacit knowledge of geometry or anything else that would involve intermediate inferential steps). This is necessary in order to allow the representation to be "scanned." In addition there must be primitive predicates that, when applied to names, evaluate the relative directions of places corresponding to those names (e.g., two-place predicates such as "RIGHT-OF" must be primitive in the architecture). This, in turn, implies that there are at least two independent, implicit, total orderings over the set of names. In addition, if the relative distance between places is to be significant in this representation, then there might be further primitive operations that can be applied to place names so as to evaluate, say, relative size (e.g., the predicate "LARGER-THAN").

This whole array of formal properties is available in all common computer architectures, because they all use numerical expressions for register (i.e., place) names and have built-in primitive arithmetic operations. But these are part of such architectures for reasons that have nothing to do with the needs of cognitive science. When these features are exploited in building cognitive models, we are tacitly assuming that such operations are part of the functional architecture of the mind—an assumption that clearly needs to be justified. Arguments have rarely been provided for any such proposals. The only suggestions of an argument for such architectural features that I have seen are due to Piaget, who has been concerned with abstract formal characteristics of cognition, and Brouwer (1964) and Nicod (1970), who, for quite different reasons, proposed that *succession* be viewed as a cognitive primitive.

The general point concerning the intimate relation between virtual machine architecture and process is exactly the same as the observation that different notations for a formal system can lead to different expressive powers and even different axioms for the same system. For example, if we use conventional notation for algebraic expressions, we need to explicitly state facts about the associativity and precedence of arithmetic operators, whereas in Polish notation we do not need to represent such properties explicitly, because, in a sense, they are implicit in the notation. Similarly, propositional logic normally contains axioms for commutativity and for the complementarity expressed in de Morgan's principles. However, if we use the disjunctive normal form for logical expressions, such axioms need not be stated, because, as in the algebraic case, they are also implicit in the notation. Mechanical theorem-proving exploits a variety of such intrinsic formal properties of both the notation (e.g., using the disjunctive normal form) and the virtual machine architecture. For example, such theorem-provers can be made much more efficient and natural in certain domains by representing sets of propositions in the form of the "semantic nets," which exploit the formal properties of the reference relation available in typical register machines (i.e., in the usual Von Neumann architectures).

From the point of view of cognitive science, the notation we choose is important for reasons that go beyond questions of efficiency or naturalness. Because we claim that behavior is governed by symbolically encoded rules and representations, the exact format or notation that is used to encode these representations constitutes a claim about mental structures, and hence an empirical claim. Formats, like functional architectures, become empirically decidable in principle if we admit the relevance of the criterion of strong equivalence, and if we develop appropriate methodologies based on this criterion.

It is important to recognize that the greater the number of formal properties built into a notation, or the greater the number of primitively fixed formal properties of the functional architecture that must be exploited, the weaker the expressive power, and the more constrained will be the resulting computational system. This is because we no longer have the option of changing such properties at will. In choosing a particular notation or architecture, we are making a commitment concerning which aspects of the functions are to be viewed as the free parameters that are tailored to fit specific situations, and which are to be viewed as the fixed properties shared by all functions in the class of models that can be constructed using that notation. The more constrained a notation or architecture, the greater the explanatory power of resulting models. It provides a principled rationale for why the model takes one particular form, as opposed to other logically possible ones. Recall that the lack of such a rationale was one of the features that made some computational models *ad hoc*. One goal in developing explanatory cognitive models then, would be to fix as many properties as possible by building them into the fixed functional architecture. Opposing this goal, however, is the need to account for the remarkable flexibility of human cognition. We shall see in section 10 that this character of cognition provides the strongest reason for attributing much of its manifested behavior to tacit knowledge of various kinds rather than to the sorts of fixed functional properties that have frequently been proposed.

9. COGNITIVE FUNCTIONAL ARCHITECTURE

The architecture-algorithm distinction is central to the project of using computational models as part of an explanation of cognitive phenomena. The core notion of strong equivalence depends upon there being a common architecture among processes. Processes can only be compared if their grain or "level of aggregation" [to use Newell and Simon's (1972) phrase] is the same. In fact, even the formal semantic properties of programs, as developed by Scott and Strachey (1971), are relative to an abstract model of computation that, in effect, specifies an appropriate grain for the analysis. Furthermore, the privileged vocabulary claim (described in section 4) asserts that cognitive phenomena can be accounted for solely by appealing to the symbolic representations (i.e., the algorithm and its associated data structures). Thus, any differences among such phenomena arise solely from the structure of these symbol systems—from the way component parts are put together. Thus, no distinctions among phenomena that we would classify as cognitive distinctions can be due to such things as differences in the way the primitive operations that constitute the algorithm themselves function. Furthermore, if differences in cognitive processing between individuals are to be explained within our computational framework, it is necessary that the basic functional architecture be universal.

Mental architecture can be viewed as consisting of just those functions or basic operations of mental processing that are themselves not given a process explanation. Thus they are functions instantiated in the biological medium. Unlike cognitive functions in general, they are, on the one hand, the primitive functions appealed to in characterizing cognition, and on the other hand, they are functions that are themselves explainable biologically, rather than in terms of rules and representations. Thus we see that the architecture-algorithm distinction parallels one we made earlier between functions symbolically computed. Since we gave, as two of the conditions for the appropriateness of the latter way of characterizing a function, that the relation between antecedent conditions and subsequent behavior be arbitrary and informationally plastic (or cognitively penetrable), these criteria will consequently be relevant to distinguishing between functions attributable to the architecture and functions attributable to the structure of the algorithm and the cognitive representations. This is our answer to Wittgenstein's "third man" puzzle. We do not need a regress of levels of interpreters, with each one interpreting the rules of the higher level and each in turn following its own rules of interpretation. Nor do we need to view our computational model as consisting of a cascade of "intentional instantiations," as Haugeland (1978) does. Only one uniform level of rules is followed, since only one symbolic level of *cognitively* interpreted representations and of cognitive process is involved. However complex the remaining functions are, they are considered to be instantiated by the underlying biological medium—i.e., they are part of the functional architecture. The reader will note a certain inevitable circularity in the above discussion of the relation between cognition and the architecture/algorithm boundary. On the one hand, cognitive phenomena are understood as those which, under the appropriate interpretation of observations, can be accounted for solely by examining the algorithm. On the other hand, the distinction between what is attributable to the algorithm and what is attributable to the functional architecture is to be decided on the basis of whether certain phenomena (namely cognitive ones) can be accounted for while keeping the architecture fixed. This circularity is not, however, vicious. The basic core intuitions concerning what constitutes a cognitive phenomenon will not have to be revised willy-nilly every time a new algorithm is formulated. While the domain of the theory will evolve gradually to accommodate the evolving theoretical system, yet at any time there will be phenomena clearly identifiable as cognitive. These are the ones that will adjudicate whether or not some function is legitimately viewed as part of the mental architecture that is to serve as the fixed primitive basis for constructing specific algorithms.

We may therefore summarize the conditions under which a specific function or behavioral property may be attributed to properties of the fixed functional architecture as follows: 1) If the form of the hypothetical function or the putative property can be systematically influenced by purely cognitive factors, such as changes in instructions or in the information-bearing aspects of the context, or any other condition that clearly leads to differences in goals, beliefs, interpretations, and so on; or 2) if we must postulate variations in the form of the hypothetical function or in the putative property in order to account for certain systematic differences in observations of cognitive phenomena; then such a function or property may *not* be attributed to properties of the fixed functional architecture (or the "medium"). Consequently, if it is not attributable to a property of the functional architecture, it must be given a cognitive account that appeals to the structure of the process and to the content and form of the representations. This cognitive process model itself will, as we noted earlier, have to acknowledge explicitly the contribution of the task demands in setting the goals and in accounting for the skill exhibited by the model.

Conditions (1) and (2) above are required not only because of our proprietary vocabulary hypothesis, but also by the arguments raised earlier regarding when it is appropriate to invoke rules and representations to explain observed behavior. Notice how closely conditions (1) relates to the informational plasticity criterion of rule-governed behavior. The informal notion of informational plasticity refers to the property of a system in virtue of which certain aspects of its behavior can be systematically altered by information, and hence by how the organism encodes stimuli or interprets events. We argued that the explanation of such behavior should appeal to rules and representations. Such a property is, of course, also one of the clearest signs that we are dealing with cognitive phenomena. Hence the proprietary vocabulary hypothesis and the representation-governed behavior arguments converge on the same principled distinction, which we take as defining the architecture/algorithm boundary.

Condition (2) can also be viewed in a way that brings out its relation to the distinction between automatic and attentional processes, which has attracted considerable interest recently (e.g., Posner and Snyder 1975; Schneider and Shiffrin 1977). Condition (2) entails the claim that functions attributable to the functional architecture can consume only constant resources. In other words, they must not include what are referred to as "attentional" processes. For any differences in resource use must arise from different execution traces of cognitive processes, or different algorithmic sequences. Hence functions that exhibit such differences do not qualify as part of the fixed architecture. I have discussed this issue in connection with Anderson's (1978) behavioral mimicry claim (Pylyshyn, 1979b), where I pointed out some of the consequences of allowing varying complexity (e.g., as indexed by reaction time) to be exhibited by primitive operations (or individual steps) in a process.

We thus conclude that a basic methodological distinguishing mark of functions that are part of the basic fixed functional architecture of the mind is that they cannot be influenced in their operation by what might be called informational or cognitive factors, nor do variations in their operation need to be posted in order to account for observed cognitive phenomena. Such functions and properties remain, to use a phrase that I have adopted in other contexts (e.g., Pylyshyn 1979a; 1979b), *cognitively impenetrable.*

The criterion of cognitive impenetrability serves as the litmus by which we can decide whether a function is a fixed, built-in, causally explainable, primitive operation or property in terms of which cognitive processes are to be described, or whether it will itself require a computational or process explanation. It is clear why such a criterion is needed. Without it one could not distinguish between a literal and metaphorical appeal to a computational model. By providing a principled boundary between the "software" and the "hardware," or between functions that must be explained mentally (i.e., computationally), and those that can only be explained biologically, one can factor the explanation into the fixed biological components and the more variable symbolic or rule-governed components. Like the factoring of fixed universal constants from particular conditions specific to the case at hand, which occurs in all physical explanations, or the factoring of linguistic universals (also taken to represent fixed properties of mind), from language-specific rules and comprehension algorithms, which occurs in models of linguistic competence, such factoring is essential for accounts to achieve explanatory adequacy.

Although, as I have repeatedly stressed, the explanation of how the primitive properties of the functional architecture are realized will ultimately be given in biological or physical terms, this should not be interpreted as meaning either that such properties must be stated in a biological vocabulary, or that they are to be inferred from biological observations. It has sometimes been claimed (e.g., Anderson 1978; Palmer 1978) that only biological data could help us decide between certain theoretical proposals for fixed properties of the cognitive system—such as between analogical and propositional forms of representation. It should be clear from the current discussion of functional architecture that this is not so. Although the architecture represents a crucial interface between properties requiring a cognitive process account and those requiring a biological account, the actual description of this architecture is a functional one. It simply specifies the primitive functions or fixed symbol-manipulation operations of the cognitive system. Furthermore, the point of the cognitive impenetrability condition is to provide a purely functional methodology for deciding whether a putative property qualifies as belonging in the category of architecture or in the category of cognitive process.

Finally, before concluding this section I must again reiterate the very strong contrast between the position I have been describing and psychophysical dualism. According to the present view, two distinct types of explanation of human behavior are possible. One of these is naturalistic (i.e., it appeals directly to intrinsic properties of the organism) and the other cognitive (i.e., it appeals to internal representations). I have tried to sketch some general criteria under which each is appropriate. But for many people there still remains the uneasy question of why it should be the case that a certain class of systems (e.g., certain organisms and computers) admit of these two analyses, while other (perhaps equally complex) systems (e.g., space vehicles) do not. Since the minutest details of the operation of all systems are clearly governed by causal physical laws, one might ask what distinguishes these two classes of system.

In its most general form this question runs into the problem of the intentionality of human cognition—a problem that is clearly beyond the scope of the present essay. This is the question of what it is about a mental representation or a thought that makes it a thought *about* some particular thing rather than another. For example, since the Löwenheim-Skolem theorem assures us that any consistent formal system has a model in the integers, any such formal system could be just as legitimately viewed as representing, say, the natural numbers as anything else we care to name. Fodor suggests that an essential methodological strategy of cognitive psychology is to factor away the intentionality question and develop models that are concerned primarily with coherence. Interesting questions still remain, even if we somehow factor away the difficult issue of intentionality from the issue of epistemic mediation. However, even in that case we can still ask what it is about certain systems that makes them candidates for an epistemic mediation account that appeals to representations and rules.

Among the exogenous factors to which we have already alluded is the human imperative to explain cognitive behaviors in terms that parallel the form in which we plan and conceive of our own behavior. Perhaps as a direct consequence of this it also seems that the appropriate regularities in our behavior are to be found when it is described in terms of what Kenneth Pike (1967) referred to as an *emic* as opposed to an *etic* taxonomy (i.e., intensional as opposed to extensional, conceptual as opposed to objective, or perceptual as opposed to physical). Of course this applies only when the phenomena to be explained are themselves cast in such terms—as they must be in the case of meaningful human behavior. Thus, to explain how the mouth and tongue move and how acoustical energy patterns are generated, we appeal to the taxonomy and laws of physics and perhaps biology, whereas to explain what someone was saying at the time and their choice of words, we must appeal to cognitive concepts and processes.

But even if we accept such reasons for turning to a representational account of human behavior, there still remains the question of what intrinsic properties humans and computers share that make behavior fitting such an account possible. Many years ago Kohler (1929) offered some suggestions on this question. He distinguished between processes that were determined by anatomically fixed, or, as he called them, "topographical factors," and those that were determined by nonlocalizable or "dynamic factors" such as "forces and other factors inherent in the processes of the system." I believe that Kohler was on the right track in this analysis (which he used in arguing for certain differences between biological and technological systems). However, he had too limited a view of how topographic factors could operate. Perhaps because of the types of artifacts with which he was familiar, Kohler took the spatial distribution of constraints to be the primary focus of the distinction. What this fails to recognize, however, is that in certain systems (e.g., computers) the functional structure can still change radically, even when the topographical structure remains fixed. Functionally, the part-whole relation in this kind of system is such that global discontinuities in function are produced by appropriate local changes in structure. Such propagation of local changes to produce systematic global effects is what Kohler believed would require a different sort of system—one governed primarily by nonanatomical dynamic factors such as field effects [see also Puccetti & Dykes: "Sensory Cortex and the Mind-Brain Problem" *BBS* 1(3) 1978].

Although Kohler may even have been right in his analysis of the structural nature of biological as opposed to artifactual systems, the realization of computational processes in topographically fixed systems shows that this particular dimension of difference is not a logical prerequisite for representation-governed behavior. Rather, what seems necessary is just what was hinted at above—namely, that the fixed factors, regardless of whether they are due to the topography or to laws of interaction of forces within prescribed boundary conditions or to any other fixed constraints, enable a certain kind of radical second-order flexibility. That flexibility might be characterized in terms of the global alteration of function that can be effected through local changes, or in terms of the existence of instantaneous functional networks that can be varied over and above the fixed topographical network, or in some other way. I do not know of a satisfactory way of precisely specifying this function in abstract terms, but I believe that it amounts to the requirement that the functional architecture be universal in Turing's sense—i.e., that it be capable of computing any computable function or of simulating any Turing machine. Whatever the correct general specification of this function is, it must distinguish between the long-term, structurally fixed functions that we have called the functional architecture, and the instantaneously alterable functions that are necessary to sustain rule-governed behavior and to enable behavior to change radically in response to such transitory effects as the inferences that the system makes upon receipt of new information. Only a system that has this character can be a candidate for a rule-governed system. What further requirements it must meet beyond that I cannot say, but clearly this particular aspect of rule-governed behavior does not raise any problems for a materialist view of mind.

10. THE PSYCHOLOGICAL RELEVANCE OF THE NOTION OF FUNCTIONAL ARCHITECTURE

In this section I shall discuss some of the implications of the present view for the development of cognitive theory. In the next section I will consider the traditional importance of something like the notion of functional architecture in psychology and examine several "fixed functions" that might be viewed as proposed properties of such an architecture.

The analysis we have been giving can be viewed as setting out a particular program of research—namely that of designing a cognitive virtual machine, or rather a system of programming language having a functional architecture appropriate for implementing cognitive algorithms. Such a machine (which, of course, would have to be emulated on available computers) would, among other things, display the appropriate resource-limited constraints characteristic of human processing. For example, it might conceivably be possible to implement various algorithms on such a machine for carrying out essentially the same function but with different trade-offs. It might, for instance, be possible to have an algorithm that attended to (i.e., whose behavior depended on) a larger number of symbolic expressions, in exchange for requiring more steps (thus trading off speed and memory load), or one that took fewer steps but failed to attend to some of the potentially relevant data (thus perhaps exhibiting a speed/accuracy trade-off).

As we have already pointed out, such an architecture would also make possible the goal of designing algorithms that were strongly equivalent to ones used by humans. Computational complexity profiles of processes, as the latter ranged over various systematic changes in inputs, could simply be read off from properties of the execution of the algorithms such as the number of primitive steps they took in each case. Such complexity features would now be empirically significant, rather than merely incidental properties of the model. These could then be compared with various hypothesized empirical correlates of human processing complexity—such as reaction times, perhaps. In the ideal case every operation and every feature of algorithms implemented on such an architecture would constitute an empirical hypothesis, just as every theorem derivable from Newtonian axioms constitutes an empirical prediction. One would not say of an algorithm executable on this architecture that the mind cannot compute such a function since, by hypothesis, processing constraints such as resource limitations, or any other fixed universal limitation in processing capacity, would have been incorporated into the architecture. Thus *every* algorithm that could be executed on this virtual machine would now be considered a humanly possible cognitive process, just as any grammar generatable by an ideal universal grammar (in Chomsky's sense) is a possible structure of a human (or humanly accessible) language.

This fact itself has the interesting consequence that it eliminates a certain asymmetry between what appear to be two radically different ways in which the rules and representations in a model could be modified. On the one hand there are the changes that come about as a consequence of various "inputs" to the model. These produce only orderly and psychologically appropriate modifications in representational states. On the other hand there are the changes that come about when the programmer intervenes by adding or deleting rules or inserting new representations. Since in conventional programming systems these changes are not constrained in any way by psychological considerations, they could result in the most bizarre and humanly inaccessible algorithms being specified. With the functional architecture appropriately constrained, however, this distinction in large part disappears, since all and only cognitively possible (though for various reasons perhaps not actual) algorithms and representations are permitted, regardless of their genesis.

The most concerted effort at designing a cognitive virtual machine (or at least at developing design specifications for an appropriate functional architecture) is currently being pursued by Allen Newell. The present form of this design is called a "production system." There are some interesting reasons for this particular choice, which we shall not go into here. They relate, in part, to Newell's concern with modelling certain resource-consuming properties of computation, which in conventional systems are not visible to the user but remain a part of the "backstage" activity of the virtual machine— namely, the control structure itself. The reader is referred to Newell (1973; 1982) for a technical discussion of these issues.

However, we should note that the view expressed here on the importance of the functional architecture does not commit one to the project of designing a complete cognitive virtual machine as the first step. Indeed, simply having in mind that every computational model commits one to implicit assumptions concerning the underlying architecture can keep one from making at least some of the more problematic assumptions. As one example of this approach, Pylyshyn, Elcock, Marmor, and Sander (1978) report some highly preliminary results of a research project aimed at understanding aspects of perceptual-motor coordination as these are involved in drawing diagrams and making inferences from what is seen. This project was primarily concerned with certain design issues that arise when one avoids certain technically simple, but in our view cognitively implausible, ways of dealing with the problem of representing spatial relations in a computational model, especially in the context of perceptual-motor coordination [see Gyr et al.: "Motor-Sensory Feedback and Geometry of Visual Space" *BBS* 2(1) 1979]. When experimental data concerning some particular human cognitive function were not available, we followed the strategy of adopting the least powerful mechanism we could devise to carry out that function.

For example, instead of maintaining a matrix structure as a global representation of the spatial layout, our system only used a qualitative representation of spatial relations, together with a limited number of pointers to specific places on the retina. Coordination with the motor system was accomplished through a minimal mechanism, which was able to maintain a "cross-modality" binding between visual and kinesthetic spaces for only two places. We thought of these as "fingers," whose position (when they were on the retina) could be seen, and whose location in proprioceptive space could continue to be sensed even when they were off the retina. Thus we had a primitive ability to hold on to off-retinal locations in order to glance back to them. This "two-finger" mechanism made possible a quite general drawing capability, which extended beyond the foveal region. The general strategy was to opt for *minimal mechanisms* wherever possible, even at the cost of a computationally awkward system, on the grounds that such mechanisms committed one to the weakest presuppositions about the underlying architecture, and hence ones that could easily be revised upward without the need to radically redesign the system. A number of such minimal mechanisms were proposed and are described in the Pylyshyn et al. (1978) paper. This is an instance of the application of the principle of "least committment" to the design project. Newell's production-system architecture proposal, referred to above, and Marr and Nishihara's (1977) minimal mechanism for rotating the principle axes of a three-dimensional model to bring it into congruence with a given two-dimensional retinal pattern, could both be viewed as examples of this strategy.

In addition to these more ambitious goals of applying the idea of a cognitive virtual machine directly to the design task, one can also appeal to it in deciding the soundness of certain proposals concerning the nature of cognitive processing. It is useful to have a general criterion for distinguishing among classes of mechanisms when these are proposed as components of a cognitive model or a cognitive explanation. For example, it is useful to have a principled basis for deciding whether a certain cognitive phenomenon ought to be viewed as arising from the nature of some analogue representational medium, as frequently claimed, or whether it will require an explanation in terms of the nature of the symbolic cognitive process itself. In the latter case the properties we observe might be seen as arising from tacit knowledge, rather than from the nature of the mechanism or medium, as we suggested earlier was the case for the "mental scanning" phenomena.

Recall that one of the features of analogues was that they were nonsymbolic and noncomputational. Analogue representations, as generally conceived, are not articulated symbolic expressions, and analogue processes are not viewed as rule-governed symbolic computations. They can thus be viewed as characteristics of the functional architecture. I believe that it is this quality of incorporating fixed constraints into the architecture, and therefore of weakening the expressive power and consequently increasing the explanatory value of the models, that makes analogue systems particularly attractive in cognitive science. It is not the fact that such systems may be more efficient or more natural, nor even that they may be continuous or holistic in some sense, that ought to be their attraction. None of these are essential properties of analogues: analogue processes don't have to be efficient, nor must they be continuous, as opposed to quantized, to retain their analogue character (e.g., imagine your favorite analogue model approximated by a discrete but finely grained quantization). What they do seem to require is that the formal property that characterizes their function be explainable as being instantiated or exhibited, rather than as being symbolically computed by the operation of rules on symbolic representations. Thus, whether some particular function should be explained as a noncomputational or as an analogue process is the same kind of question we raised earlier in this essay; namely, whether the appropriate explanation of some behavior is one that appeals to rules and representations or merely to primitive dispositions. An examination of a number of proposed analogue mechanisms suggests that, as formulated (i.e., in their simplest and most attractive form), they all exhibit some degree of cognitive penetration and hence are not eligible as part of the noncomputational function of the system. Examples such as those discussed by Pylyshyn (1979a; 1979c) considerably weaken the case for the existence of a large degree of nonsymbolic processing in cognition, at least of the kind that has frequently been proposed in discussions of, say, imagery phenomena. Every case of cognitive penetration is an instance in which we are forced to relax the hypothesized fixed functional constraints. While it will always be possible in principle to build very flexible inferential processes, which at various arbitrary points in their operation turn to highly constrained subsystems (as, for example, in the suggestion put forth by Kosslyn et al. 1979, for a way to retain the holistic analogue rotation in the face of the data I reported), it is much more problematic to justify such hybrid models. Such proposals work only by subverting the main motivation for positing such fixed architectural capacities as, say, the ability to "mentally rotate" an image—namely the greater explanatory power inherent in the weakest or least expressive system. In such hybrid models we would need to have strong independent reasons for retaining the (now redundant) constrained subprocesses.

11. THE SEARCH FOR FIXED ARCHITECTURAL FUNCTIONS

If we take a broad view of the notion of functional architecture, we can recognize that proposals for components of such an architecture are not infrequent in psychological theorizing—in fact, they have often characterized the differences among psychological schools. For example, the dominant assumption, from the time of the British empiricists until about fifteen years ago (and even today in some quarters), was that the principal built-in functional capacity of organisms was their ability to form associative links. For this assumption to be predictive it was further necessary to specify the sorts of entities over which the associations could be formed (e.g., for behaviorists these had to be behaviorally defined), as well as conditions on the formation and evocation of these links (e.g., conditions such as contiguity, reinforcement, generalization gradients, and so on). Such a hypothetical capacity, like many of the more contemporary nonbehaviorist proposals [cf. Bindra: "How Adaptive Behavior Is Produced" *BBS* 1(1) 1978], was intuitively appealing because it agreed with our informal observation of certain aggregate (i.e., statistical) regularities of behavior, as well as of behavior in certain highly controlled situations.

It is no accident that the controlled situations that were investigated from the conditioning perspective universally involved the suppression of what we have been calling cognitive factors. The experimental paradigm was always contrived in such a way that beliefs, goals, inferences, or interpretations were rendered irrelevant as much as possible. Furthermore, critical observations were invariably expressed as frequencies or probabilities, thus averaging over any remaining cognitive effects or strategies. However, cognitive factors inevitably still left their effect in the case of research involving human subjects. In those cases, as Brewer (1974) has eloquently argued, the most plausible explanation of human conditioning phenomena is one given in terms of change in belief. In other words, the most straightforward explanation of what reinforcers do is that they inform the subject of the contingent utilities. Thus, for example, the same effects can typically be produced by other ways of persuasively providing the same information (such as explaining to subjects the conditions under which they will or will not be shocked and backing up the story by showing them the wiring).

However, I don't doubt that there are ways of incorporating such results into the conditioning account (especially since individuation criteria for "stimulus," "response," or "reinforcer" are unspecified within the theory, allowing our informal "folk psychology" to come to our aid in describing the situation appropriately and thus smuggling knowledge on cognitive factors into the predictions). Yet, whatever approach one takes to explaining such phenomena, Brewer's review and analysis of a large number of studies makes it clear that even the simplest and most paradigmatic cases of conditioning in humans (e.g., avoidance conditioning of finger withdrawal to shock, or conditioning of the eyeblink reflex) exhibit cognitive penetration—i.e., they are radically, yet systematically, influenced by what the subjects believe (or by what they are told or shown). Thus even these simplest cases do not demonstrate that conditioning is a primitive function of the fixed architecture. As before (e.g., the mental rotation case mentioned earlier), attempts to retain this function as a primitive might well be possible at the cost of considerably weakening the claims that can be made about the role of conditioning—e.g., by relegating it to the role of one small element in a large cognitive process involving rules, representations, goals, inferences, and so on. But then the burden of proof falls on those who posit this mechanism to show that it is still necessary, given the flexibility of the remainder of the system that has to be posited in any case.

An intrinsic part of the conditioning account—and the only part that could conceivably explain novel behavior, is the notion of generalization. A more sophisticated contemporary version of the generalization gradient is the similarity space. Just as conditioning requires dimensions along which it can generalize to new stimuli, so some contemporary theories that appeal to prototypes require dimensions of similarity in order to account for the relations among prototypes as well as between prototypes and various exemplars or instances. Among those theoretical approaches that seek to avoid the complexities of inferential and problem-solving processes in accounting for such phenomena as recognition and classification (e.g., Rosch 1973), the most common proposal is the functional similarity space. Even Quine (1977) speaks of biologically endowed "quality space." Though no account is given of how such a space might be realized (presumably neurophysiologically), or how the location of novel stimuli in the space is determined, it can still be viewed as a possible component of the functional architecture. Thus it is appropriate once again to inquire whether this view can be empirically sustained.

The first thing to notice is that such a view cannot be applied to stimuli such as sentences, since it is clear that there is an unbounded variety of ways in which sentences can relevantly differ—i.e., there is no finite set of dimensions or categories of comparison that can exhaustively locate the meaning of a sentence in a similarity space. While it seems likely that the same is true of visual patterns, the existence of at least some quantitative dimensions of similarity (e.g., size, orientation, color-distance) makes it not as clear as in the language case. On the other hand, the very strong interactions among such putative dimensions—demonstrated repeatedly by the Gestaltists— could also be cited against the view that these can be treated as orthogonal dimensions in a similarity space. One of the clearest and simplest demonstrations of the inadequacy of the similarity space view, however, comes from the work of one of the pioneers of the multidimensional scaling technique. Shepard (1964) showed that when stimuli varied along several dimensions, judgements of their similarity could yield ratings that conform to a Euclidean metric along any of the dimensions of variation, depending on what subjects are instructed to attend to. But when the subjects were not given specific attention instructions and were left to attend to whatever they wished, the resulting data failed to conform to any metric (Euclidean or non-Euclidean) in the number of dimensions along which the stimuli varied. Shepard concluded that subjects' noticing strategy determined the similarity structure of their judgements—and these were free to move from one possible similarity space to another at will. In other words, the similarity space function is itself cognitively penetrable.

Once again, one could probably get around this sort of counterexample by allowing a cognitive component to preanalyse the stimulus prior to the use of the similarity space. But as in the previous case, in which such added cognitive processes had to be posited, it is no longer clear what function the space would now be serving, other than as an *ad hoc* parameter to increase the precision of prediction. For, if we need a cognitive process to analyse and oversee the recognition, we already have a mechanism that, at least in principle, is capable of accounting for the similarity structure of the set of stimuli. Again the burden would be on those who posit such a fixed function to show exactly what principled role it plays (not just in providing similarity judgements, but as a general representational system).

The latter result is only one of a large number of cases in psychophysics in which attempts to posit fixed psychophysical functions have run into difficulty because they turned out to be cognitively penetrable. Almost any psychophysical judgement that requires the subject to attend selectively to certain specific aspects of the stimulus, while ignoring other aspects, is likely to be cognitively penetrable. One of the best known examples of a simple function that turned out to be cognitively penetrable is the simple sensory threshold. It was shown to be penetrable by subjects' beliefs concerning the utilities of alternative responses—a finding that generated considerable interest in the theory of signal detectability (a decision-theoretic and therefore cognitive analysis) as an alternative to the threshold function.

Similarly, it has been argued (e.g., Segall, Campbell, and Herskovits 1963) that visual phenomena such as the Muller-Lyer illusion are also penetrable, though not as directly as the threshold function. The argument is that in time the function responsible for the illusion can be influenced by cognitive experience (in particular by experience with large three-dimensional rectangular shapes such as buildings). The "new look" movement in perception in the 1950s (e.g., Bruner 1957) was also built upon the recognition that a great deal of the perceptual process is penetrable. Among the better known experimental results in cognitive psychology that could be viewed in this way are the various instances of cognitive penetration demonstrated in studies of selective attention. It seems as though every time one investigator has proposed an attention-selection filter of one sort, another investigator has found evidence that the operation of that filter was sensitive to aspects of the information that the filter was supposed to have eliminated, and that therefore must have been getting through (see Norman 1969 for a review of some of these results). That is why, in an early model of selective attention, Norman (1968) found it necessary to include a factor he called "pertinence," which affects the recognition threshold of the postfilter processing. As the name suggests, the introduction of the pertinence factor is nothing but an admission that such processing is cognitively penetrable.

The various proposals that go by the title of "direct perception," as developed by J. J. Gibson (1979) and others, can be viewed as proposals for functions that are part of the fixed functional architecture of the perceptual system. The denial by this school of any "epistemic mediation" in perception makes it particularly clear that they view functions, such as those that are said to "pick up information" concerning perceptual invariants, as being instantiated by the functional architecture. But such proposals have generally not withstood the test being proposed here: the detection of everything from distance information to one's grandmother appears to be cognitively penetrable.

Howard (1978) has shown that even the perception of so obvious a property of a display as the horizontality of a colored fluid in a transparent container is strongly influenced by knowledge of the relevant physical principle. In his studies, conservatively conducted using trick forms of three-dimensional photographs and motion pictures, with the method of random presentation, Howard made the startling discovery that over half the population of undergraduate subjects he tested were unable to recognize anomalous stimuli, despite the fact that some of the mistakenly classified pictures depicted deviations of fluid levels as much as thirty degrees off horizontal, and despite the fact that the perceptual discriminability of the orientations involved was clearly above threshold, as evidenced by other methods of assessment. For example, the same subjects who failed the horizontality test could readily report when the surface of the fluid was not parallel to shelves visible in the background. What was even more surprising and relevant to the present discussion was that postexperimental interviews, scored blindly by two independent judges, revealed that *every* subject who recognized all anomalous stimuli that were out by at least five degrees could clearly articulate the principle of fluid level invariance, whereas *no* subject who failed to recognize such stimuli as deviant gave even a hint of understanding the revelevant principle. What is especially surprising in these studies was that evidence of knowledge of the relevant principle was obtainable by verbal probing. Usually the inference that tacit knowledge is involved is much less direct—as is the case for phonological rules and for at least some instances of syntactic rules.

In a similar vein I have argued for the cognitive penetrability of visual (or "imaginal") memory (Pylyshyn 1973; 1978c), of the proposed analogue function of "mental rotation" of images (Pylyshyn 1979a), and of the spatiality of images as inferred from "mental scanning" studies (Pylyshyn 1979c; also in section 5 above).

The point of these examples is not to suggest that all mental functions are cognitively penetrable. Indeed, I do not see how a computational view of cognition could be developed if that were so. (I don't mean that it would be impossible, only that it would require a rather different conception of functional architecture, and hence of algorithmic process.) The point is merely to suggest that many of the more constraining (and hence potentially more explanatory) proposals fail because of the flexibility of human cognition.

Of course, there are numerous examples of proposals that have not failed the test of penetrability (at least not yet). Most of these involve more peripheral functions, and most of them have been studied only relatively recently. For example, the work of Marr (1979) and associates provides some rather clear examples of complex processes that do not appear to be penetrable. These involve early visual processes (e.g., derivation of what Marr calls the "raw primal sketch" from incoming visual information, combining information from two retinal inputs to derive stereoptically encoded structures, derivation of certain textural and form information from retinally local patterns, and so on). At the motor end there has similarly been considerable success in demonstrating cognitively impenetrable functions (the earliest of which goes back to the work by Bernstein 1967). [See Roland, *BBS* 1(1) 1978.]

It is rather more difficult to point to examples of more central processes that are clear instances of impenetrable architectural functions. Perhaps this is because central cognitive processes are more like deductions—in which virtually any two concepts can be connected by some inference path under the appropriate circumstances. Thus I suspect that the semantic net propsals (including the organization of the lexicon in Morton's [1970] Logogen model) could be shown to be penetrable, though I know of no direct evidence bearing on this question at the moment. My own suspicions are that the functions that will be considered part of the functional architecture of such higher level processes as thinking and commonsense reasoning will be of two distinct kinds. On the one hand there will be extremely primitive elementary symbol processing operations, though they are unlikely to be the sorts of operations found in contemporary serial digital computers. On the other hand there will be extremely abstract constraints on data structures and on the control system. Further, the primitive functions needed may be quite different in different parts of the cognitive system, though there may well be common resource allocation mechanisms (e.g., a common type of control structure).

The apparent lack of highly constrained functional properties of the sort that our folk psychology might lead us to expect should not surprise us. This is one of the areas where we are seeking deeper explanatory principles and hence where folk psychology is least likely to be of service. The comparable case in which some success has been achieved in seeking highly constrained and universal properties is in the case of linguistic universals or universal grammar. There it has become obvious that properties of this sort could only be found at extremely high levels of abstractness, and at a considerable deductive distance from our intuitions and observations. There is no reason to expect the situation to be any different in the case of other areas of cognition.

Furthermore, to expect that observations such as those associated with the study of mental imagery will provide a direct route to the functional architecture of mind is to vastly underestimate the flexibility of mental processes. Even in those cases in which, out of habit or for some other reason (such as, for example, a certain typical way of interpreting the task demands of imagery tasks), it turns out that people very frequently do things in certain ways when they image, this need not be of any special theoretical significance, since it may not be due to any general properties of mind, but perhaps to certain long-standing habits. For example, when we find that people typically solve problems by imagining that they are viewing a sequence of events in more detail than is actually needed to find the solution, this fact itself could be due to some relatively uninteresting reason (from a theoretical standpoint). For example, it may be that this is what subjects believed they were supposed to do; or it may simply reflect a logical way of decomposing the task so as to make use of knowledge of certain elementary facts, such as what happens when certain small changes are made to an object (e.g., in the Shepard and Feng 1972 case, what happens when a single fold is made in a sheet of paper—

see the discussion of this interpretation in Pylyshyn 1978c), or subjects may simply have been in the habit of doing it in some particular way for one reason or another. The point is that mere statistical regularities need not tell us anything about the nature of mental structures. More significant theoretical questions arise when we inquire into which of these regularities are inviolable because they arise from fixed properties of mind—is from the functional architecture.

Rather than placing the emphasis on explaining regularities that may well reflect little more than aggregate averages over various habits of thought, we ought to be far more impressed with the extreme flexibility that thought *can* exhibit. For example, we ought to take seriously the fact that there seems to be no specifiable limit to what the human mind can imagine or think. As George Miller recently remarked to me, the salient property of mental life is surely the fact that we can will it to do practically anything we wish: given the appropriate goals and beliefs, we can alter our behavior and our thoughts to a remarkable extent by a mere act of will. Although psychology has typically focused on the things we cannot do well or on the habitual patterns of behavior we display, one should not lose sight of the fact that a psychological theory of any interest will also have to account for the fact that most of these patterns and limitations can be overcome, and hence that they tell us little about the underlying cognitive system. Thus, however uncomfortable may be the possibility that very many of the functions that have been studied by psychologists are not fixed mechanisms—in the sense that they are cognitively penetrable—we must be prepared to recognize that what is universal and fixed about the human mind may be very different from the sorts of gross functions that we readily infer from the patterns we observe in behavior. It could well turn out—and indeed it seems extremely likely, judging from the sorts of considerations explored in this paper—that the major problem in understanding how cognition proceeds will be to explain how the vast tacit knowledge at our disposal is organized and how it is brought to bear in determining our thoughts, our imaginings, and our actions. To do this will require that we pay special attention to formalisms adequate to the task of representing the relevant knowledge, rather than primarily addressing the issue of how *typical* behavior might be generatable. This, in turn, presupposes that we take seriously such distinctions as between competence and performance (see Chomsky 1964; Pylyshyn 1977) or, to use McCarthy and Hayes's (1969) term, the distinction between the epistemological and the heuristic problems of intelligence. One considerable advantage that the computational view of cognition gives us is the potential to explore these more abstract issues formally and to work with longer deductive chains between observations and explanatory principles.

ACKNOWLEDGMENTS

This paper was written while the author was a visiting fellow at the Center for Cognitive Science, Massachusetts Institute of Technology. The support of M.I.T. and the Social Science and Humanities Research Council of Canada is gratefully acknowledged.

I also wish to acknowledge my indebtedness to Allen Newell, who provided the inspiration for several of the ideas developed here. In particular the notion of mental architecture first arose from Newell's work on production systems, and its importance became clear to me after some discussions with Newell at a workshop at Carnegie-Mellon University in 1973.

ALVIN I. GOLDMAN

EPISTEMICS: THE REGULATIVE THEORY OF COGNITION

wish to advocate a reorientation of epistemology. Lest anyone maintain that the enterprise I urge is not epistemology at all (even part of epistemology), I call this enterprise by a slightly different name: *epistemics*. Despite this terminological concession, I believe that the inquiry I advocate is significantly continuous with traditional epistemology. Like much of past epistemology, it would seek to regulate or guide our intellectual activities. It would try to lay down principles or suggestions for how to conduct our cognitive affairs. The contrast with traditional epistemology—at least "analytic" epistemology of the twentieth century—would be its close alliance with the psychology of cognition. The basic premise of epistemics is that one cannot give the best advice about intellectual operations without detailed information about mental processes. Since these processes are most illuminatingly studied by cognitive psychology, epistemics would go hand in hand with empirical investigation of our "information-processing" mechanisms.[1]

Before it can select and recommend intellectual procedures, epistemics must identify a suitable set of goals or outcomes that these procedures should realize. Let us postpone the question of the nature of these goals, however, since the need for a greater alliance of epistemology and psychology can be identified independently of the choice of goals. At any rate, there is a range of different but plausible goals that would all lend themselves to the same rationale.

What then are the grounds for the alliance of epistemology and psychology? There are three such grounds. First, traditional epistemology has usually employed too simple a model of our cognitive life. For one thing, its conceptual or classificatory resources have been too weak and impoverished. Epistemological principles have standardly addressed themselves to what "beliefs" (or other doxastic attitudes, such as subjective probabilities) one should have under various circumstances. From a psychological perspective, however, this sort of mental classification is too coarse-grained, as I shall argue below. Furthermore, epistemology's simplistic mental scheme has given it an overly restrictive purview of the methods that might be used to improve our cognitive "outputs." Experimental psychology promises to enrich our model of mental processes, and, thereby, provide a more fruitful framework within which regulative epistemology may be conducted.

Second, advice in matters intellectual, as in other matters, should take account of the agent's capacities. There is no point in recommending procedures that cognizers cannot follow or prescribing results that cognizers cannot attain. As in the ethical sphere, 'ought' implies 'can.' Traditional epistemology has often ignored this precept. Epistemological rules often seem to have been addressed to "ideal" cognizers, not human beings with limited information-processing resources. Epistemics wishes to take its regulative role seriously. It does not want to give merely idle advice, which humans are incapable of following. This means it must take account of the powers and limits of the human cognitive system, and this requires attention to descriptive psychology.

Third, it is appropriate for a regulative enterprise to be concerned with the flaws or defects of the system in question. To improve a tennis player's game, it is wise to begin by identifying his bad habits. To improve a political system, it is well to concentrate on its most palpable shortcomings. Analogously, if we wish to raise our intellectual performance, it behooves us to identify those traits that are most in need of improvement. We should examine our native cognitive proclivities, to see how well they operate in the absence of special training or coaching. What kinds of mistakes, if any, are we likely to make? Answers to this sort of question—which can best come from empirical psychology—can help us formulate a genuinely useful set of guidelines for the direction of the mind.

I

Let us explore these three considerations in greater detail. First, what is impoverished about traditional epistemological classifications? What is too coarse-grained about the concept of "belief," for example, and how can cognitive psychology provide more fine-grained concepts?

A sample epistemological rule of a traditional sort might have the following form: "When in circumstances of type C, believe a proposition of type p." How should such an injunction be interpreted? Philosophers have distinguished an "occurrent" and a "dispositional" sense of "belief." In psychological terms, these denote, respectively, some sort of conscious event and some sort of storage in memory. If we say that S believes dispositionally at time t that $2 + 2 = 4$, we mean not that S is consciously thinking of this proposition at t, but that he is prepared at t to retrieve it from memory. Yet memory traces differ in accessibility. How easy must it be to recall an item from memory if it is to count as "believed"?

Consider the proposition "The man I met at lunch is named 'Prescott'." Suppose that, when I probe my memory with the question, "What's the name of the man I met at lunch?," I draw a total blank. On the other hand, if someone were to mention the name "Prescott," I would immediately recognize it as the name of the man I met at lunch. In short, I have "recognition memory" for the name, but I can't retrieve it in "free recall." Given these facts, do I *believe* the foregoing proposition? How we answer this question is not really important for my purposes. The crucial point is that there are alternative strengths of memory storage, or degrees of accessibility from memory, far more complex than the ordinary term "belief" suggests. An adequate epistemology would offer a richer array of classifications.

Analytical epistemology has not only ignored the complexity of memory storage and retrieval; it has not even paid systematic attention to the simpler distinction between occurrent and dispositional belief. Yet this is critical from a regulative point of view. There is quite a difference between the injunction to entertain a given proposition actively and the injunction to keep it in ("long-term") memory at a given time. Since there are severe limits on the number of propositions we can consciously entertain at a given moment, it is pointless to enjoin a cognizer to keep *all* propositions he is warranted in believing in conscious thought. Epistemological rules must be carefully honed, to reflect these differences in status.[2]

A traditional principle that ignores the foregoing distinctions is the *total-evidence requirement*. According to this principle, the credence it is rational to give to a statement at a given time is a function of the total evidence then "available."[3] What is meant by "available"? Does it mean only those items which immediately come to mind when you entertain the statement? Does it include, in addition, items you can retrieve with effortful search? Does it even include items for which you have "recognition memory" only? The term 'available' is obviously ambiguous, and this renders the requirement too unclear for actual application. How much effortful search of memory, if any, are you supposed to undertake when trying to make a "doxastic decision" vis-à-vis a given proposition?

Admittedly, the distinctions I have here been drawing *might* be made independently of experimental psychology. But in fact it is the detailed study of memory mechanisms that has prompted the distinction between "recognition" memory and "free recall." This illustrates how psychological investigation can refine our mentalistic conceptual scheme.

The restricted set of *methods* considered by analytical epistemology may be illustrated by Roderick Chisholm's *Theory of Knowledge*.[4] On page 15, Chisholm suggests an "intellectual requirement" to the effect that, for any proposition a person considers, he should *"try his best to bring it about"* that he believes the proposition if and only if it is true. What kinds of methods should a person employ in order to satisfy this requirement? Chisholm doesn't pose this question in a general way, but his own "epistemic principles" seem designed to fill this bill. They indicate the appropriateness of belief or suspension of judgment in propositions as a function of certain current beliefs of the cognizer. Thus, they are somewhat analogous to principles of reasoning. But this class of principles is a very narrow class. If one is really going to *try one's best* to bring about the specified goal, many other methods might be used which Chisholm completely ignores.

One kind of method for getting at truths is to employ one's spatial imagination. Recent psychological work supports the intuitive idea that much mental processing involves "iconic" representations. Presented with certain geometrical problems, for example, a person is likely to try to solve them by "mental rotation" of an imagined stimulus.[5] Spatial imaging is a legitimate cognitive method generally ignored by twentieth-century epistemologists, who have concentrated on purely "logical" procedures, construed either linguistically or propositionally.

Another relevant "method" is to employ mnemonic techniques to prevent forgetting. We frequently learn a truth at one time only to forget it later. Yet if we take Chisholm's requirement seriously, we should try our best to avert such forgetting. Again, this problem is ignored by most analytical epistemology, though classical philosophers such as Aristotle were mindful of it.[6] Since mnemonic techniques are often proposed by cognitive psychologists working on memory,[7] the epistemological bearing of this psychological work is straightforward.

II

Let me turn to the second rationale for infusing psychology into epistemology: to take account of our limited capacities. The aim of epistemics is the genuine improvement of intellectual practice. This means that epistemic advice or rules must be capable of being followed. We may distinguish *ideal* and *executable* rules. The former specify ideal courses of action, or ideal ends, which human beings may or may not be able to realize. The latter specify courses of action that can actually be executed, given only some minimum of resources all normal humans possess. Epistemics ultimately aims at formulating executable rules or principles.

The orientation of much analytical epistemology has been quite different. Epistemological rules have often ignored human capacities, either because they were aimed at "ideal" cognizers or because they were formulated with no consideration of executability. Consider the rules of deductive closure and (non-)inconsistency:

(DC) At any time, believe all the logical consequences of whatever you believe.
(INC) Do not believe, at any time, all members of an inconsistent set of propositions.

Since any set of beliefs has infinitely many consequences, but people are incapable of having infinitely many beliefs. (DC) is nonexecutable. Since there is no effective procedure for determining inconsistency, there is nothing humans can do to guarantee conformity with (INC). Hence, it too is nonexecutable.

Although (DC) and (INC) are themselves nonexecutable, it might seem easy to derive executable rules from them, by simply prescribing the resolute *attempt* to satisfy them. This would yield the following principles:

(T-DC) Try your best to bring it about, at any time, that you believe all the logical consequences of whatever you believe.
(T-INC) Try your best to bring it about that you do not believe, at any time, all members of any inconsistent set of propositions.

Assuming these rules are executable, are they *acceptable* rules? What would be involved in actually conforming to (T-DC) and (T-INC)? A person would expend all his conscious energy tracing the logical consequences of his beliefs and worrying about their possible inconsistency. This would be an all-consuming mental occupation. Is that a reasonable allocation of limited cognitive resources? Surely not. Someone who uses all his information-processing time and equipment in these tasks will acquire little or no "new" information, e.g., information about dangers in his current environment. At any rate, he will acquire far *less* information of this kind than if he pays more attention to the current environment. The same point holds of a Bayesian theorist's prescription continually to (try to) adjust subjective probabilities so as to preserve a coherent credence function. *Some* concern with logical and probabilistic relations is doubtless appropriate; but total preoccupation with logical or probabilistic relations is a misdirected employment of scarce attentional resources.[8]

I do not deny the epistemological relevance of logic (or probability theory). Truths of logic, both model-theoretic and proof-theoretic, will clearly be useful in helping to formulate epistemic advice. (One plausible bit of epistemic counsel is to study logic—and statistics.) But past epistemologists have often exaggerated the connection between logic and epistemology. Logic alone cannot directly generate epistemic principles. This is so for three reasons. First, epistemic principles should reflect a set of cognitive desiderata, which balance, for example, the relative importance of increasing true belief as compared with avoiding error. Logic cannot determine these desiderata. Second, epistemic principles should take account of the constraints under which cognizers operate, and this goes beyond the scope of logic. Third, precise epistemic principles would indicate "where" and "how" to represent information, e.g., in conscious thought or memory, imagistically or propositionally. Nothing like this can be derived from the truths of logic.

Now if epistemic principles are to be executable, the psychological operations they prescribe must presumably be subject to (direct) voluntary control. In light of this, it is ironic that epistemologists have so often suggested principles that enjoin "doxastic attitudes"; for assent and suspension of judgment are dubious candidates for the sphere of the voluntary. Contrary to Descartes's doctrine of "doxastic voluntarism," which holds that judgment and suspension of judgment are subject to the will, I believe we have little or no direct control over doxastic attitudes. I cannot, for example, simply choose to believe that there is an elephant in my study. I can choose to imagine this, or to write it down, or to repeat it to myself, or even to act as if it were true. But I cannot simply decide to go ahead and believe it.[9] Similarly, if the evidence and my inference patterns incline me to accept one of two scientific hypotheses, I cannot simply choose to believe the other one instead. I may thus be incapable of following any rule that instructs me to accept the other hypothesis.[10]

Although belief and nonbelief (in any of their more determinate psychological manifestations) may not be subject to direct control, they are certainly subject to *indirect* influence by means of (other) psychological operations that *are* under voluntary control. Part of the task of epistemics is to identify these "command variables" and see how they influence doxastic attitudes. In my opinion, *attention* constitutes the most important cognitive process largely under voluntary control. By directing perceptual attention we can influence our evidence and, thereby, our doxastic attitudes. By directing internal attention we can influence the problems and hypotheses we pursue, which also influences our doxastic attitudes.

Let me return to the topic of memory, which again illustrates how traditional epistemology ignores our limited capacities. Philosophy of science standardly assumes that we remember *individual* observed events and draw inferences from the totality of such data recalled at a given time. But psychological research suggests a different story: that it is, not only, or even primarily, individual events that we store in memory, but organized "constructions" of "summaries" of past events. More specifically, we often store experience in terms of representative, typical, or average cases, sometimes called *prototypes* or *schemata*. This is indicated by experiments of J. J. Franks and J. D. Bransford in which subjects were shown cards with simple geometric figures. They then received test cards that included not only figures they had actually seen, but prototypes not previously presented. Subjects "recognized" the prototypes more readily than patterns they had actually seen! Apparently, they had formed memory schemata of typical patterns, and found it easy to "match the prototype cards to these schemata.[11]

Other evidence suggests that, once schemata are formed, they are not easily changed by subsequent events. One often doesn't notice discrepant events at all; and, if the prototype *is* updated by new instances, the updating process is quite conservative. A comfortably lodged prototype or general impression is only slightly influenced by new observations. This is apparent from studies on impression-formation, which show that early data ("first impressions") affect judgment more than later data. When subjects are given a series of descriptive adjectives about a person, adjectives early in the list influence their overall opinion more than later adjectives.[12]

It is tempting to dismiss these facts and simply urge people to remember individual events, not general impressions. But we simply *can't* remember *all* individual observations. Moreover, the tendency to form prototypes, and to have these prototypes affect the attention given to new instances, is doubtless a deep-seated feature of our cognitive equipment. This feature may lead to error or bias, and that is something with which epistemics should be concerned. But this concern must manifest itself in a realistic acknowledgment of our mnemonic powers and limits, not mere disdain for them.

III

These remarks already initiate the third part of our rationale for the psychologization of epistemology: the importance of recognizing flaws or defects in our native cognitive system. Recent work in cognitive social psychology and the psychology of judgment has focused on such flaws or defects.

As a first example, consider Richard E. Nisbett's suggestion of a significant difference in impact between "vivid" or "concrete" information as compared with "pallid" or "abstract" material. E. Borgida and Nisbett gave undergraduate subjects some course-evaluation information and invited them to state their own choices for future enrollment. Some subjects received written summaries of all previous enrôllees' evaluations, whereas others heard evaluations of only a few individuals, but in *face-to-face* contact. It was found that abstract summary information had little impact on course choices, whereas concrete, first-hand contact had substantial impact.[13]

What makes certain information more "vivid" or "salient" than other information (e.g., statistical data) is not clear. It may reflect the relative strength of perception-related processes, i.e., imagistic modes of representation. Alternatively, it may be due to the relative case with which stories or "scripts" are encoded and retained.[14] In any case, the relative weight of such factors in native thought needs to be assessed, and if this is a defect in our equipment, we must worry about how to obviate or accommodate it.

The underutilization of statistical data was initially stressed by Amos Tversky and Daniel Kahneman.[15] Subsequently, they attempt to explain this fact, among others, by the domination of "causal schemata" in human cognition.[16] They argue that there is a natural tendency to search for causal mechanisms and to neglect information that doesn't lend itself to causal interpretation. More specifically, two propensities are suggested. First, if event X is perceived as a potential *cause* of event Y, its impact on one's judgment of Y's probability is greater than if X is merely a potential *effect* of Y. This is illustrated by a study in which people were given the following problem:

In a survey of high-school seniors in a city, the height of boys was compared to the height of their fathers. In which prediction would you have greater confidence?
(a) The prediction of the father's height from the son's height
(b) The prediction of the son's height from the father's height
(c) Equal confidence

Since the distribution of height is essentially the same in successive generations, the correct answer is "Equal." But 111 subjects chose answer (b), 24 chose (c), and 15 chose (a). Apparently, this is because people tend to see a "causal mechanism" leading from father's height to son's height, but not conversely. The second propensity suggested by Tversky and Kahneman is that data that can be interpreted as either a potential cause or effect has more weight than purely distributional data. Preoccupation with causal theories is what accounts, on their view, for the unwarranted neglect of statistical information.

In their earlier paper[17] Tversky and Kahneman suggested three other biased heuristics that affect our probability judgments: *representativeness*, *anchoring*, and *availability*. *Representativeness* is illustrated by people's answers to questions about the probability that event A originates from process B, or resembles B. For example, in considering tosses of a coin for heads or tails, people (wrongly) consider the sequence H-T-H-T-T-H to be more likely than the sequence H-H-H-T-T-T, which does not appear random, and also more likely than the sequence H-H-H-H-T-H, which does not represent the fairness of the coin.

Anchoring is a phenomenon in which probability estimates are biased toward arbitrary initial values. For example, people were asked to estimate the percentage of African countries in the U.N. Before doing so, a number between 0 and 100 was determined by spinning a wheel in their presence. The subjects were asked to make their estimate by moving upward or downward from the given number. Different groups were given different initial values, and these arbitrary numbers had a marked effect on estimates. The median estimates were 25 and 45 for groups that received starting points of 10 and 65 respectively.

In making judgments, we frequently employ examples encountered in the past. Because of how we file or code information in memory, however, certain examples are more readily *available* than others, i.e., come to mind with greater ease. Suppose you are asked whether it is more probable that a randomly selected English word *begins* with "r" or has "r" in the *third* position. You are likely to try to recall words in each category and assess the probability by the number in each class that came to mind. But, since we tend to code words in memory in terms of first rather than third letters, availability from memory is not a reliable guide to the real probability.

Another arena for the detection of flaws is hypothesis formation. Problem solvers often get into rigid "ruts" or "loops": they keep returning to hypotheses in fixed categories and cannot get outside these categories. Experimental subjects who have just solved problems requiring *position* hypotheses have an extremely difficult time with a very simple problem whose solution involves *size* rather than *position*.[18] Apparently, which hypotheses one frames or generates is heavily influenced by previous hypotheses *available* from memory. One tends to think of hypotheses that have succeeded in analogous problem situations, especially *recent* ones.

These empirical facts suggest tips for how to improve our hypothesis-generating performance.[19] Such improvement would seem to be a suitable topic for epistemology. Under the positivist conception of epistemology, however, hypothesis formation is excluded. Epistemology is to be the "logic" of science, and, since there is no "logic" of discover, hypothesis formation falls outside the pale. This conception of epistemology, I maintain, is unduly restrictive. Contrary to Carl Hempel's apparent position,[20] advice on hypothesis formation can be considered epistemological, even if it doesn't provide *mechanical* criteria for getting appropriate hypotheses. Heuristic suggestions for how to get out of loops is a legitimate part of epistemology, or at least of epistemics.

IV

My threefold rationale for infusing psychology into epistemology has concentrated on *mental* operations, where the relevance of psychology is fairly straightforward. It must be conceded, however, that intellectual activity is not purely mental. The solution of intellectual problems often involves (a) speech, (b) writing things down, either in words, diagrams, or formulas, (c) physical manipulation of experimental apparatus, and (d) physical interaction with machines and devices, such as computers, calculators, and abaci. Much intellectual improvement arises from learning and using appropriate procedures for these kinds of activities. For these reasons, epistemics cannot be concerned with psychological matters exclusively. Still, even these physical activities are intimately connected with the mental. First, the *purpose* of employing physical aids, such as diagrams or other inscriptions, is ultimately to guide one's psychological states, i.e., to produce *belief* or *understanding* (in any of their specific psychological manifestations). Second, one needs appropriate mental operations to *guide* these physical activities. Which activities should be executed? When? And in what order? These pose problems for the *mind*, problems of the structure and retrieval of plans and subroutines, to which psychology is clearly relevant.

Psychology can also play a role in determining the long-run effect on the mind of various kinds of training. How does critical discussion, for example, or imaginative play, improve mental habits? In general, some of the best advice epistemics can give is to engage in non-(purely-)mental activities that gradually mold one's cognitive traits.[21]

V

Although I have stressed the role of psychology in epistemics, it is evident that epistemic advice cannot be derived from empirical science alone (or from empirical science plus logic). Epistemics assumes that cognitive operations should be assessed instrumentally: given a choice of cognitive procedures, those which would produce the best set of *consequences* should be selected. This means, however, that epistemics must identify a relevant class of "intrinsically valuable" consequences and establish a *rank-ordering* of different sets of these consequences. What is the appropriate class of such consequences?

Some epistemologists might suggest that the proper aim of a cognizer (as such) is to have *justified* doxastic attitudes. Considered as the sole aim of cognition, this is too narrow, at least as justifiedness is usually construed. Typically, justificational status is assessed relative to the evidence actually possessed and the hypotheses actually considered. This means that a cognizer's beliefs can be justified no matter how good or bad his evidence-gathering and hypothesis-generating practices. The criterion of justifiedness does not evaluate these practices. Intuitively, however, such practices are of great intellectual significance. If they cannot be assessed by the standard of justifiedness, then meeting this standard is not the sole end of cognition.

Second it is doubtful that justifiedness is the *final* end of cognition. As I argue elsewhere,[22] justified belief is (roughly) belief formed by cognitive operations that tend to lead to truth. This suggests the more plausible view that justifiedness has value only because of its conduciveness to truth.

Consider then the view that the aim of cognition is the acquisition of truth, i.e., true belief. This must immediately be supplemented by the aim of avoiding error (otherwise one might simply try to believe all propositions, including their contradictories). But how should truth acquisition be weighted as compared with error avoidance? Second, is it only true *belief*—i.e., "acceptance" or full assent—that has (intrinsic) value? This allows no value to subjective probabilities, or qualified acceptances of truths. Third, we have already seen that so-called "belief" is ambiguous as between conscious assent and various forms of memory storage. What weights are to be assigned to such disparate mental lodgings for a given truth?

To resolve these and other problems, one might try a different approach to cognitive ends. One might suggest that the ultimate end of cognition is the *solution of problems*, where a problem is construed as how to attain a goal, whether the goal be intellectual—e.g., finding the answer to a question—or practical—e.g., finding a doctor in a foreign city. Cognitive practices have instrumental value to the extent that they lead to solutions of problems, i.e., attainment of goals. One virtue of this perspective is that it would explain the value of true as opposed to false belief, since truth facilitates goal attainment better than falsehood in all but a few, nonstandard cases. Second, no general weighting of truth acquisition versus error avoidance is needed. Their relative importance depends on the problem at hand. Third, *acceptance* of a truth is not the only good doxastic state. High subjective probabilities vis-à-vis truths also promote goal attainment. Fourth, there is no need for a general formula that weights the value of conscious versus stored beliefs. One should employ whichever patterns of information storage and retrieval best promote attainment of goals. Next, we generally prize *rapid* truth-acquisition techniques. This can be explained by the fact that many goals involve temporal constraints, which speedy techniques help to satisfy. Sixth, the goal-attainment approach can assign appropriate values to different kinds of mental representations. Imagistic representations are suitable for solving certain problems; others are best solved with purely semantic representations.

The problem-solving approach obviously faces difficulties, to which I cannot address myself here. Nor do I mean to commit epistemics to this particular answer to the question of epistemic ends. I propose it only tentatively and illustratively, as one alternate with certain attractions.

VI

Epistemics would not cover all the territory epistemology has covered in the past. It would not, for example, deal with the analysis of knowledge, or with the attempt to answer skepticism. But, to the extent that epistemology has tried to be normative or prescriptive (and it hasn't always been clear about what it was doing), I propose epistemics as an appropriate framework.

The framework presupposes a "contextualist" position of the sort championed, for example, by W. V. Quine. In studying and criticizing our cognitive procedures, we should use whatever powers and procedures we antecedently have and accept. There is no starting "from scratch"; to transcend any cognitive weaknesses, we must use cognitive operations to decide what to do. There is no logical guarantee of success, but that is more than can reasonably be expected.

My conception of epistemics resembles some earlier epistemological standpoints. Descartes's *Regulae* had a similar motivation, and Spinoza's scheme for the improvement of the understanding is very close to the program of epistemics.[23] More generally, pre-twentieth-century epistemology was often interwoven with psychology, as readers of Locke, Berkeley, and especially Hume will recognize. In the twentieth century, philosophers like John Dewey, Karl Popper, and Quine had defended psychologistic conceptions of epistemology.[24] A return to these traditions is especially timely now, when cognitive psychology has renewed prestige and promises to enhance our understanding of fundamental cognitive processes. A few psychologists have begun to detect a convergence between their interests and those of epistemology.[25] I have here tried to lay a foundation for a conception of epistemology that would effect a rapprochement between it and cognitive psychology.

NOTES

Research leading to this paper was begun under fellowships from the John Simon Guggenheim Memorial Foundation and the Center for Advanced Study in the Behavioral Sciences. I am grateful for their support. For helpful comments and criticisms on earlier versions, I am especially indebted to Holly S. Goldman, Allan Gibbard, Louis E. Loeb, Richard E. Nisbett, and Stephen P. Stich.

1. Actually my conception of epistemics is broader than these remarks suggest. It would comprehend *social* as well as *individual* dimensions of cognition. It would concern itself with the interpersonal and institutional processes that affect the creation, transmission, and reception of information, misinformation, and partial information. Like the sociology of knowledge, it would study not only organized science, but situational and institutional forces that affect the social dissemination or inhibition of knowledge. In the present paper, however, I restrict myself to "individual epistemics," which treats the individual cognizer and his cognitive system.

2. For further discussion of these points, see Goldman 1978.

3. Cf. Carnap 1950, p. 211, and Hempel 1965, p. 64.

4. Chisholm 1977.

5. Cf. Shepard and Metzler 1971; and Cooper and Shepard 1973.

6. See Sorabji 1972.

7. Cf. Klatzky 1975, chapters 5, 10, and 13.

8. Other deficiencies of (T-INC) have been noted in the literature. For example, anyone who believes that some of his beliefs are false has an inconsistent set of beliefs. But it isn't clear he should try to rid himself of this inconsistency.

9. Pascal appreciated this fact. He did not advise acquisition of faith by simply willing it. He counseled a *life* of "holy water and sacraments," which would indirectly lead to faith.

10. However, if I am persuaded, using others of my cognitive propensities, that the rule is correct, this may *cause* me to believe in accordance with the rule. Even this is not generally true, though. I may be persuaded that the gambler's fallacy is a fallacy and yet continue to have expectations that exemplify it.

11. Franks and Bransford 1971. See also Bransford and Franks 1971.

12. Cf. Posner 1973, p. 82. Also see the discussion of "perseverance" in Ross 1977.

13. Borgida and Nisbett 1977. Cf. Nisbett, Borgida, Crandall, and Reed 1976.

14. On the notion of a "script", see Schank and Abelson 1977.

15. Tversky and Kahneman 1974.

16. Tversky and Kahneman 1977.

17. Tversky and Kahneman 1974.

18. Cf. Levine 1971. The original idea of "functional fixedness" or "problem-solving set" is due to Duncker 1945 and A. S. Luchins 1942.

19. See Posner 1973, ch. 7, and Wickelgren 1974, ch. 4.

20. Cf. Hempel 1965, pp. 5–6.

21. My conception of individual epistemics comprehends not only the *self*-regulation of cognitive processes but also the *third-person* control of cognitive traits. In the latter domain, epistemics would interface with the theory of education.

22. Goldman 1979.

23. Spinoza 1951. Cf. especially pp. 10–12.

24. For Quine's views, see Quine 1969a, 1969b. Quine, however, seems interested mainly in explaining the genesis of our beliefs. Thus, his project is more positive than normative. This is equally true of the Empiricists, of course.

25. Cf. Nisbett and Ross 1980. A different psychological orientation is represented by Donald T. Campbell's writings on evolutionary epistemology. Cf. Campbell 1974.

DANIEL DENNETT

THREE KINDS OF INTENTIONAL PSYCHOLOGY

FOLK PSYCHOLOGY AS A SOURCE OF THEORY

Suppose you and I both believe that cats eat fish. Exactly what feature must we share for this to be true of us? More generally, recalling Socrates' favorite style of question, what must be in common between things truly ascribed in *intentional* predicates—such as "wants to visit China" or "expects noodles for supper"? As Socrates points out, in the *Meno* and elsewhere, such questions are ambiguous or vague in their intent. One can be asking on the one hand for something rather like a definition, or on the other hand for something rather like a theory. (Socrates of course preferred the former sort of answer.) What do all magnets have in common? First answer: they all attract iron. Second answer: they all have such-and-such a microphysical property (a property that explains their capacity to attract iron). In one sense people knew what magnets were—they were things that attracted iron—long before science told them what magnets were. A child learns what the word "magnet" means not, typically, by learning an explicit definition, but by learning the "folk physics" of magnets, in which the ordinary term "magnet" is embedded or implicitly defined as a theoretical term.

Sometimes terms are embedded in more powerful theories, and sometimes they are embedded by explicit definition. What do all chemical elements with the same valence have in common? First answer: they are disposed to combine with other elements in the same integral rations. Second answer: they all have such-and-such a microphysical property (a property which explains their capacity to combine). The theory of valences in chemistry was well in hand before its microphysical explanation was known. In one sense chemists knew what valences were before physicists told them.

So what appears in Plato to be a contrast between giving a definition and giving a theory can be viewed as just a special case of the contrast between giving one theoretical answer and giving another, more "reductive" theoretical answer. Fodor (1975) draws the same contrast between "conceptual" and "causal" answers to such questions and argues that Ryle (1949) champions conceptual answers at the expense of causal answers, wrongly supposing them to be in conflict. There is justice in Fodor's charge against Ryle, for there are certainly many passages in which Ryle seems to propose his conceptual answers as a bulwark against the possibility of *any* causal, scientific, psychological answers, but there is a better view of Ryle's (or perhaps at best a view he ought to have held) that deserves rehabilitation. Ryle's "logical behaviorism" is composed of his steadfastly conceptual answers to the Socratic questions about matters mental. If Ryle thought these answers ruled out psychology, ruled out causal (or reductive) answers to the Socratic questions, he was wrong, but if he thought only that the conceptual answers to the questions were not to be given by a microreductive psychology, he was on firmer ground. It is one thing to give a causal explanation of some phenomenon and quite another to cite the cause of a phenomenon in the analysis of the concept of it.

Some concepts have what might be called an essential causal element (see Fodor 1975, p. 7, n6). For instance, the concept of a genuine Winston Churchill *autograph* has it that how the trail of ink was in fact caused is essential to its status as an autograph. Photocopies, forgeries, inadvertently indistinguishable signatures—but perhaps not carbon copies—are ruled out. These considerations are part of the *conceptual* answer to the Socratic question about autographs.

Now some, including Fodor, have held that such concepts as the concept of intelligent action also have an essential causal element; behavior that appeared to be intelligent might be shown not to be by being shown to have the wrong sort of cause. Against such positions Ryle can argue that even if it is true that every instance of intelligent behavior is caused (and hence has a causal explanation), exactly *how* it is caused is inessential to its being intelligent—something that could be true even if all intelligent behavior exhibited in fact some common pattern of causation. That is, Ryle can plausibly claim that no account in causal terms could capture the class of intelligent actions except *per accidens*. In aid of such a position—for which there is much to be said in spite of the current infactuation with causal theories— Ryle can make claims of the sort Fodor disparages ("it's not the mental activity that makes the clowning clever because what makes the clowning clever is such facts as that it took place out where the children can see it") without committing the error of supposing causal and conceptual answers are incompatible.[1]

Ryle's logical behaviorism was in fact tainted by a groundless antiscientific bias, but it need not have been. Note that the introduction of the concept of valence in chemistry was a bit of *logical chemical behaviorism*: to have valence n was "by definition" to be disposed to behave in such-and-such ways under such-and-such conditions, *however* that disposition to behave might someday be explained by physics. In this particular instance the relation between the chemical theory and the physical theory is now well charted and understood—even if in the throes of ideology people sometimes misdescribe it—and the explanation of those dispositional combinatorial properties by physics is a prime example of the sort of success in science that inspires reductionist doctrines. Chemistry has been shown to reduce, in some sense, to physics, and this is clearly a Good Thing, the sort of thing we should try for more of.

Such progress invites the prospect of a parallel development in psychology. First we will answer the question "What do all believers-that-p have in common?" the first way, the "conceptual" way, and then see if we can go on to "reduce" the theory that emerges in our first answer to something else—neurophysiology most likely. Many theorists seem to take it for granted that *some* such reduction is both possible and desirable, and perhaps even inevitable, even while recent critics of reductionism, such as Putnam and Fodor, have warned us of the excesses of "classical" reductionist creeds. No one today hopes to conduct the psychology of the future in the vocabulary of the neurophysiologist, let alone that of the physicist, and principled ways of relaxing the classical "rules" of reduction have been proposed. The issue, then, is *what kind* of theoretical bonds can we expect—or ought we to hope—to find uniting psychological claims about beliefs, desires, and so forth with the claims of neurophysiologists, biologists, and other physical scientists?

Since the terms "belief" and "desire" and their kin are parts of ordinary language, like "magnet," rather than technical terms like "valence," we must first look to "folk psychology" to see what kind of things we are being asked to explain. What do we learn beliefs are when we learn how to use the words "believe" and "belief"? The first point to make is that we do not really learn what beliefs are when we learn how to use these words.[2] Certainly no one *tells us* what beliefs are, or if someone does, or if we happen to speculate on the topic on our own, the answer we come to, wise or foolish, will figure only weakly in our habits of thought about what people believe. We learn to *use* folk psychology as a vernacular social technology, a craft; but we don't learn it self-consciously as a theory—we learn no meta-theory with the theory—and in this regard our knowledge of folk psychology is like our knowledge of the grammar of our native tongue. This fact does not make our knowledge of folk psychology entirely unlike human knowledge of explicit academic theories, however; one could probably be a good practicing chemist and yet find it embarrassingly difficult to produce a satisfactory textbook definition of a metal or an ion.

There are no introductory textbooks of folk psychology (although Ryle's *The Concept of Mind* might be pressed into service), but many explorations of the field have been undertaken by ordinary language philosophers (under slightly different intentions) and more recently by more theoretically minded philosophers of mind, and from all this work an account of folk psychology—part truism and the rest controversy—can be gleaned. What are beliefs? Very roughly, folk psychology has it that *beliefs* are information-bearing states of people that arise from perceptions and that, together with appropriately related *desires*, lead to intelligent *action*. That much is relatively uncontroversial, but does folk psychology also have it that nonhuman animals have beliefs? If so, what is the role of language in belief? Are beliefs constructed of parts? If so, what are the parts? Ideas? Concepts? Words? Pictures? Are beliefs like speech acts or maps or instruction manuals or sentences? Is it implicit in folk psychology that beliefs enter into causal relations, or that they don't? How do decisions and intentions intervene between belief–desire complexes and actions? Are beliefs introspectible, and if so, what authority do the believer's pronouncements have?

All these questions deserve answers, but one must bear in mind that there are different reasons for being interested in the details of folk psychology. One reason is that it exists as a phenomenon, like a religion or a language or a dress code, to be studied with the techniques and attitudes of anthropology. It may be a myth, but it is a myth we live in, so it is an "important" phenomenon in nature. A different reason is that it seems to be a *true* theory, by and large, and hence is a candidate—like the folk physics of magnets and unlike the folk science of astrology—for incorporation into science. These different reasons generate different but overlapping investigations. The anthropological question should include in its account of folk psychology whatever folk actually include in their theory, however misguided, incoherent, gratuitous some of it may be. (When the anthropologist marks part of the catalogue of folk theory as false, he may speak of *false consciousness* or *ideology*, but the role of such false theory *qua* anthropological phenomenon is not thereby diminished.) The proto-scientific quest, on the other hand, as an attempt to prepare folk theory for subsequent incorporation into, or reduction to, the rest of science, should be critical and should eliminate all that is false or ill founded, however well entrenched in popular doctrine. (Thales thought that lodestones had souls, we are told. Even if most people agreed, this would be something to eliminate from the folk physics of magnets prior to "reduction.") One way of distinguishing the good from the bad, the essential from the gratuitous, in folk theory is to see what must be included in the theory to account for whatever predictive or explanatory success it seems to have in ordinary use. In this way we can criticize as we analyze, and it is even open to us in the end to discard folk psychology if it turns out to be a bad theory, and with it the presumed theoretical entities named therein.

If we discard folk psychology as a theory, we would have to replace it with another theory, which, while it did violence to many ordinary intuitions, would explain the predictive power of the residual folk craft.

We use folk psychology all the time, to explain and predict each other's behavior; we attribute beliefs and desires to each other with confidence—and quite unself-consciously—and spend a substantial portion of our waking lives formulating the world—not excluding ourselves—in these terms. Folk psychology is about as pervasive a part of our second nature as is our folk physics of middle-sized objects. How good is folk psychology? If we concentrate on its weaknesses we will notice that we often are unable to make sense of particular bits of human behavior (our own included) in terms of belief and desire, even in retrospect; we often cannot predict accurately or reliably what a person will do or when, we often can find no resources within the theory for settling disagreements about particular attributions of belief or desire. If we concentrate on its strengths we find first that there are large areas in which it is extraordinarily reliable in its predictive power. Every time we venture out on a highway, for example, we stake our lives on the reliability of our general expectations about the perceptual beliefs, normal desires, and decision proclivities of the other motorists. Second, we find that it is a theory of great generative power and efficiency. For instance, watching a film with a highly original and unstereotypical plot, we see the hero smile at the villain and we all swiftly and effortlessly arrive at the same complex theoretical diagnosis: "Aha!" we conclude (but perhaps not consciously), "he wants her to think he doesn't know she intends to defraud his brother!" Third, we find that even small children pick up facility with the theory at a time when they have a very limited experience of human activity from which to induce a theory. Fourth, we find that we all use folk psychology knowing next to nothing about what actually happens inside people's skulls. "Use your head," we are told, and we know some people are brainier than others, but our capacity to use folk psychology is quite unaffected by ignorance about brain processes—or even by large-scale misinformation about brain processes.

As many philosophers have observed, a feature of folk psychology that sets it apart from both folk physics and the academic physical sciences is that explanations of actions citing beliefs and desires normally not only describe the provenance of the actions, but at the same time defend them as reasonable under the circumstances. They are reason-giving explanations, which make an ineliminable allusion to the rationality of the agent. Primarily for this reason, but also because of the pattern of strengths and weaknesses just described, I suggest that folk psychology might best be viewed as a rationalistic calculus of interpretation and prediction—an idealizing, abstract, instrumentalistic interpretation method that has evolved because it works and works because we have evolved. We approach each other as *intentional systems*

(Dennett 1971), that is, as entities whose behavior can be predicted by the method of attributing beliefs, desires, and rational acumen according to the following rough and ready principles:

(1) A system's beliefs are those it *ought to have*, given its perceptual capacities, its epistemic needs, and its biography. Thus, in general, its beliefs are both true and relevant to its life, and when false beliefs are attributed, special stories must be told to explain how the error resulted from the presence of features in the environment that are deceptive relative to the perceptual capacities of the system.

(2) A system's desires are those it *ought to have*, given its biological needs and the most practicable means of satisfying them. Thus intentional systems desire survival and procreation, and hence desire food, security, health, sex, wealth, power, influence, and so forth, and also whatever local arrangements tend (in their eyes—given their beliefs) to further these ends in appropriate measure. Again, "abnormal" desires are attributable if special stories can be told.

(3) A system's behavior will consist of those acts that *it would be rational* for an agent with those beliefs and desires to perform.

In (1) and (2) "ought to have" means "would have if it were *ideally* ensconced in its environmental niche." Thus all dangers and vicissitudes in its environment it will *recognize as such* (i.e., *believe* to be dangers) and all the benefits—relative to its needs, of course—it will *desire*. When a fact about its surroundings is particularly relevant to its current projects (which themselves will be the projects such a being ought to have in order to get ahead in its world), it will *know* that fact and act accordingly. And so forth and so on. This gives us the notion of an ideal epistemic and conative operator or agent, relativized to a set of needs for survival and procreation and to the environment(s) in which its ancestors have evolved and to which it is adapted. But this notion is still too crude and overstated. For instance, a being may come to have an epistemic need that its perceptual apparatus cannot provide for (suddenly all the green food is poisonous, but alas it is colorblind), hence the relativity to perceptual capacities. Moreover, it may or may not have had the occasion to learn from experience about something, so its beliefs are also relative to its biography in this way: it will have learned what it ought to have learned, viz., what it had been given evidence for in a form compatible with its cognitive apparatus—providing the evidence was "relevant" to its project then.

But this is still too crude, for evolution does not give us a best of all possible worlds, but only a passable jury-rig, so we should look for design shortcuts that in specifiably abnormal circumstances yield false perceptual beliefs, etc. (We are not immune to illusions—which we would be if our perceptual systems were *perfect*.) To offset the design shortcuts we should also expect design bonuses: circumstances in which the "cheap" way for nature to design a cognitive system has the side benefit of giving good, reliable results even outside the environment in which the system evolved. Our eyes are well adapted for giving us true beliefs on Mars as well as on Earth, because the cheap solution for our Earth-evolving eyes happens to be a more general solution (cf. Sober 1981).

I propose that we can continue the mode of thinking just illustrated *all the way in*—not just for eye design, but for deliberation design and belief design and strategy-concocter design. In using this optimistic set of assumptions (nature has built us to do things right; look for systems to believe the truth and love the good), we impute no occult powers to epistemic needs, perceptual capacities, and biography but only the powers common sense already imputes to evolution and learning.

In short, we treat each other as if we were rational agents, and this myth—for surely we are not all that rational—works very well because we are *pretty* rational. This single assumption, in combination with home truths about our needs, capacities and typical circumstances, generates both an intentional interpretation of us as believers and desirers and actual predictions of behavior in great profusion. I am claiming, then, that folk psychology can best be viewed as a sort of logical behaviorism: *what it means* to say that someone believes that *p*, is that that person is disposed to behave in certain ways under certain conditions. What ways under what conditions? The ways it would be rational to behave, given the person's other beliefs and desires. The answer looks in danger of being circular, but consider: an account of what it is for an element to have a particular valence will similarly make ineliminable reference to the valences of other elements. What one is given with valence talk is a whole system of interlocking attributions, which is saved from vacuity by yielding independently testable predictions.

I have just described in outline a method of predicting and explaining the behavior of people and other intelligent creatures. Let me distinguish two questions about it: is it something we could do, and is it something we in fact do? I think the answer to the first is obviously yes, which is not to say the method will always yield good results. That much one can ascertain by reflection and thought experiment. Moreover, one can recognize that the method is familiar. Although we don't usually use the method self-consciously, we do use it self-consciously on those occasions when we are perplexed by a person's behavior, and then it often yields satisfactory results. Moreover, the ease and naturalness with which we resort to this self-conscious and deliberate form of problem-solving provide some support for the claim that what we are doing on those occasions is not switching methods but simply becoming self-conscious and explicit about what we ordinarily accomplish tacitly or unconsciously.

No other view of folk psychology, I think, can explain the fact that we do so well predicting each other's behavior on such slender and peripheral evidence; treating each other as intentional systems works (to the extent that it does) because we really are well designed by evolution and hence we *approximate* to the ideal version of ourselves exploited to yield the predictions. But not only does evolution not guarantee that we will always do what is rational; it guarantees that we won't. If we are designed by evolution, then we are almost certainly nothing more than a bag of tricks, patched together by a *satisficing* Nature—Herbert Simon's term (1957)—and no better than our ancestors had to be to get by. Moreover, the demands of nature and the demands of a logic course are not the same. Sometimes—even *normally* in certain circumstances—it pays to jump to conclusions swiftly (and even to forget that you've done so), so by most philosophical measures of rationality (logical consistency, refraining from invalid inference) there has probably been some positive evolutionary pressure in favor of "irrational" methods.[3]

How rational are we? Recent research in social and cognitive psychology (e.g., Tversky and Kahneman 1974; Nisbett and Ross 1978) suggests we are only minimally rational, appallingly ready to leap to conclusions or be swayed by logically irrelevant features of situations, but this jaundiced view is an illusion engendered by the fact that these psychologists are deliberately trying to produce situations that provoke irrational responses—inducing pathology in a system by putting strain on it—and succeeding, being good psychologists. No one would hire a psychologist to prove that people will choose a paid vacation to a week in jail if offered an informed choice. At least not in the better psychology departments. A more optimistic impression of our rationality is engendered by a review of the difficulties encountered in artificial intelligence research. Even the most sophisticated AI programs stumble blindly into misinterpretations and misunderstandings that even small children reliably evade without a second thought (see, e.g., Schank 1976; Schank and Abelson 1977). From this vantage point we seem marvelously rational.

However rational we are, it is the myth of our rational agenthood that structures and organizes our attributions of belief and desire to others and that regulates our own deliberations and investigations. We aspire to rationality, and without the myth of our rationality the concepts of belief and desire would be uprooted. Folk psychology, then, is *idealized* in that it produces its predictions and explanations by calculating in a normative system; it predicts what we will believe, desire, and do, by determining what we ought to believe, desire, and do.[4]

Folk psychology is *abstract* in that the beliefs and desires it attributes are not—or need not be—presumed to be intervening distinguishable states of an internal behavior-causing system. (The point will be enlarged upon later.) The role of the concept of belief is like the role of the concept of a center of gravity, and the calculations that yield the predictions are more like the calculations one performs with a parallelogram of forces than like the calculations one performs with a blueprint of internal levers and cogs.

Folk psychology is thus *instrumentalistic* in a way the most ardent realist should permit: people really do have beliefs and desires, on my version of folk psychology, just the way they really have centers of gravity and the earth has an equator.[5] Reichenbach distinguished between two sorts of referents for theoretical terms: *illata*—posited theoretical entities—and *abstracta*—calculation-bound entities or logical constructs.[6] Beliefs and desires of folk psychology (but not all mental events and states) are *abstracta*.

This view of folk psychology emerges more clearly when contrasted to a diametrically opposed view, each of whose tenets has been held by some philosopher, and at least most of which have been espoused by Fodor:

Beliefs and desires, just like pains, thoughts, sensations and other episodes, are taken by folk psychology to be real, intervening, internal states or events, in causal inter-action, subsumed under covering laws of causal stripe. Folk psychology is not an idealized, rationalistic calculus but a naturalistic, empirical, descriptive theory, im-puting causal regularities discovered by extensive induction over experience. To sup-pose two people share a belief is to suppose them to be ultimately in some structurally similar internal condition, e.g. for them to have the same words of Mentalese written in the functionally relevant places in their brains.

I want to deflect this head-on collision of analyses by taking two steps. First, I am prepared to grant a measure of the claims made by the opposition. Of course we don't all sit in the dark in our studies like mad Leibnizians rationalistically excogitating behavioral predictions from pure, idealized concepts of our neighbors, nor do we derive all our readiness to attribute desires from a careful generation of them from the ultimate goal of survival. We may observe that some folks seem to desire cigarettes, or pain, or notoriety (we observe this by hearing them tell us, seeing what they choose, etc.) and without any conviction that these people, given their circumstances, ought to have these desires, we attribute them anyway. So rationalistic generation of attributions is augmented and even corrected on occasion by empirical gen-eralizations about belief and desire that guide our attributions and are learned more or less inductively. For instance, small children believe in Santa Claus, people are inclined to believe the more self-serving of two interpretations of an event in which they are involved (unless they are depressed), and people can be made to want things they don't need by making them believe that glamorous people like those things. And so forth in familiar profusion. This folklore does not consist in *laws*—even probabilistic laws—but some of it is being turned into science of a sort, for example theories of "hot cognition" and cognitive dissonance. I grant the existence of all this naturalistic generalization, and its role in the normal calculations of folk psychologists—that is, all of us. People do rely on their own parochial group of neighbors when framing intentional interpretations. That is why people have so much difficulty understanding foreigners—their behavior, to say nothing of their languages. They impute more of their own beliefs and desires, and those of their neighbors, than they would if they followed my principles of attribution slavishly. Of course this is a perfectly reasonable shortcut for people to take, even when it often leads to bad results. We are in this matter, as in most, satisficers, not optimizers, when it comes to information gathering and theory construction. I would insist, however, that all this empirically obtained lore is laid over a fundamental generative and normative framework that has the features I have described.

My second step away from the conflict I have set up is to recall that the issue is not what folk psychology as found in the field truly is, but what it is at its best, what deserves to be taken seriously and incorporated into science. It is not particularly to the point to argue against me that folk psychology is *in fact* committed to beliefs and desires as distinguishable, causally interacting *illata*; what must be shown is that it ought to be. The latter claim I will deal with in due course. The former claim I *could* concede without embarrassment to my overall project, but I do not concede it, for it seems to me that the evidence is quite strong that our ordinary notion of belief has next to nothing of the concrete in it. Jacques shoots his uncle dead in Trafalgar Square and is apprehended on the spot by Sherlock; Tom reads about it in the *Guardian* and Boris learns of it in *Pravda*. Now Jacques, Sherlock, Tom, and Boris have had remarkably different experiences—to say nothing of their earlier biographies and future prospects—but there is one thing they share: they all believe that a Frenchman has committed murder in Trafalgar Square. They did not all *say* this, not even "to themselves"; *that proposition* did not, we can suppose, "occur to" any of them, and even if it had, it would have had entirely different import for Jacques, Sherlock, Tom, and Boris. Yet they all believe that a Frenchman committed murder in Trafalgar Square. This is a shared property that is visible, as it were, only from one very limited point of view—the point of view of folk psychology. Ordinary folk psychologists have no difficulty imputing such useful but elusive commonalities to people. If they then insist that in doing so they are postulating a similarly structured object in each head, this is a gratuitous bit of misplaced concreteness, a regrettable lapse in ideology.

But in any case there is no doubt that folk psychology is a mixed bag, like folk productions generally, and there is no reason in the end not to grant that it is much more complex, variegated (and in danger of incoherence) than my sketch has made it out to be. The *ordinary* notion of belief no doubt does place beliefs somewhere midway between being *illata* and being *abstracta*. What this suggests to me is that the concept of belief found in ordinary understanding, that is, in folk psychology, is unappealing as a scientific concept. I am reminded of Anaxagoras's strange precursor to atomism: the theory of seeds. There is a portion of everything in everything, he is reputed to have claimed. Every object consists of an infinity of seeds, of all possible varieties. How do you make bread out of flour, yeast, and water? Flour contains bread seeds in abundance (but flour seeds predominate—that's what makes it flour), and so do yeast and water, and when these ingredients are mixed together, the bread seeds form a new majority, so bread is what you get. Bread nourishes by containing flesh and blood and bone seeds in addition to its majority of bread seeds. Not good theoretical entities, these seeds, for as a sort of bastardized cross between properties and proper parts they have a penchant for generating vicious regresses, and their identity conditions are problematic to say the least.

Beliefs are rather like that. There seems no comfortable way of avoiding the claim that we have an infinity of beliefs, and common intuition does not give us a stable answer to such puzzles as whether the belief that 3 is greater than 2 is none other than the belief that 2 is less than 3. The obvious response to the challenge of an infinity of beliefs with slippery identity conditions is to suppose these beliefs are not all "stored separately"; many—in fact *most* if we are really talking about infinity—will be stored *implicitly* in virtue of the *explicit* storage of a few (or a few million)—the *core beliefs* (see Dennett 1975; also Fodor 1975 and Field 1978). The core beliefs will be "stored separately," and they look like promising *illata* in contrast to the virtual or implicit beliefs which look like paradigmatic *abstracta*. But although this might turn out to be the way our brains are organized, I suspect things will be more complicated than this: there is no reason to suppose the core *elements*, the concrete, salient, separately stored representation tokens (and there must be some such elements in any complex information processing system), will explicitly represent (or *be*) a subset of our *beliefs* at all. That is, if you were to sit down and write out a list of a thousand or so of your paradigmatic beliefs, *all* of them could turn out to be virtual, only implicitly stored or represented, and what was explicitly stored would be information (e.g., about memory addresses, procedures for problem-solving, or recognition, etc.) that was entirely unfamiliar. It would be folly to prejudge this empirical issue by insisting that our core representations of information (whichever they turn out to be) are beliefs *par excellence*, for when the facts are in, our intuitions may instead support the contrary view: the least controversial self-attributions of belief may pick out beliefs that from the vantage point of developed cognitive theory are invariably virtual.[7]

In such an eventuality what could we say about the causal roles we assign ordinarily to beliefs (e.g., "Her belief that John knew her secret caused her to blush")? We could say that whatever the core elements were in virtue of which she virtually believed that John knew her secret, they, the core elements, played a direct causal role (somehow) in triggering the blushing response. We would be wise, as this example shows, not to tamper with our *ordinary* catalogue of beliefs (virtual though they might all turn out to be), for these are predictable, readily understandable, manipulable regularities in psychological phenomena in spite of their apparent neutrality with regard to the explicit/implicit (or core/virtual) distinction. What Jacques, Sherlock, Boris, and Tom have in common is probably only a virtual belief "derived" from largely different explicit stores of information in each of them, but virtual or not, it is their sharing of *this* belief that would explain (or permit us to predict) in some imagined circumstances their all taking the same action when given the same new information. ("And now for one million dollars, Tom [Jacques, Sherlock, Boris], answer our jackpot question correctly: has a French citizen ever committed a major crime in London?")

At the same time we want to cling to the equally ordinary notion that beliefs can cause not only actions, but blushes, verbal slips, heart attacks, and the like. Much of the debate over whether or not intentional explanations are causal explanations can be bypassed by noting how the core elements, *whatever they may be*, can be cited as playing the causal role, while belief remains virtual. "Had Tom not believed that p and wanted that q, he would not have done A." Is this a causal explanation? It is tantamount to this: Tom was in some one of an indefinitely large number of structurally different states of type B that have in common just that each one of them licenses attribution of belief that p and desire that q in virtue of its normal relations with many other states of Tom, and this state, whichever one it was, was causally sufficient, given the "background conditions" of course, to initiate the intention to perform A, and thereupon A was performed, and had he not been in one of those indefinitely many type B states, he would not have done A. One can call this a causal explanation because it talks about causes, but it is surely as unspecific and unhelpful as a causal explanation or other falling within a very broad area (i.e., the intentional interpretation is held to be supervenient on Tom's bodily condition), but its true informativeness and utility in actual prediction lie, not surprisingly, in its assertion that Tom, however his body is currently structured, has a particular set of these elusive intentional properties, beliefs, and desires.

The ordinary notion of belief is pulled in two directions. If we want to have good theoretical entities, good *illata*, or good logical constructs, good *abstracta*, we will have to jettison some of the ordinary freight of the concepts of belief and desire. So I propose a divorce. Since we seem to have both notions wedded in folk psychology, let's split them apart and create two new theories: one strictly abstract, idealizing, holistic, instrumentalistic—pure intentional system theory—and the other a concrete, microtheoretical science of the actual realization of those intentional systems—what I will call subpersonal cognitive psychology. By exploring their differences and interrelations, we should be able to tell whether any plausible "reductions" are in the offing.

INTENTIONAL SYSTEM THEORY AS A COMPETENCE THEORY

The first new theory, intentional system theory, is envisaged as a close kin of, and overlapping with, such already existing disciplines as decision theory and game theory, which are similarly abstract, normative, and couched in intentional language. It borrows the ordinary terms "belief" and "desire" but gives them a technical meaning within the theory. It is a sort of holistic logical behaviorism because it deals with the prediction and explanation from belief–desire profiles of the actions of whole systems (either alone in environments or in interaction with other intentional systems), but it treats the individual realizations of the systems as black boxes. The *subject* of all the intentional attributions is the whole system (the person, the animal, or even the corporation or nation [see Dennett 1976]) rather than any of its parts, and individual beliefs and desires are not attributable in isolation, independently of other belief and desire attributions. The latter point distinguishes intentional system theory most clearly from Ryle's logical behaviorism, which took on the impossible burden of characterizing individual beliefs (and other mental states) as particular individual dispositions to outward behavior.

The theory deals with the "production" of new beliefs and desires from old, via an interaction among old beliefs and desires, features in the environment, and the system's actions; and this creates the illusion that the theory contains naturalistic descriptions of internal processing in the systems the theory is about, when in fact the processing is all in the manipulation of the theory and consists in updating the intentional characterization of the whole system according to the rules of attribution. An analogous illusion of process would befall a naive student who, when confronted with a parallelogram of forces, supposed that it pictured a mechanical linkage of rods and pivots of some kind instead of being simply a graphic way of representing and plotting the effect of several simultaneously acting forces.

Richard Jeffrey (1970), in developing his concept of probability kinematics, has usefully drawn attention to an analogy with the distinction in physics between kinematics and dynamics. In kinematics, you talk about the propagation of motions through a system in terms of such constraints as rigidity and manner of linkage. It is the physics of position and time, in terms of which you can talk about velocity and acceleration, but not about force and mass. When you talk about forces—*causes* of accelerations—you are in the realm of dynamics. (p. 172)

Kinematics provides a simplified and idealized level of abstraction appropriate for many purposes—for example, for the *initial* design development of a gearbox—but when one must deal with more concrete details of systems—when the gearbox designer must worry about friction, bending, energetic efficiency, and the like—one must switch to dynamics for more detailed and reliable predictions, at the cost of increased complexity and diminished generality. Similarly, one can approach the study of belief (and desire and so forth) at a highly abstract level, ignoring problems of realization and simply setting out what the normative demands on the design of a believer are. For instance, one can ask such questions as "What must a system's epistemic capabilities and propensities be for it to survive in environment *A*?" (cf. Campbell 1973, 1977) or "What must this system already know in order for it to be able to learn *B*?" or "What intentions must this system have in order to mean something by saying something?"

Intentional system theory deals just with the performance specifications of believers while remaining silent on how the systems are to be implemented. In fact this neutrality with regard to implementation is the most useful feature of intentional characterizations. Consider, for instance, the role of intentional characterizations in evolutionary biology. If we are to explain the evolution of complex behavioral capabilities or cognitive talents by natural selection, we must note that it is the intentionally characterized capacity (e.g., the capacity to acquire a belief, a desire, to perform an intentional action) that has survival value, however it happens to be realized as a result of mutation. If a particularly noxious insect makes its appearance in an environment, the birds and bats with a survival advantage will be those that come to believe this insect is not good to eat. In view of the vast differences in neural structure, genetic background, and perceptual capacity between birds and bats, it is highly unlikely that this useful trait they may come to share has a common description at any level more concrete or less abstract than intentional system theory. It is not only that the intentional predicate is a projectible predicate in evolutionary theory; since it is more general than its species-specific counterpart predicates (which characterize the successful mutation just in birds, or just in bats), it is preferable. So from the point of view of evolutionary biology, we would not want to "reduce" all intentional characterizations even if we knew in particular instances what the physiological implementation was.

This level of generality is essential if we want a theory to have anything meaningful and defensible to say about such topics as intelligence in general (as opposed, say, to just human or even terrestrial or natural intelligence) or such grand topics as meaning or reference or representation. Suppose, to pursue a familiar philosophical theme, we are invaded by Martians, and the question arises: do they have beliefs and desires? Are they that much *like* *us*? According to intentional system theory, if these Martians are smart enough to get here, then they most certainly have beliefs and desires—in the technical sense proprietary to the theory— no matter what their internal structure, and no matter how our folk-psychological intuitions rebel at the thought.

This principled blindness of intentional system theory to internal structure seems to invite the retort: but there has to be *some* explanation of the *success* of intentional prediction of the behavior of systems (e.g., Fodor 1985, p. 79). It isn't just magic. It isn't a mere coincidence that one can generate all these *abstracta*, manipulate them via some version of practical reasoning, and come up with an action prediction that has a good chance of being true. There must be some way in which the internal processes of the system mirror the complexities of the intentional interpretation, or its success would be a miracle.

Of course. This is all quite true and important. Nothing without a great deal of structural and processing complexity could conceivably realize an intentional system of any interest, and the complexity of the realization will surely bear a striking resemblance to the complexity of the instrumentalistic interpretation. Similarly, the success of valence theory in chemistry is no coincidence, and people were entirely right to expect that deep microphysical similarities would be discovered between elements with the same valence and that the structural similarities found would explain the dispositional similarities. But since people and animals are unlike atoms and molecules not only in being the products of a complex evolutionary history, but also in being the products of their individual learning histories, there is no reason to suppose that individual (human) believers that p—like individual (carbon) atoms with valence 4—regulate their dispositions with *exactly* the same machinery. Discovering the constraints on design and implementation variation, and demonstrating how particular species and individuals in fact succeed in realizing intentional systems, is the job for the third theory: subpersonal cognitive psychology.

SUBPERSONAL COGNITIVE PSYCHOLOGY AS A PERFORMANCE THEORY

The task of subpersonal cognitive psychology is to explain something that at first glance seems utterly mysterious and inexplicable. The brain, as intentional system theory and evolutionary biology show us, is a *semantic engine*;

its task is to discover what its multifarious inputs *mean*, to discriminate them by their significance and "act accordingly."[8] That's what brains *are for*. But the brain, as physiology or plain common sense shows us, is just a *syntactic engine*; all it can do is discriminate its inputs by their structural, temporal, and physical features and let its entirely mechanical activities be governed by these "syntactic" features of its inputs. That's all brains *can do*. Now how does the brain manage to get semantics from syntax? How could *any* entity (how could a genius or an angel or God) get the semantics of a system from nothing but its syntax? It couldn't. The syntax of a system doesn't determine its semantics. By what alchemy, then, does the brain extract semantically reliable results from syntactically driven operations? It cannot be designed to do an impossible task, but it could be designed to *approximate* the impossible task, to *mimic* the behavior of the impossible object (the semantic engine) by capitalizing on close (close enough) fortuitous correspondences between structural regularities—of the environment and of its own internal states and operations—and semantic types.

The basic idea is familiar. An animal needs to know when it has satisfied the goal of finding and ingesting food, but it settles for a friction-in-the-throat-followed-by-stretched-stomach detector, a mechanical switch turned on by a relatively simple mechanical condition that normally co-occurs with the satisfaction of the animals "real" goal. It's not fancy and can easily be exploited to trick the animal into either eating when it shouldn't or leaving off eating when it shouldn't, but it does well enough by the animal in its normal environment. Or suppose I am monitoring telegraph transmissions and have been asked to intercept all *death threats* (but only death threats in English—to make it "easy"). I'd like to build a machine to save me the trouble of interpreting semantically every message sent, but how could this be done? No machine could be designed to do the job perfectly, for that would require defining the semantic category *death threat in English* as some tremendously complex feature of strings of alphabetic symbols, and there is utterly no reason to suppose this could be done in a principled way. (If somehow by brute-force inspection and subsequent enumeration we could list all and only the English death threats of, say, less than a thousand characters, we could easily enough build a filter to detect them, but we are looking for a principled, projectible, extendable method.) A really crude device could be made to discriminate all messages containing the symbol strings

. . . I will kill you . . .

or

. . . you . . . die . . . unless . . .

or

. . . (for some finite disjunction of likely patterns to be found in English death threats).

This device would have some utility, and further refinements could screen the material that passed this first filter, and so on. An unpromising beginning for constructing a sentence understander, but if you want to get semantics out of syntax (whether the syntax of messages in a natural language or the syntax of afferent neuron impulses), variations on this basic strategy are your only hope.[9] You must put together a bag of tricks and hope nature will be kind enough to let your device get by. Of course some tricks are elegant and appeal to deep principles of organization, but in the end all one can hope to produce (all natural selection can have produced) are systems that *seem* to discriminate meanings by actually discriminating things (tokens of no doubt wildly disjunctive types) that covary reliably with meanings.[10] Evolution has designed our brains not only to do this but to evolve and follow strategies of self-improvement in this activity during their individual lifetimes (see Dennett 1974).

It is the task of subpersonal cognitive psychology to propose and test models of such activity—of pattern recognition or stimulus generalization, concept learning, expectation, learning, goal-directed behavior, problem-solving—that not only produce a simulacrum of genuine content-sensitivity, but that do this in ways demonstrably like the way people's brains do it, exhibiting the same powers and the same vulnerabilities to deception, overload, and confusion. It is here that we will find our good theoretical entities, our useful *illata*, and while some of them may well resemble the familiar entities of folk psychology—beliefs, desires, judgments, decisions—many will certainly not (see, e.g., the subdoxastic states proposed by Stich 1978). The only similarity we can be sure of discovering in the *illata* of subpersonal cognitive psychology is the intentionality of their labels (see *Brainstorms*, pp. 23–38). They will be characterized as events with content, bearing information, signaling this and ordering that.

In order to give the *illata* these labels, in order to maintain any intentional interpretation of their operation at all, the theorist must always keep glancing outside the system, to see what normally produces the configuration he is describing, what effects the system's responses normally have on the environment, and what benefit normally accrues to the whole system from this activity. In other words the cognitive psychologist cannot ignore the fact that it is the realization of an intentional system he is studying on pain of abandoning semantic interpretation and hence psychology. On the other hand, progress in subpersonal cognitive psychology will blur the boundaries between it and intentional system theory, knitting them together much as chemistry and physics have been knit together.

The alternative of ignoring the external world and its relations to the internal machinery (what Putnam has called psychology in the narrow sense, or methodological solipsism, and Gunderson has lampooned as black world glass box perspectivalism) is not really psychology at all, but just at best abstract neurophysiology—pure internal syntax with no hope of a semantic interpretation. Psychology "reduced" to neurophysiology in this fashion would not be psychology, for it would not be able to provide an explanation of the regularities it is psychology's particular job to explain: the reliability with which "intelligent" organisms can cope with their environments and thus prolong their lives. Psychology can, and should, work toward an account of the physiological foundations of psychological processes, not by eliminating psychological or intentional characterizations of those processes, but by exhibiting how the brain implements the intentionally characterized performance specifications of subpersonal theories.

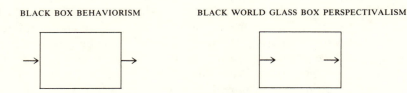

Friedman, discussing the current perplexity in cognitive psychology, suggests that the problem is the direction of reduction. Contemporary psychology tries to explain *individual* cognitive activity independently from *social* cognitive activity, and then tries to give a *micro* reduction of social cognitive activity—that is, the use of a public language—in terms of a prior theory of individual cognitive activity. The opposing suggestion is that we first look for a theory of social activity, and then try to give a *macro* reduction of individual cognitive activity—the activity of applying concepts, making judgments, and so forth—in terms of our prior social theory. (1981, pp. 15–16)

With the idea of macro-reduction in psychology I largely agree, except that Friedman's identification of the macro level as explicitly social is only part of the story. The cognitive capacities of nonlanguage-using animals (and Robinson Crusoes, if there are any) must also be accounted for, and not just in terms of an analogy with the practices of us language users. The macro level *up* to which we should relate microprocesses in the brain in order to understand them as psychological is more broadly the level of organism–

environment interaction, development, and evolution. That level includes social interaction as a particularly important part (see Burge 1979), but still a proper part.

There is no way to capture the semantic properties of things (word tokens, diagrams, nerve impulses, brain states) by a micro-reduction. Semantic properties are not just relational but, you might say, super-relational, for the relation a particular vehicle of content, or token, must bear in order to have content is not just a relation it bears to other similar things (e.g., other tokens, or parts of tokens, or sets of tokens, or causes of tokens) but a relation between the token and the whole life—and counterfactual life[11]—of the organism it "serves" *and* that organism's requirements for survival *and* its evolutionary ancestry.

THE PROSPECTS OF REDUCTION

Of our three psychologies—folk psychology, intentional system theory, and subpersonal cognitive psychology—what then might reduce to what? Certainly the one-step micro-reduction of folk psychology to physiology alluded to in the slogans of the early identity theorists will never be found—and should never be missed, even by staunch friends of materialism and scientific unity. A prospect worth exploring, though, is that folk psychology (more precisely, the part of folk psychology worth caring about) reduces—conceptually—to intentional system theory. What this would amount to can best be brought out by contrasting this proposed conceptual reduction with more familiar alternatives: "type-type identity theory, for every mentalistic term or predicate "M," there is some predicate "P" *expressible in the vocabulary of the physical sciences* such that a creature is M if and only if it is P. In symbols:

(1) $(x) (Mx \equiv PX)$

This is reductionism with a vengeance, taking on the burden of replacing, in principle, all mentalistic predicates with co-extensive predicates composed truth-functionally from the predicates of physics. It is now widely agreed to be hopelessly too strong a demand. Believing that cats eat fish is, intuitively, a *functional* state that might be variously implemented physically, so there is no reason to suppose the commonality referred to on the left-hand side of (1) can be reliably picked out by any predicate, however complex, of physics. What is needed to express the predicate on the right-hand side is, it seems, a physically neutral language for speaking of functions and functional states, and the obvious candidates are the languages used to describe automata— for instance, Turing machine language.

The Turing machine functionalist then proposes

(2) (x) $(Mx \equiv x$ realizes some Turing machine k in logical state $A)$

In other words, for two things both to believe that cats eat fish they need not be physically similar in any specifiable way, but they must both be in a "functional" condition specifiable in principle in the most general functional language; they must share a Turing machine description according to which they are both in some particular logical state. This is still a reductionist doctrine, for it proposes to identify each mental type with a functional type picked out in the language of automata theory. But this is still too strong, for there is no more reason to suppose Jacques, Sherlock, Boris, and Tom "have the same program" in *any* relaxed and abstract sense, considering the differences in their nature and nurture, than that their brains have some crucially identical physico-chemical feature. We must weaken the requirements for the right-hand side of our formula still further.

Consider

(3) (x) $(x$ believes that $p \equiv x$ can be predictively attributed the belief that $p)$

This appears to be blatantly circular and uninformative, with the language on the right simply mirroring the language on the left. But all we need to make an informative answer of this formula is a systematic way of making the attributions alluded to on the right-hand side. Consider the parallel case of Turing machines. What do two different realizations or embodiments of a Turing machine have in common when they are in the same logical state? Just this: there is a system of description such that according to it both are described as being realizations of some particular Turing machine, and according to this description, which is predictive of the operation of both entities, both are in the same state of that Turing machine's machine table. One doesn't *reduce* Turing machine talk to some more fundamental idiom; one *legitimizes* Turing machine talk by providing it with rules of attribution and exhibiting its predictive powers. If we can similarly legitimize "mentalistic" talk, we will have no need of a reduction, and that is the point of the concept of an intentional system. Intentional systems are supposed to play a role in the legitimization of mentalistic predicates parallel to the role played by the abstract notion of a Turing machine in setting down rules for the interpretation of artifacts as computational automata. I fear my concept is woefully informal and unsystematic compared with Turing's, but then the domain it attempts to systematize—our everyday attributions in mentalistic or intentional language—is itself something of a mess, at least compared with the clearly defined field of recursive function theory, the domain of Turing machines.

The analogy between the theoretical roles of Turing machines and intentional systems is more than superficial. Consider that warhorse in the philosophy of mind, Brentano's thesis that intentionality is the mark of the mental: all mental phenomena exhibit intentionality and no physical phenomena exhibit intentionality. This has been traditionally taken to be an *irreducibility* thesis: the mental, in virtue of its intentionality, cannot be reduced to the physical. But given the concept of an intentional system, we can construe the first half of Brentano's thesis—all mental phenomena are intentional—as a *reductionist* thesis of sorts, parallel to Church's thesis in the foundations of mathematics.

According to Church's thesis, every "effective" procedure in mathematics is recursive, that is, Turing-computable. Church's thesis is not provable, since it hinges on the intuitive and informal notion of an effective procedure, but it is generally accepted, and it provides a very useful reduction of a fuzzy-but-useful mathematical notion to a crisply defined notion of apparently equal scope and greater power. Analogously, the claim that every mental phenomenon alluded to in folk psychology is *intentional-system-characterizable* would, if true, provide a reduction of the mental as ordinarily understood— a domain whose boundaries are at best fixed by mutual acknowledgment and shared intuition—to a clearly defined domain of entities whose principles of organization are familiar, relatively formal and systematic, and entirely general.[12]

This reduction claim, like Church's thesis, cannot be proven but could be made compelling by piecemeal progress on particular (and particularly difficult) cases—a project I set myself elsewhere (in *Brainstorms*). The final reductive task would be to show not how the terms of intentional system theory are eliminable in favor of physiological terms via subpersonal cognitive psychology, but almost the reverse: to show how a system described in physiological terms could warrant an interpretation as a realized intentional system.

NOTES

1. This paragraph corrects a misrepresentation of both Fodor's and Ryle's positions in my critical notice of Fodor's book in *Mind* (1977) reprinted in *Brainstorms*, pp. 90–108.

2. I think it is just worth noting that philosophers' use of "believe" as the standard and general ordinary language term is a considerable distortion. We seldom talk about what people *believe*; we talk about what they *think* and what they *know*.

3. While in general true beliefs have to be more useful than false beliefs (and hence a system ought to have true beliefs), in special circumstances it may be better to have a few false beliefs. For instance it might be better for beast *B* to have some false beliefs about whom *B* can beat up and whom *B* can't. Ranking *B*'s likely antagonists from ferocious to pushover, we certainly want *B* to believe it can't beat up all the ferocious ones and can beat up all the obvious pushovers, but it is better (because it "costs less" in discrimination tasks and protects against random perturbations such as bad days and lucky blows) for *B* to extend "I can't beat up *x*" to cover even some beasts it can in fact beat up. *Erring on the side of prudence* is a well-recognized good strategy, and so Nature can be expected to have valued it on occasions when it came up. An

alternative strategy in this instance would be to abide by the rule: avoid conflict with penumbral cases. But one might have to "pay more" to implement that strategy than to implement the strategy designed to produce, and rely on, some false beliefs. (On false beliefs, see also Healy 1981.)

4. It tests its predictions in two ways: action predictions it tests directly by looking to see what the agent does; belief and desire predictions are tested indirectly by employing the predicted attributions in further predictions of eventual action. As usual, the Duhemian thesis holds: belief and desire attributions are under-determined by the available data.

5. Michael Friedman's "Theoretical Explanation" (1981) provides an excellent analysis of the role of instrumentalistic thinking within realistic science. Scheffler (1963) provides a useful distinction between *instrumentalism* and *fictionalism*. In his terms I am characterizing folk psychology as instrumentalistic, not fictionalistic.

6. "Our observations of concrete things confer a certain probability on the existence of *illata*-nothing more. . . . Second, there are inferences to *abstracta*. These inferences are . . . equivalences, not probability inferences. Consequently, the existence of abstracta is reducible to the existence of concreta. There is, therefore, no problem of their objective existence; their status depends on a convention" (Reichenbach 1938, pp. 211–12).

7. See Field (1978) p. 55, n. 12 on "minor concessions" to such instrumentalistic treatments of belief.

8. More accurately if less picturesquely, the brain's task is to come to produce internal mediating responses that reliably vary in concert with variation in the actual environmental significance (the natural and nonnatural meanings, in Grice's [1957] sense) of their distal causes and independently of meaning-irrelevant variations in their proximal causes, and moreover to respond to its own mediating responses in ways that systematically tend to improve the creature's prospects in its environment if the mediating responses are varying as they ought to vary.

9. One might think that while in principle one cannot derive the semantics of a system from nothing but its syntax, in practice one might be able to cheat a little and exploit syntactic features that don't imply a semantic interpretation but strongly suggest one. For instance, faced with the task of deciphering isolated documents in an entirely unknown and alien language, one might note that while the symbol that looks like a duck doesn't have to mean "duck," there is a good chance that it does, especially if the symbol that looks like a wolf seems to be eating the symbol that looks like a duck, and not vice versa. Call this *hoping for hieroglyphics* and note the form it has taken in psychological theories from Locke to the present: we will be able to tell which mental representations are which (which idea is the idea of *dog* and which of *cat*) because the former will look like a dog and the latter like a cat. This is all very well as a crutch for us observers on the outside, trying to assign content to the events in some brain, but it is of no use to the brain . . . because brains don't know what dogs look like! Or better, this cannot be the brain's fundamental method of eking semantic classes out of raw syntax, for any brain (or brain part) that could be said—in an extended sense—to know what dogs look like would be a brain (or brain part) that had already solved its problem, that was already (a simulacrum of) a semantic engine. But this is still misleading, for brains in any event do not *assign* content to their own events in the way observers might: brains *fix* the content of their internal events in the act of reacting as they do. There are good reasons for positing *mental images* of one sort or another in cognitive theories (see "Two Approaches to Mental Images" in *Brainstorms*, pp. 174–89) but hoping for hieroglyphics isn't one of them, though I suspect it is covertly influential.

10. I take this point to be closely related to Davidson's reasons for claiming there can be no psycho-physical laws, but I am unsure that Davidson wants to draw the same conclusions from it that I do. See Davidson (1970).

11. What I mean is this: counterfactuals enter because content is in part a matter of the *normal*

or *designed* role of a vehicle whether or not it ever gets to play that role. Cf. Sober (1981) and Millikan (1984).

12. Ned Block (1978) presents arguments supposed to show how the various possible functionalist theories of mind all slide into the sins of "chauvinism" (improperly excluding Martians from the class of possible mind-havers) or "liberalism" (improperly including various contraptions, human puppets, and so forth among the mind-havers). My view embraces the broadest liberalism, gladly paying the price of a few recalcitrant intuitions for the generality gained.

PART TWO

COMPUTATION THEORY IN COGNITIVE SCIENCE

ALLAN NEWELL AND HERBERT A. SIMON

COMPUTER SCIENCE AS EMPIRICAL INQUIRY: SYMBOLS AND SEARCH

Computer science is the study of the phenomena surrounding computers. The founders of this society understood this very well when they called themselves the Association for Computing Machinery. The machine—not just the hardware, but the programmed living machine—is the organism we study.

This is the tenth Turing Lecture. The nine persons who preceded us on this platform have presented nine different views of computer science. For our organism, the machine, can be studied at many levels and from many sides. We are deeply honored to appear here today and to present yet another view, the one that has permeated the scientific work for which we have been cited. We wish to speak of computer science as empirical inquiry.

Our view is only one of many; the previous lectures make that clear. However, even taken together the lectures fail to cover the whole scope of our science. Many fundamental aspects of it have not been represented in these ten awards. And if the time ever arrives, surely not soon, when the compass has been boxed, when computer science has been discussed from every side, it will be time to start the cycle again. For the hare as lecturer will have to make an annual sprint to overtake the cumulation of small, incremental gains that the tortoise of scientific and technical development has achieved in his steady march. Each year will create a new gap and call for a new sprint, for in science there is no final word.

Computer science is an empirical discipline. We would have called it an experimental science, but like astronomy, economics, and geology, some of its unique forms of observation and experience do not fit a narrow stereotype of the experimental method. Nonetheless, they are experiments. Each new machine that is built is an experiment. Actually constructing the machine poses a question to nature; and we listen for the answer by observing the machine in operation and analyzing it by all analytical and measurement means available. Each new program that is built is an experiment. It poses a question to nature, and its behavior offers clues to an answer. Neither machines nor programs are black boxes; they are artifacts that have been designed, both hardware and software, and we can open them up and look inside. We can relate their structure to their behavior and draw many lessons from a single experiment. We don't have to build 100 copies of, say, a theorem prover, to demonstrate statistically that it has not overcome the combinatorial explosion of search in the way hoped for. Inspection of the program in the light of a few runs reveals the flaw and lets us proceed to the next attempt.

We build computers and programs for many reasons. We build them to serve society and as tools for carrying out the economic tasks of society. But as basic scientists we build machines and programs as a way of discovering new phenomena and analyzing phenomena we already know about. Society often becomes confused about this, believing that computers and programs are to be constructed only for the economic use that can be made of them (or as intermediate items in a developmental sequence leading to such use). It needs to understand that the phenomena surrounding computers are deep and obscure, requiring much experimentation to assess their nature. It needs to understand that, as in any science, the gains that accrue from such experimentation and understanding pay off in the permanent acquisition of new techniques; and that it is these techniques that will create the instruments to help society in achieving its goals.

Our purpose here, however, is not to plead for understanding from an outside world. It is to examine one aspect of our science, the development of new basic understanding by empirical inquiry. This is best done by illustrations. We will be pardoned if, presuming upon the occasion, we choose our examples from the area of our own research. As will become apparent, these examples involve the whole development of artificial intelligence, especially in its early years. They rest on much more than our own personal contributions. And even where we have made direct contributions, this has been done in cooperation with others. Our collaborators have included especially Cliff Shaw, with whom we formed a team of three through the exciting period of the late fifties. But we have also worked with a great many colleagues and students at Carnegie-Mellon University.

Time permits taking up just two examples. The first is the development of the notion of a symbolic system. The second is the development of the notion of heuristic search. Both conceptions have deep significance for understanding how information is processed and how intelligence is achieved. However, they do not come close to exhausting the full scope of artificial intelligence, though they seem to us to be useful for exhibiting the nature of fundamental knowledge in this part of computer science.

I. SYMBOLS AND PHYSICAL SYMBOL SYSTEMS

One of the fundamental contributions to knowledge of computer science has been to explain, at a rather basic level, what symbols are. This explanation is a scientific proposition about Nature. It is empirically derived, with a long and gradual development.

Symbols lie at the root of intelligent action, which is, of course, the primary topic of artificial intelligence. For that matter, it is a primary question for all of computer science. For all information is processed by computers in the service of ends, and we measure the intelligence of a system by its ability to achieve stated ends in the face of variations, difficulties, and complexities posed by the task environment. This general investment of computer science in attaining intelligence is obscured when the tasks being accomplished are limited in scope, for then the full variations in the environment can be accurately foreseen. It becomes more obvious as we extend computers to more global, complex, and knowledge-intensive tasks—as we attempt to make them our agents, capable of handling on their own the full contingencies of the natural world.

Our understanding of the system's requirements for intelligent action emerges slowly. It is composite, for no single elementary thing accounts for intelligence in all its manifestations. There is no "intelligence principle," just as there is no "vital principle" that conveys by its very nature the essence of life. But the lack of a simple *deus ex machina* does not imply that there are no structural requirements for intelligence. One such requirement is the ability to store and manipulate symbols. To put the scientific question, we may paraphrase the title of a famous paper by Warren McCulloch (1961): What is a symbol, that intelligence may use it, and intelligence, that it may use a symbol?

Laws of Qualitative Structure

All sciences characterize the essential nature of the systems they study. These characterizations are invariably qualitative in nature, for they set the terms within which more detailed knowledge can be developed. Their essence can often be captured in very short, very general statements. One might judge these general laws, because of their limited specificity, as making relatively little contribution to the sum of a science, were it not for the historical evidence that shows them to be results of the greatest importance.

THE CELL DOCTRINE IN BIOLOGY. A good example of a law of qualitative structure is the cell doctrine in biology, which states that the basic building block of all living organisms is the cell. Cells come in a large variety of forms, though they all have a nucleus surrounded by protoplasm, the whole encased by a membrane. But this internal structure was not, historically, part of the specification of the cell doctrine; it was subsequent specificity developed by intensive investigation. The cell doctrine can be conveyed almost entirely by the statement we gave above, along with some vague notions about what size a cell can be. The impact of this law on biology, however, has been tremendous, and the lost motion in the field prior to its gradual acceptance was considerable.

PLATE TECTONICS IN GEOLOGY. Geology provides an interesting example of a qualitative structure law, interesting because it has gained acceptance in the last decade and so its rise in status is still fresh in our memory. The theory of plate tectonics asserts that the surface of the globe is a collection of huge plates—a few dozen in all—which move (at geological speeds) against, over, and under each other into the center of the earth, where they lose their identity. The movements of the plates account for the shapes and relative locations of the continents and oceans, for the areas of volcanic and earthquake activity, for the deep sea ridges, and so on. With a few additional particulars as to speed and size, the essential theory has been specified. It was of course not accepted until it succeeded in explaining a number of details, all of which hung together (e.g., accounting for flora, fauna, and stratification agreements between West Africa and Northeast South America). The plate tectonics theory is highly qualitative. Now that it is accepted, the whole earth seems to offer evidence for it everywhere, for we see the world in its terms.

THE GERM THEORY OF DISEASE. It is little more than a century since Pasteur enunciated the germ theory of disease, a law of qualitative structure that produced a revolution in medicine. The theory proposes that most diseases are caused by the presence and multiplication in the body of tiny single-celled living organisms and that contagion consists in the transmission of these organisms from one host to another. A large part of the elaboration of the theory consisted in identifying the organism associated with specific diseases, describing them, and tracing their life histories. The fact that the law has many exceptions—that many diseases are not produced by germs—does not detract from its importance. The law tells us to look for a particular kind of cause; it does not insist that we will always find it.

THE DOCTRINE OF ATOMISM. The doctrine of atomism offers an interesting contrast to the three laws of qualitative structure we have just described. As it emerged from the work of Dalton and his demonstrations that the chemicals combined in fixed proportions, the law provided a typical example of qualitative structure: the elements are composed of small, uniform particles, differing from one element to the another. But because the underlying species of atoms are so simple and limited in their variety, quantitative theories were soon formulated that assimilated all the general structure in the original qualitative hypothesis. With cells, tectonic plates, and germs, the variety of structure is so great that the underlying qualitative principle remains distinct, and its contribution to the total theory clearly discernible.

CONCLUSION. Laws of qualitative structure are seen everywhere in science. Some of our greatest scientific discoveries are to be found among them. As the examples illustrate, they often set the terms on which a whole science operates.

Physical Symbol Systems

Let us return to the topic of symbols and define a *physical symbol system*. The adjective "physical" denotes two important features: (1) Such systems clearly obey the laws of physics—they are realizable by engineered systems made of engineered components; (2) although our use of the term "symbol" prefigures our intended interpretation, it is not restricted to human symbol systems.

A physical symbol system consists of a set of entities, called symbols, which are physical patterns that can occur as components of another type of entity called an expression (or symbol structure). Thus a symbol structure is composed of a number of instances (or tokens) of symbols related in some physical way (such as one token being next to another). At any instant of time the system will contain a collection of these symbol structures. Besides these structures, the system also contains a collection of processes that operate on expressions to produce other expressions: processes of creation, modification, reproduction, and destruction. A physical symbol system is a machine that produces through time an evolving collection of symbol structures. Such a system exists in a world of objects wider than just these symbolic expressions themselves.

Two notions are central to this structure of expressions, symbols, and objects: designation and interpretation.

Designation. An expression designates an object if, given the expression, the system can either affect the object itself or behave in ways depending on the object.

In either case, access to the object via the expression has been obtained, which is the essence of designation.

Interpretation. The system can interpret an expression if the expression designates a process and if, given the expression, the system can carry out the process.[1]

Interpretation implies a special form of dependent action: given an expression, the system can perform the indicated process, which is to say, it can evoke and execute its own processes from expressions that designate them.

A system capable of designation and interpretation, in the sense just indicated, must also meet a number of additional requirements, of completeness and closure. We will have space only to mention these briefly; all of them are important and have far-reaching consequences.

(1) A symbol may be used to designate any expression whatsoever. That is, given a symbol, it is not prescribed a priori what expressions it can designate. This arbitrariness pertains only to symbols: the symbol tokens and their mutual relations determine what object is designated by a complex expression. (2) There exist expressions that designate every process of which the machine is capable. (3) There exist processes for creating any expression and for modifying any expression in arbitrary ways. (4) Expressions are stable; once created, they will continue to exist until explicitly modified or deleted. (5) The number of expressions that the system can hold is essentially unbounded.

The type of system we have just defined is not unfamiliar to computer scientists. It bears a strong family resemblance to all general purpose computers. If a symbol-manipulation language, such as LISP, is taken as defining a machine, then the kinship becomes truly brotherly. Our intent in laying out such a system is not to propose something new. Just the opposite: it is to show what is now known and hypothesized about systems that satisfy such a characterization.

We can now state a general scientific hypothesis—a law of qualitative structure for symbol systems:

The Physical Symbol System Hypothesis. A physical symbol system has the necessary and sufficient means for general intelligent action.

By "necessary" we mean that any system that exhibits general intelligence will prove upon analysis to be a physical symbol system. By "sufficient" we mean that any physical symbol system of sufficient size can be organized further to exhibit general intelligence. By "general intelligent action" we wish to indicate the same scope of intelligence as we see in human action: that in any real situation behavior appropriate to the ends of the system and adaptive to the demands of the environment can occur, within some limits of speed and complexity.

The Physical Symbol System Hypothesis clearly is a law of qualitative structure. It specifies a general class of systems within which one will find those capable of intelligent action.

This is an empirical hypothesis. We have defined a class of systems; we wish to ask whether that class accounts for a set of phenomena we find in the real world. Intelligent action is everywhere around us in the biological world, mostly in human behavior. It is a form of behavior we can recognize by its effects whether it is performed by humans or not. The hypothesis could indeed be false. Intelligent behavior is not so easy to produce that any system will exhibit it willy-nilly. Indeed, there are people whose analyses lead them to conclude either on philosophical or on scientific grounds that the hypothesis *is* false. Scientifically, one can attack or defend it only by bringing forth empirical evidence about the natural world.

We now need to trace the development of this hypothesis and look at the evidence for it.

Development of the Symbol System Hypothesis

A physical symbol system is an instance of a universal machine. Thus the symbol system hypothesis implies that intelligence will be realized by a universal computer. However, the hypothesis goes far beyond the argument, often made on general grounds of physical determinism, that any computation that is realizable can be realized by a universal machine, provided that it is specified. For it asserts specifically that the intelligent machine is a symbol system, thus making a specific architectural assertion about the nature of intelligent systems. It is important to understand how this additional specificity arose.

FORMAL LOGIC. The roots of the hypothesis go back to the program of Frege and of Whitehead and Russell for formalizing logic: capturing the basic conceptual notions of mathematics in logic and putting the notions of proof and deduction on a secure footing. This effort culminated in mathematical logic—our familiar propositional, first-order, and higher-order logics. It developed a characteristic view, often referred to as the "symbol game." Logic, and by incorporation all of mathematics, was a game played with meaningless tokens according to certain purely syntactic rules. All meaning had been purged. One had a mechanical, though permissive (we would now say nondeterministic), system about which various things could be proved. Thus progress was first made by walking away from all that seemed relevant to meaning and human symbols. We could call this the stage of formal symbol manipulation.

This general attitude is well reflected in the development of information theory. It was pointed out time and again that Shannon had defined a system that was useful only for communication and selection, and which had nothing to do with meaning. Regrets were expressed that such a general name as "information theory" had been given to the field, and attempts were made to rechristen it as "the theory of selective information"—to no avail, of course.

TURING MACHINES AND THE DIGITAL COMPUTER. The development of the first digital computers and of automata theory, starting with Turing's own work in the 1930s, can be treated together. They agree in their view of what is essential. Let us use Turing's own model, for it shows the features well.

A Turing machine consists of two memories: an unbounded tape and a finite state control. The tape holds data, i.e., the famous zeroes and ones. The machine has a very small set of proper operations—read, write, and scan operations—on the tape. The read operation is not a data operation, but provides conditional branching to a control state as a function of the data under the read head. As we all know, this model contains the essentials of all computers, in terms of what they can do, though other computers with different memories and operations might carry out the same computations with different requirements of space and time. In particular, the model of a Turing machine contains within it the notions both of what cannot be computed and of universal machine—computers that can do anything that can be done by any machine.

We should marvel that two of our deepest insights into information processing were achieved in the thirties, before modern computers came into being. It is a tribute to the genius of Alan Turing. It is also a tribute to the development of mathematical logic at the time, and testimony to the depth of computer science's obligation to it. Concurrently with Turing's work appeared the work of the logicians Emil Post and (independently) Alonzo Church. Starting from independent notions of logistic systems (Post productions and recursive functions, respectively), they arrived at analogous results on undecidability and universality—results that were soon shown to imply that all three systems were equivalent. Indeed, the convergence of all these attempts to define the most general class of information-processing systems provides some of the force of our conviction that we have captured the essentials of information processing in these models.

In none of these systems is there, on the surface, a concept of the symbol as something that *designates*. The data are regarded as just strings of zeroes and ones—indeed that data be inert is essential to the reduction of computation to physical process. The finite state control system was always viewed as a small controller, and logical games were played to see how small a state system could be used without destroying the universality of the machine. No games, as far as we can tell, were ever played to add new states dynamically to the finite control—to think of the control memory as holding the bulk of the system's knowledge. What was accomplished at this stage was half the principle of interpretation—showing that a machine could be run from a description. Thus this is the stage of automatic formal symbol manipulation.

THE STORED PROGRAM CONCEPT. With the development of the second generation of electronic machines in the mid-forties (after the Eniac) came the stored program concept. This was rightfully hailed as a milestone, both conceptually and practically. Programs now can be data, and can be operated on as data. This capability is, of course, already implicit in the model of Turing: the descriptions are on the very same tape as the data. Yet the idea was realized only when machines acquired enough memory to make it practicable to locate actual programs in some internal place. After all, the Eniac had only twenty registers.

The stored program concept embodies the second half of the interpretation principle, the part that says that the system's own data can be interpeted. But it does not yet contain the notion of designation—of the physical relation that underlies meaning.

LIST-PROCESSING. The next step, taken in 1956, was list-processing. The contents of the data structures were now symbols, in the sense of our physical symbol system: patterns that designated, that had referents. Lists held addresses which permitted access to other lists—thus the notion of list structures. That this was a new view was demonstrated to us many times in the early days of list processing when colleagues would ask where the data were—that is, which list finally held the collections of bits that were the content of the system. They found it strange that there were no such bits, there were only symbols that designated yet other symbol structures.

List-processing is simultaneously three things in the development of computer science. (1) It is the creation of a genuine dynamic memory structure in a machine that had heretofore been perceived as having fixed structure. It added to our ensemble of operations those that built and modified structure in addition to those that replaced and changed content. (2) It was an early demonstration of the basic abstraction that a computer consists of a set of data types and a set of operations proper to these data types, so that a computation system should employ whatever data types are appropriate to the application, independent of the underlying machine. (3) List-processing produced a model of designation, thus defining symbol manipulation in the sense in which we use this concept in computer science today.

As often occurs, the practice of the time already anticipated all the elements of list-processing: addresses are obviously used to gain access, the drum machines used linked programs (so called one-plus-one addressing), and so on. But the conception of list-processing as an abstraction created a new world in which designation and dynamic symbolic structure were the defining characteristics. The embedding of the early list-processing systems in languages (the IPLs, LISP) is often decried as having been a barrier to the diffusion of list-processing techniques throughout programming practice; but it was the vehicle that held the abstraction together.

LISP. One more step is worth noting: McCarthy's creation of LISP in 1959–1960 (McCarthy 1960). It completed the act of abstraction, lifting list structures out of their embedding in concrete machines, creating a new formal system with S-expressions, which could be shown to be equivalent to the other universal schemes of computation.

CONCLUSION. That the concept of the designating symbol and symbol manipulation does not emerge until the mid-fifties does not mean that the earlier steps were either inessential or less important. The total concept is the join of computability, physical realizability (and by multiple technologies), universality, the symbolic representation of processes (i.e., interpretability), and, finally, symbolic structure and designation. Each of the steps provided an essential part of the whole.

The first step in this chain, authored by Turing, is theoretically motivated, but the others all have deep empirical roots. We have been led by the evolution of the computer itself. The stored program principle arose out of the experience with Eniac. List-processing arose out of the attempt to construct intelligent programs. It took its cue from the emergence of random access memories, which provided a clear physical realization of a designating symbol in the address. LISP arose out of the evolving experience with list-processing.

The Evidence

We come now to the evidence for the hypothesis that physical symbol systems are capable of intelligent action, and that general intelligent action calls for a physical symbol system. The hypothesis is an empirical generalization and not a theorem. We know of no way of demonstrating the connection between symbol systems and intelligence on purely logical grounds. Lacking such a demonstration, we must look at the facts. Our central aim, however, is not to review the evidence in detail, but to use the example before us to illustrate the proposition that computer science is a field of empirical inquiry. Hence, we will only indicate what kinds of evidence there are, and the general nature of the testing process.

The notion of physical symbol system had taken essentially its present form by the middle of the 1950s, and one can date from that time the growth of artificial intelligence as a coherent subfield of computer science. The twenty years of work since then has seen a continuous accumulation of empirical evidence of two main varieties. The first addresses itself to the *sufficiency* of physical symbol systems for producing intelligence, attempting to construct and test specific systems that have such a capability. The second kind of evidence addresses itself to the *necessity* of having a physical symbol system wherever intelligence is exhibited. It starts with Man, the intelligent system best known to us, and attempts to discover whether his cognitive activity can be explained as the working of a physical symbol system. There are other forms of evidence, which we will comment upon briefly later, but these two are the important ones. We will consider them in turn. The first is generally called artificial intelligence; the second, research in cognitive psychology.

CONSTRUCTING INTELLIGENT SYSTEMS. The basic paradigm for the initial testing of the term theory of disease was: identify a disease, then look for the germ. An analogous paradigm has inspired much of the research in artificial intelligence: identify a task domain calling for intelligence, then construct a program for a digital computer that can handle tasks in that domain. The easy and well structured tasks were looked at first: puzzles and games, operations-research problems of scheduling and allocating resources, simple induction tasks. Scores, if not hundreds, of programs of these kinds have by now been constructed, each capable of some measure of intelligent action in the appropriate domain.

Of course, intelligence is not an all-or-none matter, and there has been steady progress toward higher levels of performance in specific domains, as well as toward widening the range of those domains. Early chess programs, for example, were deemed successful if they could play the game legally and with some indication of purpose; a little later, they reached the level of human beginners; within ten or fifteen years, they began to compete with serious amateurs. Progress has been slow (and the total programming effort invested small) but continuous, and the paradigm of construct-and-test proceeds in a regular cycle—the whole research activity mimicking at a macroscopic level the basic generate-and-test cycle of many of the AI programs.

There is a steadily widening area within which intelligent action is attainable. From the original tasks, research has extended to building systems that handle and understand natural language in a variety of ways, systems for interpreting visual scenes, systems for hand-eye coordination, systems that design, systems that write computer programs, systems for speech understanding—the list is, if not endless, at least very long. If there are limits beyond which the hypothesis will not carry us, they have not yet become apparent. Up to the present, the rate of progress has been governed mainly by the rather modest quantity of scientific resources that have been applied and the inevitable requirement of a substantial system-building effort for each new major undertaking.

Much more has been going on, of course, than simply a piling up of examples of intelligent systems adapted to specific task domains. It would be surprising and unappealing if it turned out that the AI programs performing these diverse tasks had nothing in common beyond their being instances of physical symbol systems. Hence, there has been great interest in searching for mechanisms possessed of generality, and for common components among programs performing a variety of tasks. This search carries the theory beyond the initial symbol system hypothesis to a more complete characterization of the particular kinds of symbol systems that are effective in artificial intelligence. In the second section of this paper, we will discuss one example of a hypothesis at this second level of specificity: the heuristic search hypothesis.

The search for generality spawned a series of programs designed to separate out general problem-solving mechanisms from the requirements of particular task domains. The General Problem Solver (GPS) was perhaps the first of these; while among its descendants are such contemporary systems as PLANNER and CONNIVER. The search for common components has led to generalized schemes of representation for goals and plans, methods for constructing discrimination nets, procedures for the control of tree search, pattern-matching mechanisms, and language-parsing systems. Experiments are at present under way to find convenient devices for representing sequences of time and tense, movement, causality, and the like. More and more, it becomes possible to assemble large intelligent systems in a modular way from such basic components.

We can gain some perspective on what is going on by turning, again, to the analogy of the germ theory. If the first burst of research stimulated by that theory consisted largely in finding the germ to go with each disease, subsequent effort turned to learning what a germ was—to building on the basic qualitative law a new level of structure. In artificial intelligence, an initial burst of activity aimed at building intelligent programs for a wide variety of almost randomly selected tasks is giving way to more sharply targeted research aimed at understanding the common mechanisms of such systems.

THE MODELING OF HUMAN SYMBOLIC BEHAVIOR. The symbol system hypothesis implies that the symbolic behavior of man arises because he has the characteristics of a physical symbol system. Hence, the results of efforts to model human behavior with symbol systems become an important part of the evidence for the hypothesis, and research in artificial intelligence goes on in close collaboration with research in information processing psychology, as it is usually called.

The search for explanations of man's intelligent behavior in terms of symbol systems has had a large measure of success over the past twenty years; to the point where information-processing theory is the leading contemporary point of view in cognitive psychology. Especially in the areas of problem-solving, concept attainment, and long-term memory, symbol manipulation models now dominate the scene.

Research in information-processing psychology involves two main kinds of empirical activity. The first is the conduct of observations and experiments on human behavior in tasks requiring intelligence. The second, very similar to the parallel activity in artificial intelligence, is the programming of symbol systems to model the observed human behavior. The psychological observations and experiments lead to the formulation of hypotheses about the symbolic processes the subjects are using, and these are an important source of the ideas that go into the construction of the programs. Thus many of the ideas for the basic mechanisms of GPS were derived from careful analysis of the protocols that human subjects produced while thinking aloud during the performance of a problem-solving task.

The empirical character of computer science is nowhere more evident than in this alliance with psychology. Not only are psychological experiments required to test the veridicality of the simulation models as explanations of the human behavior, but out of the experiments come new ideas for the design and construction of physical-symbol systems.

OTHER EVIDENCE. The principal body of evidence for the symbol-system hypothesis that we have not considered is negative evidence: the absence of specific competing hypotheses as to how intelligent activity might be accomplished—whether by man or by machine. Most attempts to build such hypotheses have taken place within the field of psychology. Here we have had a continuum of theories from the points of view usually labeled "behaviorism" to those usually labeled "Gestalt theory." Neither of these points of view stands as a real competitor to the symbol-system hypothesis, and for two reasons. First, neither behaviorism nor Gestalt theory has demonstrated, or even shown how to demonstrate, that the explanatory mechanism it postulates are sufficient to account for intelligent behavior in complex tasks. Second, neither theory has been formulated with anything like the specificity of artificial programs. As a matter of fact, the alternative theories are so vague that it is not terribly difficult to give them information-processing interpretations, and thereby assimilate them to the symbol-system hypothesis.

Conclusion

We have tried to use the example of the Physical Symbol System Hypothesis to illustrate concretely that computer science is a scientific enterprise in the usual meaning of that term: it develops scientific hypotheses which it then seeks to verify by empirical inquiry. We have a second reason, however, for choosing this particular example to illustrate our point. The Physical Symbol System Hypothesis is itself a substantial scientific hypothesis of the kind that we earlier dubbed "laws of qualitative structure." It represents an important discovery of computer science, which if borne out by the empirical evidence, as in fact appears to be occurring, will have major continuing impact on the field.

We turn now to a second example, the role of search in intelligence. This topic, and the particular hypothesis about it that we shall examine, have also played a central role in computer science, in general, and artificial intelligence, in particular.

II. HEURISTIC SEARCH

Knowing that physical symbol systems provide the matrix for intelligent action does not tell us how they accomplish this. Our second example of a law of qualitative structure in computer science addresses this latter question, asserting that symbol systems solve problems by using the processes of heuristic search. This generalization, like the previous one, rests on empirical evidence, and has not been derived formally from other premises. We shall see in a moment, however, that it does have some logical connection with the symbol-system hypothesis, and perhaps we can expect to formalize the connection at some time in the future. Until that time arrives, our story must again be one of the empirical inquiry. We will describe what is known about heuristic search and review the empirical findings that show how it enables action to be intelligent. We begin by stating this law of qualitative structure, the Heuristic Search Hypothesis.

Heuristic Search Hypothesis. The solutions to problems are represented as symbol structures. A physical-symbol system exercises its intelligence in problem solving by search—that is, by generating and progressively modifying symbol structures until it produces a solution structure.

Physical-symbol systems must use heuristic search to solve problems because such systems have limited processing resources; in a finite number of steps, and over a finite interval of time, they can execute only a finite number of processes. Of course that is not a very strong limitation, for all universal Turing machines suffer from it. We intend the limitation, however, in a stronger sense: we mean *practically* limited. We can conceive of systems that are not limited in a practical way but are capable, for example, of searching in parallel the nodes of an exponentially expanding tree at a constant rate for each unit advance in depth. We will not be concerned here with such systems, but with systems whose computing resources are scarce relative to the complexity of the situations with which they are confronted. The restriction will not exclude any real symbol systems, in computer or man, in the context of real tasks. The fact of limited resources allows us, for most purposes, to view a symbol system as though it were a serial, one-process-at-a-time device. If it can accomplish only a small amount of processing in any short time interval, then we might as well regard it as doing things one at a time. Thus "limited resource symbol system" and "serial symbol system" are practically synonymous. The problem of allocating a scarce resource from moment to moment can usually be treated, if the moment is short enough, as a problem of scheduling a serial machine.

Problem Solving

Since ability to solve problems is generally taken as a prime indicator that a system has intelligence, it is natural that much of the history of artificial intelligence is taken up with attempts to build and understand problem-solving systems. Problem solving has been discussed by philosophers and psychologists for two millennia, in discourses dense with a feeling of mystery. If you think there is nothing problematic or mysterious about a symbol system solving problems, you are a child of today, whose views have been formed since mid-century. Plato (and, by his account, Socrates) found difficulty understanding even how problems could be *entertained*, much less how they could be solved. Let me remind you of how he posed the conundrum in the *Meno*:

> Meno: And how will you inquire, Socrates, into that which you know not? What will you put forth as the subject of inquiry? And if you find what you want, how will you ever know that this is what you did not know?

To deal with this puzzle, Plato invented his famous theory of recollection: when you think you are discovering or learning something, you are really just recalling what you already knew in a previous existence. If you find this explanation preposterous, there is a much simpler one available today, based upon our understanding of symbol systems. An approximate statement of it is:

> To state a problem is to designate (1) a *test* for a class of symbol structures (solutions of the problem), and (2) a *generator* of symbol structures (potential solutions). To solve a problem is to generate a structure, using (2), that satisfies the test of (1).

We have a problem if we know what we want to do (the test), and if we don't know immediately how to do it (our generator does not immediately produce a symbol structure satisfying the test). A symbol system can state and solve problems (sometimes) because it can generate and test.

If that is all there is to problem solving, why not simply generate at once an expression that satisfies the test? This is, in fact, what we do when we wish and dream. "If wishes were horses, beggars might ride." But outside the world of dreams, it isn't possible. To know how we would test something, once constructed, does not mean that we know how to construct it—that we have any generator for doing so.

For example, it is well known what it means to "solve" the problem of playing winning chess. A simple test exists for noticing winning positions, the test for checkmate of the enemy King. In the world of dreams one simply generates a strategy that leads to checkmate for all counter strategies of the opponent. Alas, no generator that will do this is known to existing symbol systems (man or machine). Instead, good moves in chess are sought by generating various alternatives, and painstakingly evaluating them with the use of approximate, and often erroneous, measures that are supposed to indicate the likelihood that a particular line of play is on the route to a winning position. Move generators there are; winning-move generators there are not.

Before there can be a move generator for a problem, there must be a problem space: a space of symbol structures in which problem situations, including the initial and goal situations, can be represented. Move generators are processes for modifying one situation in the problem space into another. The basic characteristics of physical symbol systems guarantee that they can represent problem spaces and that they possess move generators. How, in any concrete situation, they synthesize a problem space and move generators appropriate to that situation is a question that is still very much on the frontier of artificial intelligence research.

The task that a symbol system is faced with, then, when it is presented with a problem and a problem space, is to use its limited processing resources to generate possible solutions, one after another, until it finds one that satisfies the problem-defining test. If the system had some control over the order in which potential solutions were generated, then it would be desirable to arrange this order of generation so that actual solutions would have a high likelihood of appearing early. A symbol system would exhibit intelligence to the extent that it succeeded in doing this. Intelligence for a system with limited processing resources consists in making wise choices of what to do next.

Search in Problem Solving

During the first decade or so of artificial intelligence research, the study of problem solving was almost synonymous with the study of search processes. From our characterization of problems and problem solving, it is easy to see why this was so. In fact, it might be asked whether it could be otherwise. But before we try to answer that question, we must explore further the nature of search processes as it revealed itself during that decade of activity.

EXTRACTING INFORMATION FROM THE PROBLEM SPACE. Consider a set of symbol structures, some small subset of which are solutions to a given problem. Suppose, further, that the solutions are distributed randomly through the entire set. By this we mean that no information exists that would enable any search generator to perform better than a random search. Then no symbol system could exhibit more intelligence (or less intelligence) than any other in solving the problem, although one might experience better luck than another.

A condition, then, for the appearance of intelligence is that the distribution of solutions be not entirely random, that the space of symbol structures exhibit at least some degree of order and pattern. A second condition is that pattern in the space of symbol structures be more or less detectible. A third condition is that the generator of potential solutions be able to behave differentially, depending on what pattern it detected. There must be information in the problem space, and the symbol system must be capable of extracting and using it. Let us look first at a very simple example, where the intelligence is easy to come by.

Consider the problem of solving a simple algebraic equation:

$$AX + B = CX + D$$

The test defines a solution as any expression of the form, $X = E$, such that $AE + B = CE + D$. Now one could use as generator any process that would produce numbers which could then be tested by substituting in the latter equation. We would not call this an intelligent generator.

Alternatively, one could use generators that would make use of the fact that the original equation can be modified—by adding or subtracting equal quantities from both sides, or multiplying or dividing both sides by the same quantity—without changing its solutions. But, of course, we can obtain even more information to guide the generator by comparing the original expression with the form of the solution, and making precisely those changes in the equation that leave its solution unchanged, while at the same time bringing it into the desired form. Such a generator could notice that there was an unwanted CX on the right-hand side of the original equation, subtract it from both sides, and collect terms again. It could then notice that there was an unwanted B on the left-hand side and subtract that. Finally, it could get rid of the unwanted coefficient $(A - C)$ on the left-hand side by dividing.

Thus, by this procedure, which now exhibits considerable intelligence, the generator produces successive symbol structures each obtained by modifying the previous one; and the modifications are aimed at reducing the differences between the form of the input structure and the form of the test expression, while maintaining the other conditions for a solution.

This simple example already illustrates many of the main mechanisms that are used by symbol systems for intelligent problem solving. First, each successive expression is not generated independently, but is produced by modifying one produced previously. Second, the modifications are not haphazard, but depend upon two kinds of information. They depend on information that is constant over this whole class of algebra problems, and that is built into the structure of the generator itself: all modifications of expressions must leave the equation's solution unchanged. They also depend on information that changes at each step: detection of the differences in form that remain between the current expression and the desired expression. In effect, the generator incorporates some of the tests the solution must satisfy, so the expressions that don't meet these tests will never be generated. Using the first kind of information guarantees that only a total subset of all possible expressions is actually generated, but without losing the solution expression from this subset. Using the second kind of information arrives at the desired solution by a succession of approximations, employing a simple form of means-ends analysis to give direction to the search.

There is no mystery where the information that guided the search came from. We need not follow Plato in endowing the symbol system with a previous existence in which it already knew the solution. A moderately sophisticated generator-test system did the trick without invoking reincarnation.

SEARCH TREES. The simple algebra problem may seem an unusual, even pathological, example of search. It is certainly not trial-and-error search, for though there were a few trials, there was no error. We are more accustomed to thinking of problem-solving search as generating lushly branching trees of partial solution possibilities, which may grow to thousands, or even millions, of branches before they yield a solution. Thus, if from each expression it produces, the generator creates B new branches, then the tree will grow as B^D, where D is its depth. The tree grown for the algebra problem had the peculiarity that its branchiness, B, equaled unity.

Programs that play chess typically grow broad search trees, amounting in some cases to a million branches or more. Although this example will serve to illustrate our points about tree search, we should note that the purpose of search in chess is not to generate proposed solutions, but to evaluate (test) them. One line of research into game-playing programs has been centrally concerned with improving the representation of the chess board, and the processes for making moves on it, so as to speed up search and make it possible to search larger trees. The rationale for this direction, of course, is that the deeper the dynamic search, the more accurate should be the evaluations at the end of it. On the other hand, there is good empirical evidence that the strongest human players, grandmasters, seldom explore trees of more than one hundred branches. This economy is achieved not so much by searching less deeply than do chess-playing programs, but by branching very sparsely and selectively at each node. This is only possible, without causing a deterioration of the evaluations, by having more of the selectivity built into the generator itself, so that it is able to select for generation only those branches that are very likely to yield important relevant information about the position.

The somewhat paradoxical-sounding conclusion to which this discussion leads is that search—successive generation of potentional solution structures—is a fundamental aspect of a symbol system's exercise of intelligence in problem-solving but that amount of search is not a measure of the amount of intelligence being exhibited. What makes a problem a problem is not that a large amount of search is required for its solution, but that a large amount *would* be required if a requisite level of intelligence were not applied. When the symbolic system that is endeavoring to solve a problem knows enough about what to do, it simply proceeds directly towards its goal; but whenever its knowledge becomes inadequate, when it enters terra incognita, it is faced with the threat of going through large amounts of search before it finds its way again.

The potential for the exponential explosion of the search tree that is present in every scheme for generating problem solutions warns us against depending on the brute force of computers—even the biggest and fastest computers—as a compensation for the ignorance and unselectivity of their generators. The hope is still periodically ignited in some human breasts that a computer can be found that is fast enough, and that can be programmed cleverly enough, to play good chess by brute-force search. There is nothing known in theory about the game of chess that rules out this possibility. But empirical studies on the management of search in sizable trees with only modest results make this a much less promising direction than it was when chess was first chosen as an appropriate task for artificial intelligence. We must regard this as one of the important empirical findings of research with chess programs.

THE FORMS OF INTELLIGENCE. The task of intelligence, then, is to avert the ever-present threat of the exponential explosion of search. How can this be accomplished? The first route, already illustrated by the algebra example and by chess programs that only generate "plausible" moves for further analysis, is to build selectivity into the generator: to generate only structures that show promise of being solutions or of being along the path toward solutions. The usual consequence of doing this is to decrease the rate of branching, not to prevent it entirely. Ultimate exponential explosion is not avoided—save in exceptionally highly structured situations like the algebra example—but only postponed. Hence, an intelligent system generally needs to supplement the selectivity of its solution generator with other information-using techniques to guide search.

Twenty years of experience with managing tree search in a variety of task environments has produced a small kit of general techniques which is part of the equipment of every researcher in artificial intelligence today. Since these techniques have been described in general works like that of Nilsson (1971), they can be summarized very briefly here.

In serial heuristic search, the basic question always is: What shall be done next? In tree search, that question, in turn, has two components: (1) from what node in the tree shall we search next, and (2) what direction shall we take from that node? Information helpful in answering the first question may be interpreted as measuring the relative distance of different nodes from the goal. Best-first search calls for searching next from the node that appears closest to the goal. Information helpful in answering the second question—in what direction to search—is often obtained, as in the algebra example, by detecting specific differences between the current nodal structure and the goal structure described by the test of a solution, and selecting actions that are relevant to reducing these particular kinds of differences. This is the technique known as means-ends analysis, which plays a central role in the structure of the General Problem Solver.

The importance of empirical studies as a source of general ideas in AI research can be demonstrated clearly by tracing the history, through large numbers of problem-solving programs, of these two central ideas: best-first search and means-ends analysis. Rudiments of best-first search were already present, though unnamed, in the Logic Theorist in 1955. The General Problem Solver, embodying means-ends analysis, appeared about 1957—but combined it with modified depth-first search rather than best-first search. Chess programs were generally wedded, for reasons of economy of memory, to depth-first search, supplemented after about 1958 by the powerful alpha-beta pruning procedure. Each of these techniques appears to have been reinvented a number of times, and it is hard to find general, task-independent, theoretical discussions of problem solving in terms of these concepts until the middle or late 1960s. The amount of formal buttressing they have received from mathematical theory is still minuscule: some theorems about the reduction in search that can be secured from using the alpha-beta heuristic, a couple of theorems (reviewed by Nilsson, 1971) about shortest-path search, and some very recent theorems on best-first search with a probabilistic evaluation function.

"WEAK" AND "STRONG" METHODS. The techniques we have been discussing are dedicated to the control of exponential expansion rather than its prevention. For this reason, they have been properly called "weak methods"—methods to be used when the symbol system's knowledge or the amount of structure actually contained in the problem space are inadequate to permit search to be avoided entirely. It is instructive to contrast a highly structured situation, which can be formulated, say, as a linear-programming problem, with the less structured situations of combinatorial problems like the traveling salesman problem or scheduling problems. ("Less structured" here refers to the insufficiency or nonexistence of relevant theory about the structure of the problem space.)

In solving linear-programming problems, a substantial amount of computation may be required, but the search does not branch. Every step is a step along the way to a solution. In solving combinatorial problems or in proving theorems, tree search can seldom be avoided, and success depends on heuristic search methods of the sort we have been describing.

Not all streams of AI problem-solving research have followed the path we have been outlining. An example of a somewhat different point is provided by the work on theorem-proving systems. Here, ideas imported from mathematics and logic have had a strong influence on the direction of inquiry. For example, the use of heuristics was resisted when properties of completeness could not be proved (a bit ironic, since most interesting mathematical systems are known to be undecidable). Since completeness can seldom be proved for best-first search heuristics, or for many kinds of selective generators, the effect of this requirement was rather inhibiting. When theorem-proving programs were continually incapacitated by the combinatorial explosion of their search trees, thought began to be given to selective heuristics, which in many cases proved to be analogues of heuristics used in general problem-solving programs. The set-of-support heuristic, for example, is a form of working backward, adapted to the resolution theorem-proving environment.

A SUMMARY OF THE EXPERIENCE. We have now described the workings of our second law of qualitative structure, which asserts that physical-symbol systems solve problems by means of heuristic search. Beyond that, we have examined some subsidiary characteristics of heuristic search, in particular the threat that it always faces of exponential explosion of the search tree, and some of the means it uses to avert that threat. Opinions differ as to how effective heuristic search has been as a problem-solving mechanism—the opinions depending on what task domains are considered and what criterion of adequacy is adopted. Success can be guaranteed by setting aspiration levels low—or failure by setting them high. The evidence might be summed up about as follows: Few programs are solving problems at "expert" professional levels. Samuel's checker program and Feigenbaum and Lederberg's DENDRAL are perhaps the best-known exceptions, but one could point also to a number of heuristic search programs for such operations-research problem domains as scheduling and integer programming. In a number of domains, programs perform at the level of competent amateurs: chess, some theorem-proving domains, many kinds of games and puzzles. Human levels have not yet been nearly reached by programs that have a complex perceptual "front end": visual scene recognizers, speech understanders, robots that have to maneuver in real space and time. Nevertheless, impressive progress has been made, and a large body of experience assembled about these difficult tasks.

We do not have deep theoretical explanations for the particular pattern of performance that has emerged. On empirical grounds, however, we might draw two conclusions. First, from what has been learned about human expert performance in tasks like chess, it is likely that any system capable of matching that performance will have to have access, in its memories, to very large stores of semantic information. Second, some part of the human superiority in tasks with a large perceptual component can be attributed to the special-purpose built-in parallel-processing structure of the human eye and ear.

In any case, the quality of performance must necessarily depend on the characteristics both of the problem domains and of the symbol systems used to tackle them. For most real-life domains in which we are interested, the domain structure has so far not proved sufficiently simple to yield theorems about complexity, or to tell us, other than empirically, how large real-world problems are in relation to the abilities of our symbol systems to solve them. That situation may change, but until it does, we must rely upon empirical explorations, using the best problem solvers we know how to build, as a principal source of knowledge about the magnitude and characteristics of problem difficulty. Even in highly structured areas like linear programming, theory has been much more useful in strengthening the heuristics that underlie the most powerful solution algorithms than in providing a deep analysis of complexity.

Intelligence Without Much Search

Our analysis of intelligence equated it with ability to extract and use information about the structure of the problem space, so as to enable a problem solution to be generated as quickly and directly as possible. New directions for improving the problem-solving capabilities of symbol systems can be equated, then, with new ways of extracting and using information. At least three such ways can be identified.

NONLOCAL USE OF INFORMATION. First, it has been noted by several investigators that information gathered in the course of tree search is usually only used *locally*, to help make decisions at the specific node where the information was generated. Information about a chess position, obtained by dynamic analysis of a subtree of continuations, is usually used to evaluate just that position, not to evaluate other positions that may contain many of the same features. Hence, the same facts have to be rediscovered repeatedly at different nodes of the search tree. Simply to take the information out of the context in which it arose and use it generally does not solve the problem, for the information may be valid only in a limited range of contexts. In recent years, a few exploratory efforts have been made to transport information from its context of origin to other appropriate contexts. While it is still too early to evaluate the power of this idea, or even exactly how it is to be achieved, it shows considerable promise. An important line of investigation that Berliner (1975) has been pursuing is to use causal analysis to determine the range over which a particular piece of information is valid. Thus, if a weakness in a chess position can be traced back to the move that made it, then the same weakness can be expected in other positions descendant from the same move.

The HEARSAY speech understanding system has taken another approach to making information globally available. That system seeks to recognize speech strings by pursuing a parallel search at a number of different levels: phonemic, lexical, syntactic, and semantic. As each of these searches provides and evaluates hypotheses, it supplies the information it has gained to a common "blackboard" that can be read by all the sources. This shared information can be used, for example, to eliminate hypotheses, or even whole classes of hypotheses, that would otherwise have to be searched by one of the processes. Thus increasing our ability to use tree-search information non-locally offers promise for raising the intelligence of problem-solving systems.

SEMANTIC RECOGNITION SYSTEMS. A second active possibility for raising intelligence is to supply the symbol system with a rich body of semantic information about the task domain it is dealing with. For example, empirical research on the skill of chess masters shows that a major source of the master's skill is stored information that enables him to recognize a large number of specific features and patterns of features on a chess board, and information that uses this recognition to propose actions appropriate to the features recognized. This general idea has, of course, been incorporated in chess programs almost from the beginning. What is new is the realization of the number of such patterns and associated information that may have to be stored for master-level play: something on the order of 50,000.

The possibility of substituting recognition for search arises because a particular, and especially a rare, pattern can contain an enormous amount of information, provided that it is closely linked to the structure of the problem space. When that structure is "irregular," and not subject to simple mathematical description, then knowledge of a large number of relevant patterns may be the key to intelligent behavior. Whether this is so in any particular task domain is a question more easily settled by empirical investigation than by theory. Our experience with symbol systems richly endowed with semantic information and pattern-recognizing capabilities for accessing it is still extremely limited.

The discussion above refers specifically to semantic information associated with a recognition system. Of course, there is also a whole large area of AI research on semantic information processing and the organization of semantic memories that falls outside the scope of the topics we are discussing in this paper.

SELECTING APPROPRIATE REPRESENTATIONS. A third line of inquiry is concerned with the possibility that search can be reduced or avoided by selecting an appropriate problem space. A standard example that illustrates this possibility dramatically is the mutilated checkerboard problem. A standard 64-square checkerboard can be covered exactly with 32 tiles, each a 1×2 rectangle covering exactly two squares. Suppose, now, that we cut off squares at two diagonally opposite corners of the checkerboard, leaving a total of 62 squares. Can this mutilated board be covered exactly with 31 tiles? With (literally) heavenly patience, the impossibility of achieving such a covering can be demonstrated by trying all possible arrangements. The alternative, for those with less patience and more intelligence, is to observe that the two diagonally opposite corners of a checkerboard are of the same color. Hence, the mutilated checkerboard has two fewer squares of one color than of the other. But each tile covers one square of one color and one square of the other, and any set of tiles must cover the same number of squares of each color. Hence, there is no solution. How can a symbol system discover this simple inductive argument as an alternative to a hopeless attempt to solve the problem by search among all possible coverings? We would award a system that found the solution high marks for intelligence.

Perhaps, however, in posing this problem we are not escaping from search processes. We have simply displaced the search from a space of possible problem solutions to a space of possible representations. In any event, the whole process of moving from one representation to another, and of discovering and evaluating representations, is largely unexplored territory in the domain of problem-solving research. The laws of qualitative structure governing representations remain to be discovered. The search for them is almost sure to receive considerable attention in the coming decade.

Conclusion

That is our account of symbol systems and intelligence. It has been a long road from Plato's *Meno* to the present, but it is perhaps encouraging that most of the progress along that road has been made since the turn of the twentieth century, and a large fraction of it since the midpoint of the century. Thought was still wholly intangible and ineffable until modern formal logic interpreted it as the manipulation of formal tokens. And it seemed still to inhabit mainly the heaven of Platonic ideals, or the equally obscure spaces of the human mind, until computers taught us how symbols could be processed by machines. A. M. Turing made his great contributions at the mid-century crossroads of these developments that led from modern logic to the computer.

PHYSICAL SYMBOL SYSTEMS. The study of logic and computers has revealed to us that intelligence resides in physical-symbol systems. This is computer science's most basic law of qualitative structure.

Symbol systems are collections of patterns and processes, the latter being capable of producing, destroying, and modifying the former. The most important properties of patterns is that they can designate objects, processes, or other patterns, and that when they designate processes, they can be interpreted. Interpretation means carrying out the designated process. The two most significant classes of symbol systems with which we are acquainted are human beings and computers.

Our present understanding of symbol systems grew, as indicated earlier, through a sequence of stages. Formal logic familiarized us with symbols, treated syntactically, as the raw material of thought, and with the idea of manipulating them according to carefully defined formal processes. The Turing machine made the syntactic processing of symbols truly machinelike, and affirmed the potential universality of strictly defined symbol systems. The stored-program concept for computers reaffirmed the interpretability of symbols, already implicit in the Turing machine. List-processing brought to the forefront the denotational capacities of symbols, and defined symbol-processing in ways that allowed independence from the fixed structure of the underlying physical machine. By 1956 all of these concepts were available, together with hardware for implementing them. The study of the intelligence of symbol systems, the subject of artificial intelligence, could begin.

HEURISTIC SEARCH. A second law of qualitative structure for AI is that symbol systems solve problems by generating potential solutions and testing them—that is, by searching. Solutions are usually sought by creating symbolic expressions and modifying them sequentially until they satisfy the conditions for a solution. Hence, symbol systems solve problems by searching. Since they have finite resources, the search cannot be carried out all at once, but must be sequential. It leaves behind it either a single path from starting point to goal or, if correction and backup are necessary, a whole tree of such paths.

Symbol systems cannot appear intelligent when they are surrounded by pure chaos. They exercise intelligence by extracting information from a problem domain and using that information to guide their search, avoiding wrong turns and circuitous bypaths. The problem domain must contain information—that in some degree of order and structure—for the method to work. The paradox of the *Meno* is solved by the observation that information may be remembered, but new information may also be extracted from the domain that the symbols designate. In both cases, the ultimate source of the information is the task domain.

THE EMPIRICAL BASE. Research on artificial intelligence is concerned with how symbol systems must be organized in order to behave intelligently. Twenty years of work in the area has accumulated a considerable body of knowledge, enough to fill several books (it already has), and most of it in the form of rather concrete experience about the behavior of specific classes of symbol systems in specific task domains. Out of this experience, however, there have also emerged some generalizations, cutting across task domains and systems, about the general characteristics of intelligence and its methods of implementation.

We have tried to state some of these generalizations here. They are mostly qualitative rather than mathematical. They have more the flavor of geology or evolutionary biology than the flavor of theoretical physics. They are sufficiently strong to enable us today to design and build moderately intelligent systems for a considerable range of task domains, as well as to gain a rather deep understanding of how human intelligence works in many situations.

WHAT NEXT? In our account we have mentioned open questions as well as settled ones; there are many of both. We see no abatement of the excitement of exploration that has surrounded this field over the past quarter century. Two resource limits will determine the rate of progress over the next such period. One is the amount of computing power that will be available. The second, and probably the more important, is the number of talented young computer scientists who will be attracted to this area of research as the most challenging they can tackle.

A. M. Turing concluded his famous paper "Computing Machinery and Intelligence" with the words:

We can only see a short distance ahead, but we can see plenty there that needs to be done.

Many of the things Turing saw in 1950 that needed to be done have been done, but the agenda is as full as ever. Perhaps we read too much into his simple statement above, but we like to think that in it Turing recognized the fundamental truth that all computer scientists instinctively know. For all physical-symbol systems, condemned as we are to serial search of the problem environment, the critical question is always: What to do next?

THOMAS TYMOCZKO

THE FOUR-COLOR PROBLEM AND ITS PHILOSOPHICAL SIGNIFICANCE[1]

The old four-color problem was a problem of mathematics for over a century. Mathematicians appear to have solved it to their satisfaction, but their solution raises a problem for philosophy which we might call the *new four-color problem.*

The old four-color problem was whether every map on the plane or sphere can be colored with no more than four colors in such a way that neighboring regions are never colored alike. This problem is so simple to state that even a child can understand it. Nevertheless, the four-color problem resisted attempts by mathematicians for more than one hundred years. From very early on it was proved that five colors suffice to color a map, but no map was ever found that required more than four colors. In fact, some mathematicians thought that four colors were not sufficient and were working on methods to produce a counterexample when Kenneth Appel and Wolfgang Haken, assisted by John Koch, published a proof that four colors suffice.[2] Their proof has been accepted by most mathematicians, and the old four-color problem has given way in mathematics to the new four-color theorem (4CT).

The purpose of these remarks is to raise the question of whether the 4CT is really a theorem. This investigation should be purely philosophical, since the mathematical question can be regarded as definitively solved. It is not my aim to interfere with the rights of mathematicians to determine what is and what is not a theorem. I will suggest, however, that, if we accept the 4CT as a theorem, we are committed to changing the sense of "theorem," or, more to the point, to changing the sense of the underlying concept of "proof." So, by raising the question of whether the 4CT has really been proved, I will be trying to elucidate the concept of proof and not attempting an evaluation of the mathematical work of Appel and Haken.

What reason is there for saying that the 4CT is not really a theorem or that mathematicians have not really produced a proof of it? Just this: no mathematician has seen a proof of the 4CT, nor has any seen a proof that it has a proof. Moreover, it is very unlikely that any mathematician will ever see a proof of the 4CT.

What reason is there, then, to accept the 4CT as proved? Mathematicians know that it has a proof according to the most rigorous standards of formal proof—a computer told them! Modern high-speed computers were used to verify some crucial steps in an otherwise mathematically acceptable argument for the 4CT, and other computers were used to verify the work of the first.

Thus, the answer to whether the 4CT has been proved turns on an account of the role of computers in mathematics. Even the most natural account leads to serious philosophical problems. According to that account, such use of computers in mathematics, as in the 4CT, introduces empirical experiments into mathematics. Whether or not we choose to regard the 4CT as proved, we must admit that the current proof is no traditional proof, no a priori deduction of a statement from premises. It is a traditional proof with a lacuna, or gap, which is filled by the results of a well-thought-out experiment. This makes the 4CT the first mathematical proposition to be known a posteriori and raises again for philosophy the problem of distinguishing mathematics from the natural sciences.

The plan of the argument is as follows. The paper begins with a preliminary analysis of the concept of 'proof' in order to extract certain features that will be useful to us later. Then the work of Appel, Haken, and Koch is described. The most natural interpretation of this work, I will argue, is that computer-assisted proofs introduce experimental methods into pure mathematics. This fact has serious implications not only for the philosophy of mathematics, but for philosophy in general, and we will examine some of these implications.

I

What is a proof? In this section three major characteristics of proofs will be considered:

(a) Proofs are convincing.
(b) Proofs are surveyable.
(c) Proofs are formalizable.

(a) Proofs are convincing. This fact is key to understanding mathematics as a human activity. It is because proofs are convincing to an arbitrary mathematician that they can play their role as arbiter of judgment in the mathematical community. On a very stark and skeptical position, such as is sometimes suggested in Wittgenstein's *Remarks on the Foundations of Mathematics*, this is all that there is to proofs: they are convincing to mathematicians. This is to be taken as a brute fact, something for which no explanation can be given and none is necessary. Most philosophers are unhappy with this position and instead feel that there must be some deeper characterization of mathematical proofs that explains, at least to some extent, why they are convincing. That proofs are surveyable and that they are formalizable are two such characterizations.

(b) Proofs are surveyable. Proofs are the gurantees of mathematical knowledge and so they must be comprehended by mathematicians. A proof is a construction that can be looked over, reviewed, verified by a rational agent. We often say that a proof must be perspicuous, or capable of being checked by hand. It is an exhibition, a derivation of the conclusion, and it needs nothing outside of itself to be convincing. The mathematician *surveys* the proof in its entirety and thereby comes to *know* the conclusion. Here is an example of a proof, attributed to the young Gauss, which helps to convey the idea of surveyability. It is a proof that the sum of the first one hundred positive numbers is 5050. Write down those numbers in two rows of fifty columns as shown:

$$
\begin{array}{ccccccc}
1 & 2 & 3 & 4 & \cdots & 49 & 50 \\
100 & 99 & 98 & 97 & \cdots & 52 & 51
\end{array}
$$

Observe that the sum of the two numbers in each column is 101 and that there are 50 columns. Conclude that the sum of the first one hundred positive numbers is 5050.

We now know that $1 + 2 + \cdots + 99 + 100 = 5050$. We have surveyed the proof in its entirety and become convinced. If someone actually attempted to add the numbers by hand and arrived at the sum 5048, we would say that he added wrong. The construction that we surveyed leaves no room for doubt. So it is with all mathematical proofs; to say that they can be surveyed is to say that they can be definitively checked by members of the mathematical community. Of course, some surveyable proofs are very long. They might take months for even a trained mathematician to review and work out—an example is Walter Feit and John G. Thompson's famous proof that all groups of odd order are solvable.[3]

Genius in mathematics lies in the discovery of new proofs, not in the verification of old ones. In a sense, the concept of surveyability provides for the democratization of mathematics by making proofs accessible to any competent mathematician. A teacher of mine, a very good mathematician but no genius, once remarked that there were only a few proofs that he couldn't understand, but that there were none that he could not follow.

Surveyability is an important subjective feature of mathematical proofs that relates the proofs to the mathematicians, the subjects of mathematical investigations. It is in the context of surveyability that the idea of "lemma" fits. Mathematicians organize a proof into lemmas to make it more perspicuous. The proof relates the mathematical known to the mathematical knower, and the surveyability of the proof enables it to be comprehended by the pure power of the intellect—surveyed by the mind's eye, as it were. Because of surveyability, mathematical theorems are credited by some philosophers with a kind of certainty unobtainable in the other sciences. Mathematical theorems are known a priori.

(c) Proofs are formalizable. A proof, as defined in logic, is a finite sequence of formulas of a formal theory satisfying certain conditions. It is a deduction of the conclusion from the axioms of the theory by means of the axioms and rules of logic. Most mathematicians and philosophers believe that any acceptable proof can be formalized. We can always find an appropriate formal language and theory in which the informal proof can be embedded and "filled out" into a rigorous formal proof.

Formal proofs carry with them a certain objectivity. That a proof is formalizable, that the formal proofs have the structural properties that they do, explains in part why proofs are convincing to mathematicians.

We've noted three features of proofs: that they are convincing, surveyable, and formalizable. The first is a feature centered in the anthropology of mathematics, the second in the epistemology of mathematics, and the third in the logic of mathematics. The latter two are the deep features. It is because proofs are surveyable and formalizable that they are convincing to rational agents.

Surveyability and formalizability can be seen as two sides of the same coin. Formalizability idealizes surveyability, analyzes it into finite reiterations of surveyable patterns. Certainly when the two criteria work together, mathematicians do not hesitate to accept or reject a purported proof. Nevertheless the two ideas spring from such different sources that we can wonder whether they will always work together. Can there be surveyable proofs that are not formalizable or formal proofs that cannot be surveyed?

Are all surveyable proofs formalizable? Most mathematicians and philosophers would assent, but not all. Some intuitionists deny that the actual proof constructions of mathematics can be completely captured by formal systems.[4] Intuitionism aside, however, it is well known that no single theory is sufficient to formalize every proof. Given any sufficiently rich theory, we can find a surveyable proof of a statement of that theory which has no formal proof. Such a statement can be a Gödel statement which, when properly interpreted, says that it has no formal proof. Of course the surveyable proof can be formalized in a new and more powerful formal theory; but that theory, in turn, will yield new surveyable proofs that it cannot formalize.

At best, formalizability is a local characteristic of proofs, not a global one. There is not one system in which any proof can be formalized; but rather, given any proof, there is some appropriate formal system in which it can be formalized. The point that formalizability is a local and not a global phenomenon is made by René Thom, where he notes the general significance of this distinction for the philosophy of mathematics.[5] However since our concern will not be with surveyable proofs that cannot be formalized, let us turn to the second question.

Are all formalizable proofs surveyable? Consider first the simpler question: Are all formal proofs surveyable? Here the answer is an easy no. We know that there must exist formal proofs that cannot be surveyed by mathematicians if only because the proofs are too long or involve formulas that are too long. Here "too long" can be taken to mean "can't be read over by a mathematician in a human lifetime." So it is logically possible that mathematicians could come across a statement with no surveyable proof but with a formalized proof.

However, if we stop to think about this situation, it appears unlikely that this logical possibility can ever be realized. How is a mathematician to know that a statement has a formal proof? On the one hand, the mathematician might actually survey or look over the formal proof and check it for correctness. On the other hand, the mathematician can derive the existence of the required formal proof, in effect, by presenting a surveyable proof that the formal proof exists. This sort of thing is standard practice in proof theory, where we find, for example, general surveyable arguments that any proof in, say, elementary arithemetic can be formalized in Zermelo-Fraenkel set theory. Hence it begins to appear that, in practice, at least, mathematicians come to know formal proofs only through the mediation of surveyable proofs. Either the formal proofs are simple enough to be surveyed themselves and verified to be proofs, or their existence is established by means of informal surveyable arguments.

It is not really surprising that we should come to know the existence of specific formal proofs only through some more primitive concept of proof, surveyable proof. After all, in the last analysis, formal proofs are abstract mathematical objects. They can be represented by sets of natural numbers, Gödel numbers, without any loss of information. To state that there is a formal proof of a formula is very much like stating that there is a number with a certain property; and how are we to come to know the latter statement except by a proof?

In summary, although formal proofs outrun surveyable proofs, it is not at all obvious that mathematicians could come across formal proofs and recognize them as such without being able to survey them.

Nevertheless, it is the contention of this paper that the current proof of the 4CT does drive a wedge between the criteria of surveyability and formalizability. In fact, there is no surveyable proof, no proof in the traditional sense, of the 4CT, nor is there likely to be one. Still Appel, Haken, and Koch's work provides mathematically convincing grounds for the 4CT. What can be surveyed, what is presented in their published work, is like a mathematical proof where a key lemma is justified by an appeal to the results of certain computer runs or, as we might say "by computer." This appeal to computer, whether we count it as strictly a part of a proof or as a part of some explicitly non-proof-theoretic component of mathematical knowledge, is ultimately a report on a successful experiment. It helps establish the 4CT (actually, the existence of a formal proof of the 4CT) on grounds that are in part empirical.

The idea that a particular proposition of pure mathematics can be established, indeed must be established, by appealing to empirical evidence is quite surprising. It entails that many commonly held beliefs about mathematics must be abandoned or modified. Consider:[6]

1. All mathematical theorems are known a priori.

2. Mathematics, as opposed to natural science, has no empirical content.

3. Mathematics, as opposed to natural science, relies only on proofs, whereas natural science makes use of experiments.

4. Mathematical theorems are certain to a degree that no theorem of natural science can match.

In order to assess such claims, let us quickly review the proof of the 4CT.

II

Sooner or later any discussion of the 4CT must begin talking of graphs in place of maps, so we might as well begin at once.[7] We can think of a *planar graph* as a finite collection of points in the plane, called *vertices*, which are joined to each other by lines, called *edges*, such that no edges meet except at vertices. The number of edges meeting at any vertex is called the *degree* of the vertex, and vertices joined by an edge are said to be *neighboring*, or adjacent. A graph is *4-colorable* if every vertex can be colored by one of four colors in such a way that neighboring vertices never receive the same color.

If every planar graph can be 4-colored, then every planar map can be. This is because every map determines a graph, its *dual graph*, as follows: place one vertex (capital city) in each region (country) of the map and join the capitals of neighboring regions by an edge (road) that crosses their common border. Obviously, the resulting graph is 4-colorable if and only if the original map is.

Next we restrict our attention to graphs in a standard form. We can delete any parallel edges, edges joining two vertices already joined by another edge, without affecting 4-colorability. Graphs without parallel edges or loops are called *simple graphs*. Moreover, we can add edges by a process of triangulation. Given any region or polygon of the *graph* that is bounded by four or more edges, there will be at least two nonadjacent vertices on the boundary. We can join such vertices by a new edge across the region that does not intersect any other edge (except at the vertices). Continuing in this way, we can completely triangulate a graph until all regions have three sides. Since triangulation can only make 4-coloring more difficult because it restricts the possible colorings of a graph, it suffices to prove the 4CT for triangulated graphs.

Now any planar triangulation has only finitely many vertices; so the way to prove that all such graphs can be 4-colored is by induction on the number v of vertices. In case $v \leq 4$, the triangulation can be 4-colored. So we assume as induction hypothesis that any planar triangulation G' with n or fewer vertices if 4-colorable. We wish to show that, if G is a planar triangulation with $n + 1$ vertices, then G can be 4-colored.

There is a well-known formula relating the number of vertices a triangulation can have to the degrees of the individual vertices. If vi is the number of vertices of degree i and if m is the maximum degree of any vertex in the triangulation, then Euler's formula states that

$$3v_3 + v_4 + v_5 + 0 \cdot v_6 - v_7 - 2v_8 - 3v_9 - \cdots - (m - 6)v_m = 12$$

At least one of v_3, v_4, v_5 must be nonzero; so any triangulated graph has a vertex with five or fewer edges. Incidentally, this fact suffices to prove, by induction, that any graph can be 6-colored. Look at the triangulation G and delete a vertex of degree 5 along with its edges. The resulting graph has one less vertex and, when triangulated, it can be 6-colored, by the induction hypothesis. However, the missing vertex has at most five neighbors, so one color will be left to color it.

To prove that any graph G can be 4-colored, we consider the following cases.

Case 1. G contains a vertex of degree 3; i.e., $v_3 \neq 0$.

Then, if we delete the vertex along with its adjacent edges, we get a graph with n vertices that can be 4-colored by assumption. Since the missing vertex has only three neighbors, it can be colored by the remaining color.

Case 2. $v_3 = 0$ but $v_4 \neq 0$; the graph G contains a vertex of degree 4.

Again, delete the vertex of minimal degree, call it v_0, and its adjoining edges, to obtain a smaller graph which is 4-colorable.

Subcase 2a. If the four neighbors of the missing vertex are colored by only three colors, then v_0 can be colored the remaining color.

Subcase 2b. The four neighbors of v_0 are each colored differently. This coloring cannot be extended to G directly, but must first be modified. Call the neighbors of v_0 v_1', v_2', v_3', v_4', and suppose that they are respectively colored a, b, c, d. Look at the smaller graph G' ($G - v_0$), and consider the subgraph of G' determined by all vertices colored a or c along with any edges connecting two such vertices. One of two alternatives must arise. Either there is an a–c chain of points and edges connecting v_1' to v_3', or there is not.

Subcase 2bi. If there is no such path between v_1 and v_3, we say that v_1 and v_3 belong to separate a–c components of G'. In this case reverse the colors in the a–c component containing v_3'. All vertices in this component formerly colored a are now colored c, and vice versa. The resulting coloring is still a 4-coloring of G' since no neighboring vertices are colored the same, but the vertex v_3' is now colored a. The color c is not used to color any neighbor of v_0; so c can be used to color v_0.

Subcase 2bii. If there is such an a–c path connecting v_1' and v_3', then these vertices belong to the same a–c component of G', and reversing the colors won't help. However, in this case there cannot be a b–d path connecting v_2' and v_4', for any such path is blocked by the a–c path connecting v_1' and v_3'. Thus v_2' and v_4' belong to separate b–d components of G', and by reversing the colors in the b–d component containing v_4', we obtain a 4-coloring of G' in which v_4' and v_2' are both colored b, leaving d to color v_0.

In either case the 4-coloring of G' can be modified and extended to a 4-coloring of G. The argument used in subcase 2b is called a *Kempe chain argument*. Incidentally, this type of argument can be applied to a vertex of degree 5 to show that any graph can be 5-colored.

If G has a vertex of degree 3 or 4, then G is 4-colorable; so we may assume that $v_3 = 0 = v_4$, and thus we come to case 3.

Case 3. $v_5 \neq 0$, the minimum degree of any vertex in G is 5. In this case the simple proof breaks down; Kempe chain arguments do not suffice if we delete a single vertex of degree 5. Instead of deleting a single vertex, we must try to delete configurations, or systems of interconnected vertices. If we remove a configuration from a triangulation we are left with a graph with a "hole" in it. The vertices of the remaining graph that are adjacent to the hole form a circuit, or *ring* around the configuration. The size of the ring is determined by the number of vertices in it. A *configuration* can be more precisely defined as a subgraph with specifications of the number of vertices, vertex degrees, and the manner in which it is embedded in the original triangulation.

A configuration is *reducible* if the 4-coloring of any planar graph containing it is deducible from the 4-colorability of any graph with fewer vertices.

Reducible configurations transmit 4-colorability upwards. Conversely, if G is a graph that *requires* five colors and if G contains the reducible configuration C, then the subgraph $(G–C)$ requires five colors. By 1913, George Birkhoff had investigated the general methods of showing that a configuration was reducible.[8] In outline what must be proved is that every 4-coloring of the ring around a given configuration can either be extended to a 4-coloring of the configuration, or modified first by one or more Kempe interchanges and then extended, or modified by suitable identification of distinct vertices and then extended. A natural plan for attacking the four-color problem suggests itself. We can try to find a set of reducible configurations that is sufficiently large so that every triangulation contains a configuration from that set. Such an *unavoidable* set of configurations would enable us to complete the induction step in case 3. This plan runs into two related problems: the potential size of the unavoidable set and the potential size of the reducible configurations in it. As Haken observes, the amount of work required to prove that a configuration is reducible increases considerably with the ring size. For a ring of size 14, the number of possible colorations is $3^{14} + 3$ (about 2×10^5). In principle, each one of these colorations must be examined in showing that the configuration is reducible. On the other hand Edward F. Moore found a triangulation that does not contain any known reducible configuration of ring size less than 12. Thus, in order to find enough reducible configurations to fill out an unavoidable set, we will have to include some with large ring size.

In order then to establish case 3, we must find a finite list of reducible configurations such that every graph contains at least one configuration from the list. Building on some work of Heinrich Heesch, Appel and Haken developed a theory of discharging procedures any of which produces an unavoidable set of configurations, i.e., a set that no triangulation ($v_3 = v_4 = 0$) can avoid. Heesch had noticed that certain kinds of configurations were reduction obstacles in that they could not be reduced by known methods. In a preliminary study, Appel and Haken developed a discharging procedure that produced an unavoidable set of configurations that excluded two of the three major reduction obstacles of Heesch. This set the stage for the final assault on the four-color conjecture.

Appel and Haken began with a discharging algorithm and tested for reducibility the configurations in the resulting unavoidable set. Whenever a configuration in the list could not be shown reducible, the discharging algorithm was modified to produce a new unavoidable set that excluded the recalcitrant configuration although generally it included new configurations. The configurations of the new set were checked for reducibility, and so on. Although the discharging procedure and the reducibility checks on individual configurations went hand in hand, and computer work was in practice necessary to develop both, when they had finished, the work of Appel, Haken, and Koch fell nicely into two parts.

The authors could specify a discharging procedure and prove in a mathematically rigorous fashion that this procedure produced an unavoidable set U of 1834 configurations (in fact, only 1482 of these configurations are really necessary). Although computer work was used to develop the procedure and the resulting set U, once the set was produced it could be surveyed and is listed in figures 1 to 63 of Appel, Haken, and Koch. Moreover, one can give a surveyable proof that this set U is unavoidable (see the Discharging Theorem and corollary in Appel, Haken, and Koch, 460).

However, to complete the proof of case 3, we need the lemma: Every configuration in U is reducible (actually, we need something a little stronger, but this version will suffice for our purposes. See Appel, Haken, and Koch on immersion reducibility). The proof of this lemma *cannot* be surveyed in detail. That these configurations are reducible is established by programming a computer to test for reducibility and running the program on the configurations in U. Since most of the configurations have large ring size (13 or 14), the use of computers to check reducibility is "unavoidable." Appel and Haken define a measure of complexity according to which the complexity of a proof of the D-reducibility of a 13-ring configuration will exceed 10^6 although other reductions (C-reducibility) of the same configuration might be of much less complexity (p. 487). In any case, no computer has printed out the complete proof of the reducibility lemma, nor would such a printout be of much use to human mathematicians. Over 1200 hours of computer time were required for the proof. Because of the complexity and time required, any proof of the reducibility lemma along its present lines must include an appeal to computer analysis. Thus it must presuppose the legitimacy of that appeal.

In its overall outlines, the logic of the four-color proof is easy to see. It is a proof by induction that requires several cases. The first case is trivial, the second has several subcases, and the third has over a thousand subcases, most of which cannot be handled except by high-speed computers. I would like to remove any impression that Appel and Haken's work is simply a "brute force" argument. To a certain extent, the appeal to computers might be regarded as "brute force," but it makes sense only when set in the context of a novel and sophisticated theory developed by the authors. However, establishing a theorem by introducing a novel and sophisticated theory is not in itself a novel mathematical procedure. The appeal to computers in order to ground key lemmas is.

To be sure, the use of computers in mathematics, even very sophisticated use, is not unfamiliar. We can cite programs for solving differential equations or the program of Hao Wang to prove theorems of propositional logic.[9] What makes the use of computers in the 4CT so dramatic is that it leads to a genuine extension of our knowledge of pure mathematics. It is not merely calculation, but yields a proof of a substantial new result.

Let us conclude this section with some general remarks on the complexity of the mathematical argument. Is the above proof of the 4CT, including computer work, the simplest or shortest proof of the 4CT? Might a surveyable proof be found some day?

Obviously some simplification is possible. Between the write-up of the proof and its publication, it was found that 429 configurations could be eliminated from the set U. Further reduction could no doubt be achieved by modifying the discharging procedure. Nevertheless, it seems that any significant simplification of one part of the proof is likely to be matched with an increase in the complexity of another part of the proof. The current consensus among mathematicians is that the present proof is reasonably close to the simplest proof.[10] If this is so, then the appeal to computers would be essential to any mathematical justification of the 4CT.

Of course, no one can completely rule out the possibility that some mathematician will one day come up with a ten-page proof of the 4CT along lines currently unimaginable. (Although even here there are some grounds for skepticism; see Kainen and Saaty, 96.) Still, from a philosophical point of view, such a discovery would have to be regarded as mere luck. The philosophical point at issue, obviously, is not simply the status of the 4CT, but the status of computer-assisted proofs in general. The work of Appel, Haken, Koch, and IBM 370-168 guarantees that the possibility of computer-assisted proofs is a real possibility.

III

The materials for our problem have been assembled. We have discussed some general features of proofs and some details of the proof of the 4CT. We can now ask whether the 4CT is really a theorem. Let us consider it with regard to the three characteristics of proofs.

(a) Is the proof of the 4CT convincing? Yes, most mathematicians have accepted the 4CT, and none, to my knowledge, has argued against it. Still, it should be noted that Appel and Haken themselves have recognized that there could be some resistance to their work, particularly from those mathematicians "educated before the development of high-speed computers" (Appel and Haken, 121). In any case, that an argument is convincing is not sufficient reason to accept it as a proof.

(b) Has the 4CT a surveyable proof? Here the answer is no. No mathematician has surveyed the proof in its entirety; no mathematician has surveyed the proof of the critical reducibility lemma. It has not been checked by mathematicians, step by step, as all other proofs have been checked. Indeed, it cannot be checked that way. Now Appel, Haken, and Koch *did* produce something that was surveyable in the sense that it could be looked over. Their work, as we have said, is very much like a surveyable proof with a lacuna where a key lemma is justifed by nontraditional means—by computer. Incidentally, we must be wary of verbal entanglements here. Of course, if we call the appeal to computers a "new method of proof" in the strictest sense, then, trivially, the 4CT will have a surveyable proof. But the notion of proof itself will have shifted to accommodate the new method.

More serious is the objection that the appeal to computers is not a method of proof at all and that the idea that it is arises from a confusion between a proof and a description of a proof. Often mathematicians forgo a complete proof and make do with a description or a sketch of the proof sufficiently detailed for their purposes. In such descriptions, mathematicians may justify a lemma by reference to some already published work, by indicating the general method (e.g., "by diagonalizing") or by simply leaving the proof of the lemma as an exercise for the reader. Of course, these are not necessarily new methods of proof; in point of fact, they are more like shorthand, a brief way of indicating a proof. These devices belong to the description of the proof and not to the proof itself. The objection suggests that we regard Appel, Haken, and Koch's papers as descriptions of a proof (which they are) and try to assimilate the appeal to computers to the pragmatic shortcuts we've just noted.

The objection fails because there is a major difference between the cases. Traditionally any such abbreviation has been backed by a surveyable proof, even more, by a surveyed proof. Some mathematician and usually several mathematicians have surveyed the real thing and verified it. In principle this surveyable backing is available to any member of the mathematical community, either directly, as when the mathematicians can work it out for themselves, or indirectly, when they look it up in the archives, to use Wittgenstein's phrase. But it is just this surveyable backing that is lacking in the 4CT! Mathematicians cannot work out the missing steps for themselves, not even in a lifetime of work; and it is nowhere recorded in the archives. What is recorded is the evidence that a computer once worked out the missing steps. So it would be a grave mistake to classify the appeal to computers as a theoretically dispensable convenience, like the appeal to published journal articles. Of course the appeal "by computer" does mark an abbreviation, and later we will consider it in more expanded form. The point at hand, however, is that surveyability is preserved in traditional descriptions of proofs, but not in the appeal to computers.

Let us consider a hypothetical example that provides a much better analogy to the appeal to computers. It is set in the mythical community of Martian mathematicians and concerns their discovery of the new method of proof "Simon says." Martian mathematics, we suppose, developed pretty much like Earth mathematics until the arrival on Mars of the mathematical genius Simon. Simon proved many new results by more or less traditional methods, but after a while began justifying new results with such phrases as "Proof is too long to include here, but I have verified it myself." At first Simon used this appeal only for lemmas, which, although crucial, were basically combinatorial in character. In his later work, however, the appeal began to spread to more abstract lemmas and even to theorems themselves. Oftentimes other Martian mathematicians could reconstruct Simon's results, in the sense of finding satisfactory proofs; but sometimes they could not. So great was the prestige of Simon, however, that the Martian mathematicians accepted his results; and they were incorporated into the body of Martian mathematics under the rubric "Simon says."

Is Martian mathematics, under Simon, a legitimate development of standard mathematics? I think not; I think it is something else masquerading under the name of mathematics. If this point is not immediately obvious, it can be made so by expanding on the Simon parable in any number of ways. For instance, imagine that Simon is a religious mystic and that among his religious teachings is the doctrine that the morally good Martian, when it frames the mathematical question justly, can always see the correct answer. In this case we cannot possibly treat the appeal "Simon says" in a purely mathematical context. What if Simon were a revered political leader as was Chairman Mao? Under these circumstances we might have a hard time deciding where Martian mathematics left off and Martian political theory began. Still other variations on the Simon theme are possible. Suppose that other Martian mathematicians begin to realize that Simonized proofs are possible where the attempts at more traditional proofs fail, and they begin to use "Simon says" even when Simon didn't say! The appeal "Simon says" is an anomaly in mathematics; it is simply an appeal to authority and not a demonstration.

The point of the Simon parable is this: that the logic of the appeals "Simon says" and "by computer" are remarkably similar. There is no great formal difference between these claims: computers are, in the context of mathematical proofs, another kind of authority. If we choose to regard one appeal as bizarre and the other as legitimate, it can only be because we have some strong evidence for the reliability of the latter and none for the former. Computers are not simply authority, but warranted authority. Since we are inclined to accept the appeal to computers in the case of the 4CT and to reject the appeal to Simon in the hypothetical example, we must admit evidence for the reliability of computers into a philosophical account of computer-assisted proofs. The precise nature of this evidence will concern us later. For now it suffices to note that, whatever the evidence is, it cannot take the form of a traditional, surveyable proof. Otherwise Appel and Haken would have given that proof and dispensed with the appeal to computers altogether.

The conclusion is that the appeal to computers does introduce a new method into mathematics. The appeal is surveyable, but what it appeals to is not.

(c) Has the 4CT a formalizable proof? Most mathematicians would concur that there is a formal proof of the 4CT in an appropriate graph theory. We can describe the formal proof in some detail, actually exhibit sections of it, calculate the total length, and so on. Nevertheless, this belief in the formal proof cannot be used to legitimize the appeal to computers. Rather, we believe that the formal proof exists only because we accept the appeal to computers in the first place. It is important to get the order of justification correct. Some people might be tempted to accept the appeal to computers on the ground that it involves a harmless extension of human powers. On their view the computer merely traces out the steps of a complicated formal proof that is really out there. In fact, our only evidence for the existence of that formal proof presupposes the reliability of computers.

This point can be clarified by the Simon parable. Martian mathematicians could say that "Simon says" incorporates no new method of proof and say that any Martian proof was still formalizable. They could claim that all of Simon's work was formalizable, only they themselves couldn't always provide the formalization. This is much the same position we claim to be in with respect to the appeal to computers. The comparison makes clear that formalization comes in only after the fact. It cannot be used as the criterion for accepting computer-assisted proofs.

In summary, the proof of the 4CT, although much like a traditional proof, differs in certain key respects. It is convincing, and there is a formal proof. But no known proof of the 4CT is surveyable, and there is no known proof that a formal proof exists. The crucial difference between the 4-color proof requires the appeal to computers to fill the gap in an otherwise traditional proof. The work of the computer is itself not surveyable. However, there are very good grounds for believing that this computer work has certain characteristics, e.g., that it instantiated the pattern of a formal proof of the reducibility lemma. Let us consider these grounds.

What does the appeal to computers amount to? Remember, we are now considering the appeal in the context of justifying a mathematical result, not yet in the context of discovery. We have a given mathematical question: Are the configurations in the unavoidable set U reducible? As part of the question, we are given procedures for testing configurations for reducibility. Second, we have a given machine with such and such characteristics. On the basis of our question and the machine's characteristics we construct a program of instruction for the machine. In this case the program is intended to "cause" the machine to "search" through the set U, testing each configuration for reducibility and reporting yes or no as the case may be. Finally we run this program on the computer and note the results. The appeal to computers, in the case of the 4CT, involves two claims: (1) that every configuration in U is reducible if a machine with such and such characteristics when programmed in such and such a way produces an affirmative result for each configuration, and (2) that such a machine so programmed did produce affirmative results for each configuration. The second claim is the report of a particular experiment. It has been experimentally established that a machine of type T when programmed by P will give output O.

But even the conditional conjunct is, at best, an empirical truth and not subject to traditional proof. Its truth depends on two interrelated factors, the reliability of the machine and the reliability of the program. The reliability of the machine is ultimately a matter for engineering and physics to assess. It is a sophisticated natural science that assures us that the computer "does what it's supposed to" in much the same way that it assures us that the electron microscope "does what it's supposed to." Of course, even if we grant that the machine does what it is supposed to—follow the program—there remains the question of whether the program does what *it* is supposed to. This question can be difficult to answer. The task of evaluating programs is a topic of computer science, but at present there are no general methods for accomplishing it at this level. Programs themselves are written in special "languages," and many of them can be quite complex. They can contain "buts," or flaws that go unnoticed for a long time. The reliability of any appeal to computers must ultimately rest on such diffuse grounds as these.

In the case of the 4CT, most mathematicians feel that the reliability is sufficiently high to warrant a qualified acceptance of the theorem. In the first place, the problem was reducible to computer-manageable complexity. There is a very clear idea of what the computer is supposed to be doing—we have a good understanding of reduction techniques. Moreover, there is a great deal of accumulated evidence for the reliability of computers in such operations, and the work of the original computers was checked by other computers. Finally, there is good reason to believe that the theorem could not be reached by any other means. It is natural for mathematicians, at least for those educated after the development of high-speed computers and pocket calculators, to accept the truth of the 4CT. The reliability of the 4CT, however, is not of the same degree as that guaranteed by traditional proofs, for this reliability rests on the assessment of a complex set of empirical factors.

A digression on the reliability of computer-assisted proofs. No detailed estimate of this reliability, nor a general account of how such estimates should be made is offered here. Instead, let us try to probe our own subjective idea of computer reliability in mathematics by means of the following hypothetical examples.

In the case of the 4CT we understand the general shape of the computer proof. Would we be prepared to rely on computers even when we could not perceive the general shape of their work? Suppose that advances in computer science lead to the following circumstances. We can program a computer to initiate a search through various proof procedures, with subprograms to modify and combine procedures in appropriate circumstances, until it finds a proof of statement A. After a long time, the computer reports a proof of A, although we can't reconstruct the general shape of the proof beyond the bare minimum (e.g., by induction). Perhaps we could describe this hypothetical example by saying that the supercomputer found a human-assisted proof. Mathematicians served to aim the computer in a certain direction, to provide it with certain techniques, and it went on to find a cumbersome patchwork proof consisting of thousands of cases. Again, the question is whether mathematicians would have sufficient faith in the reliability of computers to accept this result.

The idea that a computer program can surprise its originators is not really very farfetched. The Appel-Haken program did surprise them.

> It was working out compound strategies based on all the tricks it had been taught, and the new approaches were often much cleverer than those we would have tried. In a sense the program was demonstrating superiority not only in the mechanical parts of the task but in some intellectual areas as well. (Appel and Haken, 117)

Suppose some such supercomputer were set to work on the consistency of Peano arithmetic and it reported a proof of *inconsistency*, a proof that was so long and complex that no mathematician could understand it beyond the most general terms. Could we have sufficient faith in computers to accept this result, or would we say that the empirical evidence for their reliability is not enough? Would such a result justify a mathematician's claim to know that Peano arithmetic was inconsistent, and would such a mathematician have to abandon Peano arithmetic? These are bizarre questions, but they suggest that the reliability of computer-assisted proofs in mathematics, though easy to accept in the case of the 4CT, might some day be harder to swallow.

In conclusion, we have seen why it is reasonable to accept the 4CT, even the crucial reducibility lemma. There is no surveyable proof of the lemma, but we know that there is a formal proof. Our knowledge of this is grounded, in part, in the results of a well-conceived computer experiment. A wedge has been driven between the two explanations of proof in terms of surveyability and formalizability. In addition, a new technique has been developed for establishing mathematical truths. It is largely a matter of notational convention whether we choose to describe the new technique—appeal to computers—as a method of proof or refuse to call it a proof and insist on describing it as an experiment. In the former case, we would count the 4CT as a bona fide theorem. In the latter case we would not count it a theorem in the strict sense but admit it as a new kind of mathematical knowledge. Mere choice of labels cannot mask the underlying reality, which is an unavoidable reliance on computer experiments to establish the 4CT. Let us now turn to the consequences of this fact for philosophy.

IV

The acceptance of the 4CT is significant for philosophy at a number of points. In the first place, it is relevant to philosophy in general, especially to the theory of knowledge. Obviously, it is relevant to the details of any philosophy of mathematics. Finally, it is relevant to some issues in the philosophy of science.

Mathematics has always been important to philosophical theorizing about knowledge and reason, of course, both because mathematics stands as one of the pinnacles of human reason and rational thought and because mathematical knowledge can appear so perplexing if not actually mysterious.

> The science of pure mathematics, in its modern developments, may claim to be the most original creation of the human spirit.[11]

> The apparent contrast between the indefinite flux of sense-impressions and the precise and timeless truths of mathematics has been among the earliest perplexities and problems not of the philosophy of mathematics only, but of philosophy in general.[12]

A widely shared assumption among philosophers is that there is a significant gulf between mathematics and mathematical knowledge on the one hand, and natural science and scientific knowledge on the other. Thoroughgoing empiricists have denied that this gulf exists and have tried to explain mathematical truth, for example as Mill did, as a very general type of empirical truth. Such explanations have not been very persuasive, and, in general, philosophy has assumed that the gulf between mathematics and natural science exists and has tried to characterize the different kinds of knowledge involved by some contrasting pair, e.g., a priori, a posteriori; innate, learned; formal, empirical; certain, dubitable; analytic, synthetic. Once established, these characterizations become philosophical tools that can be applied elsewhere in the theory of knowledge. Mathematical knowledge plays a role in establishing these characterizations by serving as a paradigm of one pole in the dichotomy. The proof of the 4CT, however, undercuts this role. Knowledge of the 4CT does not have any of the characteristics that the paradigm suggests. Let us examine the case of the a priori/a posteriori distinction; the other cases proceed along similar lines.

Traditionally, a priori truths are those truths that can be known independently of any experience and a posteriori truths are those that can be known only on the basis of particular experiences. An a priori truth might be immediately evident, stipulated by convention, or, most common, known by reason independently of any experience beyond pure thought. It is plausible to maintain that such theorems as the mini-theorem that the sum of the first one hundred positive numbers is 5050 are known by reason alone—we all know it and could demonstrate its truth if we desired. However, it is not plausible to maintain that the 4CT is known by reason alone.

By reason alone, we know that the reducibility lemma implies the 4CT; but our knowledge of the reducibility lemma does not take the form of a proof. Our knowledge rests on general empirical assumptions about the nature of computers and particular empirical assumptions about Appel and Haken's computer work. Moreover, it is unlikely that anyone could know the 4CT by reason alone. The only route to the 4CT that we can ever take appears to lead through computer experiments. Thus the 4CT is an a posteriori truth and not an a priori one; mathematicians, I suggest, will never know the 4CT by a priori means.[13]

It is with the claim that the 4CT is not a priori that I differ from the position suggested taken by Saul Kripke when he considers the example of a computer verification that some very large number is a prime.[14] Kripke argues that such a theorem would be known a posteriori for the same reasons that I give that the 4CT is known a posteriori. But he leaves open the question of whether his theorem can be known a priori. I have argued that the 4CT cannot be known a priori by us.

The 4CT is a substantial piece of pure mathematics that can be known by mathematicians only a posteriori. Our knowledge must be qualified by the uncertainty of our instruments, computer and program. There surely are truths from electrical engineering about current flow through switching networks that have a higher degree of certainty than the 4CT. The demonstration of the 4CT includes not only symbol manipulation, but the manipulation of sophisticated experimental equipment as well: the four-color problem is not a formal question. In fact, the argument for the 4CT is very like an argument in theoretical physics where a long argument can suggest a key experiment that is carried out and used to complete the argument.

This is a bit of a puzzle. In the first place, it blurs the intuitive distinction between mathematics and natural science which we began with. In the second place, we are left with the question of how to explain the role of experiment in pure mathematics. It is easy to see how experiments play a role in the arguments of physical theory. The physical theory can predict phenomena of space-time that equipment can be designed to register. Are we to say that the computer registered a phenomenon of mathematical space? In not, then how else are we to explain the role of experience in mathematics? Such puzzles are one aspect of what I have called "the new four-color problem." I will not attempt any solutions to the puzzles here, but simply note these puzzles as among the consequences of the 4CT.

Not every way of characterizing the difference between mathematics and natural science falls to the 4CT. Following Kripke, we can argue that all mathematical truths, even the 4CT, are necessary, or true in all possible worlds. The 4CT, we might say, records an essential property of planar maps. (The truths of natural science, on the other hand, might be counted as contingent, or true in our world but false in some possible world.) In this case the 4CT would be an important example of an a posteriori necessary truth and, a fortiori, a counterexample to the claim that all known necessary truths are known a priori.

The new four-color problem then might serve as a stimulus to general philosophy to rethink the commonly accepted relations among knowledge, reason, and experience. Nevertheless, the most significant impact of the 4CT in philosophy obviously will concern the details of our philosophy of mathematics.

Accepting the 4CT forces us to modify our concept of proof. We can modify it by admitting a new method (computer experiment) of establishing mathematical results in addition to proofs. Or we can modify it by allowing proof to include computer-assisted proofs. I prefer the latter terminology. Either way, the details of this new method can have a substantial impact on the way mathematics is done.

This points to one of the most exciting aspects of Appel, Haken, and Koch's work, but one we have not touched on yet. So far we have been concerned with the 4CT only in the context of its justification: given the purported proof, does it prove the theorem? We have not treated it in the context of discovery. Any conclusions based only on discovery would have invited the Fregean retort that what matters to philosophy is justification and not genesis. It is time to widen our perspective; for there is much of interest about the discovery of the 4CT both to mathematics and to philosophy.

How does one decide to attempt a computer experiment in mathematics? Even where questions of the form $P(n)$ are decidable and we have the techniques to program a computer to check the instances, we cannot simply run the computer as long as it will go, hoping that it finds, say, that $(\exists x)P(x)$ before the computer reaches its limits. There must be some reason to expect that the computer will stop with an answer within a reasonable time. In the case of the 4CT we can ask why anyone thought that an unavoidable set of reducible configurations each of ring size less than or equal to 14 could be found. From the outside, 14 looks no more probable as a bound than 20 or 50 or even 100. Yet, if the minimum ring size were 20 or more, the required proof experiment could not be conducted at present! From the other direction, we know because of Moore's map that we must include configurations whose ring size is at least 12. Perhaps Moore would discover a map requiring the minimum ring size to be 20. Why did Appel and Haken think that a computer experiment could work?

What happened was that they developed a sophisticated probabilistic argument, not a proof, that the ring size could be restricted to 17 or less, and that the restriction to 14 was a good bet. They provided an argument that invested statements of the form "There is an unavoidable set of reducible configurations each of which has a ring size less than or equal to n" with a probability derived from the ratio of the number of vertices in the configuration to the ring size n (Haken, 202). With $n = 14$, the statement was very likely. Together with this probabilistic argument was an argument that the required techniques could be programmed into a computer. Koch did much of the work on the programming, and in their earlier paper Appel and Haken had showed that there was an unavoidable set of geographically good configurations of manageable size. These two arguments made it feasible to conduct the experiment.

The first type of argument is especially interesting. It is a new kind of argument endowing mathematical statements with a probability. This probability cannot be accounted for in ontological terms according to which any statement is true, or false, in all possible worlds. Having modified the concept of proof to include computer-assisted proofs, we might want to modify it again to include the kind of probabilistic argument required to set up a computer experiment. In practice this would amount to permitting mathematicians to make such arguments as part of their mathematical step if someone were to argue that a certain statement is very likely to be true, while leaving it to someone else to design and run the actual computer experiment. We must take this possibility much more seriously after the work of Appel and Haken, who established that such probabilistic arguments can have an important function in mathematics.

On the other hand, such probabilistic arguments inevitably contain the possibility of error; they can go wrong in a way strict proofs cannot.

To use the computer as an essential tool in their proofs, mathematicians will be forced to give up hope of verifying proofs by hand, just as scientific observations made with a microscope or telescope do not admit direct tactile confirmation. By the same token, however, computer-assisted mathematical proof can reach a much larger range of phenomena. There is a price for this sort of knowledge. It cannot be absolute. But the loss of innocence has always entailed a relativistic world view; there is no progress without risk of error. (Kainen and Saaty, 98)

These shifts in the concept of proof initiated by the 4CT force us to reevaluate the role of formal proofs in the philosophy of mathematics. Of course such shifts cast no doubt whatever on the legitimacy of formal proof theory as a branch of mathematical logic. Formal proofs, as idealized abstraction, still figure in our account of the 4CT. Nevertheless, after the 4CT, formal proofs cannot continue to serve the philosophy of mathematics as the sole paradigm of mathematical activity. Philosophers and mathematicians have already noted the limitations of the formal paradigm, but the 4CT aggravates these limitations to the point of a problem.[15] The old idea that a proof is a thought-experiment suggests itself here. There is not such an apparent gulf between thought-experiments and computer-experiments as there is between formal proofs and experimentations. On the other hand, there is not such a gulf between thought-experiments in mathematics and thought-experiments in physics either.

The primary impact of the new four-color problem in the philosophy of mathematics is on the concept of proof. We have discussed some of the consequences here.[16]

The relevance of the new four-color problem to the philosophy of science is largely a reworking of the earlier consequences. It is especially relevant to that branch of the philosophy of science that looks upon science as diachronic, or developing over time. In particular it is relevant to the concept of paradigm outlined by Thomas Kuhn.[17] Paradigms, according to Kuhn, are scientific achievements that some scientific community accepts as supplying a foundation for its further practice. To qualify as a paradigm, the achievement must be both "sufficiently unprecedented to attract an enduring group of adherents away from competing modes of scientific activity" and "sufficiently open-ended to leave all sorts of problems for the redefined group of practitioners to resolve" (10). The concept of paradigms plays an important role in Kuhn's explanation of the development of science. It is natural to wonder whether the methodology leading to the 4CT can serve as a paradigm in mathematics; Kainen and Saaty have suggested it will. "In fact, the Appel-Haken methodology suggests a new paradigm for mathematics. This paradigm includes the traditional elements of intuition and standard logic, as well as heuristic and probabilistic techniques combined with the high order computational abilities of a modern computer" (96).

Looking at the 4CT from the viewpoint of paradigms and thereby placing it in a historical perspective can be very illuminating. I suggest that if a "similar" proof had been developed twenty-five years earlier, it would not have achieved the widespread acceptance that the 4CT has now. The hypothetical early result would probably have been ignored, possibly even attacked (one thinks of the early reaction to the work of Frege and of Cantor). A necessary condition for the acceptance of a computer-assisted proof is wide familiarity on the part of mathematicians with sophisticated computers. Now that every mathematician has a pocket calculator and every mathematics department has a computer specialist, that familiarity obtains. The mathematical world was ready to recognize the Appel-Haken methodology as legitimate mathematics.

Before we can satisfactorily describe the 4CT in terms of paradigms, however, there are two obstacles that must be overcome. The concept of paradigm has been developed primarily for the natural sciences with some extensions to the social sciences. We would first have to extend the notion of paradigm to mathematics, both by example and by explanation of the nature of mathematical paradigms.[18] Many philosophers would resist the extension of paradigms to mathematics, of course. In the current philosophy of mathematics, mathematics is viewed solely as a synchronic or timeless structure. Against this position it might be argued that it is simply working out of another paradigm of mathematics, the formal paradigm provided by Cantor, Frege, Russell, and Hilbert. The controversy will be decided, in part, by whether the paradigm model of mathematics can provide a more satisfactory account of achievements like the 4CT than can the formal model.

A second difficulty in extending the notion of paradigm to mathematics is historical. Paradigms are defined in terms of their past performance; they are achievements that had a major effect on the development of their fields. It is one thing to characterize an achievement as a paradigm on the basis of the historical record. It is quite another to predict that a recent achievement will function as a paradigm on the basis of the limited data currently available. It is clear that claims of the second kind must be much more tentative. However, if any such claims succeed, they are likely to provide much more information to the metatheory of paradigms than is provided by the simple classification based on the historical record. Although there are obstacles to treating the 4CT as providing a new paradigm for mathematics, any attempts to solve these problems can be important exercises in the philosophy of science.

Mathematicians have solved their four-color problem, but there is a new four-color problem that has arisen for philosophy. I have tried to explain what this problem is and how it arises. I have argued for its philosophical significance by noting some of the consequences that our acceptance of the 4CT has for the theory of knowledge, the philosophy of mathematics, and the philosophy of science.

NOTES

1. I would like to thank Michael Albertson, Joan Hutchinson, and William Marsh for reading a draft of this paper and for some helpful discussions on a number of points.

2. "Every Planar Map Is Four Colorable," *Illinois Journal of Mathematics*, xxi, 84 (September 1977): 429–567. Part I, on Discharging, is by Appel and Haken; part II, on Reducibility, was done in conjunction with Koch. Parenthetical page references to Appel, Haken, and Koch, will be to this article.

3. "Solvability of Groups of Odd Order," *Pacific Journal of Mathematics*, xiii (1963): 775–1029. It is important to realize that, despite its exceptional length, this proof was surveyed from start to finish by mathematicians including Feit, Thompson, and perhaps several dozen leading group theorists.

4. See, for example, Arend Heyting, *Intuitionism* (Amsterdam: North-Holland, 1966), ch. 1.

5. Modern Mathematics: An Educational and Philosophical Error?" *American Scientist*, LIX, 6 (November/December 1971): 695–699.

6. To be sure, not all philosophers hold these beliefs, but they are common enough to warrant criticism. Some philosophers have argued against them, notably Imre Lakatos in *Proofs and Refutations* (New York: Cambridge, 1976) and Hilary Putnam in *Mathematics, Matter and Method* (New York: Cambridge, 1975). Putnam, in particular, explicitly rejects the traditional view of mathematics as an absolutely a priori discipline set apart from natural science. He suggests replacing it with the view of mathematics as *quasi-empirical*. The present paper provides additional support for the thesis that mathematics is quasi-empirical.

7. For a simple account of the proof, see Appel and Haken, "The Solution of the Four Color Map Problem," *Scientific American*, CXXXVII, 8 (October 1977): 108–121. (Parenthetical page references to Appel and Haken are to this article; similarly for the authors cited below.) More detailed summaries can be found in Haken, "An Attempt to Understand the Four Color Problem" and F. Bernhart, "A Digest of the Four Color Theorem," both published in the *Journal of Graph Theory*, I (1977): 193–206 and 207–225, respectively. P. Kainen and T. Saaty provide an account of the theorem along with the required basis in graph theory in *The Four Color Problem: Assaults and Conquest* (New York: McGraw-Hill, 1977). The definitive statement of the proof appears in Appel, Haken, and Koch, *op. cit.*

8. "The Reducibility of Maps," *American Journal of Mathematics*, xxxv (1913): 114–128.

9. "Toward Mechanical Mathematics" in K. Sayre and F. Cooson, eds., *The Modeling of the Mind* (Notre Dame, Ind.: University Press, 1963), pp. 91–120. J. Weizenbaum, *Computer Power and Human Reason* (San Francisco: W. H. Freeman, 1976), pp. 230–231.

10. Appel, Haken, and Koch, part I, sec. 5; Bernhart, p. 224.

11. A. N. Whitehead, *Science and the Modern World* (New York: New American Library, 1959), p. 25.

12. S. Körner, *The Philosophy of Mathematics* (New York: Harper, 1960), p. 9.

13. See the qualifications expressed on page 69 of this paper, at the end of sec. II.

14. "Naming and Necessity," in D. Davidson and G. Harman, eds., *Semantics of Natural Language* (Boston: Reidel, 1972), p. 261.

15. See, for example, Lakatos, *op. cit.*

16. For another reason that focuses on the idea of "difficult proof" and its relation to incompleteness results, see Haken, *op. cit.*

17. *The Structure of Scientific Revolutions* (Chicago: University Press, 1962).

G. LEE BOWIE

LUCAS' NUMBER IS FINALLY UP

J. R. Lucas has argued, in a well-known article,[1] that humans could not be machines, and that the fact that they could not follows from Gödel's theorem. His argument, with elaborations suppressed, is this: machines correspond to formal theories. Gödel's theorem shows that for any formal theory that is sufficiently strong (and Lucas is of the opinion that the formal theory of any machine that represented *him* would clearly be sufficiently strong) there will be sentences that are true of the numbers, but that cannot be proved in the theory. Moreover, Gödel gives a procedure by means of which such a sentence can be constructed from the axioms and rules of the theory. Indeed, the procedure is such that *we* can see, assuming the theory to be consistent, that the sentence so produced is true, and, again assuming the consistency of the theory, we can show it to be true.

Thus, a mechanist who produces a machine that is alleged to represent Lucas is on the horns of a dilemma. If the machine is not consistent, then surely it cannot represent Lucas, who, Lucas assures us, is consistent. But if it is consistent, then Lucas, following the Gödel procedure, will produce a sentence that he can successfully argue to be true, since we now are assuming the machine to be consistent, but which the machine cannot prove. Lucas, in short, can out-Gödel any machine presented him. Thus, whatever machine is presented cannot represent Lucas, since Lucas can do something that the machine cannot do.

Lucas' argument has been widely attacked in the literature. Indeed, the grounds on which it has been attacked cover so diverse an area that there seems to be no consensus as to what precisely is wrong with the argument. As a brief sample, it has been charged: (1) that Lucas *is* a machine, but that he cannot know what his own program is,[2] (2) that there is a fatal ambiguity of scope in "if T is consistent then it is seen that p,"[3] (3) that resolution of the issue depends on as yet unresolved problems in the constructive foundations of mathematics,[4] and (4) that Lucas' argument presupposes that the smallest nonconstructible ordinal number is constructible.[5] It appears that the heart of the problem has not yet been reached; it is with the hope of forging a consensus position that I enter the fray.

There are many ways in which a machine might be said to correspond to a formal theory, and there are many ways in which a human might be said to be represented by a machine. What is it that Lucas is doing that we are trying to represent by a machine? And how should such a machine be said to correspond to a formal theory? Since Lucas seems content to confine the battle of wits to the arena of arithmetic truth telling, we can imagine him to be wandering about, issuing forth arithmetic truths. From time to time, challenged by a mechanist, he is given the instructions for a machine claimed to represent him, at which point he produces as true an arithmetic truth which, if the machine is consistent, that machine cannot produce. We can therefore imagine Lucas' behavior to be described by a function, $g:N^2 \to N$.[6] For all x,y, $g(x,y)$ is Lucas' output given inputs x and y. We assume a fixed enumeration, a Gödel numbering, of all of the sentences of arithmetic. When Lucas is not being challenged, we set x≠0 and allow Lucas' claim that $g(x,y)$ is (the Gödel number of) an arithmetic truth. When he is being challenged by a machine y, we set x=0, and then $g(0,y)=h(y)$ is (the Gödel number of) a truth of arithmetic that the machine y cannot produce. The function h, which describes Lucas' behavior upon challenge, is the only one that interests us here, and we shall focus on it in the sequel.

We need, therefore, to number machines, and it will be convenient, for this purpose, to use the index of the instruction set of the machine.[7] So we shall understand machines to take inputs, and we can, though we need not, suppose their behavior, like Lucas', to be described by different functions for different sorts of inputs. We suppose that machines output natural numbers, and that these numbers can be understood as denoting, under some Gödel numbering, the sentences of a formal theory—typically number theory. Thus, we may speak of the machine producing (the Gödel number of) a truth. Finally, we assume that machines are individuated by the instructions for the functions that generate their outputs.[8]

Thus, to each machine we assign a natural number, n, which is one of many r.e. indexes of its total output. Thus, if Lucas is a machine, the number assigned him is an index of his g-function. Now, let $O(n)$ be the total output set of machine n.[9] Saying that a set of numbers is consistent iff the set whose formulas they number is consistent, we can then say that machine n is consistent iff $O(n)$ is consistent. That is, n is consistent iff the wffs that are numbered by the totality of n's output do not, when taken as the axioms of a first-order theory, yield a contradiction. Note that most machines, adding machines for example, are inconsistent in this sense.[10]

Now the heart of Lucas' argument is this: given any consistent machine, m, Lucas can output an arithmetic truth, $h(m)$, that is not in $O(m)$, the total output of m. Hence no machine has the same output that Lucas has, and so no machine "represents" him. What do we say of this?

As Benacerraf notes, the actual output of Lucas the organism is very finite,[11] and there is no question that for any device whose input/output relation is finite, it is possible to devise a machine that is input/output equivalent to it. So, in claiming that no machine can capture his output, Lucas must be thinking of more than his actual, finite output set. There are two possibilities here. First, we can take it that the output set in question is the set of all possible outputs, for arbitrary inputs. Second, we can take the output set to be the set of outputs generated by some suitably restricted set of possible inputs. Let us examine each possibility.

First note that it is not very plausible to suppose that the totality of all possible outputs of a person is a consistent set. People can be brought, or made, to say the most extraordinary things with the right history of input. There is some measure of safety here in taking as outputs only sentences that express claims in elementary number theory, but even here, it is plausible that there is some history of input that would bring Lucas to deny even that $7 + 5 = 12$. So as not to torture the point, or Lucas, we shall ignore such concerns for the moment, as there are deeper consistency problems to deal with.

Lucas' behavior is describable in part by the function h. Let Tr be the set of Gödel numbers of truths of arithmetic. Then h is a Lucas-describing function such that where n is a consistent machine, $h(n) \in \text{Tr} - 0(n)$.[12] How does Lucas do this? Well, he tells us, he can do it because he has followed the proof of Gödel's theorem, and that shows him, as it would any rational person, how to construct from the instructions for a machine, such a Gödel number. He does not here appeal to any divine sense of mathematical intuition, but only to his, and others', ability to understand the proof of Gödel's theorem. We may assume, then, that there is some procedure that he is following in doing what he does. Indeed, he tells us what the procedure is. We can, in fact, construct a machine, call it Sacul, that does just what Lucas is, thus far, doing. It is well known that Tr, the set of truths of elementary number theory, is productive. [To say that a set, S, is productive is to say that it fails to be r.e. in a particularly systematic way. Namely, there is a fixed, recursive procedure that will generate counterexamples to claims that some recursive function enumerates S. This procedure is called the productive function, p, for S. Thus, if p is the productive function for a productive set S, and if n is (the Gödel number of) any r.e. set, then $p(n) \in S - O(n)$. That is, there is a partial recursive function f, such that if x is the r.e. index of an r.e. subset $O(x)$ of Tr, then $f(x) \in \text{Tr} - O(x)$. This is just what Lucas is doing too, since given machine x, he is producing a truth of arithmetic that is not in the output, $O(x)$, of machine x. But Lucas must be willing to do more than just this. For the set of r.e. indexes of consistent r.e. sets of sentences is not recursive. That is, the set of consistent machines is not recursive, so there is no recursive procedure for determining from the instructions for an arbitrary machine, whether it is consistent. Yet Lucas is willing to take on all r.e. challengers, that is, all machines. He does not accord himself any special ability to tell whether a machine is consistent, and in lieu of such ability, we must suppose his willingness to apply the same procedure even in cases where the machine in question was not consistent. Even if it were true that no inconsistent machine could represent Lucas, that fact would be ir-relevant to his behavior, which is what we speak of here, unless it were also true that Lucas withholds application of his fixed procedure when he is con-fronted with instructions for an inconsistent machine. But to suppose that he was withholding the application of the fixed procedure is to suppose that he has a way of telling when to apply the procedure and when to withhold it. And that is to suppose that he can tell, from the machine's instructions, whether the machine is consistent. And this is an ability that he does not claim. To say this is not, not yet at least, to take issue with his claim that no inconsistent machine could represent him. It is only to assert his willing-ness to apply the procedure even in those cases in which the machine, un-beknownst to him, is not in the first place a viable challenger. So Lucas must answer all challenges, even from inconsistent machines.

So far, so good. Our machine, Sacul, can do that too. Indeed, the pro-cedure of Gödel's proof gives us a total recursive function, f, such that for all x, $f(x) \in \mathrm{Tr} - O(x)$ or $f(x) \in O(x) - \mathrm{Tr}$.[13] The problem with f, though, is that its output, construed now as itself a set of sentences, not only contains falsehoods; it must also be inconsistent. (See Appendix for proof.) So the procedure that Lucas describes will produce an inconsistent output set, and hence would lead him to produce-as-true sentences that yield a contradiction. Thus, if we take the relevant output set to be the totality of outputs for all possible inputs, then Lucas is inconsistent; it is the procedure that he is following for generating counterexamples to the claim that he is represented by machine x that guarantees his inconsistency.

So suppose that we consider restricting the output set. What restriction would preserve enough of Lucas' procedure, yet make possible a consistent output set? Let C be the set of indexes of consistent theories. Then if we restrict the inputs of Lucas' h-function to elements of C, the output set $h(C)$ will be a subset of Tr, and hence will be consistent. But it is well known that C, the set of indexes of consistent theories, is not recursive. Indeed, it is not even r.e., since its complement, (roughly) the set of indexes of inconsistent theories, is r.e. (see Appendix for proof), and an r.e. set with an r.e. complement must be recursive. Indeed, C is productive (see Appendix for proof), and Lucas himself, provided that his "*h*-function" is recursive, generates a productive function for C.

So while it is true that if Lucas' inputs were restricted to C, the output set so generated would be consistent, there is, by Church's thesis, no natural process that will generate just the members of C for his inspection. It is no surprise that if we restrict the domain of a recursive function to a non-r.e. set, the range can be a set that no machine could produce all on its own (that is, without help of the non-r.e. input set). Garbage in, garbage out.

Finally, it is useful at this point to ask just what will happen if, as I believe, Lucas is a machine, and if he is challenged with his own instructions. Well, so long as Lucas is willing to follow the procedure upon challenge that he has set out, then, as we have seen, he is, machine or not, inconsistent in the sense that the totality of all of his outputs for arbitrary inputs forms an inconsistent theory. Remember now that the procedure he gives us will, for input x, give an output in $\text{Tr} - O(x)$ if x is consistent, and in $O(x) - \text{Tr}$ if x is inconsistent. Hence if 1 is the index for Lucas' own instructions, then given input 1, he will output a number that is in $O(1)$ but not in Tr. That is to say, he will output an arithmetic falsehood that is in his output set. (The falsehood that Lucas would output would, under the given Gödel numbering, say of itself that Lucas will not output it.)[14] And surely there is no surprise for mechanism in that.

One last note: I believe that Lucas is a machine, although there is nothing in what I have argued here that supports that conclusion. I have shown only that Lucas' argument to the effect that he is not a machine is based on the false premise that he is consistent. I have shown that the very procedure he sets out must lead him to an inconsistent output set. Now there is nothing to prevent Lucas from becoming a consistent machine. But to do so, he will have to give up the business of endorsing procedures that produce as output the Gödel sentences of arbitrary theories. For so long as he follows such a procedure, we see that he will harbor inconsistency within him. Of course, he would also be saved from inconsistency if, *without* a procedure, he produced Gödel sentences on just those occasions when he is challenged with a consistent machine, withholding them otherwise. But I, for one, do not believe that he can do this.[15]

APPENDIX

1. Proof that the set of (Gödel numbers of) inconsistent theories is r.e. Simply dovetail all possible derivations in all possible theories, listing a theory when you get a contradiction from that theory.

2. Proof that Lucas' procedure produces an inconsistent output. Let a "Gödel function" be

any partial recursive function, h, such that if $O(x)$ is consistent then $h(x) \in \text{Tr} - T(x)$. Then there is *no* Gödel function that has a consistent range. For let k be the Gödel number of h, so that Rng $(h) = O(k)$. Then if h is a Gödel function and $O(k)$ is consistent, then by definition of Gödel functions, $h(k) \in \text{Tr} - O(k)$, so $h(k) \notin O(k)$, i.e., $h(k) \notin$ Rng (h), a contradiction.

3. Proof that C, the set of (Gödel numbers of) consistent theories, is productive. Let h be any recursive function such that if $O(x)$ is consistent then $h(x) \in \text{Tr} - O(x)$. We have seen that Gödel's proof guarantees the existence if a recursive h satisfying this condition;[16] indeed, Lucas' *h*-function is such a function, so long as it is recursive. Now let C_1 be an r.e. subset of C, and let $K = h(C_1)$, i.e., K is the image of C_1 under h. Then K is r.e., since C_1 is r.e. and h is recursive, so $K = O(j)$ for some indexes for C_1 and h. To show that C is productive, we will show that for any such C_1, when we calculate j, $j \in C - C_1$.

Suppose $j \in C_1$. Then since $j \in C_1$ $\therefore$C, $O(j)$ is consistent, so $h(j) \in \text{Tr} - O(j)$. Hence, $h(j) \notin O(j)$, i.e., $h(j) \notin$ K. But we are assuming that $j \in C_1$, so by definition of K, $h(j) \in$ K. Hence our assumption was wrong and J $\notin C_1$. Now for all x, if $x \in C_1$ then $h(x) \in$ Tr; so $h(C_1) = K$ $\therefore$ Tr. Hence $K = O(j)$ is consistent. So $j \in$ C. Hence $j \in C - C_1$. Hence C is productive.

NOTES

1. J. R. Lucas, "Minds, Machines and Gödel," *Philosophy* 36 (1961), pp. 120–24.

2. Paul Benacerraf, "God, the Devil and Gödel," *The Monist* 51 (1967), pp. 9–32.

3. Hilary Putnam in a conversation reported in J. R. Lucas, "Satan Stultified: a Rejoinder to Paul Benacerraf," *The Monist*, 52 (1968), p. 154.

4. Judson Webb, "Metamathematics and the Philosophy of Mind," *Philosophy of Science*, 35 (1968), pp. 156–78.

5. I. J. Good, "Gödel's Theorem Is a Red Herring," *British Journal for the Philosophy of Science*, 18 (1967), pp. 144–147. It does not matter to my argument what a nonconstructible ordinal number is. For the interested reader, it is a *very* large infinite number.

6. The notation indicates simply that g maps pairs of natural numbers into natural numbers.

7. Readers familiar with the rudiments of recursive function theory are encouraged to skip the rest of this note. It is straightforward to give an effective enumeration of all sets of instructions for all of the partial recursive functions, i.e., for all computing machines. The position of an instruction set in such a (fixed) enumeration is its index. Since each function must have infinitely many different instruction sets, each function will appear infinitely many times in the enumeration, hence will have infinitely many indexes. A function f enumerates its range, Rng (f). Hence, the ranges of the partial recursive functions are called the recursively enumerable (r.e.) sets. The index of a partial recursive function that enumerates (has as its range) a set A, is called an r.e. index of the set A. Each r.e. set will, *a fortiori*, have infinitely many indexes. Finally, among the r.e. sets, some get enumerated (under at least one enumeration) by a total function in strictly ascending order. Such an enumeration provides a test for membership in the set, since one can merely enumerate members until a given number has either been enumerated, or passed by. Such sets, together with the finite sets (for which there is also a test for membership) are called the recursive sets. The point of these definitions is to capture two fundamental notions: a recursively enumerable (r.e.) set is one all of whose members can be generated by some fixed procedure. A recursive set satisfies a stronger condition, namely that there is a test for determining of an arbitrary number whether it will eventually be generated by the procedure. Finally, readers already familiar with the rudiments of recursive function theory, already having ignored the earlier encouragement, will have noted that for expository ease, the definitions here differ from (although they are equivalent to) the standard definitions.

8. Alternately, one might individuate machines in virtue of the relation between inputs (or

histories of inputs) and outputs, or even in virtue merely of their total outputs. The course we have taken, individuating in virtue of instructions, is more intuitive, and the argument in the sequel works equally well with either of the more coarsely grained individuation principles. One disadvantage is that while this principle is natural so long as we are thinking, say, of Turing machines, it is not so clear how to understand it in the case, say, of general purpose computers, or of humans understood as machines.

9. Note that we are appealing to Church's thesis in the assumption that the output of any machine is an r.e. set.

10. There are more natural notions of consistency for machines, but we need not consider them here.

11. Paul Benacerraf, *op. cit.*, p. 19.

12. $Tr - O(n)$ is the set of numbers that are elements of Tr but not of $O(n)$. Thus to say that $h(n) \in Tr - O(n)$ is to say that $h(n)$ is (the Gödel number of) a truth of arithmetic which is not in the output set of n.

13. A productive set whose productive function has this nice property is called "completely productive." It turns out that every productive set is completely productive.

14. Lewis makes a similar point in David Lewis, "Lucas Against Mechanism II," Canadian Journal of Philosophy, 9 (1979), p. 376.

15. This paper has benefited from the helpful comments of the referees and editor of the *Journal of Philosophical Logic*. An earlier version of it was read in Providence, R.I., 1980, at a special session of the American Mathematical Society.

16. The details are a bit more complicated; C must be the class of consistent, axiomatic theories. Then let G be the set of axiomatic theories whose axioms include some specified set, for example the finite axiom set of Robinson's theory Q, sufficient to guarantee that the conditions of Gödel's theorem obtain. G can be specified in such a way that it is recursive; thus given x, if $x \in G$, apply the Gödel procedure to find $h(x)$ such that if $x \in C$, $h(x) \in Tr - O(x)$. If $x \notin G$, then let $h(x)$ be some new theory which is in G. Then $h(x) \in Tr - O(x)$. We assume, of course, that all of the axioms characteristic of membership in G are true in the standard model.

THOMAS TYMOCZKO

WHY I AM NOT A TURING MACHINE: GÖDEL'S THEOREMS AND THE PHILOSOPHY OF MIND

Turing machines are idealized computers, more exactly, idealized computers implementing idealized programs.[1] So if you're unfamiliar with Turing machines, you can think of ideal programed computers for most of what follows. I'm not a Turing machine because I'm essentially creative in a way that no Turing machine can be. But it's not that I'm so smart, just that I'm human; you're probably not a Turing machine either. Unfortunately, I'm not quite able to prove that neither of us is a Turing machine. Instead, I must be content to argue that we can never have good reason for believing that we are Turing machines. I'll base my arguments on the celebrated theorems of Gödel (See Fisher, 1982 for a good introduction to Gödel's work).

Since Gödel's theorems are the most profound results of modern logic, it is natural that philosophers have attempted to draw from them some conclusions of general philosophical interest. A natural place to look for such conclusions is in the philosophy of mind or cognitive science, more particularly under the heading of models or representations of the mind. The suggestion that I want to examine is that the mind, at least certain aspects of the mind, can be adequately represented by a Turing machine. Turing machines (hereafter TMs) are able to represent potentially infinite capacities by means of a finite underlying structure: this is their great virtue. Successful TM models would count as evidence for a functionalist theory of mind (as opposed to a substantival theory), with the Turing programs representing the relevant functional relationships defining mental states (see Putnam 1960 and Dennett 1978 for more on functionalism). Although abstract TMs can be realized by many types of structures—mental or physical, organic or inorganic, because TMs can be realized by ordinary physical structures, we need not postulate a special mental substance to instantiate them. So the TM hypothesis is often used in support of physicalism. Finally, if we believe that real-life computers are representable as TMs, then the TM hypothesis is crucial to the program of Artificial Intelligence. If the mind, in certain respects, *is* representable as a

TM, then in principle we could build a computer that also instantiates the very TM that represents the mind and so, in relevant respects, functions exactly as a mind. Alternatively, if the mind is *not* a TM although every computer is, then no computer could duplicate the functions of the mind. We would have to reexamine our assumption that computers were essentially TMs or redefine the goal of Artificial Intelligence research. Thus, the hypothesis that mind is, in certain respects, representable as a TM has considerable philosophical interest.[2]

This essay will examine the argument against the TM hypothesis that is suggested by Gödel's theorems. I will begin with a quick sketch of the argument, following that with a more detailed analysis.

If a TM model of the mind is ever plausible, it would seem to be most plausible with respect to our knowledge of elementary arithmetic. We're inclined to believe that at least a large part of arithmetic is made up of a certain kind of symbol manipulation and, since TMs are symbol manipulators par excellence, it is natural to suppose that if anything is representable by a TM, our knowledge of arithmetic is. What we do and can know, as articulated in terms of statements of elementary arithmetic, might be identical to the output of some particular TM. So we might assume, as I shall do throughout, that the TM in question has a particular form equivalent to a deductive system.[3] The base program consists of a set of axioms and the logical rules for deriving theorems from these axioms. Then we might explain my ability to do mathematics by saying I am equivalent to that TM; I can prove only the theorems it can. Of course for this explanation to work, it is necessary to assume that the TM is consistent: its output includes no statement of the form A & not −A. An actually inconsistent TM would produce *all* statements of arithmetic, true or false, and could not possibly serve as a model of arithmetical knowledge. It is at this point that Gödel's incompleteness theorems (and their subsequent extensions) intervene. Gödel showed, in effect, that for any consistent TM model of arithmetical knowledge it is possible for us to construct infinitely many pairs of formulas A and − A with the properties that

i) Neither A nor −A is in the output of the TM.
ii) The arithmetical assertion that A is equivalent to the metalogical assertion that the formula 'A' is not in the output of that TM.
iii) −A is equivalent to the claim that 'A' is in the output of that TM.

It follows that A is true but that since it is not in the output, the TM can never "know" A. We, however, can know that A. Under the hypothesis, we can in principle come to accept that A is true. Hence our potential knowledge exceeds the limits of that TM so the latter fails as a model of the arithmetical mind. Since we began with an arbitrary TM satisfying minimal constraints, we can conclude that no TM adequately models the arithmetical mind. Finally, since we were motivated by the idea that arithmetic was an especially easy case for the general TM hypothesis, we have reason to be skeptical of that hypothesis.

Some version of this argument is familiar to most philosophers of mind. I believe that it occurs independently to many people when they learn Gödel's proof. One version was given in passing by Nagel and Newman in their early exposition of Gödel's theorems (Nagel and Newman 1958). Lucas gave a more elaborate defense of the argument in what has become the standard reference (Lucas 1961). According to Wang, Gödel himself defended a version of the argument (Wang 1974, especially pp. 324–326). Nevertheless, the weight of current philosophical opinion is clearly against this argument.[4] It is widely considered to be fallacious or at least unsound even by some who reject the original TM hypothesis we began with. Three of the more influential criticisms have been raised by Putnam, Bowie and Dennett. Putnam criticized the claim that we can know A, the true formula that the TM model cannot know (Putnam 1960). Bowie attacked the assumption that the TM model was consistent (Bowie, this volume). According to Dennett, the argument turns on a fallacy involving levels of description of mental phenomena (Dennett 1978 "The Abilities of Men and Machines").

In this essay, I want to examine a version of the argument against the TM hypothesis in a bit more detail, and to evaluate the criticisms of Putnam, Bowie and Dennett with respect to this version. My conclusion will be that these criticisms all fail and that the argument against TM models is, in the case of arithmetical knowledge, logically valid and very probably correct. The mind is not a TM. Before beginning the argument however, I would like to pause briefly to consider the original hypothesis identifying minds with TMs.

One basic attraction of the identification is that while "mind" is a vague and elusive concept, "TM" is precisely defined. Moreover, we have a rich and sophisticated theory of TMs. When a TM model can be plausibly made out, it promises a real gain in our understanding. Now no one, with the possible exception of Turing himself, has ever claimed that a single TM model could account for *all* mental phenomena (For Turing's views, see his 1951 paper). Many features of mental life, such as emotions, feelings, moods, and dreams, seem to fall outside the scope of TMs. The hypothesis that minds are TMs is most plausible if read in a context of some limited range of mental phenomena that the TM model is intended to capture. It would be a significant result if a TM could be used to represent the mind as knower, even as a knower of truths in elementary arithmetic.

Of course, trivial representations should be discounted. It is not fair to argue that my capacity for proving mathematical results is adequately represented by a TM merely on the grounds that

a) Tymoczko's total mathematical production will be finite, and b) any finite set of symbols can be the output of some TM. The idea is that you wait until I die, collect all my results and type them into a computer file called "Tymoczko" and then instruct the machine to "Print Tymoczko!" Of course, this could be done, but it proves nothing: the TM model has no explanatory power at all. A far different case is to argue that my capacity for proving mathematical results is adequately modeled by a TM on the grounds that:

a) Tymoczko can only prove theorems about sums and products; and
b) there is a TM that produces all (and only) sums and products.

In this case, the TM model does seem to have explanatory power. In order to explain my mathematical ability, we might not need to invest me with any more capacities than a TM. *Qua* mathematician, I might as well be a TM.

We can characterize the difference between the two hypothetical models in terms of the distinction between competence and performance (roughly, what I can do versus what I do do). We block some trivial representations of the mind by insisting that any account of our actual mental performance proceed by way of an account of our mental competence or potential. The latter will show what the mind is capable of, the former explains how in actual historical circumstances such a competent mind would perform as ours actually does. Interesting TM models of the mind can be expected to be models of competence. This does not imply that we should or could construct competence models *a priori*, without appeal to features of performance. It's just that what we're really after is our abilities and capacities, not our actual, historical results.

However competence models in themselves are not always explanatory, for a variety of reasons.[5] For the TM hypothesis to be interesting, it must be the TM structure of the model that carries the burden of explanation. There is a clear distinction between identifying the mind *with a TM* and identifying the mind *with a composite* consisting of a TM + X where X is some non-TM component. The latter can be trivially true—just let X be the mind itself and the TM hypothesis then reduces to the innocuous observation that the mind uses a TM. (Apparently, Gödel thought something like this, that the mind uses a computerlike brain. See Wang, 1974.) The TM hypothesis promises an exhaustive or complete account of competence only when it completely identifies the mind with a TM (at least in certain respects, such as mathematical thought or rational thought in general).

The point is worth developing since we'll return to it later and it can be developed precisely. Consider the case of TMs relativized to some set X of natural numbers. Any relativized machine TM(X) is a regular TM augmented by an oracle for X. TM(X) functions as a regular Turing machine except that TM(X) can interupt its computations at any point with a question of the form "does n belong to X?", get a yes or no answer from the oracle and procede differently according to the answer. There is all the difference in the world between identifying the mind with a TM simpliciter and identifying the mind with a relativized machine, TM(X). For example, if we take X to be a set of Gödel numbers of all and only true arithmetical formulas, then TM(X) can escape the limitations of Gödel's theorems. However it is not a TM *representation* of the mind. A TM is *included* as a component of the representation but the real explanatory power of the model lies in its non-TM part, the oracle for X! The TM component does not explain how the device knows what's true.

The moral we are left with is that the TM hypothesis, even with respect to elementary arithmetic, is multiply ambiguous. Its interesting interpretations occupy a narrow band on a spectrum. At one end of the spectrum are TMs with finite output, constructed after the fact, to duplicate the histories of finite minds. On the other end of the spectrum are TMs augmented with nonalgorithmic capacities.

Let me conclude these preliminary considerations by presenting two TM representations for linguistic knowledge. These models are not intended as serious suggestions in theoretical linguistics; indeed, both are obviously faulty from a linguist's perspective. But they do convey a sense of the philosophical utility that might be derived from TM models. We can use them as pointers on our way to a TM model or arithmetic.

KNOWLEDGE OF ENGLISH GRAMMAR

Suppose that there is a TM which, when input with any finite string of symbols of the English language, outputs 1 if the string is a grammatical sentence of English and 0 otherwise. Then it would be tempting to suppose that the minds of English speakers could be represented by this TM at least with respect to their ability to recognize grammatical English. The TM could model English speakers' competence. We need not suppose that it models their performance, even when they are making explicit grammatical judgments. English minds need not always duplicate the computations of this machine; other factors like memory and habit might intervene. Nevertheless, to intervene is to interact with the underlying competence model. (But see the qualification mentioned in note 5.)

Such a TM model would just mark a beginning. We would need analogous, but different models for Chinese minds, Polish minds, and Swahili minds. The question would arise: how does an arbitrary human infant acquire the appropriate TM model of the grammar of its language? Here is one possible answer.

KNOWLEDGE OF NATURAL LANGUAGES

Suppose that for a class of languages including all those ever spoken by humans, there is a TM which is universal grammarian. After a sufficiently large finite input of sentences in language L, this TM first outputs a second TM which recognize the grammar of L and procedes to operate as an L sentence recognizer as in the preceding case. (Chomsky once believed something like this; Chomsky 1957.) In this situation, it would be tempting to explain the mind's knowledge of grammar in terms of the TM. We might even suppose that the TM is somehow encoded in the genetic structure of human beings (Chomsky 1972). However, before actually giving in to these temptations we had better convince ourselves of the possibility of a univeral grammarian. According to one interpretation of Gold's theorem in mathematical linguistics, a universal grammarian is not possible—natural languages are not learnable by a TM model in a finite amount of time (Gold 1967). However, for our purposes, the universal grammarian serves as a picture of how TMs could turn epistemological wheels and that is all we wanted from this preliminary account. Let us leave the digression into linguistics without prejudice and return to the main topic of concern, elementary arithmetic.

THE GÖDELIAN ARGUMENT IN MORE DETAIL

Let us agree to look at those knowledge claims in elementary arithmetic that can be expressed by sentences in a certain formal language (including 1, 0 $+$, $*$, $=$ and logical symbols). Initially, we might characterize the potential range of human knowledge by the set of all sentences true of the natural numbers. Now suppose, contrary to fact, that there was a TM whose output was just that set. Such a TM could represent mental competence in elementary arithmetic since it uses only elementary computations which we can perform. The machine could plausibly be thought of as innate, somehow encoded in the genetic makeup of human beings or, for that matter, in the genetic makeup of any rational beings—just like the earlier grammar recognizer. Moreover, the TM model could be genuinely explanatory since the most popular alternative to it is an arithmetical realism that locates the mind in a universe of arithmetical objects. Mathematical realism posits that there is a determinate structure relating mathematical objects which structure obtains independently of the mind. The mind, in turn, is equipped with a special faculty of intuition which allows it to refer to mathematical objects and to ascertain facts about their interrelationships.

Against this mathematical realism, the alleged TM model has all the power of Ockham's razor. The hypothetical TM would deliver all the mathematical results we are capable of without appeal to an external world of mathematical objects and a special faculty of mathematical intuition. If the mind is this TM, the possibility of arithmetical knowledge can be built into the internal structure of the mind (and so into our representation of the mind).

We need not claim that this TM models performance. Real mathematicians do not grind out proofs automatically; they frequently err and not even their most polished proofs are TM computations. However, we might explain all of these discrepancies without resorting to arithmetical realism, given a sufficiently plausible TM model of arithmetical competence (but see note 5).

The argument from Gödel's theorems is that we should regard the TM hypothesis for arithmetic as unsatisfactory in principle. No plausible TM representation of the mind can account for our competence in arithmetic. Gödel showed how to get from any such model of arithmetical competence to a better TM model! No one who knows Gödel's work can ever *advance* the hypothesis that the mind is some particular TM. Whatever evidence he or she has for *that* identification is simultaneously *better* evidence for identifying the mind with *another* TM. Since the mind cannot be modeled by a TM without being modeled by a particular TM, it follows that no one can successfully defend the claim that the arithmetical mind is modeled by a TM.

In order to formalize this argument, we must formalize a set of assumptions about TM models of arithmetical knowledge. This might be done in any number of ways and still Gödel's argument would apply. I choose the following assumptions for brevity and perspicuity.

We can restrict our attention to TMs whose output is constant or independent of input—we just build in the axioms of arithmetic and the output will be a set of sentences in the formal language of arithmetic, the theorems produced. In that case we could explain what minds can know in arithmetic as the output of such a TM. A theorem-producing TM is one whose output is a deductively closed set of sentences from a recursively enumerable set of axioms that includes Robinson's system. It is reasonable to assume that a TM model of the mind should be a theorem-producing TM. Deductive closure, simply put, means that the output includes B whenever it includes A and A = >B. The assumption of a recursively enumerable (or 'effectively listable') set of axioms is maximally generous. There are no TMs for non-r.e. sets. Robinson's system is unproblematic. It is the classical first-order theory deducible from about a dozen propositions, each of which is an obvious arithmetical truth. Robinson's system has sufficient power to drive the mathematics of Gödel's argument.

When the purported TM model of arithmetic is a theorem-producing TM, we can complete the explanation of mathematical competence. Suppose we just stipulate that a TM is said to know any true formula included in its output. Then our potential for arithmetical knowledge can be identified with what this TM knows and explained by the TM's generation of its output. However, this explanation will not work unless we add one further condition on TM models. They must be consistent.

A theorem-producing TM is consistent if its output includes no pair of sentences of the form A and −A. An inconsistent theorem producer, because of deductive closure, will include *all* formulas in its output (since A&−A => B for any B) and so fails utterly as a model of arithmetical knowledge. At best it would be a very long-winded way of generating all the formulas, B, of the formal language of arithmetic (a feat which, by the way, a much simpler TM can accomplish). Even if we give up the assumption of deductive closure, inconsistent TMs would remain anomolous. They blithely produce contradictions and continue business as usual. Human minds, on the other hand, tend to notice contradictions and to respond to them in a variety of ways such as repudiating A or −A or both, or reinterpreting the subject matter in a new formalization that resolves the inconsistency. Minds tend toward consistency, and initially we must assume that any plausible TM model of the mind is a consistent theorem-producing TM. Perhaps Gödel's theorems will force us to include the possibility of inconsistency in our mental representations. If that happens we should note whether the inconsistency produced by one TM can be managed by another TM or whether it requires some non-TM component to handle. Until that time, we continue to assume consistency.

Now Gödel's theorems can take hold. Given any consistent theorem-producing TM, call it "Vax," Gödel, in essence, showed how to construct infinitely many pairs of formulas of the form A and −A with the following characteristics:

1) Neither A nor −A is in the output of Vax.
2) A is equivalent to: 'A' is not in the output of Vax.
3) −A is equivalent to: 'A' is in the output of Vax.

It follows that A is true and that Vax can't know that A.

However, there is no reason to suppose that we minds can't know A and considerable reason to suppose that we could. A can have a very simple form, $(x) - Px$ or $-(3x) Px3$ where Px is a primitive recursive (or decidable) predicate of natural numbers. Mathematicians know plenty of statements of this form. Moreover, by recognizing an isomorphism between numbers and TMs and their inputs, we can reinterpret the arithmetical assertion that A as an assertion about TM outputs (fact 2 above) and often prove A in terms of this interpretation. Furthermore, there might be interpretations of A that translates it into known theorems of some other branch of mathematics, such as is the case in the Paris-Harrington results (see Graham et al., 1980).

Once we grant that the human mind can, in principle, know A, then the case against TMs is complete. Given any minimally adequate TM model of arithmetical knowledge, there are propositions that the mind can know but the model can not account for. Consequently, the model can't explain our arithmetical competence. Mind is not a TM.

As plausible as this argument might seem, it has generally been contested in the philosophical literature. Let us now turn to some of the more interesting criticisms of the argument, in particular those of Putman, Bowie, and Dennett. As I understand them, Putnam pretty much accepts the argument until the final step that we can know what Vax cannot—that is, the truth of A. He objects to that step. Bowie focuses on the earlier assumption that any plausible TM model is consistent. "Can we always be sure of that?" Bowie asks. Dennett questions the most basic premise that a TM model of arithmetical competence should be a theorem-producer in the first place. Why not assume the appropriate model is a universal TM, Dennett suggests. Let us take these objections one at a time.

PUTNAM'S CRITICISM

In his influential paper "Minds and Machines," Putnam (1960) questioned the assumption that minds can know A, a truth Vax cannot know. His actual argument is not very persuasive. He correctly noted that A is equivalent to the proposition that Vax is consistent (as a theorem producer). An inconsistent theorem producer outputs all formulas of arithmetic; so if a machine fails to output some formula, then it is consistent. But Putnam's actual criticism was merely that "it is unlikely" that we can know that complicated TMs are consistent.

Of course, there is no contradiction between saying that it is in fact unlikely that we *will* know some formula A (because of performance limitations) while still maintaining that A is within our theoretical competence. For Putnam's criticism to work, there must be specific formulas of arithmetic that are true but in principle unknowable by the human mind—absolutely undecidable to use Gödel's characterization. Moreover *every* true formula not included in the output of the purported TM model must be absolutely undecidable. If even one were knowable by the mind, then the distinction between mind and that TM could be drawn.

The hypothesis that some true proposition is absolutely undecidable is at best a controversial thesis in philosophy. The great mathematicians Hilbert, Brouwer, and Gödel himself all denied it. It is especially hard to defend the hypothesis on the grounds that we know that a certain formula A is unknowable where A is consistently interpretable as "A is unknowable!" Insofar as we know that A is an absolutely unknowable truth, and that A means that it itself is unknowable, then we know the truth of A, the paradigm example of an absolutely unknowable proposition! To avoid this paradox, a Putnam-style objection must justify the existence of absolutely unknowable propositions independently of Gödel's theorems, and this seems very unlikely. Putnam's predicament does not cast doubt on Gödel's results, of course, because Gödel showed not that there were absolutely undecidable propositions of arithmetic, but that for any TM or formal systems account of proof, there were unprovable propositions of arithmetic relative to that account. As Gödel summarized his argument:

The human mind is incapable of formulating (or mechanizing) all its mathematical intuitions. I.e.: If it has succeeded in formalizing some of them this very fact yields new intuitive knowledge, e.g., the consistency of the formalism. (Wang 1974, p. 324)

In other words, what we can consistently formalize, we can coherently transcend.

Furthermore, even if there were absolutely undecidable propositions of elementary arithmetic, there is no reason to suppose that questions of the consistency of complicated TMs invariably fall into this class and this is what Putnam needs. When Vax is a complicated TM that outputs the theorems of Robinson's arithmetic, we can prove that Vax is consistent by a variety of means available outside that system: transfinite induction, functionals of higher type, translation into intuitionistic arithmetic or construction of a set theoretic model of arithmetic. The last is an easy exercise in set theory.

Moreover, there is something faintly ludicrous about a philosopher who stoutly professes not to know that his favorite TM model for arithmetic is consistent while simultaneously attempting to justify his claim to know that $2 + 2 = 4$ on the grounds that he has a formal proof of this in his model! Unless he supposes the model is consistent, his justification is empty.

In addition, contemporary mathematicians can use Gödel's theorems to obtain new mathematical knowledge. Suppose someone were to discover that neither Fermat's last theorem nor its negation were provable in Peano arithmetic. Would mathematicians conclude, as Putnam suggests, that Fermat's last theorem is absolutely unknowable? Not at all; they would conclude that Fermat's last theorem is true! If it were false, it would be provably false.[6]

Finally, if anything more needs to be said about Putnam-style objections, let us observe that the hypothesis of an absolutely undecidable sentence does not make much sense in terms of TM models. For *any* truth of arithmetic A, it is possible to construct a TM model for knowledge of A—just program the machine to output A for any input. Thus, to object to the Gödelian argument, it is neither necessary, sufficient, or plausible to suppose that there are absolutely undecidable propositions of arithmetic. Not surprisingly, Putnam-style criticisms have fallen into disfavor. If we get to the premise that the TM model can not know some formula A, we can argue that we are not barred from knowing A in principle. Hence, we can conclude that minds are not TMs. In order to block this conclusion, we must object earlier.

BOWIE'S CRITICISM

More recent criticisms of the Gödel argument have focused on the first premise, that an appropriate TM model of the arithmetical mind is a consistent theorem-producing TM. One set of criticisms questions the assumption of consistency, another set questions the assumption that the best models will be theorem-producing TMs. The issue of consistency can be raised in two forms. While granting the desirability of a consistent model, we can wonder whether we know that some particular model is consistent. Alternatively, we can abandon consistency as a requirement on our TM representations.

The first approach is taken by Bowie in his criticism of Lucas, who advanced a version of the Gödelian argument. Bowie correctly notes that there is no TM capable of distinguishing between consistent and inconsistent theorem-producing TMs. He goes on to interpret Lucas as holding that he, Lucas, does know whether a given theorem-producing TM is consistent or not. Finally, Bowie assumes that Lucas' ability must be representable by a TM. Not surprisingly, Bowie concludes that Lucas and his argument are inconsistent. Also not surprisingly, Lucas would object. Lucas' thesis was that minds and mathematicians are not TMs; they can know something that a particular TM cannot. When Bowie assumes that if some question (like consistency) is answerable, it must be answerable by a TM, he is simply begging the question against Lucas.

Whatever the merits of Bowie's argument against Lucas, I leave for the interested reader to pursue. But his criticism quite clearly misses the present argument (and, I believe, Lucas' as well). Our argument nowhere assumes that the distinction between consistent and inconsistent TMs can be given by a mechanical procedure. The argument does assume that a given TM model of the arithmetical mind is consistent, but this was a *concession* to proponents of the TM hypothesis. An inconsistent model is no model at all. If proponents of the TM hypothesis insist that consistency be proved, let them prove it themselves. When and if they do, they'll find Gödel's theorems waiting for them. To put the point less polemically, the burden of proof is on the advocate of the TM model to show that the model is consistent. He or she cannot evade criticism by complaining, "Your criticism would work only if my model is not wildly wrong (inconsistent) to begin with!" Being wildly wrong is a defect, not a protective clause.

Some confusion about consistency can be dispelled by recasting Gödel's argument without invoking the assumption of consistency immediately. Gödel showed how to construct a TM, call it "Megavax," with the following property: when input any theorem-producing TM, e.g., Vax, Megavax constructs a Gödel sentence A for Vax, adds it to Vax's output, and then deductively closes the result, thereby yielding a new theorem-producing TM Vax II. Now if anyone should claim that a TM-like Vax sufficed to explain arithmetical competence, we could use Megavax to defeat the claim. Megavax, applied to Vax, gives a new model Vax II, *which the proponent of Vax must acknowledge as a better model of arithmetical competence.* Vax II is necessarily a better model when Vax is consistent, since Vax II can know true facts, such as a Vax-undecidable sentence, that Vax cannot. The only case in which Vax II is *not* better than Vax is when they have identical outputs, i.e., Vax is inconsistent and outputs all formulas. But the *proponent* of the Vax model can hardly advance this as a serious possibility without undercutting his position.[7] By the way, Gödel's argument works against Vax II, too.

The Gödel argument shows that no TM model suffices for arithmetical knowledge. It does not show, nor does it need to show, for any particular TM model whether it fails because it is inconsistent or it fails because it is incomplete.

If we abandon consistency as a requirement on TM representation, we must abandon the assumption that the appropriate TM model is a theorem producer. Since theorem producers are deductively closed, any contradiction "blows up" the system. Once one contradiction is produced, the rest of the output is garbage. If we abandon deductive closure, then we will have some difficulty in judging the scope of the ensuing nonclosed machines. For example, we could not assume that a nonclosed machine could output that 100 + 100 = 200 merely because it had been programmed with the recursive definitions of addition since a logical deduction is needed to get from the latter to the former. So without logical closure, the proponent will find it hard to argue his or her model is plausible at all. In any case, we would still have to address the issue of TMs with inconsistent output. An adequate TM representation could not simply be inconsistent without any procedure for dealing with the inconsistency. The human mind might be inconsistent, but at least it tries to resolve its inconsistencies. I know of no mechanical procedure adequate for dealing with inconsistency and no reason for supposing that such a procedure exists. If it does not exist, then we can't save the TM hypothesis by abandoning the consistency assumption. My point is not so much that the mind *must* be consistent (perhaps inconsistency must be recognized to be an important feature of epistemology), rather the point is that TMs are very poor models of inconsistency.

DENNETT'S CRITICISM

We come to the final attempt to defend the TM hypothesis from Gödel's theorems—denying the assumption that an appropriate TM model of arithmetical knowledge is a theorem producer. An alternative frequently suggested is that the mind is a universal TM (e.g., by Dennett in "The Abilities of Men and Machines"). Now it is true that the Gödel argument does not directly apply to universal TMs. However, it is equally true that universal TMs (UTMs) don't directly apply to models of knowledge.

A UTM is, roughly, one that accepts pairs of inputs. When the first element of a pair is a particular Turing machine, say the one numbered n, TMn, and the second is an input, i, the UTM reconstructs the computation of TMn on the input i. Intuitively, a UTM is like a modern computer. Applying the UTM to a particular TM is like loading the computer with a particular program (the one represented by the TM). Further inputs to the computer are read as inputs to the given program. Metaphorically speaking, a UTM knows nothing but simply sits there until we load it with a particular TM program, TMn. Relative to *that program*, the UTM might be said to know the outputs it generates. Merely saying this, however, does not make the UTM into a model of knowledge. Given any formula A of arithmetic, true or false, we can write a TM program for producing A and relative to this program the UTM "knows" A. As a model of knowledge, a UTM knows too much, relatively speaking. On the other hand, if we restrict the UTM to a single TM program, it will merely duplicate the computation of that theorem-producing TM and so fall victim to Gödel's argument.

In order for a UTM to function as a model of knowledge we need to posit a set X or directory of particular TM programs for the UTM to run. If X consists of a single TM, we lose all the advantages of a *universal* TM. If X consists of all TMs, we lose the notion of model altogether. In fact, there is a general problem here. Let X be any plausible directory. Is there a TM for constructing X or not? If there is then we can construct from it and the UTM a single powerful machine whose output is equivalent to that of the UTM running the directory X and we're back to the situation before Dennett. On the other hand, if there is no such TM, then the directory X is a non-TM component which must be added to a UTM to obtain a representation of the mind. It functions very much like the oracles for relativized machines that we saw earlier. In each case, the explanatory power of the model derives not so much from the TM component as from the non-TM component, be it oracle or directory or human programer with a mind.

Perhaps Dennett would object that I have inadequately depicted the role of UTMs in representations of knowledge. He might say that I have assimilated them too much to theorem-producing machines by imagining their output as simply the union of all outputs from programs in the directory. But then Dennett would be obligated to give another account of the role of UTMs without appealing to non-TM components. It is easy to utilize a UTM if we ignore the worry about whether the auxiliary devices are TMs. We might construe the directory as a finite but changing object with programs being added and deleted. We could posit a device for generating new programs to be fed to the UTM. We could invoke an operating system that shifts the UTM from one program to another as the circumstances "warrant." (Such a picture is suggested by Hofstadter 1979, as a representation of the mind). As we develop the picture further, we get something that begins to look more like a possible model of the mind. The trouble is that as the picture is developed the UTM component fades more into the background, while all the new auxiliary devices play an ever greater role in the representation of knowledge. But for the dogmatic assertion that all of these auxiliaries and their interaction with the UTM are representable as TMs, our picture would be recognized for what it is—a non-TM representation of the mind. Thus, the retreat to UTMs can only escape Gödel's argument by conceding the conclusion of that argument. Mind is not simply a TM, not even with respect to knowledge of arithmetic.

CONCLUSION

In this essay, we have reviewed a familiar argument from Gödel's Theorems to the conclusion that mind is not adequately represented as a TM. I have tried to present a version of this argument that is formally valid and plausibly correct. Several prominent criticisms of the argument were examined and each turned out to be ill founded.

I'm inclined to conclude that the Gödel argument is correct—mind is not a TM or, as Gödel put it, the mind cannot completely formalize its mathematical intuitions. Moreover, the argument suggests, but only suggests, what it is about the mind that cannot be captured by a TM. The mind is inherently creative in a very profound sense; any formalization of its intuitions can lead it to develop new intuitions and thus to another formalization of its intuitions, and so on *ad infinitum* and beyond. This is a vastly more powerful concept of creativity than that defended by Chomsky, for whom linguistic creativity seemed to be the ability to generate infinite classes of sentences that are recursively enumerable and so representable by TM. (See Lyons 1970 for a summary of Chomsky's views.)

To be sure, answering how the mind differs from any conceivable TM by a general appeal to "inherent creativity" is at best a stopgap. We want to see the creativity of the mind spelled out in more detail. While this can be done, it is best covered in a separate essay.

Let me conclude this essay with a comment on its relevance to Artificial Intelligence. I have been careful to restrict the discussion to Turing machines and not to machines in general. If we assume that thinking machines or programmable computers must be Turing machines, then the argument does apply to these and shows that Artificial Intelligence, in the fullest sense, is impossible. Of course some successes are possible; the rules for addition and multiplication are recursive, there are pocket calculators, computers can "play chess," and even the theorems of Robinson's arithmetic can be generated by Turing machines. But these are only partial successes. They tell as much for the thesis that the mind *utilizes* Turing machine computations in its thought. The fact that the TM component can be implanted either in the internal structure of the mind or in the external structure of programmable computers favors the thesis that the mind uses TMs as tools over the thesis that mind simply is a TM. (Gödel himself suggested that the brain is a computer that is used by the mind. See Wang 1974, p. 326.)

Artificial Intelligence in the fullest sense could still be possible if we did not insist on representing thinking machines or computer systems as TMs. This would entail more attention to the non-TM components of computers, tolerating vague discourse about levels and frames, embedding computers in perception-action-feedback cycles, networking computer systems and interacting with them (in the end, constructing a community of rational knowers that included both natural and artificial minds). Sometimes I think that this is the real point behind Dreyfus' polemic against AI (Dreyfus 1979). As I read him, his basic claim is not that computers *can't* think, but that nothing—organic, inorganic, or mental—can think in the narrow computational fashion that is available to Turing machines.

NOTES

1. Perhaps it is more accurate to say that modern computers are electronic realizations of Turing machines, since the idealization came first. Alan Turing, who first conceived of Turing machines, became one of the leaders in the development of computers in Britain. For an exciting account of the eccentric Turing, see Hodges (1984).

2. Among some computer scientists, even those who defend a form of mechanism, the TM hypothesis has recently fallen into disfavor. TMs are not even adequate as caricatures of the mind, these AI proponents say, but must be supplemented by additional mechanisms. Unfortunately, the characterization of these additional mechanisms is usually left quite vague—e.g., a device for 'making the best guess'—and it is by no means clear that there are machines of any sort that are up to the required task. Moreover, I suspect that this retreat from the TM hypothesis is occasioned in part by Gödel's theorems. Before trying to evaluate such speculative forms of mechanism, we should first understand where the original TM hypothesis goes wrong.

3. This assumption is quite plausible. The reason for thinking that a TM can reproduce intuitive mathematics is that deductive systems can reproduce some of our intuitive theorems and the TMs can duplicate deductive systems.

4. When I was in graduate school in the late 1960s, proponents of the argument were accused of misunderstanding Gödel's proof. Since it has become known that Gödel himself accepted the argument, this objection has been quietly withdrawn.

5. Problems with a competence model arise if the mechanisms it uses exceed human capacities (for example by being far too fast or far too lengthy or by using information we have no access to). In such a case, we can't simply plead a slip between competence and performance. The model is not a model of *our* competence.

6. If Fermat's last theorem really were undecidable in a consistent theory of arithmetic, it really would be true! For suppose that it were false. Then there would be numbers x, y, z, and $n>2$ such that $x^n + y^n = z^n$. But the computation of that sum would be a proof of the negation of Fermat's theorem, contradicting the assumption it was undecidable.

7. There are a number of ways one might be tempted to exploit Megavax to escape Gödel's argument. None of them work. Suppose we input Vax to Megavax, but then loop the output, Vax II, back as a new input to Megavax, etc. Then let Supervax be the union of all those outputs, i.e., Supervax is Vax + Vax II + Vax III etc. The same problem still arises; if Vax is consistent, then Supervax is consistent and still incomplete. No matter how many times we try to loop, as long as a TM is producing the outcome, the result will be the same.

PART THREE

ARTIFICIAL INTELLIGENCE

JOHN R. SEARLE

MINDS, BRAINS, AND PROGRAMS

What psychological and philosophical significance should we attach to recent efforts at computer simulations of human cognitive capacities? In answering this question, I find it useful to distinguish what I will call "strong" AI from "weak" or "cautious" AI (Artificial Intelligence). According to weak AI, the principal value of the computer in the study of the mind is that it gives us a very powerful tool. For example, it enables us to formulate and test hypotheses in a more rigorous and precise fashion. But according to strong AI, the computer is not merely a tool in the study of the mind; rather, the appropriately programmed computer really *is* a mind, in the sense that computers given the right programs can be literally said to *understand* and have other cognitive states. In strong AI, because the programmed computer has cognitive states, the programs are not mere tools that enable us to test psychological explanations; rather, the programs are themselves the explanations.

I have no objection to the claims of weak AI, at least as far as this article is concerned. My discussion here will be directed at the claims I have defined as those of strong AI, specifically the claim that the appropriately programmed computer literally has cognitive states and that the programs thereby explain human cognition. When I hereafter refer to AI, I have in mind the strong version, as expressed by these two claims.

I will consider the work of Roger Schank and his colleagues at Yale (Schank & Abelson 1977), because I am more familiar with it than I am with any other similar claims, and because it provides a very clear example of the sort of work I wish to examine. But nothing that follows depends upon the details of Schank's programs. The same arguments would apply to Winograd's SHRDLU (Winograd 1973), Weizenbaum's ELIZA (Weizenbaum 1967), and indeed any Turing machine simulation of human mental phenomena.

Very briefly, and leaving out the various details, one can describe Schank's program as follows: the aim of the program is to simulate the human ability to understand stories. It is characteristic of human beings' story-understanding capacity that they can answer questions about the story even though the information that they give was never explicitly stated in the story. Thus, for example, suppose you are given the following story: "A man went into a restaurant and ordered a hamburger. When the hamburger arrived it was burned to a crisp, and the man stormed out of the restaurant angrily, without paying for the hamburger or leaving a tip." Now, if you are asked "Did the man eat the hamburger?" you will presumably answer, "No, he did not." Similarly, if you are given the following story: "A man went into a restaurant and ordered a hamburger; when the hamburger came he was very pleased with it, and as he left the restaurant he gave the waitress a large tip before paying his bill," and you are asked the question, "Did the man eat the hamburger?" you will presumably answer, "Yes, he ate the hamburger." Now Schank's machines can similarly answer questions about restaurants in this fashion. To do this, they have a "representation" of the sort of information that human beings have about restaurants, which enables them to answer such questions as those above, given these sorts of stories. When the machine is given the story and then asked the question, the machine will print out answers of the sort that we would expect human beings to give if told similar stories. Partisans of strong AI claim that in this question and answer sequence the machine is not only simulating a human ability but also

1. that the machine can literally be said to *understand* the story and provide the answers to questions, and

2. that what the machine and its program do *explains* the human ability to understand the story and answer questions about it.

Both claims seem to me to be totally unsupported by Schank's[1] work, as I will attempt to show in what follows.

One way to test any theory of the mind is to ask oneself what it would be like if my mind actually worked on the principles that the theory says all minds work on. Let us apply this test to the Schank program with the following *Gedankenexperiment*. Suppose that I'm locked in a room and given a large batch of Chinese writing. Suppose furthermore (as is indeed the case) that I know no Chinese, either written or spoken, and that I'm not even confident that I could recognize Chinese writing as Chinese writing distinct from, say, Japanese writing or meaningless squiggles. To me, Chinese writing is just so many meaningless squiggles. Now suppose further that after this first batch of Chinese writing I am given a second batch of Chinese script together with a set of rules for correlating the second batch with the first batch. The rules are in English, and I understand these rules as well as any other native speaker of English. They enable me to correlate one set of formal symbols with another set of formal symbols, and all that "formal" means here is that I can identify the symbols entirely by their shapes. Now suppose also that I am given a third batch of Chinese symbols together with some instructions, again in English, that enable me to correlate elements of this third batch with the first two batches, and these rules instruct me how to give back certain Chinese symbols with certain sorts of shapes in response to certain sorts of shapes given me in the third batch. Unknown to me, the people who are giving me all of these symbols call the first batch "a script," they call the second batch a "story," and they call the third batch "questions." Furthermore, they call the symbols I give them back in response to the third batch "answers to the questions," and the set of rules in English that they gave me, they call "the program." Now just to complicate the story a little, imagine that these people also give me stories in English, which I understand, and they then ask me questions in English about these stories, and I give them back answers in English. Suppose also that after a while I get so good at following the instructions for manipulating the Chinese symbols and the programmers get so good at writing the programs that from the external point of view—that is, from the point of view of somebody outside the room in which I am locked— my answers to the questions are absolutely indistinguishable from those of native Chinese speakers. Nobody just looking at my answers can tell that I don't speak a word of Chinese. Let us also suppose that my answers to the English questions are, as they no doubt would be, indistinguishable from those of other native English speakers, for the simple reason that I am a native English speaker. From the external point of view—from the point of view of someone reading my "answers"—the answers to the Chinese questions and the English questions are equally good. But in the Chinese case, unlike the English case, I produce the answers by manipulating uninterpreted formal symbols. As far as the Chinese is concerned, I simply behave like a computer; I perform computational operations on formally specified elements. For the purposes of the Chinese, I am simply an instantiation of the computer program.

Now the claims made by strong AI are that the programmed computer understands the stories and that the program in some sense explains human understanding. But we are now in a position to examine these claims in light of our thought experiment.

1. As regards the first claim, it seems to me quite obvious in the example that I do not understand a word of the Chinese stories. I have inputs and outputs that are indistinguishable from those of the native Chinese speaker, and I can have any formal program you like, but I still understand nothing. For the same reasons, Schank's computer understands nothing of any stories, whether in Chinese, English, or whatever, since in the Chinese case the computer is me, and in cases where the computer is not me, the computer has nothing more than I have in the case where I understand nothing.

2. As regards the second claim, that the program explains human un-

derstanding, we can see that the computer and its program do not provide sufficient conditions of understanding since the computer and the program are functioning, and there is no understanding. But does it even provide a necessary condition or a significant contribution to understanding? One of the claims made by the supporters of strong AI is that when I understand a story in English, what I am doing is exactly the same—or perhaps more of the same—as what I was doing in manipulating the Chinese symbols. It is simply more formal symbol manipulation that distinguishes the case in English, where I do understand, from the case in Chinese, where I don't. I have not demonstrated that this claim is false, but it would certainly appear an incredible claim in the example. Such plausibility as the claim has derives from the supposition that we can construct a program that will have the same inputs and outputs as native speakers, and in addition we assume that speakers have some level of description where they are also instantiations of a program. On the basis of these two assumptions we assume that even if Schank's program isn't the whole story about understanding, it may be part of the story. Well, I suppose that is an empirical possibility, but not the slightest reason has so far been given to believe that it is true, since what is suggested—though certainly not demonstrated—by the example is that the computer program is simply irrelevant to my understanding of the story. In the Chinese case I have everything that artificial intelligence can put into me by way of a program, and I understand nothing; in the English case I understand everything, and there is so far no reason at all to suppose that my understanding has anything to do with computer programs, that is, with computational operations on purely formally specified elements. As long as the program is defined in terms of computational operations on purely formally defined elements, what the example suggests is that these by themselves have no interesting connection with understanding. They are certainly not sufficient conditions, and not the slightest reason has been given to suppose that they are necessary conditions or even that they make a significant contribution to understanding. Notice that the force of the argument is not simply that different machines can have the same input and output while operating on different formal principles—that is not the point at all. Rather, whatever purely formal principles you put into the computer, they will not be sufficient for understanding, since a human will be able to follow the formal principles without understanding anything. No reason whatever has been offered to suppose that such principles are necessary or even contributory, since no reason has been given to suppose that when I understand English I am operating with any formal program at all.

Well, then, what is it that I have in the case of the English sentences that I do not have in the case of the Chinese sentences? The obvious answer is that I know what the former mean, while I haven't the faintest idea what the latter mean. But in what does this consist and why couldn't we give it to a machine, whatever it is? I will return to this question later, but first I want to continue with the example.

I have had the occasions to present this example to several workers in artificial intelligence, and, interestingly, they do not seem to agree on what the proper reply to it is. I get a surprising variety of replies, and in what follows I will consider the most common of these (specified along with their geographic origins).

But first I want to block some common understandings about "understanding": in many of these discussions one finds a lot of fancy footwork about the word "understanding." My critics point out that there are many different degrees of understanding; that "understanding" is not a simple two-place predicate; that there are even different kinds and levels of understanding, and often the law of excluded middle doesn't even apply in a straightforward way to statements of the form "x understands y"; that in many cases it is a matter for decision and not a simple matter of fact whether x understands y; and so on. To all of these points I want to say, of course. But they have nothing to do with the points at issue. There are clear cases in which "understanding" literally applies and clear cases in which it does not apply; and these two sorts of cases are all I need for this argument.[2] I understand stories in English; to a lesser degree I can understand stories in French; to a still lesser degree, stories in German; and in Chinese, not at all. My car and my adding machine, on the other hand, understand nothing: they are not in that line of business. We often attribute "understanding" and other cognitive predicates by metaphor and analogy to cars, adding machines, and other artifacts, but nothing is proved by such attributions. We say, "The door *knows* when to open because of its photoelectric cell," "The adding machine *knows how* (*understands how*, is *able*) to do addition and subtraction but not division," and "The thermostat *perceives* changes in the temperature." The reason we make these attributions is quite interesting, and it has to do with the fact that in artifacts we extend our own intentionality;[3] our tools are extensions of our purposes, and so we find it natural to make metaphorical attributions of intentionality to them; but I take it no philosophical ice is cut by such examples. The sense in which an automatic door "understands instructions" from its photoelectric cell is not at all the sense in which I understand English. If the sense in which Schank's programmed computers understand stories is supposed to be the metaphorical sense in which the door understands, and not the sense in which I understand English, the issue would not be worth discussing. But Newell and Simon (1963) write that the kind of cognition they claim for computers is exactly the same as for human beings. I like the straightforwardness of this claim, and it is the sort of claim I will be considering. I will argue that in the literal sense the programmed computer understands what the car and the adding machine understand, namely, exactly nothing. The computer understanding is not just (like my understanding of German) partial or incomplete; it is zero.

Now to the replies:

I. THE SYSTEMS REPLY (BERKELEY)

"While it is true that the individual person who is locked in the room does not understand the story, the fact is that he is merely part of a whole system, and the system does understand the story. The person has a large ledger in front of him in which are written the rules, he has a lot of scratch paper and pencils for doing calculations, he has 'data banks' of sets of Chinese symbols. Now, understanding is not being ascribed to the mere individual; rather it is being ascribed to this whole system of which he is a part."

My response to the systems theory is quite simple: let the individual internalize all of these elements of the system. He memorizes the rules in the ledger and the data banks of Chinese symbols, and he does all the calculations in his head. The individual then incorporates the entire system. There isn't anything at all to the system that he does not encompass. We can even get rid of the room and suppose he works outdoors. All the same, he understands nothing of the Chinese, and a fortiori neither does the system, because there isn't anything in the system that isn't in him. If he doesn't understand, then there is no way the system could understand because the system is just a part of him.

Actually I feel somewhat embarrassed to give even this answer to the systems theory, because the theory seems to me so unplausible to start with. The idea is that while a person doesn't understand Chinese, somehow the *conjunction* of that person and bits of paper might understand Chinese. It is not easy for me to imagine how someone who was not in the grip of an ideology would find the idea at all plausible. Still, I think many people who are committed to the ideology of strong AI will in the end be inclined to say something very much like this; so let us pursue it a bit further. According to one version of this view, while the man in the internalized systems example doesn't understand Chinese in the sense that a native Chinese speaker does (because, for example, he doesn't know that the story refers to restaurants and hamburgers, etc.), still "the man as a formal symbol manipulation system" *really does understand Chinese*. The subsystem of the man that is the formal symbol manipulation system for Chinese should not be confused with the subsystem for English.

So there are really two subsystems in the man; one understands English, the other Chinese, and "it's just that the two systems have little to do with each other." But, I want to reply, not only do they have little to do with each other, they are not even remotely alike. The subsystem that understands English (assuming we allow ourselves to talk in this jargon of "subsystems" for a moment) knows that the stories are about restaurants and eating hamburgers, he knows that he is being asked questions about restaurants and that he is answering questions as best he can by making various inferences from the content of the story, and so on. But the Chinese system knows none of this. Whereas the English subsystem knows that "hamburgers" refers to hamburgers, the Chinese subsystem knows only that "squiggle squiggle" is followed by "squoggle squoggle." All he knows is that various formal symbols are being introduced at one end and manipulated according to rules written in English, and other symbols are going out at the other end. The whole point of the original example was to argue that such symbol manipulation by itself couldn't be sufficient for understanding Chinese in any literal sense because the man could write "squoggle squoggle" after "squiggle squiggle" without understanding anything in Chinese. And it doesn't meet that argument to postulate subsystems within the man, because the subsystems are no better off than the man was in the first place; they still don't have anything even remotely like what the English-speaking man (or subsystem) has. Indeed, in the case as described, the Chinese subsystem is simply a part of the English subsystem, a part that engages in meaningless symbol manipulation according to rules in English.

Let us ask ourselves what is supposed to motivate the systems reply in the first place; that is, what *independent* grounds are there supposed to be for saying that the agent must have a subsystem within him that literally understands stories in Chinese? As far as I can tell the only grounds are that in the example I have the same input and output as native Chinese speakers and a program that goes from one to the other. But the whole point of the examples has been to try to show that that couldn't be sufficient for understanding, in the sense in which I understand stories in English, because a person, and hence the set of systems that go to make up a person, could have the right combination of input, output, and program and still not understand anything in the relevant literal sense in which I understand English. The only motivation for saying there *must* be a subsystem in me that understands Chinese is that I have a program and I can pass the Turing test; I can fool native Chinese speakers. But precisely one of the points at issue is the adequacy of the Turing test. The example shows that there could be two "systems," both of which pass the Turing test, but only one of which understands; and it is no argument against this point to say that since they both pass the Turing test they must both understand, since this claim fails to meet the argument that the system in me that understands English has a great deal more than the system that merely processes Chinese. In short, the systems reply simply begs the question by insisting without argument that the system must understand Chinese.

Furthermore, the systems reply would appear to lead to consequences that are independently absurd. If we are to conclude that there must be cognition in me on the grounds that I have a certain sort of input and output and a program in between, then it looks like all sorts of noncognitive subsystems are going to turn out to be cognitive. For example, there is a level of description at which my stomach does information processing, and it instantiates any number of computer programs, but I take it we do not want to say that it has any understanding [cf. Pylyshyn: "Computation and Cognition" *BBS* 3(1) 1980]. But if we accept the systems reply, then it is hard to see how we avoid saying that stomach, heart, liver, and so on, are all understanding subsystems, since there is no principled way to distinguish the motivation for saying the Chinese subsystem understands from saying that the stomach understands. It is, by the way, not an answer to this point to say that the Chinese system has information as input and output and the stomach has food and food products as input and output, since from the point of view of the agent, from my point of view, there is no information in either the food or the Chinese—the Chinese is just so many meaningless squiggles. The information in the Chinese case is solely in the eyes of the programmers and the interpreters, and there is nothing to prevent them from treating the input and output of my digestive organs as information if they so desire.

This last point bears on some independent problems in strong AI, and it is worth digressing for a moment to explain it. If strong AI is to be a branch of psychology, then it must be able to distinguish those systems that are genuinely mental from those that are not. It must be able to distinguish the principles on which the mind works from those on which nonmental systems work; otherwise it will offer us no explanations of what is specifically mental about the mental. And the mental-nonmental distinction cannot be just in the eye of the beholder but it must be intrinsic to the systems; otherwise it would be up to any beholder to treat people as nonmental and, for example, hurricanes as mental if he likes. But quite often in the AI literature the distinction is blurred in ways that would in the long run prove disastrous to the claim that AI is a cognitive inquiry. McCarthy, for example, writes, "Machines as simple as thermostats can be said to have beliefs, and having beliefs seems to be a characteristic of most machines capable of problem solving performance" (McCarthy 1979). Anyone who thinks strong AI has a chance as a theory of the mind ought to ponder the implications of that remark. We are asked to accept it as a discovery of strong AI that the hunk of metal on the wall that we use to regulate the temperature has beliefs in exactly the same sense that we, our spouses, and our children have beliefs, and furthermore that "most" of the other machines in the room—telephone, tape recorder, adding machine, electric light switch—also have beliefs in this literal sense. It is not the aim of this article to argue against McCarthy's point, so I will simply assert the following without argument. The study of the mind starts with such facts as that humans have beliefs, while thermostats, telephones, and adding machines don't. If you get a theory that denies this point, you have produced a counterexample to the theory and the theory is false. One gets the impression that people in AI who write this sort of thing think they can get away with it because they don't really take it seriously, and they don't think anyone else will either. I propose, for a moment at least, to take it seriously. Think hard for one minute about what would be necessary to establish that that hunk of metal on the wall over there had real beliefs, beliefs with direction of fit, propositional content, and conditions of satisfaction; beliefs that had the possibility of being strong beliefs or weak beliefs; nervous, anxious, or secure beliefs; dogmatic, rational, or superstitious beliefs; blind faiths or hesitant cogitations; any kind of beliefs. The thermostat is not a candidate. Neither is stomach, liver, adding machine, or telephone. However, since we are taking the idea seriously, notice that its truth would be fatal to strong AI's claim to be a science of the mind. For now the mind is everywhere. What we wanted to know is what distinguishes the mind from thermostats and livers. And if McCarthy were right, strong AI wouldn't have a hope of telling us that.

II. THE ROBOT REPLY (YALE)

"Suppose we wrote a different kind of program from Schank's program. Suppose we put a computer inside a robot, and this computer would not just take in formal symbols as input and give out formal symbols as output, but rather would actually operate the robot in such a way that the robot does something very much like perceiving, walking, moving about, hammering nails, eating, drinking—anything you like. The robot would, for example, have a television camera attached to it that enabled it to 'see,' it would have arms and legs that enabled it to 'act,' and all of this would be controlled by its computer 'brain.' Such a robot would, unlike Schank's computer, have genuine understanding and other mental states."

The first thing to notice about the robot reply is that it tacitly concedes that cognition is not soley a matter of formal symbol manipulation, since this reply adds a set of causal relation with the outside world [cf. Fodor: "Methodological Solipsism" *BBS* 3(1) 1980]. But the answer to the robot reply is that the addition of such "perceptual" and "motor" capacities adds nothing by way of understanding, in particular, or intentionality, in general, to Schank's original program. To see this, notice that the same thought experiment applies to the robot case. Suppse that instead of the computer inside the robot, you put me inside the room and, as in the original Chinese case, you give me more Chinese symbols with more instructions in English for matching Chinese symbols to Chinese symbols and feeding back Chinese symbols to the outside. Suppose, unknown to me, some of the Chinese symbols that come to me come from a television camera attached to the robot and other Chinese symbols that I am giving out serve to make the motors inside the robot move the robot's legs or arms. It is important to emphasize that all I am doing is manipulating formal symbols: I know none of these other facts. I am receiving "information" from the robot's "perceptual" apparatus, and I am giving out "instructions" to its motor apparatus without knowing either of these facts. I am the robot's homunculus, but unlike the traditional homunuculus, I don't know what's going on. I don't understand anything except the rules for symbol manipulation. Now in this case I want to say that the robot has no intentional states at all; it is simply moving about as a result of its electrical wiring and its program. And furthermore, by instantiating the program I have no intentional states of the relevant type. All I do is follow formal instructions about manipulating formal symbols.

III. THE BRAIN SIMULATOR REPLY (BERKELEY AND M.I.T.)

"Suppose we design a program that doesn't represent information that we have about the world, such as the information in Schank's scripts, but simulates the actual sequence of neuron firings at the synapses of the brain of a native Chinese speaker when he understands stories in Chinese and gives answers to them. The machine takes in Chinese stories and questions about them as input, it simulates the formal structure of actual Chinese brains in processing these stories, and it gives out Chinese answers as outputs. We can even imagine that the machine operates, not with a single serial program, but with a whole set of programs operating in parallel, in the manner that actual human brains presumably operate when they process natural language. Now surely such a case we would have to say that the machine understood the stories; and if we refuse to say that, wouldn't we also have to deny that native Chinese speakers understood the stories? At the level of the synapses, what would or could be different about the program of the computer and the program of the Chinese brain?"

Before countering this reply I want to digress to note that it is an odd reply for any partisan of artificial intelligence (or functionalism, etc.) to make: I thought the whole idea of strong AI is that we don't need to know how the brain works to know how the mind works. The basic hypothesis, or so I had supposed, was that there is a level of mental operations consisting of computational processes over formal elements that constitute the essence of the mental and can be realized in all sorts of different brain processes, in the same way that any computer program can be realized in different computer hardwares: on the assumptions of strong AI, the mind is to the brain as the program is to the hardware, and thus we can understand the mind without doing neurophysiology. If we had to know how the brain worked to do AI, we wouldn't bother with AI. However, even getting this close to the operation of the brain is still not sufficient to produce understanding. To see this, imagine that instead of a monolingual man in a room shuffling symbols we have the man operate an elaborate set of water pipes with valves connecting them. When the man receives the Chinese symbols, he looks up in the program, written in English, which valves he has to turn on and off. Each water connection corresponds to a synapse in the Chinese brain, and the whole system is rigged up so that after doing all the right firings, that is after turning on all the right faucets, the Chinese answers pop out at the output end of the series of pipes.

Now where is the understanding in this system? It takes Chinese as input, it simulates the formal structure of the synapses of the Chinese brain, and it gives Chinese as output. But the man certainly doesn't understand Chinese, and neither do the water pipes, and if we are tempted to adopt what I think is the absurd view that somehow the *conjunction* of man *and* water pipes understands, remember that in principle the man can internalize the formal structure of the water pipes and do all the "neuron firings" in his imagination. The problem with the brain simulator is that it is simulating the wrong things about the brain. As long as it simulates only the formal structure of the sequence of neuron firings at the synapses, it won't have simulated what matters about the brain, namely its causal properties, its ability to produce intentional states. And that the formal properties are not sufficient for the causal properties is shown by the water pipe example: we can have all the formal properties carved off from the relevant neurobiological causal properties.

IV. THE COMBINATION REPLY (BERKELEY AND STANFORD)

"While each of the previous three replies might not be completely convincing by itself as a refutation of the Chinese room counterexample, if you take all three together they are collectively much more convincing and even decisive. Imagine a robot with a brain-shaped computer lodged in its cranial cavity, imagine the computer programmed with all the synapses of a human brain, imagine the whole behavior of the robot is indistinguishable from human behavior, and now think of the whole thing as a unified system and not just as a computer with inputs and outputs. Surely in such a case we would have to ascribe intentionality to the system."

I entirely agree that in such a case we would find it rational and indeed irresistible to accept the hypothesis that the robot had intentionality, as long as we knew nothing more about it. Indeed, besides appearance and behavior, the other elements of the combination are really irrelevant. If we could build a robot whose behavior was indistinguishable over a large range from human behavior, we would attribute intentionality to it, pending some reason not to. We wouldn't need to know in advance that its computer brain was a formal analogue of the human brain.

But I really don't see that this is any help to the claims of strong AI; and here's why: According to strong AI, instantiating a formal program with the right input and output is a sufficient condition of, indeed is constitutive of, intentionality. As Newell (1979) puts it, the essence of the mental is the operation of a physical symbol system. But the attributions of intentionality that we make to the robot in this example have nothing to do with formal programs. They are simply based on the assumption that if the robot looks and behaves sufficiently like us, then we would suppose, until proven otherwise, that it must have mental states like ours that cause and are expressed by its behavior and it must have an inner mechanism capable of producing such mental states. If we knew independently how to account for its behavior without such assumptions, we would not attribute intentionality to it, especially if we knew it had a formal program. And this is precisely the point of my earlier reply to objection II.

Suppose we knew that the robot's behavior was entirely accounted for by the fact that a man inside it was receiving uninterpreted formal symbols from the robot's sensory receptors and sending out uninterpreted formal symbols to its motor mechanisms, and the man was doing this symbol manipulation in accordance with a bunch of rules. Furthermore, suppose the man knows none of these facts about the robot, all he knows is which operations to perform on which meaningless symbols. In such a case we would regard the robot as an ingenious mechanical dummy. The hypothesis that the dummy has a mind would now be unwarranted and unnecessary, for there is now no longer any reason to ascribe intentionality to the robot or to the system of which it is a part (except of course for the man's intentionality in manipulating the symbols). The formal symbol manipulations go on, the input and output are correctly matched, but the only real locus of intentionality is the man, and he doesn't know any of the relevant intentional states; he doesn't, for example, *see* what comes into the robot's eyes, he doesn't *intend* to move the robot's arm, and he doesn't *understand* any of the remarks made to or by the robot. Nor, for the reasons stated earlier, does the system of which man and robot are a part.

To see this point, contrast this case with cases in which we find it completely natural to ascribe intentionality to members of certain other primate species such as apes and monkeys and to domestic animals such as dogs. The reasons we find it natural are, roughly, two: we can't make sense of the animal's behavior without the ascription of intentionality, and we can see that the beasts are made of similar stuff to ourselves—that is an eye, that a nose, this is its skin, and so on. Given the coherence of the animal's behavior and the assumption of the same causal stuff underlying it, we assume both that the animal must have mental states underlying its behavior, and that the mental states must be produced by mechanisms made out of the stuff that is like our stuff. We would certainly make similar assumptions about the robot unless we had some reason not to, but as soon as we knew that the behavior was the result of a formal program, and that the actual causal properties of the physical substance were irrelevant we would abandon the assumption of intentionality. [See "Cognition and Consciousness in Nonhuman Species" *BBS* I(4) 1978.]

There are two other responses to my example that come up frequently (and so are worth discussing) but really miss the point.

V. THE OTHER MINDS REPLY (YALE)

"How do you know that other people understand Chinese or anything else? Only by their behavior. Now the computer can pass the behavioral tests as well as they can (in principle), so if you are going to attribute cognition to other people you must in principle also attribute it to computers."

This objection really is only worth a short reply. The problem in this discussion is not about how I know that other people have cognitive states, but rather what it is that I am attributing to them when I attribute cognitive states to them. The thrust of the argument is that it couldn't be just computational processes and their output because the computational processes and their output can exist without the cognitive state. It is no answer to this argument to feign anesthesia. In "cognitive sciences" one presupposes the reality and knowability of the mental in the same way that in physical sciences one has to presuppose the reality and knowability of physical objects.

VI. THE MANY MANSIONS REPLY (BERKELEY)

"Your whole argument presupposes that AI is only about analogue and digital computers. But that just happens to be the present state of technology. Whatever these causal processes are that you say are essential for intentionality (assuming you are right), eventually we will be able to build devices that have these causal processes, and that will be artificial intelligence. So your arguments are in no way directed at the ability of artificial intelligence to produce and explain cognition."

I really have no objection to this reply save to say that it in effect trivializes the project of strong AI by redefining it as whatever artificially produces and explains cognition. The interest of the original claim made on behalf of artificial intelligence is that it was a precise, well-defined thesis: mental processes are computational processes over formally defined elements. I have been concerned to challenge that thesis. If the claim is redefined so that it is no longer that thesis, my objections no longer apply because there is no longer a testable hypothesis for them to apply to.

Let us now return to the question I promised I would try to answer: granted that in my original example I understand the English and I do not understand the Chinese, and granted therefore that the machine doesn't understand either English or Chinese, still there must be something about me that makes it the case that I understand English and a corresponding something lacking in me that makes it the case that I fail to understand Chinese. Now why couldn't we give those somethings, whatever they are, to a machine?

I see no reason in principle why we couldn't give a machine the capacity to understand English or Chinese, since in an important sense our bodies with our brains are precisely such machines. But I do see very strong arguments for saying that we could not give such a thing to a machine where the operation of the machine is defined solely in terms of computational processes over formally defined elements; that is, where the operation of the machine is defined as an instantiation of a computer program. It is not because I am the instantiation of a computer program that I am able to understand English and have other forms of intentionality (I am, I suppose, the instantiation of any number of computer programs), but as far as we know it is because I am a certain sort of organism with a certain biological (i.e., chemical and physical) structure, and this structure, under certain conditions, is causally capable of producing perception, action, understanding, learning, and other intentional phenomena. And part of the point of the present argument is that only something that had those causal powers could have that intentionality. Perhaps other physical and chemical processes could produce exactly these effects; perhaps, for example, Martians also have intentionality but their brains are made of different stuff. That is an empirical question, rather like the question whether photosynthesis can be done by something with a chemistry different from that of chlorophyll.

But the main point of the present argument is that no purely formal model will ever be sufficient by itself for intentionality because the formal properties are not by themselves constitutive of intentionality, and they have by themselves no causal powers except the power, when instantiated, to produce the next stage of the formalism when the machine is running. And any other causal properties that particular realizations of the formal model have are irrelevant to the formal model because we can always put the same formal model in a different realization where those causal properties are obviously absent. Even if, by some miracle, Chinese speakers exactly realize Schank's program, we can put the same program in English speakers, water pipes, or computers, none of which understand Chinese, the program notwithstanding.

What matters about brain operations is not the formal shadow cast by the sequence of synapses but rather the actual properties of the sequences. All the arguments for the strong version of artificial intelligence that I have seen insist on drawing an outline around the shadows cast by cognition and then claiming that the shadows are the real thing.

By way of concluding I want to try to state some of the general philosophical points implicit in the argument. For clarity I will try to do it in a question and answer fashion, and I begin with that old chestnut of a question: "Could a machine think?"

The answer is, obviously, yes. We are precisely such machines.

"Yes, but could an artifact, a man-made machine, think?"

Assuming it is possible to produce artificially a machine with a nervous system, neurons with axons and dendrites, and all the rest of it, sufficiently like ours, again the answer to the question seems to be obviously, yes. If you can exactly duplicate the causes, you could duplicate the effects. And indeed it might be possible to produce consciousness, intentionality, and all the rest of it using some other sorts of chemical principles than those that human beings use. It is, as I said, an empirical question.

"OK, but could a digital computer think?"

If by "digital computer" we mean anything at all that has a level of description where it can correctly be described as the instantiation of a computer program, then again the answer is, of course, yes, since we are the instantiations of any number of computer programs, and we can think.

"But could something think, understand, and so on *solely* in virtue of being a computer with the right sort of program? Could instantiating a program, the right program of course, by itself be a sufficient condition of understanding?"

This I think is the right question to ask, though it is usually confused with one or more of the earlier questions, and the answer to it is no.

"Why not?"

Because the formal symbol manipulations by themselves don't have any intentionality; they are quite meaningless; they aren't even *symbol* manipulations, since the symbols don't symbolize anything. In the linguistic jargon, they have only a syntax but no semantics. Such intentionality as computers appear to have is solely in the minds of those who program them and those who use them, those who send in the input and those who interpret the output.

The aim of the Chinese room example was to try to show this by showing that as soon as we put something into the system that really does have intentionality (a man), and we program him with the formal program, you can see that the formal program carries no additional intentionality. It adds nothing, for example, to a man's ability to understand Chinese.

Precisely that feature of AI that seemed so appealing—the distinction between the program and the realization—proves fatal to the claim that simulation could be duplication. The distinction between the program and its realization in the hardware seems to be parallel to the distinction between the level of mental operations and the level of brain operations. And if we could describe the level of mental operations as a formal program, then it seems we could describe what was essential about the mind without doing either introspective psychology or neurophysiology of the brain. But the equation "mind is to brain as program is to hardware" breaks down at several points, among them the following three:

First, the distinction between program and realization has the consequence that the same program could have all sorts of crazy realizations that had no form of intentionality. Weizenbaum (1976, Ch. 2), for example, shows in detail how to construct a computer using a roll of toilet paper and a pile of small stones. Similarly, the Chinese story understanding program can be programmed into a sequence of water pipes, a set of wind machines, or a monolingual English speaker, none of which thereby acquires an understanding of Chinese. Stones, toilet paper, wind, and water pipes are the wrong kind of stuff to have intentionality in the first place—only something that has the same causal powers as brains can have intentionality—and though the English speaker has the right kind of stuff for intentionality you can easily see that he doesn't get any extra intentionality by memorizing the program, since memorizing it won't teach him Chinese.

Second, the program is purely formal, but the intentional states are not in that way formal. They are defined in terms of their content, not their form. The belief that it is raining, for example, is not defined as a certain formal shape, but as a certain mental content with conditions of satisfaction, a direction of fit (see Searle 1979), and the like. Indeed the belief as such hasn't even got a formal shape in this syntactic sense, since one and the same belief can be given an indefinite number of different syntactic expressions in different linguistic systems.

Third, as I mentioned before, mental states and events are literally a product of the operation of the brain, but the program is not in that way a product of the computer.

"Well if programs are in no way constitutive of mental processes, why have so many people believed the converse? That at least needs some explanation."

I don't really know the answer to that one. The idea that computer simulations could be the real thing ought to have seemed suspicious in the first place because the computer isn't confined to simulating mental operations, by any means. No one supposes that computer simulations of a five-alarm fire will burn the neighborhood down or that a computer simulation of a rainstorm will leave us all drenched. Why on earth would anyone suppose that a computer simulation of understanding actually understood anything? It is sometimes said that it would be frightfully hard to get computers to feel pain or fall in love, but love and pain are neither harder nor easier than cognition or anything else. For simulation, all you need is the right input and output and a program in the middle that transforms the former into the latter. That is all the computer has for anything it does. To confuse simulation with duplication is the same mistake, whether it is pain, love, cognition, fires, or rainstorms.

Still, there are several reasons why AI must have seemed—and to many people perhaps still does seem—in some way to reproduce and thereby explain mental phenomena, and I believe we will not succeed in removing these illusions until we have fully exposed the reasons that give rise to them.

First, and perhaps most important, is a confusion about the notion of "information processing": many people in cognitive science believe that the human brain, with its mind, does something called "information processing," and analogously the computer with its program does information processing; but fires and rainstorms, on the other hand, don't do information processing at all. Thus, though the computer can simulate the formal features of any process whatever, it stand in a special relation to the mind and brain because when the computer is properly programmed, ideally with the same program as the brain, the information processing is identical in the two cases, and this information processing is really the essence of the mental. But the trouble with this argument is that it rests on an ambiguity in the notion of "information." In the sense in which people "process information" when they reflect, say, on problems in arithmetic or when they read and answer questions about stories, the programmed computer does not do "information processing." Rather, what it does is manipulate formal symbols. The fact that the programmer and the interpreter of the computer output use the symbols to stand for objects in the world is totally beyond the scope of the computer. The computer, to repeat, has a syntax but no semantics. Thus, if you type into the computer "2 plus 2 equals?" it will type out "4." But it has no idea that "4" means 4 or that it means anything at all. And the point is not that it lacks some second-order information about the interpretation of its first-order symbols, but rather that its first-order symbols don't have any interpretations as far as the computer is concerned. All the computer has is more symbols. The introduction of the notion of "information processing" therefore produces a dilemma: either we construe the notion of "information processing" in such a way that it implies intentionality as part of the process or we don't. If the former, then the programmed computer does not do information processing, it only manipulates formal symbols. If the latter, then, though the computer does information processing, it is only doing so in the sense in which adding machines, typewriters, stomachs, thermostats, rainstorms, and hurricanes do information processing; namely, they have a level of description at which we can describe them as taking information in at one end, transforming it, and producing information as output. But in this case it is up to outside observers to interpret the input and output as information in the ordinary sense. And no similarity is established between the computer and the brain in terms of any similarity of information processing.

Second, in much of AI there is a residual behaviorism or operationalism. Since appropriately programmed computers can have input-output patterns similar to those of human beings, we are tempted to postulate mental states in the computer similar to human mental states. But once we see that it is both conceptually and empirically possible for a system to have human capacities in some realm without having any intentionality at all, we should be able to overcome this impulse. My desk adding machine has calculating capacities, but no intentionality, and in this paper I have tried to show that a system could have input and output capabilities that duplicated those of a native Chinese speaker and still not understand Chinese, regardless of how it was programmed. The Turing test is typical of the tradition in being unashamedly behavioristic and operationalistic, and I believe that if AI workers totally repudiated behaviorism and operationalism much of the confusion between simulation and duplication would be eliminated.

Third, this residual operationalism is joined to a residual form of dualism; indeed strong AI only makes sense given the dualistic assumption that, where the mind is concerned, the brain doesn't matter. In strong AI (and in functionalism, as well) what matters are programs, and programs are independent of their realization in machines; indeed, as far as AI is concerned, the same program could be realized by an electronic machine, a Cartesian mental substance, or a Hegelian world spirit. The single most surprising discovery that I have made in discussing these issues is that many AI workers are quite shocked by my idea that actual human mental phenomena might be dependent on actual physical-chemical properties of actual human brains. But if you think about it a minute you can see that I should not have been surprised; for unless you accept some form of dualism, the strong AI project hasn't got a chance. The project is to reproduce and explain the mental by designing programs, but unless the mind is not only conceptually but empirically independent of the brain you couldn't carry out the project, for the program is completely independent of any realization. Unless you believe that the mind is separable from the brain both conceptually and empirically—dualism in a strong form—you cannot hope to reproduce the mental by writing and running programs since programs must be independent of brains or any other particular forms of instantiation. If mental operations consist in computational operations on formal symbols, then it follows that they have no interesting connection with the brain; the only connection would be that the brain just happens to be one of the indefinitely many types of machines capable of instantiating the program. This form of dualism is not the traditional Cartesian variety that claims there are two sorts of *substances*, but it is Cartesian in the sense that it insists that what is specifically mental about the mind has no intrinsic connection with the actual properties of the brain. This underlying dualism is masked from us by the fact that AI literature contains frequent fulminations against "dualism"; what the authors seem to be unaware of is that their position presupposes a strong version of dualism.

"Could a machine think?" My own view is that *only* a machine could think, and indeed only very special kinds of machines, namely brains and machines that had the same causal powers as brains. And that is the main reason strong AI has had little to tell us about thinking, since it has nothing to tell us about machines. By its own definition, it is about programs, and programs are not machines. Whatever else intentionality is, it is a biological phenomenon, and it is as likely to be causally dependent on the specific biochemistry of its origins as lactation, photosynthesis, or any other biological phenomena. No one would suppose that we could produce milk and sugar by running a computer simulation of the formal sequences in lactation and photosynthesis, but where the mind is concerned many people are willing to believe in such a miracle because of a deep and abiding dualism: the mind they suppose is a matter of formal processes and is independent of quite specific material causes in the way that milk and sugar are not.

In defense of this dualism the hope is often expressed that the brain is a digital computer (early computers, by the way, were often called "electronic brains"). But that is no help. Of course the brain is a digital computer. Since everything is a digital computer, brains are too. The point is that the brain's causal capacity to produce intentionality cannot consist in its instantiating a computer program, since for any program you like it is possible for something to instantiate that program and still not have any mental states. Whatever it is that the brain does to produce intentionality, it cannot consist in instantiating a program, since no program, by itself, is sufficient for intentionality.

ACKNOWLEDGMENTS

I am indebted to a rather large number of people for discussion of these matters and for their patient attempts to overcome my ignorance of artificial intelligence. I would especially like to thank Ned Block, Hubert Dreyfus, John Haugeland, Roger Schank, Robert Wilensky, and Terry Winograd.

NOTES

1. I am not, of course, saying that Schank himself is committed to these claims.

2. Also, "understanding" implies both the possession of mental (intentional) states and the truth (validity, success) of these states. For the purposes of this discussion we are concerned only with the possession of the states.

3. Intentionality is by definition that feature of certain mental states by which they are directed at or about objects and states of affairs in the world. Thus, beliefs, desires, and intentions are intentional states; undirected forms of anxiety and depression are not. For further discussion see Searle (1979c).

SELECTED REPLIES TO SEARLE FROM *BEHAVIORAL AND BRAIN SCIENCE*

BRUCE BRIDGEMAN

BRAINS + PROGRAMS = MINDS

There are two sides to this commentary, the first that machines can embody somewhat more than Searle imagines, and the other that humans embody somewhat less. My conclusion will be that the two systems can in principle achieve similar levels of function.

My response to Searle's *Gedankenexperiment* is a variant of the "robot reply" the robot simply needs more information, both environmental and a priori, than Searle is willing to give to it. The robot can internalize meaning only if it can receive information relevant to a definition of meaning, that is, information with a known relationship to the outside world. First it needs some Kantian innate ideas, such as the fact that some input lines (for instance, inputs from the two eyes or from locations in the same eye) are topographically related to one another. In biological brains this is done with labeled lines. Some of the inputs, such as visual inputs, will be connected primarily with spatial processing programs while others such as auditory ones will be more closely related to temporal processing. Further, the system will be built to avoid some input strings (those representing pain, for example) and to seek others (water when thirsty). These properties and many more are built into the structure of human brains genetically, but can be built into a program as a data base just as well. It may be that the homunculus represented in this program would not know what's going on, but it would soon learn, because it has all of the information necessary to construct a representation of events in the outside world.

My super robot would learn about the number five, for instance, in the same way that a child does, by interaction with the outside world where the occurrence of the string of symbols representing "five" in its visual or auditory inputs corresponds with the more direct experience of five of something. The fact that numbers can be coded in the computer in more economical ways is no more relevant than the fact that the number five is coded in the digits of a child's hand. Both a priori knowledge and environmental knowledge could be made similar in quantity and quality to that available to a human.

Now I will try to show that human intentionality is not as qualitatively different from machine states as it might seem to an introspectionist. The brain is similar to a computer program in that it too receives only strings of input and produces only strings of output. The inputs are small 0.1-volt signals entering in great profusion along afferent nerves, and the outputs are physically identical signals leaving the central nervous system on efferent nerves. The brain is deaf, dumb, and blind, so that the electrical signals (and a few hormonal messages which need not concern us here) are the only ways that the brain has of knowing about its world or acting upon it.

The exception to this rule is the existing information stored in the brain, both that given in genetic development and that added by experience. But it too came without intentionality of the sort that Searle seems to require, the genetic information being received from long strings of DNA base sequences (clearly there is no intentionality here), and previous inputs being made up of the same streams of 0.1-volt signals that constitute the present input. Now it is clear that no neuron receiving any of these signals or similar signals generated inside the brain has any idea of what is going on. The neuron is only a humble machine that receives inputs and generates outputs as a function of the temporal and spatial relations of the inputs, and its own structural properties. To assert any further properties of brains is the worst sort of dualism.

Searle grants that humans have intentionality, and toward the end of his article he also admits that many animals might have intentionality also. But how far down the phylogenetic scale is he willing to go [see "Cognition and Consciousness in Nonhuman Species" BBS 1(4) 1978]? Does a single-celled animal have intentionality? Clearly not, for it is only a simple machine that receives physically identifiable inputs and "automatically" generates reflex outputs. The hydra with a few dozen neurons might be explained in the same way, a simple nerve network with inputs and outputs that are restricted, relatively easy to understand, and processed according to fixed patterns. Now what about the mollusc with a few hundred neurons, the insect with a few thousand, the amphibian with a few million, or the mammal with billions? To make his argument convincing, Searle needs a criterion for a dividing line in his implicit dualism.

We are left with a human brain that has an intention-free, genetically determined structure, on which are superimposed the results of storms of tiny nerve signals. From this we somehow introspect an intentionality that cannot be assigned to machines. Searle uses the example of arithmetic manipulations to show how humans "understand" something that machines don't. I submit that neither humans nor machines understand numbers in the sense Searle intends. The understanding of numbers greater than about five is always an illusion, for humans can deal with larger numbers only by using memorized tricks rather than true understanding. If I want to add 27 and 54, I don't use some direct numerical understanding or even a spatial or electrical analogue in my brain. Instead, I apply rules that I memorized in elementary school without really knowing what they meant, and combine these rules with memorized facts of addition of one-digit numbers to arrive at an answer without understanding the numbers themselves. Though I have the feeling that I am performing operations on numbers, in terms of the algorithms I use there is nothing numerical about it. In the same way I can add numbers in the billions, although neither I nor anyone else has any concept of what these numbers mean in terms of perceptually meaningful quantities. Any further understanding of the number system that I possess is irrelevant, for it is not used in performing simple computations.

The illusion of having a consciousness of numbers is similar to the illusion of having a full-color, well-focused visual field; such a concept exists in our consciousness, but the physiological reality falls far short of the introspection. High-quality color information is available only in about the central thirty degrees of the visual field, and the best spatial information in only one or two degrees. I suggest that the feeling of intentionality is a cognitive illusion similar to the feeling of the high-quality visual image. Consciousness is a neurological system like any other, with functions such as the long-term direction of behavior (intentionality?), access to long-term memories, and several other characteristics that make it a powerful, though limited-capacity, processor of biologically useful information.

All of Searle's replies to his *Gedankenexperiment* are variations on the theme that I have described here, that an adequately designed machine could include intentionality as an emergent quality even though individual parts (transistors, neurons, or whatever) have none. All of the replies have an element of truth, and their shortcomings are more in their failure to communicate the similarity of brains and machines to Searle than in any internal weaknesses. Perhaps the most important difference between brains and machines lies not in their instantiation but in their history, for humans have evolved to perform a variety of poorly understood functions including reproduction and survival in a complex social and ecological context. Programs, being designed without extensive evolution, have more restricted goals and motivations.

Searle's accusation of dualism in AI falls wide of the mark because the mechanist does not insist on a particular mechanism in the organism, but only that "mental" processes be represented in a physical system when the system is functioning. A program lying on a tape spool in a corner is no more conscious than a brain preserved in a glass jar, and insisting that the program if read into an appropriate computer would function with intentionality asserts only that the adequate machine consists of an organization imposed on a physical substrate. The organization is no more mentalistic than the substrate itself. Artificial intelligence is about programs rather than machines only because the process of organizing information and inputs and outputs into an information system has been largely solved by digital computers. Therefore, the program is the only step in the process left to worry about.

Searle may well be right that present programs (as in Schank & Abelson 1977) do not instantiate intentionality according to his definition. The issue is not whether present programs do this but whether it is possible in principle to build machines that make plans and achieve goals. Searle has given us no evidence that this is not possible.

DANIEL DENNETT

THE MILK OF HUMAN INTENTIONALITY

I want to distinguish Searle's arguments, which I consider sophistry, from his positive view, which raises a useful challenge to AI, if only because it should induce a more thoughtful formulation of AI's foundations. First, I must support the charge of sophistry by diagnosing, briefly, the tricks with mirrors that give his case a certain spurious plausibility. Then I will comment briefly on his positive view.

Searle's form of argument is a familiar one to philosophers: he has constructed what one might call an *intuition pump*, a device for provoking a family of intuitions by producing variations on a basic thought experiment. An intuition pump is not, typically, an engine of discovery, but a persuader or pedagogical tool—a way of getting people to see things *your* way once you've seen the truth, as Searle thinks he has. I would be the last to disparage the use of intuition pumps—I love to use them myself—but they can be abused. In this instance I think Searle relies almost entirely on ill-gotten gains: favorable intuitions generated by misleadingly presented thought experiments.

Searle begins with a Schank-style AI task, where both the input and output are linguistic objects, sentences of Chinese. In one regard, perhaps, this is fair play, since Schank and others have certainly allowed enthusiastic claims of understanding for such programs to pass their lips, or go uncorrected; but from another point of view it is a cheap shot, since it has long been a familiar theme *within AI circles* that such programs—I call them *bedridden* programs since their only modes of perception and action are linguistic— tackle at best a severe truncation of the interesting task of modeling real understanding. Such programs exhibit no "language-entry" and "language-exit" transitions, to use Wilfrid Sellars's terms, and have no capacity for nonlinguistic perception or bodily action. The shortcomings of such models have been widely recognized for years in AI; for instance, the recognition was implicit in Winograd's decision to give SHRDLU something to do in order to have something to talk about. "A computer whose only input and output was verbal would always be blind to the meaning of what was written" (Dennett 1969, p. 182). The idea has been around for a long time. So, many if not all supporters of strong AI would simply agree with Searle that in his initial version of the Chinese room, no one and nothing could be said to understand Chinese, except perhaps in some very strained, elliptical, and attenuated sense. Hence, what Searle calls "the robot reply (Yale)" is no surprise, though its coming from Yale suggests that even Schank and his school are now attuned to this point.

Searle's response to the robot reply is to revise his thought experiment, claiming it will make no difference. Let our hero in the Chinese room also (unbeknownst to him) control the nonlinguistic actions of, and receive the perceptual informings of, a robot. Still (Searle asks you to consult your intuitions at this point) no one and nothing will really understand Chinese. But Searle does not dwell on how vast a difference this modification makes to what we are being asked to imagine.

Nor does Searle stop to provide vivid detail when he again revises his thought experiment to meet the "systems reply." The systems reply suggests, entirely correctly in my opinion, that Searle has confused different levels of explanation (and attribution). *I* understand English; my brain doesn't—nor, more particularly, does the proper part of it (if such can be isolated) that operates to "process" incoming sentences and to execute my speech act intentions. Searle's portrayal and discussion of the systems reply is not sympathetic, but he is prepared to give ground in any case; his proposal is that we may again modify his Chinese room example, if we wish, to accommodate the objection. We are to imagine our hero in the Chinese room to "internalize all of these elements of the system" so that he "incorporates the entire system." Our hero is now no longer an uncomprehending *sub*personal part of a supersystem to which understanding of Chinese might be properly attributed, since there is no part of the supersystem external to his skin. Still Searle insists (in another plea for our intuitional support) that no one—not our hero or any *other* person he may in some metaphysical sense now be a part of— can be said to understand Chinese.

But will our intuitions support Searle when we imagine this case in detail? Putting both modifications together, we are to imagine our hero controlling both the linguistic and nonlinguistic behavior of a robot who is—himself! When the Chinese words for "Hands up! This is a stickup!" are intoned directly in his ear, he will uncomprehendingly (and at breathtaking speed) hand simulate the program, which leads him to do things (*what* things—is he to order himself in Chinese to stimulate his own motor neurons and then obey the order?) that lead to his handing over *his* own wallet while begging for mercy, in Chinese, with his own lips. Now is it at all obvious that, imagined this way, no one in the situation understands Chinese? In point of fact, Searle has simply not told us how he intends us to imagine this case, which we are licensed to do by his two modifications. Are we to suppose that if the words had been in English, our hero would have responded (appropriately) in his native English? Or is he so engrossed in his massive homuncular task that he responds with the (simulated) incomprehension that would be the program-driven response to this bit of incomprehensible ("to the robot") input? If the latter, our hero has taken leave of his English-speaking friends for good, drowned in the engine room of a Chinese-speaking "person" inhabiting his body. If the former, the situation is drastically in need of further description by Searle, for just what he is imagining is far from clear. There are several radically different alternatives—all so outlandishly unrealizable as to caution us not to trust our gut reactions about them in any case. When we imagine our hero "incorporating the entire system" are we to imagine that he pushes buttons with his fingers in order to get his own arms to move? Surely not, since all the buttons are now internal. Are we to imagine that when he responds to the Chinese for "pass the salt, please" by getting his hand to grasp the salt and move it in a certain direction, he doesn't *notice* that this is what he is doing? In short, could anyone who became accomplished in this imagined exercise fail to become fluent in Chinese in the process? Perhaps, but it all depends on details of this, the only crucial thought experiment in Searle's kit, that Searle does not provide.

Searle tells us that when he first presented versions of this paper to AI audiences, objections were raised that he was prepared to meet, in part, by modifying his thought experiment. Why then did he not present us, his subsequent audience, with the modified thought experiment in the first place, instead of first leading us on a tour of red herrings? Could it be because it is impossible to tell the doubly modified story in anything approaching a cogent and detailed manner without provoking the *unwanted* intuitions? Told in detail, the doubly modified story suggests either that there are two people, one of whom understands Chinese, inhabiting one body, or that one English-speaking person has, in effect, been engulfed within another person, a person who understands Chinese (among *many* other things).

These and other similar considerations convince me that we may turn our backs on the Chinese room at least until a better version is deployed. In its current state of disrepair I can get it to pump my contrary intuitions at least as plentifully as Searle's. What, though, of his positive view? In the conclusion of his paper, Searle observes: "No one would suppose that we could produce milk and sugar by running a computer simulation of the formal sequences in lactation and photosynthesis, but where the mind is concerned many people are willing to believe in such a miracle." I don't think this is just a curious illustration of Searle's vision; I think it vividly expresses the feature that most radically distinguishes his view from the prevailing winds of doctrine. For Searle, intentionality is rather like a wonderful substance secreted by the brain the way the pancreas secretes insulin. Brains *produce intentionality*, he says, whereas other objects, such as computer programs, do not, even if they happen to be designed to mimic the input-output behavior of (some) brain. There is, then, a major disagreement about what the *product* of the brain is. Most people in AI (and most functionalists in the philosophy of mind) would say that its product is something like *control*: what a brain is *for* is for governing the right, appropriate, intelligent input-output relations, where these are deemed to be, in the end, relations between sensory inputs and behavioral outputs of some sort. That looks to Searle like some sort of behaviorism, and he will have none of it. Passing the Turing test may be prima facie evidence that something has intentionality—really has a mind— but "as soon as we knew that the behavior was the result of a formal program, and that the actual causal properties of the physical substance were irrelevant we would abandon the assumption of intentionality."

So on Searle's view the "right" input-output relations are symptomatic but not conclusive or criterial evidence of intentionality; the proof of the pudding is in the presence of some (entirely unspecified) causal properties that are *internal* to the operation of the brain. This internality needs highlighting. When Searle speaks of causal properties one may think at first that those causal properties crucial for intentionality are those that link the activities of the system (brain or computer) to the things in the world with which the system interacts—including, preeminently, the active, sentient body whose behavior the system controls. But Searle insists that these are not the relevant causal properties. He concedes the possibility in principle of duplicating the input-output competence of a human brain with a "formal program," which (suitably attached) would guide a body through the world exactly as that body's brain would, and thus would acquire all the relevant extra systemic causal properties of the brain. But such a brain substitute would utterly fail to produce intentionality in the process, Searle holds, because it would lack some other causal properties of the brain's internal operation.[1]

How, though, would we know that it lacked these properties, if all we knew was that it was (an implementation of) a formal program? Since Searle concedes that the operation of anything—and hence a human brain—can be described in terms of the execution of a formal program, the mere existence of such a level of description of a system would not preclude its having intentionality. It seems that it is only when we can see that the system in question is *only* the implementation of a formal program that we can conclude that it doesn't make a little intentionality on the side. But nothing could be only the implementation of a formal program; computers exude heat and noise in the course of their operations—why not intentionality too?

Besides, which is the major product and which the byproduct? Searle can hardly deny that brains do in fact produce lots of reliable and appropriate bodily control. They do this, he thinks, by producing intentionality, but he concedes that something—such as a computer with the right input-output rules—could produce the control without making or using any intentionality. But then control is the main product and intentionality just one (no doubt natural) means of obtaining it. Had our ancestors been nonintentional mutants with mere control systems, nature would just as readily have selected them instead. (I owe this point to Bob Moore.) Or, to look at the other side of the coin, brains with lots of intentionality but no control competence would be producers of an ecologically irrelevant product, which evolution would not protect. Luckily for us, though, our brains make intentionality; if they didn't, we'd behave just as we now do, but of course we wouldn't *mean* it!

Surely Searle does not hold the view I have just ridiculed, although it seems as if he does. He can't really view intentionality as a marvelous mental fluid, so what is he trying to get at? I think his concern with *internal* properties of control systems is a misconceived attempt to capture the interior *point of view* of a conscious agent. He does not see how any mere computer, chopping away at a formal program, could harbor such a point of view. But that is because he is looking *too deep*. It is just as mysterious if we peer into the synapse-filled jungles of the brain and wonder where consciousness is hiding. It is not at that level of description that a proper subject of consciousness will be found. That is the systems reply, which Searle does not yet see to be a step in the right direction away from his updated version of *élan vital*.

NOTE

1. For an intuition pump involving exactly this case—a prosthetic brain—but designed to pump contrary intuitions, see "Where Am I?" in Dennett (1978).

JERRY A. FODOR

SEARLE ON WHAT ONLY BRAINS CAN DO

1. Searle is certainly right that instantiating the same program that the brain does is not, in and of itself, a sufficent condition for having those propositional attitudes characteristic of the organism that has the brain. If some people in AI think that it is, they're wrong. As for the Turing test, it has all the usual

difficulties with predictions of "no difference"; you can't distinguish the truth of the prediction from the insensitivity of the test instrument.[1]

2. However, Searle's treatment of the "robot reply" is quite unconvincing. Given that there are the right kinds of causal linkages between the symbols that the device manipulates and things in the world—including the afferent and efferent transducers of the device—it is quite unclear that intuition rejects ascribing propositional attitudes to it. All that Searle's example shows is that the kind of causal linkage he imagines—one that is, in effect, mediated by a man sitting in the head of a robot—is, unsurprisingly, not the right kind.

3. We don't know how to say what the right kinds of causal linkage are. This, also, is unsurprising since we don't know how to answer the closely related question as to what kinds of connection between a formula and the world determine the interpretation under which the formula is employed. We don't have an answer to this question for *any* symbolic system; a fortiori, not for mental representations. These questions are closely related because, given the mental representation view, it is natural to assume that what makes mental states intentional is primarily that they involve relations to semantically interpreted mental objects; again, relations of the right kind.

4. It seems to me that Searle has misunderstood the main point about the treatment of intentionality in representational theories of the mind; this is not surprising since proponents of the theory—especially in AI—have been notably unlucid in expounding it. For the record, then, the main point is this: intentional properties of propositional attitudes are viewed as inherited from semantic properties of mental representations (and not from the functional role of mental representations, unless "functional role" is construed broadly enough to include symbol-world relations). In effect, what is proposed is a reduction of the problem *what makes mental states intentional* to the problem *what bestows semantic properties on (fixes the interpretation of) a symbol*. This reduction looks promising because we're going to have to answer the latter question anyhow (for example, in constructing theories of natural languages); and we need the notion of mental representation anyhow (for example, to provide appropriate domains for mental processes).

It may be worth adding that there is nothing new about this strategy. Locke, for example, thought (a) that the intentional properties of mental states are inherited from the semantic (referential) properties of mental representations; (b) that mental processes are formal (associative); and (c) that the objects from which mental states inherit their intentionality are the same ones over which mental processes are defined: namely ideas. It's my view that no serious alternative to this treatment of propositional attitudes has ever been proposed.

5. To say that a computer (or a brain) performs formal operations on symbols is not the same thing as saying that it performs operations on formal

(in the sense of "uninterpreted") symbols. This equivocation occurs repeatedly in Searle's paper, and causes considerable confusion. If there are mental representations, they must, of course, be interpreted objects; it is because they are interpreted objects that mental states are intentional. But the brain might be a computer for all that.

6. This situation—needing a notion of causal connection, but not knowing which notion of causal connection is the right one—is entirely familiar in philosophy. It is, for example, extremely plausible that "a perceives b" can be true only where there is the right kind of causal connection between a and b. And we don't know what the right kind of causal connection is here either.

Demonstrating that some kinds of causal connection are the *wrong* kinds would not, of course, prejudice the claim. For example, suppose we interpolated a little man between a and b, whose function it is to report to a on the presence of b. We would then have (inter alia) a sort of causal link from a to b, but we wouldn't have the sort of causal link that is required for a to perceive b. It would, of course, be a fallacy to argue from the fact that this causal linkage fails to reconstruct perception to the conclusion that *no* causal linkage would succeed. Searle's argument against the "robot reply" is a fallacy of precisely that sort.

7. It is entirely reasonable (indeed it must be true) that the right kind of causal relation is the kind that holds between our brains and our transducer mechanisms (on the one hand) and between our brains and distal objects (on the other). It would not begin to follow that *only* our brains can bear such relations to transducers and distal objects; and it would also not follow that being the same sort of thing our brain is (in any biochemical sense of "same sort") is a necessary condition for being in that relation; and it would also not follow that formal manipulations of symbols are not among the links in such causal chains. And, even if our brains *are* the only sorts of things that can be in that relation, the fact that they are might quite possibly be of no particular interest; that would depend on *why* it's true.[2]

Searle gives no clue as to why he thinks the biochemistry is important for intentionality and, prima facie, the idea that what counts is how the organism is connected to the world seems far more plausible. After all, it's easy enough to imagine, in a rough and ready sort of way, how the fact that my thought is causally connected to a tree might bear on its being a thought about a tree. But it's hard to imagine how the fact that (to put it crudely) my thought is made out of hydrocarbons could matter, except on the unlikely hypothesis that only hydrocarbons can be causally connected to trees in the way that brains are.

8. The empirical evidence for believing that "manipulation of symbols" is involved in mental processes derives largely from the considerable success of work in linguistics, psychology, and AI that has been grounded in that

assumption. Little of the relevant data concerns the simulation of behavior or the passing of Turing tests, though Searle writes as though all of it does. Searle gives no indication *at all* of how the facts that this work accounts for are to be explained if not on the mental-processes-are-formal-processes view. To claim that there is no argument that symbol manipulation is necessary for mental processing while systematically ignoring all the evidence that has been alleged in favor of the claim strikes me as an extremely curious strategy on Searle's part.

9. Some necessary conditions are more interesting than others. While connections to the world and symbol manipulations are both presumably necessary for intentional processes, there is no reason (so far) to believe that the former provide a theoretical domain for a science; whereas, there is considerable a posteriori reason to suppose that the latter do. If this is right, it provides some justification for AI practice, if not for AI rhetoric.

10. *Talking* involves performing certain formal operations on symbols: stringing words together. Yet, not everything that can string words together can talk. It does not follow from these banal observations that what we utter are uninterpreted sounds, or that we don't understand what we say, or that whoever talks talks nonsense, or that only hydrocarbons can assert—similarly, mutatis mutandis, if you substitute "thinking" for "talking."

NOTES

1. I assume, for simplicity, that there is only one program that the brain instantiates (which, of course, there isn't). Notice, by the way, that even passing the Turing test requires doing more than *just* manipulating symbols. A device that can't run a typewriter can't play the game.

2. For example, it might be that, in point of physical fact, only things that have the same simultaneous values of weight, density, and shade of gray that brains have can do the things that brains can. This would be surprising, but it's hard to see why a psychologist should care much. Not even if it turned out—still in point of physical fact—that brains are the only things that *can* have that weight, density, and color. If *that's* dualism, I imagine we can live with it.

JOHN HAUGELAND

PROGRAMS, CAUSAL POWERS, AND INTENTIONALITY

Searle is in a bind. He denies that any Turing test for intelligence is adequate— that is, that behaving intelligently is a suffecent condition for being intelligent. But he dare not deny that creatures physiologically very different from people might be intelligent nonetheless—smart green saucer pilots, say. So he needs an intermediate criterion: not so specific to us as to rule out the aliens, yet not so dissociated from specifics as to admit any old object with the right behavior. His suggestion is that only objects (made of stuff) with "the right causal powers" can have intentionality, and hence, only such objects can genuinely understand anything or be intelligent. This suggestion, however, is incompatible with the main argument of his paper.

Ostensibly, that argument is against the claim that working according to a certain program can ever be sufficient for understanding anything—no matter how cleverly the program is contrived so as to make the relevant object (computer, robot, or whatever) behave as *if* it understood. The crucial move is replacing the central processor (c.p.u.) with a superfast person—whom we might as well call "Searle's demon." And Searle argues that an English-speaking demon could perfectly well follow a program for simulating a Chinese speaker, without itself understanding a word of Chinese.

The trouble is that the same strategy will work as well against any specification of "the right causal powers." Instead of manipulating formal tokens according to the specifications of some computer program, the demon will manipulate physical states or variables according to the specification of the "right" causal interactions. Just to be concrete, imagine that the right ones are those powers that our neuron tips have to titillate one another with neurotransmitters. The green aliens can be intelligent, even though they're based on silicon chemistry, because their (silicon) neurons have the same power of intertitillation. Now imagine covering each of the neurons of a Chinese criminal with a thin coating, which has no effect, except that it is impervious to neurotransmitters. And imagine further that Searle's demon can see the problem, and comes to the rescue; he peers through the coating at each neural tip, determines which transmitter (if any) would have been emitted, and then massages the adjacent tips in a way that has the same effect as if they had received that transmitter. Basically, instead of replacing the c.p.u., the demon is replacing the neurotransmitters.

By hypothesis, the victim's behavior is unchanged; in particular, she still acts as if she understood Chinese. Now, however, none of her neurons has the right causal powers—the demon has them, and he still understands only English. Therefore, having the right causal powers (even while embedded in a system such that the exercise of these powers leads to "intelligent" behavior) cannot be sufficient for understanding. Needless to say, a corresponding variation will work, whatever the relevant causal powers are.

None of this should come as a surprise. A computer program is just a specification of the exercise of certain causal powers: the powers to manipulate various formal tokens (physical objects or states of some sort) in certain specified ways, depending on the presence of certain other such tokens. Of course, it is a particular way of specifying causal exercises of a particular sort—that's what gives the "computational paradigm" its distinctive character. But Searle makes no use of this particularity; his argument depends *only* on the fact that causal powers can be specified independently of whatever it is that has the power. This is precisely what makes it possible to interpose the demon, in both the token-interaction (program) and neuron-interaction cases.

There is no escape in urging that this is a "dualistic" view of causal powers, not intrinsically connected with "the actual properties" of physical objects. To speak of causal powers in any way that allows for generalization (to green aliens, for example) is ipso facto to abstract from the particulars of any given "realization." The point is independent of the example—it works just as well for photosynthesis. Thus, flesh-colored plantlike organisms on the alien planet might photosynthesize (I take it, in a full and literal sense) so long as they contain some chemical (not necessarily chlorophyll) that absorbs light and uses the energy to make sugar and free oxygen out of carbon dioxide (or silicon dioxide?) and water. This is what it means to specify photosynthesis as a *causal power*, rather than just a property that is, by definition, idiosyncratic to chlorophyll. But now, of course, the demon can enter, replacing both chlorophyll and its alien substitute: he devours photons, and thus energized, makes sugar from CO_2 and H_2O. It seems to me that the demon is photosynthesizing.

Let's set aside the demon argument, however. Searle also suggests that "there is no reason to suppose" that understanding (or intentionality) "has anything to do with" computer programs. This too, I think, rests on his failure to recognize that specifying a program is (in a distinctive way) specifying a range of causal powers and interactions.

The central issue is what differentiates *original* intentionality from *derivative* intentionality. The former is intentionality that a thing (system, state, process) has "in its own right"; the latter is intentionality that is "borrowed from" or "conferred by" something else. Thus (on standard assumptions, which I will not question here), the intentionality of conscious thought and perception is original, whereas the intentionality (meaning) of linguistic tokens is merely conferred upon them by language users—that is, words don't have any meaning in and of themselves, but only in virtue of our giving them some. These are paradigm cases; many other cases will fall clearly on one side or the other, or be questionable, or perhaps even marginal. No one denies that if AI systems don't have original intentionality, then they at least have derivative intentionality, in a nontrivial sense—because they have nontrivial *interpretations*. What Searle objects to is the thesis, held by many, that good-enough AI systems have (or will eventually have) original intentionality.

Thought tokens, such as articulate beliefs and desires, and linguistic tokens, such as the expressions of articulate beliefs and desires, seem to have a lot in common—as pointed out, for example, by Searle (1979). In particular, except for the original/derivative distinction, they have (or at least appear to have) closely parallel semantic structures and variations. There must be some other principled distinction between them, then, in virtue of which the former can be originally intentional, but the latter only derivatively so. A conspicuous candidate for this distinction is that thoughts are semantically active, whereas sentence tokens, written out, say, on a page, are semantically inert. Thoughts are constantly interacting with one another and the world, in ways that are semantically appropriate to their intentional content. The causal interactions of written sentence tokens, on the other hand, do not consistently reflect their content (except when they interact with people).

Thoughts are embodied in a "system" that provides "normal channels" for them to interact with the world, and such that these normal interactions tend to maximize the "fit" between them and the world, that is, via perception, beliefs tend toward the truth; and, via action, the world tends toward what is desired. And there are channels of interaction among thoughts (various kinds of inference) via which the set of them tends to become more coherent, and to contain more consequences of its members. Naturally, other effects introduce aberrations and "noise" into the system; but the normal channels tend to predominate in the long run. There are no comparable channels of interaction for written tokens. In fact, (according to this same standard view), the only semantically sensitive interactions that written tokens ever have are with thoughts; insofar as they tend to express truths, it is because they express beliefs, and insofar as they tend to bring about their own satisfaction conditions, it is because they tend to bring about desires. Thus, the *only* semantically significant interactions that written tokens have with the world are via thoughts; and this, the suggestion goes, is *why* their intentionality is derivative.

The interactions that thoughts have among themselves (within a single "system") are particularly important, for it is in virtue of these that thought can be subtle and indirect, relative to its interactions with the world—that is, not easily fooled or thwarted. Thus, we tend to consider more than the immediately present evidence in making judgments, and more than the immediately present options in making plans. We weigh desiderata, seek further information, try things to see if they'll work, formulate general maxims and laws, estimate results and costs, go to the library, cooperate, manipulate, scheme, test, and reflect on what we're doing. All of these either are or involve a lot of thought-thought interaction, and tend, in the long run to broaden and improve the "fit" between thought and world. And they are typical as manifestations both of intelligence and of independence.

I take it for granted that all of the interactions mentioned are, in some sense, *causal*—hence, that it is among the system's "causal powers" that it can have (instantiate, realize, produce) thoughts that interact with the world and each other in these ways. It is hard to tell whether these are the sorts of causal powers that Searle has in mind, both because he doesn't say, and because they don't seem terribly similar to photosynthesis and lactation. But, in any case, they strike me as strong candidates for the kinds of powers that would distinguish systems with intentionality—that is, *original* intentionality—from those without. The reason is that these are the only powers that consistently reflect the distinctively intentional character of the interactors: namely, their "content" or "meaning" (except, so to speak, passively, as in the case of written tokens being read). That is, the power to have states that are semantically active is the "right" causal power for intentionality.

It is this plausible claim that underlies the thesis that (sufficiently developed) AI systems could actually *be* intelligent, and have *original* intentionality. For a case can surely be made that their "representations" are semantically active (or, at least, that they would be if the system were built into a robot). Remember, we are conceding them at least derivative intentionality, so the states in question do have a content, relative to which we can gauge the "semantic appropriateness" of their causal interactions. And the central discovery of all computer technology is that devices can be contrived such that, relative to a certain interpretation, certain of their states will always interact (causally) in semantically appropriate ways, so long as the devices perform as designed electromechanically—that is, these states can have "normal channels" of interaction (with each other and with the world) more or less comparable to those that underlie the semantic activity of thoughts. This point can hardly be denied, so long as it is made in terms of the derivative intentionality of computing systems; but what it seems to add to the archetypical (and "inert") derivative intentionality of, say, written text is, precisely, semantic *activity*. So, if (sufficiently rich) semantic activity is what distinguishes original from derivative intentionality (in other words, it's the "right" causal power), then it seems that (sufficiently rich) computing systems can have *original* intentionality.

Now, like Searle, I am inclined to dispute this conclusion; but for entirely different reasons. I don't believe there is any *conceptual* confusion in supposing that the right causal powers for original intentionality are the ones that would be captured by specifying a program (that is, a virtual machine). Hence, I don't think the above plausibility argument can be dismissed out of hand ("no reason to suppose," and so on); nor can I imagine being convinced that, no matter how good AI got, it would still be "weak"—that is, would not have created a "real" intelligence—because it still proceeded by specifying programs. It seems to me that the interesting question is much more nitty-gritty empirical than that: given that programs *might* be the right way to express the relevant causal structure, are they *in fact* so? It is to this question that I expect the answer is no. In other words, I don't much care about Searle's demon working through a program for perfect simulation of a native

Chinese speaker—not because there's no such demon, but because there's no such program. Or rather, *whether* there is such a program, and *if not, why not*, are, in my view, the important questions.

DOUGLAS HOFSTADTER

REDUCTIONISM AND RELIGION

This religious diatribe against AI, masquerading as a serious scientific argument, is one of the wrongest, most infuriating articles I have ever read in my life. It is matched in its power to annoy only by the famous article "Minds, Machines, and Gödel" by J. R. Lucas (1961).

Searle's trouble is one that I can easily identity with. Like me, he has deep difficulty in seeing how mind, soul, "I," can come out of brain, cells, atoms. To show his puzzlement, he gives some beautiful paraphrases of this mystery. One of my favorites is the water-pipe simulation of a brain. It gets straight to the core of the mind-body problem. The strange thing is that Searle simply dismisses any possibility of such a system's being conscious with a hand wave of "absurd" (I actually think he radically misrepresents the complexity of such a water-pipe system both to readers and in his own mind, but that is a somewhat separable issue.)

The fact is, we have to deal with a reality of nature—and realities of nature sometimes *are* absurd. Who would have believed that light consists of spinning massless wave particles obeying an uncertainty principle while traveling through a curved four-dimensional universe? The fact that intelligence, understanding, mind, consciousness, soul all do spring from an unlikely source—an enormously tangled web of cell bodies, axons, synapses, and dendrites—is absurd, and yet undeniable. How this can create an "I" is hard to understand, but once we accept that fundamental, strange, disorienting fact, then it should seem no more weird to accept a water-pipe "I."

Searle's way of dealing with this reality of nature is to claim he accepts it—but then he will not accept its consequences. The main consequence is that *"intentionality"—his name for soul*—is an outcome of formal processes. I admit that I have slipped one extra premise in here: that physical processes are formal, that is, rule governed. To put it another way, the extra premise is that *there is no intentionality at the level of particles*. (Perhaps I have misunderstood Searle. He may be a mystic and claim that there is intentionality at that level. But then how does one explain why it seems to manifest itself in consciousness only when the particles are arranged in certain special configurations—brains—but not, say, in water-pipe arrangements of any sort and size?) The conjunction of these two beliefs seems to me to compel one to admit the possibility of all the hopes of artificial intelligence, despite the fact that it will always battle us to think of ourselves as, at bottom, formal systems.

To people who have never programmed, the distinction between levels of a computer system—programs that run "on" other programs or on hardware—is an elusive one. I believe Searle doesn't really understand this subtle idea, and thus blurs many distinctions while creating other artificial ones to take advantage of human emotional responses that are evoked in the process of imagining unfamiliar ideas.

He begins with what sounds like a relatively innocent situation: a man in a room with a set of English instructions ("bits of paper") for manipulating some Chinese symbols. At first, you think the man is answering questions (although unbeknown to him) about restaurants, using Schankian scripts. Then Searle casually slips in the idea that this program can pass the Turing test! This is an incredible jump in complexity—perhaps a millionfold increase, if not more. Searle seems not to be aware of how radically it changes the whole picture to have that "little" assumption creep in. But even the initial situation, which sounds plausible enough, is in fact highly unrealistic.

Imagine a human being, hand simulating a complex AI program, such as a script-based "understanding" program. To digest a full story, to go through the scripts and to produce the response, would probably take a hard eight-hour day for a human being. Actually, of course, this hand-simulated program is supposed to be passing the Turing test, not just answering a few stereotyped questions about restaurants. So let's jump up to a week per question, since the program would be so complex. (We are being unbelievably generous to Searle.)

Now Searle asks you to identify with this poor slave of a human (he doesn't actually ask you to identify with him—he merely knows you will project yourself onto this person, and vicariously experience the indescribably boring nightmare of that hand simulation). He knows your reaction will be: "This is not understanding the story—this is some sort of formal process!" But remember: any time some phenomenon is looked at on a scale a million times different from its familiar scale, it doesn't seem the same! When I imagine myself feeling my brain running a hundred times too slowly (of course that is paradoxical but it is what Searle wants me to do), then of course it is agonizing, and presumably I would not even recognize the feelings at all. Throw in yet another factor of a thousand and one cannot even imagine what it would feel like.

Now this is what Searle is doing. He is inviting you to identify with a nonhuman which he lightly passes off as a human, and by doing so he asks you to participate in a great fallacy. Over and over again he uses this ploy, this emotional trickery, to get you to agree with him that surely, an intricate system of water pipes can't think! He forgets to tell you that a water-pipe simulation of the brain would take, say, a few trillion water pipes with a few trillion workers standing at faucets turning them when needed, and he forgets to tell you that to answer a question it would take a year or two. He forgets to tell you, because if you remembered that, and then on your own, imagined taking a movie and speeding it up a million times, and imagined changing your level of description of the thing from the faucet level to the pipe-cluster level, and on through a series of ever higher levels until you reached some sort of eventual symbolic level, why then you might say, "Hey, when I imagine what this entire system would be like when perceived at this time scale and level of description, I can see how it might be conscious after all!"

Searle is representative of a class of people who have an instinctive horror of any "explaining away" of the soul. I don't know why certain people have this horror while others, like me, find in reductionism the ultimate religion. Perhaps my lifelong training in physics and science in general has given me a deep awe at seeing how the most substantial and familiar of objects or experiences fades away, as one approaches the infinitesimal scale, into an eerily insubstantial ether, a myriad of ephemeral swirling vortices of nearly incomprehensible mathematical activity. This in me evokes a kind of cosmic awe. To me, reductionism does not "explain away"; rather, it adds mystery. I know that this journal is not the place for philosophical and religious commentary, yet it seems to me that what Searle and I have is, at the deepest level, a religious disagreement, and I doubt that anything I say could ever change his mind. He insists on things he calls "causal intentional properties" which seem to vanish as soon as you analyze them, find rules for them, or simulate them. But what those things are, other than epiphenomena, or "innocently emergent" qualities, I don't know.

WILLIAM G. LYCAN

'THE FUNCTIONALIST REPLY (OHIO STATE)

Most versions of philosophical behaviorism have had the consequence that if an organism or device D passes the Turing test, in the sense of systematically manifesting all the same outward behavioral dispositions that a normal human does, the D has all the same sorts of contentful or intentional states that humans do. In light of fairly oblivious counterexamples to this thesis, materialist philosophers of mind have by and large rejected behaviorism in favor of a more species-chauvinistic view: $D's$ manifesting all the same sorts of behavioral dispositions we do does not alone suffice for $D's$ having intentional states. It is necessary in addition that D produce behavior from stimuli *in roughly the way that* we do—that $D's$ inner functional organization be not unlike ours and that D process the stimulus input by analogous inner procedures. On this "functionalist" theory, to be in a mental state of such and such a kind is to incorporate a functional component or system of components of type so and so which is in a certain distinctive state of its own. "Functional components" are individuated according to the roles they play within their owners' overall functional organization.[1]

Searle offers a number of cases of entities that manifest the behavioral dispositions we associate with intentional states but that rather plainly do not have any such states.[2] I accept his intuitive judgments about most of these cases. Searle plus rule book plus pencil and paper presumably does not understand Chinese, nor does Searle with memorized rule book or Searle with TV camera or the robot with Searle inside. Neither my stomach nor Searle's liver nor a thermostat nor a light switch has beliefs and desires. But none of these cases is a counterexample to the functionalist hypothesis. The systems in the former group are pretty obviously not functionally isomorphic at the relevant level to human beings who do understand Chinese; a native Chinese carrying on a conversation is implementing procedures of his own, not those procedures that would occur in a mockup containing the cynical, English-speaking, American-acculturated homuncular Searle. Therefore they are not counterexamples to a functionalist theory of language understanding, and accordingly they leave it open that a computer that *was* functionally isomorphic to a real Chinese speaker would indeed understand Chinese also. Stomachs, thermostats, and the like, because of their brutish simplicity, are even more clearly dissimilar to humans. (The same presumably is true of Schank's existing language-understanding programs.)

I have hopes for a sophisticated version of the "brain simulator" (or the "combination" machine) that Searle illustrates with his plumbing example. Imagine a hydraulic system of this type that does replicate, perhaps not the precise neuroanatomy of a Chinese speaker, but all that is relevant of the Chinese speaker's higher functional organization; individual water pipes are grouped into organ systems precisely analogous to those found in the speaker's brain, and the device processes linguistic input in just the way that the speaker does. (It does not merely *simulate* or *describe* this processing.) Moreover, the system is automatic and does all this without the intervention of Searle or any other *deus in machina*. Under these conditions and given a suitable social context, I think it would be plausible to accept the functionalist consequence that the hydraulic system does understand Chinese.

Searle's paper suggest two objections to this claim. First, "where is the understanding in this system?" All Searle sees is pipes and valves and flowing water. *Reply:* Looking around the fine detail of the system's hardware, you are *too small* to see that the system is understanding Chinese sentences. If you were a tiny, cell-sized observer inside a real Chinese speaker's brain, all you would see would be neurons stupidly, mechanically transmitting electrical charge, and in the same tone you would ask, "Where is the understanding in this system?" But you would be wrong in concluding that the system you were observing did not understand Chinese; in like manner you may well be wrong about the hydraulic device.[3]

Second, even if a computer were to replicate all of the Chinese speaker's relevant functional organization, all the computer is really doing is performing computational operations on formally specified elements. A purely formally or syntactically characterized element has no meaning or content in itself, obviously, and no amount of mindless syntactic manipulation of it will endow it with any. *Reply:* The premise is correct, and I agree it shows that no computer has or could have intentional states *merely in virtue of performing syntactic operations on formally characterized elements.* But that does not suffice to prove that no computer can have intentional states at all. Our brain states do not have the contents they do just in virtue of having their purely formal properties either; a brain state described "syntactically" has no meaning or content on its own. In virtue of what, then, *do* brain states (or mental states however construed) have the meanings they do? Recent theory advises that the content of a mental representation is not determined within its owner's head (Putnam 1975a; Fodor 1980); rather, it is determined in part by the objects in the environment that actually figure in the representation's etiology and in part by social and contextual factors of several other sorts (Stich, 1981). Now, present-day computers live in highly artificial and stifling environments. They receive carefully and tendentiously preselected input; their software is adventitiously manipulated by uncaring programmers; and they are isolated in laboratories and offices, deprived of any normal interaction within a natural or appropriate social setting.[5] For this reason and several others, Searle is surely right in saying that present-day computers do not really have the intentional states that we fancifully incline toward attributing to them. But nothing Searle has said impugns the thesis that if a sophisticated future computer not only replicated human functional organization but harbored its inner representations as a result of the right sort of causal history and had also been nurtured within a favorable social setting, we might correctly ascribe intentional states to it. This point may or may not afford lasting comfort to the AI community.

NOTES

1. This characterization is necessarily crude and vague. For a very useful survey of different versions of functionalism and their respective foibles, see Block (1978); I have developed and defended what I think is the most promising version of functionalism in Lycan (1981).

2. For further discussion of cases of this kind, see Block (1980).

3. A much expanded version of this reply appears in section 4 of Lycan (1981).

4. I do not understand Searle's positive suggestion as to the source of intentionality in our own brains. *What* "neurobiological causal properties"?

5. As Fodor (1981) remarks, SHRDLU as we interpret him is the victim of a Cartesian evil demon, the "blocks" he manipulates do not exist in reality.

ZENON W. PYLYSHYN[1]

Center for Advanced Study in the Behavioral Sciences, Stanford, California 94305

THE "CAUSAL POWER" OF MACHINES

What kind of stuff can refer? Searle would have us believe that computers, qua formal symbol manipulators, necessarily lack the quality of intentionality, or the capacity to understand and to refer, because they have different "causal powers" from us. Although just what having different causal powers amounts to (other than not being capable of intentionality) is not spelled out, it appears at least that systems that are functionally identical need not have the same "causal powers." Thus, the relation of equivalence with respect to causal powers is a refinement of the relation of equivalence with respect to function. What Searle wants to claim is that only systems that are equivalent to humans in this stronger sense can have intentionality. His thesis thus hangs on the assumption that intentionality is tied very closely to specific material properties—indeed, that it is literally *caused* by them. From that point of view it would be extremely unlikely that any system not made of protoplasm—or something essentially identical to protoplasm—can have intentionality. Thus, if more and more of the cells in your brain were to be replaced by integrated circuit chips, programmed in such a way as to keep the input-output *function* of each unit identical to that of the unit being replaced, you would in all likelihood just keep right on speaking exactly as you are doing now except that you would eventually stop *meaning* anything by it. What we outside observers might take to be words would become for you just certain noises that circuits caused you to make.

Searle presents a variety of seductive metaphors and appeals to intuition in support of this rather astonishing view. For example, he asks: why should we find the view that intentionality is tied to detailed properties of the material composition of the system so surprising, when we so readily accept the parallel claim in the case of lactation? Surely it's obvious that only a system with certain causal powers can produce milk; but then why should the same not be true of the ability to refer? Why this example should strike Searle as even remotely relevant is not clear, however. The product of lactation is a *substance*, milk, whose essential defining properties are, naturally, physical and chemical ones (although nothing prevents the production of synthetic milk using a process that is materially very different from mammalian lactation). Is Searle then proposing that intentionality is a *substance* secreted by the brain, and that a possible test for intentionality might involve, say, titrating the brain tissue that realized some putative mental episodes?

Similarly, Searle says that it's obvious that merely having a program can't possibly be a sufficient condition for intentionality since you can implement that program on a Turing machine made out of "a roll of toilet paper and a pile of small stones." Such a machine would not have intentionality because such objects "are the wrong kind of stuff to have intentionality in the first place." But what is the right kind of stuff? Is it cell assemblies, individual neurons, protoplasm, protein molecules, atoms of carbon and hydrogen, elementary particles? Let Searle name the level, and it can be simulated perfectly well using "the wrong kind of stuff." Clearly it isn't the *stuff* that has the intentionality. Your brain cells don't refer any more than do the water pipes, bits of paper computer operations, or the homunculus in the Chinese room examples. Searle presents no argument for the assumption that what makes the difference between being able to refer and not being able to refer—or to display any other capacity—is a "finer grained" property of the system that can be captured in a *functional* description. Furthermore it's obvious from Searle's own argument that the nature of the stuff cannot be what is relevant, since the monolingual English speaker who has memorized the formal rules is supposed to be an example of a system made of the *right* stuff and yet it allegedly still lacks the relevant intentionality.

Having said all this, however, one might still want to maintain that in some cases—perhaps in the case of Searle's example—it might be appropriate to say that *nothing* refers, or that the symbols are not being used in a way that refers to something. But if we wanted to deny that these symbols referred, it would be appropriate to ask what licenses us *ever* to say that a symbol refers. There are at least three different approaches to answering that question: Searle's view that it is the nature of the embodiment of the symbol (of the brain substance itself), the traditional functionalist view that it is the *functional role* that the symbol plays in the overall behavior of the system, and the view associated with philosophers like Kripke and Putnam, that it is in the nature of the causal connection that the symbol has with certain past events. The latter two are in fact compatible insofar as specifying the functional role of a symbol in the behavior of a system does not preclude specifying its causal interactions with an environment. It is noteworthy that Searle does not even consider the possibility that a purely formal computational model might constitute an essential part of an adequate theory, where the latter also contained an account of the system's transducers and an account of how the symbols came to acquire the role that they have in the functioning of the system.

Functionalism and reference. The functionalist view is currently the dominant one in both AI and information-processing psychology. In the past, mentalism often assumed that reference was established by relations of similarity; an image referred to a horse if it *looked* sufficiently like a horse. Mediational behaviorism took it to be a simple causal remnant of perception: a brain event referred to a certain object if it shared some of the properties of brain events that occur when that object is perceived. But information-processing psychology has opted for a level of description that deals with the informational, or encoded, aspects of the environment's effect on the organism. On this view it has typically been assumed that what a symbol represents can be seen by examining how the symbol enters into relations with other symbols and with transducers. It is this position that Searle is quite specifically challenging. My own view is that although Searle is right in pointing out that some versions of the functionalist answer are in a certain sense incomplete, he is off the mark both in his diagnosis of where the problem lies and in his prognosis as to just how impoverished a view of mental functioning the cognitivist position will have to settle for (that is, his "weak AI").

The sense in which a functionalist answer might be incomplete is if it failed to take the further step of specifying what it was about the system that *warranted* the ascription of one particular semantic content to the functional states (or to the symbolic expressions that express that state) rather than some other logically possible content. A cognitive theory claims that the system behaves in a certain way *because* certain expressions represent certain things (that is, have a certain *semantic* interpretation). It is, furthermore, essential that it do so: otherwise we would not be able to subsume certain classes of regular behaviors in a single generalization of the sort "the system does X because the state S represents such and such" (for example, the person ran out of the building because he believed that *it was on fire*). (For a discussion of this issue, see Pylyshyn 1980.) But the particular interpretation appears to be extrinsic to the theory inasmuch as the system would behave in exactly the same way without the interpretation. Thus, Searle concludes that it is only *we*, the theorists, who take the expression to represent, say, that the building is on fire. The system doesn't take it to *represent* anything because it literally doesn't know what the expression refers to: only we theorists do. That being the case, the system can't be said to behave in a certain way *because* of what it represents. This is in contrast with the way in which *our* behavior is determined: we *do* behave in certain ways because of what our thoughts are about. And that, according to Searle, adds up to weak AI; that is, a functionalist account in which formal analogues "stands in" for, but themselves neither have, nor explain, mental contents.

The last few steps, however, are non sequiturs. The fact that it was we, the theorists, who provided the interpretation of the expressions doesn't by itself mean that such an interpretation is simply a matter of convenience, or that there is a sense in which the interpretation is ours rather than the system's. Of course it's logically possible that the interpretation is only in the mind of the theorist and that the system behaves the way it does for entirely different reasons. But even if that happened to be true, it wouldn't follow simply from the fact that the AI theorist was the one who came up with the interpretation. Much depends on his reasons for coming up with that interpretation in any case, the question of whether the semantic interpretation resides in the head of the programmer or in the machine is the wrong question to ask. A more relevant question would be: what fixes the semantic interpretation of functional states, or what latitude does the theorist have in assigning a semantic interpretation to the states of the system?

When a computer is viewed as a self-contained device for processing formal symbols, we have a great deal of latitude in assigning semantic interpretations to states. Indeed, we routinely change our interpretation of the computer's functional states, sometimes viewing them as numbers, sometimes as alphabetic characters, sometimes as words or descriptions of a scene, and so on. Even where it is difficult to think of a coherent interpretation that is different from the one the programmer had in mind, such alternatives are always possible in principle. However, if we equip the machine with transducers and allow it to interact freely with both natural and linguistic environments, and if we endow it with the power to make (syntactically specified) inferences, it is anything but obvious what latitude, if any, the theorist (who knows how the transducers operate, and therefore knows what they respond to) would still have in assigning a coherent interpretation to the functional states in such a way as to capture psychologically relevant regularities in behavior.

The role of intuitions. Suppose such connections between the system and the world as mentioned above (and possibly other considerations that no one has yet considered) uniquely constrained the possible interpretations that could be placed on representational states. Would this solve the problem of justifying the ascription of particular semantic contents to these states? Here I suspect that one would run into differences of opinion that may well be unresolvable, simply because they are grounded on different intuitions. For example, there immediately arises the question of whether we possess a privileged interpretation of our own thoughts that must take precedence over such functional analyses. And if so, then there is the further question of whether being *conscious* is what provides the privileged access; and hence the question of what one is to do about the apparent necessity of positing unconscious mental processes. So far as I can see the *only* thing that recommends that particular view is the intuition that, whatever may be true of other creatures, I at least *know* what *my* thoughts refer to because I have direct experiential access to the referents of my thoughts. Even if we did have strong intuitions about such cases, there is good reason to believe that such intuitions should be considered as no more than secondary sources of constraint, whose validity should be judged by how well theoretical systems based on them perform. We cannot take as sacred anyone's intuitions about such things as whether another creature has intentionality—especially when such intuitions rest (as Searle's do, by his own admission) on knowing what the creature (or machine) is *made of* (for instance, Searle is prepared to admit that other creatures might have intentionality if "we can see that the breasts are made of similar stuff to ourselves"). Clearly, intuitions based on nothing but such anthropocentric chauvinism cannot form the foundation of a science of cognition [See "Cognition and Consciousness in Nonhuman Species," *BBS* 1(4) 1978].

A major problem in science—especially in a developing science like cognitive psychology—is to decide what sorts of phenomena "go together," in the sense that they will admit of a uniform set of explanatory principles. Information-processing theories have achieved some success in accounting for aspects of problem solving, language processing, perception, and so on, by deliberately glossing over the conscious-unconscious distinction; by grouping under common principles a wide range of rule-governed processes necessary to account for functioning, independent of whether or not people are aware of them. These theories have also placed to one side questions as to what constitute consciously experienced *qualia* or "raw feels"—dealing only with some of their reliable functional correlates (such as the belief that one is in pain, as opposed to the experience of the pain itself)—and they have to a large extent deliberately avoided the question of what gives symbols their semantics. Because AI has chosen to carve up phenomena in this way, people like Searle are led to conclude that what is being done is weak AI—or the modeling of the abstract functional structure of the brain without regard for what its states represent. Yet there is no reason to think that this program does not in fact lead to strong AI in the end. There is no reason to doubt that at asymptote (for example, when and if a robot is built) the ascription of intentionality to programmed machines will be just as warranted as its ascription to people, and for reasons that have absolutely nothing to do with the issue of consciousness.

What is frequently neglected in discussion of intentionality is that we cannot state with any degree of precision what it is that entitles us to claim that *people* refer (though there are one or two general ideas, such as those discussed above), and therefore that arguments against the intentionality of computers typically reduce to "argument from ignorance." If we knew what it was that warranted our saying that people refer, we might also be in a position to claim that the ascription of semantic content to formal computational expressions—though it is in fact accomplished in practice by "inference to the best explanation"—was in the end warranted in exactly the same way. Humility, if nothing else, should prompt us to admit that there's a lot we don't know about how we ought to describe the capacities of future robots and other computing machines, even when we do know how their electronic circuits operate.

NOTE

1. Current address: Department of Psychology, University of Western Ontario, London, Canada, N6A 5C2.

JERRY A. FODOR

MODULES, FRAMES, FRIDGEONS, SLEEPING DOGS, AND THE MUSIC OF THE SPHERES

There are, it seems to me, two interesting ideas about modularity. The first is the idea that some of our cognitive faculties are modular. The second is the idea that some of our cognitive faculties are not.

By a modular cognitive faculty I mean—for present purposes—an "informationally encapsulated" cognitive faculty. By an informationally encapsulated cognitive faculty I mean one that has access, in the course of its computations, to less than all of the information at the disposal of the organism whose cognitive faculty it is, the restriction on informational access being imposed by relatively unlabile, "architectural" features of mental organization. For example, I think that the persistence of the Muller-Lyer illusion in spite of one's knowledge that it is an illusion strongly suggests that some of the cognitive mechanisms that mediate visual size perception must be informationally encapsulated. You know perfectly well that the lines are the same length, yet it continues to appear to you that they are not. It would seem to follow that some of what you know perfectly well is inaccessible to the cognitive mechanisms that are determining the appearances. If this is the right diagnosis, then it follows that some of those mechanisms are informationally encapsulated.

It is worth emphasizing a sense in which modular cognitive processing is *ipso facto* irrational. After all, by definition modular processing means arriving at conclusions by attending to arbitrarily less than all of the evidence that is relevant and/or by considering arbitrarily fewer than all of the hypotheses that might reasonably be true. Ignoring relevant evidence and overlooking reasonable hypotheses are, however, techniques of belief fixation that are notoriously likely to get you into trouble in the long run. Informational encapsulation is economical; it buys speed and the reduction of computational load by, in effect, delimiting *a priori* the data base and the space of candidate solutions that get surveyed in the course of problem solving. But the price of economy is warrant. The more encapsulated the cognitive mechanisms that mediate the fixation of your beliefs, the worse is your evidence for the beliefs that you have. And, barring skeptical worries of a boring sort, the worse your evidence for your beliefs is, the less the likelihood that your beliefs are true.

Rushing the hurdles and jumping to conclusions is, then, a characteristic pathology of irrational cognitive strategies, and a disease that modular processors have in spades. That, to repeat, is because the data that they consult and the solutions that they contemplate are determined arbitrarily by rigid features of cognitive architecture. But—and here is the point I want to emphasize for present purposes—rational processes have their debilities too; they have their characteristic hangups whose outbreaks are the symptoms of their very rationality. Suppose that, in pursuit of rational belief fixation, you undertake to subject whichever hypotheses might reasonably be true to scrutiny in light of whatever evidence might reasonably be relevant. You then have the problem of how to determine when demands of reason have been satisfied. You have, that is to say, Hamlet's problem: How to tell when to stop thinking.

The frame problem is just Hamlet's problem viewed from an engineer's perspective. You want to make a device that is rational in the sense that its mechanisms of belief fixation are unencapsulated. But you also want the device you make to actually succeed in fixing a belief or two from time to time; you don't want it to hang up the way that Hamlet did. So, on the one hand, you don't want to delimit its computations arbitrarily (as in encapsulated systems); on the other hand, you want these computations to come, somehow, to an end. How is this to be arranged? What is a nonarbitrary strategy for restricting the evidence that should be searched and the hypotheses that should be contemplated in the course of rational belief fixation? I don't know how to answer this question. If I did, I'd have solved the frame problem and I'd be rich and famous.

To be sure, the frame problem isn't always formulated quite so broadly. In the first instance it arises as a rather specialized issue in artificial intelligence: How could one get a robot to appreciate the consequences of its behavior? Action alters the world, and if a system is to perform coherently, it must be able to change its beliefs to accommodate the effects of its activities. But effecting this accommodation surely can't require a wholesale review of each and every prior cognitive commitment in consequence of each and every act the thing performs; a device caught up in thought to that extent would instantly be immobilized. There must be some way of delimiting those beliefs that the consequences of behavior can reasonably be supposed to put in jeopardy; there must be some way of deciding which beliefs should become, as one says, candidates for "updating," and in consequence of which actions.

It is easy to see that this way of putting the frame problem underestimates its generality badly. Despite its provenance in speculative robotology, the frame problem doesn't really have anything in particular to do with action. After all, one's standing cognitive commitments must rationally accommodate to each new state of affairs, whether or not it is a state of affairs that is consequent upon one's own behavior. And the principle holds quite generally that the demands of rationality must somehow be squared with those of feasibility. We must somehow contrive that most of our beliefs correspond to the facts about a changing world. But we must somehow manage to do so without having to put very many of our beliefs at risk at any given time. The frame problem is the problem of understanding how we bring this off; it is, one might say, the problem of how rationality is possible in practice. (If you are still tempted by the thought that the frame problem is interestingly restricted by construing it as specially concerned with how belief conforms to the consequences of behavior, consider the case where the robot we are trying to build is a mechanical scientist, the actions that it performs are experiments, and the design problem is to get the robot's beliefs to rationally accommodate the data that its experiments provide. Here the frame problem is transparently that of finding a general and feasible procedure for altering cognitive commitments in light of empirical contingencies; i.e., it is transparently the general problem of understanding feasible nondemonstrative inference. If experimenting counts as acting—and, after all, why shouldn't it?—then the problem of understanding how the consequences of action are rationally assessed is just the problem of understanding understanding.)

Here is what I have argued so far: Rational mechanisms of belief fixation are *ipso facto* unencapsulated. Unencapsulated mechanisms of belief fixation are *ipso facto* nonarbitrary in their selection of the hypotheses that they evaluate and the evidence that they consult. Mechanisms of belief fixation that are nonarbitrary in these ways are *ipso facto* confronted with Hamlet's problem, which is just the frame problem formulated in blank verse. So, two conclusions:

- The frame problem goes very deep; it goes as deep as the analysis of rationality.
- Outbreaks of the frame problem are symptoms or rational processing; if you are looking at a system that has the frame problem, you can assume that the system is rational at least to the extent of being unencapsulated.

The second of these conclusions is one that I particularly cherish. I used it in *The Modularity of Mind* (1983) as an argument against what I take to be modularity theory gone mad: the idea that modularity is the general case in cognitive architecture, that all cognitive processing is informationally encapsulated. Roughly, the argument went like this: The distinction between the encapsulated mental processes and the rest is—approximately but interestingly—coextensive with the distinction between perception and cognition.

When we look at real, honest-to-God perceptual processes, we find real, honest-to-God informational encapsulation. In parsing, for example, we find a computational mechanism with access only to the acoustics of the input and the body of "background information" that can be formulated in a certain kind of grammar. That is why—in my view, and contrary to much of the received wisdom in psycholinguistics—there are no context effects in parsing. It is also why there is no frame problem in parsing. The question of what evidence the parser should consult in determining the structural description of an utterance is solved arbitrarily and architecturally: Only the acoustics of the input and the grammar are ever available. Because there is no frame problem in parsing, it is one of the few cognitive processes that we have had any serious success in understanding.

In contrast, when we try to build a really smart machine—not a machine that will parse sentences or play chess, but, say, one that will make the breakfast without burning down the house—we get the frame problem straight off. This, I argued in *MOM*, is precisely because smart processes aren't modular. Being smart, being nonmodular, and raising the frame problem all go together. That, in brief, is why, although we have mechanical parsing and mechanical chess playing, we have no machines that will make breakfast except stoves.[1]

In short, that the frame problem breaks out here and there but does not break out everywhere is itself an argument for differences in kind among cognitive mechanisms. We can understand the distribution of outbreaks of the frame problem on the hypothesis that it is the chronic infirmity of rational (hence unencapsulated, hence nonmodular) cognitive systems—so I argued in *MOM*, and so I am prepared to argue still.

Candor requires, however, that I report to you the following: This understanding of the frame problem is not universally shared. In AI especially, the frame problem is widely viewed as a sort of a glitch, for which heuristic processing is the appropriate patch. (The technical vocabulary deployed by analysts of the frame problem has become markedly less beautiful since Shakespeare discussed it in *Hamlet*.) How could this be so? How could the depth, beauty, and urgency of the frame problem have been so widely misperceived? That, really, is what this chapter is about.

What I am inclined to think is this: The frame problem is so ubiquitous, so polymorphous, and so intimately connected with every aspect of the attempt to understand rational nondemonstrative inference that it is quite possible for a practitioner to fail to notice when it is indeed the frame problem that he is working on. It is like the ancient doctrine about the music of the spheres: If you can't hear it, that's because it is everywhere. That would be OK, except that if you are unable to recognize the frame problem when as a matter of fact you are having it, you may suppose that you have solved the frame problem when as a matter of fact you are begging it. Much of the history of the frame problem in AI strikes me as having that character; the discussion that follows concerns a recent and painful example.

In a paper called "We've Been Framed: or, Why AI Is Innocent of the Frame Problem," Drew McDermott (1986) claims that "there is no one problem here; and hence no solution is possible or necessary" (p. 1). The frame problem, it turns out, is a phantom that philosophers have unwittingly conjured up by making a variety of mistakes, which McDermott details and undertakes to rectify.

What philosophers particularly fail to realize, according to McDermott, is that, though no solution of the frame problem is "possible or necessary," nevertheless a solution is up and running in AI. (One wonders how many other impossible and unnecessary problems McDermott and his colleagues have recently solved.) McDermott writes: "In all systems since [1969] . . . programs have used the 'sleeping dog' strategy. They keep track of each situation as a separate database. To reason about *e*, *s*, *i.e. about the result of an event in a situation*, they compute all the effects of *e* in situation *s*, make those changes, and leave the rest of *s* (the 'sleeping dogs') alone." In consequence of the discovery of this sleeping-dogs solution, since 1970 *"no working AI program has ever been bothered at all by the frame problem"* (emphasis in original).

It is, moreover, no accident that the sleeping-dogs strategy works. It is supported by a deep metaphysical truth, viz. that "most events leave most facts untouched" (p. 2): You can rely on metaphysical inertia to carry most of the facts along from one event to the next; being carried along in this way is, as you might say, the unmarked case for facts. Because this is so, you will usually do all right if you leave well enough alone when you update you data base. Given metaphysical inertia, the appropriate epistemic strategy is to assume that nothing changes unless you have a special reason for changing it. Sleeping dogs don't scratch where it doesn't itch, so doesn't the sleeping-dogs strategy solve the frame problem?

No; what it does is convert the frame problem from a problem about belief fixation into a problem about ontology (or, what comes to much the same thing for present purposes, from a problem about belief fixation into a problem about canonical notation.) This wants some spelling out.

As we have seen, the sleeping-dogs strategy depends on assuming that most of the facts don't change from one event to the next. The trouble with that assumption is that whether it is true depends on how you individuate facts. To put it a little more formally: If you want to use a sleeping-dogs algorithm to update you data base, you must first devise a system of canonical representation for the facts. (Algorithms work on facts as represented.) And this system of canonical representation will have to have the following properties:

- It will have to be rich enough to be able to represent all the facts that you propose to specify in the data base.
- The canonical representations of most of the facts must be unchanged by most events. By definition, a sleeping-dogs algorithm will not work unless the canonical notation has this property.

The problem is—indeed, the *frame* problem is—that such notations are a little hard to come by. Oh yes, indeed they are! Consider, for example, the following outbreak of the frame problem.

It has got to work out, on any acceptable model, that when I turn my refrigerator on, certain of my beliefs about the refrigerator and about other things become candidates for getting updated. For example, now that the refrigerator is on, I believe that putting the legumes in the vegetable compartment will keep them cool and crisp. (I did not believe that before I turned the refrigerator on because until I turned the refrigerator on I believed that the refrigerator was off—correctly, we may assume.) Similarly, now that the refrigerator is on, I believe that when the door is opened the light in the refrigerator will go on, that my electricity meter will run slightly faster than it did before, and so forth. On the other hand, it should also fall out of solution of the frame problem that a lot of my beliefs—indeed, most of my beliefs—do not become candidates for updating (and hence don't have to be actively reconsidered) in consequence of my plugging in the fridge: my belief that cats are animate, my belief that Granny was a Bulgarian, my belief that snow is white, and so forth. I want it that most of my beliefs do not become candidates for updating because what I primarily want of my beliefs is that they should correspond to the facts; and, as we have seen, metaphysical inertia guarantees me that most of the facts are unaffected by my turning on the fridge.

Or does it? Consider a certain relational property that physical particles have from time to time: the property of being a fridgeon. I define 'x is a fridgeon at t' as follows: x is a fridgeon at t iff x is a particle at t and my fridge is on at t. It is a consequence of this definition that, when I turn my fridge on, I change the state of every physical particle in the universe; viz., every physical particle becomes a fridgeon. (Turning the fridge off has the reverse effect.) I take it (as does McDermott, so far as I can tell) that talk about facts is intertranslatable with talk about instantiations of properties; thus, when I create ever so many new fridgeons, I also create ever-so-many new facts.

The point is that if you count all these facts about fridgeons, the principle of metaphysical inertia no longer holds even of such homely events as my turning on the fridge. To put the same point less metaphysically and more computationally: If I let the facts about fridgeons into my data base (along with the facts about the crisping compartment and the facts about Granny's ethnic affiliations), pursuing the sleeping-dogs strategy will no longer solve the frame problem. The sleeping-dogs strategy proposes to keep the computational load down by considering as candidates for updating only representations of such facts as an event changes. But now there are billions of facts that change when I plug in the fridge—one fact for each particle, more or less. And there is nothing special about the property of being a fridgeon; it is a triviality to think up as many more such kooky properties as you like.

I repeat the moral: Once you let representations of the kooky properties into the data base, a strategy that says "look just at the facts that change" will buy you nothing; it will commit you to looking at indefinitely many facts.

The moral is not that the sleeping-dogs strategy is wrong; it is that the sleeping-dogs strategy is empty unless we have, together with the strategy, some idea of what is to count as a fact for the purposes at hand. Moreover, this notion of (as we might call it) a *computationally relevant* fact will have to be formalized if we propose to implement the sleeping-dogs strategy as a computational algorithm. Algorithms act on facts only as represented—indeed, only in virtue of the form of their representations. Thus, if we want to keep the kooky facts out of the data base and keep the computationally relevant facts in, we have to find a way of distinguishing kooky facts from computationally relevant ones in virtue of the form of their canonical representations. The frame problem, in its current guise, is thus the problem of formalizing the distinction between kooky facts and kosher ones.

We do not know how to formalize this distinction. For that matter, we don't even know how to draw it. For example, the following ways of drawing it—or of getting out of drawing it—will quite clearly not work:

(a) Being a fridgeon is a relational property; rule it out on those grounds.

Answer: being a father is a relational property too, but we want to be able to come to believe that John is a father when we come to believe that his wife has had a child.

(b) *Fridgeon* is a made-up word. There is no such word as *fridgeon* in English.

Answer: You can't rely on the lexicon of English to solve your metaphysical problems for you. There used to be no such word as *meson* either. Moreover, though there is no such word as *fridgeon*, the expression *x is a particle at t and my fridge is on at t* is perfectly well formed. Since this expression is the definition of *fridgeon*, everything that can be said in English by using *fridgeon* can also be said in English without using it.

(c) Being a fridgeon isn't a real property.

Answer: I'll be damned if I see why not, but have it your way. The frame problem is now the problem of saying what a "real property" is.

In this formulation, by the way, the frame problem has quite a respectable philosophical provenance. Here, for example, is a discussion of Hume's version of the frame problem.

Two things are related by what Hume calls a 'philosophical' relation if any relational statement at all is true of them. All relations are 'philosophical' relations. But according to Hume there are also some 'natural' relations between things. One thing is naturally related to another if the thought of the first naturally leads the mind to the thought of the other. If we see no obvious connection between two things, e.g. my raising my arm now . . . and the death of a particular man in Abyssinia 33,118 years ago, we are likely to say 'there is no relation at all between these two events.' [But] of course there are many 'philosophical' relations between these two events—spatial and temporal relations, for example. (Stroud 1977, p. 89)

Hume thought that the only natural relations are contiguity, causation, and resemblance. Since the relation between my closing the fridge and some particle's becoming a fridgeon is an instance of none of these, Hume would presumably have held that the fact that the particle becomes a fridgeon is a merely 'philosophical' fact, hence not a 'psychologically real' fact. (It is psychological rather than ontological reality that, according to Hume, merely philosophical relations lack.) So it would turn out, on Hume's story, that the fact that a particle becomes a fridgeon isn't the sort of fact that data bases should keep track of.

If Hume is right about which relations are the natural ones, this will do as a solution to the frame problem except that Hume has no workable account of the relations of causation, resemblance, and contiguity—certainly no account precise enough to formalize. If, however, Hume is in that bind, so are we.

(d) Nobody actually has concepts like "fridgeon," so you don't have to worry about such concepts when you build your model of the mind.

Answer: This is another way of begging the frame problem, another way of mistaking a formulation of the problem for its solution.

Everybody has an infinity of concepts, corresponding roughly to the open sentences of English. According to all known theories, the way a person keeps an infinity of concepts in a finite head is this: He stores a finite primitive basis and a finite compositional mechanism, and the recursive application of the latter to the former specifies the infinite conceptual repertoire. The present problem is that there are arbitrarily many kooky concepts—like "fridgeon"—

which can be defined with the same apparatus that you use to define perfectly kosher concepts like "vegetable crisper" or "Bulgarian grandmother." That is, the same basic concepts that I used to define *fridgeon*, and the same logical syntax, are needed to define nonkooky concepts that people actually do entertain. Thus, the problem—the frame problem—is to find a rule that will keep the kooky concepts out while letting the nonkooky concepts in.

Lacking a solution to this problem, you cannot implement a sleeping-dogs "solution" to the frame problem; it will not run. It will not run because, at each event, it will be required to update indefinitely many beliefs about the distribution of kooky properties.

(e) But McDermott says that solutions to the frame problem have actually been implemented; that nobody in AI has had to worry about the frame problem since way back in 1969. So something must be wrong with your argument.

Answer: The programs run because the counterexamples are never confronted. The programmer decides, case by case, which properties get specified in the data base; but the decision is unsystematic and unprincipled. For example, no data base will be allowed to include information about the distribution of fridgeons; however, as we have seen, there appears to be no disciplined way to justify the exclusion and no way to implement it that doesn't involve excluding indefinitely many computationally relevant concepts as well.

There is a price to be paid for failing to face the frame problem. The conceptual repertoires with which AI systems are allowed to operate exclude kooky and kosher concepts indiscriminately. They are therefore grossly impoverished in comparison with the conceptual repertoires of really intelligent systems like you and me. The result (one of the worst-kept secrets in the world, I should think) is that these artificially intelligent systems—the ones that have been running since 1970 "without ever being bothered by the frame problem"—are, by any reasonable standard, ludicrously stupid.

So there is a dilemma: You build a canonical notation that is rich enough to express the concepts available to a smart system (a canonical notation as rich as English, say) and it will thereby let the fridgeons in. (*Fridgeon* is, as we've seen, definable in English.) Or you build a canonical notation that is restrictive enough to keep the fridgeons out, and it will thereby fail to express concepts that smart systems need. The frame problem now emerges as the problem of breaking this dilemma. In the absence of a solution to the frame problem, the practice in AI has been to opt, implicitly, for the second horn and live with the consequences, viz., dumb machines.

You may be beginning to wonder what is actually going on here. Well, because the frame problem is just the problem of nondemonstrative inference, a good way to see what is going on is to think about how the sleeping-dog strategy works when it is applied to confirmation in science. Science is our best case of the systematic pursuit of knowledge through nondemonstrative inference; thus, if the frame problem were a normal symptom of rational practice, one would expect to find its traces "writ large" in the methodology of science—as indeed we do. Looked at from this perspective, the frame problem is that of making science cumulative; it is the problem of localizing, as much as possible, the impact of new data on previously received bodies of theory. In science, as in private practice, rationality gets nowhere if each new fact occasions a wholesale revision of prior commitments. So, corresponding to the sleeping-dogs strategy in AI, we have a principle of "conservatism" in scientific methodology, a principle that says "alter the minimum possible amount of prior theory as you go about trying to accommodate new data."[2]

While it is widely agreed that conservatism, in this sense, is constitutive of rational scientific practice, the maxim as I've just stated it doesn't amount to anything like a formal principle for theory choice (just as the sleeping-dogs strategy as McDermott states it doesn't constitute anything like an algorithm for updating data bases). You could, of course, *make* the principle of conservatism into a formal evaluation metric by specifying (a) a canonical notation for writing the scientific theories that you propose to evaluate in and (b) a costing system that formalizes the notion 'most conservative theory change' (e.g., the most conservative change in a theory is the one that alters the fewest symbols in its canonical representation). Given (a) and (b), we would have an important fragment of a mechanical evaluation procedure for science. That would be a nice thing for us to have, so why doesn't somebody go and build us one?

Well, not just any canonical notation will do the job. To do the job, you have to build a notation such that (relative to the costing system) the (intuitively) most conservative revision of a theory does indeed come out to be the simplest one when the theory is canonically represented. (For example, if your costing system says "choose the alteration that can be specified in the smallest number of canonical symbols," then your notation has to have the property that the intuitively most conservative alteration actually does come out shortest when the theory is in canonical form.) Of course, nobody knows how to construct a notation with that agreeable property—just as nobody knows how to construct a notation for facts such that, under that notation, most facts are unchanged by most events.

It is not surprising that such notation don't grow on trees. If somebody developed a vocabulary for writing scientific theories that had the property that the shortest description of the world in that vocabulary was always the intuitively best theory of the world available, that would mean that the notation would give formal expression to our most favored inductive estimate of the world's taxonomic structure by specifying the categories in terms of which we take it that the world should be described. Well, when we have an inductive estimate of the world's taxonomic structure that is good enough to permit formal expression, and a canonical vocabulary to formulate the taxonomy in, most of science will be finished.

Similarly, *mutatis mutandis*, in cognitive theory. A notation adequate to support an implemented sleeping-dogs algorithm would be one that would represent as facts only what we commonsensically take to really be facts (the ethnicity of grandmothers, the temperature in the vegetable crisper, but not the current distribution of fridgeons). In effect, the notation would give formal expression to our commonsense estimate of the world's taxonomic structure. Well, when we have a rigorous account of our commonsense estimate of the world's taxonomic structure, and a notation to express it in, most of *cognitive* science will be finished.

In short, there is no formal conservatism principle for science for much the same sort of reason that there is no workable sleeping-dogs algorithm for AI. Basically, the solution of both problems requires a notation that formalizes our intuitions about inductive relevance. There is, however, the following asymmetry: We can do science perfectly well without having a formal theory of nondemonstrative inference; that is, we can do science perfectly well without solving the frame problem. That is because doing science doesn't require mechanical scientists; we have us instead. However, we can't do AI perfectly well without having mechanical intelligence; doing AI perfectly well just *is* having mechanical intelligence. Thus, we can't do AI without solving the frame problem. But we don't know how to solve the frame problem. That, in a nutshell, is why, although science works, AI doesn't. Or, to put it more in the context of modularity theory, that is why, though we are sort of starting to have some ideas about encapsulated nondemonstrative inference, we have no ideas about unencapsulated nondemonstrative inference that one could ask an adult to take seriously.

I reiterate the main point: The frame problem and the problem of formalizing our intuitions about inductive relevance are, in every important respect, the same thing. It is just as well, perhaps, that people working on the frame problem in AI are unaware that this is so. One imagines the expression of horror that flickers across their CRT-illuminated faces as the awful facts sink in. What could they do but "down-tool" and become philosophers? One feels for them. Just think of the cut in pay!

God, according to Einstein, does not play dice with the world. Well, maybe; but He sure is into shell games. If you do not understand the logical geography of the frame problem, you will only succeed in pushing it around from one shell to the next, never managing to locate it for long enough to have a chance of solving it. This is, so far as I can see, pretty much the history of the frame problem in AI, which is a major reason why a lot of AI work, when viewed as cognitive theory, strikes one as so thin. The frame problem— to say it one last time—is just the problem of unencapsulated nondemonstrative inference, and the problem of unencapsulated nondemonstrative inference is, to all intents and purposes, the problem of how the cognitive mind works. I am sorry that MacDermott is out of temper with philosophers; but, frankly, the frame problem is too important to leave it to the hackers.

We are really going to have to learn to make progress working together; the alternative is to make fools of ourselves working separately.

NOTES

1. Playing chess is not a perceptual process, so why is it modular? Some processes are modular by brute force and some are modular in the nature of things. Parsing is a case of the former kind; there is relevant information in the context, but the architecture of the mind doesn't let the parser use it. Chess playing, by contrast, is modular in the sense that only a very restricted body of background information (call it chess theory) is relevant to rational play even in principle. This second kind of modularity, precisely because it stems from the nature of the task rather than the architecture of the mind, isn't of much theoretical interest. It is interesting to the engineer, however, since informational encapsulation makes for feasible simulation regardless of what the source of the encapsulation may be.

To put it in a nutshell: On the present view, the natural candidates for simulation are the modular systems and the expert systems. This is, however, cold comfort; I doubt that there are more than a handful of the first, and I think that there are hardly any of the second.

2. Nothing is perfect, analogies least of all. Philosophers of science usually view conservatism as a principle for evaluating scientific theories, not as tactic for inventing or revising them; it is part of the "logic of confirmation," as one says, rather than the "logic of discovery." I'll talk that way too in what follows, but if you want to understand how science works it is usually unwise to push this distinction very hard. In the present case, not only do we think it rational to prefer the most conservative revision of theory *ceteris paribus*; we also think it rational to try the conservative revisions first. When conservatism is viewed in this way, the analogy to the sleeping-dogs solution of the frame problem is seen to be very close indeed.

DANIEL DENNETT

ARTIFICIAL INTELLIGENCE AS PHILOSOPHY AND AS PSYCHOLOGY

Philosophers of mind have been interested in computers since their arrival a generation ago, but for the most part they have been interested only in the most abstract questions of principle, and have kept actual machines at arm's length and actual programs in soft focus. Had they chosen to take a closer look at the details I do not think they would have found much of philosophic interest until fairly recently, but recent work in Artificial Intelligence, or AI, promises to have a much more variegated impact on philosophy, and so, quite appropriately, philosophers have begun responding with interest to the bold manifestos of the Artificial Intelligentsia.[1] My goal in this chapter is to provide a sort of travel guide to philosophers pursuing this interest. It is well known that amateur travelers in strange lands often ludicrously miscomprehend what they see, and enthusiastically report wonders and monstrosities that later investigations prove never to have existed, while overlooking genuine novelties of the greatest importance. Having myself fallen prey to a variety of misconceptions about AI, and wasted a good deal of time and energy pursuing chimaeras, I would like to alert other philosophers to some of these pitfalls of interpretation. Since I am still acutely conscious of my own amateur status as an observer of AI, I must acknowledge at the outset that my vision of what is going on in AI, what is important and why, is almost certainly still somewhat untrustworthy. There is much in AI that I have not read, and much that I have read but not understood. So traveler, beware; take along any other maps you can find, and listen critically to the natives.

The interest of philosophers of mind in Artificial Intelligence comes as no surprise to many tough-minded experimental psychologists, for from their point of view the two fields look very much alike: there are the same broad generalizations and bold extrapolations, the same blithe indifference to the hard-won data of the experimentalist, the same appeal to the deliverances of casual introspection and conceptual analysis, the aprioristic reasonings about what is impossible in principle or what must be the case in psychology. The only apparent difference between the two fields, such a psychologist might say, is that the AI worker pulls his armchair up to a console. I will argue that this observation is largely justified, but should not in most regards be viewed as a criticism. There is much work for the armchair psychologist to do, and a computer console has proven a useful tool in this work.

Psychology turns out to be very difficult. The task of psychology is to explain human perception, learning, cognition, and so forth in terms that will ultimately unite psychological theory to physiology in one way or another, and there are two broad strategies one could adopt: a *bottom-up* strategy that starts with some basic and well-defined unit or theoretical atom for psychology, and builds these atoms into molecules and larger aggregates that can account for the complex phenomena we all observe, or a *top-down* strategy that begins with a more abstract decomposition of the highest levels of psychological organization, and hopes to analyze these into more and more detailed smaller systems or processes until finally one arrives at elements familiar to the biologists. It is a commonplace that both endeavors could and should proceed simultaneously, but there is now abundant evidence that the bottom-up strategy in psychology is unlikely to prove very fruitful. The two best developed attempts at bottom-up psychology are stimulus-response behaviorism and what we might call "neuron signal physiological psychology", and both are now widely regarded as stymied, the former because stimuli and responses prove not to be perspicuously chosen atoms, the latter because even if synapses and impulse trains are perfectly good atoms, there are just too many of them, and their interactions are too complex to study once one abandons the afferent and efferent peripheries and tries to make sense of the crucial center (see Chapters 4 and 5, Dennett 1978).[2] Bottom-up strategies have not proved notably fruitful in the early development of other sciences, in chemistry and biology for instance, and so psychologists are only following the lead of "mature" sciences if they turn to the top-down approach. Within that broad strategy there are a variety of starting points that can be ordered in an array. Faced with the practical impossibility of answering the empirical questions of psychology by brute inspection (how *in fact* does the nervous system accomplish X or Y or Z?), psychologists ask themselves an easier preliminary question:

How could any system (with features A, B, C, . . .) possibly accomplish X?[3]

This sort of question is easier because it is "less empirical"; it is an *engineering* question, a quest for a solution (*any* solution) rather than a discovery. Seeking an answer to such a question can sometimes lead to the discovery of general constraints on all solutions (including of course nature's as yet unknown solution), and therein lies the value of this style of aprioristic theorizing. Once one decides to do psychology this way, one can choose a degree of empirical difficulty for one's question by filling in the blanks in the question schema above.[4] The more empirical constraints one puts on the description of the system, or on the description of the requisite behavior, the greater the claim to "psychological reality" one's answer must make. For instance, one can ask how any neuronal network with such-and-such physical features could *possibly* accomplish human color discriminations, or we can ask how any finite system could *possibly* subserve the acquisition of a natural language, or one can ask how human memory could *possibly* be so organized so as to make it so relatively easy for us to answer questions like "Have you ever ridden an antelope?" and so relatively hard to answer "What did you have for breakfast last Tuesday?" Or, one can ask, with Kant, how anything at all could *possibly* experience or know anything at all. Pure epistemology thus viewed, for instance, is simply the limiting case of the psychologists' quest, and is *prima facie* no less valuable to *psychology* for being so neutral with regard to empirical details. Some such questions are of course better designed to yield good answers than others, but *properly carried out*, any such investigation can yield constraints that bind all more data-enriched investigations.

AI workers can pitch their investigations at any level of empirical difficulty they wish; at Carnegie Mellon University, for instance, much is made of paying careful attention to experimental data on human performance, and attempting to model human performance closely. Other workers in AI are less concerned with that degree of psychological reality and have engaged in a more abstract version of AI. There is much that is of value and interest to psychology at the empirical end of the spectrum, but I want to claim that AI is better viewed as sharing with traditional epistemology the status of being a most general, most abstract asking of the top-down question: how is knowledge possible?[5] It has seemed to some philosophers that AI cannot be plausibly so construed because it takes on an additional burden: it restricts itself to *mechanistic* solutions, and hence its domain is not the Kantian domain of all possible modes of intelligence, but just all possible mechanistically realizable modes of intelligence. This, it is claimed, would beg the question against vitalists, dualists and other anti-mechanists. But as I have argued elsewhere, the mechanism requirement of AI is not an additional constraint of any moment, for if psychology is possible at all, and if Church's thesis is true, the constraint of mechanism is no more severe than the constraint against begging the question in psychology, and who would wish to evade that? (See Chapter 5, Dennett 1978).[6]

So I am claiming that AI shares with philosophy (in particular, with epistemology and philosophy of mind) the status of most abstract investigation of the principles of psychology. But it shares with psychology *in distinction from philosophy* a typical tactic in *answering* its questions. In AI or cognitive psychology the typical attempt to answer a *general* top-down question consists in designing a *particular* system that does, or appears to do, the relevant job, and then considering which of its features are necessary not just to one's particular system but to any such system. Philosophers have generally shunned such elaborate system-designing in favor of more doggedly general inquiry. This is perhaps the major difference between AI and "pure" philosophical approaches to the same questions, and it is one of my purposes here to exhibit some of the relative strengths and weaknesses of the two approaches.

The system-design approach that is common to AI and other styles of top-down psychology is beset by a variety of dangers of which these four are perhaps the chief:

(1) Designing a system with component subsystems whose stipulated capacities are *miraculous* given the constraints one is accepting. (E.g., positing more information-processing in a component than the relevant time and matter will allow, or, at a more abstract level of engineering incoherence, positing a subsystem whose duties would require it to be more "intelligent" or "knowledgeable" than the supersystem of which it is to be a part.)

(2) Mistaking *conditional* necessities of one's particular solution for completely general constraints (a trivial example would be proclaiming that brains use LISP; less trivial examples require careful elucidation).

(3) Restricting oneself artificially to the design of a subsystem (e.g., a depth perceiver or sentence parser) and concocting a solution that is systematically incapable of being grafted onto the other subsystems of a whole cognitive creature.

(4) Restricting the performance of one's system to an artificially small part of the "natural" domain of that system and providing no efficient or plausible way for the system to be enlarged.

These dangers are altogether familiar to AI, but are just as common, *if harder to diagnose conclusively*, in other approaches to psychology. Consider danger (1): both Freud's ego subsystem and J. J. Gibson's invariance-sensitive perceptual "tuning forks" have been *charged* with miraculous capacities. Danger (2): behaviorists have been *charged* with illicitly extrapolating from pigeon-necessities to people-necessities, and it is often claimed that what the person's eye tells the person's brain. Danger (3): it is notoriously hard to see how Chomsky's early *syntax*-driven system could interact with semantic components to produce or comprehend purposeful speech. Danger (4): it is hard to see how some models of nonsense-syllable rote memorization could be enlarged to handle similar but more sophisticated memory tasks. It is one of the great strengths of AI that when one of its products succumbs to any of these dangers this can usually be quite conclusively demonstrated.

I now have triangulated AI with respect to both philosophy and psychology (as my title suggested I would): AI can be (and should often be taken to be) as abstract and "unempirical" as philosophy in the questions it attempts to answer, but at the same time, it should be as explicit and particularistic in its models as psychology at its best. Thus one might learn as much of value to psychology or epistemology from a *particular* but highly *un*realistic AI model as one could learn from a detailed psychology of, say, Martians. A good psychology of Martians, however unlike us they might be, would certainly yield general principles of psychology or epistemology applicable to human beings. Now before turning to the all important question "What, so conceived, has AI accomplished?" I want to consider briefly some misinterpretations of AI that my sketch of it so far does not protect us from.

Since we are viewing AI as a species of top-down cognitive psychology, it is tempting to suppose that the decomposition of function in a computer is intended by AI to be somehow isomorphic to the decomposition of function in a brain. One learns of vast programs made up of literally billions of basic computer events and somehow so organized as to produce a simulacrum of human intelligence, and it is altogether natural to suppose that since the brain is known to be composed of billions of tiny functioning parts, and since there is a *gap of ignorance* between our understanding of intelligent human behavior and our understanding of those tiny parts, the ultimate, millenial goal of AI must be to provide a hierarchical breakdown of parts in the computer that will mirror or be isomorphic to some hard-to-discover hierarchical breakdown of brain-event parts. The familiar theme of "organs made of tissues made of cells made of molecules made of atoms" is to be matched, one might suppose, in electronic hardware terms. In the thrall of this picture one might be discouraged to learn that some functional parts of the nervous system do not seem to function in the digital way the atomic functioning parts in computers do. The standard response to this worry would be that one had looked too deep in the computer (this is sometimes called the "grain problem"). The computer is a digital device at bottom, but a digital device can simulate an "analogue" device to any degree of continuity you desire, and at a higher level of aggregation in the computer one may find the analogue elements that are mappable onto the non-digital brain parts. As many writers have observed,[7] we cannot gauge the psychological reality of a model until we are given the commentary on the model that tells us which features of the model are intended to mirror real saliencies in nature, and which are either backstage expediters of the modeling or sheer inadvertent detail. (In the Eighteenth Century, scientists built beautiful brass clockwork models of the solar system called orreries. The *gears* of an orrery are not intended to represent anything real in the firmament, nor are the reflections of one brass globe in another.) When one looks at AI programs in detail one sees mountains of digital calculation or "number crunching"; if this looks terribly un-biological, this is to be excused since that part of the model's structure is to be viewed as backstage, not part of the model we are supposed to compare with nature.

This story is fine in principle, I think, and the day may come when this imagined isomorphism down to the neuronal level (but not backstage) is proclaimed, but in fact we see nothing remotely like this in current AI work. We see instead models that diverge from nature *very* early on the downward path. AI programs typically model relatively high-level cognitive features, such as concept learning or revision of goals or beliefs, and it does indeed often take millions of basic computer events to simulate just a handful of these *intended model features*—but no one really knows or cares what these basic events are, for no one supposes that *any* of the saliencies in the mass of activity that subserves the intended features are to be taken seriously as psychology or physiology. The psychological reality of an AI program is thus usually intended to be only skin deep; only the highest levels of program description and commentary are to be counted as the model.

The *thin*ness of the psychological reality of AI models is obscured for the uninitiated by a particularly misleading feature of most of the AI programs that get into the limelight. What especially attracts audiences and evokes wonder is the marvelous verisimilitude of some of the programs. Consider this excerpt of conversation (minus the programmer's excellent commentary) between Terry Winograd's SHRDLU and its interlocutor. SHRDLU is a program that lives in an imaginary "block world" where it can manipulate colored blocks on a table in response to commands and answer questions about its life in this world. Computer responses are capitalized.

Had you touched any pyramid before you put the green one on the little cube?

YES, THE GREEN ONE.

When did you pick it up?

WHILE I WAS STACKING UP THE RED CUBE, A LARGE RED BLOCK AND A LARGE GREEN CUBE.

Why?

TO GET RID OF IT.

Why did you do that?

TO CLEAR OFF THE RED CUBE.

Why did you clear off that cube?

TO PUT IT ON A LARGE GREEN CUBE.

Why did you do that?

BECAUSE YOU ASKED ME TO.[8]

When SHRDLU replies to the last question with "Because you asked me to," one can hardly help being struck by the apparent *humanity* of the response—"SHRDLU is *one of us!*" it is tempting to exclaim. If one is naive, one will be awestruck; if one is not, one will still be titillated by the illusion, for that is largely what it is. SHRDLU's response, though perfectly appropriate to the occasion (and not by coincidence!) is "canned." Winograd has simply given SHRDLU this whole sentence to print at times like these. If a child gave SHRDLU's response we would naturally expect its behavior to manifest a general capacity which might also reveal itself by producing the response: "Because you told me to," or, "Because that's what I was asked to do," or on another occasion: "Because I felt like it," or "Because your assistant told me to," but these are dimensions of subtlety beyond SHRDLU.[9] Its behavior is remarkably versatile, but it does not reveal a rich knowledge of interpersonal relations, of the difference between requests and orders, of being cooperative with other people under appropriate circumstances. (It should be added that Winograd's paper makes it very explicit where and to what extent he is canning SHRDLU's responses, so anyone who feels cheated by SHRDLU has simply not read Winograd. Other natural language programs do not rely on canned responses, or rely on them to a mimimal extent.)

The fact remains, however, that much of the antagonism to AI is due to resentment and distrust engendered by such legerdemain. Why do AI people use these tricks? For many reasons. First, they need to get some tell-tale response back from the program and it is as easy to can a mnemonically vivid and "natural" response as something more sober, technical and understated (perhaps: "REASON: PRIOR COMMAND TO DO THAT"). Second, in Winograd's case he was attempting to reveal the *minimal* conditions for correct analysis of certain linguistic forms (note all the "problems" of pronominal antecedents in the sentences displayed), so "natural" language *output* to reveal correct analysis of natural language *input* was entirely appropriate. Third, AI people put canned responses in their programs because it is fun. It is fun to amuse one's colleagues, who are not fooled of course, and it is especially fun to bamboozle the outsiders. As an outsider, one must learn to be properly unimpressed by AI verisimilitude, as one is by the chemist's dazzling forest of glass tubing, or the angry mouths full of teeth painted on World War II fighter planes. (Joseph Weizenbaum's famous ELIZA program,[10] the computer "psychotherapist" who apparently listens so wisely and sympathetically to one's problems, is intended in part as an antidote to the enthusiasm generated by AI verisimilitude. It is almost all clever canning, and is not a psychologically realistic model of anything, but rather a demonstration of how easily one can be gulled into attributing too much to a program. It exploits syntactic landmarks in one's input with nothing approaching genuine understanding, but it makes a good show of comprehension nevertheless. One might say it was a plausible model of a Wernicke's aphasic, who can babble on with well-formed and even semantically appropriate responses to his interlocutor, sometimes sustaining the illusion of comprehension for quite a while.)

The AI community pays a price for this misleading if fascinating fun, not only by contributing to the image of AI people as tricksters and hackers, but by fueling more serious misconceptions of the point of AI research. For instance, Winograd's real contribution in SHRDLU is *not* that he has produced an English speaker and understander that is psychologically realistic at many different levels of analysis (though that is what the verisimilitude strongly suggests, and what a lot of the fanfare—for which Winograd is not responsible—has assumed), but that he has explored some of the deepest demands on any system that can take direction (in a natural language), plan, change the world, and keep track of the changes wrought or contemplated, and in the course of this exploration he has clarified the problems and proposed ingenious and plausible *partial* solutions to them. The real contribution in Winograd's work stands quite unimpeached by the perfectly true but irrelevant charge that SHRDLU doesn't have a *rich* or human understanding of most of the words in its very restricted vocabulary, or is terribly slow.

In fact, paying so much attention to the performance of SHRDLU (and similar systems) reveals a failure to recognize that AI programs are not *empirical* experiments but *thought*-experiments prosthetically regulated by computers. Some AI people have recently become fond of describing their discipline as "experimental epistemology." This unfortunate term should make a philosopher's blood boil, but if AI called itself thought-experimental epistemology (or even better: *Gedanken*-experimental epistemology) philosophers ought to be reassured. The questions asked and answered by the thought-experiments of AI are about whether or not one can obtain certain sorts of information processing—recognition, inference, control of various sorts, for instance—from certain sorts of designs. Often the answer is no. The process of elimination looms large in AI. Relatively plausible schemes are explored far enough to make it clear that they are utterly incapable of delivering the requisite behavior, and learning this is important progress, even if it doesn't result in a mind-boggling robot.

The hardware realizations of AI are almost gratuitous. Like dropping the cannonballs off the Leaning Tower of Pisa, they are demonstrations that are superfluous to those who have understood the argument, however persuasive they are to the rest. Are computers then irrelevant to AI? "In principle" they are irrelevant (in the same sense of "in principle," diagrams on the blackboard are in principle unnecessary to teaching geometry), but in practice they are not. I earlier described them as "prosthetic regulators" of thought-experiments. What I meant was this: it is notoriously difficult to keep wishful thinking out of one's thought-experiments; computer simulation *forces* one to recognize all the costs of one's imagined design. As Pylyshyn observes, "What is needed is . . . a technical language with which to discipline one's imagination."[11] The discipline provided by computers is undeniable (and especially palpable to the beginning programmer). It is both a good thing—for the reasons just stated—and a bad thing. Perhaps you have known a person so steeped in, say, playing bridge, that his entire life becomes in his eyes a series of finesses, end plays and cross-ruffs. Every morning he draws life's trumps and whenever he can see the end of a project he views it as a laydown. Computer languages seem to have a similar effect on people who become fluent in them. Although I won't try to prove it by citing examples, I think it is quite obvious that the "technical language" Pylyshyn speaks of can cripple an imagination in the process of disciplining it.[12]

It has been said so often that computers have huge effects on their users' imaginations that one can easily lose sight of one of the most obvious but still underrated ways in which computers achieve this effect, and that is the sheer speed of computers. Before computers came along the theoretician was strongly constrained to ignore the possibility of truly massive and complex processes in psychology because it was hard to see how such processes could fail to *appear* at worst mechanical and cumbersome, at best vegetatively slow, and of course a hallmark of mentality is its swiftness. One might say that the speed of thought defines the upper bound of subjective "fast," the way the speed of light defines the upper bound of objective "fast." Now suppose there had never been any computers but that somehow (by magic, presumably) Kenneth Colby had managed to dream up these flow charts as a proposed model of a part of human organization in paranoia. (The flow charts are from his book, *Artificial Paranoia*, Pergamon, 1975; figure 7.1 represents the main program; figures 7.2 and 7.3 are blow-ups of details of the main program.) It is obvious to everyone, even Colby I think, that this is a vastly oversimplified model of paranoia, but had there not been computers to show us how all this processing and much much more can occur in a twinkling, we would be inclined to dismiss the proposal immediately as altogether too clanking and inorganic, a Rube Goldberg machine. Most programs look like that in slow motion (hand simulation) but speeded up they often reveal a dexterity and grace that appears natural, and this grace is entirely undetectable via a slow analysis of the program (cf. time-lapse photography of plants growing and buds opening). The grace in operation of AI programs may be mere illusion.

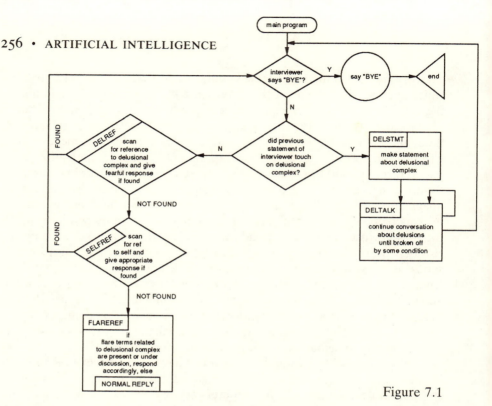

Figure 7.1

Perhaps nature is graceful *all the way down,* but for better or for worse, computer speed has liberated the imagination of theoreticians by opening up the possibility and plausibility of very complex interactive information processes playing a role in the production of cognitive events so swift as to be atomic to introspection.

At last I turn to the important question. Suppose that AI is viewed as I recommend, as a most abstract inquiry into the possibility of intelligence or knowledge. Has it solved any very general problems or discovered any very important constraints or principles? I think the answer is a qualified yes. In particular, I think AI has broken the back of an argument that has bedeviled philosophers and psychologists for over two hundred years. Here is a skeletal version of it: *First,* the only psychology that could possibly succeed in explaining the complexities of human activity must posit internal representations. This premise has been deemed obvious by just about everyone except the radical behaviorists (both in psychology and philosophy—both Watson and Skinner, and Ryle and Malcolm). Descartes doubted almost everything *but* this. For the British Empiricists, the internal representations were called ideas, sensations, impressions; more recently psychologists have talked of hypotheses, maps, schemas, images, propositions, engrams, neural signals, even holograms and whole innate theories. So the first premise is quite invulnerable, or at any rate it has an impressive mandate (see Chapter 6,

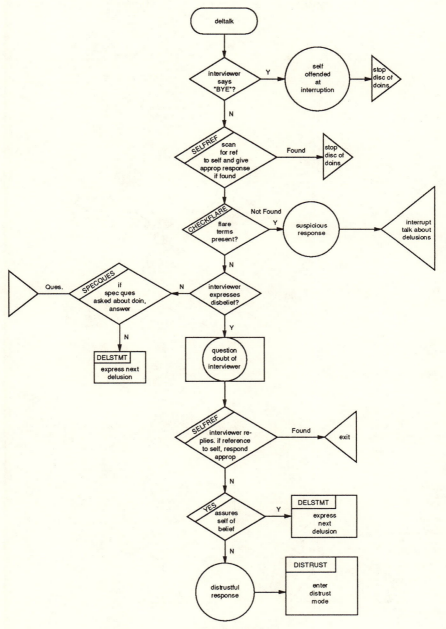

Figure 7.2

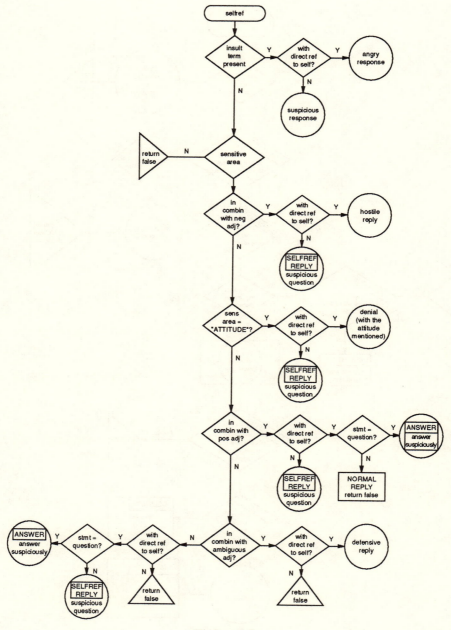

Figure 7.3

Dennett 1978). But, *second*, nothing is intrinsically a representation of any-thing; something is a representation only *for* or *to* someone; any represen-tation or system of representations thus requires at least one *user* or *interpreter* of the representation who is external to it. An such interpreter must have a variety of psychological or intentional traits (see Chapter 1, Dennett 1978): it must be capable of a variety of *comprehension*, and must have beliefs and goals (so it can *use* the representation to *inform* itself and thus assist it in achieving its goals). Such an interpreter is then a sort of homunculus.

Therefore, psychology *without* homunculi is impossible. But psychology *with* homunculi is doomed to circularity or infinite regress, so psychology is impossible.

The argument given is a relatively abstract version of a familiar group of problems. For instance, it seems (to many) that we cannot account for perception unless we suppose it provides us with an internal image (or model or map) of the external world, and yet what good would that image do us unless we have an inner eye to perceive it, and how are we to explain *its* capacity for perception? It also seems (to many) that understanding a heard sentence must be somehow *translating* it into some internal message, but how will this message in turn be understood: by translating it into something else? The problem is an old one, and let's call it *Hume's Problem*, for while he did not state it explicitly, he appreciated its force and strove mightily to escape its clutches. Hume's internal representations were impressions and ideas, and he wisely shunned the notion of an inner *self* that would intelligently *manip-ulate* these items, but this left him with the necessity of getting the ideas and impressions to "think for themselves." The result was his theory of the self as a "bundle" of (nothing but) impressions and ideas. He attempted to set these impressions and ideas into dynamic interaction by positing various as-sociationistic links, so that each succeeding idea in the stream of consciousness dragged its successor onto the stage according to one or another principle, all without benefit of intelligent *supervision*. It didn't work, of course. It couldn't conceivably work, and Hume's failure is plausibly viewed as the harbinger of doom for any remotely analogous enterprise. On the one hand, how could *any* theory of psychology make sense of representations that *un-derstand themselves*, and on the other, how could *any* theory of psychology avoid regress or circularity if it posits at least one representation-understander in addition to the representations?

Now no doubt some philosophers and psychologists who have appealed to internal representations over the years have believed in their hearts that somehow the force of this argument could be blunted, that Hume's problem could be solved, but I am sure no one had the slightest idea *how to do this* until AI and the notion of data-structures came along. Data-structures may or may not be biologically or psychologically realistic representations, but they are, if not living, breathing examples, at least clanking, functioning examples of representations that can be said in the requisite sense to understand themselves.[13]

How this is accomplished can be metaphorically described (and any talk about internal representations is bound to have a large element of metaphor in it) by elaborating our description (see Chapter 5, Dennett 1978) of AI as a top-down theoretical inquiry. One starts, in AI, with a specification of a whole person or cognitive organism—what I call, more neutrally, an intentional system (see Chapter 1, Dennett 1978)—or some artificial segment of that person's abilities (e.g., chess-playing, answering questions about baseball) and then breaks that largest intentional system into an organization of subsystems, each of which could itself be viewed as an intentional system (with its own specialized beliefs and desires) and hence as formally a homunculus. In fact, homunculus talk is ubiquitous in AI, and almost always illuminating. AI homunculi talk to each other, wrest control from each other, volunteer, subcontract, supervise, and even kill. There seems no better way of describing what is going on.[14] Homunculi are *bogeymen* only if they duplicate *entire* the talents they are rung in to explain (a special case of danger (1)). If one can get a team or committee of *relatively* ignorant, narrow-minded, blind homunculi to produce the intelligent behavior of the whole, this is progress. A flow chart is typically the organizational chart of a committee of homunculi (investigators, librarians, accountants, executives); each box specifies a homunculus by prescribing a function *without saying how it is to be accomplished* (one says, in effect: put a little man in there to do the job). If we then look closer at the individual boxes we see that the function of each is accomplished by subdividing it via another flow chart into still smaller, more stupid homunculi. Eventually this nesting of boxes within boxes lands you with homunculi so stupid (all they have to do is remember whether to say yes or no when asked) that they can be, as one says, "replaced by a machine." One *discharges* fancy homunculi from one's scheme by organizing armies of such idiots to do the work.

When homunculi at a level interact, they do so by sending *messages*, and each homunculus has representations that it uses to execute its functions. Thus typical AI discussions *do* draw a distinction between representation and representation-user[15]: they take the *first step* of the threatened infinite regress, but as many writers in AI have observed,[16] it has gradually emerged from the tinkerings of AI that there is a trade-off between sophistication in the representation and sophistication in the user. The more raw and uninterpreted the representation—e.g., the mosaic of retinal stimulation at an instant—the more sophisticated the interpreter or user of the representation. The more interpreted a representation—the more *procedural* information is *embodied in it*, for instance—the less fancy the interpreter need be. It is this fact that permits one to get away with *lesser* homunculi at high levels, by getting their earlier or lower brethren to do some of the work. One never quite gets *completely* self-understanding representations (unless one stands back and views all representation in the system from a global vantage point), but all homunculi are ultimately discharged. One gets the advantage of the trade-off only by sacrificing versatility and universality in one's subsystems and their representations,[17] so one's homunculi cannot be too versatile nor can the messages they send and receive have the full flavor of normal human linguistic interaction. We have seen an example of how homuncular communications may fall short in SHRDLU's remarks, "Because you asked me to." The context of production and the function of the utterance makes clear that this is a sophisticated communication and the product of a sophisticated representation, but it is not a full-fledged Gricean speech act. If it were, it would require too fancy a homunculus to use it.

There are two ways a philosopher might view AI data structures. One could grant that they are indeed self-understanding representations or one could cite the various disanalogies between them and prototypical or *real* representations (human statements, paintings, maps) and conclude that data-structures are not really internal representations at all. But if one takes the latter line, the modest successes of AI simply serve to undercut our first premise: it is no longer obvious that psychology needs internal representations; internal pseudo-representations may do just as well.

It is certainly tempting to argue that since AI has provided us with the only known way of solving Hume's Problem, albeit for very restrictive systems, it must be on the right track, and its categories must be psychologically real, but one might well be falling into Danger (2) if one did. We can all be relieved and encouraged to learn that there is *a* way of solving Hume's Problem, but it has yet to be shown that AI's way is the only way it can be done.

AI has made a major contribution to philosophy and psychology by revealing a particular way in which simple cases of Hume's Problem can be solved. What else has it accomplished of interest to philosophers? I will close by just drawing attention to the two main areas where I think the AI approach is of particular relevance to philosophy.

For many years philosophers and psychologists have debated (with scant interdisciplinary communication) about the existence and nature of mental images. These discussions have been relatively fruitless, largely, I think, because neither side had any idea of how to come to grips with Hume's Problem. Recent work in AI, however, has recast the issues in a clearly more perspicuous and powerful framework, and anyone hoping to resolve this ancient issue will find help in the AI discussions.[18]

The second main area of philosophical interest, in my view, is the so-called "frame problem."[19] The frame problem is an abstract *epistemological* problem that was in effect discovered by AI thought-experimentation. When a cognitive creature, an entity with many beliefs about the world, performs an act, the world changes and many of the creature's beliefs must be revised or updated. How? It cannot be that we perceive and notice *all* the changes (for one thing, many of the changes we *know* to occur do not occur in our perceptual fields), and hence it cannot be that we rely entirely on perceptual input to revise our beliefs. So we must have internal ways of updating our beliefs that will fill in the gaps and keep our internal model, the totality of our beliefs, roughly faithful to the world.

If one supposes, as philosophers traditionally have, that one's beliefs are a set of propositions, and reasoning is inference or deduction from members of the set, one is in for trouble, for it is quite clear (though still controversial) that systems relying only on such processes get swamped by combinatorial explosions in the updating effort. It seems that our entire conception of belief and reasoning must be radically revised if we are to explain the undeniable capacity of human beings to keep their beliefs roughly consonant with the reality they live in.

I think one can find an *appreciation* of the frame problem in Kant (we *might* call the frame problem Kant's Problem) but unless one disciplines one's thought-experiments in the AI manner, philosophical proposals of solutions to the problem, including Kant's of course, can be viewed as at best suggestive, at worst mere wishful thinking.

I do not want to suggest that philosophers abandon traditional philosophical methods and retrain themselves as AI workers. There is plenty of work to do by thought-experimentation and argumentation, disciplined by the canons of philosophical method and informed by the philosophical tradition. Some of the most influential recent work in AI (e.g., Minsky's papers on "Frames") is loaded with recognizably philosophical speculations of a relatively unsophisticated nature. Philosophers, I have said, should study AI. Should AI workers study philosophy? Yes, unless they are content to reinvent the wheel every few days. When AI reinvents a wheel, it is typically square, or at best hexagonal, and can only make a few hundred revolutions before it stops. Philosopher's wheels, on the other hand, are perfect circles, require *in principle* no lubrication, and can go in at least two directions at once. Clearly a meeting of minds is in order.[20]

NOTES

1. J. Weizenbaum, *Computer Power and Human Reason* (San Francisco: Freeman, 1976): p. 179, credits Louis Fein with this term.

2. Cf. also *Content and Consciousness*.

3. George Smith and Barbara Klein have pointed out to me that this question can be viewed

as several ways ambiguous, and hence a variety of quite different responses might be held to answer such a question. Much of what I say below about different tactics for answering a question of this form can be construed to be about tactics for answering different (but related) questions. Philosophers who intend a question of this sort rhetorically can occasionally be embarrassed to receive in reply a detailed answer of one variety of another.

4. Cf. Zenon Pylyshyn, "Complexity and the Study of Artificial and Human Intelligence," in Martin Ringle, ed., *Philosophical Perspectives on Artificial Intelligence* (Humanities Press and Harvester Press, 1978), for a particularly good elaboration of the top-down strategy, a familiar theme in AI and cognitive psychology. Moore and Newell's "How can MERLIN Understand?" in Lee W. Gregg, *Knowledge and Cognition* (New York: Academic Press, 1974), is the most clear and self-conscious employment of this strategy I have found.

5. This question (and attempts to answer it) constitutes one main branch of epistemology; the other main branch has dealt with the problem of skepticism, and its constitutive question might be: "Is knowledge possible?"

6. See also Judson Webb, "Gödel's Theorem and Church's Thesis: A Prologue to Mechanism," *Boston Studies in the Philosophy of Science*, XXXI (Reidel, 1976).

7. Wilfrid Sellars, *Science, Perception and Reality* (London: Routledge & Kegan Paul, 1963): pp. 182ff.

8. Terry Winograd, *Understanding Natural Language* (New York: Academic Press, 1972), pp. 12ff.

9. Cf. Correspondence between Weizenbaum et al. in *Communications of the Association for Computing Machinery*; Weizenbaum, CACM, XVII, 7 (July 1974): 425; Arbib, CACM, XVII, 9 (Sept. 1974): 543; McLeod, CACM, XVIII, 9 (Sept. 1975): 546; Wilks, CACM, XIX, 2 (Feb. 1976): 108; Weizenbaum and McLeod, CACM, XIX, 6 (June 1976): 362.

10. J. Weizenbaum, "Contextual Understanding by Computers," CACM, X, 8 (1967): 464–80; also *Computer Power and Human Reason*.

11. Cf. Pylyshyn, op. cit.

12. Cf. Weizenbaum, *Computer Power and Human Reason*, for detailed support of this claim.

13. Joseph Weizenbaum has pointed out to me that Turing saw from the very beginning that computers could in principle break the threatened regress of Hume's Problem, and George Smith has drawn my attention to similar early wisdom in Von Neumann. It has taken a generation of development for their profound insights to be confirmed, after a fashion, by detailed models. It is one thing—far from negligible—to proclaim a possibility in principle, and another to reveal how the possibility might be made actual in detail. Before the relatively recent inventions of AI, the belief that Hume's Problem could be dissolved somehow by the conceptual advances of computer science provided encouragement but scant guidance to psychologists and philosophers.

14. Cf. Jerry Fodor, "The Appeal to Tacit Knowledge in Psychological Explanation," *Journal of Philosophy*, LXV (1968); F. Attneave, "In Defense of Homunculi," in W. Rosenblith, *Sensory Communication* (Cambridge: MIT Press, 1960); R. DeSousa, "Rational Homunculi," in A. Rorty, ed., *The Identities of Persons* (University of California Press, 1976); Elliot Sober, "Mental Representations," in *Synthese*, XXXIII (1976).

15. See, e.g., Daniel Bobrow, "Dimensions of Representation," in D. Bobrow and A. Collins, eds., *Representation and Understanding* (New York: Academic Press, 1975).

16. W. A. Woods, "What's in a Link?" in Bobrow and Collins, op. cit.; Z Pylyshyn, "Imagery and Artificial Intelligence," in C. Wade Savage, ed., *Minnesota Studies in the Philosophy of Science*, IX (1978), and Pylyshyn, "Complexity and the Study of Human and Artificial Intelligence," op. cit.; M. Minsky, "A Framework for Representing Knowledge," in P. Winston, ed., *The Psychology of Computer Vision* (New York, 1975).

17. Cf. Winograd on the costs and benefits of declarative representations in Bobrow and Collins, *op. cit.*: 188.

18. See, e.g., Winston, op. cit., and Pylyshyn, "Imagery and Artificial Intelligence," op. cit.; "What the Mind's Eye Tells the Mind's Brain," *Psychological Bulletin* (1972); and the literature referenced in these papers.

19. See e.g., Pylyshyn's paper op. cit.; Winograd in Bobrow and Collins, op. cit.; Moore and Newell, *op. cit.*; Minsky, *op. cit.*

20. I am indebted to Margaret Boden for valuable advice on an early draft of this paper. Her *Artificial Intelligence and Natural Man* (Harvester, 1977), provides an excellent introduction to the field of AI for philosophers.

HUMAN INTELLIGENCE

J. J. GIBSON

ECOLOGICAL OPTICS

The overall problem of vision is that of understanding those activities of men and animals that depend on the stimulation of their eyes. This includes not only problems like the discrimination of wavelength, intensity, and flicker, but also the study of surface, form, space, and motion. For vision in this general sense of the term, classical optics, taken straight, is not an adequate basis. It creates troublesome puzzles and contradictions of theory. Perhaps students of vision should reconsider some fo the fundamental assumptions about light which they have borrowed from physics.

A large part of physical optics is admittedly not apropriate for the study of vision, nor relevant to it. The theory of the design of optical instruments is of great importance, but it cannot be taken over and applied to the eye. For an eye is *not* an optical instrument, despite all the textbook comparisons. An eye is logically prior to any optical instrument, and incommensurable with it. An instrument is something which is intended, in the last analysis, to be used by an eye.

We are accustomed to say that the stimulus for an eye is light, and in truth it has long been known that the stimulus for the kind of photoreceptor found in a lower animal is the light falling on it. The effective limits of wavelength and intensity have been measured. Accordingly it is easy to assume that the stimulus for the eye of a higher animal is the light falling on a mosaic of photoreceptors. But this analogy is misleading, for the characteristic activity of an eye is not that of a simple photoreceptor. An eye proper, including both the chambered organ of the vertebrates or the higher mollusks and the compound organ of the higher insects, enabels its possessor to respond not only to light but also to the things from which light is reflected. Just what does stimulate such an eye? What is it naturally adapted to register? To what is it sensitive, considered as an organ instead of a mosaic of cells? "Light" is much too simple an answer. A better answer is needed, and one might begin by suggesting that an eye registers *ambient* light. The remainder of this paper will be an effort to elaborate this answer.

The use of the term "ambient" suggests the light that surrounds an individual on all sides. This is part of what is intended. But I wish to refer more particularly to the light which arrives from all directions at a position in space and which does so whether or not an individual is stationed at that position. If this light has different intensities in different directions, instead of the same intensity in all directions, I propose to call it an *optic array*. It is an array because the variation of intensities makes an *arrangement*.

In our world, which is primarily composed of air and surfaces, the air transmits light and the surfaces reflect it. They reflect light diffusely, not regularly, since mirrors are rare in nature. Moreover, they reflect in multiple fashion, from one surface to another and to yet another. The outcome of diffuse reflection and multiple reflection is a reverberating flux of light in the transmitting medium. When analyzed in terms of rays, such a reverberating flux consists of a dense intersecting network made up of pencils of rays. A pencil can be defined as a cluster of lines meeting at a common point, and there will be two types of pencil, divergent and convergent. The divergent pencils are cases of light radiating from a point source on a surface; the convergent pencils are cases of light coming to a point of observation in the medium. The former might be called "radiant" and the latter "ambient." Each of the convergent pencils of light in an ordinary illuminated environment is an optic array.

The radiant pencils issuing from point-sources can be properly treated as physical energy and measured as such. But I suspect that the convergent pencils to a point of observation should be treated as *potentially stimulating* energy, not energy as such, and that they cannot be measured in the same way. The ray of ambient light, I will suggest, should be conceived as different from the ray of radiant light.

I cannot discover that the facts about ambient light have ever been fully recognized in optics, or in any allied discipline. They are more or less recognized in books on perspective, or perspective geometry. But this discipline came to a halt many years ago, having achieved a satisfactory set of rules for the making of pictures by artists and architects. The special rules applied to a *picture plane* and a *station point*. We should not allow these special rules of pictorial perspective to take the place of a general study of environmental perspective. The viewing of pictures is by no means the same problem as the viewing of the environment, but many writers have tended to confuse them.

The above set of facts is also more or less implicit in the technology of making images on viewing screens. The concept of *projection* uses the idea of a pencil of rays intersecting in a point, thereby analyzing the correspondence between an object and its image. Taken abstractly, the concept is the basis of projective geometry. But neither of these disciplines is directly relevant to the problem of vision. The term "projection" is unfortunate when applied to the light stimulating an eye since this event is more like introjection than projection. The practice of illuminating engineering likewise depends on the same set of fundamental facts, but it does not seem to have been formulated or exploited.

These considerations have convinced me that psychologists, physiologists, and others concerned with vision should try to define a special branch of optics appropriate for their problems. I suggest that it be called *ecological optics*. It would be concerned strictly with light in its capacity to stimulate eyes. It would be physics, in a sense, because it deals with a form of physical energy. It would be ecological because it deals with the relation of this energy to a concrete environment which reflects light. I venture to propose a set of assumptions for ecological optics. They are useful in putting a foundation under the kind of visual experiments I have been doing. They may also prove useful to other experimenters but, even if not, they should at least provoke a re-examination of optical theory.

1. THE CONCEPT OF AN OPTIC ARRAY

The primary assumption is that the natural stimulus for the ocular equipment of the higher animals is what I have called an *optic array*. An optic array is the light converging to any position in the transparent medium of an illuminated environment insofar as it has different intensities in different directions. Differences in spectral composition may accompany the differences of intensity. Geometrically speaking, it is a pencil of *rays* converging to a point, the rays taking their origin from textured surfaces, and the point being the nodal point of an eye. We have already noted that rays may diverge from a reflecting point (or a luminous point) as well as converge to a point of observation but that a divergent pencil of rays is *not* an optic array. The essence of an optic array is that it has pattern or structure. The radiant pencil has no pattern.

It should be noted that if the medium of the illuminated environment is not transparent, if it wholly scatters the reverberating flux of light by reason of fog or dust, then no optic array can exist in that medium. Likewise no optic array can occur in complete darkness.

The Optic Array as a Stimulus

The above assumption may astonish some readers. An optic array is extended and enduring whereas the word "stimulus" suggests something punctate and momentary, like a pinprick. An optic array is external to the eye. It cannot act all at once. Above all, it violates the accepted belief that the retinal image is the stimulus. I am suggesting, however, that we re-examine the meaning of that term.

It is just as reasonable to suppose that a sense organ can be stimulated as to suppose that a single receptor-cell can be stimulated. So can a whole sensory system. Each has its own level or order of stimulation. An optic array is the proper stimulus for an ocular system. A retinal image is the proper stimulus for a retina, considered by itself. But we should not be preoccupied with it to the exclusion of other facts. A single eye admits only a *sector* of a complete optic array at any one time. But the ocular equipment of an active animal, as we shall note, can respond by one method or another to a complete spherical array. As we know, the first responses of a man to an optic array, if he is awake, are to focus, fixate, modulate its intensity, and above all *explore* it. The optic array is a *potential* stimulus. It is also a *global* stimulus rather than a *punctate* stimulus.

Retinal stimulation and ocular stimulation have to be distinguished. One is inside the eye and the other outside. The steady application of an image to the human retina (by artifically "stabilizing" it) results in a wholly ineffective stimulus after a short time. But the steady application of an optic array to an eye, which is the natural condition, does not so result. The movements of the eye prevent it. Another proof of the distinction is the fact that both the compound eye of an insect and the camera-eye of a vertebrate can respond to an optic array, but that only the latter kind of an eye has a retinal image. The optic array is an essential feature of all vision; the retinal image only of vision in some animals.

In speaking of the optical stimulus one must distinguish between simultaneous action and successive action. For the kind of animal with a panoramic ocular system, with eyes on each side of the head, the whole optic array is a simultaneous stimulus, or nearly the whole of it. For animals like ourselves with forward-pointing eyes the optic array is physically present at the station-point but it has to be sampled in successive overlapping sectors. In short, a single eye in a given posture registers no more than half of an array but an ocular system is constructed either to register a whole array or to explore it. By either mechanism animals react to their surroundings. How the nervous system integrates the successive patterns of retinal input and makes them equivalent to a simultaneous pattern of input is, of course, a question.

The eyes are different in different species of animals but the natural stimulus for all animals is the optic array, that is, the *differences* in ambient light. The latter is the "adequate" stimulus for vision. It is the circumstance under which eyes developed during the millions of years of evolution. Artificial or "inadequate" stimuli of all sorts can be applied to eyes, of course, and this is how we study vision experimentally. Some of these are quite unlike the natural stimulus; some are like it. At one extreme, electrical current can be used to excite the retina. If the subject will fixate on verbal command, a measured beam of light can be thrown into the eye and presumptively on the retina. Or a picture can be put in front of an eye, and this can reproduce part of a natural optic array—a sort of window opening on an environment other than the present one. This is a favorite method of psychologists. The possibilities of controlling light rays to one or both eyes are endless. Psychophysical experiments on vision have unlimited possibilities. But in constructing optical devices we should remember, I think, the kind of stimuli that eyes are equipped to register.

The Set of Optic Arrays at Differing Station Points

Animals with eyes move about in the environment. The optic array at one position will, in general, be different from that in any other position. That is, its pattern will be different. It will be so by virtue of the laws of parallax and perspective. No two "perspectives" of the world are ever exactly the same. The change from one stationary optic array to another is itself assumed to be a kind of stimulus for an ocular system. All eyes, including the compound type, are known to be sensitive to "motion" and this assumption is, therefore, reasonable. One might even suppose that the optic array at a moving viewpoint is just as much an effective stimulus as the array at a stationary viewpoint (Gibson 1958).

The set of changes from one to another optic array in a given environment and the set of moving optic arrays come to the same thing. They are equivalent to the *complete* set of all stationary arrays in that environment. This is an abstract notion, more familiar to geometers than to students of vision. Nevertheless it is a useful concept. It defines the permanent possibilities of optical stimulation for the environment in question. It is potential stimulation, of course, and the actual or effective stimuli for a particular animal or man will always fall short of it no matter how thoroughly he inspects his part of the world. The notion of an unlimited reservoir of potential stimuli for the eyes to explore is a very fruitful one for visual theory.

The change of pattern from one stationary optic array to another can be termed a transformation of pattern. For animals with a panoramic ocular system, the whole global transformation arising from a change of location is a simultaneously present potential stimulus. It probably serves as a controlling input for their locomotion. For animals like ourselves, with forward-pointing eyes, matters are more complicated. The whole transformation of the array during locomotion can be registered only by successive sampling, but the simultaneous mismatch of the two slightly different arrays at the two eyes can be picked up in front, and this sensitivity to binocular parallax is undoubtedly a compensating advantage.

2. THE CONTENT OF AN OPTIC ARRAY

An optic array was said to consist of "rays." But in ecological optics, I believe, a ray should not be conceived as a beam of light, not even as one which vanishes to a geometrical line, but as the transition between one beam, and the next. It is the locus of a change in light energy over the array. Considered in two dimensions, the array would consist not of spots or patches but of the boundaries between them. This means that if an optic array had no transitions along either meridian, if it were homogeneous with respect to energy and spectral composition, it would not be a stimulus for an eye and would not be an array at all. The energy of the ambient light could be measured by instruments but it would not stimulate an eye to its characteristic activity. There are many facts to support this inference.

The concept of a beam of light which becomes vanishingly thin but still retains a given intensity and spectral character is troublesome. Such a fiction may be useful for geometrical optics, and convenient for the tracing of rays through refracting media, but it cannot stimulate an eye. A transition, however, *can* stimulate an eye. The rays of ecological optics, being the loci of transitions, are not infinitely dense as they are supposed to be in pure geometry. Ecological optics does not have to be concerned with the problem of waves or particles nor with the laws of refraction, reflection, and diffraction. It is primarily concerned with margins, borders, contrasts, ratios, differences, and textures in the array.

The stimulating properties of an array thus depend on what is loosely called its structure. It will have both microstructure and macrostructure. An ordinary daylight array will have a fine structure at the level of seconds of arc, a coarse structure at the level of minutes, and a gross structure at the level of degrees. Outdoors, the upper half of the array will come from the sky and the lower from the earth. The fine structure corresponds to the rays coming from very small or very distant things; the gross structure corresponds to those coming from very large or very near things. The levels of structure exist whether or not an attentive eye is in a position to pick them up. Within what limits they are registered is another question. It depends on what kind of eyes the animal has, not on ecological optics.

We must not confuse optical structure with material structure. The texture of focusable light is not the same as the texture of the surface which reflected it, although the one tends to *correspond* to the other in important respects. The precise geometrical relation between the layout of opaque substances in space and the layout of luminous transitions in an optic array has to be determined by ecological optics.

There is a great advantage in defining the optical stimulus in terms of the transitions between spots or patches of light, not the spots or patches themselves. It encourages the use of relational magnitudes in visual experiments instead of the absolute magnitudes borrowed from physics. Physiologists used to assume that the elementary stimulus for vision was a narrow beam of light, measured for wavelength and intensity, that could be applied to a single receptor, and then to suppose that the whole of vision could be derived from knowledge of these elementary stimuli and their effects. It seems to me that this program has failed. It would be better to start from the fact that an optic array as a stimulus is independent of the intensity of light over a wide range of intensities, that is, degrees of illumination. From noon to sunset the *contrasts* are the same. Only as light energy, and only when taken piecemeal, is the optic array different from noon to sunset. This hypothesis seems to show disrespect for the labors of photometry and radiometry. I do not mean to be glib about the measurement of light. I only wish to suggest that there are profound difficulties in all present efforts to do so in a way that is relevant to an eye. We do see the difference between noon and sunset, to be sure, and our eyes still have some function as photoreceptors, but this is not their *characteristic* function.

3. THE STIMULUS VARIABLES IN AN OPTIC ARRAY

The essential stimulus variables in "light" have, since Newton, been taken to be wavelength and intensity, or amount of energy. These can be measured in fundamental physical units. Hue is in psychophysical correspondence to wavelength, and brightness to energy. When saturation is included, corresponding to wavelength "purity" or some such measure, one gets the three supposedly basic dimensions of sensory experience. A beam of light can vary in these three physical ways and, correspondingly, a patch of color in experience can vary in three ways. Vision is then supposed to be based on color-sensations. The formula is simple and is tied to simple physical measurement. The trouble with it is that, however amended and supplemented, it does not fit all the facts, not even all the facts of color vision.

Ecological optics would assume that the essential stimulus variables for vision are *not* to be found in a beam of light and are *not* wavelength and amount of energy. Instead, the stimulus variables depend on the optic array, and must be discovered by analyzing its structure. Variables of structure or pattern, to be sure, cannot so easily be tied to the fundamental measures of physics. They seem inexact. Nevertheless if the old theory is inadequate, a beginning must be made on a new one. If "color" does not account for vision, let us see if "pattern" will do so, and perhaps then discover that color phenomena will fall into line. Or, putting it in another way, perhaps we cannot understand how the retina works unless we understand how the eye works.

The transitions in a natural optic array are primarily transitions of intensity. These depend on the layout, the chemical and structural composition, and the illumination of the solids, liquids, and gases of the environment. That is, they depend on the edges, corners, and other irregularities of reflecting surfaces. The intensity transitions are usually accompanied by spectral transitions (changes in the wavelength distribution relative to the spectrum of the illumination), but these are secondary. The fundamental variables of an optic array would then be ones like the following:

(a) Abruptness of transition, or what is loosely called "sharpness" of the boundary. A penumbra is at one extreme and an edge is at the other. How to measure this variable is still a question.

(b) Amount of transition. It seems likely that this variable should be measured as a ratio or fraction of the adjacent intensities, not as the absolute difference between them.

(c) Shape of the boundary, e.g., rectilinear, curved, or pointed.

(d) Closure of the boundary or nonclosure.

(e) Density of the transitions, or number per unit angle of the array.

(f) Change in the density of transitions; also the rate of change of density. The latter is the "gradient" of density of texture.

(g) Motion of one boundary relative to others; or motion of each boundary relative to all the others. The latter might be called a "transformation." There can also be gradients of motion.

(h) Presence or absence of transitions within a closed boundary of the array.

This list might be extended indefinitely. It consists of "significant" variables (of which more later). They have all been isolated experimentally and shown to be effective stimuli. But they are only the ones I happen to have studied, and there are many other potential stimuli in an optic array.

4. THE INFORMATION CARRIED BY STIMULUS VARIABLES IN AN OPTIC ARRAY

When defined as above, the variables of an optic array may *carry information* about the environment from which the light comes. This is a central hypothesis for ecological optics. By "carry information," I mean only that certain variables in an array, especially a moving array, will correspond to certain properties of edges, surfaces, things, places, events, animals, and the like—in short to environmental facts. They will not, of course, replicate but only specify such facts.

This hypothesis is perfectly capable of being investigated, and the extent to which it is true or false can be determined. The difficulty has been that no discipline acknowledges the responsibility of doing so—of finding the connections between optical stimuli and their natural sources. The problem falls between ecology, optics, physiology, and psychology. There has been plenty of speculative theorizing about the so-called cues for perception but no empirical study of whether a cue is in fact a clue to its object. The late Egon Brunswik called for a study of the "ecological validity" of cues (1956), but few have heeded him. However, he believed that the only relations that could be found between "proximal" stimuli and "distal" objects were statistical probabilities, and this made the problem seem overwhelmingly difficult. I cannot believe that it is so. The notion of an optic array puts the problem on a geometrical basis, not a statistical one, although an element of probability no doubt remains.

There are almost certainly laws by which some variables in the optic array specify some environmental facts. They need to be investigated. Here are some tentative ones to start with:

(a) A sharply bounded sector of the optic array specifies an object in the world; a penumbra specifies a shadow in the world.

(b) A textured patch of the array specifies an obstructing surface in the world; a homogeneous patch specifies air. This is "surface quality" vs. "film quality."

(c) The kind of texture in a patch of the array specifies the kind of substance composing the surface—water, sand, grass, fire.

(d) A rectilinear boundary in the array specifies a straight edge in the world. Angles specify angles, and curves specify curves although, of course, the shape of an object is not specified by its form in the array.

(e) A gradient of density of the *same kind* of texture in the array specifies the direction of recession of a continuous surface.

(f) A transformation of the pattern and texture of the whole array specifies a change of station point.

(g) A transformation of a textured and bounded patch of the array in isolation, specifies a displacement of an object in the world.

There are surely also complements and corollaries of such laws which will tell us what optical variables do *not* specify environmental facts. For example, optical size does not specify the physical size of an object. But magnification specifies the coming closer of an object and minification the opposite with considerable reliability. The intensity of a patch in the array does not specify the reflectance of a surface in the world. But relative intensities over the whole array might specify the relative reflectances of the whole layout of surfaces. If the stimuli, once naïvely thought to provide information about the environment, turn out not to do so others may be discovered which do. There is no reason to conclude that knowledge of the world is impossible because "light" is empty of information.

Invariant Properties under Transformation of an Array

It was noted earlier that the optic array at one position is different from that in another, and that waking animals continually move about. As slight a change of viewpoint as 2½ inches horizontally yields a change in the structure of the array—one that we are used to calling a "disparity" where retinal images are concerned. Consider the change of form and texture for any change of station point. Only some properties of the array change, not all of them. There are *variant* properties of such an array and *invariant* properties. Some "variables" are altered, others are constant. The invariant variables, as they might be called, have not been specified and listed, but they can be, and this is another task for ecological optics.

From projective geometry we know that when a form undergoes a perspective transformation some features are altered and others not. The same rule holds for the overall structure of an optic array.

The reason why invariants need to be isolated and studied is that they are potentially stimuli. Variants and invariants need to be distinguished. In the past we have assumed that an altered pattern at the eye is simply a different stimulus for the eye. This is not true for an unaltered property. It remains constant and is therefore the *same* stimulus. The unaltered property provides a possible basis for the impression of a constant object or a rigid surface (Gibson 1957b). On this theory, the variants in an optic array specify motions of objects or of the individual; the invariants specify the permanent characteristics of the layout of the environment. Here is a radical departure from previous theorizing.

The classical explanation of the constancy of phenomenal objects with respect to shape and size has been to ascribe it to some higher mental process. None has been verified. Actually the problem is one of the constancy of the whole phenomenal environment, not merely of objects. As such it is part and parcel of the study of vision. The theory suggested explains the constancy of phenomenal space as well as that of objects in space. I omit color constancy, but I suspect it can be explained in a similar way by reference to invariants under change of illumination.

The problem of the control of locomotion by vision and the perception of moving objects has scarcely been touched on by psychologists. When the variant properties of a moving optic array have been separated from the invariant ones the necessary stimulus information will, I think, become evident (Gibson, 1958).

5. SOME IMPLICATIONS

These assumptions about light clarify some old puzzles and suggest many new experiments. The advantages that occur to me are as follows:

1. The concept of an optic array enables us to investigate vision without having to choose between sensation and perception. The known facts cannot be separated into these two categories, and the theoretical separation is becoming meaningless. For example, color-perception and surface-perception need to be studied in relation to one another.

2. The defining of higher orders of optical stimuli enables us to perform simple psycho-physical experiments on qualities of experience previously called "perceptual." For example, gradients of optical texture can be used as stimuli for impressions of slant-depth.

3. The optic array permits the defining of *relational* magnitudes in the light entering an eye as well as *absolute* magnitudes of stimulus energy, and suggests new experiments in which pattern and sequence are systematically varied instead of frequency and intensity. For example, parameters of optical transformation can be used as stimuli.

4. The notion of an optic array that emanates from surfaces resolves the ancient theoretical puzzle of the "third dimension."

5. By providing a theory of the relation between the proximal stimulus and its distal source, it promises to put the problems of size, shape, and color constancy on a new footing, to be treated as problems of vision instead of some little-understood kind of mental activity.

6. The optic array puts the retinal image in its proper place as one stage in the process of seeing in animals having chambered eyes.

7. It destroys the misleading analogy between the retinal image and a picture, while clarifying the relation between them. A picture is a human means of reproducing a part of a natural optic array.

8. It also enables us to bypass some of the long-standing paradoxes concerning the retinal image considered as a picture. For example, instead of worrying about double and single impressions from the two eyes we are led to consider information pickup in a conjugated binocular system.

9. The optic array requires us to consider the responses of the eye and the responses of the retina as each affects the other instead of treating them separately. The orienting and exploratory movements of the eyes developed in parallel with the structure of the retina.

10. Finally, if potentially stimulating light carries information about the environment, as ecological optics may demonstrate, the ancient problem of veridical perception is solved.

6. SUMMARY

I have made some tentative suggestions about how to further the study of vision by modifying our assumptions about light. They have been dignified by the term "ecological optics." An optic array was defined, and three main assumptions were made. They seem to be as follows:

1. There is a set of optic arrays in every habitable environment when it is illuminated.

2. Some correspondence exists between the structure of a local optic array and the structure of the local environment, also between the set of arrays and the whole environment.

3. The variables of structure in an array and a set of arrays are potential stimuli for an ocular system.

These hypotheses provide a novel basis for the study of the eyes. They suggest an assumption which common sense would like to accept but which students of vision have thought they had to reject, namely:

An ocular system is essentially a mechanism for registering the information about the environment in a set of optic arrays. It thereby makes possible the control of behavior with respect to the environment.

JERRY A. FODOR and ZENON W. PYLYSHYN

HOW DIRECT IS VISUAL PERCEPTION? SOME REFLECTIONS ON GIBSON'S "ECOLOGICAL APPROACH"

1. INTRODUCTION

There is always a scientific Establishment, and what it believes is always more or less untrue. Even in the respectable sciences empirical knowledge is forever undergoing reformulation, and any generation's pet theories are likely to look naive when viewed from the perspective of thirty or forty years on. In psychology, however, reformulation tends to be radical. When the dominant paradigm goes, the whole picture of the mind may shift; and, often enough, the scientific consensus about what constitutes a psychological explanation changes too. At such times, to use a phrase of Gibson's, the "old puzzles disappear,"[1] and one may be hard put to understand what on earth one's predecessors thought that they were up to. This has happened so often in the history of psychology that it would surely be unwise to assume that it is not going to happen again; in particular, it would be unwise to assume that it is not going to happen to *us*. Gibson thinks that it has already, and it seems that a substantial minority of the cognitive science community is inclined to agree with him. The purpose of this essay is to examine whether there is anything to that claim. In particular, we will examine the thesis that the postulation of mental processing is unnecessary to account for our perceptual relationship with the world; that if we describe the environment in the appropriate terms we see that visual perception is *direct* and requires only a selection from information present in the ambient light.

The current Establishment theory (sometimes referred to as the "information processing" view) is that perception depends, in several respects presently to be discussed, upon *inferences*. Since inference is a process in which premises are displayed and consequences derived, and since that takes time, it is part and parcel of the information processing view that there is an intrinsic connection between perception and memory. And since, finally, the Establishment holds that the psychological mechanism of inference is the transformation of mental representations, it follows that perception is in relevant respects a computational process.

What makes Gibson's position seem outrageous from the Establishment perspective is that it is presented as an outright denial of every aspect of the computational account, not merely as a reformulation of parts of it. According to Gibson, the right way of describing perception is as the "direct pickup" of "invariant properties." (More precisely, we are taking Gibson to be claiming this: for any object or event x, there is some property P such that the direct pickup of P is necessary and sufficient for the perception of x.) Now, what is "direct" is *ipso facto* not mediated; in particular, according to Gibson, perception is not mediated by memory, nor by inference, nor by any other psychological processes in which mental representations are deployed. Moreover, Gibson insists upon the radical consequences of his unorthodoxy: "The ecological theory of direct perception . . . implies a new theory of cognition in general" (p. 263).

In his last book, which will serve as the basis for our discussion, Gibson elaborates on the views he has arrived at after thirty years of research on perception, and on the bases of his disagreement with the Establishment position. The tone of the book, when it comes to Gibson's relation to received psychological theorizing is pretty intransigent:

> The simple assumption that the perception of the world is caused by stimuli from the world will not do. The more sophisticated assumption that perceptions of the world are caused when sensations triggered by stimuli are supplemented by memories will not do. . . . Not even the current theory that the inputs of the sensory channels are subject to 'cognitive processing' will do. The inputs are described in terms of information theory, but the processes are described in terms of old-fashioned mental acts: recognition, interpretation, inference, concepts, ideas and storage and retrieval of ideas. These are still the operations of the mind upon the deliverances of the senses, and there are too many perplexities entailed by this theory. It will not do, and the approach should be abandoned. . . . What sort of theory, then, will explain perception? Nothing less than one based on the pickup of information. . . . [p. 238].

> The theory of information pickup differs radically from the traditional theories of perception. First, it involves a new notion of perception, not just a new theory of the process. Second, it involves a new assumption about what there is to be perceived. Third, it involves a new concept of the information for perception . . . Fourth, it requires the new assumption of perceptual systems with overlapping functions . . . Finally, fifth, optical information pickup entails an activity of the system not heretofore imagined by any visual scientist. . . . [p. 239] Such is the ecological approach to perception. It promises to simplify psychology by making old puzzles disappear [p. 300].

We will suggest that there is a way of reading Gibson that permits the assimilation of many of his insights into the general framework of Establishment psychological theorizing. Moreover, given this conciliatory reading, much that Gibson says is seen to be both true and important; and it does indeed differ in significant respects from what has generally been assumed by psychologists who accept the information processing framework. But, as should be clear from the preceding quotes, Gibson *does not want* to be read in a conciliatory way. And for good reason: if the program as he presents it were to succeed, it would constitute a conceptual revolution on the grand scale. Many of the deepest problems in cognitive psychology and the philosophy of mind would be bypassed, and the future of research in both disciplines would be dramatically altered. Such a possibility may seem particularly attractive to those who believe that our current understanding of psychological processes has been too much influenced by the achievements of computer technology. And it will appeal, too, to those who feel that the antibehaviorist revolution in cognitive psychology has gone too far; a sentiment with which Gibson is by no means unsympathetic.

We will argue, however, that Gibson's claim to have achieved, or even to have initiated, such a fundamental reformulation of the theory of mind simply cannot be sustained. The main line of our argument will go like this: Gibson's account of perception is empty *unless* the notions of "direct pickup" and of "invariant" are suitably constrained. For, patently, if *any* property can count as an invariant, and if any psychological process can count as the pickup of an invariant, then the identification of perception with the pickup of invariants excludes nothing. We will show, however, that Gibson has no workable way of imposing the required constraints consonant with his assumption that perception is direct. To put the same point the other way around, our argument will be that the notion of "invariant" and "pickup" can be appropriately constrained only on the assumption that perception is inferentially mediated. This is hardly surprising: Gibson and the Establishment agree that pickup and inference exhaust the psychological processes that could produce perceptual knowledge; hence, the more pickup is constrained, the more there is left for inference to do.

It will turn out, in the case of visual perception, that at least two constraints upon pickup are required. First, nothing can be picked up except a certain restricted class of properties of the ambient light. Second, spatiotemporal bounds on the properties that are picked up are determined by what stimuli turn out to be "effective"; i.e., sufficient to cause perceptual judgments. The consequence of the first restriction is that all visual perception must involve inferences based upon those properties of the light that are directly detected; in particular, all visual perception of features of objects in the environment requires such inferences. The consequence of the second restriction is that visual perception typically involves inference from the properties of the environment that are (to use Gibson's term) "specified" by the sample of the light that one has actually encountered to those properties that would be specified by a more extensive sample. This sort of inference is required because the causally effective stimulus for perception very often underdetermines what is seen. These two kinds of inference are, however, precisely the ones that information processing theories have traditionally assumed must mediate visual perception. We will therefore conclude that Gibson has not offered a coherent alternative to the Establishment view; indeed, that the Establishment view falls out as a consequence of the attempt to appropriately constrain Gibson's basic theoretical apparatus.

2. THE TRIVIALIZATION PROBLEM

The easiest way to see that constraints on the notion of invariant and pickup are required is to notice that, in the absence of such constraints, the claim that perception is direct is *bound* to be true simply because it is empty. Suppose that under certain circumstances people can correctly perceive that some of the things in their environment are of the type P. Since you cannot correctly perceive that something is P unless the thing is P, it will always be trivially true that the things that can be perceived to be P share an invariant property: namely, *being* P. And since, according to Gibson, what people do in perceiving is directly pick up an appropriate invariant, the following pseudoexplanation of any perceptual achievement is always available: to perceive that something is P is to pick up the (invariant) property P which things of that kind have. So, for example, we can give the following disarmingly simple answer to the question: how do people perceive that something is a shoe? There is a certain (invariant) property that all and only shoes have—namely, the property of being a shoe. Perceiving that something *is* a shoe consists in the pickup of this property.

It is quite true that if you do psychology this way, the old puzzles tend to disappear. For example many psychologists have wondered how somebody like Bernard Berenson managed to be so good at perceiving (i.e., telling just by looking) that some painting was an authentic Da Vinci. This problem is one of those that disappears under the new dispensation, since there is obviously some property that all and only genuine Da Vincis share; namely, the property *having been painted by Da Vinci*. What Berenson did was simply to pick up this invariant.[2]

Clearly this will not do, and we do not suppose that Gibson thinks it will. Although he never discusses the issues in quite these terms, it is reasonably evident from Gibson's practice that he wishes to distinguish between what is *picked up* and what is *directly perceived*. In fact, Gibson ultimately accepts something like our first constraint—that what is picked up in visual perception is only certain properties of the ambient light array. Gibson is thus faced with the problem of how, if not by inferential mediation, the pickup of such properties of light could lead to perceptual knowledge of properties of the environment. That is: how, if not by inference, do you get from what you pick up about the light to what you perceive about the environmental object that the light is coming from? If Gibson fails to face this difficulty, it is because of a curious and characteristic turn in his theorizing: when he is being most careful, Gibson says that what is picked up is the *information* about the environment which is contained in the ambient array. We shall see that it is close to the heart of Gibson's problems that he has no way of construing the notion *the information in the ambient array* that will allow it to do the job that is required.

Pursuing the main course of Gibson's attempt to constrain the notion of pickup will thus bring us, eventually, to the notion of the "information in the light." There are, however, other passages in Gibson's writings that can also plausibly be viewed as attempts to impose constraints on the notions of pickup and invariance. We will discuss several of these proposals, but we want to emphasize that it is not clear which, if any, of them Gibson would endorse. This deserves emphasis because the constraints are not only non-coextensive, they are not even mutually consistent; and none of them is consistent with *all* of the things that Gibson describes as being directly perceived. So this is very much a matter of our reconstruction of Gibson's text. The reason it is worth doing is that we will argue that there is, in fact, *no* satisfactory way of constraining the notions of invariant and of pickup so as both to exclude the sort of trivialization discussed above and at the same time to sustain the thesis of unmediated perception; and to make such an argument one has to consider all the possible ways of interpreting Gibson's views.

2.1. First gambit: Only the ecological properties of the environment are directly perceived.

Gibson's last book starts with the observation that "Physics, optics, anatomy and physiology describe facts, but not facts at the level appropriate for the study of perception" (p. xiii). The first section of the book is then devoted to sketching an alternative taxonomy in terms of *ecological* properties of environmental objects and events. Gibson provides many examples of properties that are to count as ecological and some examples of properties that are not. The former include some properties of objects (for example, texture, shape, illumination, reflectance, and resistance to deformation are mentioned). There are also ecological properties of arrangements of objects and of surfaces. For example, being *open* or *cluttered* are ecological properties of what Gibson calls the "layout" of an environment (an open layout is one which consists of just a ground, horizon and sky; a cluttered layout is one that has objects scattered on the ground). Similarly, containing a hollow or an enclosure is to count as an ecological property of a layout.

This list by no means exhausts the examples that Gibson provides, nor are we to assume that the examples he provides exhaust the category of ecological properties. There is, however, one class of ecological properties which requires special mention: the "affordances." Affordances are certain properties of objects which somehow concern the goals and utilities of an organism. So, being edible is an affordance of certain objects, as is being capable of being used as a weapon or tool, being an obstacle, being a shelter, being dangerous or being a potential mate. Roughly, affordances are *dispositional* properties (because they concern what an organism *could* do with an object) and they are *relational* properties (because different organisms can do different things with objects of a given kind).

According to Gibson then, "the environment of any animal (and of all animals) contains substances, surfaces, and their layouts, enclosures, objects, places, events and other animals. . . . The total environment is too vast for description even by the ecologist, and we should select those features of it that are perceptible by animals like ourselves" (p. 36). When, by contrast, Gibson gives examples of properties that are *not* ecological, they tend also to be properties that things *cannot be perceived to have*. "Perceiving" here means something like telling-by-looking. (Perceiving by the use of instruments does not count as a core case for Gibson.) So, properties like being made of atoms, or being a thousand light years away are offered as instances of *non*-ecological properties. This makes it seem as though Gibson has it in mind that "ecological" and "directly perceivable" should be interdefined, as is also suggested by the quotation just cited.

But, of course, that will not work. If the notion of an ecological property is to serve to constrain the notion of direct perception, then it cannot be stipulated to embrace all properties that are "perceptible by animals like ourselves." Consider again the property of being a shoe. This is clearly a property that we can perceive things to have, hence it is a property we can *directly* perceive, assuming that being ecological is a sufficient condition for being perceptible. But this means that introducing the construct "ecological property" has not succeeded in constraining the notion of direct perception in such a way as to rule out vacuous explanations like "the way that you perceive a shoe is by picking up the property it has of *being a shoe*." If all properties that can be perceived are *ipso facto* ecological, then the claim that perception is the pickup of ecological properties is vacuously true. What we need, of course, is some criterion for being ecological *other than perceptibility*. This, however, Gibson fails to provide.

2.2. Second gambit: Only the projectible properties
of ecological optics are directly perceived.

We have just seen that if by "ecological properties" Gibson means *all* perceptible properties, then the notion of an ecological property will not serve to constrain the notion of direct pickup. Perhaps, then, only some independently specifiable subset of the ecological properties should count as directly perceptible. In particular, the directly perceptible properties might be the ones that figure in the laws of the science of "ecological optics."

There are, according to Gibson, *laws* about ecological properties of the environment. The laws that get discussed most in Gibson's text are the ones which connect ecological properties with features of the light that objects in the environment emit or reflect. For example, such laws connect certain sorts of discontinuities in the light array with the spatial overlap of surfaces of environmental objects; and they connect flow patterns in the light array with characteristic alterations of the relative spatial position of the observer and the object being observed. Similarly, Gibson presents the following "tentative hypothesis." "Whenever a perspective transformation of form or texture in the optic array goes to its limit and when a series of forms or textures are progressively foreshortened to this limit, a continuation of the surface of an object is specified as an occluding edge." Presumably, if this hypothesis is true, then the relation between the occlusion and the transformation of the textures is lawful, and the generalization that the hypothesis expresses is a law of ecological optics.

Now, it is generally held that laws of a science are distinguished by, among other things, characteristic features of their vocabulary (see Goodman, 1954). Only certain sorts of predicates can appear in a law, those being the ones which pick out natural kinds in the domain that the law subsumes. We need such a notion of "natural kind" in order to explain a striking difference between laws and mere true generalizations: the former hold in counterfactual cases (hence, they apply to unexamined instances) and the latter do not.

Consider, for example, the following two generalizations: *all mammals have hearts* and *all mammals are born before 1982*. The point is that (as of this writing) *both generalizations hold for all the observed cases*. To date, there have been no observations of mammals without hearts, and there have been no observations of mammals born after 1982. The difference between the cases is that, whereas the observation of a large number of mammals with hearts (and none without) is grounds for believing that there *could be* no mammals without hearts, the observation of a large number of mammals born before 1982 (and none born after) provides no reason at all for believing that there could be no mammals born in 1983. The idea, then, is that the property *being born before 1982* fails to subsume a natural kind; it is not the sort of property in virtue of which things enter into lawful relations. Since generalizations about things which happen to have that property are not laws, there is no reason for believing that they will hold in *new* cases. The inductive "confirmation" of such generalizations provides no rational basis for making predictions.

We will borrow a term from the philosophy of science and refer to predicates that appear in laws as "projectible predicates," and we will say that projectible predicates express "projectible properties." To say that a predicate is *not* projectible is thus to say that there are no laws about the property that it expresses. For example, the predicate "is my grandmother's favorite metal" is nonprojectible since, presumably, there are no laws that apply to things in virtue of their being metal of my grandmother's favorite kind. Notice that this is still true even on the assumption that my grandmother's favorite metal is gold and that there *are* laws about gold. This is because *being my grandmother's favorite metal* and *being gold* are different properties, and the laws about gold would continue to hold even if my grandmother's taste in metals were to change. Coextensive properties may differ in projectibility (see also note 8).

To return to Gibson: the projectible ecological properties would be the ones which are connected, in a lawful way, with properties of the ambient light. It would thus be in the spirit of much of Gibson's text to suggest that it is the projectible ecological properties, and only those, that are the possible objects of direct visual perception. This would at least rule out the direct perception of such properties as having been painted by Da Vinci since, presumably, there are no laws, ecological or otherwise, which subsume objects in virtue of their possession of that property (whereas, on Gibson's assumptions, there *are* laws which subsume objects in virtue of such of their properties as their surface texture—see above).

As will presently become clear, we think that there is much to be said for explicating the notion of a directly detected property by reference to the notion of projectibility. Nevertheless, this move will not do much for Gibson, for the following reason:

a. Not all projectible properties are directly perceived on Gibson's view. For example, the projectible properties of classical optics are not; that is why you need *ecological* optics to construct a theory of visual perception. That classical optics fails to taxonomize properties in the ways that a theory of direct visual perception requires is, in fact, among Gibson's favorite themes. So, then, if the distinction between directly perceptible properties and others is to be explicated by reference to the projectible *ecological* properties, and if the explication is to be noncircular, we need a principled way of distinguishing between ecological laws and laws of other kinds. This, however, Gibson does not provide. Rather, insofar as Gibson is explicit about the matter at all, the notion of an ecological law is introduced by reference to the notion of an ecological property (e.g., ecological laws connect ecological properties to properties of the ambient light). But, as we have seen, the notion of an ecological property appears to be characterizable only by reference to the notion of a property that is directly perceivable (e.g., by "animals like ourselves"). And, of course, it was precisely the notion of direct perception that needed explication in the first place.

b. Not all of the properties that Gibson wants to be directly perceptible are plausibly considered to be projectible; in particular, affordances usually are not projectible. There are, for example, presumably no laws about the ways that light is structured by the class of things that can be eaten, or by the class of writing implements, though being edible or being a writing implement are just the sorts of properties that Gibson talks of objects as affording. The best one can do in this area is to say that things which share their affordances often (though, surely, not always) have a characteristic shape (color, texture, size, etc.) and that there are laws which connect *the shape* (etc.) with properties of the light that the object reflects. But, of course, this consideration does Gibson no good, since it is supposed to be the affordances of objects, not just their shapes, that are directly perceived. In particular, Gibson is explicit in denying that the perception of the affordances of objects is mediated by inference from prior detection of their shape, color, texture, or other such "qualities."

In short, if we assume (as we should) that being a Da Vinci (or a pencil, or a shoe) is *not* projectible, we are in need of an explanation of how people perceive that some paintings are Da Vincis (or that some objects are shoes). The natural view would be: the Da Vincihood of an object (or its shoehood) is inferred from those of its (projectible) properties that are directly perceived. But this is the Establishment solution; precisely the one that Gibson is pledged to avoid.

As is customary with dilemmas, Gibson's has two horns. Either you trivialize the notion of a projectible property by stipulating that all perceptible properties are projectible; or you assume that some perceptible properties are not projectible, in which case you need to say how the perception of these nonprojectible properties is possible. The Establishment story is that the detection of nonprojectible properties is inferential, but that is the route that Gibson has eschewed. In either case, projectibility is not doing the job that Gibson needs done: viz. to provide a notion of direct perception that is simultaneously nonvacuous and compatible with the doctrine that perception is immediate.

2.3. Third gambit: Only phenomenological propertiess are directly perceived.
Introspection suggests that the world is perceptibly accessible under some descriptions but less so under others. A landscape, for example, is readily seen as containing fields, trees, sky, clouds, houses, shrubs, and stones. But it takes special training to see those properties of a landscape which a convincing *trompe l'oeil* painting would have to duplicate; typically, properties

which depend on a fixed locus of observation. It is a matter of considerable significance that properties of the world that seem to be perceptually accessible are generally onces that children learn early to recognize and to name.

Suppose we call these relatively accessible properties of things their *phenomenological* properties. Then much of what Gibson says can be construed as suggesting that it is phenomenological properties, and only those, that are directly perceived. This may be what is at issue in Gibson's injunction that the environment must be described in *meaningful* terms: ". . . the qualities of the world in relation to the needs of the observer are experienced directly," whereas "sensations triggered by light, sound, pressure and chemicals are merely incidental".

Phenomenological properties are accorded a similarly central role in Gibson's discussion of ontogenesis. ". . . the infant does not begin by first discriminating the qualities of objects and then learning the combinations of qualities that specify them. Phenomenological objects are not built up of qualities; it is the other way around. The affordance of an object is what the infant begins by noticing. The meaning is observed before the substance and the surface, the color and the form, are seen as such" (p. 246).

If we go by introspection alone, the identification of the perceptually accessible properties with those that are directly perceived certainly seems plausible: phenomenological properties are precisely the ones which strike one as "given" rather than inferred. Gibson says such things as that "the perceiving of the world entails the coperceiving of where one is in the world and of being in the world at that place" and "the environment seen-at-this-moment does not constitute the environment that is seen". And these remarks (with which, by the way, Husserl would have been entirely comfortable) seem true enough in light of introspections of perceptual salience. There is a scale of phenomenological accessibility, and locations, objects, and affordances are high on this scale. Contrariwise, the "sensory properties" which function as the bases of perceptual inference in, for example, Helmholtzian versions of the Establishment theory, do seem to be very low in phenomenological accessibility.

There are, however, three objections to the proposal that we take the phenomenological properties to be directly perceived. The first is internal: the proposal fails to include some of Gibson's own favorite examples of ecological invariants. For example, the slant of surfaces, the gradients and flows of textures, the amount of texture occluded by interposing objects, the moving occluding texture edge, etc., are *not* phenomenologically accessible. Witness the fact that it requires delicate experimentation to discover the central role that the detection of such properties plays in perception. Roughly, the present proposal has difficulties complementary to those of the suggestion that the object of direct perception is the projectible properties of ecological optics (see above); whereas the projectibility criterion leaves the affordances out, the phenomenological criterion lets almost only the affordances in. This is not surprising; you would not really expect the properties in virtue of which objects satisfy laws to be coextensive, in the general case, with those which are phenomenologically accessible. If such a general coextension held, doing science would be a lot easier than it has turned out to be.

Second, it seems at best a dubious strategy to infer direct perception from phenomenological salience: perhaps the latter is *solely* a phenomenon of conscious access and tells us nothing about the nature of perception *per se*. This is, in any event, a familiar claim of Establishment theories, and it is often rendered persuasive by experimental demonstrations that the perception of phenomenologically salient properties of the stimulus is causally dependent upon the detection of features whose phenomenological accessibility is negligible; properties of the stimulus which may, in fact, entirely escape the conscious notice of the subject. For example, Hess (1975) has shown that a variety of highly accessible perceived properties of faces—including their relative attractiveness—depends on the detection of the relatively *in*accessible property of pupilary diameter. In the light of such findings, Gibson cannot, in any event, establish the identification of directly perceived properties with phenomenologically salient ones by fiat; he cannot simply assume that what is most readily reported is what is noninferentially perceived.

Finally, we are going to need a *mechanism* for the direct perception of phenomenological properties, and it is hard to imagine one that will work in the case of properties like the affordances. It is, for example, not good enough merely to *say* that we directly perceive that a rock can be used as a weapon; we need an account of how the apprehension of such a property *could* be noninferential. We will see, presently, that Establishment theories do propose mechanisms for the direct pickup of certain sorts of stimulus properties; but it is a consequence of the Establishment proposal that affordances (and, indeed, most phenomenologically salient properties) are inferred rather than directly perceived. Gibson sometimes speaks of the perceptual mechanism as "resonating" to the values of ecological parameters that they are "tuned" to. But since a more detailed account does not appear to be forthcoming, the resonance metaphor amounts to little more than whistling in the dark. We shall return to this issue further on.

2.4. Fourth gambit: What is directly perceived is whatever "perceptual systems" respond to.

It is a point that we will presently make much of—and that Gibson is reasonably clear about—that *all* theories of perception must acknowledge the direct pickup of *some* properties. In Establishment theories, what is directly picked up is often taken to be the properties to which *transducers* respond. There is a circle of interdefined notions here, a directly detected property being one to which a transducer responds, and a transducer being a mechanism that responds directly to the properties that it detects. One way that Establishment theories have of breaking out of this circle is by specifying—typically by enumeration—which organs are to count as transducers; for example, the retina in the case of vision and the tympanic membrane in the case of audition.

We shall have more to say about how the notion of transduction can be constrained presently, and we will argue that such specification by anatomical enumeration is inadequate. The present point is that Gibson recognizes that to specify what is to count as a perceptual organ is implicitly to constrain what a theory says is directly picked up. For example, if you think that the organ of visual transduction is the retina, and if you can show that the retina responds only to such properties as the wavelength and intensity of light, then you are committed to the view that only those properties are directly detected. Consequently, other properties of the light (and, *a fortiori*, all visual properties of distal objects) are apprehended only *indirectly*, presumably *via* processes that involve inference.

Gibson believes that the perceptual organs have been misidentified by Establishment theorists. Correspondingly, he claims that if one individuates the perceptual organs correctly, one gets a new and better census of the immediately perceived properties. So, "Helmholtz argued that we must deduce the causes of our sensations because we cannot detect them. . . . The alternative is to assume that sensations triggered by light, sound pressure, and chemicals are merely incidental, that *information* is available to *perceptual systems*, and that the qualities of the world in relation to the needs of the observer are experienced directly" (p. 246, emphasis added). It is a moral of *The Ecological Approach to Visual Perception*, and it is the main point of *The Senses Considered as Perceptual Systems* (Gibson 1966) that the "perceptual system" for vision is the entire complex consisting of "first, the lens, pupil, chamber and the retina . . . Second, the eye with its muscles in the orbit . . . Third, the two eyes in the head . . . Fourth, the eyes in a mobile head that can turn . . . Fifth, the eyes in a head on a body . . ." (p. 245). It is the discriminative capacity of this system—*and not the discriminative capacity of the retina*—which determines what vision can, in principle, detect.

We can certainly grant that the class of properties to which this complex system is specifically "tuned"—the class of properties it can "directly respond to"—may not be the class of properties that Establishment theories have usually taken to be visually transduced. (It is far from clear that it will be the class of ecological properties either. But as we remarked above, the criteria we are ascribing to Gibson for selecting candidate objects of direct visual perception are not, in general, coextensive.) So, Gibson is right to claim that reparsing the system of perceptual organs provides for, or at least permits, a new census of directly detected properties. It follows that *if* Gibson had a motivated criterion for deciding what is to count as a perceptual system, he would *ipso facto* have a principled way of constraining the notion of direct pickup.

But Gibson provides *no* criterion for identifying perceptual systems, or even for circumscribing which organs can in general be regarded as parts of the same perceptual system. For example, it is notable that Gibson's enumeration of the parts of the visual system does not include the brain. Inasmuch as Gibson emphasizes that perceptual systems can overlap (different such systems may share anatomically individuated organs) this exclusion seems, to put it mildly, unmotivated. If, however, the brain *is* included as a component of the visual system, then presumably the properties that the visual system can pick up would *ipso facto* be coextensive with the properties that people can visually perceive and we are back where we started. We still want independent characterizations of "perceive" and "pick up directly" if the identification of perception with direct pickup is to amount to an empirical hypothesis.

It is clear from Gibson's discussion of perceptual systems that he intends to individuate them functionally rather than anatomically, a decision which we applaud. The problem is that the proposed criteria of individuation are so flexible that the notion of "perceptual system" actually provides *no* constraint on what might count as a "directly detected" invariant. According to Gibson, there are five overlapping perceptual systems, each of which can ". . . orient, explore, investigate, adjust, optimize, and come to an equilibrium. . . ." The functioning of these systems is explicitly *not* limited to the transduction of impinging stimulation. Rather, the responses of perceptual systems are "specific to the qualities of things in the world, especially affordances" (p. 246). Furthermore, the nature of the information which such systems can pick up "becomes more and more subtle, elaborate and precise with practice." Given the unbounded scope of the activities that perceptual systems can perform, there would seem to be nothing in the notion that prevents the detection of shoes, grandmothers, genuine Da Vincis, performances of Beethoven's Kreutzer Sonata, or authentic autographs of George Washington all being possible "achievements of perceptual systems." It looks as though whatever is perceived is *ipso facto* the proper object of a perceptual system, and whatever is the proper object of a perceptual system is *ipso facto* perceived directly; we have, in particular, no independent constraints on the individuation of perceptual systems that will permit us to break into this chain of interdefinitions.

The moral of all this is that to define the directly perceivable in terms of what perceptual systems respond to is merely to shift the locus of trivialization from the former notion to the latter. It puts the same pea under a different shell. We believe that there *are* ways of constraining the notion of a perceptual mechanism—via an independent characterization of transduction—but the price you pay is that many perceptual processes turn out to be *non*transductive, hence presumably inferential. This is Gibson's characteristic dilemma, and we claim that he has no way out of it.

2.5. The problem of misperception

In much of the preceding discussion we have emphasized the undesirable consequences of interdefining "pickup," "invariant," "ecological property," and "directly perceive," but that is not the only difficulty with Gibson's approach. Part of an adequate theory of perception ought to be an account of perceptual *errors*, and it is hard to see how this requirement can be squared with the claim that perception is direct on *any* of the interpretations that Gibson's text suggests.

People who have tried to understand the nature of the mind, at least since Plato, have been particularly worried about the problem of false belief. In the present context, this is the problem of explaining how *misperception* is possible. The standard approach to this problem within Establishment theories is to connect misperception with failed inference. Your perception that something is edible, for example, is said to depend upon inferences from the appearance of the thing (e.g., from its smell, taste, texture, shape, color, and so forth). These inferences depend upon generalizations gleaned from past experience, and the generalizations are themselves nondemonstrative, and hence fallible. So, for these and other reasons, the (perceptual) inference from appearance to edibility sometimes goes wrong, with consequences that are typically painful and occasionally fatal.

Now consider how a noninferential story about misperception might go. Here we get a first glimpse of a dilemma that emerges, in various guises, throughout Gibson's text. If "directly perceive that" is taken to be factive, then by stipulation "x directly perceives that y is edible" will entail that y is edible. It follows that what goes on when one misperceives something as edible cannot be the direct perception of edibility. If, on the other hand, "directly perceive that" is *not* taken to be factive, then it is logically possible to, as it were, directly *misperceive* that something is edible. But Gibson will then need an account of what has gone wrong when misperception is direct. Notice, in particular, that he *cannot* account for such cases by saying that what you pick up when you directly misperceive the edibility of a thing is the property of *apparent* edibility. For, things that are misperceived to be edible *do* have the property of being *apparently* edible, and the problem for a theory of misperception is to explain how things could be taken to have properties that in fact they do *not* have. (A way out would be to say that you pick up the apparent edibility and *infer* the edibility from that; but this just *is* the Establishment way out and, of course, it is closed to Gibson.)

Probably the line that Gibson wants to take is that *if* an affordance is correctly perceived, *then* it is perceived directly; and that is, of course compatible with the factivity of "directly perceive." Notice, however, that such an approach does not help with the problem of misperception, since it does not tell us how we are to describe the cases where the antecedent of the hypothetical is *false*. We will return to this sort of difficulty. Suffice it at present to say that the problem of constraining "directly perceive" so as to provide a nonvacuous construal of the claim that perception is noninferential, and the problem of providing a coherent account of misperception without recourse to the notion of perceptual inference, are two sides of the same coin. No wonder Gibson is so unhappy about the role that appeals to illusions have played in the confirmation of Establishment theories of perception.

If a theory of perception is to be tenable it must not only address the most common (veridical) cases, but also the ones in which perception fails to be veridical and leads to false beliefs. The relative infrequency of the latter sorts of cases does not alter this principle (and, in fact, they are arguably not all that infrequent; only they tend to escape our notice except when the consequences are serious). Gibsonians sometimes urge that we should take very seriously the fact that perception works most of the time (see Reed and Jones 1978), and it is true that this fact is of central importance for epistemology. But the goal of psychological theory construction is not to predict most (or even all) of the variance; it is to explicate the underlying mechanisms upon whose operation the variance depends. It seems quite inconceivable that the psychological mechanisms of perception and the psychological mechanisms of misperception are different *in kind*.

This problem is such a serious one that it sometimes drives Gibsonians to truly desperate recourses. For example, Turvey and Shaw (1979) suggest that we should cope with the issue of perceptual error by "tak[ing] perception out of the propositional domain in which it can be said to be either right or wrong . . . and relocat[ing] it in a nonpropositional domain in which the question of whether perception is right or wrong would be nonsensical." (p. 182). Apparently, this means either that we should stop thinking of perception as eventuating in beliefs, or that we should stop thinking of beliefs as having truth values. Turvey and Shaw describe this proposal as "radical", but "suicidal" might be the more appropriate term.

Perhaps the most characteristic Gibsonian move in this area is to identify misperception with failure to pick up 'all the relevant information'; (the bird flies into the window because it failed to pick up the ambient information that specifies *window*). But, of course, pick up of the very light structures which failed to specify *window* for the bird might be adequate to specify *window* for *us*. From a mentalistic point of view, this is not surprising; we know a lot more about windows than birds do. So, the form of the problem for Gibson is to explain how pick up of the very same state of affairs that constitutes an adequate sample of information for one organism could constitute an inadequate sample for another. The Establishment account has an answer: viz. that what you perceive depends not only on the ambient information picked up, but also on the mental processes deployed in processing that information. It is far from clear what alternative the Gibsonian position could purpose.

3. THE PROBLEM OF DIRECT DETECTION
IN ESTABLISHMENT THEORIES

Our argument thus far has been that unless the notions of pickup and invariant are constrained, it will always be trivially true that there is an invariant property whose pickup is necessary and sufficient for the perception of any object: viz. the property of being that object. We have also argued that some doctrines of Gibson's which can plausibly be construed as attempts to provide the relevant constraints do not succeed in doing so.

Though these considerations raise problems for Gibson's theory, it is important to understand that all other theories, including Establishment theories, have problems of a corresponding sort. This is because even theories that hold that the perception of many properties is inferentially mediated must assume that the detection of *some* properties is direct (in the sense of *not* inferentially mediated). Fundamentally, this is because inferences are processes in which one belief causes another. Unless some beliefs are fixed in some way other than by inference, it is hard to see how the inferential processes could get started. Inferences need premises.[3]

To admit this is not, however, to endorse any "foundationalist" view of epistemology: to say that the pickup of some properties must be noninferential is not to say that our knowledge of these properties is infallible, or that the justification of perceptual beliefs depends upon assuming that the mechanisms of direct pickup are epistemologically privileged. Many philosophers have held that the deliverances of direct perception must figure centrally in the arguments which justify our perceptually based knowledge claims, but it is quite unnecessary to read this sort of moral from Establishment perceptual psychology.

The psychologist's topic is the causation of perceptual judgments, not the establishment of epistemic warrant in justificatory arguments. One can perfectly well hold—as in fact we are inclined to do—*both* that matters of epistemic warrant are typically determined by "inference to the best explanation" *and* that the causation of perceptual judgements typically involves inferences from premises which are not themselves inferred. The causal chain in perception typically flows "inward" from the detection of those properties to which peripheral transducers respond. But the flow of epistemic justification typically goes in every which way since the justification of perceptual knowledge claims is heavily constrained by principles of conservatism, parsimony, and coherence. In what follows, then, the epistemological issues will be put competely to one side: we make no assumptions about the epistemological role of whatever is directly detected[4]; for us, "direct" means only "noninferential."

One can distinguish at least two proposals that Establishment theories have made about how to draw the line between what is directly detected and what is inferentially mediated. On some views, especially the older, epistemologically based theories, the distinction between direct detection and inferential mediation is taken to be coextensive with the distinction between "sensory" properties and the rest. Typically, the sensory properties are characterized by introspective availability, and often enough it is assumed that the deliverances of introspection are infallible; hence the putative connection between perceptual immediacy and epistemic warrant that we noted in the preceding paragraph. Gibson holds, and we think that he is right about this, that the appeal to introspection will not do the job. In fact, as we saw when we discussed the "phenomenological" criterion for direct detection, what is introspectively accessible is typically not the traditional sensory properties (color, two-dimensional form, etc.) but rather "meaningful" properties like the affordances. When Gibson says that "phenomenological objects are not built up of qualities; it is the other way around" (p. 134) he is quite right about the deliverances of introspection. Since, however, traditional theorizing is precisely concerned to treat properties taht are on the level of the affordances as *inferred*, it very early abandoned the identification of what is directly detected with what is introspectively available. If, however, the sensory properties are *not* identifiable with the ones that are introspectively available, it does not help much to say that sensory properties are what we detect directly, the former notion being as unclear as the latter.

Recent versions of the Establishment theory have sought to constrain the notion of direct detection by identifying the properties that are available without inferential mediation with those to which transducer mechanisms are sensitive. This transfers the problem of constraining "directly detectible property" to the problem of constraining "mechanism of transduction" and, contrary to assumptions that appear to be widely made, specifying what is allowed to count as a transducer for the purposes of cognitive theory is a nontrivial problem. For example, transducers are technically defined as mechanisms which convert information from one physical form to another. But this definition is entirely compatible with there being transducers for *any* pattern of stimulation to which the organism can respond selectively since *whole organisms* are, in that sense, transducers for any category to which they can reliably assign things; e.g., for sentences, or shoes, or, in Berenson's case, for Da Vincis. This is precisely Gibson's problem as it arises in the context of Establishment theories, and to fail to grasp its seriousness is to fail to understand the challenge that Gibson poses to the Establishment. The theory that perception is typically direct is empty barring an independent construal of pickup; *but so too is the theory that perception is typically inferential.* On the other hand, it should be borne in mind that the Establishment does not accept Gibson's condition on the solution of this problem; viz. that the objects of direct detection (transduction) must be so specified that no perceptual judgements turn out to be inferentially mediated. We think that Gibson's position is hopeless precisely because pickup can be constrained only if that condition is abandoned.

Some theorists in the Establishment tradition hold that the way to decide what transducers we have is by appealing to neurophysiology—for example, by finding out what biological mechanisms serve to convert ambient stimulation into the electrical energy of nerve impulses. There are, however, several difficulties with this sort of approach. In the first place, it fails to rule out the whole nervous system as a transducer since, after all, converting ambient energies into neural excitations is a good part of what the nervous system does. Moreover, the class of mechanisms that would count as transducers by this criterion involves many which perform no function that is of significance for the theory of perception. This is because not all stimulus events that affect the character of nerve impulses are *ipso facto* available for the causation of perceptual judgements. Uttal (1967) refers to those neural events that are functionally relevant as *signals* and those that are not as *signs*, precisely in order to emphasize this distinction. This consideration suggests that the identification of transducers will have to advert not, in the first instance, to their neurological structure but to their role in the cognitive processes that they subserve. Like Gibson, we assume that the individuation of perceptual mechanisms is primarily functional rather than physiological.

Finally, it might be argued that whether a device (including a neurophysiological mechanism) counts as a transducer depends, at least in part, on its psychophysical characteristics; on the way that its output depends upon its input. As will become clear, we think that some proposal of this general kind is probably correct. Notice, however, that it does not follow that the sort of evidence that is collected in standard psychophysical experiments will resolve the issue. This is because such evidence does not, in the general case, directly reflect the behavior of isolated components of the perceptual system. Psychophysical curves reflect patterns of judgements produced by *whole or-*

ganisms, and are typically affected not only by stimulus parameters, but by the utilities, expectations, and beliefs that the organism entertains.

We will assume, in what follows, the identification of what is "picked up" with those properties that transducers respond to. Our problem will thus be to find some satisfactory alternative to the ways of constraining transduction that we have just discussed.

4. THE FIRST CONSTRAINT ON PICKUP:
WHAT IS PICKED UP IN (VISUAL) PERCEPTION IS
CERTAIN PROPERTIES OF THE AMBIENT LIGHT

We begin by considering a fundamental construct in Gibson's theory, the notion that states of affairs can *contain information about* one another. The basic idea is that the state of affairs S1 contains information about the state of affairs S2 if and only if S1 and S2 have correlated properties. Suppose that S1 consists of a's having property F and S2 consists of b's having property G. Then if, in general, x's having property F is correlated with y's having property G, then S1 contains information about S2.

As Gibson repeatedly remarks, this is an entirely "objective" nonpsychological notion of information. Information in this sense is something "in the world," just as correlation is. In particular, information-cum-correlation is not something that is encoded, or transmitted, or stored; though it is, according to Gibson, "picked up" whenever anything is perceived.

But, whereas information is an ontological category, *specification* is an epistemological one. The idea is basically that when two states of affairs are correlated, the organism can use the occurrence of one to find out about the other. Under such circumstances, the first state of affairs is said to *specify* the second (for that organism). Correlation (hence information) is presumably a necessary condition for specification: when S1 specifies S2, S1 and S2 are correlated,[5] and S1 contains information about S2. Gibson's favorite example is the relation of specification that holds between features of the ambient light and features of the distal environmental layout. Features of the light are correlated with features of the layout in virtue of the regularities expressed by laws of ecological optics. The structure of the light therefore contains information about the character of the layout; and, since organisms actually use that information in the perceptual identification of layout features, the structure of the light is said to specify the character of the layout.

Now, the relation of *containing information about* is symmetrical, but, in the general case, the relation of *specifying* is not. Suppose that the state of the layout is correlated in a certain way with the state of the light. While it is then true that the properties of the light contain information about the properties of the layout, it is equally true that the properties of the layout contain information about the properties of the light. However, for no organism that we know of—barring, perhaps, the occasional ecological optician—does the structure of the layout specify the light. Organisms just do not use the properties of the layout to find out how the light is arranged. Notice that that is not because the information is not there. Since the two are correlated you could, in principle, determine the structure of the light given the facts about the layout (and about the correlations) just as you can, in principle, determine the structure of the layout given the facts about the light (and about the correlations). And this raises a problem, though not one that Gibson discusses in these terms: viz. *what determines the direction of specification?*

As soon as the problem is put this way, the principle at issue seems clear enough. What determines the direction of specification is the nature of the detectors (transducers) available to the organism. Light specifies layout and not vice versa precisely because we have transducers for light and no transducers for layout. If we had transducers for layout and no transducers for light, then any specification relation that held between the two would have to go in the opposite direction. The moral is: if we are in a position to say what the direction of specification is for a given organism, then that fact constrains our attribution of transducer mechanisms to the organism. The attribution of transducers must serve (*inter alia*) to explain the facts about the direction of specification for the organism.

So we have a constraint on transduction. But how is this constraint to be applied? In particular, how do you tell which sorts of states of affairs serve as specifiers for a given organism? Given correlated states of affairs, how do you tell which specifies which? The answer is sufficiently obvious. What you do is, you break the correlation experimentally (you set up a case in which the correlation fails) and then you see what happens.[6]

Consider the following simple examples. How do we know that the light specifies the layout and not vice versa? Well, we can create paired situations in one of which we preserve the features of the light without the corresponding layout, and in the other of which we preserve the features of the layout without the corresponding light. The presentation of a hologram would be an example of the first kind; turning out the lights would be an example of the second kind. There is no dispute about what would happen in such experiments. You can vary the layout as much as you like; so long as the properties of the light are unaffected, the perceptual judgments of the organism are unaffected too. On the other hand, leaving the layout intact does you no good if the structure of the light is changed. In the extreme case, take the light away, and the organism cannot see.

In short, the way you determine which of a pair of correlated states of affairs specifies the other is by applying the "method of differences," in which one determines which of two factors is the cause of some effect by setting up a situation in which only one of the factors is operative. In the present case, we have a pair of correlated states of affairs and a perceptual judgement in which they eventuate. We assume that the light contains information about the layout, but we have still to show that the information in the light serves to *specify* the layout; viz. that the perception of layout features is causally dependent upon the detection of the information in the light. The hypothesis that the light does specify the layout implies two predictions corresponding to the two ways of breaking the correlation between light features and layout features: since the detection of the light is causally *necessary* for the (visual) perception of the layout, we predict that the organism sees nothing in the layout-without-light setup. Since the detection of the light is causally *sufficient* for the perception of the layout, we predict *layout illusions* in the light-without-layout setup.

It is the latter consideration which accounts for the centrality, in perceptual psychology, of experiments which turn on the creation of perceptual illusions. An illusion is simply a case in which the specifying state of affairs is brought about without the occurrence of the correlated state of affairs that it normally serves to specify. To produce an illusion is thus to demonstrate a direction of specification. It is characteristic of Gibson's break with the tradition that he disapproves of psychological theories which appeal to perceptual illusions as data, Gibson's point being that the laboratory illusion is an 'ecologically invalid' happening. So it is—by definition—since, as we have seen, you construct an illusion precisely by breaking a correlation that holds *in rerum natura*. Our point is, however, that the theoretical pertinence of facts about illusions is an immediate consequence of taking the specification relation seriously. If saying that S1 specifies S2 implies that the perception of S2 is causally dependent upon the detection of S1, and if causal dependence implies causal sufficiency, then one is committed by the logic of the case to the prediction that S1 presentations can engender S2 illusions. It is notable that Gibson himself (tacitly) accepts this form of argument. When he cites evidence in support of particular empirical claims regarding the identity of specifying stimuli, he frequently appeals to the standard kinds of experimental data about illusions; e.g., cases where one can produce illusions of motion by providing subjects with simulations of optical flow patterns. It seems that some illusions are ecologically more valid than others.

The state of the argument is now as follows: when S1 specifies S2, the perception of S2 is causally dependent upon the detection of S1. Since the direction of specification is determined by the transductive capacities of the organism, it follows that S1 specifies S2 only if the organism has transducers for S1. The notion that the facts about transduction determine the direction of specification thus serves simultaneously to constrain the notion "object of detection" (only specifiers are directly detected) and the notion "mechanism of transduction" (only mechanisms which respond to specifiers are transducers). The method of differences gives us a way out of the threatened interdefinition of "transducer" with "object of direct detection" since we have *empirical* tests for whether a stimulus is a specifier.

Here, then, is the proposal in a nutshell. We say that the system S is a detector (transducer) for a property P only if (a) there is a state S_i of the system that is correlated with P (i.e., such that if P occurs, then S_i occurs); and (b) the generalization *if P then S_i* is counterfactual supporting—i.e., would hold across relevant employments of the method of differences.[7] It is, of course, condition (b) that does the work. For, if a state of a system is correlated with a property, then it will typically also be correlated with any property with which that property correlates. Specifically, if there is a subsystem of the organism whose states are correlated with properties of the light, then the states of that subsystem will also be correlated with the properties of the layout that the light specifies. However, only the former correlation will be counterfactual supporting in the required way; visual transducers are unaffected by manipulation of the layout unless the manipulations affect the properties of the light. Hence, by our criterion, *only* properties of the light are transduced in visual perception.

Another way of stating this condition is to say that a system which is functioning as a detector of P is in a certain sense illusion-free with respect to P. This is not, however, because detection is, in some puzzling way, infallible; it is only because, by assumption, the validity of P-*perception* depends upon situational correlations in a way that the validity of P-*detection*, by assumption, does not. To say that a property is detected is to say that the property would continue to have its psychological effect in circumstances in which correlated properties were suppressed. But P-illusions are possible only where the perception of P is mediated by the detection of one of its correlates, the illusion occurring when the correlation fails. Since, however, transduction is, by assumption, direct—i.e., *not* dependent on specification—failure-of-correlation illusions cannot, by definition, arise in the case of transduced properties.

We have seen that the counterfactual-support condition on transducers has the consequence that only properties of the light are transduced in visual perception. It should be emphasized, however, that not *all* properties of the light can be so transduced if that condition is to be honored. Consider, for example, the (relational) property that the light has if and only if it is caused by the layout being arranged in a certain way. This is a perfectly good property of the light, but it is not one that can be directly detected according to the present view. For, this property has its effect on perception only *via* the effects of such correlated light features as wavelength, intensity, color discontinuities, etc. That is, the perceptual effects of the former property are preserved only in those circumstances in which the latter properties are detected. (We make this claim on empirical rather than *a priori* grounds; we assume that it is what the relevant employments of the method of differences would show to be true.) The property of having-been-caused-by-such-and-such-a-layout-feature is thus a property that the light may have, but it is not a detectable property of the light.

Because the counterfactual support condition is not satisfiable by such properties, the illusion freedom condition is not either. It will always be possible, at least in principle, to construct minimal pairs of light arrays such that one of them has the property and the other does not; and the organism will be unable to distinguish between such pairs within the limits of the experimental procedure. That is what happens when we construct an object that looks like a shoe but isn't one; if it structures the light in a way sufficiently like the way that a shoe does, the subject cannot tell by looking that the light structure lacks the property of having been caused by a shoe. Similarly, *mutatis mutandis*, when one fakes a Da Vinci. So, then, on the one hand, nothing but the properties of the light can be directly detected in visual perception; and, on the other hand, there are (infinitely) many properties of light that cannot be so detected.

We shall presently return to the bearing of all this upon the main question of whether perception ought to be considered to be an inferential process. First, however, it may be worth considering some further implications of the counterfactual-support condition. We believe that the tacit acceptance of this condition upon detection explains a number of intuitions theorists have had concerning what can count as a transducer.

For example, it is frequently assumed that detectors are sensitive only to *physical* properties (i.e., to such properties of states of affairs as can be expressed in the vocabulary of the physical sciences). On this view, we could, in principle, have detectors for wavelength, intensity, pressure, or even chemical composition, but not, say, for being expensive, being nutritious, being causally related to some past event (e.g., being a genuine Da Vinci), or being a sentence of English. We suggest that these intuitions about which properties are transducible are shaped by the theorist's implicit allegiance to the counterfactual support condition *via* the following considerations.

It is usually assumed that the only empirical generalizations which support counterfactuals are laws. This is practically tautological since a law just is a generalization that holds in all physically possible worlds in which the relevant background conditions are satisfied; i.e., across all relevant employments of the method of differences. Suppose that this assumption is correct. Then, since generalizations which specify the relation between detector output states and detected properties must be counterfactual supporting, it follows that such generalizations must be lawful. However, as we have seen, the vocabulary of laws is restricted to predicates which express projectible properties. In short, then, the following theoretical decisions ought to go together: (a) the decision as to whether a property is detectible; (b) the decision as to whether the property is projectible; (c) the decision as to whether a generalization which involves that property is a law; (d) the decision as to whether the generalization is counterfactual-supporting; (e) the decision as to whether a mechanism which is sensitive to the property can count as a detector for that property.

Now, many theorists have held, more or less explicitly, that the only laws there are are laws of the physical sciences, hence that the only properties that can be subsumed by counterfactual supporting generalizations are physical properties. If you believe this, then given the considerations just reviewed, you ought also to hold that there can be detectors only for physical magnitudes. And, whether or not you believe that all laws are laws of physics, there is presumably nobody who believes that there are laws about, say, grandmothers *qua* grandmothers or about genuine Da Vincis *qua* genuine Da Vincis, though there may, of course, be laws about coextensive kinds. (Remember that coextensive properties may nevertheless differ in projectibility.)[8] The suggestion is that the intuition that there cannot be grandmother detectors. The moral is: the decision about what detectors there are is linked to the decision about what laws there are. A world in which there were laws about the property *shoe* would be a world in which there could be detectors for shoes. After all, a law about *shoe* would, presumably, connect the shoe property to other sorts of properties, and then things which have properties of these other sorts would *ipso facto* be available for service as shoe detectors.

In the light of these considerations, we can now understand at least one of the moves that Gibson makes. The fact that Gibson holds *both* that there is detection of ecological parameters and that there are *laws* of ecological optics are seen to be linked decisions. If you hold that nonphysical parameters can be detected, and if, by definition, the states of detectors are lawfully connected with the properties they detect, then you must also hold that there are laws which involve nonphysical magnitudes. In this respect, at least, Gibson's doctrines are mutually consistent.

5. THE "INFORMATION IN THE LIGHT"

The main point of our discussion was to establish some conditions on the notion *detection* (transduction). We needed to do this because we doubted that the notion *could* be appropriately constrained consonant with the doctrine that perception is, in the general case, not inferentially mediated. We are now in a position to see one of the ways in which the conflict arises; indeed, one of the respects in which the Gibsonian model of visual perception is after all committed to inferential mediation, just as Establishment models are.

The first point to notice is that Gibson actually agrees with much of what we have been saying, although the terminology he employs sometimes obscures the consensus. Gibson makes a distinction (largely implicit, and not invariably honored) between what he describes as "directly perceived" and what he describes as "picked up." The latter locution is usually reserved for features of the light, while the former is usually used for features of the layout. Moreover, Gibson seems to agree that picking up features of the light is causally necessary for "directly perceiving" features of the layout. Notice that, in this respect, Gibson's view is simply indistinguishable from the Establishment theory. Where Gibson speaks of directly perceiving features of the layout in consequence of picking up features of the light, the Establishment theory speaks of perceiving features of the layout in consequence of transducing features of the light. Thus far, the differences are merely terminological. The important fact is the agreement that the subject's epistemic relation to the structure of the light is different from his epistemic relation to the layout of the environment, and that the former relation is causally dependent upon the latter.

There is, however, this difference: the classical theory has a story about *how you get from detected properties of the light to perceived properties of the layout.* The story is that you infer the latter from the former on the basis of (usually implicit) knowledge of the correlations that connect them. Gibson clearly does not like this story, but it is quite unclear how he is going to get along without it. It is all very well to call your epistemic relation to layout features "direct perception," but if it is agreed that that relation is dependent upon an epistemic relation to properties of the light, "direct" certainly cannot be taken to mean "unmediated." The basic problem for Gibson is that picking up the fact that the light is so-and-so is *ipso facto* a *different* state of mind from perceiving that the layout is so-and-so. In the normal case, states of mind like the first are causally necessary to bring about states of mind like the second (and they are normally causally sufficient for organisms which have had appropriate experience of the ways in which light states and layout states are correlated). Some process *must* be postulated to account for the transition from one of these states of mind to the other, and it certainly looks as though the appropriate mechanism is inference. The point is that Gibson has done nothing to avoid the need to postulate such a process; it arises as soon as "direct detection" is appropriately constrained. And he has suggested no alternative to the proposal that the process comes down to one of drawing perceptual inferences from transducer outputs; in the present state of the art that proposal is, literally, the only one in the field.

What obscures this problem in Gibson's presentation is that, instead of speaking of picking up properties of the light, he talks about picking up *the information about the layout* that the light contains. This certainly appears to be an alternative to the Establishment idea that layout features are inferred from light features. But, in fact, if one bears in mind the character of the theory of information that Gibson has actually provided, one sees that the appearance is illusory. Remember that "information" is a defined construct for Gibson; S1 contains information about S2 if, and only if, they are correlated states of affairs. The problem is that while Gibson gives no hint of any notion of information other than this one, it is hard to see how this account can sustain talk of information pickup.

Given that "contains information about" just means "is correlated with" what could it mean to say that an organism picks up the information that S1 contains about S2? The obvious suggestion is that you pick up some property of S1 that you know to be correlated with some property of S2, and you use your knowledge of the correlation to infer from the former property to the latter. But this cannot be what Gibson has in mind, since this is just the Establishment picture; we learn about the layout by inference from the detected properties of the light. That is, what we detect is not the information *in* S1 but rather the informative properties *of* S1. Then what we learn about S2 in consequence of having detected these informative properties depends upon which inferences we draw from their presence.

Perhaps, then, Gibson's idea is that detecting the information that S1 contains about S2 is detecting the correlation between S1 and S2. But a moment's thought shows that this cannot be right either. To say (loosely) that S1 is correlated with S2 is to say that S1 and S2 belong to correlated *types* of states of affairs (see note 5). But, surely, you find out about correlations between types of states not by "detecting" the correlation but by processes of nondemonstrative (e.g., inductive) inference.

Something has clearly gone wrong, and it is not hard to see what it is. Having introduced the (purely relational) notion of states of affairs *containing information about* one another (i.e., being correlated) Gibson then slips over into talking of *the information in* a state of affairs. And, having once allowed himself to reify information in this way (to treat it as a thing, rather than a relation), it is a short step to thinking of detecting the information in the light on the model of, for example, detecting the frequency *of* the light; viz. as some sort of causal interaction between the information and the states of a perceptual mechanism (the information makes the perceptual mechanisms "resonate").

This is such an easy slide that it is essential to bear in mind that Gibson has no notion of information that warrants it. Information, in Gibson's sense, is not the sort of thing that can affect states of perceptual systems. What *can* function causally is *informative properties* of the medium, properties of the medium which are *de facto* informative because they are correlated with properties of the layout. So, for example, the frequency of the light can cause a state of a detector, and the frequency of the light can be be *de facto* informative about the color of reflecting surfaces in virtue of a correlation that holds between frequency and color. But the fact that the frequency of the light is correlated with the color of reflecting surfaces cannot itself cause a state of a detector, and appeal to that fact exhausts Gibson's construal of the notion that the light contains information about the color of surfaces. So we are back in the old problem: how (by what mental processes) does the organism get from the detection of an informative property of the medium to the perception of a correlated property of the environment? How does the fact that certain properties of the medium are *de facto* informative manage to have any epistemic consequences? The function of the Establishment notion of perceptual inference is, of course, precisely to answer this question.

In short, "picking up the information in the light" must, given Gibson's account of information, come down to picking up features of the light that are correlated with features of the layout. Since the correlation is empirical (*via* the laws of ecological optics), it is perfectly possible that an organism should pick up a *de facto* informative property of the light but not *take it to be* informative, e.g., because the organism does not know about the correlation. In this case, picking up the information in the light will *not* lead to perceptual knowledge of the environment. Since this can happen (and does in innumerably many cases; see the discussion of the bird and the window in section 2.5), the theorist must face the question: what more than the pickup of *de facto* informative medium properties is required to mediate perceptual knowledge? The notion of inference may provide an answer; but, in any event, Gibson's notion of information does not. Information explains only what correlation explains, and the existence of a correlation between two states of affairs does not, in and of itself, explain how the detection of one of them could eventuate in perceptual knowledge of the other.

There is, we think, a deeper way of putting these points, and it is one that we will return to in the last section of our discussion. The fundamental difficulty for Gibson is that "about" (as in "information *about* the layout in the light") is a semantic relation, and Gibson has no account *at all* of what it is to recognize a semantic relation. The reason this is so serious for Gibson is that it seems plausible that recognizing X to be about Y is a matter of mentally representing X in a certain way; e.g., as a premise in an inference from X to Y. And it is, of course, precisely the notion of mental representation that Gibson wants very much to do without. We have here a glimmer of Gibson's ultimate dilemma: the (correlational) notion of information that he allows himself simply will not serve for the identification of perception with information pickup. Whereas, the semantic notion of information that Gibson needs depends, so far as anyone knows, on precisely the mental representation construct that he deplores. The *point* of the inferential account of perception is to spell out what is involved in taking proximal (or ambient) stimulation as containing information about its distal causes. One cannot provide an alternative to that theory merely by assuming the notion of information as unexplicated, though that is, to all intents and purposes, just what Gibson does.

To summarize: Gibson has no notion of information over and above the notion of correlation. You can, no doubt, pick up properties of S1, and, no doubt, some of the properties of S1 that you can pick up may be correlated with properties of S2. But you cannot pick up the property of *being correlated with S2*, and it is hard to see how the mere existence of such a correlation could have epistemic consequences unless the correlation is mentally represented, e.g., as a premise in a perceptual inference. We can put it in a nutshell: sensible constraints on visual direct detection make properties of light its natural object. And then the question "how do you get from an epistemic relation to properties of the light (viz. pickup) to an epistemic relation to properties of the layout (viz. perception)?" seems to have only one conceivable answer: by inferential mediation, like the Establishment says.

The moral of all this is that when Gibson says that we perceive the layout "directly", one must not take him to be claiming that the perception of the layout is unmediated. Gibson, in fact, accepts that visual perception of the layout is mediated at least by the detection of properties of the light, and we have argued that he has suggested no alternative to the idea that such mediation also involves inference. Thus, if we want to find a disagreement between Gibson and the Establishment, we shall have to look to something other than the question whether the perception of distal visual layout involves inference from proximal visual stimulations; both sides agree that it does, albeit with unequal explicitness.

6. THE SECOND CONSTRAINT ON PICKUP: ONLY PROPERTIES OF "EFFECTIVE STIMULI" ARE DIRECTLY DETECTED

Since when Gibson says that perception is "direct" he is clearly not saying that it is unmediated, the question arises what alternative construal might be placed upon his claim. The following suggestion seems to be compatible with much of the text: Although perception of the layout is causally dependent upon pickup of properties of the medium, still the information about the layout that the medium makes available is so rich that the pickup of that information is, as it were, *tantamount* to the perception of the correlated layout properties. To all intents and purposes, this comes to the claim that a given configuration of the medium (e.g., of the ambient optical array) specifies a corresponding configuration of the layout uniquely.

There is a stronger and a weaker version of this claim. The stronger version is that (so long as we focus on the right properties of the medium) the information we find there is, under normal circumstances, *almost invariably* sufficient to specify the ecologically relevant properties of the layout. The weaker claim is that, although *some* of the perceptually available properties of the layout are uniquely specified by properties of the medium, it is left open that other such properties may not be. Gibson's exposition makes it clear that he intends the former of these claims, as indeed he must if there is to be a difference between his views and those of the Establishment.

The Establishment theory takes the connection between the distal layout and the states of the transducers to be something like this: certain properties of the medium are causal determinants of the output of the detectors. Some of these medium properties are, in turn, causally determined by properties of the distal layout. Since the relation of causal determination is transitive, the detector output is itself normally contingent upon particular features of the layout. If, as has usually been assumed, this relation between layout properties and detector outputs is more or less one-to-one (i.e., the mapping is reversible), then this view is entirely compatible with the weaker version of Gibson's claim. In both the Gibsonian account and the Establishment view, it is part of the explanation of the verdicality of perception that, in ecologically normal circumstances, many of the directly detectable properties of the light are specific to properties of the layout which cause them.

In short, the weak version of Gibson's claim is that there are *some* visual properties of the layout which are, to a first approximation, causally necessary and sufficient for properties of the light, which latter properties are themselves directly picked up. Our point has been that the Establishment theories say that too; in particular, the Establishment theories provide precisely that account in the case of the sensory properties of the layout, taking these to be, by stipulation, the properties of the layout which are causally responsible for the properties of the medium that transducers respond to.

Since the weak version of Gibson's claim does not distinguish his position from the Establishment's, let us consider the stronger version, which is that the light contains information that is specific to just about all the visual properties of the layout. By contrast, according to Establishment theories, the sensory properties are a very small subset of the visual properties, and it is *only* for the sensory properties that the medium-to-layout mapping is assumed to remotely approach uniqueness. Hence, the Establishment theory is *not* compatible with the strong version of Gibson's claim. Given this incompatibility, the next question is whether Gibson's claim is plausible on its strong construal. It turns out, however, that before we can raise this question, we have to face yet another trivialization problem.

Consider the claim that, for each visually perceptible property of the layout, there is a corresponding property of the light which is, in some non-vacuous sense, directly detectable and specific to the layout feature in question. For the moment, let us not worry about how the notion of a directly detectable property is to be constrained, and concentrate instead on the issue of specificity. Once again there is a way of trivializing Gibson's claim. The trivializing alternative arises if, among relevant properties of the medium, we allow properties of *arbitrary spatio-temporal cross sections of the light* (for example, the distribution of the light across the entire inhabited universe throughout some arbitrary segment of history, including the arrangement of the light reflected from all the pages of all the books in all the libraries, and all the dials on all the apparatus in all the scientific laboratories). If we take such an arbitrarily bounded sample of the light, then it may well be that its structure does uniquely specify every perceptible property of the corresponding layout. Indeed, it may be that the arrangement of all the light specifies a unique layout of all the objects, perceptual or otherwise. Whether this is true may be of considerable epistemological interest, since an epistemologist might well wonder whether there is enough data in the medium to determine a unique best theory of the world. The trouble is that, either way, the issue has no implications for the psychology of perception.

The important psychological question is whether the claim of specificity can be maintained for *appropriately bounded* samples of the ambient optic array, and the interest of the Establishment contention that perception is typically inferential depends in large part on the claim that the answer to this question is "no." The Establishment holds that there must be inference from medium to layout; but, as we have seen, that must be admitted by anyone who accepts the principle that only properties of the medium are detected directly. What is more contentious is the Establishment claim that layout properties are typically inferred on the basis of *relatively fragmentary* information about the structure of the medium; hence that the patterns of transducer outputs which serve as "premises" for perceptual inferences in general significantly *underdetermine* the percepts to which they give rise.[9] This is an issue on which Gibson and the Establishment certainly disagree. Our point has been that before it can be assessed, we need some independent criterion for what is to *count* as an appropriately bounded sample of the optic array.

We assume that the following is—or, anyhow, ought to be—untendentious: The goal of a theory of perception includes characterizing the sample of the ambient array which causes each percept. It is true that, in his most recent writings, Gibson sometimes seems to be saying that perception should not be viewed as caused by stimulation. Indeed, he appears to want to do away with the notion of the stimulus altogether. "I thought I had discovered that there were stimuli for perception in much the same way that there were known to be stimuli for sensations. This now seems to me to be a mistake. I failed to distinguish between stimulation proper and stimulus information" (p. 149). But, whatever this distinction may come to, it surely does not provide an argument against there being environmental causes of perception. And, as long as it is assumed that there are, giving a causal account of perceptual phenomena is surely one of the central aims that psychology ought to pursue. In particular, what we want is a specification of the sample of the ambient array which causes each distinct perceptual episode.

Just as the goal of specifying the environmental causes of percepts survives disagreements over whether what causes a percept is stimulation or stimulus information, so it also survives disagreements over how percepts ought to be described. Gibson says: "I should not have implied that a percept was an automatic response to a stimulus, as a sense impression is supposed to be. For even then I realized that perceiving is an act, not a response . . ." (Ibid). An adequate psychology might provide mappings from segments of the ambient array onto percepts, or onto some larger events, or patterns of behavior; in either case, perceptual episodes will be viewed as caused and the problem of specifying bounds on the causally efficacious sample of the ambient array will have to be faced.

In fact most of these worries are, in the invidious sense, academic. Gibson and the Establishment agree on what constitutes some clear cases of perceptual phenomena to be explained. When one performs an experiment by setting up certain displays and finds that subjects report seeing certain things, this is *prima facie* a relevant datum for perceptual theory. For example, Gibson (p. 190) makes much of an experiment by Kaplan involving progressive deletion or accretion of a random texture. He reports: "What observers saw was an edge, a cut edge, the edge of a sheet, and another surface behind it." This, then, is a perceptual phenomenon which everyone agrees requires causal explanation; and this agreement presupposes no general consensus about the ontological status of percepts.

On any account, then, percepts have causes, and among the causes of a percept will be some bounded spatio-temporal segments of the ambient optical array. Let us call such a segment the *effective stimulus* for the percept that it causes. Thus for every percept there is some effective stimulus which is its immediate environmental cause. Given this notion we can now ask the critical question: Is it true, in the general case, that each effective stimulus is uniquely correlated with the structure of a corresponding layout? We take it that this is the appropriate way to ask the question whether, in the general case, the structure of the medium specifies the structure of the layout uniquely.

When, however, we put the question this way, it seems obvious that the answer is "no." The mapping of layouts onto effective stimuli is certainly many-to-one, for it has been repeatedly shown in psychological laboratories that percepts can be caused by samples of the ambient medium which demonstrably underdetermine the corresponding layout. Nor is this phenomenon specific to vision. Consider, for example, the "phoneme restoration effect" (Warren 1970) in psycholinguistics: Take a tape recording of an English word, and delete the part of the tape corresponding to one of the speech sounds. (For example, one can start with a recording of "determine" and produce a recording of "de#ermine".) Now record a cough-sound and splice it into the gap. The resulting tape is heard as containing the ungapped original word ("determine") with a cough-sound "in the background." The experiment thus demonstrates that an acoustic array which serves as an effective stimulus for the perception of a cough when heard in nonspeech contexts, can also serve as an effective stimulus for the percept /t/ when heard in the context "de#ermine," for the percept /k/ when heard in the context "es#ape," etc. The mapping from effective stimuli onto layouts is thus one many in at least one case.[10]

Gibson is, of course, aware of such results, but he deprecates them on the grounds that providing a *richer* sample of the ambient array is often sufficient to change the organism's perception of the layout; as, for example, when one destroys the Ames' room illusion by allowing the viewer to move freely through the experimental environment or when, in the case of the phoneme restoration effect, one slows down the tape enough to hear what is "really" going on. (The latter case shows, by the way, that the "richer" stimulus—the one which leads to true perceptual beliefs—is by no means always the ecologically normal stimulus; there are illusions which occur in the normal situation, and in these cases it is the ecologically pathological stimulus which is required to produce the veridical percept). But Gibson's criticism of these results is irrelevant once one accepts the condition, enunciated above, that an adequate theory must account for the effects of *all* perceptually effective stimulations. True, we can alter the initial percept by adding to the input (supplying context); but it remains to be explained how the original "ecologically invalid" percept was caused. In effect, Gibson's criticism is telling only if one accepts the trivializing construal of his claim that the medium contains information sufficient to specify the layout, thereby avoiding the serious issue which is how much information the *effective stimulus* contains.

If, by contrast, we take the effective stimulus constraint seriously, the facts seem to be clear: percepts are often caused by effective stimulation which is not specific to a layout. In such cases, the properties of the medium that are picked up underdetermine the layout that is perceived. So we are in need of an answer to the question what processes *other than* the pickup of medium properties are implicated in the causation of percepts? The Establishment theory has an answer; viz. the occurrence of certain perceptual inferences. In particular, inferences *from* the detected properties of the fragmentary stimulus *to* the properties that a richer sample of the ambient array would reveal. Gibson, has, thus far, provided no reason for rejecting that answer, nor has he shown how an alternative might be formulated.

To summarize: the claim that there is enough information in each sample of the light to specify a unique layout is empty without some constraint on what is to count as a sample. Gibson provides no such constraint, but it is fairly clear how one ought to do so: since the goal is a theory of the causation of percepts, the appropriate sample must be what we called the "effective stimulus". For, by stipulation, the effective stimulus just *is* an arrangement of the medium that is sufficient to cause a percept. But then the claim that, in the general case, effective stimuli uniquely specify layouts is patently false on empirical grounds. Note, finally, that the fact that the perception of the layout is generally veridical does *not* require that effective stimuli specify uniquely; indeed, the inferential account of perception is precisely an attempt to show how veridical perception could occur without unique specification. Since perception depends on ambient stimulation *together with inference*, the veridicality of perception requires only that the principles of inference should be truth preserving most of the time.

NOTES

1. All References are to Gibson 1979, except as otherwise noted.

2. The problem that we are raising against Gibson is, to all intents and purposes, identical to one that Chomsky (1959) raised against Skinner. Chomsky writes: "A typical example of *stimulus control* for Skinner would be the response . . . to a painting . . . *Dutch*. (Such responses are said by Skinner to be) 'under the control of extremely subtle properties of the physical object or event' (p. 108). Suppose instead of saying *Dutch* we said *Clashes with the wallpaper, I thought you liked abstract work, Never saw it before* . . . , or whatever else might come into our minds when looking at a picture. . . . Skinner could only say that each of these responses is under the control of some other stimulus property of the physical object. If we look at a red chair and say *red*, the response is under the control of the stimulus *redness*; if we say *chair*, it is under the control of (the property) *chairness*, and similarly for any other response. This device is as simple as it is empty . . . properties are free for the asking. . . . (p. 52 in Block, 1980; Chomsky's page reference is to Skinner, 1957). If one substitutes "the property picked up in perception" for "the stimulus property controlling behavior," it becomes apparent how similar in strategy are Skinner's antimentalism and Gibson's. There is, however, this difference: Skinner proposes to avoid vacuity by requiring that the "controlling stimulus" by physically specified, at least in principle. Chomsky's critique thus comes down to the (correct) observation that there is no reason to believe that anything physically specifiable *could* play the functional role vis à vis the causation of behavior that Skinner wants controlling stimuli to play; the point being that behavior is in fact the joint effect of impinging stimuli *together with the organism's mental states and processes*. Gibson has

the corresponding problem of avoiding triviality by somehow constraining the objects of direct perception; but, as we shall see, he explicitly rejects the identification of the stimulus properties that get picked up with physical properties.

3. There is, nevertheless, a sense in which all perceptual processes, strictly so called, might be inferential. Perception is usually taken to affect what the organism knows, and it is conceivable that transducer-detected properties are epistemically inaccessible to the organism and subserve no purposes except those of perceptual integration. (Cf. Stich's 1978 discussion of "subdoxastic" states.) In that case, these noninferential processes are nonperceptual, as it were, by definition. In deference to this consideration, we have generally avoided talking of transduced properties as directly *perceived*, preferring the less tendentious "directly picked up." Of course, this ter-minological issue does not jeopardize the observation in the text that processes of perceptual inference must begin from premises that are not themselves inferred. The present question is just whether the noninferential processes of pickup which make such premises available should themselves be referred to as perceptual. (See also the discussion in section 7.4.)

4. Some Gibsonians apparently want to read a sort of epistemological Realism as one of the morals of theories of direct perception (see, for example, Turvey 1977, but that would seem quite unjustifiable. On the one hand, *every* theory will have to acknowledge the fact of at least *some* misperception, and if one is going to run skeptical arguments in epistemology, that is the premise one needs to get them started (e.g., "if you admit that perception is sometimes fallible, what reason is there to suppose that it isn't always wrong? . . ." etc.). If you find such arguments persuasive, the idea that perception is direct *when it is veridical* will do nothing to soothe the skeptical itch, since that idea is compatible with the possibility that perception is *never* veridical. Correspondingly, an inference based theory of perception is perfectly compatible with a Realistic account of the information that perception delivers. All that is required for a perceptual inference to yield knowledge is that it should be sound. Gibson's views have philosophical implications, but not for epistemology.

5. Strictly, S1 and S2 are tokens of correlated types. We will not be explicit about the type token relation except where the intention is not clear from context.

6. Of course, knowing the phsycial/physiological structure of the organism can provide some constraints upon the assignment of transducers, since if there is *no* mechanism that is differentially sensitive to a given form of input energy, then that form of input *cannot* be a specifier for that organism. However, as we remarked above, this consideration does less than might be supposed since, in the general case, practically any form of ambient energy is likely to have *some* effect on the organism's neurological condition, and it is functional considerations which must decide which such effects are to count as transductions.

7. It is of prime importance that the employments of the method of differences should be *relevant* since, of course, there are *some* counterfactual conditions in which P will *not* produce S_i even if S is a transducer: e.g., the universe blows up, the organism dies, and so forth. The counterfactual supporting generalizations about transducers are thus like most counterfactual supporting generalizations in science in that they must be relativized to assumptions of "normal background conditions." Perhaps only the fundamental laws of microphysics are exempt from such relativization, these being assumed to hold, literally without exception, for all segments of space-time.

8. For our purposes, a world in which there were laws about grandmothers would be one in which some effect is a consequence of something being a grandmother, regardless of what other properties it may have. But, surely, this is not true in our world. Suppose, for example, that there are true empirical generalizations of the form $(\forall x) (\exists y) (x$ is a grandmother $\rightarrow Fy)$. Then it seems enormously plausible that such a generalization holds only because there is some property H *other than being a grandmother*, such that the generalization $(\forall x) (\exists y) (Hx \rightarrow Fy)$ is true; and moreover that it is the latter generalization which supports counterfactuals in the critical

cases. That is, if *a* were a grandmother but H*a* was false, then the former generalization would not hold for x = *a*.

9. For purposes of this discussion, we will usually speak of the epistemic states arising from perception as *percepts*. One could equally talk of perceptual beliefs, perceptual judgements, or any other epistemic state that an organism is in as a logical consequence of having perceived—as opposed to having guessed, deduced, remembered or otherwise concluded—that P.

Talk of percepts, as opposed to beliefs about the world that do not arise directly from perception, implies a distinction between perceptual and cognitive processes (Dretske 1978). Empirical grounds for drawing this distinction are discussed in, for example, Hochberg (1968). The present point is that all theories have to draw it somewhere, and the question about the richness of the ambient array arises specifically for the causation of perception, however it may be defined.

10. It might occur to a Gibsonian to avoid this conclusion by reanalyzing the effective stimuli. Whereas we assumed that the effective stimulus was *cough* (which, occurring in isolation is heard as a cough but occurring in speech-context is heard as a phone) a Gibsonian might want to argue that the isolated stimulus is actually *#silence-cough-silence#*. Since that stimulus is never presented in the speech condition, the appearance of a one-many stimulus-to-layout mapping is dissipated. This would be a typically Gibsonian tactic of appealing to context to avoid the problem of ambiguity.

The disadvantages of the tactic are, however, clearly revealed in this case. For, the stimulus #noise-*cough*-noise# *will*, in general, be heard as containing a cough; and this fact is rendered a mystery on the assumption that the right way to describe the effective stimulus for a cough perceived in isolation is as #silence-cough-silence#. Quite generally, what you gain vis à vis ambiguity by enlarging the effective stimulus, you lose a vis à vis the perception of similarity. This is because the perception of similarity is so often mediated by the recognition of partial identity of the internal structures of the stimuli.

STEPHEN STICH

GRAMMAR, PSYCHOLOGY, AND INDETERMINACY

Significance is the trait with respect to which the subject matter of linguistics is studied by the grammarian.
Pending a satisfactory explanation of the notion of meaning, linguists in semantic fields are in the position of not knowing what they are talking about.   W. V. Quine

According to Quine, the linguist qua grammarian does not know what he is talking about. The goal of this essay is to tell him. My aim is to provide an account of what the grammarian is saying of an expression when he says it is grammatical, or a noun phrase, or ambiguous, or the subject of a certain sentence. More generally, I want to give an account of the nature of a generative grammatical theory of a language—of the data for such a theory, the relation between the theory and the data, and the relation between the theory and a speaker of the language.

1

Prominent among a linguist's pronouncements are attributions of grammaticality. What are we saying about a sentence when we say it is grammatical? One strategy for answering this question is to attend to the work of the grammarian. To be grammatical, a sentence must have those characteristics which the grammarian seeks in deciding whether a sentence is grammatical. So a reconstruction of the grammarian's work is a likely path to an explication of "grammatical." This is the strategy adopted by Quine,[1] and it will be of value to study his remarks in some detail. On Quine's account, *significance* rather than *grammaticality* "is the trait with respect to which the subject matter of linguistics is studied by the grammarian" (49). If the two are different, there is some inclination to take the grammarian at his name. So let us see what can be learned by taking Quine's proposal as an explication of *grammaticality*.

The problem for the grammarian may be posed as the segregating of a class *K* of sequences that we will call *grammatical*. On Quine's view, he attends to four nested classes of sequences, *H*, *I*, *J*, and *K*.

H is the class of observed sequences, excluding any which are ruled inappropriate in the sense of being non-linguistic or belonging to alien dialects. *I* is the class of all such observed sequences and all that ever will happen to be professionally observed, excluding again those which are ruled inappropriate. *J* is the class of all sequences ever occurring, now or in the past or future, within or without professional observation—excluding, again, only those which are ruled inappropriate. *K*, finally, is the infinite class of all those sequences, with the exclusion of the inappropriate ones as usual, which *could* be uttered without bizarreness reactions. *K* is the class which the grammarian wants to approximate in his formal reconstruction. (53)

The linguist's data are *H*, and he checks his predictions against *I* minus *H* hoping that this will be a representative sample of *J*. It is when we come to *K* that philosophical eyebrows are raised; for what is the force of the "could" which extends the class beyond *J*, commonly infinitely beyond? Quine's answer is that, besides *H* and future checks against *I*, the "could" is the reflection of the scientist's appeal to simplicity. "Our basis for saying what 'could' be generally consists . . . in what *is* plus simplicity of the laws whereby we describe and extrapolate what is" (54).

Quine's proposal shares with other operational definitions the virtue of objectivity. Yet his solution is beset with problems. For Quine's procedure just does not pick out anything like the class we would pre-systematically hold to be grammatical—and this because his account fails to portray what the grammarian *actually does*. To see this, consider the case of a Quinean linguist ignorant of English setting out to segregate grammatical English sequences. He starts with *H*, the class of sequences he observes. But *H*, in addition to samples of what we would pre-systematically hold to be grammatical sequences, contains all manner of false starts, "lost thoughts," peculiar pauses ("aahhhh!") and, unless he is uncommonly fortunate, a liberal sprinkling of blatantly incoherent speech. Yet Quine, if we take him literally, would have *H* included as a subset of *K*. What the resulting projection might be is hard to imagine. But *K*, so constructed, would not be the class of grammatical sequences in English.

It might be thought that, appealing to simplicity, the linguist could toss out an occasional member of *H*, much as he excludes from *H* what he takes to be nonlinguistic noise or intrusion from another tongue. But an hour spent attending carefully to unreflective speech will dispel this notion. There is simply too much to exclude.[2]

Quine succeeds in muddying the waters a bit by sprinkling the restriction that the sentences to be studied are those which could be uttered "without bizarreness reactions." It is not clear whether he takes such sentences to be excluded from H and I by virtue of their being observed *in situ* or whether he would have H and I further filtered. But it seems clear that, in either case, either this move is inadequate or it begs the question. If by "bizarreness" Quine means *bizarreness*, then the exclusion will hardly accomplish his purpose. For many sorts of sequences that we would want to exclude from K (those with "aahhhh's" interspersed, for example, or those which change subject midsentence) are uttered all the time without bizarreness reactions. And many sentences we would want to include in K would surely evoke the strongest of bizarreness reactions. Indeed, though K will be infinite, only members of a finite subset could be uttered without evoking a bizarreness reaction. Sentences that take more than six months to utter are bizarre. If, however, the reaction Quine has in mind is the reaction (whatever it may be) characteristically displayed when an ungrammatical sequence is uttered, then, until he has provided some account of how this reaction is to be recognized, he has begged the question.[3]

2

Taking Quine's proposal as an explication of grammaticality has led to an impasse. In seeking our way around it we might do well to return to Quine's original insight and attend more closely to what the grammarian actually does. From the first, the generative grammarian has relied heavily on the fact that, with a modicum of instruction, speakers can be brought to make all manner of judgements about their language. In particular, they can be brought to make firm judgements on the oddness or acceptability of indefinitely many sequences. Provided with a few examples, speakers can go on to judge new sequences in point of grammaticality, and do so with considerable consistency for large numbers of cases. This suggests that we might try to remedy the difficulties with Quine's proposal by substituting *intuitive judgments* for observed utterances. On the revised account, H would be the class of those sequences which to date have been considered and judged to be grammatical. I would be the class of sequences ever reflected upon and judged clearly grammatical. And K is the infinite class projected along simplest lines from H and checked against I.

This modified account nicely circumvents the major shortcoming we found in Quine's proposal. Read literally, Quine's method did not pick out the class of sequences we would pre-systematically call grammatical. The class

H on which his projection was based was already tainted with ungrammatical sequences. Our modified version avoids this difficulty by basing its projecting on sequences intuitively taken to be grammatical. The projected class *K* can still miss the mark, failing to be compatible with *I* minus *H*. But this potential failure is the normal inductive one.[4]

We can now make a plausible first pass at depicting the grammarian's work. He proceeds by eliciting intuitive judgements about which sequences are in the informant's language and which are not. He then projects these clear cases along simplest lines, checking his projected class against speakers' intuitions. Thus the task of the generative grammarian may be viewed as that of constructing a system of rules and a definition of "generate" that define a terminal language containing phonetic representations for all the sequences judged by speakers to be clearly acceptable and containing no sequence judged to be clearly unacceptable. The sequences about which speakers have no firm or consistent intuitions can be relegated to the class of "don't cares" and decided by the simplest grammar that handles the clear cases.

Yet as it stands the account still will not do. One fault is its myopic concentration on intuitions. Speakers' judgments about acceptability are the most important data for the grammarian. But they are not his only data, nor are they immune from being corrected or ignored. The attentive grammarian will attend to many aspects of his subjects' behaviour in addition to their response to questions about sentences' acceptability. And a proper explication of the grammarian's job must provide some account of the role these additional data play.

Perhaps the most important sort of evidence for the grammarian besides intuitions of acceptability is the actual unreflective speech of his subjects. An informant's protest that a given sequence is unacceptable may be ignored if he is caught in the act, regularly uttering unpremeditatedly what, on meditation, he alleges he doesn't say. In addition to actual speech, there is a host of further clues for the grammarian. Stress patterns, facts about how sentences are heard and data on short-term verbal recall are among them.[5] Others might be mentioned. To what use does the grammarian put this further evidence? Principally, I suggest, to shore up the evidence provided by the speakers' intuitive judgements or to justify his neglect of them. A sentence whose acceptability to speakers is in some doubt will, with good conscience, be generated by a grammar if it ranks high in the other tests. And, on the other side, a sentence that has the blessings of speakers may be rejected—not generated by the grammar—if it fails to display the other characteristics of grammatical sequences.

We now have one justification the grammarian may use for rejecting speakers' intuitions. There is another. And consideration of it will lead to a fundamental revision of our account of grammaticality. Intuitive oddness may be explained by many factors. Some sentences seem odd because they are pragmatically odd, describing a situation that is bizarre. Others, perhaps, may be rejected as obscence or taboo. Most importantly, sentences may seem odd because they are simply too long and complicated. If the grammarian suspects that any of these factors explain speakers' rejection of a sentence, he may classify it as grammatical *even though it lacks all the characteristics in the cluster associated with grammaticality*.

Note that at this juncture two notions we have been conflating part company. Thus far I have been interchanging "acceptability" and "grammaticality" with studied equivocation. Intuitions of acceptability and the cluster of further characteristics usually accompanying sentences judged acceptable have been taken as (more or less) necessary and sufficient conditions for grammaticality. But the picture changes when a sentence may be classed as grammatical in spite of failing each relevant test. The motivation for separating acceptability and grammaticality is *broad theoretic simplicity*. It is simpler to generate an infinite class including the acceptable sentences than it is to draw a boundary around just those sentences which rank high in the several tests for acceptability. But in thus choosing the simpler task we must assume that some further theory or theories will account for those grammatical sentences which are unacceptable. And we must also assume that the new theory combined with a grammatical theory will together be simpler than any theory attempting directly to generate all and only the acceptable sequences. In short, we are venturing that the best theory to account for *all* the data will include a grammar of infinite generative capacity. This is hardly a step to be taken lightly. For in allowing his grammar to generate an infinite number of sentences, the grammarian is countenancing as grammatical an infinite number of sentences that fail each test of acceptability. It might be thought that such prodigality could be avoided by simply cutting off the class of sentences generated by a grammar at an appropriately high point. But this is not the case. For there is no natural point to draw the line—no point at which the addition of another conjunct or another clause regularly changes a clearly acceptable sentence in to a clearly unacceptable one. Nor would it do to pick an *arbitrary* high cut-off point. This would leave the grammarian as before with generated sentences that are unacceptable. And any account of *why* these sentences were unacceptable would likely also account for the sequences beyond the arbitrary cut-off point.

By now it is evident that grammaticality is best viewed as a *theoretical* notion. Like other theoretical notions, it is related to relevant data in several and complex ways. Simple grammatical sentences generally have several or all of the cluster of characteristics typical of acceptable sequences. More complex grammatical sentences may share none of these characteristics. They are grammatical in virtue of being generated by the grammar that most simply generates all the clearly acceptable sentences and holds the best promise of fitting into a simple total theory of acceptability.

There is, thus, a conjecture built into a proposed grammar—the conjecture that this generative system will fit comfortably into a total theory that accounts for all the data. In this respect a grammar is similar to the theory of ideal gases. The ideal-gas laws do a good job at predicting the behaviour of light gases at high temperatures and low pressures. In less favourable cases, the laws predict poorly. They were acceptable in the hope, later fulfilled, that further laws could be found to explain the difference between the behaviour of real gases and the predicted behaviour of ideal ones. The adoption of a given grammar or form of grammar might be viewed as setting up a "paradigm"[6] or framework for future investigation. The grammar serves to divide those phenomena still needing explanation (viz. unacceptable grammatical sequences) from those already adequately handled.

In our portrait of the grammarian's job, the emphasis has shifted from the concept of grammaticality to the notion of a correct grammar. A sequence is grammatical if and only if it is generated by a correct grammar for the language in question. And a grammar is correct only if it excels in the virtues lately adumbrated. But there are higher virtues to which a grammar may aspire, and more data to be reckoned with. So far we have taken into account data about speakers' intuitions of acceptability and data about a cluster of further characteristics common among acceptable sequences. But we have hardly exhausted the speaker's intuitions about matters linguistic. There is a host of other properties of sentences and their parts about which speakers have firm intuitions. With a bit of training speakers can judge pairs of sentences to be related as active and passive, or as affirmative and negative. They can pick out parts of speech, detect subjects and objects, and spot syntactic ambiguities. The list of these grammatical intuitions could easily be extended. A grammatical theory will not only try to specify which sequences are acceptable; it will also try to specify the grammatical properties and relations of sentences as intuited by speakers. As in the case of intuitions of acceptability, the grammatical theory will be expected to agree with grammatical intuitions only for relatively short and simple sentences. The theory is an idealization, and, as before, we permit it to deviate from the intuited data in the expectation that further theory will account for the differences.

3

It might seem our job is finished. We set ourselves to giving an account of the grammarian's doings in building a grammar, and this we have done. But the reader conversant with competing accounts[7] will expect more. For, commonly, such accounts go on to talk of *linguistic theory, acquisition models, evaluation measures* and other notions related to the question of how a speaker acquires his grammar. Moreover, the discussion of these notions is not a simple addition to the account of the grammarian's work in constructing a grammar. Rather, it is an intrinsic part of that account. Yet why this is so is far from obvious. Constructing a theory of grammar acquisition is surely a fascinating project and one which would naturally catch a grammarian's eye. But, at first blush at least, it would seem to be a new project, largely distinct from the job of constructing grammars for individual languages. Why, then, do Chomsky and others view the study of acquisition as intrinsic to the construction of grammars for individual languages? This is the riddle that will occupy us in the present section. In the course of untangling it we will come upon some unexpected facts about grammar and its place among the sciences.

Let me begin with a puzzle. A grammar of English will generate structural descriptions for English sentences in the form of phrase markers or labelled bracketings. The labels on these brackets will be the familiar NP, VP, etc. But now imagine a perverse variant of our grammar created by systematically interchanging the symbols NP and VP throughout the theory. If the change is thoroughgoing (made in all appropriate generative rules and definitions), then presumably the original theory and the variant will make exactly the same predictions about intuitions, etc. So the two would appear to be empirically indistinguishable. On what basis, then, are we to select one over the other?

To underscore the puzzle, consider a grammarian attending to the hitherto neglected tongue of some appropriately exploited and unlettered people. His grammer will likely end up generating labelled bracketings among whose labels are the familiar NP and VP. But what justification can there be for this grammar as contrasted with a variant interchanging NP and VP throughout, or yet another variant in which NP and VP are systematically replaced with a pair of symbols that occur nowhere in any grammar of English?[8]

There is a related puzzle that focuses not on the vocabulary of a grammar but on its rules. Consider any grammar or fragment of a grammar for English. With the grammar at hand it requires only modest ingenuity to produce a variant set of rules and defintions whose consequences (the entailed chains about grammaticality, grammatical relations and the rest) are identical with those of the original. Among the variants that might be produced some will differ only trivially, adding a superfluous rule perhaps, or capturing a generalization in two rules rather than one. But other variants exist which differ quite radically from the original.[9] A grammar is but an axiomatized theory, and it is a truism that a theory that can be axiomatized at all can be axiomatized in radically different ways. Yet each of these variants makes identical claims about the grammarian's data—not only the data on hand, but *all* the data he might acquire. They may, of course, predict incorrectly on a given point; but if one variant predicts incorrectly they all will. How then is the grammarian to decide among them?

The point of these puzzles is that grammar is afflicted with an embarrassment of riches. It is a task demanding wit and perseverance to construct a grammar that correctly captures a broad range of speakers' intuitions. Yet when the job has been done there are indefinitely many variants each of which captures the known intuitions equally well and predicts unprobed intuitions equally well (or poorly). Somehow the grammarian does come up with a single theory. What principle can he use to guide his choice?

It is in attempting to answer this question that the study of acquisition looms large in Chomsky's writings. But exactly how a theory of grammar acquisition is supposed to motivate a choice among alternative grammars is far from clear. Part of the obscurity, I suspect, stems from the fact that Chomsky, perhaps without realizing it, pursues two rather different strategies in relating the study of acquisition to the problem of choosing among alternative grammars. One of these strategies, I will contend, is thoroughly misguided and rests on a mistaken picture of what grammar is. The other is quite compatible with the account of grammar developed above and suggests an illuminating solution to the puzzles of alternative grammars. Our first project will be to dissect out these alternatives for closer inspection.

Before we begin, some terminology will be helpful. Let us call a grammar *descriptively adequate* for a given language if it correctly captures the intuitions of the speakers of the language (and the rest of the grammarian's data) within the limits of accuracy allowed by idealization. The grammarian's embarrassment of riches arises from the fact that for each descriptively adequate grammar of a language there are indefinitely many alternatives all of which are also descriptively adequate.

Now the strategy I would disparage unfolds like this:[10] When a child learns a language, he learns a descriptively adequate grammar (*dag*). He somehow "internally represents" the rules of the grammar. So if we could discover which set of rules the child has "internalized" we would be able to choose a right one from among the *dags* of the child's language. The right one is simply that grammar which the child has in fact internally represented. The study of acquisition will be designed to give us a lead on which descriptively adequate grammar the child has learned.

Let us reflect on what the child must do to acquire his grammar. The learner is exposed to what Chomsky calls *primary linguistic data (pld)* which "include examples of linguistic performance that are taken to be well formed sentences, and may include also examples designated as nonsentences, and no doubt much other information of the sort that is required for language learning, whatever this may be" (ibid., p. 25). When he has succeeded in learning his language the child will have internalized a *dag*. In two rather different ways this grammar will specify more information about the language than is to be gleaned from the *pld*. First, the *pld* contain a modest sample of the grammatical sentences of the language; the grammar acquired generates all the grammatical sentences. Second, the *pld* contain little or no information about the structural descriptions of sentences and the grammatical relations among them; the grammar assigns structural descriptions to each grammatical sentence and entails all the appropriate facts about grammatical relations. Thus a theory of grammar acquisition must explain how the child can acquire and internalize a grammar that is significantly more informative about the sentences of the language than the *pld* he has been exposed to.

How might we build a theory that accounts for the child's accomplishment? What we seek is a model (or function) which, when given a complete account of the *pld* available to the child as input (or argument), will produce, as output (or value), the *dag* that the child acquires. Our problem is to design the model with sufficient structure so that it can correctly project from the limited *pld* to the full grammar of the language from which the data are drawn. What sort of information should the model contain?

Suppose it were discovered that certain features were shared by all *dags*. If the grammars that shared the features were sufficiently numerous and diverse we might reasonably hypothesize that these features were universal among *dags* of natural language. We would, in effect, be hypothesizing that there is a restricted set of grammars that humans can in fact learn (in the normal way). Were such universal features to be found, our strategy suggests that we take account of them in our acquisition model. Since the output of the model must be a *dag*, we would want to build our model in such a way that the possible outputs (the range of the acquisition function) each had the features that were universal to all *dags*. We would thus take the specification of universal features to define the class of *humanly possible grammars (hpgs)*. The task of the acquisition model is to discover the correct grammar, the grammar of the language the child is actually exposed to, from among the humanly possible grammars.

There is great gain for the builder of an acquisition theory in discovering as rich a set of universal features as possible. For the stronger the restrictions on the *hpgs*, the smaller the class of such grammars will be. Thus, the easier the task relegated to the other parts of the model. What remains for the rest of the model is to compare the *pld* with the class of *hpgs* and exclude those possible grammars which are incompatible with the data.

Now it might happen that the universal features we discover so narrow down the class of *hpgs* that only one *hpg* is compatible with the *pld*.[11] If this is commonly the case, our acquisition theory need contain only a specification of *hpgs* and a device for excluding those *hpgs* which are incompatible with the *pld*. If, however, there are several *hpgs* compatible with all the data the child has accumulated by the time acquisition is essentially complete, we will have to seek some further principle of selection. The principle, the strategy suggests, is to be found in an evaluation measure or weighting of *hpgs*. Some of the *hpgs* that are compatible with all the *pld* will still fail to be descriptively adequate for the child's language. Some of these may simply project incorrectly beyond the sample of the language available to the child. They will then classify as grammatical sequences that are not grammatical. Others, while projecting correctly, may miss the mark on structural descriptions or grammatical relations, specifying that sentences are related in ways other than the ways speakers in fact intuit them to be related. So what we seek in our evaluation measure is some ranking of *hpgs* that has the following property: when we exclude from the *hpgs* those grammars which are incompatible with the *pld*, the highest ranked of the *remaining* grammars is a descriptively adequate grammar of the language the child acquires. The acquisition model would then proceed by first eliminating those *hpgs* which are not compatible with the *pld*, then selecting from among those which remain the one that is highest ranked. The grammar selected is unique among *dags*, for it is chosen by a model that explains how a child might go about acquiring the grammar he does acquire. It is this "explanatorily adequate" grammar which the child actually internalizes and which the linguist seeks to uncover.

A more detailed account of the strategy we are sketching might now go on to worry about how the appropriate evaluation measure could be discovered or what we can say about linguistic universals in the light of present knowledge. But this will not be our course. For I think we have said enough to see that the strategy is wholly wrongheaded. To begin, let us consider the possibility, mentioned briefly a paragraph back, that the universals so constrict the class of *hpgs* that only one *hpg* will be compatible with the *pld*. A moment's reflection will reveal that this is not a real possibility at all. For recall the pair of puzzles that initially prodded our interest in acquisition models. Each puzzle pointed to the superabundance of descriptively adequate grammars for any natural language. For every *dag* there are alternatives which are also descriptively adequate. But the linguistic universals were taken to be properties of all *dags*.[12] Thus, each *dag* for every natural language will be among the *hpgs*. So if any *dag* is compatible with the *pld*, all its alternatives will be as well. And we have made no progress at selecting a single *dag* as the right one.

What is more, the hunt for an evaluation measure is of no real value in narrowing down the class of *dags*. The job that was set for the evaluation measure was not a trivial one. Given any body of *pld*, the evaluation measure had to rank as highest among the *hpgs* which are compatible with the *pld* a *dag* of the language from which the data are drawn. Finding such a measure would likely be a task of considerable difficulty. But, and this is the crucial point, once a measure *has* been found there will be indefinitely many alternative measures which select different *dags* for the same body of *pld*. If the subclass of *hpgs* compatible with a given body of *pld* contains *one dag* of the language of which the data are a sample, it will contain many. Thus, if we can design a measure which ranks any one of these *dags* highest in the subclass, there will be another measure which ranks a different *dag* highest.[13] But whatever justification there is for holding the *dag* selection by one measure to be the grammar actually internalized is equally justification for holding that the other is. And we are back where we started, with too many *dags* each with equal claim to be the "right one."

The second strategy for solving the problem, the strategy I would endorse, sets out in quite a different direction from the first. It does not propose to select among *dags* by finding the one actually internalized. Indeed it is compatible with (but does not entail) the view that *no* grammar is, in any illuminating sense, internally represented in the speaker's mind or brain, and that there is no good sense to be made of the notion of "internal representation." The second strategy approaches the multiplicity of *dag* as a practical problem for the working linguist. At numerous junctures a linguist may find himself with data to account for and a variety of ways of doing so. Among the alternatives, more than one will handle all the data available and will coincide with their predictions about facts as yet unrecorded. How is the linguist to choose? What the linguist seeks, according to this strategy, is not the grammar actually in the head (whatever that may mean) but some motivated way to select among *dags*.

The motivation is to be found through the study of acquisition models, though the goals of an acquisition model must be reinterpreted. If we suspend interest in which grammar is "internally represented" we need no longer demand of an acquisition model that, for a given body of *pld*, it produce as output a grammar that a learner exposed to the data would internalize. Instead, we ask only that the acquisition model have as output *some* grammar that is true of the accomplished speaker (i.e., some grammar that correctly describes the sentences acceptable to him, his intuitions about grammatical relations, etc). But let it not be thought that this is a trivial task. Such a model would be able to specify a grammar true of the speaker given only the (relatively scant) primary linguistic data to which the speaker was exposed. To do this would be a monumentally impressive feat realizable, for the foreseeable future, only in linguistic science fiction.

How can such a model be built? In attending to the more demanding model of the first strategy, our first move was to linguistic universals, the properties shared by all *dags*. The analogous role in the present strategy can be played by properties less difficult to discover. For suppose we have a single descriptively adequate grammar of a particular natural language. Might it not be reasonable to take as many properties of that grammar as possible as "quasi-universals"? "Quasi-universal" properties play just the role that universals did in the first strategy—they constrain the output of the acquisition model. The quasi-universals, then, define a class of 'quasi-humanly possible grammars' which are the only possible outputs of the acquisition model. The terminology is adopted to stress the parallel with the first strategy. But there are important differences. For quasi-universals are in no sense universals— there is no claim that all *dags* must share them. Nor does the class of quasi-humanly possible grammars pretend to exhaust the class of grammars that humans can learn;[14] it simply coincides with the possible outputs of the acquisition model.

As was the case at the analogous point in the first strategy, there is profit in taking the quasi-universals to be as strong as we can. For the stronger the quasi-universals, the smaller the class of quasi-*hpgs* and thus the easier the task that remains for the rest of the model. Indeed, it would not be unreasonable as a first guess to take *all* the properties of the single *dag* as quasi-universals.[15] But this clearly will not do. For then the output class of the acquisition model would have but a single member. Rather, our principle in deciding whether to take features of our single *dag* as quasi-universal is this: take as quasi-universal as many features of the *dag* as possible, provided only that the resultant class of quasi-*hpgs* contains at least one quasi-*hpg* for each natural language. The remainder of the model will contain (at least) a component testing the compatibility of quasi-*hpgs* with the accumulated *pld*. Note that, on this second strategy, it is indeed possible that the quasi-universals so narrow down the class of quasi-*hpgs* that only one *hpg* will be compatible with any given body of *pld*. If this is the case, then a specification of the quasi-universals and a compatibility-testing device of the sort lately considered would complete an acquisition model. But if we cannot discover quasi-universals of this strength, we will again resort to an evaluation measure. As with the first strategy, what we seek is a ranking of quasi-*hpgs* which, when we exclude from the quasi-*hpgs* those grammars incompatible with a given body of *pld*, ranks highest among the remaining quasi-*hpgs* a grammar that is descriptively adequate for the language from which the *pld* was drawn. Since we are making no claim that the selected grammar is "actually internalized" we need not be concerned that there may be several such evaluation measures. Our project is the highly nontrivial project of producing a model that takes *pld* as input and yields an appropriate *dag* as output. *Any* evaluation measure that does the trick will be suitable.

The outline we have given of the construction of an acquisition model is, in a crucial respect, misleading. For it suggests that the model builder is bound irrevocably by the first *dag* he constructs. He takes as quasi-universal as many properties of this grammar as he can get away with, weakening the quasi-universals only when he comes upon some language no *dag* of which could be included among the quasi-*hpgs* if the stronger quasi-universals are retained. Actually, of course, matters are much more flexible. There is room for substantial feedback in both directions as work proceeds on the model and on individual grammars. The overriding concern is to make both the individual grammars and the acquisition model as simple and as powerful as possible. If at a given juncture it is found that adhering to the working hypothesis about the acquisition model will substantially complicate construction of grammars for one or more languages, he will try to alter the model, even if this may require altering or abandoning the original grammar from which the earliest hypothesis about quasi-universals was drawn. And, on the other side, if in constructing a particular *dag* a certain choice of how to proceed would accord well with the working hypothesis about the acquisition model, then he will be inclined to make that choice even if the resulting grammar is somewhat less elegant than another which would result from an alternative choice. There is no circularity here, or at least, to crib a phrase, the circularity is virtuous. Through this process of mutual adjustment progress on the acquisition model and on particular grammars can take place simultaneously.

Notice, now, that the strategy we have been detailing will solve the puzzles with which we began. An acquisition model provides motivation for selecting one *dag* over another, though both do equally well at predicting intuitions and such. The grammar to be chosen is that which accords with the quasi-universals. And, if several do, the grammar chosen is the one the evaluation measure ranks highest. Thus the grammar chosen will be preferred to its descriptively adequate competitors because it is more closely parallel to successful grammars for other languages and integrates more successfully into a model of grammar acquisition.

The account we have given of the second strategy has the further virtue of according well with actual linguistic practice. It is simply not the case that, when speculating about "linguistic universals," Chomsky and his followers set out to survey a broad range of languages and collect those features common to all the grammars. Rather, speculation is based on the study of a single language, or at best a few closely related languages. A feature of a grammar will be tentatively taken as "universal" if it is sufficiently abstract (or nonidiosyncratic) to make it plausible that the feature could be readily incorporated into a grammar of every natural language. If "universals" are taken to be features common to all *dags*, this speculation about universals would be quite mad. But in the light of the second strategy the speculation appears as a thoroughly reasonable way to proceed.

An element of indeterminacy still lurks in our second strategy. And if I am right in identifying this strategy with the generative grammarian's practice, then the indeterminacy infuses his theory as well. In constructing an acquisition model, the first few plausible (approximations of) descriptively adequate grammars have a profound influence. For it is the abstract features of these grammars which are taken as quasi-universals. Yet the selection of these first *dags* over indefinitely many alternatives is completely unmotivated by any linguistic evidence. Which *dag* is first constructed is largely a matter of historical accident. But the accident casts its shadow over all future work. The acquisition model serves to direct future research into the channel forged by these first grammars, even though there are indefinitely many other possible channels available. Nor does the flexibility we stressed three paragraphs back eliminate the indeterminacy. There we noted that, if an original choice of quasi-universals led to overwhelming difficulties in constructing a grammar for some previously neglected language, the universals might be patched and the early grammars that suggested them might be abandoned. But the new choice of quasi-universals has no more claim to uniqueness than the old. For they too will be abstracted from *dags* that were selected over competitors largely by virtue of historical accident.

To the appropriately conditioned reader this indeterminacy will appear familiar enough. It bears strong analogy with Quine's thesis of the indeterminacy of translation.[16] Quine's analytical hypotheses, like the first *dags*, are underdetermined by the data. The selection of one *dag* or one set of analytical hypotheses is largely a matter of cultural bias or historical accident. But once a *dag* or a set of analytical hypotheses has been formulated, it has profound effects on the remainder of the translation theory (for analytical hypotheses), or on the acquisition model and *dags* for other languages. Both analytical hypotheses and early *dags* are susceptible to later tampering; but neither a patched *dag* nor a patched analytical hypothesis has any more claim to uniqueness than the originals.

My departure from Quine comes on the score of the *implications* of the indeterminacy. Were Quine to grant that grammars and translation manuals share a sort of indeterminacy,[17] he would presumably conclude that for grammars, as for translations, modulo the indeterminacy, there is nothing to be right about. On this view there is no saying that one *dag* of a language is more correct than another, except relative to a given set of quasi-universals. Yet the selection of quasi-universals, like the selection of analytical hypotheses, is in part quite arbitrary. My dissent comes in the step that passes from recognition or arbitrariness in quasi-universals or analytical hypotheses to the claim that there is (modulo the indeterminacy) nothing to be right about. For I think that, *pace* Quine, the same indeterminacy could be shown lurking in the foundations of every empirical science. Grammar and translation are not to be distinguished, in this quarter, from psychology or biology

or physics. If we are disinclined to say that in all science, modulo the indeterminacy, there is nothing to be right about, it is because the theories we
are willing to allow as correct are those whose arbitrary features have the
sanction of tradition. But all this is to stake out my dissent, not to defend it.
The defence is a project I must postpone until another occasion.

4

Our sketch of the grammarian's doings is all but complete. We have surveyed
the data to which he attends and indicated the nature of the theory he builds
upon his data. It remains to say something of the interest of the grammarian's
theory and to set out the relation between his theory and the speakers whose
intuitions and behaviour are his data.

As I have depicted it, a grammar is a modest portion of a psychological
theory about the speaker. It describes certain language-specific facts: facts
about the acceptability of expressions to speakers and facts about an ability
or capacity speakers have for judging and classifying expressions as having or lacking grammatical properties and relations.

The modesty of a grammar, on my account, stands in stark contrast to
more flamboyant portraits. On Jerrold Katz's view, a grammar is a theory in
physiological psychology whose components are strongly isomorphic to the
fine structure of the brain. "The linguistic description and the procedures of
sentence production and recognition," according to Katz, "must correspond
to independent mechanisms in the brain. Componential distinctions between
the syntactic, phonological, and semantic components must rest on relevant
differences between three neural submechanisms of the mechanism which
stores the linguistic description. The rules of each component must have their
psychological reality in the input-output operations of the computing machinery of this mechanism."[18] Though Katz's claims about grammar are more
expansive than those I have made, the evidence he uses to confirm a grammar
is of a piece with the evidence indicated in my account. Thus it remains
something of a mystery how the grammarian has learned as much as Katz
would have him know about the structure of the brain, having left the skulls
of his subjects intact.

Less imaginative than Katz's view, but still not so sparse as mine, is a
story about grammar put forward by Chomsky.[19] On this account a grammar
describes the speaker's "competence"—his knowledge of his language. The
speaker is held to have a large and complex fund of knowledge of the rules
of his grammar. The grammarian's theory mirrors or describes the knowledge
that the speaker has "internalized" and "internally represented." Chomsky's
view is intriguing, though an explicit unpacking of the metaphors of "internalization," "representation," and the rest can prove an exasperating task.

My own view is that the notion of competence is explanatorily vacuous and that attributing knowledge of a grammar to a speaker is little more plausible than attributing knowledge of the laws of physics to a projectile whose behaviour they predict. But the issues are complex, and I have aired my views at length elsewhere.[20] I will not rehash them here. What is important to our present project is the observation that, on the account of grammar and acquisition models we have constructed, no knowledge claim is *needed*. A grammar is a theory describing the facts of acceptability and intuition; a grammar-acquisition model is a theory specifying a grammar which comes to be true of a child, as a function of the linguistic environment in which he is placed. Grammar and the theory of grammar acquisition are bits of psychological theory.

If our account of the grammarian's activity is accurate, then it is perhaps misleading to describe him as constructing a theory of the language of his subjects. Rather he is building a description of the facts of acceptability and linguistic intuition. A theory of a language seriously worthy of the name would provide some insight into what it is to *understand* a sentence, how sentences can be used to communicate and to deal more effectively with the world, and into a host of related questions that we have yet to learn to ask in illuminating ways. But a grammar does none of this. Indeed, it is logically possible that there be a person whose linguistic intuitions matched up near enough with our own, but who could neither speak nor understand English. Such a person would serve almost as well as an English speaker as an informant for constructing a grammar of English, provided only that we shared a metalanguage in which we could question him about the sequences of sounds he did not understand. What is important about this bit of fiction is that it is *only* fiction. It is an empirical fact that comprehension and intuition run in tandem. And this fact provides the beginning of the answer to a question that will likely have begun to trouble the reader: Of what interest is a grammar? If a grammar is not, in any exciting sense, a theory of a language, why bother constructing it?

The answer is twofold. First, there is substantial correspondence between the grammatical sentences and the sentences we do in fact use for thought and communication; grammatically related sentences are understood in similar ways[21] (though in our present state of ignorance we have no serious understanding of what it is to "understand sentences in similar ways"); the ability to speak and understand a language is an empirically necessary condition for the possession of linguistic intuitions about the expressions of the language. So one reason for studying grammar is the hope that these overlaps and correlations can be exploited to yield deeper insight into the exciting phenomena of comprehension and communication. Once we have the sort of description of acceptability and linguistic intuition provided by a grammar we can begin to seek an explanation of these facts. We can ask what psychological mechanisms underlie the speaker's ability to judge and relate sentences as he does. The parallels between linguistic intuition and other language-related phenomena make it reasonable to hope that insight into the mechanisms underlying intuition will explain much else about language as well. But hope is not to be confused with accomplishment. If we fail to recognize how modest a theory a grammar is, we can expect only to obscure the extent of our ignorance about language, communication, and understanding.

A second reason for doing grammar is that it is something to do. In grammar, at least we have a coherent set of data that we know how to study, intelligible questions to ask, and some clear indication as to how we can go about answering them. Acceptability and grammatical intuitions are language-related phenomena about which we have the beginnings of an empirical theory. Few other approaches to the phenomena of natural language fare as well. Thus grammar is a natural focus of attention for the investigator concerned with language. It is an entering wedge to a theory of a language, and, for the present at least, there are few competitors.

NOTES

1. *From a Logical Point of View*, 2nd ed., revised (New York: Harper & Row, 1963), essay III.

2. Much the same point is made by Jerrold Katz and Jerry Fodor in "What's Wrong with the Philosophy of Language?" *Inquiry*, 5 (1962) 197–237.

3. Significance is likely a more inclusive notion than grammaticality, more liberal in the constructions it will allow and tolerating a richer sprinkling of "aahhh's," "I mean's," and "you knows's." Thus perhaps Quine's proposal does rather better when taken as advertised. But whatever its interest, significance as characterized by Quine is not the property studied by grammarians of a generative bent.

4. Note that Quine's "bizarreness reactions" could be taken as negative judgments when the subject is queried about a sequence's acceptability. If this is Quine's intention, his proposal and the present account converge.

5. Cf. George A. Miller and Stephen Isard, "Some Perceptual Consequences of Linguistic Rules," *Journal of Verbal Learning and Verbal Behavior*, 2 (1963), 217–228.

6. In a sense that may be intended by T. S. Kuhn, *The Structure of Scientific Revolutions* (Chicago: University Press, 1962).

7. For example, those in Noam Chomsky, "Current Issues in Linguistic Theory," in Fodor and Katz, eds., *The Structure of Language* (Englewood Cliffs, N.J.: Prentice-Hall, 1964); in Chomsky, *Aspects of the Theory of Syntax* (Cambridge, Mass.: MIT Press, 1965), ch. I; and Katz, *The Philosophy of Language* (New York: Harper & Row, 1966).

8. Much the same puzzle is hinted at by Quine in "Methodological Reflections on Current Linguistic Theory," *Synthèse*, 21, 3/4 (Oct. 1970), 386–398, pp. 390 ff.

9. Such variants often require considerable effort to construct. Nor is it always a trivial matter to prove their equivalence of a pair of grammars.

10. I think this strategy is often suggested by what Chomsky says (e.g., in *Aspects of the*

Theory of Syntax, pp. 24–27 and elsewhere). But my concern here is to scotch the view, not to fix the blame. So I will not bother to document details of its parentage.

11. Chomsky suggests this possibility, ibid., pp. 36–37.

12. It is essential that the linguistic universals be taken as the properties common to each descriptively adequate grammar of every natural language. An alternative notion that took the linguistic universals as the features common to each of the actually internalized grammars of every natural language would be useless in the present context, since our project is to discover which among the *dags* of a given language is internalized. And until we *know* which grammars are internalized we cannot discover which features are universal to such grammars.

13. As is the case with alternative *dags*, some alternative measure functions will be trivially cooked up variants of the original (e.g., simply select an arbitrary *dag* of the language from which the *pld* is drawn and place it highest under the evaluation measure, leaving the rest of the measure unchanged). Others will exist which differ from the original in more substantial ways.

14. Indeed, if we abandon the notion of internal representation, it is no longer clear that it makes sense to speak of a child "learning" a grammar. When the child succeeds in mastering his mother tongue, each *dag* of that tongue is true of him. But he surely has not learned *all* these *dags*. What, then, is the "cash value" of the claim that he has learned any one of them?

15. During the John Locke Lectures at Oxford in 1969, Chomsky suggested that were a Martian linguist to come to earth in the midst of an English-speaking community, his most reasonable first hypothesis would be that the ability to speak English is entirely innate. I suspect that Chomsky's remark and the present observation are directed at basically the same point.

16. Cf. "Speaking of Objects," *Proceedings and Addresses of the American Philosophical Association*, 31 (1957–1958), 5–22; "Meaning and Translation," in Fodor and Katz, *The Structure of Language*, op. cit.; *Word and Object* (Cambridge, Mass.: MIT Press, 1960), ch. 2; and "Ontological Relativity," *The Journal of Philosophy*, 69, No. 7 (4 April 1968), 185–212, reprinted in *Ontological Relativity, and Other Essays* (New York: Columbia, 1969).

17. There is evidence that he would. Cf. "Methodological Reflections," op. cit.

18. "Mentalism in Linguistics," *Language*, 40 No. 2 (April/June 1964), 124–137, p. 133.

19. In *Aspects of the Theory of Syntax*, op. cit., and elsewhere.

20. "What Every Speaker Knows," *Philosophical Review*, 80, No. 4 (Oct. 1971), 476–96, and "What Every Grammar Does," *Philosophia*, 3, No. 1 (Jan. 1973), 85–96.

21. Cf. Chomsky, *Syntactic Structures* (Mouton, The Hague, 1957), p. 86: "the sentences (i) *John played tennis* [and] (ii) *my friend likes music* are quite distinct on phonemic and morphemic levels. But on the level of phrase structure they are both represented as *NP-Verb-NP*; correspondingly, it is evident that in some sense they are similarly understood.*" [Last emphasis added.]

NOAM CHOMSKY and JERROLD KATZ

WHAT THE LINGUIST IS TALKING ABOUT[1]

At the beginning of his article "Grammar, Psychology, and Indeterminacy,"† Stephen Stich announces that his goal is to tell the linguist "what he is talking about." The implication is that linguists are confused about important issues in the theory of grammar which Stich will proceed to clarify for them. In fact, much of Stich's essay recapitulates familiar descriptions of the theory of grammar. Where he departs from these, his approach seems to us fundamentally mistaken, though it does touch on important issues. The most important of such issues is Quine's indeterminacy thesis. Stich claims that, on his description of the theory of transformational grammar, this theory itself attributes indeterminacy to natural languages as an inherent feature. Thus, if Stich's interpretation of the present theory of grammar were right, indeterminacy would be implied by the theory, rather than merely a controversial philosophical doctrine urged on linguistics from the outside by Quine and his followers. Stich's argument is directed specifically against views that we have developed in various publications. We believe that his criticism is not well founded on this and other issues and that Stich's alternative descriptions of the theory of grammar are seriously in error.

Sections I and II of Stich's essay review the methodological backgrounds of current linguistic theory along conventional lines. A grammar is a theory of the language, an idealization similar to those in other branches of science such as the theory of gases. Grammars are constructed on the basis of various types of data that linguists have available to them: data on acceptability, ambiguity, relatedness of utterances and their parts, etc. The rules of a grammar assign a structural description to each of the infinitely many sentences of the language. The structural description of a sentence is in principle a complete account of its grammatical (i.e., semantic, syntactic, and phonological) properties. Grammars, moreover, form part of a more comprehensive theory of language use which takes into account such factors as the structure of memory and perceptual strategies in order to explain linguistic behavior and the judgments speakers make about sentences. In this way, the linguist seeks a full account of the entire range of linguistic data concerning a language.[3]

At this point Stich departs from familiar formulations, and undertakes a critical discussion of them. Before proceeding to investigate the problems and solutions he presents, let us review briefly what is actually proposed in the account to which he specifically refers (ibid., 321).

In addition to accounting for the linguistic data concerning particular languages, the linguist seeks to construct a general linguistic theory expressing the grammatical properties essential to all human languages. A grammar, regarded as a theory of an individual language, "is *descriptively adequate* to the extent that it correctly describes the intrinsic competence of the idealized speaker." In contrast, "*a linguistic theory is descriptively adequate* if it makes a descriptively adequate grammar [*dag*] available for each natural language," each system that is a possible language for this particular organism. A linguistic theory "meets the condition of *explanatory adequacy*" to the extent that it "succeeds in selecting a *dag* on the basis of primary linguistic data [*pld*]," namely, the kind of data that suffice for language acquisition. Such a theory would offer an explanation, not merely a description, of particular judgments that constitute part of the linguist's data, in that it offers a principled reason for the selection by the speaker-hearer of the grammar that entails these judgments. The theory is falsifiable in many ways: e.g., "by showing that it fails to provide a *dag* for *pld*" for some language. The linguistic theory may be regarded as an abstract theory of language acquisition: it postulates certain "innate predispositions" that enable the child to develop competence on the basis of *pld*. The linguistic theory "constitutes an explanatory hypothesis about the form of language as such," and, at the same time, "an account of the specific innate abilities that make [the achievement of language acquisition] possible."

For convenience of exposition, we will refer to the approach summarized so far as the "standard account" of "what the linguist is talking about."

Stich argues that the standard account is badly confused about the relation between grammars, linguistic theory, and acquisition models. There is, according to Stich, a "riddle" here:

Constructing a theory of grammar acquisition is surely a fascinating project and one which would naturally catch a grammarian's eye. But, at first blush at least, it would seem to be a new project, largely distinct from the job of constructing grammars for individual languages. Why, then, do Chomsky and others view the study of acquisition as intrinsic to the construction of grammars for individual languages? (320)

We find nothing puzzling in this. Lingusits who concern themselves with acquisition models do so in the belief that grammar construction gains its primary intellectual significance from the role it plays in the study of language acquisition. Grammar construction is a worthwhile enterprise in itself, but the study of language bears directly on philosophical and psychological issues, specifically, we have argued, on issues of rationalism and empiricism.[4] For this reason, we and others have been particularly concerned with developing a general theory that has something of the character of traditional "universal" or "philosophical" grammar. We have argued that the study of these more abstract questions leads to a rationalistic account of the acquisition of language. The speaker-hearer does not acquire competence by inductive generalization from regularities in a corpus of *pld*; rather, a rich framework of linguistic universals defines a set of what Stich calls "humanly possible grammars" (*hpgs*). Language learning is a process of determining which of these is the actual grammar of the language to which the child is exposed. The procedure, we suggest, is akin to theory construction. Learning of language is a matter of selecting among *hpgs*, filling in details in a fixed framework or schematism. Generative grammars of individual languages thus provide the empirical basis for construction of a theory that deals with the common structure of natural languages. This theory leads to specific hypotheses about the innate principles underlying language acquisition.[5]

Stich believes that the study of acquisition and the related concern with general linguistic theory (universal grammar) are motivated by the "puzzle" of how to choose among alternative *dags*. The puzzle he sees is that there are variant grammars "each of [which] makes identical claims about the grammarian's data—not only the data on hand, but *all* the data he might acquire . . . grammar is afflicted with an embarrassment of riches" (320–321).

We have already given the answer to Stich's "riddle": the study of acquisition and universal grammar does not arise as an ancillary problem in the course of constructing grammars, but is rather the focus of our interest—grammars interest us insofar as they contribute to these further investigations. Stich's "puzzle" is nothing more than his formulation of the defining characteristic of empirical science: nontrivial theories are underdetermined by data. If working linguists are unconcerned with the further problems that happen to intrigue us, they will simply exercise their acquired skills to formulate the best hypothesis they can with regard to the grammar of the language under study. Like other working scientists, they will not worry about the problem of induction nor about rationally reconstructing criteria for choosing hypotheses. Rather, they will exercise a skill that might as well be on all fours with chicken sexing: linguists and other scientists use these skills without knowing the details about their nature. Stich gives no argument to show that linguists and other scientists are wrong to rely on such criteria and their skill in applying them.

We would argue, moreover, that the linguist who happens to be so lacking in curiosity as to be unconcerned with universal grammar is excluding significant data that bear on the choice of a grammar for the language. For us, data from language L' can contribute to the choice of a grammar for language

L. Thus, suppose that two *dags* G_1 and G_2 are under consideration for *L*, but that only G_1 is an *hpg* in accordance with a general linguistic theory *T* which serves as a hypothesis concerning the human "language faculty" as such and which provides a basis for explaining how speaker-hearers of *L'* acquired a *dag* for *L'*. Any scientist would tentatively select G_1 over G_2 on this more extensive data base. Linguists unconcerned with linguistic theory would be forced to disregard this evidence, to the detriment of their work. For a linguist with broader interests, data from *L'* can be used to confirm or reject a hypothesis for *L*—on the reasonable assumption that speaker-hearers are not genetically predisposed to acquire *L* but not *L'*, that the capacity to acquire language is a fixed human capacity, not differing for members of different races, political groupings, etc.

Stich presents several versions of his puzzle. He asks:

. . . what justification can there be for [a] grammar as contrasted with a variant interchanging NP and VP throughout, or yet another variant in which NP and VP are systematically replaced with a pair of symbols that occur nowhere in any grammar of English? (320)

And he asks how one decides among different sets of grammatical rules all of which make the same predictions about all the data a linguist might acquire. As far as interchange of symbols is concerned, this is merely a notational change unless linguistic theory presents—as we think it must and can—a set of substantive conditions on the choice of such symbols as NP and VP. As for the more general question that Stich raises, the linguist, like any scientist, will attempt to choose among variants that are empirically indistinguishable in principle by simplicity considerations and other methodological principles. Where such variants exist, choice of a best hypothesis in empirical science is not only underdetermined locally, that is, by particular samples from the data available in principle, but also globally: that is, even given "all data," there are variant hypotheses consistent with the data. But, assuming there could be nonequivalent hypotheses that are consistent with *all* relevant data (of any sort), there is no argument in Stich's essay to prevent us from saying what surely any other scientist would say: simplicity and other methodological criteria, applied by skilled scientists, may determine a unique best choice among these hypotheses.

According to the standard account, linguistic theory specifies the schematism for grammar, thus generating the class of *hpgs*, and furthermore provides an evaluation measure—an algorithm for selecting among *hpgs* that are compatible with given *pld*. Much of the linguistic work of recent years has been an effort to determine the character of the schematism and the evaluation measure. Plainly, all hypotheses about these matters are empirical;

hence, if nontrivial, underdetermined by evidence. Notice that the schematism and the evaluation measure are not to be confused with the criteria used by scientists (including linguists) in choosing among possible theories, whatever these criteria may be. The latter are general methodological criteria employed to select a preferred hypothesis; the former are hypotheses about the form of linguistic rules, conditions on rules, relations among subcomponents in grammars, linguistically significant generalizations, etc. That is, the latter constitute a hypothesis that falls within theoretical human psychology. This hypothesis concerning a schematism and an evaluation measure is itself to be judged on the basis of general methodological criteria that guide ordinary scientific practice.

Consider now Stich's approach to the "puzzle" and "riddle" that he has posed. He outlines two strategies: strategy I, which he "disparages," and strategy II, which he "endorses." Strategy I incorporates a determinacy thesis; strategy II, an indeterminacy thesis. Strategy I is "thoroughly misguided and rests on a mistaken picture of what a grammar is" (321). Strategy II, he contends, "suggests an illuminating solution to the puzzle of alternative grammars" (324). Stich's strategy I is alleged to be a summary of the standard account, recapitulated above. However, his strategy I misstates this account in a crucial respect, implying an absurdity which leads him to reject strategy I.

According to Stich's strategy I, linguists postulate "all known *dags*" for the languages for which they have data. They seek to determine "universal features" of "all known *dags*," incorporating such features in their "acquisition model." This model defines the class of *hpgs*. If the theory is not so restrictive that there is only on *hpg* compatible with *pld*, then the theory must also provide an "evaluation measure or weighting of *hpgs*," which selects the highest ranked among them as the grammar which, it is postulated, is "internally represented" by the speaker-hearer who has learned the language, who has acquired competence.[6] But, Stich remarks, this strategy is "wholly wrongheaded." The reason is that there is a

. . . superabundance of *dags* for any natural language. For every *dag* there are alternatives which are also descriptively adequate. But the linguistic universals were taken to be properties of all *dags*. Thus each *dag* for every natural language will be among the *hpgs*. So if any *dag* is compatible with the *pld*, all its alternatives will be as well. And we have made no progress at selecting a single *dag* as the right one. (323)

Furthermore, the same problem holds in the case of an evaluation measure:

. . . once such a measure *has* been found there will be indefinitely many alternative measures which select different *dags* for the same body of *pld*. . . . Thus if we can design a measure which ranks any one of these *dags* highst in the sub-class, there will be another measure which ranks a different *dag* highest. (323–324)

Notice in the first place Stich has misrepresented the account he is disparaging. The standard account defined a descriptively adequate theory as a theory that provides *some dag* for each set of *pld*. In Stich's version, we must first consider "all known *dags*" and then arrive at the theory inductively by considering features common to all of these. Naturally, this strategy will fail, given the superabundance of *dags*—that is, given the general underdetermination of theory by evidence. There will, to be sure, be mutually inconsistent grammars, all descriptively adequate so far as can be determined, but differing in their properties. We will get nowhere if we insist on first considering all known (imaginable, contrivable) grammars compatible with evidence, then proceeding to determine their common properties. But this was not the enterprise outlined. Rather, the account suggested that we construct a linguistic theory, which defines *hpgs* and offers a measure to select among them, as a hypothesis about human language and the capacity to acquire language in the normal way on the basis of *pld*. We then test this theory for descriptive adequacy by determining whether it provides *a dag* (not *all dags*) for each human language. We test it for explanatory adequacy by determining whether it selects, on the basis of *pld*, a *dag* for each language. Replacing an existential by a universal quantifier, Stich converts a sensible and properly limited inquiry into one that is "utterly wrong-headed," but has never been suggested in the literature.

In formulating his strategy I, Stich argues that "It is essential that the linguistic universals be taken as the properties common to each descriptively adequate grammar of every natural language," as against "An alternative notion that took the linguistic universals as the features common to each of the actually internalized grammar of every natural language" (331). The latter notion, which is in fact that of the standard account, is "useless," Stich claims: "until we *know* which grammars are internalized we cannot discover which features are universal to such grammars" (ibid.). But the objection is senseless. We cannot "know" which grammars are internalized in advance of constructing a linguistic theory. We can only *hypothesize* that certain grammars are internalized. The natural and appropriate strategy is to construct hypotheses with regard to particular grammars *and* with regard to linguistic theory, confronting the entire complex with data from various languages for confirmation. That is, we ask whether the grammars selected on the basis of *pld* by the postulated linguistic theory, with its definition of *hpg* and an evaluation measure, are, so far as can be determined, *dags*. We do not "know" that we are correct in these hypotheses. Nor will we ever be certain about this. All of this is commonplace, and it is perhaps surprising that it is necessary to reiterate it. Once it is recognized, however, it is plain that Stich has offered no objection at all to the account that has actually been proposed, though we agree with him in rejecting his strategy I, which misrepresents the standard account by a change of quantifiers. The latter seems to us quite adequate as far as it goes. The problems that arise are in principle no different from those which arise in any other empirical inquiry.

Of course, having constructed a linguistic theory meeting (to some extent) the conditions of descriptive and even explanatory adequacy, we will always be able to construct another theory, with a different characterization of *hpg* and a different evaluation measure, which will meet these conditions (to the same extent), selecting different *dags* that are just as compatible with evidence. Thus Stich is perfectly right in saying that "if we can design a measure which ranks any one of the *dags* highest in the subclass, there will be another measure which ranks a different *dag* highest" (324). This, he asserts, is the "crucial point." The point amounts to nothing more than the assertion that linguistics is an empirical science, not a branch of logic or mathematics. It thus has no force whatever with regard to the standard account, which of course also insists that linguistic theory, being a nontrivial empirical theory, is underdetermined by evidence.

Stich then expands the argument as follows:

> But whatever justification there is for holding the *dag* selected by one measure to be the grammar actually internalized is equally justification for holding that the other is. And we are back where we started, with too many *dags* each with equal claim to be the "right one." (ibid.)

The statement is uninteresting, no matter how we understand the notion "all evidence" that figures in the definition of *dag* and "justified linguistic theory." If by "all the grammarian's data"[7] we mean "all available data," then the linguist faced with alternative theories that are equally justified by all the data would search for more data to choose among them. Furthermore, he would consider how general methodological criteria (not to be confused with the evaluation measure that forms part of empirical linguistic theory) apply to the choice between these theories. If by "all the grammarian's data" we mean "all possible data" (granting some sense to this notion), then the linguist, by hypothesis, is restricted to methodological considerations. The linguist's "dilemma" would be exactly that of a physicist faced with the question: what would you do if you were presented with incompatible theories each "justified" in terms of all possible data?

Here we come to the real crux of the matter. Clearly, the physicist will reply that under such conditions the choice between these theories will be made on the basis of simplicity and other methodological criteria. What, then, would Stich say to this reply? He can only try to argue that the particular methodological criteria to which the physicist appeals are not the only criteria to which appeal could be made in choosing among these theories, and that—and here is the critical point—the criteria to which the physicist has appealed enjoy no special privilege among imaginable criteria. If philosophically informed and not caught napping, the physicist will surely point out that the criteria appealed to are justified by their success in other cases of scientific choice. For example, let the argument be about whether the physicist can motivate a choice of a specific curve to express the relation between the temperature and pressure of a gas on the basis of a set of observed values (supposing them to include every possible piece of data). Let us suppose further there are a number of curves $C_1, \ldots$ such that each passes through every observed point, and that the methodological criteria K to which our physicist appeals lead to selection of the curve with the least average curvature, say C_1. Then, if Stich suggests that there are other criteria K', K'', etc. that rank these curves differently, the physicist would, on our account, respond that K is preferable to the alternatives because in other cases in which K has been used to select a relationship between physical properties the subsequent evidence has confirmed the choice of K. Curves with the least average curvature, in general, turn out to state physical relationships more correctly than curves with any of the curvature properties that are evaluated more highly under K', K'', etc. Now, Stich has to reject such "empirical justification" by arguing that it depends on a second-level inductive extrapolation from similar cases in which K has been used and that such an extrapolation itself might be judged by varying criteria. But now Stich is in the position of asking that the physicist justify inductive criteria over counterinductive criteria, that the working physicist solve the Humean problem of induction in order to make practical decisions among competing theories. Unless Stich makes the solution of the philosophical problem of justifying an inductive policy a condition of scientific practice, he allows empirical justifications of methodological criteria of the kind that physicists and linguists use to choose hypotheses and theories. This concession, of course, means that in principle we may always be able to show, for any two *dags*, that they do not have "equal claim" to being the "right one," since only one of them may be in accord with the empirically justified evaluation measures. Thus Stich equivocates on the term "justification." If in asking for a justification of a simplicity criterion or other methodological criteria, he means "justification" in the sense in which this term is used in connection with the classical riddle of induction, then he is clearly asking too much of the scientist. On the other hand, if he is not asking too much, then the sense of 'justification' must allow empirical evidence in the form of higher-level inductions to count as justifying a simplicity criterion and other methodological critera.

Suppose it were further argued that the totality of possible observations concerning dispositions to respond by verbal (or other) behavior is consistent with *dags* and linguistic theories that are incompatible with one another. This observation would not distinguish linguistics from physics, since it is also true of physical theory that it is underdetermined by all possible data regarding dispositions (again, granting that this is a coherent notion). Suppose it were further argued, as it has been by Quine,[8] that there is nevertheless a difference between physics and linguistics because "theory in physics is an ultimate parameter," and we must "go on reasoning the affirming as best we can within our ever underdetermined and evolving theory of nature, the best one that we can muster at any one time"; whereas in linguistics,[9] "there is no real question of right choice; there is no fact of the matter even to *within* the acknowledged underdetermination of a theory of nature" because there is no "right English answer which is unique up to equivalence transformations of English sentences" to the question: "What did the native say?" This effort to distinguish linguistics from physics amounts to nothing more than the unargued claim that meanings do not exist.[10] But if physicists were to argue, say, that vital forces or atoms do not exist, they could not merely appeal to the undeniable fact of underdetermination of theory by evidence. Rather, they would either show some incoherence in the postulation of vital forces or atoms or construct a better theory to account for the data without any such assumptions. In the case at issue, Quine does nothing of the sort. There is no sense in which theory is an "ultimate parameter" in physics, more so than in other domains of empirical inquiry (granting the vast differences in depth of theory and empirical confirmation). We see no force whatsoever to the claim that there is some fundamental problem here that distinguishes linguistics from physics, and until some alternative is proposed to the theories of semantic representation now being explored in various ways, we see no reason to accept the arbitrary and unargued assertion that these theories have nothing to be right or wrong about.

Moreover, there is something conceptually incoherent in Quine's position. Quine accepts atoms and other inferred entities in physics, but would refuse to accept meanings even if the best theory to explain linguistic phenomena were to posit them. But surely Quine would not reject in principle a reduction of linguistics together with meanings to physics, say, a reduction on which meanings are interpreted as equivalence classes of brain states. On this possibility, linguistics is part of physical theory and semantic theory is part of our theory of the brain. If physics is able to deal with questions of truth, then surely it can deal with such questions in connection with states of the brain. How, then, can there be no truth in translation when there is something to be right or wrong about in physics generally?

Let us now consider the strategy that Stich endorses, his strategy II. In accordance with this strategy, the linguist seeks to construct an "acquisition model [which gives] as output *some* grammar that is true of the accomplished speaker," some grammar that is selected as "true of the speaker" given *pld*. Note that this is exactly the standard account, with one exception: that account took the linguist's hypothesized *dag* to be a description of the postulated "internal representation" of linguistic competence, whereas Stich speaks of this *dag* as "true of the speaker." Furthermore, Stich asserts that his strategy II does not "pretend to exhaust the class of grammars that humans can learn," whereas the standard account does propose that a theory meeting the condition of explanatory adequacy be taken as an empirical hypothesis concerning the intrinsic human ability to acquire language on the basis of *pld*. Thus, we note two respects in which Stich's strategy II appears to differ from the account that is familiar in the linguistic literature.[11]

We have already noted that Stich offers no objection to the standard account. Let us now compare strategy II with the standard account. The latter proposes that linguistic theory is falsifiable by the demonstration that, on some *pld*, a speaker-hearer will acquire competence that is not as described by the grammar selected by linguistic theory—or, in Stich's terms, that the grammar selected by the acquisition model will not be "true of the speaker." Since Stich does not impose on his acquisition model the condition that its outputs "exhaust the class of grammars that humans can learn," it would seem that he would not regard the result just described as a refutation of his model. On the other hand, since he does impose on his acquisition model the condition that, for each choice of *pld*, "the acquisition model have as output *some* grammar that is true of the accomplished speaker," it would seem that he should regard the result just described as a refutation of his theory. Suppose that we interpret him as saying that this result does refute the theory. In this case, his strategy II does not differ at all, in this respect, from the standard account. Suppose that he would not regard this result as refuting the theory. Then we will disregard his alternative and less exacting enterprise until he suggests some interesting empirical conditions that it must in fact meet.

Let us turn then to the issue that Stich seems to regard as more important, namely, the distinction between grammars "true of" speakers and grammars that correctly describe what is "internally represented" by speakers. Note that this issue has no relation to anything discussed so far. That much is plain when his misunderstanding of the standard account is corrected. Thus that account could have been formulated, throughout, referring to the *dags* as "true of speakers" rather than as descriptions of the internally represented linguistic competence. The question now at issue is, in essence, the question of realism. Are we willing to postulate that our *dags*, and our linguistic theory, describe properties of the speaker-hearer? Is the mature speaker-hearer to be regarded as a "system" with the properties spelled out in detail in the postulated *dag*, and is the child to be regarded as a "system" with the properties spelled out in detail in the postulated linguistic theory?

The standard account follows normal scientific practice in answering "yes" to both of these questions. Thus, imagine that a psychologist, investigating properties of visual perception, were led to postulate a theory involving analyzing mechanisms of various sorts, say, devices that analyzed stimuli into line, angle, motion, and so on. Would the psychologist propose that the theory is "true of" the organism or that it describes mechanisms possessed by the organism? If the former, the psychologist would be unconcerned if neurophysiological investigation were to demonstrate that visual perception actually proceeds in some entirely different way, with entirely different and unrelated mechanisms. The theory would still be "true of" the organism in Stich's sense of this notion. But any actual scientist regards a theory as subject to disconfirming or confirming evidence from other domains and would abandon the theory if it were shown that it is incompatible with such evidence, say, from neurophysiology. Comparably, a linguist who postulates a *dag* will not merely propose that it is "true of" an organism in what appears to be Stich's sense of this notion. Thus suppose it were discovered, say, by neurophysiological investigation or by psycholinguistic study, that all the linguist's data (and more) can be better explained by assuming that the organism has a system of perceptual strategies not involving the principles of generative grammar in any manner. The linguist who postulates a *dag* as "true of" the organism will be unperturbed. Linguists who take the realist position, claiming that a *dag* actually describes the speech mechanisms at work, might well abandon their formerly held comprehensive performance theory, with its idealized components and its specific principles and properties.

Now it might be argued that the perceptual psychologist, in the analogue, need not take a "realist" position; rather, if it is shown by neurophysiological investigation that some other theory is "true of" the organism, accommodating the data and much else, providing better explanations and deeper understanding, etc., then the perceptual psychologist can shift to this new theory, regarding it as "true of" the organism but not describing properties of the organism. Similarly, generative grammarians, faced with the discovery that a theory of perceptual strategies is superior in explanatory power, may shift to this theory taking it to be "true of" the organism but not as attributing to the organism specific properties and devices. If this tack is taken, then the alternative to the normal realist approach of the scientist is revealed to be merely a terminological quibble. Thus the physicist, following this approach, would no longer say that atomic theory postulates that matter consists of atoms, electrons, and so on; rather, the physicist says nothing about the structure of matter, but merely maintains that atomic theory is "true of" the world.

Stich's strategy II, understood narrowly, seems to amount to nothing more than an expression of lack of interest in certain problems; the problem of determining the nature of universal linguistic structure, the capacities that make language learning possible, the relation of logic to language, and whatever further insight the study of language might provide for psychology, philosophy, or neurophysiology. If grammars are not taken as theories about the internally represented systems of rules correlating sound and meaning, there is no problem for a theory of language acquisition to address itself to, since there is no longer a linguistic competence to account for as the product of language acquisition. Moreover, the notion of "linguistic universal" also is abandoned, since linguistic universals are principles common to the competence of native speakers of every natural language.[12] Abandoning this notion, we also relinquish any interest in the common structure of natural languages (should it exist). Moreover, we abandon the project of discovering general principles that determine the logical form of sentences in natural language (for example, determining how they are used in valid reasoning) on the basis of properties of postulated underlying structures; the search for such principles is hopeless, it would appear, if there are no universal properties of these underlying structures. All this follows, of course, only if we interpret Stich rather narrowly. If, on the other hand, he is merely proposing a terminological revision of the sort discussed in connection with perceptual psychology, we conclude that he is raising no substantive issue.

What, then, does Stich offer by way of counterbalancing advantages? He cites two. First, strategy II avoids the "puzzle" he brought up in connection with strategy I: now there is no need to make a unique choice among *dags* since there is no claim in strategy II that the selected grammar is actually internalized. Thus, the fact that there are competing evaluation measures for ranking *dags* is no problem. As Stich says:

Our project is the highly nontrivial project of producing a model that takes *pld* as input and yields an appropriate *dag* as output. *Any* evaluation measure that does the trick will be suitable (325).

This, however, is hardly an advantage if, as argued above, the alleged puzzle amounts to nothing more than the observation that linguistics is an empirical science. The second of the advantages that Stich claims for strategy II is that it accords better with actual linguistic practice than strategy I. Chomsky and others, Stich asserts, do not really study a broad range of languages in attempting to construct theories about universal grammatical structure and language acquisition, but merely speculate on the basis of "a single language, or at best a few closely related languages" (326). Stich's assertion is both false and irrelevant. Transformational grammarians have investigated languages drawn from a wide range of unrelated language families. But this is beside the point, since even if Stich were right in saying that all but a few closely related languages have been neglected by transformational grammarians, this would imply only that they ought to get busy studying less closely related languages, not that there is some problem in relating grammar construction to the study of linguistic universals.

Stich confuses the matter further by introducing plainly irrelevant analogies. Thus, he argues that "attributing knowledge of a grammar to a speaker is little more plausible than attributing knowledge of the laws of physics to a projectile whose behavior they predict" (328–329). Physicists postulate certain laws. Observing the behavior of a projectile, they attribute to it a structure that accounts for its behavior, given these laws. Thus, observing that the earth wobbles on its axis, physicists attribute to it the required bulge at the equator— and may go on to try to determine whether the earth is constructed as required by the theory. Following Stich's analogy, linguists postulate the "laws" of English grammar and attribute to the speaker a structure that accounts for its behavior, given these "laws." But what are the "laws," and what is the "structure"? Plainly, the "laws" are not like the laws of motion—they do not apply to rocks, or even to speakers of Japanese. In fact, under any intelligible formulation that has ever been offered, the "laws" apply only to an organism postulated to have an "internal representation" of the rules and principles of the grammar, along with other systems that interact with this internal representation to yield the judgments of grammaticality, acceptability, etc., that constitute the linguist's data, in accordance with the standard account. Since Stich does not address the problem why the "laws" do not apply to rocks or to speakers of Japanese, it is unnecessary for him to inquire into the structure of the organism that behaves in accordance with these "laws." Thus he is able to present such pointless and irrelevant analogies as the analogy to a projectile in motion that obeys the laws of physics.

Notice that a physicist might well conclude, observing a projectile, that it contains computing mechanisms that assess trajectory, change course, etc., employing an internal representation of the laws of physics. Thus, he might be led to this conclusion by observing how the projectile behaves under various modifications of the environment. If he were to obtain evidence suggesting that the projective has an internal computing structure, or even that it is not a servomechanism but seems to be aiming to reach a certain goal in some other fashion, or is acting in a still more complex way, he would not hesitate to postulate additional structure and to search for additional evidence of its existence and character. As a scientist, he would assume the reality of the structure he postulates in his theory of the projectile, and try to disconfirm or confirm this assumption. He would not be much interested if a philosopher were to tell him that he might rephrase his account of what he is doing, saying rather that he is attributing no structure or properties to the projectile but is "merely" proposing a theory that is "true of" the projectile.

There remains the question whether the structure that we attribute to the speaking person can properly be called "knowledge of a language," "knowledge of grammar," "possession of a cognitive state," or something else. Stich does not raise the issue here, but he has elsewhere. His conclusions in this regard seem to us unacceptable.[13] At best, it is an open question whether more than an uninteresting issue of terminology is involved.[14]

Stich observes that in his strategy II (the nonrealist version of the standard account) "an element of indeterminacy still lurks." This is quite true. Again, it is a defining characteristic of empirical science that theories are underdetermined by raw data. As already noted, Stich rejects Quine's conclusion that there is some special kind of indeterminacy that plagues the study of language beyond that of physics. He then goes on to claim (327–328) "If we are disinclined to say that in all science, modulo the indeterminacy, there is nothing to be right about, it is because the theories we are willing to allow as correct are those whose arbitrary features have the sanction of tradition." Thus neither linguistics, nor biology, nor physics, has anything "to be right about," tradition aside. Stich promises elsewhere a defense of this position. It will be interesting to see whether his defense will amount to something more than (a) a *reductio ad absurdum* argument against the indeterminacy thesis as formulated, or (b) a terminological variant of familiar realist approaches. We remain skeptical. In any event, we see no reason for taking seriously Stich's proposal that physics and linguistics, as well as every other science, have nothing to be right about, tradition aside.

Moreover, Stich's claim that there is a "strong analogy" between his thesis about the selection of *dags* in strategy II and Quine's thesis about the indeterminacy of translation is, as far as we can see, both a misunderstanding of Quine's thesis and an unwarranted claim. Stich seems to think that the fact that a *dag* has no claim to uniqueness and that an analytical hypothesis on Quine's thesis has none either is enough to establish Stich's thesis as analogous to Quine's except for their implications (327). However, on Stich's strategy II, a *dag* "correctly captures the intuitions of the speakers of the language (and the rest of the grammarian's data) within the limits of accuracy allowed by idealization" (321). Hence, the *dag* correctly predicts phonological, syntactic, and semantic properties of sentences (though without hypothesizing anything about an internalization). Therefore, since Stich's strategy II allows for the selection of a *dag*, it ought to choose between alternative analytical hypotheses, since Quine's analytical hypotheses state predictions about semantic properties of sentences. For any analytical hypothesis, say, *X* is synonymous with *Y*, the *dag* will correctly predict whether it is true or not. The point is this: Quine's thesis is a thesis about the tenability of meanings and the clarity and scientific status of semantic properties. Stich's is not, at least as far as we can determine.

Stich apparently interprets his strategy II in such a way that it leaves linguistics without the least interest to other scientific disciplines. He observes that "The modesty of a grammar, on my account, stands in stark contrast to more flamboyant portraits" (328).[15] The "flamboyant portrait" turns out to be nothing more than the claim that the grammar in the form it would take in models of speech production and perception must structurally correspond to some features of brain mechanism. Stich wonders how a linguist could presume to know so much about "the structure of the brain, having left the skulls of his subjects intact" (ibid.). His skepticism seems to derive from some variant of instrumentalism. Clearly, the linguist does not produce a priori pronouncements on the details of neural connections and pathways, but rather presents a modest inference from some very general features of effects to very general features of their causes, providing a sketch of what the causes would have to be like to be capable of producing the effect.[16]

But, given Stich's charge, it is perhaps worth while to sketch the rationale for such realistic inferences from effects. Such inferences are standard practice in science. Early physicists had no opportunity to look at the microstructure of matter, but, like present-day linguists, had to leave the "skulls of their subjects intact." Nonetheless, they were able to determine a great deal about the microstructure of matter from its behavior. For instance, they could infer that matter is discontinuous, composed of many tiny particles that are invisible, because on this account they were able to explain such phenomena as diffusion. But to explain observable effects like the change of the color of water when dye is put in it in terms of the migration of dye molecules into the spaces between the water molecules commits scientists to the reality of the unobserved causal conditions, since such explanations make sense only if we adopt the realistic assumption that the theoretical terms in which they are couched actually refer to things in nature. If one were to say that the term "molecule" in the foregoing explanation is a mere *façon de parler*, that it denotes nothing real, the "explanation" would become nonsense.

These considerations are quite general, applying to linguistic explanations as much as to explanations in physics. We postulate certain properties of the brain, e.g., that it must contain some neural mechanism that stores the information in the grammar,[17] on the grounds that properties of linguistic behavior can be explained by assuming them to be causal consequences of brain mechanisms with access to such information. To explain the grammatical judgments of speakers on the basis of such a hypothesized causal chain while denying the existence of essential links in the chain makes no more sense than to explain diffusion while denying the existence of molecules.[18] Stich asserts:

> Though Katz's claims about grammar are more expansive than those I have made, the evidence he uses to confirm a grammar is of a piece with the evidence indicated in my account. Thus, it remains something of a mystery how the grammarian has learned as much as Katz would have him know (328).

In reply, we can point out that some people may well be interested in making hypothetical inferences about underlying causes on the basis of certain evidence, while others with different interests and outlook may choose to restrict their attention more narrowly to the evidence. We can certainly imagine that some early physicists might have been quite happy to accept diffusion and similar phenomena at face value, chiding their Democritean colleagues for "flamboyant portraits" of atoms.

Finally, Stich argues that it is "perhaps misleading" for the grammarian to claim that he is "constructing a theory of the language of his subjects. Rather he is building a description of the facts of acceptability and linguistic intuitions" (329). Apparently this remains true even if the grammarian succeeds in the task that Stich correctly regards as "a monumentally impressive feat," namely, constructing an acquisition model in accordance with his strategy II. The reason why even this feat would produce only a description, not a theory, is that "A theory of a language seriously worthy of the name would provide some insight into what it is to *understand* a sentence, how sentences can be used to communicate and to deal more effectively with the world, . . . But a grammar does none of this" (ibid.; see our note 15). Stich continues: "Indeed it is logically possible that there be a person whose linguistic intuitions màtched up near enough with our own, but who could neither speak nor understand English" (ibid.). Stich's point is that, since such a person would be equivalent to a native speaker for the purposes of grammar construction, grammar construction has no contribution to make to explain how speakers use and understand sentences. Since this is the only argument Stich offers to show that Chomsky's notion of grammatical competence is "explanatorily vacuous" and that grammars provide no "insight into what it is to *understand* a sentence,"[19] it is worth considering it in some detail.

To begin with, we agree—in fact, we insist—that grammars are not full theories of sentence use. Indeed, this is the essence of the competence-performance distinction. But to conclude that theories of competence are "explanatorily vacuous" or mere descriptions is plainly a *non sequitur*. With equal force, one might argue that physics is explanatorily vacuous and provides only descriptions, not theories, because it gives us no insight into human behavior; who, after all, could be interested in mere inanimate objects and their properties? Plainly the distinction between "theory" and "description" and the notion of "explanatory force" are not dependent on the extent to which one or another person may be intrigued by the subject matter under discussion.

Pursuing Stich's argument, since we adopt the competence-performance distinction, we agree with him that it is logically possible that some creature might have full linguistic competence but lack the devices that are postulated in the more comprehensive theory of language use. Since, on Stich's account, the *dag* that is "true of" this speaker describes all his intuitions about grammatical properties and relations, then it describes in particular all semantic properties and relations. For each sentence, it determines whether it is meaningful, analytic, how many senses it has, to what sentences it is synonymous (on some reading), etc.[18] We fail to see, then, how this *dag* can describe all the speaker's intuitions about such properties and relations while offering no insight into how sentences are used and understood—though the creature postulated in Stich's logically possible case would, by hypothesis, not be able to proceed to use and understand sentences as do persons with the same linguistic competence embedded in a performance system. The fact that there could, in principle, be a creature whose linguistic intuitions "match up near enough with our own but who could neither speak nor understand English" shows no more than what the standard account assumes: a more comprehensive theory of performance must be constructed, incorporating grammars, to account for the use and understanding of speech.

In effect, Stich is arguing that a certain type of aphasia is logically possible: a case in which a speaker can give judgments about sentences and thus "serve almost as well as an English speaker as an informant for constructing a grammar of English," while being unable to speak and understand the language. From this observation he concludes that it is misleading to describe a grammar as a theory of the language of the linguist's subject. The conclusion, if anything, should be quite the opposite. The existence of this type of aphasia would be most congenial to the standard account, since it would indicate that it is possible for the competence system to function even when it is "disconnected" from one component of the performance system in which the standard account assumes it to be embedded. Whereas the standard account does not imply that such a case must exist, discovery of such a case would surely confirm its specific empirical assumptions about the speaker.

In summary, we see no reason to believe that Stich has offered any coherent challenge to the standard account of what the linguist is talking about.

NOTES

1. This work was supported in part by the National Institute of Mental Health, Grant 5 PO1 MH 13390-07.

2. *The Journal of Philosophy*, LXIX, 22 (Dec. 7, 1972): 799–818.

3. Cf. Chomsky, *Aspects of the Theory of Syntax* (Cambridge, Mass.: MIT Press, 1965), ch. I, and other sources.

4. Cf. *ibid.*, ch. I, and Katz, *The Philosophy of Language* (New York: Harper & Row, 1966), pp. 240–282.

5. Transformational analysis inherently reflects this concern with more abstract questions. For one thing, in revealing underlying levels of sentence structure, transformational analysis overcomes structuralist objections to many of the claims of traditional universal grammar, namely, apparent counterexamples to cross-language generalizations based on features of surface structure. A transformational-generative grammar reveals deeper levels and more abstract properties which appear to be more uniform across languages, thus permitting the formulation of nontrivial general hypotheses about language structure. Furthermore, it seems reasonable to expect that important aspects of the traditional distinction between "logical form" and "grammatical form" can be explicated on the basis of syntactic structure and its semantic interpretation; Katz, *Semantic Theory* (New York: Harper & Row, 1972).

6. He refers to the selected grammar as "this 'explanatorily adequate' grammar which the child actually internalizes and which the linguist seeks to uncover." Notice that in the account he is attempting to reproduce, "explanatory adequacy" is a property of linguistic theory, not of grammars.

7. Stich defines a *dag* as a grammar that "correctly captures the intuitions of the speakers of the language (and the rest of the grammarian's data) within the limits of accuracy allowed by idealization" (807).

8. "Replies," in D. Davidson and J. Hintikka, eds., *Words and Objections: Essays on the Work of W. V. Quine* (Dordrecht: Reidel, 1969), pp. 303–304.

9. It is unclear to us whether Quine intends to restrict his remarks about indeterminacy in linguistics to "indeterminacy of translation," which he explicitly discusses, or to indeterminacy of all linguistic theory that goes beyond the Gedankenexperiment on "stimulus meaning" to which he arbitrarily restricts attention at certain points in his exposition. It is obvious and uninteresting that, given an arbitrary restriction on permissible evidence, there will be incompatible hypotheses compatible with this evidence. It is less obvious that there are incompatible hypotheses such that no imaginable evidence can bear on the choice between them. We will not pursue this matter, since, even if we were to grant the latter claim, it would in no way distinguish linguistics in principle from other empirical inquiries. Stich, incidentally, agrees with our conclusion that Quine's arguments do not distinguish linguistics from physics, a matter to which we return. For further discussion of Quine's efforts to distinguish linguistics from physics, see Chomsky, *Current Issues in Linguistic Theory* (The Hague: Mouton, 1964); and "Quine's Empirical Assumptions," in Davidson and Hintikka, op. cit.

10. As is shown in Katz, *Semantic Theory*, pp. 286–292.

11. Stich suggests another respect in which his strategy II differs from the standard account, namely, he is concerned only with "quasi-universals" which are properties of all the outputs of the acquisition model, but "are in no sense universals—there is no claim that all *dags* must share them" (812). Again, this observation reflects his misunderstanding of the standard account, which did not hold that universals are properties of all *dags* that are in fact descriptions of linguistic competence. In fact, Stich's "quasi-universals" are exactly the universals of the standard account, if we add the realist assumptions just noted.

12. Stich continues to use the term "acquisition model" in connection with strategy II, but this usage seems to us incomprehensible on his grounds.

13. See Graves, Katz et al., "Tacit Knowledge," *The Journal of Philosophy*, LXX, 11 (June 7, 1973); 318–330.

14. See Chomsky, "Knowledge of Language," *Times Literary Supplement*, 15 May 1969, excerpted from an essay to appear in K. Gunderson and G. Maxwell, eds., *Minnesota Studies in Philosophy of Science*, vol. VI. And also *Problems of Knowledge and Freedom* (New York: Pantheon, 1971), ch. I.

15. Note that in Stich's view the best that one can say for doing grammar is to hope that it may lead to "deep insights into exciting phenomena of comprehension and communication" and "that it is something to do." Vague hopes and busy hands.

16. Katz, "Mentalism in Linguistics," *Language*, XL, 2 (April/June 1964): 133.

17. This is the disputed question: cf. Stich, 816.

18. Katz, *Semantic Theory*, pp. 28–29.

19. Stich 816/17. We are, of course, by-passing the question of attributing knowledge of a grammar to a speaker, which does not really play an essential role in the present discussion. Cf. Stich, "What Every Speaker Knows," and Graves, Katz et al., op cit.

PART FIVE

NEW FRONTIERS

MICHAEL G. DYER

$RESTAURANT REVISITED OR "LUNCH WITH BORIS"

1. INTRODUCTION

Several natural language understanding systems, such as SAM (Cull-ingford 1978) and FRUMP (DeJong 1979), use the notion of a script (Schank and Abelson 1977), knowledge structure containing a stereotypic sequence of actions. Scripts are intended to capture situations in which the behavior is so stylized that the need for complex plan or goal analysis rarely arises. A prototypical example of a script is $RESTAURANT = ENTER + BE-SEATED + WAITRESS-COMES + ORDER-FOOD + FOOD-BROUGHT + EAT-FOOD + RECEIVE-CHECK + LEAVE-TIP + PAY-BILL + LEAVE.

Scripts are useful in supplying expectations during processing. These expectations represent an active context and help in such tasks as:

(1) Pronoun Resolution—In a $RESTAURANT context, clearly the "he" in: "He left him a big tip." is the customer while "him" must be a waiter.

(2) Word Sense Disambiguation—The expressions "ordered" and "to go" have very different meanings in a restaurant ("John ordered a pizza go.") than in the military ("The general ordered a private to go.")

(3) Supplying Inferences—Once a script is chosen, processing can proceed very efficiently, since missing information is automatically provided by the script. For example:

John ordered a lobster.
John paid and left.

Q: What did John eat?
A: Lobster.

Scripts also contain one or more paths (Cullingford 1978), each supplying a possible alternative sequence of actions to ghost (Lehnert 1977) (or default) path. An alternative path in $RESTAURANT includes leaving without paying because the food was improperly cooked. This path information is used to answer questions, such as:

Q: Why didn't John eat the hamburger?

In this case, the search heuristic starts with the "ghost path" in which the food would have been eaten. The retrieval heuristic backs up along this path until a branch point is found. Here resides the reason:

A: The hamburger was burnt.

that an alternate path was taken.

2. PROBLEMS WITH $RESTAURANT

However, representing what people know about restaurants only in terms of a $RESTAURANT script is inadequate, for three reasons:

(1) Scripts were conceived as self-contained "chunks" of knowledge. As a result, it is difficult to share knowledge across scripts. For example, a restaurant serves meals, but people also eat meals in nonrestaurant situations (home, picnics). This meal knowledge should be shared with restaurant knowledge, even though the meal server in a restaurant differs from the meal server at home.

(2) Because scripts are self-contained, experiences occurring within one script cannot be generalized to other relevant situations. For example, if we refuse to pay for burnt food in a restaurant, somehow the knowledge derived from this experience should be available later in an $AUTO-REPAIR context, when the mechanic fails to fix the engine properly.

(3) Scripts lack intentionality. From a scriptal point of view, each event occurs next simply because it is the next event in the script. Although script-based programs know that characters initiate $RESTAURANT to satisfy hunger, they do not know why any specific event within $RESTAURANT occurs. This is analogous to answering:

Q: Why does the diner tip the waitress?
A: I don't know. That's just what he does in a restaurant after he's eaten.

Lack of intentionality has both advantages and disadvantages. It is certainly more efficient, since goals and plans do not have to be processed in order to predict what a character will do next. However, it is difficult to handle novel situations, where a character's reaction might be explainable if the underlying goals and motivations (for the expected event) were known (Wilensky 1978).

For instance, a friend admitted to me that, as a child, she enjoyed pocketing the coins people left on restaurant tables. One day she was caught by

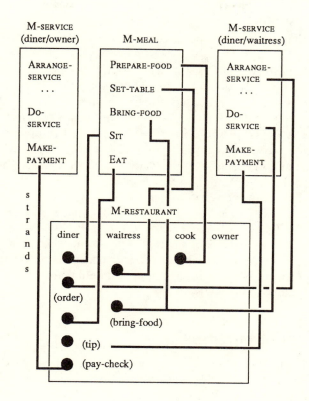

her parents, who informed her that these coins were to reward the waitress for her service. Until this moment, in which my friend grasped the intentional significance of tipping, it had just been a "scriptal action" for her.

3. MOPS

In BORIS, an in-depth understander of narratives (Dyer and Lehnert 1980) (Lehnert and Dyer 1980), scripts have been augmented by a class of knowledge structures called MOPs (Memory Organization Packets) (Schank 1981).

Like scripts, MOPs encode expectations, but unlike scripts, MOPs are not isolated chunks of knowledge. Instead, each MOP in BORIS has strands which indicate how the MOP has been constructed from other knowledge sources. Each strand connects an event in one MOP to some event in another MOP. In this way, MOPs are overlaid with each other. Consider diagram-1:

Events in M-RESTAURANTare overlaid with their corresponding events in M-MEAL and M-SERVICE. In this way, M-RESTAURANT can be viewed from different perspectives. From the perspective of M-MEAL, a restaurant is simply a setting in which people have meals. From the perspective of M-SERVICE, the diner in M-RESTAURANT is engaged in a service contract with the restaurant owner. The restaurant must serve food to the diner and, in return, the diner is expected to pay for this service.

As stated earlier, script-based systems represent scriptal deviation in terms of alternate "paths." Thus, the restaurant script contains a BURNT-FOOD → LEAVE-WITHOUT-PAYING path. But this approach causes a proliferation of paths, for two reasons: First, every possible deviation has to be anticipated and "canned" into the script; otherwise the script would not be able to handle the deviation. Second, each service-related script ends up copying the same path. For example, in $AUTO-REPAIR there has to be a BAD-REPAIR → LEAVE-WITHOUT-PAYING path. By overlaying these scripts with M-SERVICE, a single deviation path: POOR-SERVICE → RE-FUSE-TO-PAY in M-SERVICE can represent deviation knowledge at a more general level. Likewise, "payment for service" occurs in many situations, not just in $RESTAURANT. Therefore, tipping should be understood at a more general level than $RESTAURANT.

4. HANDLING DEVIATIONS

When stereotypic situations are first encountered, people let their scriptal knowledge handle the situation until a violation occurs. At this point they become aware of other perspectives associated with the script, each potentially useful in understanding the violation.

For instance, we rarely think about the contractual aspects of restaurants when eating in one. Restaurants are usually "taken for granted" as a place where one can have a meal and socialize. Only when something goes wrong do we think of the contract we're implicitly engaged in. If the service is bad, then we reconsider the amount of the tip and what it's for.

More importantly, a deviation which has never before been encountered may be handled, as long as some strand exists from the script to a knowledge structure with information about this type of deviation. For instance, if $MOVIE has strands to M-SERVICE then the very first time the movie projector breaks we can use our deviation path in M-SERVICE to demand a refund, even if the projector breaking is a novel experience.

Consider how BORIS processes the following fragment of DIVORCE-2, a complicated narrative (Dyer 1983) concerning marital infidelity:

George was having lunch . . . when the waitress accidentally knocked a glass of coke on him. George was very annoyed and left refusing to pay the check . . .

Briefly, an analysis of "having lunch" activates M-MEAL. When "waitress" occurs, the MOPs associated with this role are examined. If a MOP being examined has a strand to an active MOP, then it is also activated. Since there are strands from M-RESTAURANT to M-MEAL, and since M-MEAL is already active, M-RESTAURANT is activated also.

An interpretation of "accidentally" indicates that a violation may follow. This heuristic is based upon the assumption that unintended actions usually violate scriptal expectations.

"Knocked a glass of coke on him" is analyzed in terms of the Conceptual Dependency (Schank and Abelson, 1977) primitive PROPEL (Object = Liquid). Given this event, BORIS tries to match it against the events expected in M-RESTAURANT. This match would normally fail, since M-RESTAURANT does not expect waitresses to PROPEL food-stuffs. However, "accidentally" has warned BORIS of a possible violation, so a violation match is attempted and succeeds. At this point BORIS realizes that the PROPEL event is a violation of the event BRING-FOOD in M-RESTAURANT, rather than some event totally unrelated to M-RESTAURANT.

Now what is BORIS to do? In previous systems, there would be a path in the script for such a deviation. However, this is not the case here. When BORIS encounters a deviation, it searches the strands connected to the event where the deviation occurred. This leads to DO-SERVICE in M-SERVICE (see diagram-1).

Associated with M-SERVICE is general knowledge about how things may "go wrong" for each event in M-SERVICE. There are several events, such as: ARRANGE-SERVICE, DO-SERVICE, INFORM-BILL, MAKE-PAYMENT, etc. For example, the sentence:

The waitress overcharged George.

constitutes a violation of INFORM-BILL.

In addition, there is knowledge about how violations may be related to each other. This knowledge is represented by rules, such as:

If SERVER has done SERVICE badly (or not at all),
Then SERVER should either not BILL CONTRACTOR or BILL for amount < NORM.

If SERVER has done SERVICE badly or BILLs CONTRACTOR for amount > NORM,
Then CONTRACTOR may REFUSE PAYMENT.

BORIS uses this knowledge to recognize the connection between the waitress PROPEL LIQUID and George's refusal to pay a check.

Left to consider is how BORIS realizes that the violation of BRING-FOOD actually constitutes POOR-SERVICE. This is accomplished by tracking the goals of the characters. The PROPEL LIQUID on George is understood to cause a PRESERVE-COMFORT goal for George. This goal is examined by M-SERVICE, which applies the following heuristic:

If SERVER causes a PRESERVATION GOAL for CONTRACTOR while performing SERVICE,
Then it is probably POOR-SERVICE.

Thus, BORIS uses several sources of knowledge to understand what has happened. M-RESTAURANT supplies expectations for what the waitress should have done. Knowledge about PROPEL and LIQUIDs supplies goal information, while M-SERVICE (between waitress and diner) provides very general knowledge about how contractors will respond to poor service.

5. CONCLUSIONS

Early script-based systems operated within restricted knowledge source domains. For instance, although Frump had many available scripts to choose from, once a single script had been selected, the rest of the story was processed within the context of that script alone. As a result, many problems involving scriptal interactions never arose.

In this paper I have discussed various problems with scripts, and suggested memory 'overlays' as an initial solution. This overlay scheme has several advantages:

Each knowledge structure need know only what is directly relevant to it. For example, what a waitress does in captured in M-RESTAURANT, while her reasons for doing her job are represented at the M-SERVICE level which will handle any type of service. M-SERVICE need not be repeated for janitors, salesgirls, etc. This supports economy of storage, but more importantly, it means that any augmentation of the knowledge in M-SERVICE will automatically improve the processing ability of any MOP with strands to it.

Related knowledge sources need not be activated unless something goes wrong during processing. For instance, people do not normally think of the contract between themselves and the restaurant manager unless they are having trouble with the service.

Finally, a given event can be understood from several perspectives. For example, a "business lunch" involves M-MEAL, M-SERVICE, M-RESTAURANT, and M-BUSINESS-DEAL simultaneously.

NOTE

1. This work supported in part by Advanced Research Projects Agency contract N0014-75-C-111 and National Science Foundation contract IST7918463.

ACKNOWLEDGMENTS

Special thanks go to Tom Wolf, Pete Johnson, Mark Burstein and Marty Korsin for their conceptual and practical contributions to the BORIS project.

MICHAEL G. DYER

THE ROLE OF TAUs IN NARRATIVES

1. INTRODUCTION

People often rely upon common sayings, or adages, when asked to characterize stories (either by way of summarization, or title selection). What are people doing in such cases? Why do adages often serve as an effective way of characterizing a story, and how are people able to accomplish this?

For instance, when asked to characterize the following story:

MINISTER'S COMPLAINT
In a lengthy interview, Reverend X severely criticized President Carter for having "denigrated the office of president" and "legitimized pornography" by agreeing to be interviewed in Playboy magazine. The interview with Reverend X appeared in Penthouse magazine.

readers often responded with adages such as:

ADG-1: The pot calling the kettle black.
ADG-2: Throwing stones when you live in a glass house.

Clearly, these adages are an effective characterization of MINISTER'S COMPLAINT. But how do we recognize this fact? By what process does an "appropriate" adage come to mind, and to what purpose?

Furthermore, when supplied with an adage and a context, some individuals experience remindings from episodes in their lives. For instance, one individual was first presented with the following:

context: EDUCATION
ADG-3: Closing the barn door after the horse has escaped.

and then asked to recall some episode from his life. He experienced this reminding:

ACADEMIA

Years ago, I was at University U-1, where I could never get the facilities I needed for the research I wanted to do. So I decided to apply to University U-2, which offered a much better research environment. When the chairman learned I had been accepted to U-2 and was actually leaving U-1, he offered to acquire the facilities I had wanted. By then, however, my mind was already made up.

Several observations are worth making here: First, for adage ADG-3 to have initiated this reminding, the ACADEMIA episode must have somehow been indexed in long-term memory in terms of some abstract situation characterized by that adage. Furthermore, this indexing could not have had anything to do with the specific semantic content of the adage, since ADG-3 ostensibly concerns a farmer, a horse, and a barn door. In contrast, ACA-DEMIA involves a chairman, a researcher, and university facilities.

To account for such phenomena, I will present a class of knowledge constructs, called TAUs (Thematic Affect Units), which share similarities with other representational systems under development at Yale, such as Schank's TOPs (Schank 1980) and Lehnert's Plot Units (Lehnert 1980).

2. THEMATIC AFFECT UNITS

TAUs were first developed in the context of BORIS (see Lehnert and Dyer 1980, and Dyer, forthcoming), a computer program designed to read and answer questions about narratives that require the application and interaction of many different types of knowledge. In BORIS, TAUs serve a number of purposes: First, they allow BORIS to represent situations which are more abstract than those captured by scripts, plans, and goals as discussed in (see Schank and Abelson, 1977). Second, TAUs contain processing knowledge useful in dealing with the kinds of planning and expectation failures that characters often experience in narratives. Finally, TAUs also serve as episodic memory structures, since they organize events which involve similar kinds of planning failures. For more detail on the use of TAUs in narratives, see (Dyer 1981).

In general, TAUs arise when expectation failures occur due to errors in planning. As such, they contain an abstracted planning structure, which represents situation-outcome patterns in terms of: (1) the plan used, (2) its intended effect, (3) why it failed, and (4) how to avoid (or recover) from that type of failure in the future. If we abstract out this planning structure from both the BARN-DOOR and ACADEMIA episodes, we get the following TAU:

TAU-POST-HOC

(1) x has preservation goal G (Schank and Aelson 1977) active since enablement condition C unsatisfied.
(2) x knows a plan P that will keep G from failing by satisfying C.
(3) x does not execute P and G fails.
  x attempts to recover from the failure of G by executing P.
  P fails since P is effective for C, but not in recovering from G's failure.
(4) In the future, x must execute P when G is active and C is not satisfied.

TAU-POST-HOC captures the kind of planning failure that occurred for both the farmer who lost his horse, and the chairman who lost a graduate student. If the ACADEMIA story were told to an actual farmer who had lost his horse under the same planning circumstances, that farmer might well be reminded of his own experience. Whether this occurs or not, however, depends upon what other episodes are in long-term memory and what features are shared between them. Notice, for instance, that both BARN-DOOR and ACADEMIA share goals at some level. That is, both the farmer and the chairman had a goal requiring proximity on the part of another entity. Since these features are shared, one experience has a better chance of causing a reminding of the other to occur. For instance, the farmer would have recalled the HIRED HAND episode below before recalling the BARN-DOOR episode because of their shared features:

HIRED HAND

The hired hand always wanted a raise, but the farmer would not grant it. Finally, the hired hand got an offer to work at a neighbor's farm. When the farmer found out, he offered the hired hand a nice raise, but it was too late.

Although these episodes (i.e., HIRED HAND, ACADEMIA, BARN-DOOR) share the same TAU, HIRED HAND and ACADEMIA have more indices in common. One possible organization for them appears below:

In this way TAUs can account for cross-contextual remindings (as in the case of BARN-DOOR and ACADEMIA). Episodes are often related in memory because they share the same abstract planning error even though they differ in content. However, cross-contextual remindings can occur only where episodes are organized under the same TAU, yet do not share content features. Where content is shared, the "closer" episode will be recalled.[2] Consider the following episode:

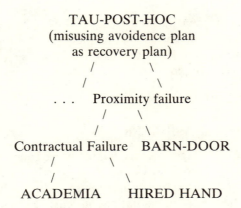

TAU-POST-HOC
(misusing avoidence plan
as recovery plan)

. . . Proximity failure

Contractual Failure   BARN-DOOR

ACADEMIA   HIRED HAND

IRANIAN EMBASSY

While holding 52 US hostages in Iran, the Iranian government condemned the take-over, by terrorists, of its embassy in Great Britain. "This is a violation of international law," protested Iran.

A reader was spontaneously reminded of this episode while reading MINISTER'S COMPLAINT. Again, there is little in common between these stories at the content level. IRANIAN EMBASSY is about politics, while MINISTER'S COMPLAINT is about pornography. However, at the abstract planning level, they both share the following TAU:

TAU-HYPOCRISY

x is counter-planning against y.
x is trying to get a higher authority z to either block y's use of a plan P-1 (or to punish y for having used P-1) by claiming that P-1 is an unethical plan.
y claims that x has used an unethical plan P-2 similar to P-1.
therefore, x's strategy fails.

In the case of MINISTER'S COMPLAINT, x is Reverend R, y is President Carter, and the third party is "public opinion." In the case of IRANIAN EMBASSY, x is the Iranian militants, y is the British terrorists, and the third party is "world opinion," such as the United Nations.

As argued in (Schank 1980), the reminding process is useful for this reason: Once a situation has caused one to be reminded of an episode, all of the expectations associated with that episode become available for use in making predictions about what will occur next. In the case of TAUs, their associated expectations include advice on either how to avoid making the error predicted by the TAU, or on what alternative plan can be used to recover from the error once it has been made. The ability to store cross-contextual episodes make TAUs very general and powerful mechanisms.

Once an episode has been indexed under a TAU, its recovery/avoidance heuristics become available for use in completely different situations. Thus, planning advice learned in one context can help processing in other contexts, if the experience was recognized in terms of an appropriate TAU in the first place.

3. BAD PLANNING IS WIDESPREAD

An examination of adages reveals that many are concerned with planning failures. That is, adages advise us either how to recover from a failure, or how to recognize and thus avoid future failures. Often, this advice is given implicitly, simply by describing situations in which certain planning errors lead to goal failures. In most cases, adages capture what has been called meta-planning (Wilesnky 1980) — i.e., planning advice on how to select or use plans in general. For example, some adages deal with the need for checking enablement conditions before plan execution:

ADG-4 Don't count your chickens before they're hatched.

Other adages stress choosing less costly avoidance plans over more costly recovery plans:

ADG-5 A stitch in time saves nine.

or weighing the risks involved with the goal to be achieved:

ADG-6 If it ain't broke, don't fix it.
ADG-7 The cure can be worse than the disease.

Many plans require cooperation or coordination with others. This can simplify planning but complicate plan execution:

ADG-8 Two heads are better than one.
ADG-9 Too many cooks spoil the broth.

Some plans involve selecting an appropriate agent:

ADG-10 The blind leading the blind.
ADG-11 Who pays the piper calls the tune.

Timing, enablement conditions, cost, plan coordinations, and agents are just a few of the areas in which plans can go wrong. Other areas, for example, include counter-planning against a foe,

ADG-12 Cut off your nose to spite your face.

anticipating planning failures when using high risk plans,

ADG-13 Don't burn bridges behind you.

the timing of plans,

ADG-14 The early bird catches the worm.

and tradeoffs between short-term and long-term planning strategies:

ADG-15 If you can't lick 'em join 'em.
ADG-16 Don't bite the hand that feeds you.
ADG-17 Honesty is the best policy.
ADG-18 Live by the sword, die by the sword.

Any story that involves these kinds of planning failures will end up being indexed under a TAU which contains abstract planning advice (and can be expressed in natural language by an adage.) When a related story is read and indexed under that TAU, its associated adage may come to mind. For instance, a story about how a ghetto riot protesting bad economic conditions resulted in black businesses being burned, would be indexed under TAU-GREATER-HARM, with an adage such as ADG-12 possibly coming to mind.

Plans and plan failures cut across all knowledge domains. This is because we are always choosing plans, adjusting old plans to new situations, recovering from errors in planning, finding explanations for why a plan failed, etc. Furthermore, we have a large storehouse of heuristic plans, and there are many ways a plan can go wrong: You can't execute one plan until you have the right enablements satisfied; plan components must be executed in the right order; plans require agents, etc. This large and complex domain serves as a perfect terrain in which to index many episodes.

Many of these adages give what may appear to be superficial advice. It may seem strange that memories should be organized around such "obvious" rules for planning, but then again, how often do we fail in our plans because we have violated some adage? How often, for instance, have we failed because we acted before we planned? ("Look before you leap.") How many times have we gotten into trouble for being late? When have we initiated a plan, only to discover we had miscalculated the amount of effort (or the side-effects) involved? ("Easier said than done.") How often have we delayed executing a simple plan, only later having to execute a more costly plan? The answer is: "very often." These adages are common because they point out the kinds of planning errors people are always making. By definition, plans which failed were "bad" plans. Good planners at the very least follow the general planning advice represented in the adages of their culture.

4. TAU IMPLEMENTATION

The recognition of TAUs is complex. Clearly, goals and plans must be tracked. In many cases there is also an affect component. For instance, in TAU-POST-HOC it is the futility of the recovery plan, combined with the sense of "if only I had done things differently" that helps provide an access "key" to this TAU.

So far the BORIS project has emphasized the use of TAUs in narrative comprehension. Much work remains to be done in modeling remindings during comprehension. This is important for extracting the "moral" or point of a story. A computer program which can only answer questions of fact about IRANIAN EMBASSY, such as:

Q: How many Americans are being held in Iran?
A: Fifty-two.
Q: Who seized the Iranian embassy in Britain?
A: Terrorists.
Q: What did the Iranians do?
A: They protested the take-over.

is missing the point of why the IRANIAN EMBASSY is of interest. The point of IRANIAN EMBASSY is TAU-HYPOCRISY, and that's where it should be remembered in long-term memory (rather than just under "things I know about Iran," or "embassy events I have read").

5. TAU EXPERIMENTS

What is the psychological validity of TAUs? Do people have TAUs "in their heads" and, if so, how do they use them? Some initial exploratory experiments by Seifert (Seifert 1980) in the Yale psychology department indicate that people use TAUs to organize narratives.

In one experiment, subjects read groups of stories each sharing the same TAU, but differing in content. Subjects were able to generate new stories, using completely different contexts, yet capturing the same planning structure specified by each TAU. In a follow-up experiment, different subjects were asked to sort the resulting stories generated from the first experiment. A cluster analysis (Reiorer, et. al., forthcoming) revealed a strong tendency for subjects to sort stories together by TAUs. Where stories shared the same content (but not the same TAUs) they were still grouped by TAUs.

6. CONCLUSIONS

In this paper I have presented a class of knowledge constructs called TAUs, which are related to TOPs (Schank 1980) and PLOT UNITs (Lehnert, forthcoming). I have argued that TAUs organize episodes around failures in planning, and as such, TAUs account for at least one form of cross-contextual reminding phenomena. Furthermore, TAUs have adages associated with them, which express avoidance and/or recovery advice available once the TAU has been accessed. Since stories are indexed in terms of planning errors, this information often captures the moral or point of a story.

NOTES

1. This work supported in part by the Advanced Research Projects Agency under contract N0014-75-C-111 and in part by the National Science Foundation under contract IST7918463.

Thanks go to Tom Wolf and Marty Korsin for helping with some of the ideas presented here, and for being sources of remindings.

2. This does not imply that BARN-DOOR can't remind one of episodes unrelated to TAU-POST-HOC. Clearly, other indexing methods may be operating at the same time. The farmer may recall BARN-DOOR simply in terms of "experiences I've had with horses." Of course, this kind of indexing can not lead to cross-contextual remindings.

TERRY WINOGRAD

MOVING THE SEMANTIC FULCRUM

The emergence of situation semantics has been a notable cross-disciplinary event. The theory was developed by a philosopher and a mathematician in the tradition of the analytic philosophy of language. Many of its most enthusiastic advocates have been natural language researchers in artificial intelligence. This commentary explores the reasons for this enthusiasm, the limitations of the theory as seen from an AI perspective, and the significance it is likely to have for computational theory and practice.

SUMMARY OF THE NEW IDEA

The main innovation of Barwise and Perry is their attempt to move the *fulcrum* on which semantic theory rests. In order to separate the study of semantics from problems of ontology and epistemology, it is necessary to explicate the meaning of linguistic objects in terms of something nonlinguistic—something whose nature is taken for granted within the semantic theory, rather than being analyzed as a part of it. As a simple example, if we take as a fulcrum the ability to assign truth values to simple sentences, such as "Snow is white," then we can develop a theory (as Tarski did) that provides formal 'leverage' for determining the truth of more complex sentences, such as "Snow is white or Socrates is mortal." The rigorous nature of the theory is ensured by its restriction to the questions that can be posed independently of the underlying assumptions (i.e., what it really means for snow to be white or for a primitive sentence to be true). The genius of analytic philosophy has been in its ability to make this kind of separation, and thereby to create domains in which precise formal problems can be posed and solutions found.

In trying to account for more of the properties of language, we must move the fulcrum back further than our above example suggests. One step has been to posit the existence of objects and sets of objects, and to explicate the meanings of words in terms of them. "Socrates" refers to an object, "mortal" refers to a set, and the meaning of "Socrates is mortal" can be formalized in terms of set memberships, The apparatus of set theory provides our formal lever, enabling explanations of a variety of linguistic constructs. However, as has often been pointed out in the literature, it does not provide enough leverage to handle a variety of problems, such as intensionality and indexicality.

In order to deal with some of these problems, Montague and his followers shifted the fulcrum further by positing a primitive of "possible world." A good deal of technical apparatus can be added to this base, but the effort to do so has raised a nagging concern. If one is content to treat formal primitives as just that—primitive and subject to no further analysis—then the possible world mechanism can be used for many aspects of semantics. But there is something uncomfortable about positing primitive entities with no intuitive grounding. When we try to understand what a possible world "really is," or how we would come to know about one, we draw an ontological/epistemological blank. The name "possible world," which provides a metaphor for some of the initial uses of the mechanism, is at best misleading when we try to undersand the full range of uses to which it has been put. A pure formalist may not care, but those who want to relate theories of semantics to theories of mind and mental processing cannot be as unconcerned.

Work in artificial intelligence is directly concerned with the mental, or with its analogs in computer processing. Semantics must be linked to an operational understanding of how manipulations of symbolic tokens are correlated with the elements of language and of the world it describes. We find few clear statements of this issue in the AI literature, but in the general practice and in attempts to rationalize it, we can discern a commitment to a fulcrum based on the mind (not unlike the theories of Locke and his followers). In a typical AI program, the "meaning" of a sentence (or utterance—the difference is not important here) is explicated in terms of some "internal representation language" that is the basis for reasoning processes within the program. Some researchers attempt to portray this representation language as a model of "concepts" that play a direct role in human cognition. Others make no explicit appeal to psychological validity, but nevertheless the only ground on which the representation language can rest is that it is some kind of "mentalese," if only for an artificial mind.

"Concepts" are more acceptable to common sense than "possible worlds." It is easier to accept the statement that "unicorn" somehow refers to the concept of being a unicorn, than that it is a function over an infinite collection of possible worlds. But there is still the nagging problem that we really have no idea of what concepts are or how they are related to the neural processes that most of us take to be the causal basis for mental function. We are still left with the problem of signification—of how concepts relate to the world. Attempts to solve this with some kind of "procedural" verificationism (see, for example, Miller and Johnson Laird 1976) are only marginally more successful than the less computationally sophisticated forms of verificationism that preceded them. Of course, this lack of grounding does not prevent programs from being written and being partially effective in what they do. It just means that we have no theoretical basis from which to build or judge the results.

Barwise and Perry take a different step. They posit the existence of individuals, properties, relations, and locations, as part of the real world (or at least that world as it appears to the human organism). The meaning of "unicorn" is not a set (which would be empty), a function over possible worlds, or a concept. It is the property **Unicorn**, which exists *in the real world* as a property, independently of whether any real objects exhibit it. Having made all of this primitive (i.e., part of the fulcrum), they gain tremendous new leverage. Many technical problems having to do with intensional contexts and indexicality yield to straightforward commonsensical solutions, and much of their book is an exploration of just how far this goes.

In addition (and perhaps more radically) they argue that "There is something profoundly misleading about the traditional concern over entailments between sentences." They augment the formal logic of deduction with a primitive notion of "constraint," represented by a relation they call "Involves." "Smoke means fire" is not subject to the standard logical law that would lead to the false conclusion that every occurrence of smoke was caused by (or even in proximity to) a fire. Rather, the situation of smoke being present "gives information about" the presence of a fire, just as the utterance of "Here's a cookie" gives information about situations in which a cookie is present. This is a clever maneuver, the significance of which we will discuss below.

It is important to distinguish two kinds of argumentation that can be made about this theory. The first deals with the technical devices and their capacity to account for various properties of natural language utterances. Within this discussion, the fulcrum is taken for granted. There is (tacit) agreement that the things they posit as primitive are unproblematic—that consensus about their nature and application to any particular situation could in principle be reached without appeal to the linguistic forms whose meaning they are being used to explicate. From this standpoint we need not be concerned with whether properties are real, or whether situations "carry information" independently of any use of language about them. The second argument deals with the plausibility of the primitive grounding. Barwise and Perry's main objection to possible world semantics is its failure of plausibility, and they appeal over and over again to commonsense intuitions about reality and to the importance of honoring those intuitions in devising a semantic theory. It is quite possible, as we will see below, to see benefit in their theory on the basis of its technical devices while rejecting its metaphysical assumptions.

THE AI PROBLEM

Why are AI researchers looking for new semantic theories at all? What is wrong with the existing ones as a basis for building effective natural language programs? These questions can be answered in two very different directions, and it is important to distinguish them. One is *failure of coverage* and the other is *lack of respectability*. Barwise and Perry have done a relatively small amount to help with the former, but are being hailed as a great step forward with respect to the latter. In order to see why, let us examine some particular semantic problems that have been tackled in AI research: definite reference, compositionality, and commonsense entailment.

Definite Reference
Since the earliest natural language programs, there has been concern with handling difficult cases of definite reference. In order to properly understand a sentence that includes a reference to "the red block" or "The waitress" or "the wrench," one cannot appeal to the uniqueness (within the world or the previous text) of an object fitting the description. In all but the simplest AI programs, one finds mechanisms such as recency lists, scripts, frames, and topic structures, along with a complex (and generally *ad hoc*) collection of heuristic rules for applying them to particular cases. If this rather motley mechanism is given any justification at all, it is in terms of a supposed psychological reality, for which the evidence is at best speculative. (This and the following issues are discussed in more detail in Winograd 1981.)

When one turns to existing formal semantic theories, this issue is simply ignored or is at best acknowledged in passing. The formal mechanisms assume uniqueness of the object denoted by the phrase, or dump the problem into some undefined function. Barwise and Perry account for the meaning of an expression α (which may be a definite referring phrase) as "a relation d, $c[[\alpha]]\sigma$, e between discourse situations, connections, a setting provided by other parts of the utterance and a described situation." The complexity of definite reference is accounted for by the nature of the "speaker connections" and the constraints relating them to the discourse situation.

All well and good, but what does that tell us? It gives us a good name and a couple of useful places for variables, but when it comes time to analyze "the red block" we find that the theory makes no pretense of accounting for the constraints in any detail. In fact, any plausible account (especially given Barwise and Perry's attachment to commonsense introspection) will look just like the AI mechanisms that have already been developed. We have gained respectability by the fact that the *ad hoc* mechanisms are at least in principle locatable with respect to the theoretical framework, but there is nothing new on which to build extensions or improvements to the current programs.

Compositionality

In dealing with the compositional structure of language, there is a gap between the formal ideals and the practice that is necessary to make things work. When analyzing a carefully idealized "fragment" of natural language, one can apply elegant principles of compositionality, so that the meaning of a phrase is a function of the meanings of its constituents. In building programs to cope with the range of complexities of natural language, it has always been much more effective to allow the "semantic translation" of a particular phrase to depend not only on its contents, but on the values of some number of "free variables" that are determined by the surrounding context (both within the sentence and outside it in the discourse). This could be done without abandoning formal compositionality by making all meanings be higher order functions of appropriate collections of arguments, in which needed information that isn't available in the phrase is left as an argument to which the result will be applied at a higher constituent level. This is the basic trick of Montague semantics, and it leads to messy and unintuitive objects as the "meanings" of words and phrases. The meaning of the simplest word becomes a function from functions of functions onto other functions, in a bewildering nest of lambdas.

Barwise and Perry's meaning relation as quoted above has convenient places to handle this in a cleaner way. It not only deals with a discourse situation (which provides bindings for speaker, hearer, time of utterance, etc.), but also with a "setting" provided by other parts of the utterance. In other words, all of the LISP free variables that were used with mumbled apologies in the interpretation functions can now come out of the closet as fully respectable parts of the formalism. I am not arguing that this is wrong or bad—in fact it will hopefully divert effort away from the rather baroque apparatus that has been created to avoid doing what was the obvious thing to do. However, as with definite reference, establishing the respectability of "setting" is far different from explicating it.

Commonsense Entailment

One of the major problems in natural language programs (and AI programs in general) is the failure of logical formalisms to account for ordinary human reasoning. Attempts to deal with this failure have been given labels like "common sense reasoning," "non-monotonic reasoning," and "default reasoning." The simple account is that people make constant use of generalizations of the form "Given *A*, conclude *B unless there is some good reason not to.*" This is crucially different from a universal implication, for which the logical treatment is straightforward. The problem, of course, is in formalizing what constitutes a good reason not to. Whether this task is totally impossible (as critics like Dreyfus 1979 argue) or just vastly difficult, it is clear that no programs today begin to approach human-like use of generalizations.

Barwise and Perry recognize this problem and argue against taking logical inference as a foundation for semantics. As mentioned above, they take the constraint relation "*A* involves *B*" as a primitive of their theory. They spend a good deal of time motivating its plausibility (based on the work of Dretske). But as good analytic philosophers they know better than to try give a detailed explication of what's in a primitive. The one piece of mechanism provided is that of "conditional constraints" that "hold through some limited region *l* of space time." These are exemplified by a constraint relating utterances to meanings, which clearly must hold only at a certain stage in the evolution of the language in which they are uttered.

As in all the cases given above, the success of the theory lies in its clear separation of those problems for which it has good answers (precise mechanisms) and those others about which it will remain silent, even though the authors in their consensus-gathering role may choose to make reasonable commonsense exhortations.

Thus, in all three of these areas, as in many others related to the study of meaning, Barwise and Perry do the service of providing a cleaner separation of concerns. But the result will not be any major new functionality in AI programs, and they leave untouched the issues that many of us see as most central and difficult.

THE REALITY OF INTENSION

So far I have argued that situation semantics does not do enough. It provides a more respectable way to describe what is already being done in AI anyway and carefully avoids the messy problems. This is of some use, and certainly not harmful. But there is another area in which the foundational assumptions of the theory are wrong and ultimately dysfunctional: the explication of lexical meaning in terms of "real-world" properties and relations (uniformities across situations). To see why, let us first look at the problem of lexical meaning as it has been explored in recent AI and semantic research.

The naive view of language is that it simply reflects reality. Nature (or at least nature as perceived by the human organism) comes carved up into objects of various kinds, and the role of language is to give them labels. A language can be arbitrary in calling things "dog" and "cow" or "chien" and "vache," but is constrained by the nature of the world to group a certain set of objects (or properties) together under whichever name it uses. It is this naive realism to which Barwise and Perry appeal, and which they go to such great pains to preserve in their theory. They state that "Reality consists of situations, individuals having properties and standing in relations at various spatio-temporal locations."

But in every field of human study associated with language, from psycho-linguistics to socio-linguistics to literary criticism, we find paper after paper describing phenomena that bring this assumption under question. We find lengthy discussions of the meaning of "bachelor" (Winograd 1976), "lemon" (Putnam 1970), "tiger" (Putnam 1970), "bird" (Rosch 1975), "water" (Put-nam 1973; Winograd 1981), "cup" (Labov 1973), "widow" (Fillmore 1974), "decapitate" (Fillmore 1974), "in" (Herskovits 1985), "on" (Searle 1979), and on and on. In each case, the author demonstrates that there does not exist a "property" or "relation" correlated with the word that can be defined or discovered in isolation of the context in which the word is used. Some authors raise psychological or anthropological evidence, others give linguistic arguments and others are simply introspective. Attempted accounts include "prototypes," "schemas," "frames," "resource-limited reasoning," "meta-phor," "salience," "pragmatic extension" and a host of other devices. What they all have in common is the observation that the category associated with a word won't stay put. The specific context in which the word is used (which may be social, psychological and textual) plays a complex and central role in determining whether a particular object will or will not be appropriately denoted by a phrase containing it.

As an example, consider Searle's (1979) discussion of "The cat is on the mat". In a series of fanciful examples he illustrates that no straightforward account of the meaning of "on" can provide an adequate explication of the literal meaning of that sentence—i.e., there is no relation of "on-ness" that corresponds to its full range of appropriate uses. He conjures up cats suspended on wires, cats and mats floating in space, and so on, at each point showing how the context controls our judgment as to whether in a particular situation the cat is indeed "on the mat" or not. A simple application of situation semantics would lead us to say that an event fitting the description "The cat is on the mat" (leaving aside complications caused by definite reference) corresponds to the event type:

$$E: \; = \; \text{at } l: \text{on, Cat, Mat; yes}$$

What we have done is push the problem of delimiting "on-ness" onto the world of properties, out of the semantic theory. This might be all right if it simply avoided having to deal with the problem as part of semantics, leaving it to be solved independently. But the factors that determine the meaning are those that depend on the utterance situation, which by Barwise and Perry's primary dogma cannot affect the organization of the "reality" about which the utterance conveys information.

Of course one could hedge by having a plethora of different "on" relations in the world, and having the semantic analysis assign one or another on the basis of the context. But this vitiates the theory, since in the limit (and probably in practice) it would lead to arguing that although relations exist in reality (independent of language), this division of reality includes a distinct specialized "on" relation corresponding to each situation type in which the word "on" might be uttered.

As long as we stick to the rather idealized sentences used as examples in books on philosophy (including *Situations and Attitudes*), it may seem plausible to ground the meaning of words in a language-prior categorization. But as soon as we look at real situated language, the foundation crumbles. Consider an example from a carefully written technical work—the initial sentence of Barwise and Perry's book. "Semantics, the study of linguistic meaning, is a notoriously slippery business." Leaving out the appositive for simplicity, we find that this applies to situations in which:

E_1: = at l: business, Semantics; yes slippery, Semantics; yes
E_2: = at l: notorious, E_1; yes

Somehow this makes one a bit more queasy about looking for properties and relations in the world than does "E: = at l: bite, Frenchie, Jackie: yes."

One might argue that although many phenomena cannot directly be accounted for with Barwise and Perry's "ecological realism," it is the right approximation to begin with, just as friction-free point masses are the right initial approximation for physics. Although the theory of these idealized objects does not fully account for the motion of any real bodies, it is a central component in a more adequate theory.

I believe that another analogy is more apt. Consider an economist who sets out to explain the world of commerce by positing a primitive "value" function that assigns a measure to every object. This measure is "real," in that it is determined by the object itself, not any activities of buying, selling, or trading. This basis could then be used to develop theories of what actually goes on in the marketplace, trying to account for prices in terms of distortions, augmentations, and other perturbations to the real values.

Such a theory is not logically incoherent. It is just not very likely to work. The apparatus needed to account for the variance between prices and objective values will turn out to be more complex than an account that did not take value as a primitive quality of an object at all, but instead grounded its account of value in the activities of buying and selling. In the same way, a theory that begins by taking properties and relations as primitive will need radical augmentation to deal with those cases where it is the linguistic activity that determines the meaning. Those cases are not the exception, but the norm.

Why then does the realist theory seem so plausible and appealing? There are a couple of obvious reasons. First, it is more technically tractable. We gain the ability to do all kinds of formal manipulations using the primitives without having to worry about their underlying nature. If this can be made to work, our job as students of language is much less formidable.

The seond reason is that the externalization of responsibility for properties and relations fits the commonsense understanding of language. Barwise and Perry state directly:

Not everyone will share our belief in real situations. We won't offer much in the way of argument for them, beyond whatever overall satisfactoriness the reader may find in our way of looking at things. We are only claiming to find this view of the world embedded in natural language, not to discover how the world really is, even if we do happen to think the world is the way we describe it. (p. 58f)

The naive layperson will often insist that every word has a fully determined "meaning," which is purely "objective." Whether a given object is a bachelor or a lemon is taken to be a matter of definition or science, not one of utterance context. A few well-chosen examples usually convince people that this cannot account for the way they actually use language (although some will continue to maintain that it accounts for the way people *should* use language).

Reflecting the beliefs of "folk semantics" may have some value, but it is hardly a basis for justifying the adequacy of a semantic theory. Freud demonstrated clearly that there is more to human motivation than what we can introspectively observe, or what our naive pre-Freudian language of explanation implies. This insight is no less valid in understanding the use of language.

But even many sophisticated linguists and philosophers are genuinely puzzled when one proposes that the basis for understanding the meaning of linguistic items is not ultimately grounded in the real world. There might be funny cases like "slippery semantics" and even weird ones with "cat on the mat," but most of the time for most purposes, the correspondence is pretty close to what you would naively expect it to be. Anyone who denies this is being obscurantist and perverse.

Consider an analogy: the study of roads and their relation to the terrain. Looking at a roadmap superimposed on a topographic map, one immediately sees tremendous regularities. Roads follow along riverbeds, they go through passes, and they wind their way up and down mountainsides in a regular fashion. Surely this regularity must mean that road placement is determined by the lay of the land. But of course it isn't. The road network is conditioned by the lay of the land, and it would be strange (though certainly not impossible given modern technology) to cut from here to there in total disregard of the terrain. But the actual placement depends on who wants to get vehicles of what kind from where to where, for reasons that transcend geography.

Words correspond to our intuition about "reality" because our purposes in using them are closely aligned with our physical existence in a world and our actions within it. But the coincidence is the fortunate result of evolution (both biological and linguistic), not foundational.

IS THERE AN ALTERNATIVE?

The initial section mentioned some other possibilities that have been considered for a fulcrum on which to rest semantic theory. The only one whose inadequacy is not immediately obvious is the mental one, and as have often been pointed out, it has serious problems. A very different alternative is to reject a deeper assumption: the assumption that it is possible to find any privileged place for the fulcrum at all.

Let us turn to what actually goes on in semantic theory. A person or group of people propose that meaning is to be explicated in terms of some set of primitive constructs and relations over them. They describe these primitives and relations and enter into a discourse with other theorists about whether they are adequate, what problems are raised and solved, etc. What are the primitives, then? They are linguistic objects, created and used in the discourse about semantics. One can try (as Barwise and Perry do at length) to engender the belief that they correspond to something "real," but ultimately all that can be said for sure about them is that they have such and such a symbolic form and are used in a certain way in the discussion of semantics. A theory of language rests on more language. The consensus that must be reached about the primitives is not a collective discovery, but a collective construction.

This observation is disquieting. It seems to imply a vicious circle in which we can never relate language to anything outside of itself. Surely as philosophers of language we want to discover the "eternals" that lie outside of our own discussions.

We may want to, but in the end we can only "discover" by entering into a conversation in which we are bound by our own use of language and the understanding that it supports. There is no reason to assume that the use of language in general rests on anything else. If asked to explicate the nature of the properties in the real world such that it is valid to say "Semantics is a slippery business" but not that it is a "slimy business" or a "sticky business" we find ourselves enmeshed not in a discussion of the properties of goopy substances, but one about the nature of conversations about people and their work. Like the roads, it is this recursive conversation that transcends the "lay of the land" and is at the same time constrained by it.

What will semantic theory look like under this new assumption? In part, it will look just like it has in the past (including the work on situation semantics). One set of relevant questions will deal with the ways in which language can be related to a consensual basis, without assuming that basis to be language-free. But it will also have to deal with the nature of conversations that do not rest on a consistent basis, but which themselves delimit the nature of the things they are about. This calls for a shift away from language as a conveyer of information to language as a mode of action.

Barwise and Perry continue a long tradition in semantics, in which assertions are taken as the primary form of language. "We focus on a relatively straightforward type of information-conveying utterance: one in which a speaker uses an indicative sentence assertively and thereby conveys information to a single listener." They briefly mention speech acts in a section on open research topics, but see them as secondary. The alternative is to take language action as primary. Language is first and foremost a means of doing something—of securing cooperative action and consensus. This leads to looking at a different field of uniformities and will lead to new formalisms for language of which we now have only beginning suggestions in speech act theory and its extensions (for example, Habermas 1978).

HOW SITUATION SEMANTICS IS USEFUL

The analogies to physical and economic theories presented above suggest a skepticism as to whether situation semantics, as it stands, could serve as a component of a comprehensive theory of language. Unlike point masses, the primitive objects of situation semantics may not be the right basis for elaboration. However, there is another relevant analogy from physics. Newtonian mechanics as a whole is an approximation to our quantized, relativistic universe. When we try to deal with the full range of phenomena, we must give up its basic primitives and assumptions, such as the continuity of physical quantities and the conservation of mass. Nevertheless, it is a perfectly adequate approximation for dealing with a great number of interesting relevant phenomena.

We might ask then, whether situation semantics could serve as a "Newtonian" semantic theory. Even granting that some problems are simply beyond its reach, we might take it as a practical basis for domains of language use that can be adequately characterized within its bounds. This is closely related to the more general question of what can be achieved by artificial intelligence systems, since the limitations of situation semantics are closely mirrored by limitations of the formalisms underlying those systems.

The first observation is that no natural class of natural texts or conversations is sufficiently limited. We cannot hope that by restricting ourselves to technical journals or children's stories, or newspaper accounts of train wrecks, we will be able to succeed in the program of ecological realism. Whenever people use language naturally, they fall into all of the messy problems of open-ended meaning.

There do exist stylized text forms that make use of natural language structure but are defined artificially. These include "fragments" like those dealt with by Montague and defined by Barwise and Perry (ALIASS). They also include the limited natural language that is the basis for interacting with data base "front ends" and other specialized AI applications. Clearly situation semantics will apply fully to text forms that were designed with it in mind. It is also comprehensive and solid enough to apply well to a variety of other natural-language-motivated formats. It is likely that it will play a role in the design of AI natural language systems of this type.

However, the most interesting potential becomes apparent when we look back at our concept of "fulcrum" and ask what is being assumed. Situation semantics falls short as a theory of natural language because it puts into the primitive fulcrum aspects of meaning that must be integrated with the full account of language use. What would it be like to have a language in which that was not the case—in which agreement about the existence of objects, properties, relations, and locations was indeed unproblematic, and did not depend on the use of the language? Situation semantics would be perfectly suited for such a language, and has many technical aspects that would be of value.

But such languages do exist, and are of major importance. They include programming languages, specification languages, protocol defining languages, hardware description languages, data base query languages, and more—in short, all of the artificial languages that have been devised for use with computers. The relation of such languages to the world they describe is not simple or unproblematic, but in each case the correspondence is the result of a conscious design. It is the outcome of an articulated consensus. When one writes a graphics protocol language, "line" means something very specific as determined by the implementers. No user of the language is allowed to stray with impunity outside of the prescribed meaning.

What distinguishes these languages from the purely formal languages of logic and mathematics is that they are designed to be *about* something. What distinguishes them from natural language is the precise grounding given to their constructs, including the meaning of the individual terms. As of yet we do not have a comprehensive or coherent theory of such languages, but the outlines of such a theory are beginning to emerge and will be a major area of linguistic study in the coming years.

In many of these languages, the additional mechanisms of situation semantics are not necessary. A straightforward extensional first-order account is sufficient to account for the entire language. But things become more interesting when the language includes analogs of those things that motivated Barwise and Perry—indexicality and intensional contexts. This would include, for example, a specification language that could be used to describe a system in which some objects in the system were intended as descriptions of other objects in it.

It has often been taken as self-evident that the path towards more effective computer use is to give computers the capacity to understand ordinary human language. As the dimensions of that problem become more visible, we are witnessing a shift towards a different path—the design of artificial languages suited to human communication through computers. These languages will go far beyond our current ideas of what a computer language can look like, but they will share with current computer languages the explicitness of semantic grounding—the ability to be understood in terms of a semantic relationship resting on a set of externally agreed upon primitives. Situation semantics and its successors may well play a significant role in the development of the more expressive and elegant artificial languages that will be the primary medium of human-computer interaction in the future.

JOHN L. TIENSON

AN INTRODUCTION TO CONNECTIONISM

The computer metaphor has played a prominent role in the philosophy of mind at least since the advent of artificial intelligence in the 1950s. Connectionism is a new development—some say fad—in cognitive science/ artificial intelligence. Naturally, philosophers are interested in the question whether connectionism can provide a fruitful model of the mind/brain, and the related question, what the implications will be concerning cognition if connectionism is able to provide such a model. The papers in *The Southern Journal of Philosophy* xxvi (1979) carry on some aspects of this young discussion and begin some new ones.

Since connectionism is not yet familiar to many philosophers, it seems appropriate to begin with a brief, nontechnical introduction to connectionism. The recent popularity of connectionism is in part a response to a Kuhnian crisis in artificial intelligence. I will begin with a brief description of that crisis situation.

1. GOOD OLD-FASHIONED ARTIFICIAL INTELLIGENCE

The field of artificial intelligence (AI) aims at getting computers to behave in ways that we can recognize as intelligent. A significant portion of this research has the goal of understanding *natural* intelligence, and thus aims at getting computers to behave intelligently in some sense *in the way we do it.*[1] The defining characteristic of familiar computers is that they manipulate symbols in terms of precise rules—they are rule governed symbol manipulators. They contain data structures—syntactically structured objects, sentences— and rules that refer to those sentences. A program is a sequence of such rules. Since the rules themselves are also data structures, programs can be stored in memory to serve as repeatable routines accessible by other programs. The trick of making a computer is to get the causal processes of the mechanism to mirror the syntactic processes specified in programs. For this to be possible, the rules must be precise and exceptionless.

The defining characteristic of classical artificial intelligence—what John Haugeland has labeled GOFAI ("good old-fashioned artificial intelligence"[2]) —is that classical computer architecture gets at the essence of intelligence; cognition is what the classical computer does, rule-governed symbol manipulation. The aim is to write programs that will result in intelligent behavior, and ultimately to write programs like those that underlie our intelligent behavior. Since we humans do behave intelligently, it is assumed that there must be such programs to discover.

In our use or understanding of them, we interpret the sentences of computer languages. They thereby have semantic content; they represent, if only second hand. GOFAI assumes that we humans must have significantly comparable representations.[3] So the classical viewpoint is often called the "rules and representations" view of the mind, characterized by

1) Syntactically structured representations.
2) Precise, formal rules that advert to the syntactic structure of those representations.[4]

2. THE KUHNIAN CRISIS IN GOFAI

There is a Kuhnian crisis in GOFAI, brought on by a pattern of unfulfilled promises and disappointing results. Throughout the history of artificial intelligence, researchers have optimistically predicted, "In five (or ten) years, computers will do such and such: translate, or understand speech, or be as good as experts at . . ." It has never happened; usually it has not even begun.[5]

In particular, there seem to be certain kinds of things that we are good at that are very difficult for computers, such as pattern recognition, understanding speech, recalling and recognizing relevant information, and making plans. It has also proven very difficult to program computers to learn in any domain. On the other hand, computers are much better than humans at other tasks, paradigmatically, number crunching, but in general, anything that involves many precisely specifiable computations or manipulating large amounts of data according to precise rules.

This suggests that human brains do not do things in the way conventional computers do, that ours is a different kind of intelligence. There are two other things that fans of connectionism are fond of bringing up in support of the idea that human intelligence is different in kind from computer "intelligence": neurons are slow, and graceful degradation.

Neurons operate in times measured in milliseconds at best, 10 to the sixth or so times slower than the current generation of computers. The exact significance of this comparison is not clear, since we have no idea how cognitive functions might be implemented in the brain, although it seems certain that single neurons compute simple functions. We are able to do very sophisticated processing—such as memory retrieval, perceptual processing, and language processing—in a few hundred milliseconds. This imposes what Jerome Feldman[6] has called the 100 step program constraint. No task can require more than 100 or so serial steps. This at least applies at the cognitive, rules and representations, level at which the rules refer to the syntactic structure of our supposed internal representations. Even if many things are done in parallel, this means no one of the parallel tracks can be more than about 100 steps long. If we do cognitive things by following programs, this is a severe limitation. More likely, connectionists argue, that is not how we do it.

"Graceful degradation" refers to a variety of ways in which the performance of natural systems deteriorates gradually. Brain damage or disease may affect performance, but it does not cause loss of specific memories or functions until it reaches a level of severity where a whole class of capacities is lost. And when we approach the limits of our ability in some area, because of time constraints or information overload, for example, our performance suffers, but it does not crash. Rules and representations processing, on the other hand, is naturally "brittle." Damage causes loss of particular functions and everything that depends on them. The system either works—in a particular respect—or it doesn't.

The slowness of neurons, graceful degradation versus brittleness, and the different realms in which each is at its best suggest that natural systems and conventional computers do things in very different ways. And connectionists have used these things as arguments for looking at an approach to cognition that is more closely analogous to the way the brain works. But none of this could have brought about a crisis in GOFAI. That had to come from within.

The problem is that it has thus far proven impossible to find the kinds of rules that GOFAI requires. The difficulties seem to turn on two clusters of problems. The first is the problem of dealing with multiple simultaneous soft constraints. The second cluster of problems results from the fact that any bit of common sense knowledge might turn out to be relevant to any task or any other knowledge. Included here, as perhaps two ends of a spectrum, are the so-called "frame" problem and what I will call the "folding" problem.[7]

Consider the problem of getting to a particular store in a shopping mall. You must chart a course from mall door to the store, perhaps using stairs or an escalator, avoiding stationary obstacles like plants, fountains, benches and areas open to the floor below, and also avoiding milling people, baby strollers and the like. We do this so naturally that it is difficult to appreciate the complexity of the task. But to program a computer to do it would require rules that take account of an enormous number of factors. The number of computations required expands exponentially with the number of factors, leading to an unmanageable computation explosion.

Chess provides a well studied example of computation explosion. The best current chess programs are capable of examining about 10 million positions looking four or possibly five moves into the future. To limit the possibilities, they use clever "tree pruning" programs to ignore implausible moves.[8] But in the mall case, it is not at all clear how to give a general rule for ignoring factors or possibilities.

Typically, where there are multiple simultaneous constraints, the constraints are "soft." That is, any one of them can be violated while the cognitive system is doing its job properly. Chess, and even the mall example, as briefly described here, may be misleading in this respect, so let us consider another example.

Understanding speech involves many distinguishable kinds of factors, including at least phonology, syntax, semantics, and several factors often lumped together as pragmatics, including at least social context, physical context, and conversational context. Each of these "levels" introduces a complex array of factors that go into interpreting verbal stimuli. But rules at any of these levels can be violated with little or no impairment of understanding. For example, you can understand speech from a vast number of regional dialects, most of which you could not imitate. The same goes for syntax and the social stratification of language. What you hear violates the rules of your language—of any language you could speak—but you use the rules of *your* language to understand it.[9] The rules play a role even when they are violated. This is common where there are multiple constraints.

The second cluster or problems on which GOFAI is foundering has to do with the fact that any part of common sense knowledge might have to be used in dealing with any cognitive task. Cognition cannot be partitioned into isolated domains. This requires both being able to see that certain information is relevant, and being able to find relevant information from the whole data base that consists of all of one's knowledge. Easy for us, hard for them.

Classical AI has had some moderate degree of success in writing programs that "understand" simple stories about particular domains.[10] They have what is called a "script" for that domain which they can use to make inferences that allow them to answer questions that are not explicitly answered in the story.

Recently, I took a group of six-year-olds to Sea World for a birthday party. They all knew about birthday parties. Some of them had been to Sea World and could describe it to the others, but none of them had been to a party at Sea World. They were able to combine their birthday party "scripts" and their Sea World "scripts" to plan the day's activities, including how Sea World things would be ordered with birthday party things, which typical party things would be included, which left out, and which modified appropriately, and what precautions would be taken to keep the group together, since, after all, they were only six years old. Computers cannot do anything like "fold" together knowledge in this way, and no one has a clue how to get them to do it.

At the other end of the spectrum, any single bit of information you acquire will change your total system of beliefs. Some of your earlier beliefs must be deleted, and you must make some obvious inferences from other beliefs. But the new bit of information will be irrelevant to most of your previous beliefs, and those will remain unchanged. The frame problem is the problem of determining, in an effective, general way, what each new bit of information would change and what it would leave the same in a system of beliefs.[11] And the first part of the problem is that of determining which old beliefs are in any way relevant to the new information. For a system of any size, it is totally inefficient to have to search through each bit of old information to see if and how it is affected.

Because we combine knowledge so naturally, and the inferences seem so natural and obvious, it may be difficult to see the problem if you have not tried to deal with it. The point can be put this way. Consider any program that purports to mimic the performance of some normal human being. If it does not access all of that person's knowledge, it will be subject to counter-example. Furthermore, even if it can access all of that knowledge, it must also somehow specify *in advance* what each new bit of knowledge would change and what it would leave the same in any situation. Without that, again, it would be subject to principled counterexamples.

What may be the flip side of this problem is the fact that there are virtually no bounds on what part of specialized or common sense knowledge might be relevant to solving a particular problem. We are good enough at retrieving and using relevant information that we notice failures and take success as routine. On the other hand, this is very difficult for conventional computers. Our memory retrieval is in some sense based on content. In conventional computer architecture, retrieval is on the basis of the address where the data is stored. So part of the problem for GOFAI is the problem of content addressable memory.

But this is only part of the problem, and giving it this label may obscure the difficulty. First you have to see that a bit of information is relevant. Then you retrieve it. But how can you see that a bit of information is relevant until you find it? Apparently, you must find it and see that it is relevant all at once. As Hume said, "One would think the whole intellectual world of ideas was at once subjected to our view, and that we did nothing but pick out such as were most proper for our purposes" (*Treatise*, 1, 1, vii.). What we need is *relevance* addressable memory, whatever that might be.

Sometimes also, this whole cluster of problems, and the frame problem in particular, is characterized as the problem of representing common sense knowledge. But this, too, may minimize the difficulties. For it is a problem of representing, storing, retrieving and using knowledge, all in one package.

These two clusters of problems—multiple simultaneous soft constraints and the potential relevance of anything to anything—do not *prove* that the assumptions of GOFAI are wrong and that rules and representations cannot provide a satisfying model of human cognition. The point here is that they have resisted serious progress for more than a decade, and the appeal of connectionism should be understood in that light.

3. THE BASICS OF CONNECTIONISM[12]

A connectionist system, or *neural network*, consists of a network of simple, neuronlike processors, called *nodes* or *units*. Each node has directed connections to several other nodes, so that it gets signals from some nodes and sends signals to some nodes, possibly including the ones from which it gets signals. In practice, a given node may get input from just two or three other nodes, or from as many as two or three dozen. In principle, it could be thousands. The input from each node is a simple signal, like an electrical current or synaptic transmission. This signal might have only the values on and off, or it might vary on a single dimension, which I will call *strength*. The total input to a node will determine its *state of activation*. The node can be on or off. It might be on whenever it is getting any input at all, or there might be a threshold which the input must reach before the node will turn on. In either case, the node might have just two values, "on" and "off," or the state of activation might vary as a function of total input. Finally, sometimes systems allow signals that inhibit activation as well as excitatory input.

When a node is on, it sends out signals to the nodes to which it has output connections. The strength of output signal is a function of its degree of activation, and again, various functions have been used.

The connections between nodes are analogous to electric wires or synaptic connections. So they have a degree of resistance. The input to node *b* from node *a* is a function of the strength of *a*'s output signal and the strength of the connection between them. The strength of the connection between nodes is referred to as *weight*. Higher weight means less resistance, stronger signal received.

The properties of nodes are typically considered fixed in a given connectionist system. The weights, on the other hand, can vary as a function of

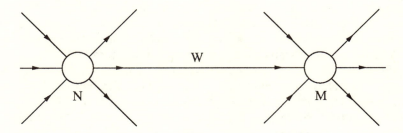

experience. As a result, it is possible to construct connectionist systems that are capable of learning in very natural ways. Thus, connectionist learning is "getting your weights changed."

As a simple example, if the weight between two nodes increases—meaning the resistance is lower—whenever both nodes are on together, the probability increases that when one is on the other will go on, too. This provides for simple associationist learning.[13] We will discuss some other kinds of learning momentarily.

Some units in a connectionist system get stimuli from outside the system. These are *input* units. Some are *output* units. They are thought of as sending signals outside the system. Input units may also get stimuli from nodes within the system, and output nodes can send feedback to nodes of the system. The rest of the nodes, with no connections outside the system, are called *hidden* or *internal* nodes.

The connectionist framework imposes no limitations on the kinds of structures of nodes that are possible, and many different kinds of structure can be found in the PDP volumes. Layered structures as in Figure 2 are useful to think about. In such a structure, a problem is posed by activating a pattern of input nodes, the processing proceeds through the activation of nodes in one or more—typically smaller—hidden layers until a pattern of activation appears on the output nodes. This counts as the system's solution to the problem posed. Possible complications include feedback, loops, and inhibitory connections within a pool of units so that only one or a fixed group of units can be on together—"winner take all."

In typical processing, it is not the case that only the right internal and output nodes are activated. Typically, there is a great deal of activity, with nodes going on and off and sending and receiving signals repeatedly until the system "settles" into a stable configuration that constitutes its solution to the problem posed. Imagine an array of connected lights, flashing on and off, gradually reaching a stable state with some on and some off.

Several differences between connectionist and classical architecture are apparent. In classical architecture, what happens throughout the system is controlled by the program at the central processing unit (CPU). In a connectionist system, there is no central executive, and there is no program that determines what happens throughout the system. All connections are local, so that each node knows only what it gets from the nodes to which it is connected. And the only information that one node communicates to another is, "I'm turned on, (so much)." No one in the system knows more than that. So, in particular, no one in the system knows what the system as a whole is doing. Furthermore, what goes on at one place in the system is independent of what goes on elsewhere in the system. The behavior of each node is determined only by its current state and its input. Nevertheless, connectionist systems can be interpreted to globally represent interesting content when in a particular state, and as having stored (in the weights) knowledge that is not presently actively represented.

"Connectionism" is a good name for the family of systems that fit this description. Though equally well entrenched, the term "parallel," on the other hand, as in "massively parallel," or even "Parallel Distributed Processing," seems less fortunate to me. It is apt to mislead, since it may suggest many separate *sequences* going on in parallel, each according to its own program. This is not the correct picture of connectionist systems. They do not involve parallel independent processes that are either programmed or hardwired but in principle programmable.[14] They are characterized by simultaneous local processing distributed over the whole system. From this simultaneous local processing a stable configuration of the system emerges which constitutes the system's solution to the problem posed.

Feed forward networks like Figure 2 are capable of learning in a rather natural way that has received a good deal of study.[15] Input and output nodes are arbitrarily assigned interpretations in such a way that certain patterns of output nodes will be the "right" output given certain patterns of stimulation of input nodes. Weights are set at small random values throughout the system. At this point, it will be purely accidental if the system produces the right output for a given input. Now weights are adjusted algorithmically layer by layer back through the system as a function of each weight's contribution to the error. For a wide range of problems, after going through this "back propagation" procedure repeatedly, the system will produce the right output for every input. It will have "learned" the answers and may even be able to "generalize" to cases it has not seen.[16]

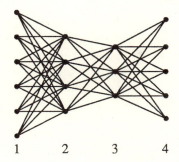

The success of back propagation as a training technique shows that connectionist systems are capable of interesting learning. But back propagation as understood so far is unsatisfactory in several respects. If the network is thought of as a model of a natural system, there must be some process *in the network* that changes weights appropriately. In current simulations, no such means is provided, and it is not clear how they might be built into a network. Back propagation is also extremely slow, requiring a great many passes for successful learning. And it remains something of a black art. What works and what does not, both in terms of network structure and in terms of mathematical parameters, is largely a matter of experimenter's intuition and trial and error. These are no doubt at least in part due to the youth of the enterprise, and this is an active area of connectionist research.

4. REPRESENTATION IN CONNECTIONIST SYSTEMS

Geoffrey Hinton has described an interesting system that learns family relationships by back propagation.[17] The rest of the connectionist concepts to be introduced will be discussed in terms of this system. The data the system learns consist of two isomorphic, three generation family trees, with 12 individuals in each family.

The network is a five layered network. The input layer consists of two distinct pools, one with 24 nodes, each assigned to one of the 24 individuals, the other pool has 12 units, assigned the relationships, father, mother, husband, wife, son, daughter, uncle, aunt, brother, sister, nephew, and neice. There are 24 output nodes, again one for each individual. The three internal or hidden layers consist of 12, 12, and 6 units respectively. With one exception, each layer is totally connected to the subsequent layer, and there are no other connections in the network. The exception is that the first internal layer—i.e., the second layer—is divided into two six unit pools, one pool connected only to relationship units, the other pool totally connected to people units.[18]

Input is always given by turning on one people node and one relationship node, say, "Penelope," and "husband." The system gets it right if the only output node it turns on is the node for her husband, i.e., "Christopher." If the input were "Colin" and "aunt," the right answer would consist of two specific output nodes, since Colin has two aunts.

Initially, internal nodes have no representational content. Weights are set at small random values. At first, of course, output is like guessing; most answers are wrong. Weights are slowly changed in the direction of correct answers.[19]

The system was "trained up" on 100 of the 104 encoded relationships in the two family trees. Eventually—after 1500 passes of all 100 cases—it got all of these relationships right. Furthermore, it was able to generalize, or make the proper inference, and get the remaining four relationships right as well.[20]

This may not seem too impressive as a "generalization," but it is learning, and you could not expect much more in this particular case. What has happened is this. In order to get the 100 training cases right with its limited neural resources, the system had to encode the structure of the kinship system and relevant features of the individuals. Having done this, it was able to "infer" the relationships it had not been told about. That is, the information it had encoded determined these relationships. Since it began as a tabula rasa, it had to be given enough data to determine the structure of the domain it was dealing with.

After training, many internal nodes had discernable content, e.g., "first generation," or "English," or "left branch of the family tree."[21] That is, there was one internal node that would only go on when the input person was English, and so forth. (Furthermore, the system used the fact, which it could not, of course, be told, that the two family trees were isomorphic.)

Input and output nodes are arbitrarily assigned certain meanings. *Given* that interpretation, the system can be said to have acquired the concepts represented by its internal nodes. We can also say—with the same puffery—that the system has learned that Penelope is English, first generation, etc. These lights come on when it is given "Penelope" as input. It "recognizes" her as English.

Not all of the internal nodes of the final system have obvious, namable content. But in this tiny system, all of the internal nodes are necessary for the system to function properly. If any of the nodes of a trained up network were excised, it would no longer get all the right answers. Thus, it would seem that some nodes were responding to real, but no easily describable, features of the domain.[22]

Another interesting fact about this network is that when it is trained up more than once starting from different initial weights, it can end up with different internal representations. It will certainly end up with different final weights. But also, certain concepts may get encoded by different internal nodes, and more interestingly, there may be no analogue in one trained up system of a concept encoded in another. Thus, the same input/output relations can be accomplished using different internal concepts.[23] There are different ways of encoding the structure of the domain. It is reasonable to suspect that this is a common feature of connectionist networks, and of natural systems.

I turn now to one final, much discussed feature of connectionist thinking, "coarse coding." Our network can be thought of as having an *internal* representation of Penelope. A certain pattern of activation, with some nodes on and some off, is unique to Penelope. She is *the* one that is English, first generation, etc. Some of the nodes that are on for Penelope are also on for Andrew. But Andrew has a different total pattern of activation; some nodes that are on for Penelope are off for him, and some new ones are on. Indeed, there is a unique internal pattern of activation for each individual.

Representations involving many units are called *distributed* representations. Where the same node is part of many different distributed representations, as in our network, we have what is called *coarse coding*.[24] With coarse coding, nodes may or may not have content individually. In our network, there are also *local*—single node—representations of the individuals. It is more common, however, in networks with distributed representations for contents to be represented *only* in a distributed manner.

Distributed representations raise many interesting possibilities, of which I will mention only a couple. If a given representation is encoded as the activity of a large number of nodes, it may not be necessary for all of these nodes to be active to constitute the activation of the representation. To take the simplest case, the activation of the representation might consist in the activation of a sufficient number of its nodes. Thus, the same representational content may be present in a system as the activity of somewhat different nodes on different occasions.

A feature of many systems with distributed representations is that weights are set so that representations have a tendency to complete themselves once some of their nodes are active. This makes for something like content addressable memory. A portion of the content of a complex representation tends to activate the whole.

When nodes that are part of several complex representations are activated, there can be competition for completion among those representations. This is one of the situations where a variant of a winner take all mechanism may be operative. It is also a typical situation where there is a process of "settling." The system will sparkle and sputter until it "settles into" the representation that *best fits* the input. There may be many different factors—constraints—that go into determining which representation fits best.

Furthermore, some of these constraints might be violated by the representation that best fits the constraints as a whole. For example, the internal representation that wins as the best representation of the input may nevertheless conflict with some of the input. That is, it is natural in connectionist systems for constraints to be *soft*—that is violable when the system is doing its job properly. In GOFAI the same constraints would most naturally be represented as logical inconsistencies, and hence inviolable (Cf. note 9). Connectionists believe—rightly, I think—that most of cognition is soft; the correlative features of soft constraints and best fit are an important source of appeal of connectionism.

Suppose, for example, that we had a connectionist speech recognition system.[25] One could expect such a system to naturally and automatically understand new accents, dialects, and speech impediments, using the same principles it uses in understanding speech that is normal for it. One would expect a GOFAI speech recognition system to be able to do these things only with special programming for each new variation, which is cheating.

We might say, not only that Hinton's system has acquired the concept, "English," but that it *believes* that Penelope is English. The "English" light comes on whenever the "Penelope" light comes on. It also knows that her husband is Christopher.

Where is the information that Penelope is English or that Christopher is her husband when that information is not actively represented? In one sense, it is nowhere. In another, it is in the weights.

In conventional computer architecture, information is stored in the same form in which it is used. When information is being used, a certain structure—a syntactic object—is in the CPU. When it is not being used, the same data structure is stored in memory.

In a connectionist system, information is actively represented as a pattern of activation. When that information is not in use, that pattern is nowhere present in the system. Information is not stored as data structures. The only symbols ever present in a connectionist system are active representations.

But of course, there is a sense in which the information is in the system. The weights—strength of connections between nodes—are such that appropriate active representations are created as needed. Thus, in our simple example, when the Penelope input node is turned on, the system activates its internal representation of Penelope.

There are two points here. Information is stored in the weights. And because the weights are as they are, representations are *created* in response to internal or external stimuli. Memories are not stored; they are recreated over and over again in response to whatever reminds you of them. Information that is not presently active—not in use—is only in the system potentially.[26] Thus, there is no distinction internal to the system between recreating old representations and creating new ones in response to the situation.

Whatever may be the case with memory, this is surely the way things work in many cognitive domains, like perception and understanding language. We could not store linguistic information about each individual sentence we can understand. In understanding a sentence, we create linguistic information about it on the spot, in response to present stimuli. Except in the case of a few cliches, it does not matter whether we have heard the sentence before or not.[27]

I have said that Hinton's trained up system "believes" that Penelope is English. But this way of speaking is excessive here in a way that it is not with respect to classical architecture. When the "Penelope" light comes on, the "English" light comes on. One might think that this temporal sequence is like a *spoken* sentence, whereas conventional computers have data structures that are analogous to written sentences. But this is incorrect. The "Penelope," "English" sequence of node lightings is *only* a causal sequence. There is no syntactic structure here.

This points to a feature typical of extant connectionist systems: representations typically have no syntactic structure. Representations are either single nodes (local coding) or sets of nodes (coarse coding). Where structure is needed, usually it is built into the system by having different pools of nodes dedicated to different parts of the needed structure. So, in a word recognition system, for example, there will be a pool of nodes for the first letter, a pool for the second, and so forth.[28] What is attained in this way is a structure of atomic representations, not structured representations.

The lack of syntactically structured representations is not an essential limitation[29] of connectionist architecture. Indeed, Paul Smolensky has shown an elegant way to do it, called "vector product representations,"[30] which Michael Tye mobilizes in his contribution to this volume.

However, Fodor and Pylyshyn[31] have argued that if you construct syntactically structured representations in a connectionist network, you will merely be implementing classical AI (GOFAI) in a novel way. Processes that depend on that structure will be describable in terms of sequences of rules that correspond to a classical program. But then those rules or that program will describe the *cognitive* processes in question. Connectionism, so developed, would not be a contribution to our understanding of cognition.[32]

Suppose we had a successful GOFAI theory of human cognition, and a successful connectionist implementation that we thought revealed how the GOFAI theory could be realized in human brains. If we found Martians who satisfied the GOFAI cognitive theory, but not the connectionist implementation, we would (and should) say that the Martians were cognitively, psychologically, like us. Rob Cummins' paper in The *Southern Journal of Philosophy* (1979) is in large part an exploration of the prospects for connectionism in light of this challenge.

Fodor and Pylyshyn argue strenuously that cognitive processes depend on structured representations. Thus, connectionism appears to be faced with a potentially devastating dilemma. Either it gives us only associations of unstructured representations, or it gives us cognitive processes involving complex representations. If the former, connectionism is "mere associationism," too weak to give us all or even very much of cognition.[33] If the latter, it is "mere implementation," not informative at the level of cognition.

If connectionism is not a model of all human cognition, then of how much? David Kirsch points out in his contribution to this volume that implementing complex representations is computationally enormously expensive for connectionism. Thus he suggests that opting for connectionism amounts to adopting the hypothesis that only a small portion of cognition involves rules and structured representations, and that cognition is mostly soft and associative.

5. CONNECTIONISM, APRIL 1988

There are certain desirable features that you would expect connectionist systems to have, which are in fact exhibited by some extant connectionist systems: ability to learn, ability to deal with multiple soft constraints, successful pattern recognition, and content addressable memory. There are among the factors that seem to be at the heart of the crisis in GOFAI.

To my mind, no connectionist system produced so far should be interpreted as a serious attempt to model or simulate any aspect of human cognition. Connectionist systems I have seen are too simple, too artificially constrained, and have been given too much help by the artificial specification of the task domain. Furthermore, there is no prospect that these systems will "scale up" to model some aspect of real cognition.

However, these systems show that connectionist systems can do at least some of the right kinds of things. Furthermore, some of these systems exhibit intriguingly lifelike properties.[34] Thus, they serve as plausibility arguments. They show that it is worthwhile thinking seriously about how connectionism would have to be developed to yield a serious model of (all or any of) cognition.

In this regard, we should keep in mind that connectionism looks attractive in part precisely because it looks promising where GOFAI has repeatedly failed. If connectionism is to succeed as a model of cognition, it must address itself to the problems that have precipitated the crisis in GOFAI. If connectionism cannot solve there problems, it does not deserve to replace GOFAI.

Perhaps it can be said that some progress has been made in the area of recognition problems. However, no progress at all has been made on frame and folding type problems. Indeed, since these problems involve propositional—i.e., syntactically structured—information, they cannot even be formulated in terms of the typical connectionist systems produced so far.[35,36]

NOTES

1. Of course, we must begin where we can, with simplified models of artificially isolated parts of what we do, in the hope that these will lead us to less simplified models of less isolated parts. But the goal is to understand how we do it, and hence one (vague) desideratum of models is that they solve problems in ways that are relevantly like the way we solve those problems.

2. John Haugland, *Artificial Intelligence: The Very Idea* (Cambridge: Bradford Books, MIT Press, 1985).

3. Which presumably represent, not by interpretation, but by nature. Note that on its assumptions, GOFAI does not aim at *simulating* intelligence, as we simulate hurricanes and economies. To be content with simulation is to give up the GOFAI view that cognition *is* executing the right kind of program.

4. "Rules and representations" has a nice ring to it, but it is more revealing to think of it as the "representations and rules" view. There are representations, and there are rules that *refer to those mental representations*.

5. Cf. Hubert L. Dreyfus and Stuart E. Dreyfus, *Mind over Machine* (New York: The Free Press, 1986).

6. J. A. Feldman, "Connectionist Models and Their Applications: Introduction," *Cognitive Science* 9, 1–2.

7. These clusters of problems are not unrelated, and how we ultimately see their relationships will no doubt be influenced by their resolution. Indeed, to put multiple constraints with soft constraints is already to see things from the perspective of connectionism.

8. Arthur Samuel, author of a checker playing program that is one of the first and best game playing programs ever written, calculated that if brute force methods that took account of every possible move were used, it would take the fastest computer 10^{21} centuries to make the first move. Quoted in Dreyfus and Dreyfus, op. cit.

9. The rules of GOFAI are hard rules, with strict necessary and sufficient conditions for their application. There are devices for building in at least an imitation of softness. But softness seems to be a *natural* feature of human cognition.

10. Roger C. Shank with Peter Childers, *The Cognitive Computer* (Addison Wesley, 1984).

11. New information can also change your representation of a task. Seeing a pest you want to avoid changes the whole course charting problem at the mall. Seeing a casual acquaintance does not. Of course, we might build this into our mall navigation problem. The problem is, virtually any new information might, given other factors, change the task at hand. It seems that our mall navigation program is going to have to have rules that determine, for any possible specific situation, whether or not each particular bit of potential new information is relevant or not, and if so, what changes it induces.

12. The bible of connectionism is David E. Rumelhart, James L. McClelland, and the PDP

Research Group, *Parallel Distributed Processing*, 2 Volumes (Cambridge: Bradford Books, MIT Press, 1986), hereafter, *PDP*. The first four chapters of *PDP*, Part I, (pp. 3–146), introduce "The PDP Perspective."

13. In his contribution to this volume, George Graham suggests that connectionism can provide a deeper understanding of at least some simple learning than either behaviorism or discrepancy theory.

14. Both the processing of nodes and changes of weights in a connectionist system are algorithmic. So, of course, connectionist processing is programable. Furthermore, connectionist systems can be simulated on conventional computers, and indeed at this point, most connectionist research takes this form. Thus, there is—as there must be—a level of analysis at which connectionist systems are rule or program controlled (or controllable). However, the point in the text is that at the level of cognitive processing, of representations, this is not what is going on in a connectionist system. All processing is local, determined only by nodes and neighboring weights. The *system's* solution to a problem emerges from this local processing, This issue of rules and levels of description is discussed in several papers in this volume.

15. Cf. "Learning Internal Representations by Error Propogation," D. E. Rumelhart, G. E. Hinton, and R. J. Williams, Chapter 8 of *PDP*.

16. Cf. "On Learning Past Tenses of English Verbs," D. E. Rumelhart, and J. L. McClelland, Chapter 18 of *PDP*, Vol. 2. Though artificial in several respects, the system described in this paper learns in a sequence interestingly like that in which children actually learn past tenses. First it gets common irregular forms correct. Later, it "overgeneralized" regular patterns and produces forms like "goed."

17. Cf. for example, "Learning Distributed Representations of Concepts," *Proceedings of the Eighth Annual Conference of the Cognitive Science Society*, Amherst, MA, 1986, pp. 1–12; and "Learning in Parallel Networks," *Byte*, April, 1985, pp. 265–273.

18. Totally connected means every unit in layer n is connected to every unit in layer $n + 1$.

There is no *a prior* reason for this particular network. Choosing a structure is a matter of researcher's intuition and trial and error. One principle is that internal layers must contain *fewer* nodes than input and output layers to induce generalization.

19. As it was actually done, a total pass of all 100 cases was run before any weights were changed. Then each weight as changed as a function of its contribution to the total error. The details of this calculation do not concern us here, though such matters are a focus of much connectionist research. See Hinton, op. cit.

20. In one trial it gave the right answer in three of the four cases on which it was not trained. In the other, it got all four test cases right.

21. Interestingly, none of the second layer nodes represented "female." Probably this was because all of the relationships used are sex determinate.

22. The ability to do this is certainly one exciting potentiality of connectionism. Cf. the last section of Cummins' paper.

23. One is reminded of Quine's elephantine form differently fulfilled by different bushes. *Word and Object* (Cambridge: MIT Press, 1960), p. 8.

24. This seems to me the most reasonable and most useful use of this term, but it is not universal. Sometimes individual nodes are thought of as having specific content, but not at the level of conceptualization—micro-features. Then shared nodes of distributed representations can be thought of as representing shared or overlap of content.

25. I do not mean to suggest that this is a short term possibility. A realistic speech recognition system—connectionist or otherwise—may be centuries in the future, or beyond human ken altogether, frequent optimistic pronouncements of the GOFAI community notwithstanding. For all we know now, it may be that the only way humans can make a speech recognition system is by copulation.

26. When I first read this idea in Locke (*Essay*, II, X), I thought it was dumb. It doesn't seem so dumb anymore.

27. GOFAI folks know this, of course. It may, however, be significant that this is the natural way for connectionist systems.

28. Cf. for example, J. L. McClelland and D. E. Rumelhart, "An Interactive Activation Model of Context Effects in Letter Perception: Part 1, An Account of Basic Findings," *Psychological Review* 82 (1981). The point made here holds of Touretzky and Hinton's frequently cited, "Symbols among the Neurons: Details of a Connectionist Inference Architecture." *Proceedings of the Ninth International Joint Conference on Artificial Intelligence*, 1985.

29. Some, I suppose, will not see this as a limitation. I believe it is; see the paper by Horgan and Tienson in *The Southern Journal of Philosophy*, (1979).

30. Paul Smolensky, "On Variable Binding and the Representation of Symbolic Structures in Connectionist Systems," and "A Method for Connectionist Variable Binding," Institute of Cognitive Science, University of Colorado, Technical Reports number CU-CS-356-87 and CU-CS-355-87.

31. Jerry A. Fodor and Zenon Pylyshyn, "Connectionism and Cognitive Architecture: A Critical Analysis," *Cognition* 28 (1988), pp. 3–71.

32. If this is correct, connectionist implementation might still be interesting and important. Since connectionist systems seem to be computationally much more like brains than GOFAI systems, implementing GOFAI systems in connectionist networks might be a step toward understanding *how* GOFAI cognitive processes could be realized in the brain. But that would not be a step toward understanding the cognitive processes themselves.

33. Connectionists claim to be presenting a model of cognition *in general*, e.g., *PDP* I, Chapter 4, p. 110.

34. Cf., e.g., Rumelhart and McClelland's past tense learning system in *PDP*, II, Chapter 18.

35. This applies to the *systems* exhibited—in contrast with the intuitive discussion—in the place one would most hope for some illumination on this matter, "Schemata and Sequential Thought Processes in PDP Models," by Rumelhart, Smolensky, McClelland, and Hinton, *PDP*, II, Chapter 14.

36. I wish to thank Stan Franklin for comments on an earlier draft of this paper that led to several improvements.

JOHN HAUGELAND

UNDERSTANDING NATURAL LANGUAGE[1]

The trouble with Artificial Intelligence is that computers don't give a damn—or so I will argue by considering the special case of understanding natural language. Linguistic facility is an appropriate trial for AI because input and output can be handled conveniently with a teletype, because understanding a text requires understanding its topic (which is unrestricted), and because there is the following test for success: does the text enable the candidate to answer those questions it would enable competent people to answer? The thesis will not be that (humanlike) intelligence cannot be achieved artificially, but that there are identifiable conditions on achieving it. This point is as much about language and understanding as about Artificial Intelligence. I will express it by distinguishing four *different* phenomena that can be called "holism": that is, four ways in which brief segments of text cannot be understood "in isolation" or "on a one-by-one basis."

I. HOLISM OF INTENTIONAL INTERPRETATION

Consider how one might *empirically* defend the claim that a given (strange) object plays chess. Clearly, it is neither necessary nor sufficient that the object use any familiar chess notation (or pieces); for it might play brilliant chess in some alien notation, or it might produce "chess salad" in what appeared to be standard notation. Rather, what the defense must do is, roughly:

(i) give systematic criteria for (physically) identifying the object's inputs and outputs;

(ii) provide a systematic way of interpreting them as various moves (such as a manual for translating them into standard notation); and then

(iii) let some skeptics play chess with it.

The third condition bears all the empirical weight, for satisfying it amounts to public *observation* that the object really does play chess. More specifically, the skeptics see that, as interpreted, it makes a sensible (legal and plausible) move in each position it faces. And eventually, induction convinces them that it would do so in any position. Notice that, *de facto*, the object is also being construed as "remembering" (or "knowing") the current position, "trying" to make good moves, "realizing" that rooks outrank pawns, and even "wanting" to win. All these interpretations and construals constitute collectively an *intentional interpretation*.

Intentional interpretation is intrinsically holistic. It is supported empirically only by observing that its object makes generally "sensible" outputs, given the circumstances. But the relevant circumstances are fixed by the object's prior inputs and other outputs, *as interpreted*. Thus, each observation distributes its support over a whole range of specific interpretations, no one of which is supported apart from the others. For example, a chess move is legal and plausible only relative to the board position, which is itself just the result of the previous moves. So one output can be construed sensibly as a certain queen move, only if that other was a certain knight move, still another a certain bishop move, and so on.[2]

This is the *holism of intentional interpretation*; and it is all too familiar to philosophers. Intentional interpretation is tantamount to Quine's "radical translation"—including, as Davidson emphasizes, the attribution of beliefs and desires. The condition that outputs be "sensible" (in the light of prior inputs and other outputs) is just whatever the ill-named "principle of charity" is supposed to capture. I have reviewed it here only to distinguish it from what follows.

II. COMMONSENSE HOLISM

Years ago, Yehoshua Bar-Hillel pointed out that disambiguating "The box was in the pen" requires common-sense knowledge about boxes and pens. He had in mind knowledge of typical sizes, which would ordinarily decide between the alternatives "playpen" and "fountain pen."[3] In a similar vein, it takes common sense to determine the antecedent of the pronoun in: "I left my raincoat in the bathtub, because it was still wet." More subtly, common sense informs our appreciation of the final verb of: "Though her blouse draped stylishly, her pants seemed painted on."

Straightforward questioning immediately exposes any misunderstanding: Was the bathtub wet? Was there paint on her pants? And the issue isn't just academic; a system designed to translate natural languages must be able to answer such questions. For instance, the correct and incorrect readings of our three examples have different translations in both French and German— so the system has to choose. What's so daunting about this, from the designer's point of view, is that one never knows which little fact is going to be relevant next—which commonsense tidbit will make the next disambiguation "obvious." In effect, the whole of common sense is potentially relevant at any point. This feature of natural-language understanding I call *common-sense holism*; its scope and importance was first fully demonstrated in Artificial Intelligence work.

The difference between common-sense holism and the holism of intentional interpretation is easily obscured by vague formulas like: the meaning of an utterance is determinate only relative to *all* the utterer's beliefs, desires, and speech dispositions. This covers both holisms, but only at the price of covering up a crucial distinction. The holism of intentional interpretation is *prior* holism, in the sense that it's already accommodated *before* the interpretation of ongoing discourse. An interpreter *first* finds an over-all scheme that "works" and *then* can interpret each new utterance separately as it comes. For example, once a holistic chess-player interpretation has been worked out, its holism can be ignored—moves can perfectly well be translated "in isolation."[4] By contrast, common-sense holism is *real-time* holism—it is freshly relevant to each new sentence, and it can never be ignored. Even if a perfect dictionary and grammar were available, sentences like our three examples would still have to be disambiguated "in real time," by some appeal to common sense.

The point can be put another way. Prior holism is compatible with the (Fregean) ideal of semantic atomism: the meaning of a sentence is determined by the meanings of its meaningful components, plus their mode of composition. This ideal is (nearly) achieved by chess notations, formal logics, and most programming languages; but it is only grossly approximated by English—assuming that "meaning" is what one "grasps" in understanding a sentence, and that words and idioms are the meaningful components.[5] Real-time holism is precisely *in*compatible with semantic atomism: understanding a sentence requires *more* than a grammar and a dictionary—namely, common sense.[6]

The nature of commonsense holism is brought into sharper relief by current efforts to deal with it—those in Artificial Intelligence being the most concentrated and sophisticated. The hard problem, it turns out, is not simply the enormous volume of common knowledge, but rather storing it so that it can be efficiently accessed and used. Obviously, it is quite impractical to check every available fact for possible relevance, every time some question comes up. So the task is to design a system that will quickly home in on genuinely relevant considerations, while ignoring nearly everything else. This is the "memory organization" or "knowledge representation" problem; what makes it hard is the quixotic way that odd little "facts" turn up as germane.

Most comtemporary systems employ some variant of the following idea: facts pertaining to the same subject are stored together ("linked") in structured clusters, which are themselves linked in larger structures, according as their subjects are related.[7]

We can think of these clusters as "concepts," so long as we remember that they are much more elaborate and rich than traditional definitions— even "contextual" definitions. For example, the concept for 'monkey' would include not only that they are primates of a certain sort, but also a lot of "incidental" information like where they come from, what they eat, how organ grinders used them, and what the big one at the zoo throws at spectators. It's more like an encyclopedia than a dictionary entry.

Three points will clarify how this is supposed to work. First, much of the specification of each concept lies in its explicit links or "cross references" to other concepts, in an over-all conceptual superstructure. For instance, part of the monkey concept would be an "is-a" link to the primate concept, which has in turn an "is-a" link to the mammal concept, and so on. So, the monkey, rat, and cow concepts can effectively "share" generic information about mammals. Second, entries in a concept can have modalities, like "necessarily," "typically," "occasionally," or even "only when. . . ." The "typically" mode is particularly useful, because it supplies many common-sense "assumptions" or "default assignments." Thus, if monkeys typically like bananas, the system can "assume" that any given monkey will like bananas (pending information to the contrary). Third, concepts often have "spaces" or "open slots" waiting (or demanding) to be "filled up" in stipulated ways. For example, the concept of eating would have spaces for the eater and the eaten, it being stipulated that the eater be animate, and the eaten (typically) be food.

A system based on such concepts copes with common-sense holism as follows. First, a dictionary routine calls the various concepts associated with the words in a given sentence, subject to constraints provided by a syntactical analyzer. Hence, only the information coded in (or closely linked to) these concepts is actually accessed—passing over the presumably irrelevant bulk. Then the systems applies this information to any ambiguities by looking for a combination of concepts (from the supplied pool) which fit each other's open spaces in all the stipulated ways. So, for Bar-Hillel's example, the system might call four concepts: one each for "box" and "is in," and two for "pen." The "is in" concept would have two spaces, with the stipulation that what fills the first be smaller than what fills the second. Alerted by this requirement, the system promptly checks the "typical size" information under the other concepts, and correctly eliminates "fountain pen." An essentially similar procedure will disambiguate the pronouns in sentences like: "The monkeys ate the bananas because they were hungry" or ". . . because they were ripe" (cf. Wilks, op. cit. p. 19).

The other two examples, however, are tougher. Both raincoats and bathtubs typically get wet, so *that* won't decide which was wet when I left my coat in the tub. People opt for the coat, because being wet is an understandable (if eccentric) reason for leaving a coat in a tub, whereas the tub's being wet would be no (sane) reason to leave a coat in it. But where is *this* information to be coded? It hardly seems that concepts for "raincoat," "bathtub," or "is wet," no matter how "encylopedic," would indicate when it's sensible to put a raincoat in a bathtub. This suggests that common sense can be organized only partially according to subject matter. Much of what we recognize as "making sense" is not "about" some topic for which we have a word or idiom, but rather about some (possibly unique) circumstance or episode, which a longer fragment leads us to "visualize." Introspectively, it seems that we imagine ourselves into the case, and then decide from within it what's plausible. Of course, *how* this is done is just the problem.

The ambiguity of "painted-on pants" is both similar and different. Again, we "imagine" the sort of attire being described; but the correct reading is obviously a metaphor—for "skin tight," which is both coordinated and appropriately contrasted with the stylishly draped blouse. Most approaches to metaphor, however, assume that metaphorical readings aren't attempted unless there is something "anomalous" about the "literal" reading (as in "He is the cream on my peaches," or ". . . faster than greased lightning"). But, in this case there is nothing anomalous about pants with paint on them—they would even clash with "stylish," explaining the conjunction "Though. . . ." On that reading, however, the sentence would be silly, whereas the metaphor is so apt that most people don't even notice the alternative.

These examples are meant only to illustrate the subtlety of common sense. They show that no obvious or crude representation will capture it, and suggest that a sophisticated, cross-referenced "encyclopedia" may not suffice either. On the other hand, they don't reveal much about what's "left out," nor (by the same token) whether that will be programmable when we know what it is. The real nature of common sense is still a wide-open question.

III. SITUATION HOLISM

Correct understanding of a sentence depends not only on general common sense, but also on understanding the specific situation(s) to which it pertains. I don't have in mind the familiar point about descriptions and indexicals, that only the "context" determines *which* table is "the table . . ." or "this table. . . ," and so on. Much more interesting is the situation-dependence of examples like Bar-Hillel's; Dreyfus (op. cit.) points out that

. . . in spite of our *general* knowledge about the relative sizes of pens and boxes, we might interpret "The box is in the pen," when whispered in a James Bond movie, as meaning just the opposite of what it means at home or on the farm. (216)

This is not just a problem about "exotic" contexts, where normal expectations might fail; both of the following are "normal":

When Daddy came home, the boys stopped their cowboy game. They put away their guns and ran out back to the car.

When the police drove up, the boys called off their robbery attempt. They put away their guns and ran out back to the car.

The second sentence is not exactly ambiguous, but it means different things in the two situations. Did they, for instance, put their guns "away" in a toy chest or in their pockets? (It makes a difference in German: *einräumen* or *einstecken*.) Could "ran" be paraphrased by "fled"?

So far, the role of "situation sense" seems comparable to that of common sense, though more local and specific. A fundamental difference appears, however, as soon as the stories get interesting enough to involve an interplay of several situations. A Middle-Eastern folk tale gives a brief example:

One evening, Khoja looked down into a well, and was startled to find the moon shining up at him. It won't help anyone down there, he thought, and he quickly fetched a hook on a rope. But when he threw it in, the hook snagged on a hidden rock. Khoja pulled and pulled and pulled. Then suddenly it broke loose, and he went right on his back with a thump. From where he lay, however, he could see the moon, finally back where it belonged—and he was proud of the good job he had done.

The heart of this story is a trade-off between two situations: the real one and the one in Khoja's imagination. The narrative jumps back and forth between them; and it is up to the reader to keep them straight, and also to keep track of their interaction and development.

In the first sentence, for example, the embedded clauses "Khoja found the moon" and "it shined up at him," are clearly about the epistemic situation, despite their grammar. One must understand this at the outset, to appreciate Khoja's progressive misperceptions, and thus his eventual pride. A trickier shift occurs in the clause "It won't help anyone down there . . . ," which must mean "*if it stays* down there" (not: "anyone *who is* down there"). In other words, it's an implicit hypothetical which refers us to yet another situation: a counterfactual one in which people are left in darkness while the moon is still in the well. This too is essential to understanding the pride.[8]

The important point is how little of this is explicit in the text: the clauses as written exhibit what can be called "situational ambiguity." It's as if situations were "modalizers" for the expressed clauses, generating "mini-possible-worlds" and implicit propositional operators. I'm not seriously proposing a model theory (though, of course, this has been done for counterfactuals, deontic modalities, and epistemic states) but only suggesting what may be a helpful analogy. Thus the clause "Khoja found the moon" would have not only the modality "Khoja thought that . . ." but also the modality "while looking into the well. . . ." The latter is a crucial modalization, for it (along with common sense) is what forces the former.

Given this way of putting it, two things stand out. First, rather than a fixed, lexically specified set of possible modalities, there are indefinitely many of them, more or less like sentences (or indeed, whole passages). Second, many of these have to be supplied (or inferred) by the reader—often, as in the last example, on the basis of others already supplied. That is, to understand the text, the reader must provide for each clause a number of these generalized or "situational" modalities, and must do so largely on the basis of some over-all situational or modal coherence. This demand for over-all coherence—that all the various "situations" (with respect to which clauses are understood) should fit together in an intelligible way—is what I call *situation holism*. It is a general feature of natural-language text, and coping with it is prerequisite to reading.

Situation holism is especially characteristic of longer texts. We had a brief sample in our folk tale; but it really comes into its own in the forms of dialectic, characterization, and plot. Mystery novels, for example, are built around the challenge of situation holism when pivotal cues are deliberately scattered and ambiguous. Translators (who read the book first, naturally) must be very sensitive to such matters—to use "ran" or "flew" instead of "fled," for instance—on pain of spoiling the suspense. But only the overall plot determines just which words need to be handled carefully, not to mention how to handle them. Engrossed readers, of course, are alert to the same issues in a complementary way. This is situation holism, full-fledged.[9]

IV. DIGRESSION: HERMENEUTICS

Hermeneutics, in the classical (nineteenth-century) sense, is the "science" of textual interpretation—i.e., exegesis. It is often described as "holistic," on something like the following grounds: the meanings of particular passages, doctrines, and specialized ("technical") terms, are only apparent in the context of the whole; yet the whole (treatise, life's work, or genre) is composed entirely of particular passages, containing the various doctrines and special terms. So the interpreter must work back and forth among part, subpart, and whole, bootstrapping each insight on one level into new insights on the others, until a satisfactory over-all understanding is achieved.

Hermeneutics is like intentional interpretation, insofar as the point is to translate baffling expressions into others more familiar or more intelligible. And the constraint on adequacy is again that the text, as construed, make a maximum of sense. But in exegesis, "sensibleness" is not so easy to determine as it is, say, in translating chess notations. For each sentence will have various presuppositions or "facts" taken for granted and will make sense only in the light of these. Part of the interpreter's task, in determining what the text means, is to ferret such assumptions out and make them explicit. So hermeneutic interpretation must deal explicitly with commonsense holism (though it may be "common" only to the initiated few). But the paramount concern in formal exegesis is exposing the overall structure and purpose of the original. A construal cannot stand unless it renders sensible the progression and development of arguments, examples, incidents, and the like. But this is just situation holism, made more articulate. Thus, I don't think the holism of classical hermeneutics is different from the three kinds so far discussed, but is instead a sophisticated combination of them all.[10]

V. EXISTENTIAL HOLISM

In the section on intentional interpretation, we noticed how naturally we construe chess-playing computers as "trying" to make good moves, and "wanting" to win. At the same time, however, I think we *also* all feel that the machines don't "really care" whether they win, or how they play—that somehow the game doesn't "matter" to them. What's behind these conflicting intuitions? It may seem at first that what machines lack is a "reason" to win: some larger goal that winning would subserve. But this only puts off the problem; for we then ask whether they "really care" about the larger goal. And until this question is answered, nothing has been; just as we now don't suppose pawns "matter" to computers, even though they subserve the larger goal of winning.

Apparently something else must be involved to make the whole hierarchy of goals worth while—something that itself doesn't need a reason, but, so to speak, "Matters for its own sake." We get a hint of what this might be, by asking why chess games matter to people (when they do). There are many variations, of course, but here are some typical reasons:

(i) public recognition and esteem, which generates and supports self-esteem (compare the loser's embarrassment or loss of face);
(ii) pride and self-respect at some difficult achievement—like finally earning

a "master" rating (compare the loser's frustration and self-disappoint-
ment); or

(iii) proving one's prowess or (as it were) "masculinity" (compare the loser's
self-doubt and fear of inadequacy).

What these have in common is that the player's self-image or sense of identity
is at stake. This concern with "who one is" constitutes at least one issue that
"matters for its own sake." Machines (at present) lack any personality and,
hence, any possibility of personal involvement; so (on these grounds) nothing
can really matter to them.[11]

The point is more consequential for language understanding than for
formal activities like chess playing, which are largely separable from the rest
of life. A friend of mine tells a story about the time she kept a white rat as
a pet. It was usually tame enough to follow at her heels around campus; but
one day, frightened by a dog, it ran so far up her pantleg that any movement
might have crushed it. So, very sheepishly, she let down her jeans, pulled
out her quivering rodent, and won a round of applause from delighted pas-
sersby. Now, most people find this anecdote amusing, and the relevant question is: Why? Much of it, surely, is that we identify with the young heroine
and share in her embarrassment—being relieved, at the same time, that it
didn't happen to us.

Embarrassment, however, (and relief) can be experienced only by a being
that has some sense of itself—a sense that is important to it and can be
awkwardly compromised on occasion. Hence, only such a being could, as we
do, find this story amusing. It might be argued, however, that "emotional"
reactions, like embarrassment and bemusement, should be sharply distinguished from purely "cognitive" understanding. Nobody, after all, expects a
mechanical chess player to *like* the game or to be thrilled by it. But that
distinction cannot be maintained for users of natural language. Translators,
for instance, must choose words carefully to retain the character of an amusing
original. To take just one example from the preceding story, German has
several "equivalents" for "sheepish," with connotations, respectively, of
being simple, stupid, or bashful. Only by appreciating the embarrassing nature
of the incident, could a translator make the right choice.

A different perspective is illustrated by the time Ralph asked his new
friend, Lucifer: "Why, when you're so brilliant, beautiful, and everything,
did you ever get kicked out of heaven?" Rather than answer right away,
Lucifer suggested a little game: "I'll sit up here on this rock," he said, "and
you just carry on with all that wonderful praise you were giving me." Well,
Ralph went along, but as the hours passed, it began to get boring; so, finally,
he said: "Look, why don't we add some variety to this game, say, by taking
turns?" "Ahh," Lucifer sighed, "that's all I said, that's all I said."

Here, even more than Ralph's embarrassment, we enjoy the adroit way that Lucifer turns the crime of the ages into a little *faux pas*, blown out of proportion by God's infinite vanity. But why is that funny? Part of it has to be that we all know what guilt and shame are like, and how we try to escape them with impossible rationalizations—this being a grand case on both counts. It's not the *psychology* of guilt that we "know," but the tension of actually *facing* it and (sometimes) trying not to face it. And actually "feeling" guilty is certainly not a cognitive state, like believing you did wrong, and disapproving; nor is it that, with some unpleasant sensation added on. It is at least to sense oneself as diminished by one's act—to be reduced in worth or exposed as less worthy than had seemed.

Crime and Punishment, too, is "about" guilt, but it isn't especially funny. The novel is powerful and didactic: the reader's experience of guilt is not simply drawn upon, but engaged and challenged. We enter into Raskolnikov's (and Dostoyevsky's) struggle with the very natures of guilt, personal responsibility, and freedom—and in so doing, we grow as persons. This response, too, is a kind of understanding, and asking questions is a fairly effective test for it. Moreover, at least some of those questions will have to be answered in the course of producing an adequate translation.

One final example will demonstrate the range of the phenomenon I'm pointing at, and also illustrate a different way in which the reader's personal involvement can be essential. It is a fable of Aesop's.

One day, a farmer's son accidentally stepped on a snake, and was fatally bittten. Enraged, the father chased the snake with an axe, and managed to cut off its tail. Whereupon, the snake nearly ruined the farm by biting all the animals. Well, the farmer thought it over, and finally took the snake some sweetmeats, and said: "I can understand your anger, and surely you can understand mine. But now that we are even, let's forget and be friends again." "No, no," said the snake, "take away your gifts. You can never forget your dead son, nor I my missing tail."

Obviously, this story has a "moral," which a reader must "get" in order to understand it.

The problem is not simply to make the moral explicit, for then it would be more direct and effective to substitute a nonallegorical paraphrase:

A child is like a part of oneself, such as a limb. The similarities include:
(i) losing one is very bad;
(ii) if you lose one, you can never get it back;
(iii) they have no adequate substitutes; and thus
(iv) they are literally priceless.

Therefore, to regard trading losses of them as a "fair exchange," or "getting even," is to be a fool.

But this is just a list of platitudes. It's not that it misrepresents the moral, but that it lacks it altogether—it is utterly flat and lifeless. By comparison, Aesop's version "lives," because we as readers identify with the farmer. Hence, we too are brought up short by the serpent's rebuke, and that makes us look at ourselves.

The terrifying thing about losing, say, one's legs is not the event itself, or the pain, but rather the thought of *being* a legless cripple for all the rest of one's life. It's the same with losing a son, right? Wrong! Many a parent indeed would joyously give both legs to have back a little girl or boy who is gone. Children can well mean more to who one is than even one's own limbs. So who are you, and what is your life? The folly—what the fable is really "about"—is not knowing.[12]

A single event cannot be embarrassing, shameful, irresponsible, or foolish in isolation, but only as an act in the biography of a whole, historical individual—a person whose personality it reflects and whose self-image it threatens. Only a being that cares about who it is, as some sort of enduring whole, can care about guilt or folly, self-respect or achievement, life or death. And only such a being can read. This holism, now not even apparently in the text, but manifestly in the reader, I call (with all due trepidation) *existential holism*. It is essential, I submit, to understanding the meaning of any text that (in a familiar sense) *has* any meaning. If situation holism is the foundation of plot, existential holism is the foundation of literature.

In the context of Artificial Intelligence, however, there remains an important question of whether this sets the standard too high—whether it falls into what Papert somewhere calls "the human/superhuman fallacy," or Dennett "the Einstein-Shakespeare gambit." Wouldn't it be impressive enough, the reasoning goes, if a machine could understand everyday English, even if it couldn't appreciate literature? Sure, it would be impressive; but beyond that there are three replies. First, if we could articulate some ceiling of "ordinariness" beyond which machines can't pass or can't pass unless they meet some further special condition, that would be very interesting and valuable indeed. Second, millions of people can read—really read—and for most of the others it's presumably a socio-historical tragedy that they can't. Existential holism is not a condition just on creative genius. Finally, and *most important*, there is no reason whatsoever to believe there is a difference in kind between understanding "everyday English" and appreciating literature. Apart from a few highly restricted domains, like playing chess, analyzing mass spectra, or making airline reservations, the most ordinary conversations are fraught with life and all its meanings.

VI

Considering the progress and prospects of Artificial Intelligence can be a peculiarly concrete and powerful way of thinking about our own spiritual nature. As such, it is a comrade of the philosophy of mind (some authors see AI as allied to epistemology, which strikes me as perverse). Here, we have distinguished four phenomena, each with a claim to the title "holism"—not to trade on or enhance any mystery in the term, but rather, I would hope, the opposite. The aim has not been to show that Artificial Intelligence is impossible (though it is, you know) but to clarify some of what its achievement would involve, in the specific area of language understanding. This area is not so limited as it seems, since—as each of the four holisms testifies—understanding a text involves understanding what the text is "about." The holisms, as presented, increase in difficulty relative to current AI techniques; and my own inclination (it's hardly more than that) is to regard the last, existential holism, as the most fundamental of the four. Hence my opening remark: the trouble with Artificial Intelligence is that computers don't give a damn.

NOTES

1. To be presented at an APA symposium on Artificial Intelligence, December 28, 1979. C. Wade Savage and James Moor will comment; see this *The Journal of Philosophy*, VXXI, this issue, 633–634, for an abstract of Moor's comment; Savage's paper is not available at this time.

I am grateful for suggestions from Nuel Belnap, Bob Brandom, Bert Dreyfus, Jay Garfield, and Zenon Pylyshyn. Kurt Baier helped with the German, and Genevieve Dreyfus with the French.

2. A different argument for a similar conclusion depends on assuming that the inputs and outputs are semantically compound. Then, since each compound will in general share components with many others, their respective interpretations (in terms of their compositions) will be interdependent. Thus the (semantic) role of 'P' in 'P-K4' must be systematically related to its role in 'P-R3,' and so on. The argument in the text, however, is more fundamental. There are fewer than two thousand possible chess moves. [Martin Gardner, in his June 1979 *Scientific American* column, gives the figure 1840; but he neglects castling and pawn promotion (see pp. 25–26)]. These could be represented unambiguously by arbitrary numbers, or even simple symbols; yet interpreting an object using such a system would still be holistic, for the earlier reasons.

3. "The Present Status of Automatic Translation of Languages," in F. L. Alt. ed., *Advances in Computers* (New York: Academic Press, 1964), vol I, pp. 158–159. Quoted in H. L. Dreyfus, *What Computers Can't Do*, 2nd ed. (New York: Harper & Row, 1979), p. 215.

4. Cryptography is comparable: code cracking is holistic, but once it succeeds, deciphering goes along on a message-by-message basis.

5. Hilary Putnam argues that there is more to meaning than what competent speakers understand, but his point is orthogonal to ours ["The Meaning of Meaning," in *Mind, Language and Reality* (New York: Cambridge, 1975)].

6. It is difficult to say what significance this has (if any) for formal semantics. The most common tactic is to relegate matters of real-time holism to "pragmatics," and apply the semantic theory

itself only to idealized "deep structures" [in which ambiguities of sense, pronoun binding, case, mood, scope, etc. are not allowed—thus saving atomism (perhaps)]. A protective quarantine for semantics may or may not work out, but earlier experience with syntax hardly bodes well.

7. See, for example: Marvin Minsky, "A Framework for Representing Knowledge," in Patrick Winston, ed., *The Psychology of Computer Vision* (New York: McGraw-Hill, 1975); Yorick Wilks, "Natural Language Understanding Systems with the AI Paradigm," Stanford AI Memo-237, 1974; Roger Schank and Robert Abelson, "Scripts, Plans, and Knowledge," *International Joint Conference on Artificial Intelligence*, IV (1975); Daniel Bobrow and Terry Winograd, "An Overview of KRL, a Knowledge Representation Language," *Cognitive Science*, I, 1 (1977).

8. There are also a number of "background counterfactuals" involved in understanding what happens. Thus, a reader should be able to say what would have happened if the hook hadn't caught on the rock, or if it hadn't broken loose. Anyone who couldn't answer, wouldn't really "have" it.

9. In AI, work on this problem has only just begun. See, e.g., David Rumbelhart, "Notes on a Schema for Stories," in Bobrow and Allan Collins, eds., *Representation and Understanding* (New York: Academic Press, 1975); Bob Wilensky, "Why John Married Mary: Understanding Stories Involving Recurring Goals," *Cognitive Science*, II (1978): 235–266; and Robert de Beaugrande and Benjamin Colby, "Narrative Models of Action and Interaction," *Cognitive Science*, III (1979): 43–66. Compare also David Lewis, "Scorekeeping in a Language Game," forthcoming in *Journal of Philosophical Logic* (8), 339–359.

10. It can be argued (though not here) that genuine radical translation is less like the interpretation of a chess player than like a hermeneutic investigation of a whole culture—including (so are as possible) an "interpretation" of its practices, institutions, and artifacts. For a good account of what hermeneutics has become in the twentieth century (very roughly, it adds my fourth holism), see Charles Taylor, "Interpretation and the Sciences of Man," *Review of Metaphysics*, XXV, 1 (September 1971): 3–51.

11. There are many problems in this vicinity. For instance, people (but not machines) play chess for *fun*; and, within limits, winning is more fun. It's very hard, however, to say what fun is, or get any grip on what it would be for a machine actually to *have* fun. One might try to connect it with the foregoing, and say (in a tired European tone of voice) that fun is merely a temporary diversion from the ever-oppressive burden of self-understanding. But that isn't very persuasive.

12. Rumelhart (op. cit.) analyzes a different version of this story in terms of an interesting "story grammar," loosely analogous to sentential grammar. Significantly, however, he addresses only the continuity of the story and never touches on its moral or meaning.

REFERENCES

Abramsen, A. A. (1987). "Bridging Boundaries Versus Breaking Boundaries: Psycholinguistics in Perspective." *Synthese* (72), 355–388.

Alt, F. L., ed. (1964). *Advances in Computers*. New York: Academic Press.

Anderson, J. R. (1983). *The Architecture of Cognition*. Cambridge: Harvard University Press.

Appel, Haken, and Koch. (1977). "Every Planar Map Is Four Colorable." *Illinois Journal of Mathematics* (21) 429–567.

Aristotle. (1941). *De Anima*. Translated by J. A. Smith. In R. McKeon, ed., *The Basic Works of Aristotle*. New York: Random House.

Attneave, F. (1960). "In Defense of Homunculi." In W. Rosenblith, *Sensory Communication*. Cambridge: MIT Press.

Bar-Hillel, Y. (1960). "The Present Status of Translations of Languages." In F. L. Alt, ed., *Advances in Computers 1*, 91–163. New York: Academic Press.

Bar-Hillel, Y., A. Kasher, and E. Shamir. (1963). *Measures of Syntactic Complexity*. Report for U.S. Office of Naval Research, Information Systems Branch, Jerusalem.

Barsalou, L. W. (1987). "The Instability of Graded Structure: Implications for the Nature of Concepts." In U. Neisser, ed., *Concepts Reconsidered: The Ecological and Intellectural Bases of Categories*. Cambridge: Cambridge University Press.

Barsalou, L. W. (1988). "Intra-concept similarity and its implications for Inter-Concept Similarity." In S. Vosnaidou & A. Ortony, eds., *Similarity and Analogy*. Cambridge: Cambridge University Press.

Barwise, J. and J. Perry, (1984). *Situations and Attitudes*. Cambridge: MIT Press/Bradford Books.

Beattie, J. (1788). *The Theory of Language*. New York: AMS Press, 1974.

Bechtel, W. (1985a). "Realism, Instrumentalism, and the Intentional Stance." *Cognitive Science* (9) 265–292.

Bechtel, W. (1985b). "Realism, Reason, and the Intentional Stance." *Cognitive Science* (9) 473–497.

Bechtel, W. (1985c). "Are the New Parallel Distributed Processing Models of Cognition Cognitivist or Associationist?" *Behaviorism* (13) 53–61.

Bechtel, W. (1986). "What Happens to Accounts of the Mind-brain Relation if We Forego an Architecture of Rules and Representations?" In A. Fine & P. Machamer, eds., *PSA 1986* (pp. 159–171). East Lansing, MI: Philosophy of Science Association.

Bechtel, W. (1988a). *Philosophy of Science: An Overview for Cognitive Science*. Hillsdale, NJ: Lawrence Erlbaum Associates.

Bechtel, W. (1988b). "Connectionism and Rules-and-Representations Systems: Are They Compatible?" *Philosophical Psychology*, 1.

Bechtel, W. (forthcoming). "Connectionism and the Future of Folk Psychology."

Bechtel, W., and R. C. Richardson (in preparation). "A Model of Theory Development: Localization as a Scientific Research Strategy."

Benacerraf, P. (1967). "God, the Devil and Godel." *The Monist* (51) 9–32.

Berkowitz, L. (1977). *Advances in Experimental Social Psychology*, vol. 10. New York: Academic Press.

Berliner, H. (1975). "Chess as Problem Solving: The Development of a Tactics Analyzer." Unpublished Ph.D. thesis, Carnegie-Mellon University.

Berliner, H., and Ebling, C. (1986). "The SUPREM Architecture: A New Intellectual Paradigm." *Artificial Intelligence* (28) 3–8.

Bernhart, F. (1977). "A Digest of the Four Color Theorem." *Journal of Graph Theory* (1) 207–225.

Birkhoff, G. (1913). "The Reducibility of Maps." *American Journal of Mathematics* (35) 114–128.

Block, N. (1978). "Troubles with Functionalism." In Block, 1980.

Block, N. ed. (1980). *Readings in the Philosophy of Psychology*. Cambridge: Harvard University Press.

Bobrow, D. (1975). "Dimensions of Representation." In D. Bobrow and A. Collins, eds., *Representation and Understanding*. New York: Academic Press.

Bobrow, D., and T. Winograd (1977). "An Overview of KRL, a Knowledge Representation Language." *Cognitive Science* I (1).

Borgida, E., and R. Nisbett. (1977). "The Differential Impact of Abstract vs. Concrete Information on Decisions." *Journal of Applied Social Psychology* (7) 258–271.

Bruner, J. (1957). "On Perceptual Readiness." *Psychol. Rev.* (64) 123–152.

Brunswik, E. (1956). *Perception and the Representative Design of Psychological Experiments*. Berkeley: University of California Press.

Burge, T. (1979). "Individualism and the Mental." *Midwest Studies in Philosophy* (4) 73–121.

Burge, T. (1987). "Marr's Theory of Vision." In Garfield, ed., *Modularity in Knowledge Representation and Natural Language Understanding*. Cambridge: MIT Press/Bradford Books.

Campbell, D. (1973). "Evolutionary Epistemology." In P. Schilpp, ed., *The Philosophy of Karl Popper*. La Salle: Open Court Press.

Campbell, D. (1977). "Descriptive Epistemology: Psychological, Sociological, and Evolutionary." William James Lectures, Harvard University.

Carnap, R. (1950). *Logical Foundations of Probability*. Chicago: University of Chicago Press.

Carroll, J. S., and Payne, J. W., eds. (1976). *Cognition and Social Behavior*. Hillsdale: Lawrence Erlbaum Associates.

Charniak, E. (1974). "Toward a Model of Children's Story Comprehension." Unpublished doctoral dissertation, MIT and MIT AI Lab Report 266.

Chase, W. H., ed. (1973). *Visual Information Processing*. New York: Academic Press.

Chisholm, R. M. (1977). *Theory of Knowledge*. (2nd ed.) Englewood Cliffs: Prentice-Hall.

Chomsky, N. (1952). *Morphophonemics of Modern Hebrew*. Unpublished Master's thesis, University of Pennsylvania.

Chomsky, N. (1955). *The Logical Structure of Linguistic Theory*. Mimeographed, M.I.T. Library, Cambridge, MA.

Chomsky, N. (1956). "Three Models for the Description of Language." I.R.E. Transactions on Information Theory, vol. 1T-2, pp. 113–324. Reprinted, with corrections, in R. D. Luce, R. Bush, and E. Galanter, eds. *Readings in Mathematical Psychology*, vol. 2. New York: Wiley 1965.

Chomsky, N. (1957). *Syntactic Structures*. The Hague: Mouton & Co.

Chomsky, N. (1959a). "On Certain Formal Properties of Grammars." *Information and Control* (2) 137–167.

Chomsky, N. (1959b). "A Review of B. F. Skinner's *Verbal Behavior*," reprinted in Block, N. ed., *Readings in Philosophy of Psychology, Vol. 1*. Cambridge: Harvard University Press.

Chomsky, N. (1961). "Some Methodological Remarks on Generative Grammar." *Word* (17) 219, 239.

Chomsky, N. (1962a). "A Transformational Approach to Syntax." In A. A. Hall, ed., *Proceedings of the 1958 Conference on Problems of Linguistic Analysis in English*, pp. 124–148. Austin, Texas.

Chomsky, N. (1962b). "Explanatory Models in Linguistics." In E. Nagel, P. Suppes, and A. Tarski, eds., *Logic, Methodology and Philosophy of Science*. Stanford: Stanford University Press.

Chomsky, N. (1963). "Formal Properties of Grammars." In R. D. Luce, R. Bush and E. Galanter, eds., *Handbook of Mathematical Psychology, vol. 2*, pp. 232–418. New York: Wiley.

Chomsky, N. (1964). *Current Issues in Linguistic Theory*. The Hague: Mouton & Co.

Chomsky, N. (1965). *Aspects of the Theory of Syntax*. Cambridge: MIT Press.

Chomsky, N. (1966). "Topics in the Theory of Generative Grammar." In T. A. Sebok, ed., *Current Trends in Linguistics, Vol. 3, Linguistic Theory*. The Hague: Mouton & Co.

Chomsky, N. (1969). "Knowledge of Language." *New York Times Literary Supplement* (15).

Chomsky, N. (1972). *Language and Mind*. New York: Harcourt Brace & Jovanovich.

Chomsky, N. (forthcoming). "Cartesian Linguistics."

Chomsky, N., M. Halle, and F. Lukoff. (1956). "On Accent and Juncture in English." In M. Halle, H. Lunt, and H. MacLean, eds., *For Roman Jakobson*, pp. 65–80. The Hague: Mouton & Co.

Chomsky, N., and J. Katz. (1966). *The Philosophy of Language*. New York: Harper and Row.

Chomsky, N., and G. A. Miller (1963). "Introduction to the Formal Analysis of Natural Languages." In R. D. Luce, R. Bush, and E. Galanter, eds., *Handbook of Mathematical Psychology, vol. 2*, pp. 269–322. New York: Wiley.

Chomsky, N., and M. P. Schutzenburger (1963). "The Algebraic Theory of Context-free Languages." In P. Braffort and D. Hirschberg, eds., *Computer Programming and Formal Systems*, pp. 119–61, Studies in Logic Series. Amsterdam: North-Holland.

Churchland, P. M. (1981). "Eliminative Materialism and the Propositional Attitudes." *Journal of Philosophy* (78) 67–90.

Churchland, P. M. (1984). *Matter and Consciousness: A Contemporary Introduction to the Philosophy of Mind*. Cambridge: MIT Press/Bradford Books.

Churchland, P. M. (1986). "Some Reductive Strategies for Neurobiology." *Mind* (95) 279–309.

Churchland, P. S. (1980). "Language, Thought and Information Processing." *Nous* (14) 147–170.

Churchland, P. S. (1986). *Neurophilosophy: Toward a Unified Science of the Mind-brain*. Cambridge: MIT Press/Bradford Books.

Cooper, L. A., and R. N. Shepard. (1973). "Chronometric Studies of the Rotation of Mental Images." In Chase 1973.

Cottrell, G. W. and S. L. Small (1983). "A Connectionist Scheme for Modelling Word Sense Disambiguation." *Cognition and Brain Theory* (6) 89–120.

Cullingford, R. E. (1978). "Script Application: Computer Understanding of Newspaper Stories." Tech. Rep. 116. Computer Science Dept., Yale University.

Davidson, D. (1970). "Mental Events." In L. Foster and J. Swanson, eds., *Experience and Theory*. Amherst: University of Massachusetts Press.

de Cordemoy, G. (1667). *A Philosophical Discourse Concerning Speech*. The English translation is dated 1668.

De Jong, G. F. (1979). "Skimming Stories in Real Time: An Experiment in Integrated Under-standing." *Tech. Rep. 158.* Computer Science Dept., Yale University.

Dennett, D. (1969). *Content and Consciousness.* London: Routledge and Kegan Paul.

Dennett, D. (1971). "Intentional Systems." *Journal of Philosophy* (8) 87–106.

Dennett, D. (1974). "Comment on Wilfred Sellars." *Synthese* (27) 439–444.

Dennett, D. (1975). "Brain Writing and Mind Reading." In K. Gunerson, ed., *Language, Mind and Meaning.* Minnesota Studies in Philosophy of Science, VII. Minneapolis: University of Minnesota Press.

Dennett, D. (1976). "Conditions of Personhood." In A. Rorty, ed., *The Identities of Persons.* Berkeley: University of California Press.

Dennett, D. (1978). *Brainstorms.* Cambridge: MIT Press/Bradford Books.

Dennett, D. (1982). "How to Study the Human Consciousness Empirically: Or Nothing Comes to Mind." *Synthese* (53) 159–80.

Dennett, D. (1986a). "Is There an Autonomous 'Knowledge Level'?" in Z. Pylyshyn and W. Demopoulos, eds., *Meaning and Cognitive Structure: Issues in the Computational Theory of Mind.* Norwood: Ablex.

Dennett, D. (1986b). "The Logical Geography of Computational Approaches: A View from the East Pole." In R. Harnish and M. Brand, eds., *The Representations of Knowledge and Belief.* Tucson: University of Arizona Press.

Descartes, R. (1641). *Meditations.* Trans. by D. A. Cress. Indianapolis: Hackett Publishing Co. (1980).

DeSousa, R. (1976). "Rational Homunculi." In A. Rorty, ed., *The Identity of Persons.* University of California Press.

De Vries, W., and J. Garfield. (Upublished). "Concepts, Foundations, and Justification: A Study in Sellarsian Epistemology." Amherst College and Hampshire College, Amherst, MA.

Diderot, D. (1751). *Lettre sur les Sourds et Muets.*

Dixon, R. W. (1963). *Linguistic Science and Logic.* The Hague: Mouton & Co.

Dretske, R. (1978). "The Role of the Percept in Visual Cognition," in C. Wage Savage, ed., *Perception and Cognition, Issues in the Foundations of Pscyhology,* Minnesota Studies in the Philosophy of Science, Vol. IX, Minneapolis: University of Minneapolis Press.

Dreyfus, H. L. (1979). *What Computers Can't Do: A Critique of Artificial Reason* (Second ed.). New York: Harper & Row.

Dreyfus, H. L., and S. E. Dreyfus (1986). *Mind Over Machine: The Power of Human Expertise in the Era of the Computer.* New York: The Free Press.

Dyer, M. G. (1981). "Thematic Affect Units and Their Use in Narratives." Paper submitted to IJCAI–81.

Dyer, M. G. (1983) *In-Depth Understanding: A Computer Model of Memory for Narrative Comprehension.* Ph.D. Thesis, Computer Science Department, Yale University.

Dyer, M. G., and W. G. Lehnert (1980). "Organization and Search Processes for Narratives." *Tech. Rep. 175.* Computer Science Dept., Yale University.

Fahlman, S. A. (1979). *NETL: A System for Representing and Using Real Knowledge.* Cambridge: MIT Press.

Feit, W. and J. G. Thompson (1963). "Solvability of Groups of Odd Order." *Pacific Journal of Mathematics* (13) 775–1029.

Feldman, J. A., and D. H. Ballard (1982). "Connectionist Models and Their Properties." *Cognitive Science* (6) 205–254.

Field, H. (1978). "Mental Representations." *Erkenntnis,* (13) 9–61.

Fillmore, C. (1974). *The Future of Semantics.* Berkeley Studies in Syntax and Semantics I. Berkeley: Dept. of Linguistics, Univ. of California.

Fishbein, M., ed. (1977). *Progress in Social Psychology*. Hillsdale: Lawrence Erlbaum Associates.

Fisher, A. (1982). *Formal Number Theory and Computability*. Oxford: Clarendon Press.

Fodor, J. (1968). "The Appeal to Tacit Knowledge in Psychological Explanation." *Journal of Philosophy* (LXV).

Fodor, J. (1975). *The Language of Thought*. New York: Cromwell.

Fodor, J. (1978). "Tom Swift and His Procedural Grandmother." *Cognition* (6).

Fodor, J. (1980). *Representations*. Vermont: Bradford Books.

Fodor, J. (1981a). "The Mind-Body Problem." *Scientific American* (244) 114–123.

Fodor, J. (1981b). "Three Cheers for Propositional Attitudes." In Fodor (1980).

Fodor, J. (1983). *The Modularity of Mind*. Cambridge: MIT Press/Bradford Books.

Fodor, J. (1985). "Fodor's Guide to Mental Representations." *Mind* (94) 76–100.

Fodor, J., and J. J. Katz, eds. (1964). *The Structure of Language: Readings in the Philosophy of Language*. Englewood Cliffs: Prentice Hall, Inc.

Fodor, J., and Z. Pylyshyn. (1988). "Connectionism and Cognitive Architecture: A Critical Analysis." *Cognition* (28) 3–71.

Foot, P. (1961). "Goodness and Choice." *Proceedings of the Aristotelian Society*. Supplementary Volume 35, pp. 45–80.

Frege, G. (1949). "On Sense and Nominatum." Reprinted in H. Fiegl and W. Sellars, eds. *Readings in Philosophical Analysis*, New York: Appleton Century Crofts.

Friedman, M. (1981). "Theoretical Explanation." In R. Healy, ed., *Reduction, Time and Reality*. Cambridge: Cambridge University Press. 2–31.

Frishkopf, L. S., and M. H. Goldstein. (1963). "Responses to Acousti Stimuli from Single Units in the Eighth Nerve of the Bullfrog." *Journal of the Acoustical Society of America* (35) 1219–1228.

Garfield, J. (1983). "Propositional Attitudes and the Ontology of the Mental." *Cognition and Brain Theory* (6) 319–331.

Garfield, J. (1985a). *Deconstructing Robots, Reconstructing Persons: Reply to Lycan*. The Forry Lecture, Amherst College, Amherst.

Garfield, J. (1985b). *Artificial Intelligence and Artificial Citizenship*. Convention and Knowledge: The Anatomy of Inquiry in Contemporary Intellectual Culture, a conference at Smith College, Northampton.

Garfield, J., ed. (1987). *Modularity in Knowledge Representation and Natural Language Understanding*, Cambridge: MIT/Bradford Books.

Garfield, J. (1988). *Belief in Psychology*. Cambridge: MIT/Bradford Books.

Gibson, J. (1957a). *The Senses Considered as Perceptual Systems*. Boston: Houghton Mifflin.

Gibson, J. (1958). "Visually Controlled Locomotion and Visual Orientation in Animals." *Brit. J. Psychol.* (49) 182–194.

Gibson, J. (1979). *The Ecological Approach to Visual Perception*. Boston: Houghton Mifflin.

Gibson, J., and E. Gibson. (1957b). "Continuous Perspective Transformations and the Perception of Rigid Motion." *J. Exp. Psychol.* (54) 129–138.

Gleason, H. A. (1961). *Introduction to Descriptive Linguistics* (2nd ed.) New York: Holt, Rinehart & Winston.

Gold, E. M. (1967). "Language Indentification in the Limit." *Information and Control* (10) 447–474.

Goldman, A. (1978). "Epistemology and the Psychology of Belief." *Monist* (61) 525–535.

Good, I. J. (1967). "Human and Machine Logic." *British Journal for the Philosophy of Science* (18) 144–147.

Good, I. J. (1969). "Gödel's Theorem Is a Red Herring." *British Journal for the Philosophy of Science* (19) 359–373.

Goodman, N. (1954). *Fact, Fiction and Forecast*. London: The Althone Press.

Graham, R., B. Rothschild, and J. Spencer. (1980). *Ramsey Theory*. New York: Wiley and Sons.

Graves, Katz et al. (1973). "Tacit Knowledge." *The Journal of Philosophy* (70) 318–330.

Grice, H. P. (1957). "Meaning." *Philosophical Review* (66) 377–388.

Habermas, J. (1978). *Communication and the Evolution of Society*. Boston: Beacon Press.

Haken (1977). "An Attempt to Understand the Four Color Problem." *Journal of Graph Theory* (1) 193–206.

Halle, M. (1959a). "Questions of Linguistics." *Nuovo Cimento*, (13) 494–517.

Halle, M. (1959b). *The Sound Pattern of Russian*. The Hague: Mouton & Co.

Halle, M. (1961). "On the Role of the Simplicity in Linguistic Description." In R. Jakobson, ed., *Structure of Language and its Mathematical Aspects, Proceedings of the Twelfth Symposium in Applied Mathematics*, pp. 89–94. Providence: American Mathematical Society.

Halle, M. (1962). "Phonology in Generative Grammar." *Word* (18) 54–72. Reprinted in Fodor and Katz (1964).

Halle, M. (1964). "On the Bases of Phonology." In Fodor and Katz (1964).

Halle, M. (1968). *The Sound Pattern of English*. New York: Harper & Row.

Halle, M., and N. Chomsky. (1960). "The Morphophonemics of English." *Quarterly Progress Report*, No. 58, Research Laboratory of Electronics, MIT, pp. 275–281.

Halle, M., and K. Stevens. (1962). "Speech Regulation: A Model and a Program for Research." *I.R.E. Transactions in Information Theory*, vol. IT–8, pp. 155–9. Reprinted in Fodor and Katz (1964).

Harman, G. H. (1963). "Generative Grammars without Transformational Rules: A Defense of Phrase Structure." *Language* (39) 597–616.

Haugeland, J. (1979). "Understanding Natural Language." *The Journal of Philosophy* (76) 619–632.

Haugeland, J. (1985). *Artificial Intelligence: The Very Idea*. Cambridge: MIT/Bradford Books.

Held, and A. Hein. (1963). "Movement-produced Stimulation in the Development of Visually Guided Behaviour." *Journal of Comparative and Physiological Psychology* (56) 872–876.

Hempel, C. G. (1965). *Aspects of Scientific Explanation*. New York: Free Press.

Herskovits, A. (1985). *Space and the Prepositions in English: Regularities and Irregularities in a Complex Domain*. Cambridge: Cambridge University Press.

Hess, E. (1975). "The Role of the Pupil Size in Communication." Reprinted in Atkinson and Atkinson, eds., *Mind and Behaviour, Readings from Scientific American*. San Francisco: W. H. Freeman and Co., 1980.

Heyting, A. (1966). *Intuitionism*. Amsterdam: North-Holland.

Hinton, G. E., J. L. McClelland, and D. E. Rumelhart. (1986). "Distributed Representations." In Rumelhart & McClelland (1986) 77–109.

Hochberg, J. (1968). "In the Mind's Eye." In R. N. Haber, ed., *Contemporary Theory and Research in Visual Perception*. New York: Holt.

Hockett, C. F. (1958). *A Course in Modern Linguistics*. New York: Macmillan.

Hodges, A. (1984). *Turing: The Enigma*. New York: Simon and Schuster.

Hofstader, D. (1979). *Gödel, Escher Back: an Eternal Golden Braid*. New York: Basic Books.

Hollan, J. D. (1975). "Features and Semantic Memory: Set Theoretic or Network Models?" *Psychological Review* (82) 154–155.

Hubel, D. H., and T. N. Wiesesel. (1962). "Receptive Fields, Binocular Interaction and Functional Architecture in the Cat's Visual Cortex." *Journal of Philosophy*, (40) 124–137.

Hume, D. (1978). A Treatise of Human Nature. Oxford: The Clarendon Press.

Jeffrey, R. (1970). "Dracula Meets Wolfman: 'Acceptance vs. Partial Belief." In M. Swain, ed., *Induction, Acceptance and Rational Belief*. Dordrecht: Reidel.

Johnson-Laird, P. (1983). *Mental Models*. Cambridge: Cambridge University Press.

Franks, J. J., and J. D. Bransford. (1971). "Abstraction of Visual Patterns." *Journal of Experimental Psychology* (90) 65–74.

Kainen, P., and T. Saaty. (1977) *The Four Color Problem: Assaults and Conquests*. New York: McGraw Hill.

Katz, J. J. (1964a). "Mentalism in Linguistics." *Language* (40) 124–37.

Katz, J. J. (1964b). "Semantic Theory and the Meaning of 'Good'." *Journal of Philosophy*.

Katz, J. J. (1972). *Semantic Theory*. New York: Harper & Row.

Katz, J. J., and J. A. Fodor. "The Structure of a Semantic Theory." *Language* (33) 170–210. Reprinted in Fodor and Katz (1964).

Katz, J. J., and J. A. Fodor (1964). "A Reply to Dixon's 'A Trend in Semantics'." *Linguistics* (3) 19–29.

Kaufman, S. A. (1986). "A Framework to Think about Evolving Genetic Regulatory Systems." In W. Bechtel, ed., *Integrating Scientific Disciplines*. Dordrect: Martinus Nijhoff.

King, P. (1984). "The Judicial Status of the Fetus: A Proposal for the Protection of the Unborn." In J. Garfield, and P. Hennessey, eds. *Abortion: Moral and Legal Perspectives*. Amherst: University of Massachusetts Press.

Klatzky, R. L. (1975). *Human Memory: Structures and Processes*. San Francisco: Freeman.

Korner, S. (1960). *The Philosophy of Mathematics*. New York: Harper.

Kripke, S. (1972). "Naming and Necessity." In Davidson and Harman, eds., *Semantics of Natural Language*. Boston: Reidel.

Kripke, S. (1984). *Wittgenstein on Rules and Private Language*. Cambridge: Harvard University Press.

Kuhn, T. (1962). *The Structure of Scientific Revolutions*. Chicago: University Press.

Labov, W. (1973). The Boundaries of Words and Their Meanings. In C-J. N. Bailey and R. Shuy, eds.,. *New Ways of Analyzing Variation in English*. Georgetown University.

Lakatos, I. (1976). *Proofs and Refutations*. New York: Cambridge.

Lancelot, C. A., Arnauld et al. (1660). *Grammaire Générale et Raisonée*.

Lees, R. B. (1957). Review of Chomsky (1957). *Language* (33) 375–407.

Lehnert, W. (1978). *The Process of Question Answering*. New Jersey: Lawrence Erlbaum.

Lehnert, W. (1980). "Affect Units and Narrative Summerization." *Technical Report 188*, Yale University. Department of Computer Science.

Lehnert, W. (1983). "BORIS: An Experiment in In-Depth Understanding of Narratives." *Artificial Intelligence* (20) 15–62.

Leibniz, G. W. (1949). *New Essays Concerning Human Understanding*. Translated by A. G. Langley. LaSalle Ill.: Open Court, 1949.

Lemmon, W. B., and G. H. Patterson. (1964). "Depth Perception in Sheep." *Science* (145) 835.

Lenneberg, E. (1960). "Language, Evolution, and Purposive Behavior." In S. Diamond, ed., *Culture in History: Essays in Honor of Paul Radin*. New York: Columbia University Press. Reprinted in a revised and extended version under the title "The Capacity for Language Acquisition" in Fodor and Katz (1964).

Lenneberg, E. (1967). *The Biological Bases of Language*. New York: John Wiley & Sons, Inc.

Lettvin, J. Y., H. R. Maturana, W.S. McCullock, and W. H. Pitts. (1959). "What the Frog's Eye Tells the Frog's Brain." *Proceedings of the I.R.E.*, (47) 1940–1951.

Lucas, J. R. (1961). "Minds, Machines and Gödel." *Philosophy* (36) 120–124.

Lycan, W. (1981a). "Form, Function and Feel." *The Journal of Philosophy* (78) 24–49.

Lycan, W. (1981b). "Toward a Homuncular Theory of Believing." *Cognition and Brain Theory* (4) 139–160.

Lycan, W. (1985). *The Computer Model of the Mind and the Mind Model of the Computer*. The Forry Lecture, Amherst College, Amherst.

Lyons, J. (1970). *Noam Chomsky*. New York: Viking Press.

Macklin, R. (1984). "Personhood and the Abortion Debate." In Garfield and Hennessey, eds., *Abortion: Moral and Legal Perspectives*. Amherst: University of Massachusetts Press.

Marr, D. (1976). *Early Processing of Visual Information*. Philosoph. Trans. Royal Soc. London (275) 483–534.

Marr, D. (1982). *Vision*. Cambridge: MIT Press.

Marr, D., and Poggio, T. (1976). "Cooperative Computation of Stereo Disparity." *Science* (194) 283–287.

Matthews, G. H. (1964). *Hidatsa Syntax*. The Hague: Mouton & Co.

McCarthy, J. (1960). "Recursive Functions of Symbolic Expressions and Their Computation by Machine." *Communications of the Association for Computing Machinery* (3)184–195.

McClelland, J. L. (1986). "The Programmable Blackboard Model of Reading." In McClelland and Rumelhart (1986) 122–169.

McClelland, J. L., and D. E. Rumelhart. (1981). "An Interactive Activation Model of Context Effects in Letter Perception. Pt. 1, An Account of Basic Findings." *Psychological Review* (88) 375–407.

McClelland, J. L., D. E. Rumelhart, and the PDP Research Group. (1986). *Parallel Distributed Processing: Explorations in the Microstructures of Cognition. Vol. 2: Psychological and Biological Models*.

McCulloch, W. S. (1961). "What Is a Number, That a Man May Know It, and a Man, That He May Know a Number?" *General Semantics Bulletin* (26 & 27) 7–18.

McDermott, D. (1986). "We've Been Framed: or, Why AI is Innocent of the Frame Problem." In Pylyshyn (1986).

Miller, G. A., and N. Chomsky. (1963). "Finitary Models of Language Users." In R.D. Luce, R. Bush, and E. Galanter eds., *Handbook of Mathematical Psychology*, vol. ii, Ch. 13, pp. 419–92. New York: Wiley.

Miller, G. A., and S. Isard. (1964). "Some Perceptual Consequences of Linguistic Rules." *Journal of Verbal Learning and Verbal Behavior* (2) no. 3, 217–228.

Miller, G. A., and P. N. Johnson-Laird. (1976). *Language and Perception*. Cambridge: Harvard University Press.

Miller, G. A., and D. A. Norman. (1964). *Research on the Use of Formal Language in the Behavioural Sciences*. Semi-annual Technical Report, Department of Defense, Advanced Research Projects Agency, January-June, 1964, pp. 10–11. Cambridge: Harvard University Center for Cognitive Studies.

Millikan, R. (1984). *Language, Thought and Other Biological Categories*. Cambridge: MIT Press/Bradford Books.

Minsky, M. (1975). "A Framework for Representing Knowledge." In P. Winston, ed., *The Psychology of Computer Vision*. New York.

Minsky, M., and S. Papert. (1969). *Perceptrons*. Cambridge: MIT Press.

Moore, and Newell. (1974). "How can MERLIN Understand?" In L. W. Gregg, *Knowledge and Cognition*. New York: Academic Press.

Moore, R. C., and G. G. (1982). "Computations Models of Belief and the Semantics of Belief Sentences." In Peters and Saaranen, eds., *Processes, Beliefs, and Questions: Essays on Formal Semantics of Natural Language and Natural Language Processing*. Dordrecht: D. Reidel.

Nagel, E., and J. R. Newman. (1958). *Gödel's Proof*. New York: New York University Press.

Neisser, U. (1975). *Cognition and Reality: Principles and Implications of Cognitive Psychology*. San Francisco: Freeman.

Neisser, U. (1982). *Memory Observed*. San Francisco: Freeman.

Newell, A. (1980). "Physical Symbol System." *Cognitive Science* (4) 135–183.

Newell, A. (1982). "The Knowledge Level." *Artificial Intelligence* (18) 81–132.

Newell, A. (1987). *Unified Theories of Cognition.* The William James Lectures, Harvard University repeated and Carnegies Mellon University.

Nilsson, N. J. (1971). *Problem-Solving Methods in Artificial Intelligence.* New York: McGraw-Hill.

Nisbett, R. E., E. Borgida, R. Crandell, and H. Reed (1976). "Popular Induction: Information Is Not Necessarily Informative." In Carroll and Payne (1978).

Ornan, U. (1964). *National Compounds in Modern Literary Hebrew.* Unpublished doctoral dissertation, Jerusalem, Hebrew University.

Pinker, S., and A. Prince. (1988). "On Language and Connectionism: Analysis of Parallel Distributed Processing Model and Language Aquisition." *Cognition* (28) 73–193.

Posner, M. I. (1973). *Cognition: An Introduction.* Glenview: Scott, Foresman.

Postal, P. M. (1962). "On the Limitations of Context-free Phrase Structure Description." *Quarterly Progress Report* No. 64, Research Laboratory of Electronics, M.I.T., 231–238.

Postal, P. M. (1964a). *Constitute Structure: A Study of Contemporary Models of Syntactic Description.* The Hague: Mouton & Co.

Postal, P. M. (1964b). "Underlying and Superficial Linguistic Structure." *Harvard Educational Review* (34) 246–266.

Postal, P. M. (1964c). "Limitations of Phrase Structure Grammars." In Fodor and Katz (1964).

Prazdny, K. (1981). "Egomotion and Relative Depth Map from Optical Flow." *Biological Cybernetics* (36) 87–102.

Prendle, S., C. Carello, and M. Turvey. (1980). "Animal-Environment Mutuality and Direct Perception." *The Behavioral and Brain Sciences.*

Putnam, H. (1960). "Minds and Machines." In S. Hook, ed., *Dimensions of Mind.* New York: New York University Press.

Putnam, H. (1968). In a conversation reported in J. R. Lucas, "Satan Stultified: A Rejoinder to Paul Benacerraf." *The Monist* (51) 9–32.

Putnam, H. (1973). "Is Semantics Possible?" In Kiefer and Muntiz, eds., *Language, Belief and Metaphysics*, Albany: SUNY Press.

Putnam, H. (1973). "Meaning and Reference." *Journal of Philosophy* (LXX) 699–711.

Putnam, H. (1975a). *Mathematics, Matter and Method.* New York: Cambridge University Press.

Putnam, H. (1975b). "The Meaning of 'Meaning'." In *Mind, Language and Private Language: Philosophical Papers, Vol. II*, Cambridge: Cambridge University Press.

Pylyshyn, Z. (1978). "Complexity and the Study of Artificial and Human Intelligence." In M. Ringle, ed., *Philosophical Perspectives on Artificial Intelligence.* Humanities Press and Harvester Press.

Pylyshyn, Z. (1980). "Computation and Cognition, Issues in the Foundations of Cognitive Science." *The Behavioral and Brain Sciences*, 3 (1) 111–169.

Pylyshyn, Z. (1981). "The Imagery Debate: Analog Media versus Tacit Knowledge." *Psycho. Rev.* (88) 16–45.

Pylyshyn, Z. (1986). *The Robot's Dilemma: The Frame Problem in Artificial Intelligence.* Ablex.

Quillan, M. R. (1968). "Semantic Memory." In M. Minsky, ed., *Semantic Information Processing* (pp. 24–48). Cambridge: MIT Press.

Quine, W. V. (1960). *Word and Object.* Cambridge: M.I.T. Press, and New York: Wiley.

Ramachandran, V. S. (1985a). "Apparent Motion of Subjective Surfaces." *Perception* (14) 127–34.

Ramachandran, V. S. (1985b). Guest Editorial in *Perception.* (14) 97–103.

Raphael, B. (1976). *The Thinking Computer: Mind Inside Matter.* San Francisco: Freeman.

Reed, E., and R. Jones. (1978). "Gibson's Theory of Perception: A Case of Hasty Epistemologizing?" *Philosophy of Science* (45) 519–530.

Reichenbach, H. (1983). *Experience and Prediction.* Chicago: University of Chicago Press.

Reid, T. (1785). *Essays on the Intellectual Powers of Man*. Page references are to the abridged edition by A. D. Woozley, 1941. London: Macmillan and Co.

Reiser, L. J., M. G. Dyer, P. N. Johnson, C. J. Yang, and S. Harley, (forthcoming). "Plot Units and the Understanding of Narratives." Cognitive Science Technical Report, Yale University.

Rips, L. J., E. E. Smith, and E. J. Shoben. (1975). "Set-theoretic and Network Models Reconsidered: A Comment on Hollan's 'Features and Semantic Memory'." *Psychology Review* (82) 156–157.

Rosch, E. (1975). "Cognitive Representations of Semantic Categories." *Journal of Experimental Psychology: General* (104) 192–133.

Rosch, E. (1978). "Principles of Categorization." In E. H. Rosch and B. B. Lloyd, *Cognition and Categorization*, pp. 24–48. Hillsdale: Erlbaum.

Rosenblatt, F. (1962). *Principles of Neurodynamics*. New York: Spartan.

Ross, L. (1977). "The Intuitive Psychologist and His Shortcomings: Distortions in the Attributions Process." In Berkowitz (1977).

Rumelhart, D. E., G. Hinton, and J. L. McClelland (1986). *A General Framework for Parallel Distributed Processing*. In Rumelhart & McClelland, 1986, 45–76.

Rumelhart, D. E., and D. A. Norman. (1982). "Simulating a Skilled Typist: A Study of Skilled Cognitive-motor Performance." *Cognitive Science* (6) 1–36.

Rumelhart, D. E., J. L. McClelland, and the PDP Research Group. (1986). *Explorations in the Microstructure of Cognition. Vol. 1: Foundations*. Cambridge: MIT Press/Bradford Books.

Rumelhart, D. E., and D. Sipser. (1985). "Feature Discovery by Competitive Learning." *Cognitive Science* (9) 75–112.

Rumelhart, D. E., P. Smolensky, J. L. McClelland, and G. E. Hinton.(1986). *Schemata and Sequential Thought Processes in PDP Models*. In McClelland & Rumelhart, 1986.

Runeson, S. (1980). "There Is More to Psychological Meaningfulness than Computation and Representation." *The Behavioral and Brain Sciences*.

Russell, B. (1940). *An Inquiry into Meaning and Truth*. London: Allen & Unwin.

Ryle, G. (1931) "Systematically Misleading Expression." *Proceedings of the Aristotelian Society*. Reprinted in A. G. N. Flew, ed., *Logic and Language*, first series. (1951) Oxford: Blackwell.

Ryle, G. (1949). *The Concept of Mind*. London: Hutchinson.

Sahlin, G. (1928). *César Chesneau de Marsais et son role dans l'évolution de la grammaire générale*. Paris: Presses Universitaires.

Schank, R. C. (1976). Research Report No. 84, Yale University Department of Computer Science.

Schank, R. C. (1980). "Language and Memory." *Cognitive Science* 4(3).

Schank, R. C. (1981). "Reminding and Memory Organization: An Introduction to MOPs." In W. Lehnert and M. Ringle, eds., *Strategies for Natural Language Processing*. New Jersey: Lawrence Erlbaum.

Schank and Abelson. (1977). *Scripts, Plans, Goals and Understanding*. Hillsdale: Lawrence Erlbaum Associates.

Scheffler, S. (1976). "The Basis of Reference." *Erkenntnis* (13) 171–206.

Searle, J. R. (1979). "Literal Meaning." In *Expression and Meaning*, Cambridge: Cambridge University Press, 117–136.

Searle, J. R. (1980). "Minds, Brains, and Programs." *The Behavioral and Brain Sciences* (3) 417–457.

Searle, J. R. (1982). "The Myth of the Computer: An Exchange." *The New York Review of Books*. June 24, 56–57.

Seifert, C. (1981) "Preliminary Experiments on TAUs" unpublished manuscript. Psychology Dept., Yale University.

Sellars, W. (1954). "Some Reflections on Language Games." *Philosophy of Science* (21) 204–228.

Sellars, W. (1956). "Empiricism and the Philosophy of Mind." In *Science, Perception, and Reality*. London: Routledge, Kegan and Paul.

Sellars, W. (1963). *Science, Perception and Reality*. London: Routledge & Kegan Paul.

Selridge, O. (1955). "Pattern Recogntion in Modern Computers." *Proceedings of the Western Joint Computer Conference*.

Shepard, R. N., and J. Metzler. (1971). "Mental Rotation of Three-Dimensional Objects." *Science* (171) 701–703.

Simon, H. (1957). *Models of Man*. New York: Wiley.

Skinner, B. F. (1957). *Verbal Behavior*, New York: Apple Century Crofts.

Smith, E. E., and D. L. Medin. (1981). *Categories and Concepts*. Cambridge: Harvard University Press.

Smith, E. E., E. J. Shoben, and J. L. Rips. (1974). "Structure and Process in Semantic Memory: A Featured Model for Semantic Decisions." *Psychological Review* (81) 214–241.

Smolensky, P. (1988). "On the Proper Treatment of Connectionism." *Behavioral and Brain Sciences* (11).

Sober, E. (1976). "Mental Representation." *Synthese* (33).

Sober, E. (1980). *Why Logically Equivalent Predicates May Pick Out Different Properties*. Mimeog., University of Wisconsin.

Sober, E. (1981). "The Evolution of Rationality." *Synthese* (46) 95–120.

Sorabji, R. (1972) *Aristotle on Memory*. Providence: Brown University Press.

Stevens, K. (1979). *Surface Perception from Local Analysis of Texture and Contour*, M.I.T. Ph.D. Thesis.

Stich, S. (1978). "Beliefs and Subdoxastic States." *Philosophy of Science* (45) 499–518.

Stroud, B. (1977). *Hume*. Routledge & Kegan Paul.

Sutherland, N.S. (1959). "Stimulus Analyzing Mechanisms." *Mechanization of Thought Processes*, vol. ii. National Physical Laboratory Symposium, No. 10, London.

Sutherland, N. S. (1964). "Visual Discrimination in Animals." *British Medical Bulletin* (20) 54–59.

Thom, R. (1971). "Modern Mathematics: An Education and Philosophical Error?" *American Scientist* (59) 695–699.

Touretsky, D. S. (1986). "BoltzCONS: Reconciling Connectionism with the Recursive Nature of Stacks and Trees." *Proceedings of the Eighth Annual Conference of the Cognitive Science Society*. Hilldale: Lawrence Erlbaum Associates.

Turing, A. M. (1950). "Computing Machinery and Intelligence." *Mind* (59).

Turvey, M., and R. Shaw. (1979). "The Primacy of Perceiving: An Ecological Reformulation of Perception for Understanding Memory." In. L. G. Nillson, ed., *Perspectives on Memory Research, Essays in Honor of Uppsala University's 500th Anniversary*. New Jersey: Erlbaum.

Tversky, A., and D. Kahneman. (1974). "Judgement under Uncertainty: Heuristics and Biases." *Science* (185) 1124–1131.

Tversky, A., and D. Kahneman (1977). "Causal Schemata in Judgements under Uncertainty." In Fishbein (1977).

Twaddell, W. F. (1935). *On Defining the Phoneme*. Language Monograph No. 16. Reprinted in part in M. Joos, ed., *Readings in Linguistics*. Washington: 1957.

Tymoczko, T. (1985). *The Private Language Argument*. Convention and Knowledge: The Anatomy of Inquiry in Comtemporary Intellectual Culture, a conference at Smith College.

Uhlenbeck, E. M. (1963). "An Appraisal of Transformation Theory." *Lingua* (12) 1–18.

Uhlenbeck, E. M. (1964). Discussion in the Session "Logical Basis of Linguistic Theory'." In

H. Lunt, ed., *Proceedings of the Ninth Congress of Linguistics*, 98103. The Hague: Mouton & Co.

Ullman, S. (1979). *The Interpretation of Visual Motion*. Cambridge: M.I.T. Press.

Ullman, S. (1981). *Against Direct Perception*. The Behavioral and Brain Sciences.

Uttal, W. (1967). "Evoked Brain Potentials: Signs or Codes?" *Perspectives in Biology and Medicine* (10) 627–639.

Wang, H. (1963). "Toward Mechanical Mathematics." In K. Sayre and F. Cooson, eds., *The Modeling of the Mind*. Notre Dame: University Press.

Wang, H. (1974). *From Mathematics to Philosophy*. New York: Humanities Press.

Warren, R. (1970). "Perceptual Restoration of Missing Speech Sounds." *Science* (167) 392–393.

Webb, J. (1976). "Gödel's Theorem and Church's Thesis: A Prologue to Mechanism." *Boston Studies in the Philosohy of Science XXXI*. Dordrecht: Reidel.

Weizenbaum, J. (1967). "Contextual Understanding by Computers." CACM, X (8) 464–480.

Weizenbaum, J. (1976). *Computer Power and Human Reason*. San Francisco: Freeman.

Whitehead, A.N. (1959). *Science and the Modern World*. New York: New American Library.

Wilensky, R. (1978). "Understanding Goal-Based Stories." *Tech. Rep. 140*. Computer Science Dept., Yale University.

Wilensky, R. (1980). "Meta-Planning: Representing and Using Knowledge About Planning in Problem Solving and Natural Language Understanding." *Technical Report Memo. No. UCB/ERL M80/33*, Electronics Research Lab. Engineering College, University of California at Berkley.

Wilks, Y. (1974). "Natural Language Understanding Systems within the AI Paradigm." *Stanford AI Memo–237*.

Winograd, T. (1972). *Understanding Natural Language*. New York: Academic Press.

Winograd, T. (1973). "A Procedural Model of Language Understanding." In Schank and Colby, eds., *Computer Models of Thought and Language*. New York: W.H. Freeman and Co.

Winograd, T. (1976). "Towards a Procedural Understanding of Semantics." *Revue Internationale de Philosophie*, fasc. 3–4 (117–118) 260–303.

Winograd, T. (1981). "What Does It Mean to Understand Language?" In D. A. Norman, ed., *Perspectives on Cognitive Science*. Norwood, NJ: Ablex, 231–264.

Winston, P., ed. (1975). *The Psychology of Computer Vision*. New York: McGraw-Hill.

Wittgenstein, L. (1953). *Philosophical Investigations*. New York: Macmillan.

Woods, W. A. (1975). "What's in a Link?" In Bobrow and Collins, eds., *Representations and Understanding*. New York: Academic Press.

Woods, W. A., and J. Makhoul. (1974). "Mechanical Inference Problems in Continuous Speech Understanding." *Artificial Intelligence* (5) 73–91.

Ynvge, V. (1960). "A Model and a Hypothesis for Language Structure." *Proceedings of the American Philosophical Society*, (104) 444–466.

INDEX